KEY TOPICS FULLY INTEGRATED

This text fully integrates key topics via the following icons, which appear in the margins throughout the book:

LEGAL ICON

refers to legal issues as they pertain to business communication.

ETHICAL ICON

refers to topics with ethical implications that lend themselves to classroom discussion.

GLOBAL ICON

refers to global issues surrounding international and intercultural business communication.

TECHNOLOGY ICON

refers to issues of technology that affect the conduct of business communication.

Business Communication

Gretchen N. Vik
Professor
San Diego State University

Jeannette Wortman Gilsdorf
Professor
California State University – Long Beach

IRWIN

Burr Ridge, Illinois
Boston, Massachusetts
Sydney, Australia

© RICHARD D. IRWIN, INC., 1994

Senior sponsoring editor:	Craig Beytien
Senior developmental editor:	Libby Rubenstein
Marketing manager:	Kurt Messersmith
Project editor:	Rita McMullen
Production manager:	Ann Cassady
Designer:	Larry J. Cope
Art coordinator:	Mark Malloy
Art studio:	Electra Graphics
Photo research coordinator:	Charlotte Goldman
Compositor:	The Clarinda Company
Typeface:	10/12 Garamond
Printer:	Von Hoffmann Press

Library of Congress Cataloging-in-Publication Data

Vik, Gretchen N.
    Business communication / Gretchen N. Vik, Jeannette Wortman
Gilsdorf.
        p.   cm.
    ISBN 0-256-11376-9
    1. Business writing.   2. Business communication.   3. English
language—Business English.   I. Gilsdorf, Jeannette Wortman.
II. Title.
    HF5718.3.V55   1994
    658.4′5—dc20   93–22405

Printed in the United States of America
1 2 3 4 5 6 7 8 9 0 VH 0 9 8 7 6 5 4 3

To my mentors, Clyde and Dorothy Wilkinson, and to Doris Sponseller, whose help and counsel are profoundly missed.

G.V.

To Ruth Wortman and Frances Figgins.

J.W.G.

About the Authors

GRETCHEN N. VIK

Dr. Gretchen N. Vik is a professor of information and decision systems in the College of Business Administration at San Diego Sate University. She has been teaching and consulting in communication for 26 years. She teaches a range of business communication courses to undergraduate and graduate students, focusing on improving writing and speaking skills needed on the job. She was named the 1991 Distinguished Faculty Member of the Department of Information and Decision Systems by the San Diego State University Alumni and Associates Board.

An active member of the Association for Business Communication, Gretchen has served on a number of committees, on the board of directors from 1978 to 1991, and as president in 1989–90. All of her degrees are in English, her B.A. from Rice University, her M.A. from the University of South Dakota, and her Ph.D. from the University of Florida.

She has written three other business communication texts, including the 9th and 10th editions of the popular Wilkinson text, *Writing and Speaking in Business,* and articles on basic communication testing programs, videodisc training package development, collaborative writing projects, internship programs, and computer screen design.

JEANNETTE W. GILSDORF

Dr. Jeannette Wortman Gilsdorf is a professor in the College of Business Administration, California State University—Long Beach, where she teaches business and managerial communication at the undergraduate and graduate levels. Her Ph.D. and M.A., both in English, are from the University of Nebraska—Lincoln; her B.A. (English with journalism minor) is from Creighton University in Omaha. Gilsdorf has served on the board of directors of the Association for Business Communication since 1986. She will be president of ABC from November 1993 to November 1994.

Jenny has published her research in *Journal of Business Communication, Public Relations Review,* and *Management Communication Quarterly,* as well as in the *Bulletin of the ABC* and numerous other periodicals. She is on the editorial review board of *Management Communication Quarterly* and is a regular presenter at meetings of the ABC. This is her second book, the first being *Business Correspondence for Today,* published by John Wiley & Sons.

Preface

Why write one more business communication book? We believe it's time for a book that's organized the way the course really unfolds—from basics of communication, to direct messages, then to reports (because they're usually direct, they take students several weeks to prepare, and they take so much time to grade), oral presentations, on to indirect messages, job résumés, letters, and interviews. We end with interpersonal communication, organizational communication, and managerial and supervisory communication, thus enabling students to understand how the principles they've learned actually come to life in the workplace.

Early Writing Application. One of our guiding principles was to get students writing early. We wanted students to realize that this course has information they can use *now* as well as later, on the job. We also include managerial and supervisory communication as it applies to new managers.

Real Life Examples. Each chapter begins with "From the desk of," a section in which a practicing manager explains both the dollar and human costs of missed or bungled communication opportunities. Within the chapters we offer many examples, most on letterheads, that *show* students how to handle communication problems.

Integrated Topics. Rather than adding chapters for the new "special" topics, we integrated legal, ethical, international, and technological issues throughout the text wherever these topics are relevant. The result is a 16-chapter book that fits a semester or a quarter course, depending on which chapters you choose to teach. Four distinct icons call students' attention to the discussions of legal, ethical, international, and technological issues. Reading lists in the instructor's manual also expand on these topics, as do some of the reports and research cases.

Checklists. For student review and writing efficiency, we've included helpful checklists throughout the text on audience analysis and revision, in addition to checklists on the different message strategies students will learn to use. The report checklist, for example, offers many final reminders of format and style tips covered in the chapter.

Application Exercises and Cases. Students learn by doing! Thus, we provide end-of-chapter exercises that help students apply the material they learned so they can retain it better. Real-life cases show how communication problems on the job interact with one another.

Readings on Chapter Topics. Most chapters include one or two short readings to give students different points of view and actual managerial comments on text topics.

Reference Appendixes. To make information easily accessible, we put it in end-of-text appendixes: model letter and memo formats and layout tips in Appendix A; a grammar and mechanics handbook with examples in Appendix B; documentation models from all three major styles, MLA, APA, and Chicago Manual of Style, in Appendix C; and collection letters in Appendix D.

INNOVATIVE CHAPTERS

Chapter One: Basics of Business Communication

After studying audience analysis, a basic model of communication, and effective communication despite cultural and personal differences, students will cover conventional strategies and learn when to use direct and indirect approaches to convey messages. Chapter One also covers the writing process from planning to writing a rough draft through revision. This chapter includes helpful checklists on audience analysis and revision, which students will use throughout the course.

Chapter Two: The Routine, Direct Business Message

Direct messages begin with the most important point to present to the reader or listener. This chapter covers providing information someone has asked for, responding to customers about a company's products, notifying people about business changes, and asking for information. We work through some direct messages from planning through drafting and revising, looking at how good document design and format can help get a message across, whether through word processing, desktop publishing, electronic mail, voice mail, or phone.

Chapter Three: Business Writing Style

Elements of style, especially word choice, influence readers' perceptions of writers and organizations. This chapter develops students' ability to write in a concise, clear, readable style. It covers the changing language of business and develops students' sensitivity to readers' language needs and preferences. A plain, inconspicuous style conveys meaning quickly and conserves readers' time. Many style decisions, made at the "micro" level of words and sentences, govern success at the "macro" or whole-message level. From this chapter, students will learn how important language mastery is and will gain motivation to pursue it.

Chapter Four: Short Reports and Proposals

Reports help people plan and make decisions. Shorter than 10 pages, less formal than longer reports, these documents, if well written, allow the recipient to understand a point quickly and with little effort. This chapter covers justification reports, feasibility studies, such periodic reports as progress reports, and proposals. Examples show how these reports can convey information quickly. Since short reports tend to be direct, they fit well at this point in the text.

Chapter Five: Secondary Research for Business Reporting

Business research is costly in itself. Business decisions based on business research have far-reaching consequences that can be much *more* costly. Secondary research, usually less expensive than primary, contains the answers to many real-world business problems, though far too few business practitioners realize it.

A business research case in this chapter leads students through the extensive planning process that precedes research. The discussion of the business library will help any student in any college or university library, whether that library relies on traditional information-finding tools or offers the latest in computer-assisted indexes and delivery systems.

Chapter Six: Primary Research for Business Reporting

Chapter Six prepares students to perform simple primary-research projects involving either observation or survey. After understanding that both validity and reliability characterize good research, students will learn how to prepare for and conduct an observation; distinguish among kinds of samples; draw a random sample; develop a questionnaire; administer a questionnaire by mail, by phone, and in person; treat their data; and interpret data and draw conclusions. Finally, they will explore the task of narrowing a broad topic into one that is useful and researchable.

Chapter Seven: Graphics

Businesspeople receive more and more of their information visually. Sometimes one or two excellent exhibits can take the place of many paragraphs or even pages of text. This chapter shows students how to construct many different kinds of effective graphics and how to incorporate them into a written text. We provide many exhibits to show students their varied options for visuals. Though many students now have access to computer graphic-drawing packages, the chapter covers low-tech graphics as well.

In preparation for using graphics in oral presentations, Chapter Seven discusses differences between graphics intended for oral presentation and those made for inclusion in a written document. Examples of effective presentation graphics are shown. Another plus in Chapter Seven is the section on computer screen design.

Chapter Eight: Report Organization and Format

This chapter covers longer, more formal reports. In addition to discussing report parts and showing partial and complete examples of real student reports, we discuss collaborative writing of reports, report style, and the importance of audience analysis to the production of a successful report.

Chapter Nine: Oral Presentations

This chapter helps students overcome apprehension, build confidence, and develop skill in giving business presentations. It explains that audiences generally support speakers and want them to succeed. Students learn to build common ground with the audience by becoming audience-centered.

Students also learn about different ways to structure a talk. Extemporaneous speaking receives in-depth attention, with manuscript, memorized, and impromptu speaking covered to a lesser extent. Other strengths of this chapter include detailed information on nonverbal signals and aspects of voice, and guidelines for preparing and using many kinds of visual and audiovisual presentation aids. Because presenting on video is more and more common today, Chapter Nine discusses presenting for the mass media, for in-house use, and for videoconferencing.

Chapter Ten: Indirect Messages: Handling Negative and Sensitive Information

This chapter covers tactful and effective messages containing negative or sensitive information, messages usually written indirectly. Indirect messages include refusals, adjustments, order problems, and personnel problems. We discuss potential problems of sending negative information by phone, fax, or E-mail. Techniques for conveying information indirectly, such as using passive voice, emphasizing the positive over the negative, and avoiding negative words, are covered, as is service attitude as a means of thoughtfully handling external negative situations.

Chapter Eleven: Writing to Persuade

Chapter Eleven covers perhaps the most challenging types of business messages—those that must influence or change what the reader thinks or does. When students need to write persuasively on the job, they will have to know much more than merely how to write a sales letter or a favor request. Most business persuasion involves gaining a needed action that is not simply a favor. Moreover, in organizations, business persuaders work more effectively by developing reasons the action is good for receiver, sender, and organization.

Chapter Twelve: Job Search

After learning about job research and personal analysis, students go on to gather background data on themselves for personal portfolios used to compile effective résumés and application letters. In addition to many partial and full résumé and letter examples used by real applicants, this chapter includes useful forms for record-keeping during the job search.

Chapter Thirteen: Job Interviews

This chapter will help students to prepare for and succeed at job interviews. In addition to discussing on-campus interviews, we look at second, on-site interviews, and videotape, computer, and group interviews. Nonverbal interview tips and sample questions in each conventional area, as well as the newer situational or critical-incident-skills questions, are also included, as are thank-you letters and salary negotiation.

Chapter Fourteen: Communicating Interpersonally

With strong emphasis on teamwork, Chapter Fourteen covers building trust and common ground. Active listening is explored in depth. High or low skill in nonverbal communication often separates successful from unsuccessful employees and managers. This chapter covers many categories of unworded signals: facial expression, posture, gesture and movement, touch, tone of voice, use of time, and use of space. Throughout, the discussion shows how to send the appropriate nonverbal signals for business success.

Chapter Fifteen: Communicating in Organizations

New to organizations, students can find themselves challenged by an immediate need for acculturation. This chapter explains corporate culture and offers a variety of ways for students to become quickly effective in the workplace. The discussion of organizational communication networks will clarify the need for information flow and coordination of efforts—and alert students to some of the common barriers. Coverage of meetings is thorough—from planning and organizing, to conducting, to following up—showing how to get the highest value for the use of members' expensive time.

Chapter Sixteen: Communication in Managing and Supervising

Students often graduate into immediate supervisory responsibility. This chapter covers interviewing to hire, to solve problems, and to appraise. The coverage of the appraisal process, which includes documenting personnel action, coaching and supporting the employees, and using progressive discipline, will help students act in the best interests of both their employer and the individuals they must supervise and evaluate. Motivating, managing and resolving conflict, and communicating with an organization's many different stakeholders round out an indispensable chapter for the beginning supervisor.

Appendix A: Formats for Business Messages

This appendix gives models for letter and memo formats, discussing letter parts and showing alternate styles common in business today.

Appendix B: Writing Handbook

This alphabetical list of symbols saves teachers time in marking papers and gives students brief explanations of common writing problems. The list covers grammar and style, spelling and diction, and other aspects of business writing, giving examples but no exercises.

Appendix C: Three Common Bibliographic Styles: APA, MLA, and University of Chicago

While students may encounter widely differing bibliographic styles in their research sources, they must make their own bibliographic entries stylistically consistent. They will be glad to see Appendix C, which gives helpful examples of each of the major bibliographic and references styles, APA, MLA, and University of Chicago. This appendix also offers common-sense formats for non-print and computerized sources. We put this material in an appendix rather than a chapter because of the lower emphasis placed upon documentation in business compared to academia.

Appendix D: Specialized Persuasion: Collecting

Although today specialized departments or agencies handle most collections, students working in small businesses may need collection skills. Accordingly, Appendix D offers principles and examples for the collection-message series. This appendix also covers collecting by telephone, with an interesting case example.

COMPREHENSIVE SUPPLEMENTS

We offer an outstanding supplement package. The **Instructor's Manual/Test Bank,** prepared by Cynthia Dudley of San Diego State University, contains the following elements:

- Sample syllabi for both quarter and semester schools.
- Chapter outlines.
- Lecture notes with suggestions for transparencies and activities to insert at specific points.
- Suggested readings and videos.
- Exercises with worksheets.
- Glossary of business communication terms.
- Helpful handouts.
- "Answers" to exercises and suggestions on what to look for in cases from the text.
- Eight to ten transparency masters per chapter.
- One sample case per chapter with good and poor answers marked as graded papers.

The **test bank** has 50 questions per chapter—both true/false and multiple choice.

A **computerized test bank** is available through Irwin's software support department.

A **teletest** is also available. Just specify which questions you want, and within a few days you will get your printed exam.

Computer Simulation Software, by management consultant Larry R. Clapper, is shrinkwrapped with the Instructor's Manual. It consists of 20 writing cases tied to chapter topics. Students can use these practice cases to prepare for in-class exams, or they can work through the simulation in a lab setting as a way of individualizing a large class section.

A package of 50 **color acetates** is available to adopters.

We also offer four **videos** from the Irwin Business Communication video library. Tapes 1 and 2 consist of four self-contained, informative segments on writing correctly, concisely, clearly, and interestingly. Tape 3 deals with listening—why many people are poor listeners, the major impediments to effective listening, and techniques for sharpening listening skills. Tape 4 introduces students to the basics of résumé writing and self-assessment, providing helpful hints and advice to those either beginning their careers or reentering the job market.

ACKNOWLEDGMENTS

Special thanks go to Larry R. Clapper, whose business experience added immeasurably to Chapters 4 and 8 on memos, proposals, and reports as well as to other sections of the book; to Ross Figgins, whose artistic eye and creative talent have enriched this book; to Alice Littlejohn, whose thoughtful and gracious critique improved Chapter 5 on secondary research; and to our colleagues, students, and business associates who have taught us much over the years.

We also thank the following reviewers, whose comments on two drafts of the manuscript helped us craft a useful and innovative textbook:

Janet G. Adams
Mankato State University

Lawrence Barton
University of Nevada, Las Vegas

Caroll J. Dierks
University of Northern Colorado

Fred W. Heidrich
Black Hills State University

Francis Hendrix
Rose State College

Rovena Hillsman
California State University,
Sacramento

Thomas Hilton
Utah State University

Linda Lawrence
Pittsburg State University, Kansas

Pat Lehrling
Kankakee Community College

Linda Loehr
Northeastern University

Rita Thomas Noel
Western Carolina University

Ken Pickard
California State University

Joan Roderick
Southwest Texas State University

Grant T. Savage
Texas Tech University

Rebecca Smith
University of California, Berkeley

Nelda Spinks
University of Southwestern
Louisiana

Jim Stull
San Jose State University

John Wuchenich
Community College of Allegheny
County—South Campus

Michael R. Wunsch
Northern Arizona University

Myron D. Yeager
Chapman University

Gretchen N. Vik
Jeannette Wortman Gilsdorf

Brief Contents

Contents

Contents | xvii

Chapter Fifteen: COMMUNICATING IN ORGANIZATIONS 492

Chapter Sixteen: COMMUNICATION IN MANAGING AND SUPERVISING 520

Business Communication

Basics of Business Communication

Effective communication skills will help you succeed in business. You will be able to get your ideas across more quickly and easily, and you will be more likely to get your audience to see ideas your way. *Communication* means the exchange of ideas using common symbols. The most important word to remember here is *exchange*. Remember: You *communicate* only when your audience understands your message—communication is a two-way street.

This chapter is an overview of the basic things you need to know about communicating in business. Most of the ideas will be discussed in detail later, but in this chapter you will learn enough to begin to communicate more effectively. After learning about *audience analysis*, you'll read about a basic *model of communication* and how we communicate, coding and decoding others' information despite cultural and personal differences.

Writing will become easier when you use *conventional strategies* to attack writing and speaking problems. Many business messages are direct: You ask or tell the important idea right at the beginning of the letter, memo, report, or speech. When you need to send negative or persuasive information, however, you usually choose to communicate indirectly, because that way your audience is more likely to accept the information and ultimately do what you want.

Becoming a good business communicator takes practice, but it's worth the trouble to know you have improved your chances of getting your point across and convincing people to take action in the way you recommend. We first cover planning and *writing* good business communication, because you can apply these same skills to preparing effective *oral* presentations. ●

Milo Turner
Assistant Manager of
Engineering

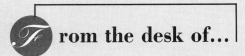

From the desk of...

The Million-Dollar Communication Problem

I work for an automotive parts company that lets each employee act as expert on his or her own job. We had a terrible communication problem on a software development project because the engineers and the management information systems people didn't communicate their needs about a large project.

The engineering department was unstructured and individual oriented, in the company style, and MIS was very rigid and tried to control information. Instead of working together to meet a tight deadline, members of the two departments actually stopped speaking. The software developer was *very* detail oriented and took way too long to develop a perfect system to automate custom parts production. As a result, our firm incurred millions of dollars in penalties and was even written up in trade publications when our client's plant opened late because of our communication problem.

This incident is an extreme example of what can happen when people can't or don't communicate at work. It also shows that different organizations value different styles of communicating, but certain communication basics are fundamental to all business communication.

COMMUNICATING AS PART OF A BUSINESS

Most of the *academic* writing you have done has probably been to an audience of one—an instructor. This audience used your writing, whether an essay test, term paper, or report, mostly to evaluate your work for a grade, since you were writing about something on which the audience was an expert. You may also have been judged on your creativity. As a result, you may have some negative feelings about these kinds of academic writing. So you probably will be glad to know that the business writing you do will be easier to do well.

Business communication, whether written or spoken, has some typical characteristics:

- It is written for an audience who will find the information useful rather than simply entertaining.
- It is written under time and money constraints. (According to the Dartnell Institute of Business Research, a letter dictated to a person costs nearly $11.00 to produce and a letter dictated to a machine costs about $8.50. Computer-produced letters are less expensive if they run several pages long.)
- It often has more than one purpose (for example, to refuse a request but retain the requester as a potential customer). Goodwill is an important aspect of most business communication.
- Its tone and attitude toward the reader are as important as the actual words used or the information conveyed.

Effective business communication fosters goodwill, develops good public relations, and convinces your audience to take the action you recommend. Because most people tend to return to businesses where they are treated well, companies need to ensure that their business communications—whether from salespeople, phone receptionists, or letter writers—treat customers well.

For most business communication, the bottom line is helping your business make money. A business can save money by using the most efficient and effective strategies to produce business messages successfully the first time around. (As Peter Drucker has pointed out, doing something *efficiently* is doing it right, but doing it *effectively* is doing it well.) One positive approach to improving business communication is paying attention to your audience.

Audience Analysis

A business audience (readers or listeners) for your letter, memo, report, or presentation can be a boss, a peer manager in another department, subordinates, laypeople, clients, or readers of annual reports. These people range from those who know a great deal about your topic to those who may be hearing of it for the first time.

While your listeners can let you know as you speak whether they understand your ideas, your readers may not tell you you've lost them. In both cases, it's better to be clear the first time than to have to repeat yourself in different words or send another memo clearing up the misunderstanding.

Checklist 1–1 on page 6 offers suggestions to help you analyze your audience so that you can provide them with the most useful information.

Analyzing your audience ahead of time will help you remember to

- *Translate* technical terms for nonbusiness audiences.
- *Adjust* the amount and tone of information for different audiences— bosses, peers, subordinates.

Of course, you should analyze your audience before you speak as well as before you write. Audience analysis for speaking also requires that you find out the physical characteristics of the place where you'll be speaking (size, noise level, availability of microphone, other speakers, audiovisual capability, etc.). Audience analysis is definitely one of the basics of business communication.

The "You" Attitude

One reason for analyzing your audience is to help you plan your message to make the audience members feel as though they are the center of attention. You can do this by using a "you" attitude. A **"you" attitude** means writing as much as possible from the other person's point of view. What is your reader interested in? If the reader has asked you a question, he or she is interested in the answer. If contemplating buying your services, the reader wants to know what you offer that's useful to him or her. Give the reader the information wanted; don't delay with extra words or use business jargon the reader won't understand.

Think in terms of how your reader will benefit by agreeing with you or from doing what you ask. Notice how the friendly tone of the memo in Exhibit 1–1 (on page 7), sent via electronic mail by the editor of a company newsletter, takes the reader's time and interest into account (and succeeds in getting the writer's questionnaire answered!). Had the editor not used a "you" attitude, the action desired might seem like too much work. Notice too that the writer avoids beginning the memo with a seeming threat (if you submit items to the newsletter, you're responsible for all sorts of future projects dealing with the newsletter). Also, the writer avoids using clichés like "your cooperation is greatly appreciated" that could distance the writer from the reader through both the hackneyed language and the passive-voice verb. Think of the image your writing creates about you!

Who is your audience? How many people? What is their education level? What is their background in your topic? What kinds and levels of jobs do they hold? The corporate culture will affect tone, word choice, and even format. If your audience is large and consists of potential customers for a product, you'll need to be clear and focused on selling points that may appeal to many people.

What information do they already have? Don't tell something your audience already knows (for example, a consultant telling a client how large the client's company is).

How much information do they need? We all have a tendency to give more details than necessary. Do you really need to start at the beginning and describe every step? Should you begin with the main point and then describe in less detail how you got there?

What technical information (such as accounting terms, computer jargon, financial ratios) do they understand? For example, if your client has hired you to provide computer assistance, he or she needs to understand what you are talking about. Resist the urge to impress with your knowledge of the jargon of the field. Use common words and explain any technical terms you need to use.

What is their attitude toward your information? If your audience is likely to agree with you or expect the information, you'll know to be direct and get right to the point. If your message is negative or unexpected, you'll need to approach your audience less directly. (We'll discuss communication strategies later in this chapter.)

What is your relationship to your audience? Of course, you will write differently to your boss than to your subordinates, and to a manager at the same level in yet another way. Answering the earlier questions will help you see why. Your boss may need to see the big picture, your subordinates may need details to be able to take action, and your peer manager may need to know how to set up a similar project in her or his department.

Business communications often carry significant power and political meaning far beyond the content. Later examples will show you how writing to people in different work ranks differs in content *and* in tone.

What action do you want your audience to take as a result of your message? Knowing this will help you focus and organize your message to get the action you desire. For example, in writing a letter to accompany your résumé, the action you want is usually an interview, since it's not likely that you'll be offered a job on the strength of even the best-written letter.

Consider whether the following letter opening sounds like one person talking to another:

> Thank you for the courtesies you extended to me recently while we discussed the transfer of the above-referenced business to Arkansas.

Is this opening thoughtful? Is it personal? Does it sound like the people have actually met each other? Did one do a favor for the other? We'll look at the specifics of this business relationship as we discuss *audience analysis*. (Because this is an example of a poorly done letter, we'll show you only the text, omitting names and addresses.)

What courtesies?

> Thank you for the courtesies you extended to me recently while we discussed the transfer of the above-referenced business to Arkansas. I have enclosed for your review and execution, the following documents:
>
> Document 1
>
> Document 2

No letterhead—
this is E-mail

February 15, 1993
To: @KUDO.DIS
From: GENVAX::HRRVM
Subject: MAGIC BULLETIN INFORMATION GATHERING

Tells reader
why he/she
received
message

Because you've submitted kudos to the Magic Bulletin over
the last few months, your input is valuable to me in
deciding if we should change that section of the
newsletter.

Tells what
action to take

I've compiled a short survey to get the needed information,
but I'd appreciate any other comments you have. This E-
mail survey seemed the easiest way to find out what you
think without taking up too much of your time.

Makes the
action easy

To help improve the company newsletter, please send me your
responses by Monday, February 22. You can send them in by
VAX or mail (06). I appreciate your help!

(Questionnaire followed: 20 of 27 employees answered it,
for a response rate of 74%.)

Kindly execute all of the enclosed documents and return them to me in the enclosed self-addressed and stamped envelope.

If you have any questions, please do not hesitate to contact me.

Now let's review the audience analysis questions in Checklist 1—1 to see where the writer made some ineffective decisions.

Who is your audience?   In this case, the audience is an officer of a corporation that has moved to another state. The corporation is an association; the officer has been called and told to expect the papers to be signed.

What information do they already have?   The reader knows that she or he needs to sign some legal papers to approve the transfer.

How much information do they need?   Since the move has taken place, all the reader needs to know is what and where to sign.

What technical information do they understand?   Certainly anyone can understand "legalese" if he or she wants to. However, artificial language such as this doesn't endear the writer to the reader. Here the overly formal language makes a simple request seem almost silly. Apparently the "courtesies extended" to the writer were a phone call asking where the papers to be signed should be sent. (The phrase sounds as though the two people had tea in the reader's office or that the reader provided the writer with a courtesy car.)

Once the reader feels talked *at* rather than talked *to,* later sections of the letter sound even sillier. "Kindly execute all of the enclosed documents" conveys an image of a firing squad! (*Execute* is a common legal term, however.)

The last paragraph includes two business clichés to avoid. "If you have any questions" implies that the writer hasn't answered *anything* yet. If your reader may have *further* questions, word the request "If you have questions" or "If you have further questions" to show that you think you have answered the earlier questions. If you believe you've covered your topic completely, you can omit any reference to questions. If your reader has a question, he or she surely will ask it.

The second cliché in the last paragraph is "do not hesitate to ask." It is friendlier to say, "please ask." "Do not hesitate" sounds neither conversational nor friendly.

Taking the audience's attitude, the relationship between writer and reader, and the desired action into account, look at this improved version of this simple letter:

Here are the documents we discussed in last week's phone call:

Document 1

Document 2

Please sign both at the X mark and return them to me in the enclosed envelope.
Please call me if you have questions; I look forward to working with you again.

This revised letter certainly is shorter and clearer than the original. Additional advantages include the elimination of the comma in the first paragraph (there is no need for a pause and a comma after *execution*), the misnamed "self-addressed" envelope (printed, no doubt, and probably addressed to the law firm, not to the recipient), and the cliché at the end ("do not hesitate to"). The

Chapter One

added reference to future work in the revised version is good business; you can't build a client base if you do just one job for each client. Finally, the revised letter is friendly and helpful.

Business audiences range in size from one (a letter to a customer answering a product question) to many (a letter to the board of directors of a company, a dues notice to the members of a club), and you will need to plan accordingly. Often you will have multiple audiences: an interview plan written for a human resources department and sent to a college recruiting office to help its staff prepare students for job interviews; a project request that needs to be approved by both the CEO and the comptroller; a report sent to a number of clients that needs an accompanying personalized letter.

    Using the audience analysis questions in Checklist 1–1, you can tailor your message to multiple as well as single audiences. Of course, the easiest audience to write for is the single-person audience, because you can obtain more specific information about that person's needs and desires. Frequently, however, your audiences will be broader, and you will need to tailor your messages to them as specifically as you can under the circumstances.

Multiple Audiences

On larger projects, you may even have multiple writers. Perhaps a team will work on a client proposal, and members will share their writing via computer groupware or networking programs. This text, for example, was written by two people who live more than 100 miles apart. We shared hard copies, disks, and faxes (and meetings and phone calls, of course) to produce the final work.

    Obviously *organization* is critical to a team project, because you don't want to have parts that overlap or that fail to provide necessary information.

    Consistency is also important, for you want your audience to be more aware of your ideas than of different writing styles in the various parts of the report or proposal. The revision checklist on page 24 includes a section on consistency in group writing projects.

    If your writing partners are from a different division, be sure that your disks are compatible in format—you don't want to send a disk that someone else can't use (or receive one that you can't use)! Word processing software versions, fonts, margins, and many other details can be specified on a style sheet for your group document or report.

    In June 1991, *Popular Science* reported on a software product called Corporate Voice, a style replicator that analyzes a text's adherence to a predetermined style model.[1] You can put several of your best documents on the disk and build a style format much as you would on a style sheet, choosing word length, number of words per sentence, number of trade words, percentage of uncommon words, and so on. The program comes with some style models built in (from newspaper writing to Tom Clancy) and highlights problem areas so that you can make revisions to achieve a more uniform document.

Multiple Writers

If your company does business in other countries, you'll need to add questions to the audience analysis list. Although you will probably still write in English, you'll need to write in a style appropriate for your expanded audience. Pre-

Globalization of Communication

---

[1]"Writing in Style," *Popular Science,* June 1991, pp. 37–38.

EXHIBIT 1-2 A Communication Model

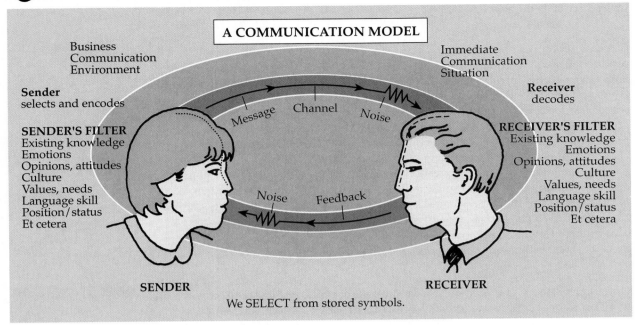

A COMMUNICATION MODEL

Business Communication Environment

Immediate Communication Situation

Sender selects and encodes

Receiver decodes

SENDER'S FILTER
Existing knowledge
Emotions
Opinions, attitudes
Culture
Values, needs
Language skill
Position/status
Et cetera

RECEIVER'S FILTER
Existing knowledge
Emotions
Opinions, attitudes
Culture
Values, needs
Language skill
Position/status
Et cetera

Message Channel Noise

Noise Feedback

SENDER **RECEIVER**

We SELECT from stored symbols.

dictably, people of different cultures write in different ways. For example, Japanese business writers tend to be less direct than those in the United States, and German writers are more formal but more direct.

If you are in this position, read all you can about corporate culture in other countries rather than relying on stereotypes. Two good sources of information are David Victor, *International Business Communication* (Harper Collins, 1992), and Robert Grosse and Duane Kujawa, *International Business: Theory and Managerial Applications,* second edition (Richard D. Irwin 1992).

After audience analysis, the second basic of business communication is understanding a *communication model.*

A COMMUNICATION MODEL

People in business send messages to get some particular kind of response. You will create better business messages if you keep in mind what you want the reader to do after reading your message. You also need to be aware of how the communication process works. As you know from experience, communication does not always take place in the way you expect.

Think of the communication process as a cycle, or loop. (Some kinds of communication are a series of cycles.) As you examine the communication model in Exhibit 1 – 2, you'll be asked to look closely at elements that influence human communication. As you will see, many barriers to successful communication exist.

Two basic elements are necessary before any communication transaction can take place: a sender and a receiver.

Sender, Receiver, and Situation

A **sender** (writer, speaker, E-mail user, etc.) puts a message together and sends the message through a communication channel to a **receiver** (reader, listener) within a business environment. Elements outside the firm, elements specific to the firm, and elements specific to the immediate situation and the two individuals communicating can influence the symbols the sender chooses and how she or he puts them together.

Outside influences include such elements as business competition and the business language of the country. Elements specific to the firm include a corporate writing manual and availability of channels of communication such as E-mail. Elements specific to the individuals and the situation include how well the two people know each other, how their jobs are related by rank, and how much background information on the topic they have already exchanged.

The **channel**—the means by which the message is transmitted—can be a telephone system, television coverage for a speech or news report, an electronic mail system, a written report, a terse handwritten memo, or even the open air in which people communicate in person. A sender chooses a channel based on where and how large the audience is, how quickly the message needs to be received and acted on, how permanent and how formal the message needs to be, and how convenient and how costly the channel is.

Channel

Feedback—the response or lack of it—can be "Mm-hmm," a nod, a criticism, a supportive phone call, new information, a laugh, a commendation six weeks later, or frozen silence instead of the return message the sender expected. Feedback can also be many other possible responses. If the feedback is what the sender hoped for, the communication has succeeded. For a successful communication, the sender must consider carefully the elements shown in Exhibit 1–2.

Feedback

The **filter** is the total of the communicator's experiences leading up to the communication. The filter consists of existing knowledge, emotions (both permanent and transitory), attitudes, cultural background, values, needs, language skill, position or status, self-knowledge, perceptiveness, intelligence, keenness of senses, and many other factors.

Filter

Calvin and **Hobbes**   by Bill Watterson

Words that have more than one meaning can easily create an unintended communication barrier. Using Hobbes's definition of *peck* certainly doesn't help Calvin understand his math problem, because he is talking about an entirely different word meaning even though the word itself certainly looks the same. The two characters have different *filters*.

Basics of Business Communication |

The filter changes or colors whatever passes through it to and from the communicator's mind. The sender has a unique filter; the receiver has a different and also unique filter. The message must pass through both filters successfully. Because individuals are unique, no message is ever received exactly as sent. If both sender and receiver are careful and attentive, however, distortions will be minimal. The message will be transmitted accurately enough to accomplish its purpose. If you think about the receiver's filter and ways it might match your own, you will tend to make more accurate assumptions about the receiver.

Other communication barriers related to people's unique filters are cultural background, language, and education; listening habits; and thinking habits that may keep people from accepting new ideas easily, such as prejudices or a tendency to see ideas as "either/or" (the last problem is called *polarization*).

Still another potential barrier to communication is a company's corporate culture. Some companies have policies that make communication among different levels of employees easy; other companies' policies are much more structured and formal.

Noise

Another barrier to communication is referred to as **noise**—anything that interferes with the free flow of information between the sender and the receiver. Noise can occur in a literal sense, such as a jackhammer digging up a parking lot outside or the static created when an electrical storm interferes with a radio or television broadcast.

Noise also refers to *interpersonal* and *intrapersonal* barriers to communication. If either the sender or the receiver is feeling sick or distracted, any resulting weakness or inaccuracy in what is sent or received is categorized as noise. Noise also occurs if the receiver is so displeased with the sender's nonverbal cues that he or she misperceives or blocks out the message. Another example is a telephone call that comes at a busy time, when the receiver may be unable to devote full attention to it.

Encoding and Decoding

Communicating through language means *decoding* the symbols contained in words, nonverbal signals, and facial expressions. From birth, and perhaps even before, you began learning and storing symbols for communication. The earliest symbols probably were nonverbal signals you heard and felt. A little later you took in meaningful symbols, both verbal and nonverbal, by sight. By age four you could use several thousand words, interpret many kinds of nonverbal messages, and put on convincing smiles and scowls yourself.

When you became an active reader, your repertoire of symbols grew to perhaps 75,000 words or more. As you watched your family and friends, television and movies, and the daily activities of various people, you kept adding to the symbols stored in your brain. You stored the meanings of different tones of voice, posture, gestures, facial expressions, and many other symbols in addition to words.

Your rich storehouse of symbols enables you to *encode* a message in many different ways. As you do so, you make many tiny, instantaneous decisions as you select from this storehouse and put the message together. Most of the decisions are automatic. Yet one small wrong signal can confuse or annoy a receiver. When the receiver's filter and your filter do not perceive the symbol the same way, what you try to encode may not be what he or she decodes.

Almost anything written or spoken can be misunderstood by a person who reads or hears the words differently than the writer or speaker intended.

One coding problem arises because words have both a *denotation* (dictionary meaning) and a *connotation* (the meaning people attach to the word). When a businessperson writes to a customer, "You claim that the entertainment center was scratched when you received it," the customer may conclude that he or she is not believed; *claim* implies, "You say this, but I don't believe it." If the writer meant to imply only that the reader had submitted evidence of damage, a less emotion-laden message would be "You have written us that the entertainment center was scratched when you received it."

Another problem with encoding a message is *cognitive dissonance*. Suppose your supervisor says, "Of course I have time to talk to you about your project," but uses nonverbal signals such as standing up from her desk, looking at her watch, or folding her arms—all signals that say to you, "I'm not open to talking about this now." Receiving two sets of conflicting signals creates cognitive dissonance and makes decoding the actual message difficult.

Successful communicators continuously increase the contents of their storehouses of symbols. Doing so permits them to communicate successfully with more kinds of people in more kinds of situations. For a specific communication, they choose from their stored symbols based on how the intended receivers will understand and react to the symbols selected. To succeed in business, you need to learn about how people who are different from yourself communicate.

As mentioned earlier, *cultural differences* may create communication barriers. As each new wave of immigrants arrived in the United States, the newcomers brought with them a different set of verbal and nonverbal symbols and a different set of attitudes and values. To be sure, the most basic human values are the same, but communicators are constantly surprised by the many things that *are* different.

Nonverbal symbols, such as ways of signaling respect or friendliness, may differ. For instance, the length of time it is acceptable for a person to look directly into another person's eyes differs greatly from culture to culture. Violating this rule can seriously offend.

Verbal symbols can be mystifying. Whereas long-time residents may know fifteen or twenty words for a particular item, the newcomer may know only one. For instance, consider the many types of bread you can buy and the potential confusion experienced by a newcomer who is asked, "How about sourdough?" especially if he or she has heard both *bread* and *dough* used as slang terms for *money.*

Cultural Differences

Basics of Business Communication

Stock Imagery/The Slide File

Intercultural communication offers possibilities for miscommunication between people with different verbal cultures.

Learning the proper words and verb endings in a language is only part of being able to communicate in that language. For example, a young Air Force lieutenant was sent to Russian-language training. After a tough year of intensive daily drill, he and his classmates asked the instructor, "So do we speak as well as Russians now?" "Yes," the instructor replied, "as well as five-year-old Russians. But you don't hold your faces right." Long years of experience with a language build our storehouses of symbols, which go beyond words.

We can tell when someone is speaking a foreign language in our presence. We *know* we are not understanding. When newcomers to the United States speak *some* English, however, we are likely to make mistaken assumptions about how much of our symbol set they know. Therefore, it's important to check for understanding if follow-up is required.

Now that you have seen some of the issues involved in communicating, let's look at **strategies** you can use to communicate different kinds of information most effectively.

STRATEGIES FOR EFFECTIVE COMMUNICATION

How you present material to your reader largely depends on what kind of material you have and how the reader will react to it. In many business situations, you will send positive, expected, or neutral information to your reader and thus can begin directly. If you are sending unexpected, negative, or persuasive information, you will be better off presenting it indirectly to prepare the reader for the information.

Most of the time, *put your main idea up front.* Then provide supporting details so the reader gets the full picture.

On the other hand, don't give *all* the details or provide them in chronological order. *Give the reader enough information to understand the issue, but not too much information.* It's easy to talk about what we know, but remember that your reader may not need to know all that information, all those examples, or all the steps you went through to get the information.

Concentrate on one or two subjects. Most people can't remember more than two or three things at once. If you have to send a great deal of information or background material, *consider using a cover letter or a memo* attached to a report on the topic.

Use emphasis and subordination of ideas to guide your reader. Strong ideas use active voice, are placed in emphatic positions, take up more space, and get emphasis through headings, lists, and other layout features. Less important ideas might be presented in passive voice in the middles of paragraphs.

Explain terms your reader may be unfamiliar with, whether an accounting term to a client or a computer term to your boss. If you must use many unfamiliar terms in a report, you might consider including a glossary. If you will use only a few technical terms, simply explain them, perhaps parenthetically, the first time each is used.

Use examples to explain. Think of how good textbooks first discuss a general principle and then use an example to show how it applies in real life. Think *show,* rather than *tell.* One reason *Reader's Digest* is so successful is that it uses stories to explain things rather than lots of dry discussion.

One overriding idea to keep in mind is: *What do I want the reader to do with this information?* What action do I want him or her to take? That way, you'll focus your message on the main idea you want to get across. In an audit report, for example, you will concentrate on the things you want the reader to do to improve operations rather than on the things the company hasn't done correctly so far.

To help your reader follow your meaning, use conventional thought patterns to shape your ideas. Successful writers and speakers have used these patterns for 2,500 years—since the Greeks wrote down the patterns communicators used in order to be most completely understood by their audiences.

Here are the most common business patterns:

Chronological: Arranges information according to time order, or reverse chronology, as in a résumé's list of jobs you have held beginning with the most recent.

Geographic: Arranges information by place, such as when you describe locations of your offices or site selection for a new plant.

Description: Tells what something looks like, feels like, and so on.

Analysis: Breaks something into its parts and discusses them, drawing conclusions.

Cause-effect: Establishes reasons for or results of something.

Definition: Explains what something is.

Classification: Groups similar things together.

Illustration by example: Provides specifics that make abstract ideas more understandable and memorable.

Narration: Tells the *what, where,* and *to whom,* as in case histories.

Process: Tells how something is done, as in a manual.

In choosing your examples, you may explain something through *comparison* (similarities) or *contrast* (differences) or through a longer *analogy* (comparing situations or things similar in some respects to better explain the unknown item).

In addition to these internal methods of organizing information, some overall organizing strategies will help you get information across to your audi-

Internal Structural Patterns

ence. Chapter 2 will discuss *direct messages* in detail; Chapters 10 and 11 will discuss indirect messages. Following is a brief discussion of how these two basic approaches differ.

Direct Messages

When you are sending information, asking for information, writing routine, repetitive messages or forms, sending transmittals, or giving instructions, you can most easily do so directly (sometimes called *deductively*). *Deductive,* or *direct, structure* allows you to begin with your main point and then provide supporting data, arguments, or information. As you will learn in more detail in Chapter 2, you can start with the most important piece of information, fill in the details, and close quickly with an action request or other appropriate ending.

DIRECT MESSAGE OUTLINE
Begin with something important to the reader.
Present the relevant details.
End with a request for action or a pleasant closing.

Exhibit 1–3 shows a memo recommending the purchase of a robot to deliver medications to nursing stations. As you can see, the writer comes directly to the point. He enumerates the advantages of using a robotic courier. The complete memo continues for two more pages, describing the maintenance of a robot, the expense of one robot compared to that of a human employee, and the time savings in using a robotic courier. It concludes with a list of recommendations to get the purchase under way quickly so that the hospital can begin taking advantage of this technology.

Indirect Messages

Chapters 10 and 11 discuss indirect messages in detail. You need to know that sending negative or persuasive messages is best done indirectly, or *inductively. Inductive,* or *indirect, structure* allows you to build your argument before revealing your conclusion. This is a good way to deal with information that may displease or startle your reader.

If you are turning down a request, you can soften the blow by easing into the information.

If you are asking someone to do something for you that the reader hasn't anticipated, lead up to the request with some information on what the reader will get out of it—a reader benefit. Otherwise, your reader may quickly think of reasons *not* to do what you ask.

INDIRECT MESSAGE OUTLINE
Begin with a buffer to set up the situation.
Explain the problem.
Embed the negative.
Get the necessary action.
End on a positive note.

The letter in Exhibit 1–4 stresses the positive solution over the problem and shows concern for the reader's needs and feelings. Clearly the writer can't promise that this oversight won't ever occur again, but she doesn't hide behind the large size of the company as an excuse. At least the reader will feel assured that someone has paid attention to his problem.

After learning how to analyze your audience, use a communication model, and choose a strategy for communicating your message, the next step is actually writing a business message.

Houston College of
Osteopathic Medicine

March 23, 1993
TO: Patricia Aldrich, Director of Pharmacy Services
FROM: Leonard Leon
SUBJECT: PURCHASE OF A "HELPMATE" ROBOTIC COURIER

Puts information in context for reader

After yesterday's site visit to Bergen Community Hospital, I agree that we should purchase a Helpmate robotic courier to deliver medications to the nursing units.

The robot is a dependable transporter of medications that:

Focuses on advantages to reader through itemizing

--doesn't take breaks, vacation, or sick days.

--can carry 100 pounds.

--can reach every nursing station in the hospital, and can operate its own elevator.

499 City Avenue
Houston, TX 77251
713 • 572•1180

July 2, 1993

Mr. Jaime Ortiz
1176 May Street
Newport, Rhode Island

Dear Mr. Ortiz:

Buffer

I certainly agree that you should have received the special
diet meal you had requested onboard your recent flight.

*Explanation of
how oversight
happened*

I have sent your letter to the assistant Vice President,
Inflight, who monitors this program closely to ensure
proper communication between the reservation for a special
meal and the implementation through catering. We
appreciate your help in letting us know that our system
doesn't always function as it should.

*Pleasant
looking-forward
ending*

We pride ourselves on our service to our patrons; we know
you chose to fly our airline over other carriers and look
forward to seeing you again soon.

Sincerely,

Janet Orcholski

Janet Orcholski
Customer Service Manager

4312 West 8th Street
Memphis, TN 54903
901 361 4700

While writing produces a *product* (letter, memo, report, speech outline), writing is a *process.* For this reason, it isn't just one step—writing is a *series* of steps. If you follow these steps, you will produce effective work more quickly and easily.

To use your writing time most efficiently, you need to divide your time into planning, writing a rough draft, and revising approximately as follows:

Planning your message: 40 percent of your time.

Writing a rough draft: 20 percent of your time.

Revising your message: 40 percent of your time.

Because you will *save* time by *spending* time planning, this method will help you produce effective written work quickly. Many technical experts have difficulty getting words down—they hesitate to make a mistake on a clean sheet of paper! If you jot down some ideas first and then write a quick rough draft, you can spend more time revising the message to make it most effective for your intended audience.

As you learned earlier in this chapter, planning a message for your intended audience is a major part of your planning process. Another planning aspect—one that's a bit harder than it looks—is deciding on your message's purpose.

Are you conveying information? Asking for action? Stating negative findings, such as in an accounting audit? Trying to persuade someone to speak at a meeting of your professional organization?

Many business messages have more than one purpose. You might think your purpose is to inform a recent college graduate that you've hired someone else, but even that message has the underlying purpose of giving the bad news nicely enough that the person will think well of your firm if he or she does business with you in the future. Even an audit report isn't just a list of negative findings. Your other purpose is to recommend better procedures *and* convince the client to use your recommendations.

For even the simplest memo, you'll need to gather information before you begin writing. If you are inviting people to a meeting, you need to know that the conference room is available, that the head of the marketing group can be there to present the new product plan, and that the desktop publishing staff will have the slides and handouts ready for you.

For a typical client letter, you might need to get the client's file to review previous correspondence, locate a similar proposal done the year before for a different client, and talk to the salesperson who has been working with this client.

As you'll learn in Chapters 5 and 6, business research can involve library research, interviews, questionnaires, and possibly even experimentation. For routine short messages such as letters and memos, you'll probably be able to get the information you need in house.

Chapters 2, 10, and 11 will give you more information about organizing your message for impact depending on the kind of information you need to convey. The strategies discussed earlier show that you should be direct when giving information and requesting positive action and indirect when conveying negative and persuasive messages.

THE WRITING PROCESS

Plan Your Message

Analyze Your Audience

Identify Your Purpose

Gather Information

Plan Organization, Emphasis, and "You" Attitude

As you plan, you can decide what information to put first, how much information you need to include, whether you need to include graphics or add attachments, and how to get the reader to take the appropriate action.

By controlling your *emphasis* (What do you spend the most time or words on? Which ideas are placed first and which last? What do headings and lists emphasize?), you can control what the reader or listener perceives as important. In a direct message, put the most important idea first. Beginnings and endings of paragraphs, sentences, and even whole letters and memos are emphatic positions. Chapter 3 discusses emphasis in detail. Other easy ways to make ideas stand out are to

- Use headings and lists.
- Underline.
- Use all capital letters, as in headings.
- Discuss the idea more fully (take up more space).

In addition to writing from the reader's point of view instead of the writer's, one way to help achieve a "you" attitude is to use *active-voice* verbs—verbs in which the subject controls the action of the verb. Using active-voice verbs helps involve the reader in your message; you can insert pronouns into your text with the active verbs and make it more "you" oriented too. *Passive-voice* verbs, in which the subject receives the action but the performer of the action is not specified, are used to downplay mistakes or negative material and to be more considerate of the reader's feelings.

For example, you would use active voice in the recommendations sections of an audit report and passive voice for describing the negative findings.

Finding: We found the guest checks *had not been tallied* weekly for the accounting report. (Passive voice does not indicate who made the mistake.)

Recommendation: We recommend that the night clerk *tally* guest checks at least twice a week to be ready for the Friday report. (Active voice forces the writer to say who will take the action.)

Similarly, you would use active voice for selling a product and passive voice for explaining why an item must be repaired.

Selling: You can produce professional-quality color graphics for your client reports as well as crisp black-and-white text with just this one Megagraphics 2 printer. (Active voice helps the writer show the reader using the product.)

Repairing: The watch back *had been pried off* with something other than the proper tool, causing the waterproof casing to leak. Our service department *can repair* the seal for the small fee of $12.95, making the watch swimproof once again. (Passive voice avoids blaming anyone specific; active voice stresses positive action.)

Passive voice can be used successfully to avoid blaming, such as when a customer returns a product damaged by customer negligence or ignorance. As a customer, would you rather read this:

Upon inspection, we found that you had taken the motor apart, something you were warned in the instruction manual not to do.

or this:

> Upon inspection, we found that the motor had been taken apart, which the instruction manual warns should not be done.

In either case you know *who* took the motor apart, but the first version blames whereas the second one merely points out factual information. The latter is a kinder way to get appropriate action, in this case the customer's willingness to pay for repairs instead of returning a "defective" product. Because passive voice is neither personal nor emphatic, it is effective for downplaying or subordinating ideas.

Active voice, on the other hand, gets people directly involved. Passive voice always contains a form of *be* (*was, were, are, have been,* etc.) and in some cases may be less effective. Look at this example:

> Your support for Mount Hamilton Observatory in the past year *has been greatly appreciated.*

How sincere does passive voice sound when expressing appreciation for something? It sounds pretty distant, as though the writer were in an ivory tower looking down at the reader—not the impression a fund-raising group wants to convey! Here is a better way to say it:

> *We appreciate* your support of the Mount Hamilton Observatory.

or

> Your support of the Mount Hamilton Observatory *has enabled* us to build a new astronomers' dormitory this year.

These versions of the message get people "talking to" people. Of course, the letter would continue with specifics about how the support is helping the observatory staff purchase a 100-inch telescope and offer Summer Star Parties for visitors.

Now that you have planned how to approach your audience to achieve your purpose, gathered the needed information, and organized your message for impact, write a *quick* rough draft of your message. It's important to write quickly for two reasons. First, your writing will sound more as if you are talking, giving a human tone to your "paper personality." Second, you won't get bogged down in details like spelling and punctuation but can concentrate on your message instead.

Your *paper personality* is how you sound on paper—in a letter, memo, or report. Many of the people who get letters and memos from you may not know you personally yet. Make sure that your paper personality sounds like one they would like to get to know!

To achieve a conversational style, you should write your rough draft quickly, without stopping to think about questions of grammar, spelling, or anything else that could slow you down. Imagine that you're explaining something by talking to whoever your audience is, because this will make your writing sound like a real person rather than stuffy or formal.

You can sound pompous if you use overly long words. Likewise, you'll waste your audience's time if you use wordy phrases and unnecessary words, or confuse your reader if you use involved noun phrases instead of powerful

Write a Quick Rough Draft

verbs. Chapter 3 discusses these style points in more detail. The general rule is to choose everyday words and use as few words as possible to get your ideas across.

Consider this example:

I hope that you will renew your membership, share in these programs, and support the important research and educational work at Mount Hamilton Observatory.

Would this weak-sounding message persuade you to renew your membership? Probably not! *I hope* sounds as if the writer doesn't even believe in the cause. The reasons given are so vague that the reader isn't motivated to act.

Similarly, would you go on reading this report?

This report is a summary of information compiled in an attempt to obtain a better understanding of multimedia.

Probably not! The writer sounds neither knowledgeable nor confident and again is so vague that it's difficult for a reader to get interested.

Fortunately, the hackneyed language in the following examples is becoming less common as communicators think more about their audiences and less about their own images:

We have your letter of December 8 and are indeed grateful for your reply.

(Why not answer the question asked in the letter and get to the point?)

This is to inform you that your application has achieved a positive result.

(Wouldn't you rather hear, "Congratulations! The job is yours"?)

Recently you received a brochure from the U.S. Postal Service concerning the coming of automated sortation and the need for proper address hygiene.

(As discussed by William Safire in an "On Language" column, what the USPS apparently meant was *automatic sorting* and use of ZIP codes.[2] Who knows why the writer chose the unlikely word *hygiene* to refer to this process? The result is confusion for the reader and probably a good laugh at the government—which wasn't the intended effect.)

Here is another example in which confusing syntax needs editing, a common problem in informal spoken communication:

My goal is an America where something or anything that is done to or for anyone is done neither because of nor in spite of any difference between them, racially, religiously, or ethnic-origin-wise.[3]

This example from a form letter sent to doctors ends up not saying what its writer intended:

Statistics show that ischemic heart disease claims over 1,000 lives each day—more lives than handguns claim in an entire year. Tragically, a significant number of these deaths may be preventable.

(Since when is it tragic for doctors to prevent disease?)

[2]William Safire, "On Language," *San Diego Union,* June 9, 1991, p. D12.

[3]Ronald Reagan, quoted in *Parade,* April 21, 1985.

The next example could confuse the regulator with the abuser (have the candidates or Garza's committee committed the abuse?):

> Candidates can, and have been, disqualified from the election if found guilty of campaign abuses by Garza and her committee.

Watch your writing for this kind of unintentional humor (the house must be huge!):

> Property on the market includes Hoover's $2.1 million Virginia house, a Washington home occupied by his estranged wife and several condominiums.

One way to gain and keep clients is to sound helpful, sincere, and clear in your written communications. A good paper personality will sound like someone people can work with easily. One of your jobs is to *translate* the technical information you are an expert in so that a customer can understand and use it.

Revision is the step in the writing process where you can get down to details. In your academic career, this is the step where you corrected punctuation and spelling and looked for other mistakes (or your teacher marked mistakes and you made the corrections). However, you will save time (and money) in the long run by first looking at the *big picture:* Have you met your planning goals related to audience, purpose, and organization? Is all the information covered? Is the message clear?

Then consider the *"you" attitude:* Have you put the reader first? Is your style appropriate for that reader? (You won't use the same style for your staff, your boss, and a client.)

Look at your *paper personality:* Do you sound stuffy? Use clichés? Too many words? The wrong words? Does your style sound like a person? Did you write conversationally? Is your style inconspicuous or does it distract from your message?

Did you design your layout for easy readability? Do you have enough or need more white space? Headings? Graphics? Attachments? Is there a clear progression of ideas?

To avoid distracting your audience from your message, strive for error-free writing: Proofread both manually and with computer software, checking for spelling; punctuation, especially apostrophes, semicolons, and commas; and agreement of subjects and verbs, nouns and pronouns. Checklist 1–2 details the steps in the revision process. It will help you prepare effective pieces of communication, and you will use it throughout this book.

Revise from the Top Down

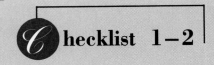

Checklist 1-2

Revising from the Top Down

First, Look at the Big Picture

Analysis Did you:

- Examine enough data to find all the relevant evidence?
- Draw appropriate conclusions from your data?
- Qualify any not-quite-proven assertions?
- Identify your assumptions?

Conviction Did you:

- Aim your argument at a decision maker's action?
- Use indirect strategy and passive voice to handle negative or questionable findings?
- Remain unbiased and base your argument on facts only?

Completeness Check for:

- Details of dates, times, numbers
- Spelling and inclusion of names, addresses
- Enough information to act on

Look for Appropriate Order and Emphasis
Audience analysis? Motivational?

Check Your Format and Layout Choices

- Sentences average 16–17 words?
- Paragraphs 6–8 typed lines?
- Beginning and ending paragraphs 4 typed lines?
- Lists itemized?
- Important items set off by placement or space?
- Emphasis on the important points?

Then You Can Check for Details

Language Choices Jargon? Technical terms? Big words? Too many words? Strong verbs?

Tone Appropriate for the reader, whether boss, peer, subordinate, or client? Good paper personality?

Mechanics

- Word choice (diction)
- Active and passive voice
- Verb tenses
- Agreement—subject/verb, noun/pronoun
- Possessives
- Punctuation
- Placement of phrases
- Complete sentences

Consistency Use a style sheet to attain consistent headings and spacing in team writing.

REVIEW

This chapter introduced you to a number of basic ideas about business communication. Communicating successfully in business will help you get promoted, obtain and retain clients and customers, and—most important—get your ideas across efficiently.

You can become a better communicator by

1. *Analyzing your audience*

   - How many readers or listeners will you have?
   - Are you writing to a global audience?
   - Have you used a *"you" attitude?*

2. *Understanding a basic communication model*

- Consider the sender as well as the receiver (more than one writer?).
- Look at the situation, channel, feedback, filter, noise, coding, and decoding.
- Analyze cultural differences and other barriers to communication.

3. *Learning which strategy to use to get your message across*

- Direct messages—forthright, often routine.
- Indirect messages—ease into negative or persuasive information.

4. *Planning and revising your message*

- Analyze your audience.
- Identify your purpose.
- Gather information.
- Plan organization and emphasis.
- Write with a "you" attitude.
- Create a quick rough draft.
- Revise from the top down.

APPLICATION EXERCISES

1. List the information you need about your potential audience to be able to analyze their needs most successfully.

2. Which of the following messages have a multiple audience?
   a. An interviewing manual written for a college dean to pass on to graduating students.
   b. An annual report.
   c. A letter answering a customer's complaint about an insurance bill.
   d. A memo to employees about the new plant opening.
   e. A memo to your boss outlining a new project on which your boss has the final decision-making power.
   f. A memo to your boss outlining a new project for which your boss needs to get approval.

3. List and define the parts of the communication model.

4. Define communication *noise.* Give two examples of noise that interfered with your communication in the past week.

5. List five characteristics of your own communication filter.

6. Pair up with another member of the class and compare your filters. What are the similarities? What are the differences?

7. Discuss cultural differences among your class members. How can you use this information to communicate better?

8. Outline the steps in writing direct and indirect messages. What is the major difference between the two processes?

9. List the steps in the writing process. Why is *planning* a time saver rather than a time waster?

10. Why do you begin revision with the big picture instead of with punctuation and spelling?

CASES

1. **Selling a New Product: Analyze Your Audience.** Choosing the best word to describe your product isn't always easy. For example, the one-use cameras made by Fuji and Kodak are often called "disposable" even though most of the material is actually recyclable. Since many people are interested in recycling, help Kodak think of a better adjective and tell it how to "sell" the new name. The cameras use 35mm film and come in versions that take wide-angle shots (the Grand Canyon), underwater shots (for diving vacations), ultrafast shots (sports events), closeups with no flash (baby pictures), fish-eye lens, and filter shots.

2. **Getting Corporate Donors for Your School: Analyze Your Audience.** In a time of budget cuts, your school needs to encourage every source of income it can. You work in the development office at your university. You know that nearly 40 percent of donated money goes to education (actually 38.5 percent, with 28.3 percent going to health and human services activities, 11.9 percent to cultural and arts organizations, and 12.4 percent to civic and community groups, according to the American Association of Fund-Raising).

   Only about 5 percent of donated money comes from corporations. How can you increase this amount? What would motivate businesses to donate to schools? What might they donate? What might they want in return? Analyze your audience and outline how you might appeal to a certain group of businesses for funds for your school.

3. **Changing Your Company's Travel Policy: Gather Information.** The large corporation you work for allows the top-level executives to fly first class but makes all you managers fly coach. A flyer came with your American Express bill explaining that 52 percent of all companies now allow only coach-class travel (up from 37 percent in 1990) and only 26 percent treat senior executives differently from other employees (down from 37 percent). What other information would you need to gather to be able to write a memo to your boss recommending a new travel policy in which everyone travels alike? Would a new policy improve productivity? Would a new policy make lower-level employees feel more empowered? Would there be intangible as well as measurable benefits of the new policy?

4. **Marketing Diapers and Detergent to Men: Choose Emphasis.** With both parents working outside the home, more men are doing the grocery shopping than ever before. You may have seen TV ads in which a man buys baby shampoo at Kmart, discusses brands of peanut butter at a playground, or chooses a brand of spaghetti sauce. People who study this trend say that men don't use coupons, but they do buy groceries (including baby food, detergent, soup, baking mixes, and lots of other traditionally non-macho products). Look at some supposedly male-oriented magazines (sports, music, health, business), and find ads for products other than cars, liquor, and electronics. Discuss two or three

of these ads. How do they differ from the same type of ad in a "women's" magazine? How do you know the ads are directed at men?

5. **Giving Consumer Advice: Choose Emphasis.** You are a newspaper consumer writer and have received a press release from the California attorney general giving the lead concentration in a liter of water from a faucet turned on after being unused overnight. Since a liter is about four big glasses of water, this concentration means that a person who drinks a glass of water in the morning would have higher lead exposure than is allowed in the industry. To avoid this problem, all a person has to do is run the water for 60 seconds before using it for cooking or drinking (and save the water for doing dishes or watering plants). Another tip is to use cold water for drinking and cooking because it will tend to hold less lead.

A chart in the press release shows how much lead each brand of faucet produces (from 2.76 micrograms of lead per liter to 124.8 micrograms per liter). Except for two very high readings, most faucets produce less than 50 micrograms; the problem is that the state standard for industrial lead content is 0.5 micrograms per day. You don't want people to panic, because even replacing *all* faucets would still give people potentially five times the acceptable exposure. Write an opening paragraph that emphasizes helping consumers rather than resorting to sensationalism.

6. **Plan for Emphasis: Interest Your Potential Audience.** The following memo includes necessary information about the event it promotes, but it fails to focus on the desired action: attending the event to help prove that the promotion effort succeeded. The memo also needs proofreading for obvious errors that detract from the positive image the group is trying to convey. What errors can you find? (Hint: Look for word endings and a run-on sentence.) List them, and try writing a new opening paragraph that will create more reader interest. Who is your audience? What might convince those people to attend your event? (The attached brochure mentions prizes, drawings for a 23-inch TV, and music and other entertainment, as well as the exhibit promoting the car.)

MEMO

DATE: November 18, 1994
TO: College of Business Faculty, Staff, and Administrators
FROM: Tom Harris, Professor
Marketing Department
SUBJECT: CAR PROMOTION EVENT

You are cordially invited to attend and participate in a new car promotion event designed by our marketing students for our students, faculty, staff, and administration. This event will be held on Thursday, December 8, 1994 from 9:00 AM to 2:30 PM at the North end of the Student Center.

This promotional event is developed by the students in Advertising Management as part of the competition for X Truck Division. In addition, the students are competing against 23 other Texas colleges and universities for scholarships and other awards granted to the three most outstanding promotional event. These students have put an incredible amount of time and effort into this project. Their efforts with the project will be evaluate by the interest and attendance it generates.

The students and I will appreciate your interest and participation in this event, I am sure you will be impressed with what the Marketing students have accomplished. Enclosed is a flyer detailing the event. Please announce this event to your students.

7. **Revise for Active Voice and Clarity: Sell Your Idea Better.** Revise the following paragraph to use more active-voice verbs (to involve the reader more closely in your proposed action) and cut down on deadwood phrases and words for clearer, more powerful writing. The paragraph appeared at the end of a memo recommending that a firm implement concurrent engineering (in which all departments involved work on product development simultaneously rather than perform development sequentially) to save time, make more money, and increase product quality. Look at tone, wordiness, clarity, paragraph division, and punctuation as well (some words are in italics to help you find areas to revise).

I hope that I have impressed upon you the benefits and challenges of concurrent engineering. Although the challenges are substantial, the risks of not changing the product development system *can be greater.* Even though changing corporate culture is a daunting *task it* doesn't *need to be accomplished in a revolutionary manner. In other words,* phasing in some of the key elements of concurrent engineering *can be done* in an evolutionary way. For example, Engineering Design News estimates that overlapping tasks that had previously been sequential can require up to five times the flow of information. *In our company this fact can be kept in mind* when designing future facilities and communication systems such as voice mail and E-mail. Additionally, the design of future database systems can be structured in such a way as to permit the transfer of large databases easily between departments.

8. **Analyze Audience and Purpose: Use a Form Effectively.** The following form post card acknowledges an order. After reading it, comment on how well you think it does its job. How might

you improve the form? Analyze your audience and purpose to help you develop your answer.

Dear Customer:

Thank you for your order for one (or more) of our record or tape treasuries as advertised in the UNION and the TRIBUNE. Your treasury is now being shipped to you and will arrive in just a few weeks. Please save this card until your shipment arrives.

If you have any questions regarding your order, please contact us at the address below.

Sincerely,

NORFOLK MARKETING, INC.
123 West Main Street
Columbus, OH 43235

9. **Revise for Clarity: Avoid Cultural Barriers.** In international business, translation can become a serious (but unintentionally hilarious) problem. "Translate" the following phrases and sentences into less confusing English (and before laughing, think about how well *you* would translate similar items into Italian, Japanese, Arabic, Dutch, or another language you do not know well!).[4] After translating, explain the English word that seemed to cause the problem.

At a ski resort: Do not perambulate the corridors in the hours of repose in the boots of ascension.

At a hotel: Please leave your values at the front desk.

[4]Based on an Associated Press article appearing in a number of newspapers around November 22, 1922.

At another hotel: It is forbidden to steal hotel towels please. If you are not a person to do such thing please not to read notice.

In a cocktail lounge: Ladies are requested not to have children in the bar.

In a busy tailor's shop: Because is big rush we will execute customers in strict rotation.

In a zoo: Please do not feed the animals. If you have any suitable food, give it to the guard on duty.

In an elevator: The elevator is being fixed for the next day. During that time we regret that you will be unbearable.

In an airport: We will take your bags and send them in all directions.

10. **Revise for Tone: Improve the Paper Personality.** Comment on the tone of the following collection letter for a product you had never subscribed to:

Dear Subscriber:

Please tell us yes or no.

Are you going to keep your word and pay for the subscription to the University Wellness Letter which you ordered?

Sincerely,

Helen Mitchell
Circulation Director

What paper personality does this writer convey? Do you feel positive about this company? How does the tone make you feel?

THE ART OF THE MEMORABLE MEMO

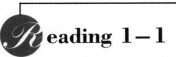 eading 1—1 | *Jim Jubak*

Most people think of the memo as an informal document, a chance to jot down a few quick thoughts or offer suggestions. But in a busy or highly stratified workplace, that innocent piece of paper may be the only chance you have to impress the powers that be. "Writing and making presentations are the two major things, other than getting along with people, that count for promotions," says Joan Minninger, Ph.D., a San Francisco–based writing consultant. Indeed, some companies—IBM, AT&T, and General Electric, for example—consider internal correspondence such an important communications tool that they hire outside experts to teach the craft of memo writing to valued executives.

You probably don't need a tutor to write a noteworthy memo. You do need to give the document some thought before putting it into circulation. The major question to ask yourself—aside from Why am I writing this?—is, What do I expect from the reader? Do I want to change her mind, impress her with my acumen, inspire action, or all three? Also determine how many people will be reading your document and how much background each has on the topic.

Most writing teachers suggest beginning with the roughest of rough drafts—just jot your thoughts on paper in the order they come to you. Don't worry about style, grammar, or structure. You might also make a list of questions your reader will ask (*Why* are we having yet another meeting on the Wombat problem? What's the purpose of bringing in three more consultants?). Then go through your random jottings and underline the important points. Organize these points into categories and put a heading on each.

In business writing, "begin at the beginning" isn't necessarily good advice. Sometimes it's best to declare your purpose and immediately follow with the conclusion. Though this tactic may feel psychologically backward, it instantly alerts readers as to why they've received a memo in the first place. If your conclusions are controversial and you want the reader to understand the reasoning that led to them, you may prefer to leave them until the end. Whatever you do, don't bury any important recommendations in the middle.

The subject line at the top serves the same function as a newspaper headline: to grab the reader's interest and summarize the contents in a few choice words. Strive for vivid, concise language. "New Expense Account Policies" is more arresting than "Accounting Department Revisions on Expense Policies."

Presentation—how the memo looks—is almost as critical as what you have to say. "My assumption is that readers are pressed for time," says Beatrice Mitchell, managing director of Sperry, Mitchell & Co., an investment banking boutique in New York City. Mitchell puts a summary at the top and then bullets or underlines her main points, keeping the "meat" to about fifteen seconds of reading time. The memo ends with an action summary. "In the worst-case scenario, someone could read the summary and the next steps, skip the whole middle and still get what I wanted to say," she says.

For the optimum in reader-friendliness, use lots of white space. Keep the margins wide and insert at least one line space between paragraphs. If you have the luxury of boldface type, use it to highlight subheads and main points.

It's best to let your prose "rest" for a spell—a day or at least an afternoon—before you send it. You might also ask for a second opinion. "A lot can happen because of a memo, and if you don't think it through you can really get burned," says Maryann Piotrowski, a principal of Corporate Writing Consultants in Cambridge, Massachusetts. At one client company, Piotrowski recalls, a junior executive who exhorted his superiors to attend a meeting in hyperurgent prose lost more than a few points. "Management was very annoyed," she says. "He was just trying to tell them how important the meeting was, but the memo came across as harsh and demanding."

And when your goal is communication, that's almost as bad as being a bore.

THE FORGETTABLE MEMO

To: Carol Baer   September 9, 1991
From: Constance Davis
Subject: Possible promotion for Julie Rhodes

Ever since Julie Rhodes began working for me as an administrative assistant almost a year ago, our department's sales have increased by 5 percent a quarter. We have consistently exceeded other departments' levels and our own projections in this time.

This employee does a very good job for us. She is always willing to do more work than is required and to take on projects before being asked. I always feel confident when she is heading up a project. Julie has taken additional training in sales techniques and plans to begin an afterhours MBA program with a specialty in sales in the fall.

I am recommending that she be promoted to associate department manager when her one-year anniversary comes up next month. Julie has shown that she can persevere in going after new clients (for example, she pursued the Burton Sofa account, which is now responsible for 22 percent of our department's annual sales, for three months). I think she should receive an 8 percent raise to go with this promotion.

THE MEMORABLE MEMO

To: Carol Baer   September 9, 1991
From: Constance Davis
Subject: Promotion for Julie Rhodes

I recommend that we promote Julie Rhodes to associate department manager, with an 8 percent raise, effective October 17, her one-year anniversary.

My reasons:

Results   Since Julie has been working for me, sales have increased by 5 percent a quarter, consistently exceeding other departments' levels and our own projections for this year.

Initiative   Julie is always willing to do more work than is required and to take on projects before being asked.

Perseverance   After three months of targeted efforts, she managed to get the Burton Sofa account, which is now responsible for 22 percent of our department's annual sales.

Skills   Julie is constantly aiming to improve her skill level. She's taken courses in sales techniques in the past and plans to begin an MBA program, specializing in sales, in October.

Jim Jubak, "The Art of the Memorable Memo," *Self*, September 1991, pp. 116, 118.

Chapter Two

The Routine, Direct Business Message

Because many business messages can be direct, you need to learn techniques for making your writing and speaking clear and to the point. If the information you are sending is neutral or positive, be direct in presenting it to your audience. A great many routine messages *should* be direct to save your audience time and achieve your desired action sooner.

Direct, or deductive, messages begin with the most important point to present to the reader or listener. You should use the direct strategy to provide information some-one has asked for, respond to customers' questions or complaints about your company's products, notify people about business changes, and ask for information.

Routine business messages such as transmittals, notifications, responses to neutral material, and inquiries need to be clear and direct to get their job done quickly and efficiently. By writing deductively, you begin with the point of your communication and then provide enough details to enable the reader to take any necessary action. Because the material you are sending is routine, neutral, or good news, your audience does not need to be convinced as much as notified.

After working through some direct messages, from planning through drafting and revising, we'll look at how effective document design and format can help get your message across, whether through word processing, desktop publishing, electronic mail, voice mail, or phone. ●

Sometimes new employees have to guess what the corporate culture is and how messages about important things are sent. But many basic business messages (to employees, customers, government agencies, stockholders, and your other audiences) can be direct. Direct messages save time and are clear, concise, and (usually) easy to take appropriate action on.

PREPARING DIRECT, NEUTRAL, POSITIVE MESSAGES

Remember that when using the direct strategy to create messages, you begin with your most important point and follow with supporting data, arguments, or information.

DIRECT MESSAGE OUTLINE
Begin with something important to the reader.
Present the relevant details.
End with a request for action or a pleasant closing.

Your business audience pays attention to something that interests them, so begin a positive or neutral message by letting the audience know what the message is about.

If you are answering someone's question or providing information someone has asked for, you can write a quick *transmittal memo* such as the following:

DATE: June 28, 1993
TO: Jane Silva
FROM: Janet Kim

Subject line gives topic directly   SUBJECT: USE OF COLOR IN PRESENTATION VISUALS

Gets directly to topic   At our last staff meeting, you asked for suggestions on improving our presentations. I believe we can use color in our presentation visuals to help us communicate more effectively.

Summarizes attachment
Asks for action   The attached report shows why, how, and when we should use color in our presentations. I look forward to hearing from you about implementing these suggestions. If you have questions, please call me at extension 2785.

This kind of transmittal memo or letter (for a report sent outside your company) quickly introduces its subject, gives enough details to prepare the reader

EXHIBIT 2–1 Daffodil Days Postcard

A MESSAGE TO OUR DAFFODIL DAY CLIENTS ...

THE BIG CHILL

Dear Daffodil Days Friends:

Since the storm wasn't the Society's fault, it probably doesn't need to apologize so profusely!

Due to a terrible Alaskan storm we're sorry to say—
Our daffodils are not ready to bloom in March.

We deeply regret this inconvenience

New Daffodil Days dates:

Daffodil Sunday, April 2
Delivery April 3 & 4
Von's Promotion April 7 & 8

For more information:
Call 299-4200 or
740-0511

Thanks to Plaza Print for the printing.

AMERICAN CANCER SOCIETY

EXHIBIT 2–2 Mail-Order Response Card

Dear Customer:

What if only one product ordered is out of stock?

The product(s) noted below is out of stock. Because our supplier is not able to tell us when we may expect shipment, it is necessary to cancel this order. Your account will not be billed for this merchandise.

Chapter 10 will tell you how to handle negatives better!

We are sorry to disappoint you, and wish to apologize for any inconvenience this may cause. We hope that we may be of service at some future time.

NOTTHINKING MAIL ORDER HOUSE

CUSTOMER SERVICE

for the message, and allows for a response, or feedback. It need not be longer or more "gimmicky" to get the job done.

Form notification messages often can be direct (but can't be too personal, since they usually go to many people in the same format). Note how the postcard from the American Cancer Society in Exhibit 2–1 notifies many people in a direct but friendly way. A postcard is an easy, inexpensive, and quick way to notify many customers that an annual fund raiser's flowers will be late.

Of course, to use a form you need to consider whether it will cover all the possible situations you can predict. A form is *not* the appropriate means of communication to use if it raises more questions than it answers. Nor is a form a good choice if it might offend someone expecting a personal response. Consider the response card from a mail-order company in Exhibit 2–2. What's wrong with it from a business response point of view? For one thing, the customer may have ordered more than one item. If only one item is out of stock, will the whole order be canceled? When you choose to use a form, make sure it doesn't create more problems than its ease of use solves! In Chapter 3 you'll learn more about good business style, and in Chapter 10 about negative messages—which this postcard certainly is.

WRITING RESPONSES THAT SELL YOUR FIRM

Realistically, when you respond to a customer about an order, you could send a one-sentence reply containing purely information: "Your printing was shipped this morning." If you are providing quick service, the customer will be inclined to return to you the next time he or she needs printing done. But since you're writing anyway, why not include more information *and* build goodwill toward your company and its services? Filling some of the space available on the postcard will make the message look friendlier and less like a telegram.

Consider the example in Exhibit 2–3 from Miles Kimball, a long-standing, successful mail-order company. Using the writing process outline in Chapter 1, let's compare how well the writers of the forms in Exhibits 2–2 and 2–3 planned and wrote their messages.

Identify the problem.   The order cancellation card in Exhibit 2–2 identifies one problem—the missing item—but does not consider whether the customer ordered more than one item. The Miles Kimball letter in Exhibit 2–3 thanks the customer (one purpose of the letter) and then explains what to do if a correction is required, offers extra envelopes, and encourages the customer to buy again next year.

Analyze the audience.   The order cancellation form assumes that everyone only orders one item or understands that only part of an order can be canceled (which is probably true, but not stated in the form). The Miles Kimball letter assumes the writer is having a conversation with a reader who is likely to be a satisfied customer and explains details (such as the availability of extra envelopes) the reader is unlikely to know.

Gather information.   The writer in Exhibit 2–2 could have sent one response form for one out-of-stock item and another for an order with more than one item indicating that some were sent and/or some were canceled. The writer in Exhibit 2–3 planned a good form letter: It includes the necessary information about the customer's order, adds information the customer might need, and sounds friendly and helpful. One form letter can't do much more than that!

Plan organization and format.   Both letters begin directly.

Write a quick, conversational rough draft.   Clearly the letter in Exhibit 2–3 is more conversational. Even though the writer doesn't mention the reader's name, the *tone* of the letter is personal and friendly.

Dear Customer--

Note how friendly and helpful the tone is.

Thanks -- much -- for your Christmas Card order.

Would you do me a favor by checking this order right away to be sure everything is just as you want it?

I am the last one to check your order before it is sent to you. I've tried to make sure that it is exactly right. We want you to be proud of our cards.

Makes action easy

Should anything be wrong, please let me know immediately so we can make it right. Send along your original order blank (enclosed) and just one copy of the card, marking the correction plainly. It's not necessary to return the entire order.

Should you need a few more envelopes, let me know. We'll send them without charge. (Tell us what card they're for.)

Looks to future business

Next August we'll send you a new catalog of exciting Christmas Card ideas.

Again -- thank you.

Cordially,
MILES KIMBALL COMPANY

Anne Ware

Revise from the top down. The cancellation form fails an early revision test—it doesn't cover all the necessary information. After that, it doesn't matter whether or not all the punctuation is correct.

Many business messages should be direct, but we've all picked up some bad habits over the years, using wordy, hackneyed phrases. Look at the following time wasters that creep in and delay transmittal of information:

Thank you for your interest in our firm. Instead, start with some information about the firm that will *sell* it to the prospective client.

Feel free to call. "Please call if you have other questions" is less of a cliché and thus sounds more sincere.

In a timely manner. Tell *when* and tell *what* to do, using active voice—you'll get action that way.

Now compare the following:

Loan documents should be processed in a timely manner.

The loan officer should process all loan documents by 4 P.M. Friday each week.

The second version names the person to do the task (remember that passive voice often makes us guess who will take the action), describes the task specifically, and tells when it should be done. Remember *who, what,* and *when.*

Rather than waste your reader's time with extra words or words that add little to your message, concentrate on conveying the message quickly and concisely but with a friendly tone and a *"you" attitude.* Sometimes called a *service attitude,* this will help you compete by placing your reader's needs above your own. A service attitude is even more important when problems arise (and you need to use an indirect strategy), but keep your reader in mind as you write direct messages, too.

WRITING MEMOS THAT GET RESULTS

In addition to writing direct letters about routine and positive matters, you will write many *routine memos* within your company.

The most obvious difference between letters and memos is what is at the top of the page (name of recipient, date, subject line, etc.). Other than that, letters and memos can cover similar subjects, but for different audiences. Letters are nearly always written to people outside your firm (e.g., clients), whereas memos are used for almost all in-house correspondence. The major exception is personnel actions, which usually call for a letter—often to the person's home address to protect his or her privacy—whether the news is good (you received the promotion you interviewed for) or bad (you didn't).

Effective Subject Lines

Many memos can be direct because the reader expects the information, as in the transmittal memo on page 37. Because memos use a *subject line,* you're not likely to keep many surprises unless you write a subject line that's deliberately neutral. A good subject line acts like a newspaper headline or magazine caption: It gets the reader's attention by mentioning both the topic and the writer's slant on it.

Try to make your subject line vivid but concise. Give your reader as much of a picture of your topic as you can—and make it a lively picture, if possible. For example, you could say "New Parking Assignments" rather than "Policy and Procedures for Assigning Parking Spaces in the New Lot." Since effective business communication strives for conversational tone, you'll want to avoid

DATE: February 17, 1993
TO: James Relyea
FROM: Holly Marcinek H.M.
SUBJECT: PREPARING SUCCESSFUL PRINTING CONTRACTS

Here is the information you requested about obtaining
printing bids, working with printers and the printing
process, and preparing printing contracts for our new
direct mail campaign.

Obtaining the Printing Bid

Working with Your Printer

Preparing a Printing Contract

Attachment: Request for Bid on Printing Costs

"businessese" phrases like *policy and procedure,* which sound stiff at best and boring at worst. Use *policy* or *procedure* alone if clear and necessary.

If you can work in a verb form, as in "Choosing a New Inventory Control Software Package," you will also give your reader an idea of the purpose of your memo and the action that may be required. A good subject line helps workers distribute a document to people who need the information and also helps workers file the document in a logical place. Remember that the subject line is one clue to the various readers of the memo about subsequent required action.

Direct Strategy Organization

In a direct message memo, you can start with your main point ("I recommend that" or "you should") and then explain your point of view with a bulleted list or short paragraphs, each with a heading to guide the reader through your argument. See how the memo outline in Exhibit 2–4 guides the reader. (Of course, the actual memo included several paragraphs after each subheading.) This two-page memo and a one-page attachment discuss the three topics listed and end with steps for writing a thorough printing specification sheet. Attaching the relevant form helps the reader take action immediately using the information in the memo.

ASKING FOR INFORMATION DIRECTLY

Using the same direct strategy, if you need to request information, you can safely begin by asking for at least some of it rather than giving a lengthy explanation of why you need the information. Compare the letters in Exhibits 2–5 and 2–6 for directness, ease of locating needed information, unnecessary repetition, and possibility of successful action. The letter in Exhibit 2–5 is more likely to get the job done and win the writer a variety of comparable proposals to choose from for her meeting. One reason this request will get results is that it uses *dated action*—giving the reader a deadline for getting the information to the writer.

REPLYING TO A READER'S COMPLAINT

A direct strategy can help you respond to a customer complaint. Even if you can't solve the problem in a letter, you can sound concerned and helpful. Exhibit 2–7 shows how Ford Motor Company uses a form (adapted to individual cases) to begin solving a customer's problem. This letter acknowledges the customer's concern and lets him or her know that the complaint is taken seriously. The objective is to let the customer know that she or he has been heard and that Ford is doing everything possible to follow up on the concern. It explains the "complaint process" so that the customer understands the time involved in servicing a complaint. It provides the customer with additional suggestions for checking into the complaint. This step prevents the customer from feeling powerless or ignored.

USING FORM MESSAGES

Like Ford, any business has communications that occur repeatedly. Think of loan application cover letters for banks, legal documents, insurance policy renewal letters, proposals to different clients on the same general topic, and tax question answers from an accountant. Your firm doesn't want to waste time having each employee draft an original version of each type of communication. Word processing allows you to write paragraphs, letters, and sections of proposals and reports, call them up from the computer's memory, and use them in appropriate locations.

The key word here is *appropriate.* You may have received an inappropriate form document and wondered whether the writer was answering the question

Spencer's Toy Closet, Inc.

May 1, 1994

Catering and Sales Manager
Broadacres Hotel
1000 Broadway
Lincoln, Nebraska   77301

Dear Catering and Sales Manager:

Puts direct question in opening paragraph

Does the Broadacres Hotel have three break-out rooms
each seating at least 50 people? I'm planning our
annual sales meeting and need at least three rooms for
concurrent meetings.

Lists requests for emphasis

Here are our other requirements:
    --150 sleeping rooms available November 3 and 4
    --a breakfast buffet set up for our group
    --a banquet room seating 300 on November 4
    --fax and copying services available on site
    --airport transportation available 24 hours
    --optional activities for spouses

Asks for dated action

Please let me know if you have the appropriate rooms
available for November 3 and 4. Since I hope to
finish our plans by June 1, please let me receive
your written proposal before then.

I look forward to hearing from you. Please call
me if you have questions about your proposal.

Sincerely,

Kjersti Eriksen

Kjersti Eriksen
Corporate Meeting Planner

18165 Gottschalk Avenue
Kansas City, MO 64124
816 • 282 • 5251

PWC

May 1, 1994

Catering and Sales Manager
Broadacres Hotel
1000 Broadway
Lincoln, Nebraska   77301

Dear Sir:

Gives reader seemingly pointless history at beginning

Piedmont Wholesaling Company has a long history of top sales in the hardware industry. Each year, we hold a sales meeting for all 150 of our salespeople and their spouses. This year, the meeting has been scheduled for November 3 and 4.

Reader must take time to figure out requirements from the narrative.

Knowing that the Broadacres Hotel is a leader in its field, we would consider having our sales meeting at your property if you have enough rooms available. We will have 150 salespeople (and potentially their spouses) staying overnight on November 3 and 4, with breakfast (buffet preferred) each day and a banquet for all on November 4. During the day on November 3 and 4 we need to have three equal-size sessions running at the same time.

Adds more requirements; passive voice makes action sound unimportant.

Please let me know if you will provide round the clock airport transportation and if you will submit a proposal for our meeting. My deadline is June 1; questions may be submitted to me at the phone number listed on this page.

Sincerely,

Joe Jones
Meeting Planner

Piedmont Wholesaling Company
16834 Minsenheimer Boulevard
Knoxville, TN 37933

Ford Motor Company

The American Road
Dearborn, Michigan 48121

Contact No._____

Dear Mr. Sample:

*Directly
expresses
concern for
reader*

Thank you for letting us know about the concerns you have with your vehicle.
We regret any inconvenience you have experienced and assure you that your
continuing satisfaction is important to us.

A summary of your concerns has been sent electronically to your servicing
dealer and to our local District Office. Normally, that will result in a
contact in a short time by the dealer or local service zone manager. If you
do not hear from one or the other soon, it may be because they have been
unable to reach you. In that case, we suggest that you contact the dealership

*Explains
complaint
process*

service manager directly and refer to the Contact Number shown above. The
service manager should be eager to assist you.

If your contact with the dealership is not fully productive, or if we can
assist you in the future, please call us toll free at the Ford Customer
Assistance Center:

        1-800-392-Ford

A Customer Service Representative will be available to assist you.

*Ends on a
friendly
note*

Again, we appreciate hearing from you. Your continuing satisfaction is
important to us.

you asked. For example, suppose you write in to change your address on a magazine subscription and you receive a form postcard saying, "Thank you for your interest in Blank Magazine. To change your subscription address, please fill out this form with your new address." Since you just sent that information, this subscription center either has too few forms to fit several possible situations or has sent you the wrong form.

You would get the same reaction from this letter from a lawyer's secretary sending some information in the lawyer's capacity as president of an alumni club. It's a classic example of inappropriate form use—legal jargon in what should be handled as a friendly situation.

March 29, 1993

Mr. Charles Luick
2245 River Run Drive, Apt. 4202
Irvine, CA 92714

Re: University Club Spring Seminar

Dear Mr. Luick:

Enclosed please find the registration forms regarding the above-captions matter.

Very truly yours,

Paying Very Little Attention
Secretary to Not Proofreading

Besides using distant language ("enclosed please find" rather than "the enclosed registration forms") and including a typo (*captioned* is doubtless what the typist meant to write), this letter illustrates the danger of using a legal formula to try to communicate about a friendlier subject.

After describing the seminar, the writer could have said, "To attend, just fill out the enclosed registration forms and mail to me with your check. I look forward to seeing you on April 5." The paper personality would have sounded friendlier and more helpful.

One of our colleagues once received an unintentionally funny form letter from her senator:

Dear Mrs. Barney:

I, like you, am concerned about human rights violations in

The omitted specifics after *in* make it obvious that this is a computerized letter—and make it sound silly. Rather than building reader goodwill, it's the slap in the face of a mechanized response.

Exhibit 2–8 is a better computerized form letter that addresses the reader's needs *and* saves time and money for the writer. It was a response to a convention and visitors' bureau's call for hotels at which to hold a meeting. Of course, it would be even more sales oriented if it dealt with specifics of the reader's proposed meeting, but it provides basic hotel information and could be followed up with a phone call scheduling the site visit to present details suited to this potential customer. The only personalized part of this letter (other than the inside address) is the name of the association at the end of the second paragraph. The letter addresses the reader's concerns about having a successful meeting, sends information about the property, and offers to schedule a site visit. One letter, form or individualized, could hardly do more.

Tara Suites
Hotel

March 23, 1994

Meeting Planner
Romance Novels Trade Association
666 Fifth Avenue
New York, NY 10022

Greetings from the Tara Suites Hotel, Jonesboro!

Directs message to specific meeting planner

We know that as a Meeting Planner you are certainly "under the gun" to produce high-quality meetings for The Romance Novels Trade Association.

Adds positive information about reader and writer

We would like to become a part of your programs in order that we can help you to continue to live up to the high standards set forth by your industry.

Gives specifics about hotel

Our beautiful property has become a favorite destination for meeting planners. Our ideal location, superior facilities, as well as complimentary services and amenities make Tara Suites-Jonesboro the perfect place for your next meeting.

Explains attachment
Asks for action

The enclosed Meeting Planner's guide outlining our services and amenities will help acquaint you with Tara Suites-Jonesboro. Please call so we can arrange for you to visit our property to experience firsthand exactly what we have to offer your association.

I look forward to hearing from you soon!

Sincerely,

Muffy Butler

Muffy Butler
Convention Services

1200 Butler Drive
Jonesboro, Georgia
41976

SAN DIEGO HUMANE SOCIETY AND S.P.C.A.
887 Sherman Street, San Diego, CA 92110-4088 ● FAX (619) 299-4269 ● (619) 299-7012

April 17, 1992

Ms. Gretchen Vik
4518 Max Dr.
San Diego, California 92115

We hope by now, Ms. Vik...

Friendly, direct opening

that you and your new pet have settled into a comfortable and rewarding relationship . . . that you're both experiencing the joys of living fuller, more meaningful lives - - because you're together! We're sure that's the way it's meant to be.

As you look back on the experience of adopting your new pet at the San Diego Humane Society, we hope you're pleased with the experience, as well as the outcome. We'd like to hear from you. Use the back of this letter, if you wish. Through your comments, we hope to improve our services for the benefit of the animals, and the people who come to adopt them.

If you're having behavior problems with your new pet, ask our "resident expert," Mr. Woods. Call him at 299-7012, ext. 250, Monday – Friday, 8:30 a.m. to 5:00 p.m. He can help.

Offers further services

And, if you are pleased with your pet, tell friends and acquaintances about the healthy, family-ready animals to be found here. We always have many worthy pets, like yours, waiting for new owners. You can help them by telling others.

In addition to adoptions, we also investigate reports of animal cruelty or neglect; teach thousands of school kids all over the county about the needs of animals; take animals into hospitals, convalescent homes, psychiatric centers and homes for abused children to help those people feel better; provide free, companion pets to senior citizens; and rescue animals whose lives are in danger. Yes, we're a lot more than an adoption agency – – though that's mighty important to us, too.

Again, if you need help with your pet, let us know. And, please tell others about the wonderful pets waiting for adoption. For the animals, thanks!

Ends on a positive note

Sincerely,

Fred Lee

Fred J. Lee, Executive Director

P.S. We've enclosed a handy, addressed envelope for you to to send us your comments . . . . or a check if you're able to assist us to help more animals. Remember, we're not tax-supported. Individual contributions and some fees for our services help us help the animals. But even if you can't send the animals a donation now, please let us hear from you. Thank you.

Mentions enclosure

EXHIBIT 2-10   Humane Society Response Envelope

Flap forms mailing list card later

Enclosed is my/our gift to support the work of the San Diego Humane Society:

☐ $10   ☐ $15   ☐ $25   ☐ $50   ☐ $100   ☐ $ _____

Name _____

Address _____

City _____ State _____ Zip _____

☐ To help keep Society expenses down, my/our check will serve as a receipt.

☐ Please do *not* send me/us your newsletter, *AnimalFare*.

☐ Send me/us information about tax-advantaged planned giving, please.

☐ Send information about including the Society in my/our will(s).

Supported by your individual contributions—No tax support is received.

Contributions to the Society are tax deductible to the full extent of the law.

Helping animals everywhere in San Diego County with five vital programs:

Envelope sells positive features

1. Receiving, sheltering and adopting,

2. Investigating reports of cruelty,

3. Educating people about animals' needs,

4. Sharing animals with the elderly, confined people and abused children,

5. Rescuing animals in emergencies.

SAN DIEGO HUMANE SOCIETY AND S.P.C.A.
887 Sherman St., San Diego, CA 92110-4088

One less thoughtful response using a form tried to sell a business communication association on using a keynote speaker to "increase profits . . . and inspire your members to take action for increased productivity at less cost." The programs touted by the speaker involved selling, management, marketing, stress, and customer service. The letter should have been directed only to corporations inquiring about scheduling meetings, eliminating associations consisting of professional speakers! Remember the first rule of using forms: A form must fit the reader's situation closely enough that it is helpful and doesn't immediately *sound* like a form.

A form can be a useful follow-up to a business interaction—and gain sales. Exhibit 2–9, a form letter from a local humane society, asks for comments, offers help, and seeks further business (since pets cost $20 to $60 to adopt). It also asks for donations, but it does so in a friendly, helpful way. The response envelope included with the letter (Exhibit 2–10) is a perfect size for checks (no folding required) and includes information on the flap that can easily be filed for a future mailing list. The remaining envelope space is used for a "mission statement" that would be appropriate to send to all potential donors.

CONVENTIONAL FORMATS

Salutations and Closings

In Appendix A, you will find layout format examples and tips on how to create professional-looking letters, memos, and reports.

Use conventional openings and closings in your letters. Let readers concentrate on your message rather than on elaborate salutations or closings. *Dear _____* is an easy, inoffensive opening. In writing to someone whose name could indicate male or female, some firms choose to write, "Dear Jody Barry" to avoid an error of gender. If the person is important to your firm, *find out* whether Jody is male or female so that you can use the appropriate courtesy title *(Ms., Mr., Miss, Mrs.)*.

If you know to whom you are writing, use the name (courtesy title and last name, unless you know the person well). If you don't, *Dear Sir* or *Dear Marketing Manager* will serve the purpose. Although some people find an implication of sexism in *Dear Sir,* it is still a common salutation and is so generic many people do not notice it.

Sincerely is a good, plain ending. You really don't need more words here (and people may not even read this part, so don't waste time thinking of alternatives). *Respectfully yours* is still sometimes used when writing to government entities such as the IRS and the SEC, but it isn't appropriate for customers or others to whom you wish to sound equal. (Appendix A discusses salutations and closings in detail.)

DESIGNING LAYOUT FOR GREATEST IMPACT

In addition to analyzing your reader, planning your content, and organizing the best strategy for delivering your message, you can improve communication by making effective format and layout decisions.

Topic sentences will help guide the reader through the material. They can even be emphasized as headings. A topic sentence doesn't always have to be the first sentence in a paragraph.

For greatest *readability,* keep sentences to 16 to 17 words and paragraphs to 6 to 8 typed lines. (Opening and closing paragraphs can be four typed lines for emphasis.) If you really want to emphasize something, a one-sentence paragraph will do it.

Headings

Headings, or captions, are an effective way to let the reader know what you think is important. They also help guide the reader. Conventional heading systems generally follow the system illustrated below. Centered headings are given more importance than left-margin headings, and left-margin headings get more emphasis than indented headings. Similarly, capital letters are more important than lowercase letters, boldface type is more important than regular type, and large-size fonts are more important than small fonts. If you don't use a larger font size or boldface to make a heading stand out, underline the heading to differentiate it from the rest of the text.

MAIN TITLE OF YOUR REPORT

Major Divisions (I, II or 1.0, 2.0)

Subdivisions (A, B or 1.1, 2.1)

Still Smaller Subdivisions (1, 2 or 1.11, 2.11) Text would follow this level of heading, not spaces on both sides as in higher levels.

The next subdivision (a, b or 1.111, 2.111) is an underlined part of a sentence.

This conventional system uses a first-degree heading for the title, second degree for main headings, third degree for subdivisions (all of these levels are separated from the text by a space before and after the heading), fourth degree for smaller subdivisions, and fifth degree for subdivisions of fourth-degree topics.

The headings in the example use underlining for emphasis, but you could use boldface instead. Just make sure the headings stand out from the text. Desktop publishing software allows for different sizes of type and different typefaces or fonts to indicate heading levels, but designers still follow the "rules" concerning heading placement.

Main Title

You will have only one centered, all-caps (capital letters) heading, because there will be only one main title. This type of heading is sometimes called a *first-degree* heading.

Major Divisions

The major divisions (I or II, 1.0 or 2.0) can be placed in the center and underlined or put in bold type. If you have only a few headings, you may prefer to begin at the left margin (as is done with the next level in the example). Just be sure to start with centered-level headings if you *do* have subdivisions, or your letter or memo will look like an outline, all indented across the page!

You can (and often should) have more than one paragraph under a heading. This type of heading is called a *second-degree* heading.

Subdivisions

A subdivision, or *third-degree* heading *(A, B, 1.1, 2.1),* is one of the most common types of heading. You don't need to indent or center it; it emphasizes the text by setting it off (as do all headings). Subdivisions are useful in letters and memos with only a few divisions.

Still Smaller Subdivisions

The next level, *fourth-degree* headings (1, 2, 1.11, 2.11), is the first level to have a structural difference. The higher levels are all placed above the text; this level is emphasized only through underlining, boldface, or capital letters. (Headings after the first level can use just initial caps, although the one shown in the example uses capital letters to begin each major word.)

The Next Subdivision

This level (a, b, 1.111, 2.111) is a *fifth-degree* heading. Its structural difference is that it merely underlines or boldfaces the first part of a sentence (or another part of the sentence, if you wish to emphasize only key words at this level). This level of heading is useful if you want to underline topic sentences in paragraphs as your lower-level headings.

Headings are useful in nearly any piece of writing longer than one page—and sometimes in one-page memos as well—because they help structure the writing for the reader. We have learned what heading placement means, even if we've never studied it, by seeing headings in newspapers, magazines, and textbooks. We have so deeply internalized the basic rule of "higher is more important than lower" that a number of people complained to the *San Diego Union-Tribune* about what they perceived as misplaced emphasis on the front page on July 14, 1992, shown in Exhibit 2–11.[1] The five-column headline "All-Star game something to cheer about" is in 30-point type, followed by a

[1]Gina Lubrano, "Democrats Lose to the All-Star Game," *San Diego Union-Tribune,* July 20, 1992, p. B7.

The San Diego Union-Tribune

Tuesday
July 14, 1992

City Final
23¢

Stricter emissions program proposed

EPA plan may cost county's drivers

By FRANK GREEN
Staff Writer

WASHINGTON — Car owners in San Diego County likely would have to drive farther for emissions tests and spend more money on car repairs under a strict new emissions inspection program proposed yesterday by the federal Environmental Protection Agency (EPA).

The EPA proposed tougher emissions standards as part of a new inspection program for 82 of the ▓▓'s most polluted

All-Star game something to cheer about

Out-of-town fans (including 2 presidents) and huge TV audience will give city a boost

By FRANK GREEN
Staff Writer

Baseball's storybook event, the All-Star game, couldn't have come to San Diego at a better time.

Despite winning their last four games, the Padres are in third place in the division standings, and tourism has been flat here as an extra-inning game between also-rans.

So when the major leagues' dream teams take to the warm, humid field at San Diego Jack Murphy Stadium this afternoon — in front of President George Bush, Mexican President Carlos Salinas de Gortari and 56,000 others — the dog days will turn

■ More coverage of All-Star festivities in Sports—**D1**

to happy ones. For a while, anyway.

"About 10,000 people are coming into town for the game, and a crowd like that can, before you know it drop $10 million," said Reint Reinders, president of the San Diego Convention and Visitors Bureau. "There are also 30 million people who'll be watching the game on television, which gives the city invaluable visibility."

It has been 14 years since the All-Star game played out on San Diego turf, and there is no comparison between that event

and this year's game in the weight of pomp and circumstance involved.

International politics will lend a new element to All-Star preliminaries. President Bush is scheduled to arrive on Air Force One in the early afternoon at Miramar Naval Air Station, then immediately go into a meeting with President Salinas at San Diego Mission de Alcala on the pending U.S.-Mexico trade agreement.

Bush and Salinas will later view the game from the owner's box at the stadium.

Padres fans should get a lift out of the emotional cellar, with five members of the team — Tony Fernandez, Tony Gwynn, Fred McGriff, Beito Santiago and

See **All-Star** on Page A-4

Democrats hoot, display hope

By GEORGE E. ▓ONDON
Copley News Servi▓

▓NEW YORK — With a scath▓ ▓▓▓ge at George ▓sh, a ▓▓

Brown loyalists so▓ ▓d a lonely

---

story about that evening's All-Star game. The next five-column headline, "Democrats hoot, display hope," is in bolder, 48-point type and followed by a story about the ongoing Democratic convention. Readers complained that the "more important" placement of the All-Star game story showed that the paper was biased toward Republicans. The real story was that the paper had changed format and used a *high-interest* story at the top of the page, but intended to show that the second story was the *main* story, with the larger and bolder-type headline. (*Both* headlines appeared above the fold in the top half of the page— the part that shows when newspapers are on display for sale.)

Apparently, the rule "higher is more important than lower" has come to overrule "big print is more important than smaller print." The news editor for the morning edition of the *San Diego Union-Tribune,* Bernie Jones, says, "if the format is misleading readers about which story is more important, then perhaps the newspaper should take another look at its design guidelines."

Lists

Lists are very emphatic, so save them for important things. *Don't* number all your lists. Numbering takes away emphasis by making everything important (so that nothing is!). Use bullets or dashes (two hyphens typed next to each other, no spaces in the middle or on either side) for most of your lists, and save numbers for the most important list—perhaps the recommendations or something similar.

Suppose you are a consultant advising a real estate office owner on motivating agents who have reached a sales plateau and seem to be suffering from "burnout." You could recommend a number of things the owner can do to motivate the agents. To make these recommendations stand out, put them in list form:

For the plateaued agent, I have several recommendations based on Erickson's work on motivation:

- Provide the top producer for the month with a special parking space closest to the office entrance.
- Take long-time salespeople and their spouses out for an appreciation dinner.
- Submit a deserving member's name to the local board for the various awards it presents annually.
- Designate long-time agents "resident experts" in their areas of specialization. Have them conduct a short training session in the real estate area in which they excel.
- Let experienced agents develop a mentor relationship with newly hired agents.
- Have them attend continuing education classes to boost their interest in the business.

Notice how much more important the items become when they are listed this way. As we discussed earlier, *emphasis* comes from physical placement as well as from type size and other elements. You don't need to number a list of six items unless you wish to emphasize the order of steps in a process or the ranked importance of the items.

White Space

White space (wide margins, spaces between paragraphs, spaces around lists) is one way to break up your copy and make it easier to read. One of the biggest problems with the desktop-published look is that it allows people to cram more information on one page—so much information that the piece becomes hard to read. Remember: Your readers can't do what you ask if they can't or won't read the information you send.

Keep margins of 1 inch on all sides of the page unless you plan to bind the document; then leave 1¼ to 1½ inches on the left side. Word processing programs like WordPerfect® will automatically give you a binding margin of 1¼ inches and will alternate it left and right if you plan to print on both sides of the page.

Fonts, Type Sizes, and Desktop Publishing Software

Now that you have so many choices of kinds and sizes of type, you can get yourself into trouble! Experts offer some tips to avoid the desktop-published look (sometimes called the "ransom note" effect). They suggest choosing only one *serif* (a typeface with thin lines projecting from the strokes that make up the letter) and one *sans serif* (a typeface with smooth strokes having no extra lines) typeface per document. Vary the look by using different sizes of these two fonts. For ease of reading, you could use the serif for text and the sans serif for headings.

Exhibit 2–12 illustrates a number of points about type:

- Combining several kinds of typefaces, as in the first line, makes the text harder to read.
- Both serif typefaces like Bookman and Times Roman and sans serif typefaces like AvantGarde are easy to read, but they give different

This is very hard to read **because the *font keeps changing.***
This is Bookman, an easy-to-read serif font.
This is AvantGarde, a modern sans serif font.
This is Zapf Chancery, a font you might use for a fancy invitation.
This is Times Roman, the most common font on personal computers.
See how you can emphasize something by typing it in **bold,** or even more in **BOLD CAPITALS? BUT IT GETS VERY DIFFICULT IF YOU WRITE VERY MUCH. IT'S JUST TOO HARD ON THE EYES.**

EXHIBIT 2–13   Examples of Right Justification

Construction on the project is expected to begin this spring. It is being designed by renowned architect Helmut Jahn and Krommenhoek/McKeown & Associates.	The very different fates of the blimps are symbolic of what's going on in the soft-drink industry. While much hoopla has been made in recent years over new cherry-flavored, orange-flavored, juice-added, even spice flavored soft drinks, the highflier of soda pops by far—even more than a decade ago—is plain old cola.

effects. A fancier typeface like Zapf Chancery is harder to read and thus is best used sparingly.

- **Bold** and **BOLD CAPITALS** both add emphasis, but overuse gives so much emphasis that the text is hard to read.

Text is said to be easier to read in a serif typeface (because that's what we have learned to read with), but visuals such as overheads and slides, as well as computer screens, are easier to read in a sans serif typeface because sans serif is more legible.

Just because your software program will automatically format a document for you (with your instructions) doesn't mean you should rely on it completely for your layout and writing decisions. Spend some time reading about type layout, and develop an eye for good placement on your own.

Right Justification

Right justification is harder to read than nonjustified (sometimes called *ragged right*) type. If you don't have proportional spacing, turn off the right justification—it leaves odd-looking spaces. (See Exhibit 2–13.) A number of researchers have found that ragged right is easier to read because of the more even spacing and logical word breaks. Steve Morgenstern points out that a justified right margin requires the writer to spend a lot of time policing the choices made by the program, such as hyphenation and spacing.[2]

Line Divisions

Line divisions can confuse your reader. One quick rule is never to divide a word at the end of a line; that way you don't have to worry whether you've

[2]*Home Office Computing,* February 1992.

done it in the right place! Avoid *widows* (last line of a paragraph appearing on the first line of a page) and *orphans* (first line of a paragraph falling on the last line of a page). Put an orphan at the top of the next column or page. Similarly, don't leave a word or part of a word with fewer than seven characters as the last line of a paragraph.

With a desktop publishing program, you can make a document look typeset (and also easier to read). However, if you use too many desktop publishing features at once, you can produce a document that is harder to read. Putting too many typefaces together, using boldface, putting boxes around text, and varying headline style and placement gives a document what is called the *ransom note* look. Compare Exhibit 2–14 to a ransom note made from cut and pasted magazine and newspaper letters and words to see where this label came from. In summary, your layout decisions should help your readers better understand your document, not confuse them.

CREATING AN EFFECTIVE BASIC BUSINESS MESSAGE
Keep it simple.
Make it concise.
Be sure it's complete.
Think of your reader first.
Run your spell-check program.
Proofread!

Electronic mail messages are messages entered into a computer and sent to another terminal or sometimes a phone system. E-mail messages are used by about one-third of all computer users. Instead of having to produce and mail paper copies of memos, you can send the same electronic message to as many people as you have addresses for with much less effort literally by touching one computer key (once the addresses are all entered). However, while they save paper, E-mail messages can still bury receivers with information as people discover how easy they are to send.

ELECTRONIC MAIL MESSAGES

The steps in writing an effective E-mail message are the same as those in composing a paper one: Analyze your audience, picturing the reader and his or her reaction to the message; plan the message; write a quick draft; and revise and *proofread* before sending your message into the electronic void.

According to the Roper Organization, 25 percent of personal computer owners use their PCs for electronic mail and facsimile transmission.[3] Electronic mail has the tremendous advantage of allowing you to notify all employees quickly about a change in hours, repairs to the building, additions to the company's library, and other information that would take stacks of paper memos to transmit.

For longer messages, E-mail may not work quite as well. A three-page electronic memo requires the same kind of planning as a hard-copy memo. Although DOS files can be transferred into E-mail systems and the length of the message (as long as it will read well in print) isn't a constraint, most E-mail messages are brief. These short messages are more like phone answering machine messages or quick notes than like printed reports. You can hear the "voice" of the writer in the E-mail message that follows on page 53.

[3]*The Wall Street Journal,* October 21, 1991, p. R15.

RANSOM NOTE NEWSLETTER

NEWS FOR NOIDS

Volume 1, Issue 1

October 1, 1992

Kidnappers get $2 million

PageMaker 4.0 for Windows-compatible computers

you have installed or are planning to install Windows type managers such as Adobe Type Manager, FaceLift, or Intellifont, please read TYPEMGR.TXT for information about using these programs with PageMaker 4.0.

Asked for used bills

For your viewing convenience, print a hard copy of this file to keep with your Page-Maker documentation. To read this document online in Notepad, choose "Word wrap" from the Edit menu for a readable text display, and use the "Search…" command when looking up particular topics.

WARNING: As a general rule, do not run more than one type manager at a time. Aldus product testing identified a number of conflicts when running Intellifont and FaceLift simultaneously.

This section explains a number of the more interesting nuances of using ATM with PCL and PostScript printers.

ATM uses about 400K of RAM, depending on the size of the font cache you have set up. If you have only 2 mega-bytes of RAM and find that Page-Maker runs slowly with ATM on, try running PageMaker with ATM off. If the difference in performance is

Get hard currency

If your purchase of PageMaker includes ATM, please note that this version of ATM uses different fonts from those available in the standard retail version. Specifically, the PageMaker version provides TimesNewRomanPS instead of Times, and GillSans instead of Helvetica. If you have already installed the retail version of ATM, you can still install the PageMaker version to add TimesNewRomanPS and GillSans to your "Font" submenu.

Another difference between the retail and PageMaker versions of ATM is that the ATM fonts Times and Helvetica map to (substitute for) the Windows fonts Tms Rmn and Helv respectively, but TimesNewRomanPS and GillSans do not. As a result, if you installed the PageMaker version only and want to treat these Windows fonts as ATM fonts, add these lines to the (Aliases) and (Synonyms) section of the ATM.INI file, which is located in your Windows directory:

Helv=GillSans
T   m   s
Rmn=TimesNewRomanPS

Howard Grey/Tony Stone Images

E-mail can't substitute for all face-to-face contact or long written communications, but it is a quick way to send many routine messages.

May 6, 1993

Staff:

Welcome to Round 2 of Let's Hire a Secretary. Even though I picked Door No. 1 in Round 1, they wouldn't give me my prize. Now I'm picking Door No. 2, and we should have someone beginning Thursday morning. Her name is Emily Yoshinaga and she has some good experience. However, this is her first job at a law firm, so please be your usual outgoing and cordial, patient selves.

Thanks.

Jim

Because the E-mail format lists full names in the address area, the writer doesn't have to use a full name and title and detract from the informal tone of the message.

Because computer screens look different from the printed page, when you prepare an E-mail message be sure to break up paragraphs, make lists, and otherwise include as much white space as possible. *Don't* right-justify or use all capital letters; your message will be harder to read. *Do* proofread before you "send" the message, because typos stand out on the screen just as strongly as on paper. Be sure to date and sign your message so the receiver will know how long it has been waiting (and you will remember in case the message comes back to you, either having been missent or attached to the reply).

E-mail has its own system of rules and etiquette, and many firms are realizing that this is one more area that needs a company policy. Here are some tips from experienced users:

- Assume your material may not be confidential. It could be sent to more people than you intend, be copied onto letterhead so that it looks like an official notice, or remain in archives that unknown persons have access to in the future. So don't call your boss names, arrange liaisons with your boyfriend, or discuss last night's happy hour electronically any more than you would on a monitored phone.

- Realize that humor, anger, or any other emotion can get lost or misinterpreted by the reader(s) of your message. Users have devised a set of symbols for happy, angry, and other feelings using common keyboard symbols. For example, :) means *happy* and :(means *sad* or *angry.*
- Realize that typeface choices make a difference even in electronic messages. All capital letters, for example, can look like "yelling" on a computer screen.
- Picture your audience just as you would in writing a paper message. This will help you avoid sounding harsher than you intend. You are addressing a person, not a machine. But remember that, like a tape recording, your electronic message may be preserved indefinitely. Think your message through and revise it rather than sending your first reaction, especially if it's an emotional one!

Ethical issues regarding E-mail are beginning to surface as more and more firms use it. According to the *Los Angeles Times,* although the Electronic Communication Privacy Act of 1986 protects against *outside* eavesdropping, E-mail is employer-employee communication and thus not covered under this act.[4]

The Los Angeles Police Department is now investigating the content of squad car messages—messages police officers thought were as temporary as a conversation. A Southern California company is being sued both by an E-mail manager fired for trying to stop other managers from reading messages between employees and by the employees whose messages were read.

The message is clear: The new technology created a new set of rules. Currently, companies take opposite views; some consider in-house messages to be like private phone calls, while others consider anything in house to be company property. From a legal point of view, the important point is to make sure employees know the specifics of the company policy on privacy.

A typical corporate policy on E-mail might include the following warnings to users:

- If you wouldn't say something in a business meeting, don't say it in an electronic message.
- Normal workplace rules of conduct apply: Don't libel or slander others, even public figures; don't make comments of a sexual, racial, or ethnic nature; don't use company time to socialize with other employees or plan nonwork activities.
- Because the computers are furnished by the firm for company use, the firm has the right to review and control this use.
- Political petitions, ethnic jokes, chain letters, activities for individual financial gain, and inappropriate disclosure of company information are prohibited in E-mail just as they are in other office activities.

Exhibit 2–15 compares E-mail to communicating in person, by memo or letter, and by phone.

[4]Amy Kubelbeck, "Getting the Message," *Los Angeles Times,* September 4, 1991, pp. E1, E2.

EXHIBIT 2–15   E-Mail Versus Traditional Business Communication Media

In-Person Communication	Phone	Memo or Letter	E-Mail
• Immediate	• Fast—if you reach the person	• Slow • Can reach hard-to-reach person	• Offers fast turnaround • Receiver must be on E-mail
• Feedback permits fixing errors	• Can recognize and fix mistakes	• One-shot—an error? Too bad!	• Can fix mistakes after the fact
• Group meeting is an option	• Conference call is an option	• Usually one message to one receiver	• Can send to many • Can replace or shorten meetings • Can forward to another receiver • Can verify message is received • Can make hard copy • Can store messages
• Low cost unless visit digresses	• Low cost unless call digresses	• Has high per-message cost	• Has low per-message cost
• Interrupts work in progress	• Interrupts work in progress	• Doesn't interrupt	• Doesn't interrupt • Facilitates group writing • Raises productivity • Equalizes status and promotes upward communication
		• High level of correctness expected	• Standards of correctness are looser
• People remain aware of receiver	• People remain aware of receiver	• People are careful	• People feel freer, less guarded • People forget human receiver • "Flaming" occurs Sarcasm, wisecracks Swearing, bad language Extreme statements
• A record is rarely made	• Few people keep phone log	• People are aware of document's legal status	• Stored messages can be subpoenaed • Users forget hard copy is possible • Users presume message is ephemeral • Security is not perfect
• Full range of visual and verbal signals	• Wide range of aural signals	• Very limited set of symbols	• Limited set of symbols
		• Good for long, complex matters	• Not good for long, complex ideas • E-mail promotes "windiness"

Reprinted by permission of J. D. Crowe.

Voice mail systems are disliked but expected today.

PHONE MESSAGES

Voice mail, phone messages, answering machines, and phone conversations form a group of communications that can cause unexpected problems. Voice mail systems seem to be one of the most disliked features of business today. Reasons include the impersonal quality of an electronic message and the confusing and seemingly endless routing a person gets from a poorly set-up system. Because so many people dislike voice mail and answering machines, you need to give some thought to audience analysis. These are areas where the audience's attitude toward the *medium* can hurt your message. Because phone communication is especially common in business, you need to be conscious of your voice mail messages, the messages you leave for others on their systems, and the impression you give over the phone.

Remember Audience Analysis

Of course, you will need to consider the content of your message. Consider the union president who left a message on an employee's answering machine that the employee would not be called back to work. The employee was so distraught that he went to his former post office job and shot eight people, killing four, and then shot himself. Although the employee was to blame, the thoughtless message certainly contributed to the tragedy. Leaving personal and potentially distressing messages on an answering machine or voice mail system is too distant a way of conveying important information.

In leaving a negative phone message, you will need to use a buffer to set up the situation but avoid giving the bad news. If you were delivering the news personally or in writing, you would use the same approach, as you'll see in Chapter 10: "This is Jennifer Slater. I'm sorry I missed you—please call me, as I have some news for you." The problem arises when people simply dump the bad news into electronic space. Perhaps we are less sensitive than we should be when we can't see people's reactions to our news. The detachment machines create can lead to rudeness if we're not careful.

Ellen Goodman has suggested that the game of **telephone tag** (calling and leaving messages for others, who then call and leave messages for you, then you call and leave more messages for them) now consists of leaving messages as quickly as possible, hoping the receiver will return the call to *your* machine.[5] In more courteous times, telephone tag consisted of leaving messages with machines and secretaries until eventually the two parties were actually able to converse. Now voice mail and answering machines are used almost as a letter used to be—as a nonpersonal way of transferring information and, as Goodman says, "with all its distance and none of its grace."

Since business consists of people, don't let your machines take over jobs that you could do better. Don't sacrifice interpersonal relations with your staff and your customers to speed and efficiency, or you may end up with a lot of time on your hands and no one to talk to!

Some companies that installed voice mail systems have removed them because the systems were alienating customers. First Union Bank in Charlotte, North Carolina, decided that "Voice mail sends a message that our time is more important than yours. That's not the message a service-oriented business should be giving out."[6]

The chief problem with voice mail is that people expect a human being to pay attention to them and give them a response rather than a machine that may shift the caller from one place to another. Because business consists of transactions among people, callers resent the difficulty of reaching a real person. Some systems offer an extensive menu of options before a caller can even use one of the options. Others offer every option except the one the caller wants.

A health maintenance plan in Concord, California, actually used people's dislike of voice mail to sell its services by advertising that "its members don't have to suffer through voice mail when they call." The ad made fun of competitors' complicated voice mail systems:

> If you have a question, press 1, now. If you would like it answered, press 2, now. If you would like to be put on hold for 10 minutes, press 3, now. If you want a membership card, please punch in Beethoven's Fifth, now, in D minor.[7]

Retain People Skills

Put the Customer First

---

[5]"In Today's Tag, Only the Losers Talk," *San Diego Tribune,* January 7, 1992, p. B-11.

[6]John Flinn, " 'To Disconnect, Press 1 Now': Human Tide Turns against Hated Voice Mail," *San Diego Tribune,* January 15, 1992, p. E-2.

[7]Ibid.

Even Miss Manners has compiled a modern list of etiquette points to smooth your way in communicating by phone.[8] The following list combines her suggestions with those of other phone users.

- Eliminate mechanical noise when possible. If your cordless phone buzzes, try relocating the base. Don't place cellular phone calls when traveling through a tunnel.
- Keep your phone message short and dignified: Give your name and number, then say, "Please leave a message."
- Get permission before forwarding your calls to someone else's office or home. Your host isn't an answering service!
- Leave your full name and number so the receiver is sure who called and doesn't have to look up your number.
- Place and receive calls so that you don't inconvenience those around you. On the commuter train, go to the vestibule; in a restaurant, leave your table; when driving, keep alert and pull off the road for a complicated conversation.

ANALYZING A CASE: HOW TO SOLVE A COMMUNICATION PROBLEM

Now that you know how to send basic business messages, you are ready to work on some cases to practice the things you are learning about successful communication. Many of the chapters in this book provide communication cases for you to solve. Here are some suggestions for writing a case answer (usually a letter or a memo).

You need to approach the case systematically, using Checklist 1–1 (Audience Analysis). Here's a slightly different version of those questions that includes some ideas on dealing with cases rather than with live communication situations. First, read the case through at least twice. Ask for clarification if you don't understand the information given. Then work through the case material, answering the following questions as part of your planning process:

1. Who are you to be? (Your role is specified or hinted at somewhere in the case.)
2. To whom are you writing, and will the information be welcome or unwelcome? Is the person familiar with the subject? What is your business relationship to this person?
3. What is the heart of the matter to be communicated? The case material may be purposely organized in a roundabout way to encourage you to analyze the situation rather than just use the facts in their order of presentation.
4. Should you use a direct or indirect strategy?
5. What data are extraneous to the case? We usually include information to help you feel as though you really work for the company described in the case, but you needn't give all this information to the reader. What does the reader *need* to know? Do you need to add as well as subtract information?
6. Do you need to organize the information to make it more understandable to the reader? Convert ounces to milliliters, for example? Put some of the numbers in chart form? Attach charts, insert graphics, or refer to attachments? (Your instructor may tell you that

[8]Judith Martin, "Be Courteous on Phone, But Wait for Sound of Beep," *San Diego Union-Tribune,* July 20, 1992.

you need not actually *attach* these materials in a timed, in-class case, but you can still refer to them to help your reader understand your communication.)

7. Would itemizing help highlight separate ideas? Would headings help organize information?

8. What response do you hope for? How can you end your letter or memo to get the action you desire?

Routine, direct business messages should get to the point quickly, cover the necessary information, and either ask for action or close quickly but in a friendly way. You can use forms or form paragraphs for many routine messages to save you and your staff time. If you can write an effective direct message for a specific reader, you can adapt the message to serve as a useful form for sending to many readers.

In this chapter, you learned how to prepare direct messages to

- Respond to a question from a prospective customer.
- Write an effective memo to convey requested information.
- Ask for information efficiently.
- Answer a frequently asked question with a form.

Using the planning, rough-draft, and revision process, you can prepare such routine messages efficiently whether you are responding in print, electronically, or by phone.

Service attitude, word choice, emphasis, and layout also contribute to the success of your communication.

APPLICATION EXERCISES

1. Look again at the Daffodil Days card in Exhibit 2–1. How can you reword the line "we deeply regret this inconvenience" to show that you're sorry and yet show *positive* concern for the reader?

2. What is a *service attitude?* Give an example from your experience of a store where employees demonstrate a service attitude. How do they make you feel important?

3. In the following pairs, which is the better subject line for a memo? Why?
   a. Parking Procedures
      Opening New Parking Lot No. 7 on March 5
   b. Payroll Office Now Open on Saturdays
      Paychecks
   c. Profits
      Profits Up 8 Percent This Quarter

4. What is *dated action?* Discuss the difference between these two requests:

   Because I need to compile the data by June 1, please send me your response before then.

   A prompt reply is appreciated.

5. Rewrite paragraph 2 in Exhibit 2–6 so that the requirements are clearer to the reader.

6. Write a paragraph addressing the potential customers' meeting in Exhibit 2–8. Make up the necessary details, and show where you would insert the paragraph in the letter.

7. Evaluate the humane society letter in Exhibit 2–9. In what ways is it a successful form?

8. Find an example of poor layout (bad-looking right justification, too many typefaces put together, type too crowded on the page, etc.). Write a paragraph or two about why the layout is poor and how you would change it to make it more effective.

9. How do you feel about telephone answering machines and voice mail? Give one or two examples of problems you have encountered when using these media.

10. Using the list for solving a communication case problem on page 58, work through the questions for one of the cases at the end of this chapter.

CASES

1. **Routine Form Letter: Revise for "You" Attitude.** The goodwill letter below is factually correct but written with little "you" attitude and lots of negatives. The effect is to make the discount card sound too difficult to use. Rewrite the letter so that customers will be encouraged to shop with the discount card.

   Welcome Senior Citizens:

   The Acme Grocery Company would like to welcome all senior citizens to take advantage of our 5 percent discount on their grocery bill.

   We have listed below some points on how the program works:

   —5 percent discount is for persons 55 years of age and older.

   —5 percent discount is available on Tuesdays and Wednesdays only.

   —Discount card obtained from courtesy counter must be presented to the cashier at the time of purchase.

   —Discount is applied before tax is calculated and before coupons.

   —Discount does not apply to tobacco products or beer.

   —Discount may not be used by dealers or on products purchased for resale.

   —Offer expires October 31, 1995.

   —Discount card is to be used by the person to whom the card is issued.

   We hope that this program will be a service to you. Please let us know if we can help in any other way.

   Thank you,

   Tom Jones and Gary Blake
   Managers, Acme Columbus and Hamilton

2. **Routine Inquiry Letter: Deciding on a Display Unit.** You have developed a home business creating and selling jewelry and scarves and want to start showing your creations at craft shows. Craft fairs are becoming big business in your part of the country, and you and your assistant could easily drive from show to show on weekends.

   Because some shows are indoors and some are outdoors, you need a display unit that looks professional but is easy to handle and adapts to different terrain (unlevel ground, a windy day). Some of the spaces you will rent will be 6 × 6, some will be 6 × 8, and some will be 10 × 10, so you will need a flexible arrangement of panels. You also need to find out if you can carry the display yourself or if two of you will have to go to every show. Some shows are held in dimly lit buildings, so extra lights might be a good accessory. Can you afford the display system? Will all of the equipment fit into your Mazda minivan?

Write a one-page inquiry to Graphic Display Systems, 31725 Williamson Parkway, Hauppauge, NY 11788, to find out if the panel display system advertised in the January issue of *Special Events* is the one for you.

3. **Routine Reply: Selling Your Display Unit.** As the marketing manager of Graphic Display Systems (see Case 2–2), answer the inquiry about the display unit. Your product is made of aluminum and has three panels, which can be carried and set up by one person in 20 minutes. It features adjustable legs, ground pegs for windy conditions, and panels either 6 × 6 or 6 × 3. For extra charges, you will include lights, panel covers made of fabric, and personalized signs that can be put on the top of a panel to identify the booth. You will pay for shipping and handling if the person orders within 30 days.

Customers can pay cash, by credit card, or in installments, and you can ship the order within two weeks of receipt. Write a response that answers all the questions about the product and makes it easy to order.

4. **Goodwill Letter: Saying Thank You.** Write a brief but specific letter to a company commending an employee who went beyond his or her job description to help you. If you haven't had a positive business experience lately, use the following anecdote for your letter (make up any necessary details).

The high heel of your shoe got stuck in an escalator and came off as you were checking in for a flight to Chicago. You were carrying only a change of shirts, as you planned to wear the same suit and shoes for both days of the trip. There wasn't time to return home and get another pair of shoes. The American Airlines counter clerk tried to find you a pair of shoes among the other employees at the counter; when that failed, she checked you in quickly and called a mechanic, who met you at the jetway and nailed the heel back on your shoe. It was a temporary fix, but he told you there was a shoe repair store inside the terminal at O'Hare, so you could get it fixed right before your business appointment.

5. **Inquiry: Selling your Product Overseas.** Write the U.S. Department of Commerce to find out if it is scheduling any trade shows this year that feature marine equipment, your specialty. Will the show be in the United States or overseas?

You are concerned that you can't afford to both pay a high fee and travel to an out-of-country show because your company is still pretty small. Can you go to a Department of Commerce office and just talk to someone? You would prefer to get an experienced exporter to do the selling for you—for a fee, of course. How can you tell if the overseas distributor is honest? You've read about firms here in the United States called *export management companies* that will sell for you on a three-year contract for 12 percent of gross sales. Would this be a better option? Can you find out in time to attend a trade conference in Denver in March? It is now February 7.

6. **Response: Becoming a Successful Exporter.** You are in charge of answering inquiries from new exporting companies (see Case 2–5). The Department of Commerce offers everything from training in export terminology to trade shows in the United States and abroad. A special service called the *agent/distributor service* takes two months, but for $125 it can help a company find overseas distributors for a product. (A credit report is available for an extra charge of $100.) Trade shows are as follows: A *catalog* show costs $100 to $300 and shows a company's catalog or video to potential buyers overseas. A *trade* show brings buyers and vendors together either overseas or in the United States (overseas fees range to $4,000 without travel expenses; U.S. shows are free, but the group of buyers is very small). Each district Commerce office (there are 68) has computerized databases on countries, markets, vendors, distributors, and so on. A person can just go to a Commerce office and look at the reports or subscribe for $360 a year. There is a trade show for marine equipment in Peru in June; the sign-up deadline is May 1.

Answer the inquiry in Case 2–5. Make this newcomer to exporting feel he or she has a chance of success in this growing market.

7. **Routine/Welcome News Memo: Improving Lunch Service.** You work in personnel at a medium-size firm that hasn't had a lunch facility up until now. Employees either had to walk or drive off site or bring a brown-bag lunch. Your firm has contracted with Service-USA for an on-site mobile lunch facility. It is a self-contained trailer with a walk-up window.

Write a memo to all personnel introducing this amenity. Describe it as much as seems necessary, and tell where to find it. You'll need to consider what types of beverages and food items, both hot and cold, a facility like this can offer, and you'll need to have some idea what they are likely to cost. You won't set up the whole menu, but tell employees approximately what they can expect.

To minimize waiting in lines, your company has decided to stagger employees' lunchtimes; one-hour lunchtimes will be at 11:30, 11:45, 12:00, 12:15, and 12:30. You'll need to devise an arrangement for which departments or sections go to lunch at what time and explain this clearly to avoid confusing anyone.

Mentally place yourself in this situation at a real organization. Try to think what questions employees will have, and include the answers in your memo. Present the information in such a way that employees will be glad to hear about it.

This message should run about one typed single-spaced page.

8. **Routine/Welcome News Memo: Borrowing Office Equipment.** Your company, Bellavista, Inc., is going to permit salaried employees to check out certain rather expensive items to take home for the purpose of completing work outside normal working hours. The employee checks an item out on his or her credit card, just as in a video store. *The item will be charged to that credit card if it is lost, damaged, or stolen.*

You will be in charge of checking the items out. You can choose your own area (notebook computers, company training videos, camcorder for practicing oral presentations). Mentally put yourself in the salaried position you'll occupy after graduation, and think about what company equipment you wish you could work with on weekends.

Devise a simple but foolproof system for checking out an item. Then write a memo announcing and explaining this arrangement. Be sure to develop the benefits to the reader. Emphasize (without talking down to the reader) that employees are responsible for the equipment or item once it leaves company premises.

Anticipate employees' questions, and answer them in advance. Where do they find you (room number, near what entrance)? What do they have to fill out? Do they need a supervisor's signature? If the item is heavy, can they drive up to the service door? Part of your grade on this assignment rides on how thoroughly you think these questions through. Also, consider how you can make this a positive benefit for employees without needing to hire a full-time employee to run the program.

This message should run about one typed single-spaced page. The *To* line should say, To: Salaried Employees of Bellavista.

9. **Routine Reply: Selling Company Services.** As licensing agent for the International Olympic Committee, answer an inquiry from a large food corporation of your choice regarding sponsorship of the 1996 Olympics in Atlanta. You want to encourage potential sponsors, and the goal of this letter is to set up an appointment to talk face to face with corporate decision makers about their sponsorship.

The food company is concerned that even if it pays a large sponsorship fee, competing firms may also sponsor certain events and dilute the effect of its expensive advertising. What is your policy on selling television time to outside sponsors? (For example, could one soft-drink company buy an official IOC sponsorship and another soft-drink company advertise during the television broadcasts?)

Your sponsorship package includes television rights, market research on sports audiences, and merchandise licensing (such as "the official cereal of the Olympic track and field events"). While costs are high ($40 million for an official sponsorship), the sponsor gets worldwide exposure and exclusive broadcast rights on the Olympics. Can you sell this potential sponsor on being one of 10 to 15 major sponsors? If you can, add specifics about sports and the company's tie-in to a particular sport.

This letter should be one typed single-spaced page with attachments giving some details. (You don't need to prepare the attachments, but you should refer to them in your letter.)

10. **Routine News to All Employees: Memo on Recycling.** You work in the administrative office of Bridges, a not-for-profit organization that provides legal mediation services to firms and individuals. Bridges is large for this kind of organization: 38 professionals and 87 support staff. An important part of your job is to monitor and purchase supplies. Since Bridges is a service rather than a product organization, it uses very large quantities of paper, some plastics (trash bags, diskettes, etc.), and other common items.

Bridges is committed to social responsibility and has had an internal recycling program for some time (for example, employees save used paper, computer printouts, and soft-drink cans from the employee lounge; each person has a personalized company coffee mug to use instead of throwaways). Realizing that recycling is creating a market for goods made of recycled materials, your boss asked you to locate suppliers of recycled and recyclable office supplies. You have already done this.

Write a memo, for your immediate supervisor's signature, directed to all employees, explaining your organization's use of recycled products. Before writing, think thoroughly about the possibilities and limitations of recycling for a situation like this. You may have to do some library reading on recycled office products.

Making up appropriate details, tell what suppliers you have located, what percentage of which of the organization's needs can be filled using recycled materials, and how the costs will compare with those of nonrecycled materials. (The organization may or may not be saving money, but it does care about recycling.) Be specific about what can be recycled: Printed forms? Computer paper? Copier paper? What else? Explain what supplies cannot be made of recycled materials. (For instance, high-quality paper has to be used for formal legal communications.) Describe how employees can recycle in their offices. Make the process sound reasonably convenient.

Be sure to make the message sound like welcome news rather than just additional daily tasks for employees. Think *reader benefits* and *goodwill*. Remember that your boss signs this memo.

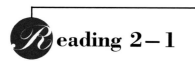

Reading 2–1

TOOLS OF THE TRADE

Cheryl Reimold

How can you use your writing to improve quality on the job? The answer is simple: tell your readers clearly and simply what they want to know.

The answer may be simple, but as most letters, memos, and reports prove, the execution of it is extremely difficult. Telling your readers what they want to know is wrenching work, when you're burning to write about what interests you.

But if you do manage to follow this simple guideline—every bit of it—you will improve the quality of work as you contribute important information effectively to those who need it to do the job well.

To see how to put it into practice, let's consider each part of this guideline.

Tell . . .

Before you put pen to paper or finger to keyboard, think: "I want to *tell* X that . . ." Do *not* think: "I want to *write* about . . ." The word *tell* is critical. It guides you to the straightforward, honest language of everyday speech.

If you start thinking *write* instead of *tell,* you'll be surprised how your words suddenly mutate and multiply. *Here is . . .* explodes into *As per your request, enclosed please find . . . When* expands into *at such time as,* if into *should the situation arise that,* and so on.

Even if you avoid the puffy polysyllabic, your attitude changes when you slip into the "write" mode. You begin to think: "How shall I write this?" instead of "What do I want to tell this person (or people)?" And before you know it, you're wondering about words and phrases instead of thinking about the message that you have to transmit.

. . . Your Readers . . .

Tell . . . led you to the right *words* and *attitude.* The next two words point you to the right *focus:* your readers. Be-fore you start writing, imagine who your readers are and what their interest in your topic might be. Then you'll have a good beginning idea of what to tell them.

. . . Clearly and Simply . . .

This is your guideline for *style.* Good style is not one that sounds "businesslike" or "formal" or "technical" or even "professional." Good style in business writing actually doesn't sound at all. You don't notice it, because it is totally in service of the message. It is clear and simple.

If you're focused on telling your reader what he wants to know, you will naturally search for the words that tell him as *clearly* and *simply* as possible.

. . . What They Want to Know . . .

This final part of the guideline gives you the *content* of an effective piece of writing. To be sure you write something that people will read, answer three questions:

1. What does the reader . . . or, if several, the primary reader . . . *already* know about the subject?
2. What else would *he want to know* about it?
3. What do *I* want to tell him?

Your answer to Question 1 will show you what you do and don't need to cover. Why waste your reader's time telling him what he already knows? Just give him enough background to explain and clarify your message.

Then answer Question 2 right away, as close to the beginning of your piece as possible. Tell your reader right up front what he wants to know.

If you're in luck, the answers to Question 2 and 3 will be the same. Sometimes fortune smiles on us, and to our delight, we find that what the reader wants to know is actually what we are burning to tell him.

But frequently, this is not the case. Hence the writer's dilemma: Which do I tell him first? Do I start with the vitally important point that I absolutely *have* to tell him? Or do I begin with the somewhat ancillary and frankly trivial thing that interests him? What if he reads that and stops there?

The answer is that busy people read only those things that they consider important. If you start with the point that interests your reader, you will get his attention. He will also feel positive about you and be willing to go on reading.

Start with his interest. Then go on to your interest. *But be sure to show him how that second point—your interest—affects him.* If you don't—he won't read it.

If you're not convinced, try stepping into the reader's place. Which would you like to find up front: the point that interests you or the one that interests the writer?

Tell your readers clearly and simply what they want to know. That's all. Simple, isn't it?

Source: Cheryl Reimold, "Communication—A Key to Quality Control. Part 5: How to Make Your Writing a Quality Improvement Tool," *IEEE Professional Communication Society Newsletter* (July/August 1992), pp. 6–7.

Business Writing Style

PREVIEW

Business executives and managers say repeatedly that they are looking for good writers. They want people who can use language well, say what they mean clearly, and move information efficiently and accurately to where it is needed. The better your business writing style, the better your writing will satisfy these needs of your business readers.

Good business style conveys the message without drawing either positive or negative attention to the style itself. Good business style is concise, clear, inconspicuous, credible, and suited to its medium and channel. It is courteous, correct, natural, positive, and interesting. It must be readable—and many of a writer's choices affect readability. It must be coherent, use emphasis appropriately, and avoid the "isms" (sexism, racism, and so on). This chapter covers all these characteristics of effective writing. It offers several generalizations about word choice and explores four areas where your educated judgment must guide your choice of words. Finally, the chapter looks at selected international aspects of writing style and at computer aids designed to improve writing style. ●

**Joel Shimerda
Branch Manager**

 rom the desk of...

I'm a branch manager in a marketing services company that operates in several southern cities. During a slow January, all branches received a memo from the boss in Mobile, Stephen Downey, saying, "Build business aggressively. Sign anyone interested and able to pay."

I'd been pitching Bolling & Co., an import-export firm that showed interest in contracting with us for radio spots and local print advertising. But then I got another memo from Stephen with strict orders *not* to do business with any company resembling Turetti Inc., another import-export company. The memo's tone discouraged discussion, and B & C was the same type of company as Turetti.

Though I hated to lose a promising contract, I called Bolling and said we could not provide the precise service they wanted. We didn't sign anybody new for the next two weeks, and suddenly Downey walked into a staff meeting, having flown in from Memphis for the sole purpose of reprimanding me. "I don't know if you're the kind of manager this company needs," he said.

In my defense, I outlined the similarities between Turetti and Bolling. "I followed your express orders," I said.

He looked sheepish. "That's not what I meant," he said, as all of us thought about the $15,000, three-month, renewable contract we'd lost.

MEETING READERS' EXPECTATIONS

The more writers know about their readers, the more writers can shape their messages to meet readers' needs.

People in business often must communicate with others whose experiences, needs, beliefs, vocabularies, educational levels, and emotions differ greatly from their own. Writers are rarely safe in assuming readers' minds are similar to their own. Assuming too much leads to reactions like "But I *told* you!," "But I didn't understand," "But I clearly said . . .," "But I thought you meant . . ." — reactions that inevitably subtract from a business's profits.

The first step needed to ensure that messages meet readers' expectations does not come naturally to most people. Writers need to get outside themselves, put themselves mentally into the reader's frame of reference, and view the message from the reader's viewpoint rather than their own.

In Chapter One, you read about reader analysis. The more you know about your reader or readers, the better you can shape messages to meet readers' needs. Ask yourself all the audience analysis questions set forth in Chapter One. Your answers to those questions will help you to write your business messages in the style best suited to individual readers' understanding.

When the message is highly important or the reader has unusual expectations, we can make additional inquiries about the reader. We might need to consider the reader's interests, biases, values, and priorities in choosing a writing style.

Other potential influences on writing style include the relationship between writer and reader, the reader's likely attitude toward the message, and even the kind of organization in which the message is sent or received. Will your readers resist what you say? If so, is it because they dislike you or the unit you represent, because the subject is distasteful to them, or perhaps because they have fixed ideas about how the matter should be presented? If you write assertively, will they dig in their heels harder? If you write deferentially, will they think you are a wimp? What will your readers find appropriate? Try not to disrupt those expectations.

Because business readers are usually rushed, with many things competing for their attention, they expect efficient, businesslike messages. A concise communication is easy to get through rapidly. The message must contain everything necessary for understanding but waste no words.

Don't repeat an idea without a reason. Don't use extra words. Redundancy is useless and irritating to a reader. Most redundancy comes from careless habit or a wish to impress. People say, "These are true facts" as though "facts" failed to express truth strongly enough. Facts *are* true; false facts aren't facts.

Redundancy is needless repetition of an idea.

Have you heard people say that ingredients are "combined together"? "Combined" *means* "put together." How about "revert back"? "Revert" *means* "go back." Here are a few more common redundancies and wordy phrases:

Instead of	Say
completely destroyed	destroyed
adequate enough	adequate *or* enough
assemble together	assemble
on an occasional basis	occasionally
a total of $945.95	$945.95
at this point in time	now, at present
each and every	each *or* every
for a period of six weeks	for six weeks

Editing out empty words will yield better emphasis for important words.

Business writers must write so clearly that the meaning won't be mistaken even if the reader's attention is divided. A variant of Murphy's Law makes clarity essential: If anything *can* be misunderstood, it *will* be misunderstood.

Nothing should be ambiguous. The language must be simple, plain, and clear.

Good business style is plain, unobtrusive, and "businesslike" rather than clever or artistic.

Anything in your writing that calls attention to itself calls attention away from the message.

"Anything" could be an overlooked error, such as an unclear expression or a sentence structure problem. It could be something that is not wrong in itself but inappropriate for business, such as a word the reader does not know, a pompous expression, a metaphor, a showy stylistic trick, a literary allusion, or any of dozens of other poor choices.

What calls attention to itself in business writing might be perfectly acceptable elsewhere. But if a business reader has to stop to figure out or think about anything conspicuous, he or she is for that instant *not* thinking about the writer's message. If the busy reader is handling many simultaneous messages, *this* message might get lost.

CREDIBILITY

A calm, balanced style raises the credibility of a business message.

Writers must be keenly aware of any personal biases or opinions so that their own "blind spots" do not weaken their messages. Even when writers attempt to persuade, their writing style must strike readers as balanced and sensible.

Precision in word choice, accuracy in facts and presentation, and full, understandable development of ideas contribute to a writer's credibility. So does avoidance of overstatement. Enthusiasm is attractive until it carries a person away. People overstate their case when their enthusiasm takes them beyond what is true. Business readers want *factual* information. When extreme terms are used carelessly or too frequently, they stop sounding true. The message is not taken seriously.

Watch out for words like *extremely, really, awfully, tremendously, terribly, such a, so much, really a lot, sky-high, wonderful, marvelous,* and *immense.* Use them infrequently enough that when you do use them they haven't been "used up." If everything is "wonderful," then nothing is. A word to watch closely is *very.* You will rarely need this word; avoid it unless you have a compelling reason to use it.

Be careful with the **superlative** degree of adjectives and adverbs—the *-est* form of a short modifier, like *newest,* or the *most* form of a longer modifier, like *most unusual.* Thrown about carelessly, these words lose their power to persuade or impress. Don't say that something is "the greatest," "the newest," or "the best" unless you can demonstrate that fact—and then do so at once.

Avoid declaring that "orders increased spectacularly" or using expressions like "a whopping" 45 percent. State the percentage and let the fact speak for itself, giving the reader a context for evaluating the number if necessary. Words like *spectacularly* and *whopping* imply that the facts are *not* substantial—that the reader has to be urged to see them as substantial.

SUITABILITY FOR MEDIUM AND CHANNEL

Style, medium, and format affect one another. The style of an electronic mail message might differ greatly from that of a formal report.

Writers need to choose medium, channel, and format with care and make style choices that work well in the channel selected. Many writing decisions relate to the level of formality.

Business letters, memos, and reports can assume a wide range of formality, depending on receiver, topic, and situation. At the formal end of the scale, consider a letter a law office might send to someone it is proceeding against in court or a mid-length memo report containing a research and development proposal. The longer documents become, the more likely they are to be formal. At the informal end of the scale would be a brief memo from a supervisor reminding subordinates of an upcoming meeting or a good-news letter from a company making a favorable adjustment for a customer.

Writers also use the medium of the letter, memo, or other written form with a view to attractive and appropriate format. Skilled business writers prevent paragraphs from getting too long and gray. They make use of white space (space containing no type, like margins, spaces between paragraphs and around headings) so that the reader's eye gets a rest between chunks of type. They employ other elements of eye appeal, like underscoring, graphs, or indented blocks, where appropriate.

A message that is attractively organized and carefully crafted for its medium represents you and your organization well. It sends a positive nonverbal message over and above the content and adds credibility to that content. Poor use of the medium sends the opposite message.

COURTESY

During the typical hectic business day, writers must remain aware of courtesy. All receivers of business messages should be treated with respect. In most cases, the necessary polite and positive words are ready in our memory, and all we have to do is remember to use them. For instance, instead of "Get these corrections back to me on the double," try "I'll appreciate having these corrections back by 5 P.M."

Sometimes you will write to someone who has annoyed you or disrupted your expectations. Using positive, courteous language in response to a negative message will be profitable. While you may be tempted to send a disrespectful or angry message, you and the business unit you represent cannot afford its cost.

Few things are free, but you can give—and receive—courtesy at no cost.

CORRECTNESS

Business readers expect error-free standard English. Your business style must show a competent grasp of businesslike usage, grammar, and word choice.

When is a word "correct English" or "incorrect English"? Many people believe that all of English falls neatly into rigid "right" and "wrong" categories. They are surprised to learn that usage experts differ over some elements. Nevertheless, unless you are sure about an individual reader, do not assume your reader prefers loose standards. You are safer taking a conservative approach to usage, so keep these points in mind:

- Business readers expect competent use of standard English.
- The way writers use the language makes an impression, good or bad.
- Business communication must be appropriate to the reader, the subject, and the situation.

Refer to your dictionary and the handbook section of this textbook when in doubt. Learn which elements of English may be changing. Some errors gradually become correct, but others will always be incorrect. Until most educated users view a changing element as correct, you will be wise to avoid the risk.

NATURALNESS
Write as you would (*carefully*) speak.

The language of your message should sound comfortable, familiar, and natural. "Write as you would (*carefully*) speak" is good advice. Think of the way you speak when the subject matter is important, your knowledge is thorough and well organized, and an influential listener is present. If your writing has that sound, it will sound natural to business readers.

However, "natural" does not mean "error filled." Do not pattern your business writing on careless, informal elements of spoken English such as "Well, like all of us, really, you know, feel like, well, our professor, you know, is just too hard." This looks ludicrous in writing and it sounds nearly as bad when uttered aloud. Readers expect complete, coherent sentences and accurate word choice. They expect you to say what you mean clearly and correctly and will be bothered if you do not.

Note Differences between Written and Spoken English

When you put your ideas in writing, you need to conform to a rather conservative set of rules. In speaking, a less strict standard applies.

For instance, many businesspersons—even highly educated ones—sometimes use "between you and I" or "on behalf of Chris and I" in speaking. Of course, these are errors. *Between* and *of* are prepositions; the object of a preposition is in the objective case. Thus, *me,* not *I,* is correct. So prevalent is this error in speaking, however, that businesspersons, even those who know it is incorrect, rarely feel very critical of the person using it. When they encounter the error in writing, though, they react quite differently.

DRABBLE reprinted by permission of UFS, Inc.

To many audiences, careless use of the language is highly irritating.

The spoken form of a language changes more rapidly than does the written form. In fact, written language acts as a brake to slow down the evolution of a language. What this means for business communicators is that in writing they must adhere to the conventions of standard English. If those writers rarely read, they will form all their language patterns on the basis of the spoken form. When those patterns are put down in writing, they are glaring errors to many business readers.

Writing is typically a more deliberate act than speaking. Unlike most listeners, readers assume writers have the opportunity to revise their work and to check for errors. Readers often keep written messages on file, and errors in those messages can come back to haunt the writers.

You may be objecting, "If the language is changing and most of us make the error in speaking, why don't they just declare it correct?" "They" are not just one decision maker but many people. Eventually a persistent error becomes standard, but meanwhile we must *write* for our business *readers'* needs. Most readers feel strongly about correctly written English, and we would be foolish to disregard their expectations.

Avoid Outdated Expressions

To sound natural and conversational, choose familiar words and normal sentence structure. Do not use stilted or outdated expressions such as "per your request" or "please find enclosed." No one speaks these phrases, so, in general, do not write them.

Most such expressions were common during the last two centuries, when businesspersons were the social inferiors of the wealthy classes they served. The language they used to address their patrons was subservient. For example, a businessman would close his letter with "Your most humble and obedient servant." A few such expressions carried over into the early 20th century. Here are examples:

Enclosed herewith is . . .

I beg to submit . . .

I offer for your kind consideration . . .

I take the liberty of sending . . .

I wish to acknowledge receipt of your letter . . .

Modern practice recommends doing away with expressions like these. If you have enclosed a price list, say simply "Enclosed is our price list." Better yet, say, "Our enclosed price list shows . . ." so that you get your reader *using* your material. If you are sending a proposal or an application, say, "Here is a proposal I hope you'll consider." The last phrase in the preceding list simply means "I have received your letter." Usually there is no need to mention that fact at all. If you are responding to a person's letter, obviously you received that letter.

Outworn expressions will strike a wrong chord with today's business reader. They are wordy and unnatural in modern communication. If an expression springs into your head that "sounds like business talk," think again; it may be one of these time-worn phrases. In general, if you wouldn't *say* it, don't *write* it.

Many words have multiple **denotations,** or dictionary meanings, and many have **connotations,** or emotional associations.

Use Accurate Denotation and Connotation

Explore the different denotations of an ordinary word like *key*. A key opens a lock. A key is also a list of answers to an exam. An island in a row offshore from the state of Florida is a key, as is the lever you turn to wind a music box. Composers write music in a key (for instance, the key of G major). Pianos and computers have keys. The top stone in an arch is a key, as is the scale-of-miles graph on a map.

All of the preceding examples are nouns, but *key* has many other meanings as a verb, adjective, or compound word, especially in idioms. A person who is keyed up is tense and excited. *Key* often means indispensable (key decision maker, key player).

These examples do not begin to exhaust the meanings of that one symbol. You know these meanings, and the people with whom you communicate know them. But you can see how misunderstandings can arise if a speaker or writer does not make clear from the context which of these many meanings he or she intends.

By estimate, the 500 most common words in the English language have a total of about 14,000 different dictionary meanings. That gives you an idea of the potential problems created by multiple *denotations*. Add to this the matter of *connotation*, the array of emotional associations that accompany some words.

A thorough grasp of connotation is one of the most useful skills a writer can develop. In informative writing, you should choose words without strong connotations. In Chapter Eleven, we'll examine techniques for writing persuasively and read about ways a persuasive writer can use word connotations to create the desired emotional appeal to the reader.

Some words have few emotional associations. It's hard to get excited about words like *building, report,* or *material*. Words like these do not create strong feelings for most people. Many words, though, have some type of emotional association, and some are heavily laden with connotations. The emotions conjured up differ widely in kind and in degree, *and they differ from person to person*. To a person who has high power, the word *power* will feel quite different than it will to a person who feels threatened and powerless.

"You say I have funny ideas. Is that funny 'ha-ha' or funny 'peculiar'?"

Consider the word *fight*, whose denotative meaning is "to struggle or contend with an opponent." But what connotative meaning does the word carry to a kindergarten teacher? To a football team? To a resident of south-central Los Angeles during the riots of May 1992? To a business competitor or a politician? To a person battling a grave illness? To you?

Consider a few more examples. What does *freedom* mean? How about *victim?* How does *blue* make you feel? What about *red?* How about *forgive, lawyer, regret, gift, vagrant, magic, fascist, snake, discount, Mercedes-Benz?* You probably do not have entirely neutral feelings about any of these words.

The fact that words evoke feelings, along with the multiple denotative meanings many of our most common words have acquired, creates a paradox for business writers. Words have denotational meanings only because users of the language agree on those meanings. Nevertheless, because of the different experiences people bring to the act of communicating, no two users agree exactly on either the denotational or connotational meanings of all symbols.

Naturalness might mean different things to different readers. Sometimes you will write for highly educated readers. These readers' expectations, based on the kind of material they read most frequently, will differ from the expectations of an uneducated audience and even those of a general audience. In meeting the expectations of an educated audience, you will sometimes use less familiar words and do less explaining. Don't assume, though, that a highly educated reader always wants to read at his or her top comprehension level. All business audiences expect and appreciate ease of reading and clarity.

Sometimes you will write for less educated readers. For these readers, you must write quite simply *without talking down to them.* Whatever their level of education and sophistication, all of your readers deserve respectful treatment. For all readers, avoid choosing odd synonyms over words they know. Do not flaunt your ability to create an ornate phrase. All business readers react negatively to obvious efforts to dazzle them.

POSITIVENESS

An old story tells of a pessimist and an optimist contemplating the same eight-ounce glass containing four ounces of milk. The pessimist remarks, "It's half empty." The optimist counters, "It's half full."

Businesspeople can make the best or the worst of a situation by the way they view it and talk about it. You are aware that people make decisions based not only on facts but also on how they feel about those facts. Using positive language can make a great deal of difference in how writers and readers feel about facts.

Business communicators are wise to keep in mind the feelings a given word can call up in a reader or listener. In business, a person who receives a letter beginning

We regret that we cannot, with existing information, honor your recent claim. You failed to provide . . .

will have an unpleasant reaction to the negative feelings that accompany the words *regret, cannot, claim,* and *failed.*

Positive words can convey the same message without the negative effect. The negative message you just read could begin

As soon as you send us the transaction number (see top right corner of invoice), we'll be glad to send you the replacement cordless phone you requested.

Although you may need to use negative words in exceptional circumstances, watch for opportunities to replace with positive language such negative expressions as these:

error	excuse	poor	reject
refuse	deny	fault	incompetent
doubt	unfortunately	guilt	ridiculous
you never . . .	you always . . .	why???	I told you so

Most readers react positively to positive language. Truthful, positive word choice is not false word choice, and it does not strike a reader as false unless it is overdone. Common sense, truth, and good taste should guide all word choice. For best effect, choose words with positive connotations whenever you can. Avoid bringing a negative note into your business writing unnecessarily.

INTEREST

Writing—and reading—about facts and figures need not be dull. A business style can have ample variety, visual appeal, and activity. You have some choices that will raise the interest level of your written messages. Where appropriate, you can

- Select active-voice instead of passive-voice verbs.
- Select action verbs such as *show, prove,* or *drive* rather than *be* verbs or weak, vague verbs such as *have, seem,* and *do.*
- Choose concrete, specific words instead of abstract, general words.
- Use the precise word needed instead of a vague word needing many modifiers.

A writing style that adds interest often makes the message more readable as well. The style used in the following memo could have "defaulted" to passive voice and weak word choice. Instead, the writing is lively and active.

The air-pump kneepad sales look good, at midquarter report. Regions 3, 4, and 6 sold, respectively, 7,218 units, 9,194 units, and 12,320 units.

At $32.74 wholesale, the pads compete on price as well as quality. Revenue for regions 3, 4, and 6 amounted to $236,317.32, $301,011.56, and $403,356.80.

At the end of the quarter, we should decide on promoting them in our other three regions.

Price can rise approximately $3.00 once our buyers recognize the value our product offers.

Sometimes, however, interesting writing might work against your goals as a writer. For instance, if you have to smooth someone's annoyance or convey unwelcome news, bland rather than colorful writing might serve you better.

A number of factors affect the readability of a message, including word counts, use of active voice, noun clumps, length of paragraphs and sentences, and use of white space.

READABILITY

Several business communication experts, including Robert Gunning, have developed numerical readability formulas.[1]

Consider "The Numbers"

To use most readability formulas, business writers take a sample of the document they want to check. They count several things: words, sentences, and number of long words. Using a simple mathematical formula, for each piece of writing they generate a reading on a scale. Gunning's formula, called the *Fog Index,* uses school grade levels—not only the usual kindergarten through high school grades but college and graduate levels as well, ending in the high 20s.

---

[1]Robert Gunning, *The Technique of Clear Writing,* rev. ed. (New York: McGraw-Hill, 1973).

Some communication experts advise you to write at a level just below your reader's education level. We say, "When in doubt, keep it simple." (Do not, of course, write so as to insult your reader's intelligence.) Few business messages are written too simply. The unreadable ones usually offend by being too long and using too complex words, sentences, and paragraphs.

Word counts tell only part of the story, however. Readable writing includes many characteristics. Some add interest to writing; others help the reader grasp quickly *who does what* or *what does what.*

Choose Active Voice

Use active rather than passive forms of verbs. Active voice and passive voice are covered in Appendix B, but let's briefly examine the difference this choice can make in business writing.

First, recall that *in **active voice**, the subject of the sentence is the doer of the verb's action.*

    subject/doer   verb   receiver of action
The manager coached the new employee.

*In **passive voice**, the subject of the sentence is the receiver of the verb's action.* The subject of the sentence does not act but instead is passive (is acted on).

    receiver of action   verb   doer
The new employee was coached by the manager.

In a passive-voice sentence, the doer either appears in a prepositional phrase late in the sentence or does not appear at all, as in this example.

    receiver   verb
The new employee was encouraged to use positive language.

As these examples show, a passive-voice verb differs from an active-voice verb in that the passive-voice verb always has the *passive participle (taken, built, chosen, shown, completed)* and some form of the verb *to be.*

Passive voice is not wrong; it has its uses, as we'll point out later. But business writers choose active voice most of the time, for several reasons.

First, active voice is shorter. Compare these active-voice verbs and their passive-voice counterparts. Note that passive voice is always at least one word longer than active voice:

Active	Passive
promotes	is promoted
has done	has been done
is fixing	is being fixed
gave	was given
did	was done
will ask	will be asked

You have been urged to cut excess words whenever you can. Sometimes you can do so simply by changing passive verbs to active verbs.

Second, active voice is livelier, more vivid, and easier for the listener or reader to picture mentally. In the sentence "Ted Farmer supervises three workers at the drilling site," the reader can easily visualize a man guiding other workers near some drilling machinery. In the sentence "Three workers are being supervised at the drilling site," the reader cannot so easily picture the action because no doer is mentioned. An action without a doer remains abstract. Even if we add the phrase "by Ted Farmer" at the end of the sentence, the reader has to wait for that detail, and chances are the detail will make little impression.

Third, overuse of passive voice makes a writing style dull and heavy. Imagine reading paragraph after paragraph in which nobody ever exactly *does* anything; things just *are done.*

> A decreased error rate *was reported* in the accounting department. The rate *was lowered* from 1.4 percent to .9 percent. The department *should be commended,* and it *is expected* that more confidence *will be placed* in any projections that *are based* on figures received from accounting.

Readers prefer to read about *people doing things,* for example, "The accounting department reports a decreased error rate." If you cannot write about people doing things, let the reader see *things doing other things,* as in "The low error rate permits increased confidence in projections."

If you see too many passives as you revise a letter, memo, or short report, ask yourself, "In this sentence, *who does what* or *what does what?*" Your answers should yield sentences with active-voice verbs to replace some of the passives.

In some cases, you might have good reason to keep some passives. Used sparingly, passive voice can add variety. In addition, using passive voice is a deemphasis technique. Business writers sometimes need to state things without drawing much attention to them. In bad-news messages, for example, negative information must be communicated, but the wise writer talks about reasons for the unwelcome news before actually giving it, uses positive language, and usually buries the bad news in a long sentence in a long paragraph. Frequently the writer also uses passive voice in that sentence to keep the reader from picturing the news vividly and becoming angry about it. For instance, the sentence "Because of heavy absenteeism caused by flu cases, the ambitious production target was not reached in February" tends to downplay and deemphasize an unwelcome piece of information.

Sometimes the doer of an action is so unimportant or routine that mentioning the doer in an active-voice sentence would overemphasize him or her and seem absurd. For example, in a routine short report, it would seem silly to say, "The men and women on the production line turned out 700 units—exactly the quota—this month" or "Our grounds workers cleared all the leaves on schedule." If the information is routine, report it without undue emphasis on the doer. The best form might be passive voice: "The production department's quota of 700 units was met"; "Ground raking around the plant was completed on schedule."

Passive voice tends to spread in business writing because businesspeople are interested in facts, numbers, quotas, trends, and accomplishments—more sometimes than they are in knowing who produced them. That doesn't mean businesspeople are unfeeling. They care about data because they must make decisions based on it. Though facts may occupy more of a typical businessperson's attention than people do, it's a rare businessperson who prefers to read long strings of passive-voice sentences.

English lets us use a noun to modify another noun. We do this daily: "The *parking-lot machine* wouldn't take my coins"; "The *evening accounting class*

Using active voice lets you show people doing things or things doing other things.

Avoid Noun Clumps

is full." Short "stacks" of nouns modifying other nouns create few problems. However, business, industry, government, law, and many academic disciplines have generated a long-winded, pompous, intimidating, official-sounding style of writing.

This undesirable style is heavy on long words, noun clumps, long sentences and paragraphs, unnecessary abstractions, technical jargon, and excessive prepositional phrases. The style overuses passive voice and **nominalizations** (nouns made out of verbs by adding one or more suffixes—for example, the verb *stratify* becomes the noun *stratification*). Such devices can make a two-page memo or policy statement virtually impossible to read. The reader wearies and perhaps desires no further exchanges with the writer.

In the following example, a daily metropolitan newspaper quotes a scholarly business journal:[2]

> In another case, a high *technology composites design house* chose to expand out of the protected *Class 1 custom aerospace market* into the competitive *Class 2 automotive adhesives business.*

Those four-noun clumps make for hard reading. Watch out for "noun abuse" as you write and revise. If you find yourself overusing noun clumps or writing tall "stacks," break them apart.

Shorten Sentences and Paragraphs

When you write, try to help the reader see the "skeleton" of the sentence,

$$S \rightarrow V$$

the subject and the main verb. Also, the reader should be able to see immediately which phrases and other modifiers belong to which words. If that succeeds, your idea will take shape in the reader's mind with no struggle.

Shorter is easier.

The longer a sentence is, the harder it can be for a reader to find its "backbone." Long sentences, even when perfectly grammatical, slow a reader down. Most experts say a business writer's sentences should *average* no more than 16 to 17 words. Sentence length can comfortably vary between 5 and 25 words.

Paragraphs in business letters and memos should be fairly short; a good average is six to eight lines. Paragraphs in reports, especially lengthy reports, can be longer. Even then, you should consider the reader's eyes and divide paragraphs that have become very long.

A paragraph is long enough when it contains the material the reader expects to find there. A typical paragraph contains

- A topic sentence.
- Sentences that develop the idea in the topic sentence (the number varies).
- A sentence that sums up and provides a transition to the next paragraph.

Exceptions to this outline exist. You might see a very brief paragraph whose sole purpose is to provide a transition between sections, or a one-line paragraph placed alone for emphasis, or a long paragraph containing a narrative. Business readers are accustomed to standard-length paragraphs, though. In general, you should meet their expectations.

[2]"Stephen King It's Not," *Los Angeles Times,* July 13, 1992, p. D-1.

When in doubt, keep a paragraph short. No paragraph should be stretched out or padded to make it seem more important.

On a page of a business message, all the space that contains no type is called *white space*. It includes margins, space between paragraphs, space around tabulated material, and the like. Picture the appearance of a page without white space, a page filled solidly with type. Such a page makes most people resist even starting to read. Readers like white space for several reasons:

- It lessens eye fatigue.
- It makes a message seem easy to read.
- It lets the eyes travel rapidly and determine a message's meaning quickly.
- It makes a page more attractive graphically.

Use white space thoughtfully. A page should look full and developed but still invite the eye.

What makes a message coherent? Basically, good standard English and sound sentence structure are necessary for all coherent business messages. If writing is flawed at this basic level, coherence is impossible.

In addition to using correct English and good sentence structure, a writer can do the following to help a reader understand the links among ideas:

1. Put the ideas in an order that makes sense.
2. Repeat key words as necessary.
3. Use synonyms for key words.
4. Use appropriate pronoun substitutes for key nouns.
5. List or enumerate key ideas. (The list you are reading makes use of this coherence device.)
6. Use conjunctions and transitional expressions to show relationships among ideas.
7. Use parallel structure to show equality among ideas.

The following memo body uses several of these devices. Italics highlight some of the repeated key words, synonyms, and pronouns.

When *Trident Computers'* fine *sales staff* hits its highest *energy* level, *previous sales records* tumble. *Holiday season* is coming, and all of *us* would like to see *another record* year.

We'd like, therefore, to ask *you* what *sales incentives* would make *you* feel most like outdoing *yourselves.*

Here are *some* of the *incentives* being considered for different levels of achievement. (Keep in mind that the larger the award, the fewer persons would be eligible.)

- Rotating engraved plaque for Salesperson of the Month.
- 2 percent added commission above a set level.
- 14-karat-gold lapel pins, with more valuable gemstones for higher levels of sales.
- Added days of paid vacation.
- One-week trip to Hawaii.

Please tell *your* manager by August 12 which of *these* would *energize your sales* the most. And if *you* have other ideas, please pass them on as well.

Trident is shooting for the happiest *holidays* ever—for all of *us*.

Repetition with variation can often improve coherence.

Study the effect of the key word repetition. *Holiday* at the beginning ties in with *holidays* at the end. Some form of *record* appears more than once. The same is true of *Trident Computers, incentive,* and *energy. Sales* is repeated in *sales staff* and *sales incentives.* The writer is careful not to repeat a word too often. In addition, she varies the form of the key word. Too frequent or unvarying repetition can strike a reader as odd or monotonous.

The indented list uses parallel structure. The pronouns *some* and *these* refer to the incentives on the list. Other pronouns—*we, us, you, your,* and *yourselves*—recall the nouns *Trident Computers* and *sales staff.*

Reviewing Transitional Expressions

The memo uses only two transitional expressions: *therefore* and *and.* Also, the sentence *Here are . . .* that introduces the list is a transitional sentence. When other coherence devices work as they should, a writer may not need many explicit transitions.

Following are some frequently used transitional words and phrases.

Transitional Adverbs

Most in the first list are ***transitional adverbs.*** Consider what each one means and how it is used:

therefore	for example	accordingly	furthermore
thus	on the other hand	next	hence
nevertheless	alternatively	however	in contrast
meanwhile	consequently	moreover	then
also	otherwise		

Transitional expressions help explain relationships among ideas.

Notice that some of these words, like *alternatively* and *nevertheless,* express contrast. Others, like *meanwhile* and *then,* indicate a time relationship among the ideas they link. Still others, like *thus, consequently,* and *accordingly,* show that the idea coming after them follows logically from the idea preceding them.

Coordinating Conjunctions

Coordinating conjunctions can express the same kinds of links among ideas that transitional adverbs do. Remember that conjunctions can "conjoin" clauses in sentences; adverbs cannot. Coordinating conjunctions are few enough to remember easily: *and, but, or, nor, yet,* and, in very informal writing, *so.* One of these can connect two independent clauses with only a comma between the clauses.

Subordinating Conjunctions

A ***subordinating conjunction*** makes a clause dependent. It signals a reader to look for another clause to complete the sentence. Here are some subordinating conjunctions:

before	after	that	in order that	who (whom)
though	where	unless	as long as	whoever (whomever)
although	wherever	why	as though	what (whatever)
if	when	since	whether	which (whichever)
as	whenever	because	whose	how (however)
as if	until	while		

TABLE 3–1 Techniques for Emphasis and Deemphasis

To Emphasize	To Deemphasize
Short sentence with one idea	Longer sentence with several ideas
Independent clause	Dependent clause
Beginning or end of sentence	Middle position in either sentence
Beginning or end of paragraph	or paragraph
Parallel structure	Avoidance of parallel structure
Parallel structure, indented, sometimes with numbers, letters, or bullets	Parallel structure, paragraph style
White space around idea	Inclusion of idea in paragraph
Repetition	Single statement or implication
Concrete, specific language	Abstract, general language
Active voice	Passive voice
Second person *(you)*	Third person *(he, they)*
Full development	Sparse development
Mechanical signals such as all caps, color, underlining, italics, boldface	No mechanical signals
Verbal "flags" *(most important, above all)*	No verbal flags

Elements receive emphasis when they differ from an established pattern. Make sure emphasis always works in your favor. Errors receive emphasis too, but you don't want that kind of attention in your writing!

Once you have learned how to use transitional adverbs, coordinating and subordinating conjunctions, and other means of achieving unity and coherence, you will have mastered an important business-writing skill.

EFFECTIVE EMPHASIS

When your message is neutral or favorable, consider using one or more emphasis techniques for the main idea. When your message calls for sensitivity or indirectness, one or more deemphasis techniques are appropriate. Table 3–1 lists techniques for emphasizing and deemphasizing.

One principle of emphasis is making an element *different* from what precedes and follows it. For this reason, emphasizing many elements has the effect of emphasizing nothing. Overuse of emphasis techniques also makes a message seem rough and jerky.

AVOIDANCE OF "ISMS"

The "isms"—sexism, racism, ageism, and so on—are enemies of business productivity. Nevertheless, some people feel threatened when those they perceive as unlike them seem likely to gain in power or economic success.

In the early part of the 20th century, nearly all business and professional leaders—managers, doctors, politicians, bankers, salespeople, executives— were white males. Language, including business language, promoted this assumption. Over the decades, the business world has assimilated many new or underrepresented worker populations and has supported their gains in power and economic security. Examples of these groups are women, minorities, elderly persons, and workers with disabilities.

Reading only about white male managers, executives, bankers, and the like tends to reinforce in a reader's mind the idea that only white males can hold these positions. For changes to occur, people have had to change the way they think and talk about these groups. Not everyone has changed. In addition, discrimination has become more subtle.

A group that lacks power can do little to prevent others from applying negative labels. Meanwhile, the labels create negative images in the minds of people who hire, train, evaluate, and promote workers.

A rigid and unchangeable negative image of a group of people is called a **stereotype.** Stereotypes appear in forms like these:

- You have to expect old Ted to be set in his ways. He must be at least 50.
- Ming is shy and unassertive—Chinese women are like that.
- Japanese men are evasive and sly.
- Latino men are hot tempered.
- If you hire workers with disabilities, you'll have to pick up a lot of slack.

Often stereotypes take the form of jokes, sometimes jokes told in the presence of a member of the targeted group. The target is supposed to "join in the fun" and "be a good sport." Or he or she hears, "Of course we don't mean *you.*" Jokes containing stereotypes have no place in business communication.

We encounter at least two kinds of "labeling" offenses. The first suggests that the status or accomplishment of a person who belongs to a certain group is unusual for that group. For example, when a newspaper reports, "Gerald Lanham, an African-American banker, said today that . . . ," it subtly implies that there is something strange about an African-American being a banker. The article should say simply, "Gerald Lanham, a banker, said. . . ."

The second type of labeling applies a racial, ethnic, gender, or other label with nearly every mention of the individual, whether or not the label is relevant to the matter being discussed. Phrases like "my Jewish friend says" or "our Latina sales associate" may seem to send a subtle signal that the labeled individual is not really "one of us" in the mind of the speaker.

One of the most damaging kinds of stereotype is the sweeping generalization. Like most of the other offenses, these inclusive and rigid statements can hit an individual in any category—sex, race, ethnic group, age, and so on.

"Soft" Categories: Generalizations with Growing Room

Generalizations and categories
are useful as long as new
information prompts us to
revise them. Stereotypes, which
do not change, are harmful.

Think for a moment about generalizing and categorizing. Are they wrong in themselves? Certainly not. They are natural and necessary functions of the human mind. If we do not make generalizations on the basis of our experience, we cannot learn. For example, from getting burned once by touching a hot radiator, we would not be able to predict that a second hot radiator would burn us. Similarly, categories serve a useful purpose. When we alphabetize a list of names, we create a useful category. When we tell a child, "Do not talk to strangers," we use a category to ensure the child's life and safety.

Categories and generalizations can become harmful stereotypes when they are created too quickly, when their scope is too inclusive, or when new, different experiences cannot modify them. As perceptive people gain more experience with members of a group different from themselves, they learn that these individuals are different from them in some ways, similar to them in other ways, but also quite different among themselves. Individuals are seen as individuals, and differences among groups become less meaningful. In other words, the categories and generalizations "soften." They resist becoming set in concrete. Revision is not only possible; it is constant. Responses are more rational. The individual using the categories and generalizations is able to grow.

Sexism

You have probably heard people say things like "Women are emotional and vindictive. They shouldn't try to manage. They especially shouldn't manage other women." The proportion of female managers who are not good at managing is probably the same as the proportion of ineffective male managers.

Labels, Descriptors, and Sexism

Another kind of sexism occurs when a male executive writes in a memo, "We're meeting with a lady construction engineer today. . . ." That executive may be implying a warning or a hint that the "lady" isn't to be taken seriously. Remarks of this kind should be avoided and discouraged.

We need to use sex-neutral word choices: *firefighter, police officer,* and *mail carrier* have replaced *fireman, policeman,* and *mailman; stewardess, male nurse,* and *foreman* have given way to *flight attendant, nurse,* and *supervisor.* The person who chairs a meeting might be the *chairperson, presiding officer,* or, simply, *chair.* We can use *synthetic* instead of *manmade* and *humankind* or *people* instead of *mankind.*

We need to avoid words and phrases that make women seem small, weak, or trivial. Avoid using and discourage the use of expressions like "the little woman," "the gals," "little lady," "the gentler sex," or "a small but mighty voice."

Details of physical appearance are irrelevant in speaking of a woman or a minority group member. For instance, since you would not write, "John Brown, the burly corporate executive," it is equally inappropriate to write "Mary Ward, the diminutive vice president." Similarly, expressions like "she's too mannish" or "she's too feminine" are impossible to interpret objectively. They convey someone's value judgment based on taste (which is in no way objective). They are not meaningful but are certainly prejudicial.

Singulars, Plurals, and Sexism

One language difficulty is the need for a singular pronoun to refer to a mixed group or to an individual whose sex is not known to us at the time we write. We have several options; clarity and gracefulness of style determine which to select.

- If the reference will be made only once, no problem. Say *he or she* or *him or her.* ("Each manager has selected his or her assistant.") If used more than once, however, the phrase will begin to call attention to itself and away from the message.
- Change to plural. ("All the managers have selected their assistants.")
- If you know the message will not be read aloud, *he/she, his/her,* and *him/her* are acceptable (though ungraceful).

- If you can ascertain the sex of the recipient of a letter or memo, do so. If you can determine your recipient's level of sensitivity on the "he or she" issue, do so, and write with that in mind.
- Some readers still find *him* and *he* perfectly acceptable as common gender. Use them only if you are certain you will not offend.
- In a long document with examples ("Manager A," "Manager B"), alternate sexes in your examples: Let Manager A be a woman, Manager B a man. Let some subordinates be women, some men.

In colloquial spoken English, many people use *they* or *them* to rename a singular. This is still an error in *writing*.

Racial and Ethnic Prejudice

Another offense is discrimination against ethnic and racial minorities. Hateful language, with racial, ethnic, sexual, and other slurs is still alive; in fact, recent court cases have shown it to be protected by the First Amendment. Examples are not necessary; this kind of language is easy to identify. It has no place in business writing or speaking.

Not all prejudicial language is blatant. Some takes the form of adverse assumptions and generalizations. ("Wouldn't fit in"; "Our customers just wouldn't take to him"; "Too brassy"; "Wouldn't be able to hold his own in our fast-moving organization.") Sometimes a stereotype takes the form of a "back-handed compliment"—an ostensibly positive comment setting an individual apart from what "everyone knows" about a group. ("You'd never expect someone named Juana to be five minutes early for work all the time, but she is!"; "Krisha is the most productive African-American worker I've ever seen.") No group is "always" or "never" or even "usually" anything. Across sexes, races, and ethnic and other groups, we see the whole range of human types and behaviors. Some Americans are evasive and sly, as are some Japanese, some Swedes, some Australians, and so on. Negative labels for Caucasian males are as inappropriate as negative labels for any other group.

Business communicators should avoid any wording suggesting that the presence and accomplishments of minority members, women, or any other single group are unusual for that group. For business persons to make such remarks, even in ignorance and with good intentions, is bad humanity and bad business. We all need awareness of *receivers'* perceptions of what we say. Sometimes those perceptions are surprisingly different from ours.

Bias Against Workers with Disabilities

Of the many groups seeking to find a productive place in the economy, persons with disabilities have faced some of the more serious language and labeling barriers. For example, a phrase like "wheelchair victim" creates a mental image of helplessness. That image, not the fact of the trained worker who uses a wheelchair, often blocks opportunity for the worker.

Workers with disabilities often face insensitive language and treatment daily, some of it absurd. For instance, a worker who uses a wheelchair sometimes finds people talking very loudly to him as though he were hard of hearing as well. People with disabilities also may bear unnecessary labels, such as "Curtis Baxter, the handicapped vice president of Warwick Inc., announced ground-breaking ceremonies. . . ." Baxter's disability has no bearing on the subject. There is no need to mention it.

In offering guidance to help remove language barriers, writing experts say, "Put the person first," that is, make the mention of the disability, if needed at all, secondary to the person and his or her abilities or accomplishments. If you need to, say "a person who has a partial hearing loss" or "a worker who uses braces." Most of the time, the disability will be irrelevant and you will need no descriptor at all.

We have not devoted space to all the groups who can be harmed by adverse word choice in the business communication environment. Stereotypical images and language directed against any group, however, must be discouraged. Stereotypes do great harm because they sustain negative images. People who hold stereotypes see what they think they are going to see, even if it is untrue. Even more stubbornly, they tend to exaggerate the importance of a negative and ignore a much more important positive.

Other "Isms" and Writers' Responsibility

Members of certain groups are becoming increasingly active in discouraging the language of discrimination. Older workers know they do not have to put up with "old coot" or "bluehair." The American Association of Retired Persons (AARP) is a large and influential group. Ethnic groups have formed antidiscrimination societies to protest language that denigrates them. Several associations of women executives and managers speak out against sexism.

Discriminatory labels are less frequent than they used to be, but attitudes change slowly and sometimes grudgingly. It is important to avoid discriminatory language yourself and to challenge it if you see or hear it from others. This does not mean that you can never say a person has a disability, is female, is Asian-American, and so on. If you use the descriptor only when it is relevant, though, it will not create an image of "differentness" or inferiority in a receiver's mind. Suppose Curtis Baxter in our earlier example was invited to join the governor's advisory group on making buildings accessible to people with disabilities. Baxter's being himself a member of this group makes the fact relevant.

Avoid using discriminatory language yourself. Challenge it if you see or hear it from others.

The language we use in business can help make the mix of people around us work for the prosperity of everyone. We all need all of us, working productively.

Writers about business communication agree on five basic principles governing word choice:

WORD CHOICE: SOME GENERAL PRINCIPLES

1. Choose short words over long words.
2. Choose plain words over pompous words.
3. Choose familiar words over unfamiliar words.
4. Use concrete, specific words rather than abstract, general words.
5. Choose precise nouns and verbs over adjectives, adverbs, and prepositional phrases.

When you write—and when you revise—follow these principles unless you have good reason not to (we'll point out some exceptions as we go along).

Modern English abounds with synonyms, as a scan of your thesaurus will reveal. Often we have a choice between a short word and one or more long synonyms. In general, choose the short word unless it's odd, unfamiliar, or

Choose Short Words over Long Words

imprecise. (You don't want your word choice to call attention to itself, make your reader stop to decipher meaning, or cause other problems.) Here are some examples.

Instead of	Try This
advise	tell
endeavor	try
transpire	occur, happen
substantial	large
insufficient	not enough
subsequently	later

Consider, however, that some long words are necessary. A short word for what you mean may not exist, or the connotation of a shorter word may be wrong for your purpose. Especially as you revise, if you find a string of long words, try to substitute shorter words for some of them. Strings of long words discourage a reader and slow comprehension.

Other considerations might suggest choosing a longer word sometimes. Some longer words are not at all difficult. Also, using too many short words makes a writing style seem childish.

Choose Plain Words over Pompous Ones

Weed out wordiness and pretentiousness, as in the following examples:

Instead of	Try This
along the lines of	like, such as
above-mentioned	these
ascertain the data	get the facts
at all times	always
conceptualize	think of
eliminate the possibility of	prevent
the manner in which	how
until such time as	until

Choose Familiar Words over Unfamiliar Words

"I hear you talking, but the words are so big they don't leave any room for the ideas."

Some short words are unfamiliar. For example, instead of *gaffe* you'd choose the synonym *mistake* or *blunder* for most audiences.

Unfamiliar words are even harder on a reader than long words are. Readers can often figure out what a long word means if they are familiar with some of it. If a word is unfamiliar, though, readers have no choices other than stopping to look it up or skipping over it and trying to guess from the context what it means. As the writer, you don't want readers to stop or skip, because that interrupts the logic of your presentation. You don't want readers to guess what you mean, because they might guess wrong. And you don't want to irritate readers, because you want to build and preserve a good business relationship.

Here are some examples of possible unfamiliar words and suggested substitutes:

Instead of	Try This
concomitant	accompanying
stratum	layer
malfeasance	wrongdoing
dissimulate	pretend
controvert	dispute
vigilant	watchful

Observe caution in using familiar words. Sometimes the familiar word is not the right one. For instance, an *envoy* is usually a messenger with high status. To call an *envoy* a mere *messenger* could give offense. Be certain of the connotations of the words you choose.

A few people really enjoy thinking mostly in abstractions. Though readers can manage some abstractions, most would rather read about concrete, specific things—things they have actually seen and known about. Concrete words permit readers to visualize meaning and thus remember more easily. The following example illustrates abstract, general language:

> Woodleigh and Sons intends to seek a growth pattern by encouragement of capital investment and intelligent use of leverage, while holding to its ideals of community service and corporate citizenship.

It's hard to sustain interest at this level of abstraction. Readers can't pin this kind of writing down. They wonder just what constitutes "a growth pattern." Does "encouragement of capital investment" mean they should expect a new public stock offering? Which of the several ways to use leverage (corporate debt) will be chosen? And what will be done for the community?

Abstractions are sometimes useful in business writing. Sometimes a writer can begin a piece abstractly and get down to concrete examples soon after. If writing becomes laden with abstractions, however, readers grow bored and sometimes suspicious. Abstractions, even more than ordinary words, mean different things to different people. Business writers can hide in abstractions.

Abstractions and generalities are sometimes misused to blur meaning. Some business writers, when in doubt about whether a statement can be made, simply state their facts more generally. Then no one can exactly say they're wrong. This amounts to evasion, however, and no business writer does well to arouse distrust in a reader.

In the example just given, stockholders who bought stock expecting dividend income might suspect that "a growth pattern" means profits will be reinvested instead of paid out to stockholders. Readers can't really tell what the statement means. It sounds vaguely good, appropriate, and sound, and it doesn't tell readers a thing.

Here are a few examples of concrete, specific words and some abstract, general categories to which they might belong:

Concrete and Specific	More Abstract and General	Still More Abstract and General
Scanlon Plan	gain-sharing plan	employee benefit
union demand for $2 raise	wage dispute	disagreement
June 16 sales for Southeast Valley	sales figures	data

It's possible, of course, to overspecify. A cafeteria manager writing a short report for the accounting department wouldn't name all the cafeteria workers, dishes offered, and employees served. A writer should be as specific as the reader will find meaningful.

Abstractions and general language also *deemphasize.* Sometimes a business writer needs to report something without drawing attention to it. For example, suppose a minor mistake was made, discovered, and corrected. Use of concrete, specific detail and active voice (who did what) would tend to inflate the importance of the mistake, and the mistake has already been corrected. The business writer's best decision in this case is simply to state the event in general language and passive voice and move on to more important and positive things.

Choose Precise Nouns and Verbs over Adjectives and Adverbs

Weak, general, imprecise nouns and verbs need describers—adjectives for the nouns, adverbs for the verbs. Choosing strong nouns and verbs will permit you to cut many adjectives and adverbs. Examples of weak verbs are *go, make, do, have,* and any form of *be.* Instead of "Model P-614 will be a good seller for us," write "Model P-614 will sell well." Rather than "Volume went upward," write "Volume rose" or "Volume climbed," and then say by how much.

Let the verbs in your sentences work hard. Don't overwork the nouns. And especially don't put the whole burden on the adjectives and adverbs.

A major noun problem occurs when a writer chooses inexact nouns and then has to nail them down with descriptors. Avoid words like *area, situation, concept,* and *progress,* which say little in themselves. Such "empty" words require more words before a reader can determine their meaning. What "area"? Name it: "Word processing needs. . . ." What "situation"? Say "The electrical short on the cutter. . . ." State the "concept." Delineate the "progress." Pin these abstractions down.

Watch for *-tion, -ance,* and *-ment* nouns. Often you can change a noun phrase to a single strong verb. Here are a few examples:

Instead of	Try This
make an examination of	examine
for alignment of	to align
the preparation of proposals	preparing proposals

VARIABLES AND JUDGMENT CALLS

Use a given slang term, euphemism, jargon word, or new term only if your audience knows it and will receive it well.

The last element of word choice concerns several "judgment-call" language categories, including slang, euphemisms, jargon, and a category best called "new language." Your judgment must guide you here, because all these categories contain some useful and some useless words. The criterion for judging whether to use a given slang term, euphemism, jargon word, or new term is whether your audience knows it and will be receptive to it.

Slang

Slang is highly informal, nonstandard English. Closed groups that guard their closeness generate slang. You're "in" if you know it; you're "out" if you don't. Slang has come from junior high school student cliques, soldiers, the drug subculture, truckers with CB radios, and dozens of other groups. Much of it disappears rapidly and is replaced by other short-lived slang.

Ms. Dog could be "best of show" or a major disappointment. With slang, audiences can't always tell.

Some slang enters the mainstream of language. For example, *far out* was— but is no longer—a popular expression. You'll recognize *dudes, punch him out, cool, dis,* and many others. Rarely would any of these belong in a business message. Take a word like *guys* however. This word might appear in a memo to someone the writer knows quite well. Or the writer might use *vanilla* to refer to a plain version of something (a car, a computer) that could have extra features but does not, or say that the car or computer that does have the extras comes in *flavors* or even *tasty flavors.*

People might argue that these words are not slang but are instead colloquial, though highly informal. But this distinction is not the point—the point is *the reader's expectations.* If the reader will appreciate your saying "It blew me away!" when something has astonished you, go ahead and write it. If you have any doubt whether the reader will accept a slang expression, simply find a more conventional way to say what you mean.

People are uncomfortable with some basic facts of life, among them death, old age, sex, mental or physical disability, and drug abuse. Most of the world's languages have generated euphemisms for these and other "taboo" subjects. **Euphemisms** are words and expressions intended to soften the impact of these ideas (at least until the euphemisms become too closely associated with the subjects themselves and new ones must be found). Ideas that make businesspeople uncomfortable include failures, financial losses, emotional outbursts, bad debts, and lies, to name just a few.

Euphemisms

Euphemisms soften shock. For instance, a corpse is *the loved one,* a widow is *the bereaved. Undertaker* and *mortician* are former euphemisms that began to sound too harsh; now we have *funeral directors, grief therapists,* and vendors of cemetery lots who offer *preneed planning.*

No one suggests that you call all uncomfortable ideas by their real names. If you do, you will offend many people. In many cases, a euphemism keeps people from being disturbed unnecessarily, and that's good. It's hard to object, for example, to the "Special Olympics" held for "special children" (children with disabilities). Likewise, if a newly bereaved person says a "loved one passed away," most people understand and sympathize.

Closely related to euphemisms are **dysphemisms.** These are unfavorable, ugly, shocking, sometimes disgusting words and phrases for uncomfortable ideas. Some dysphemisms for *drunk* include *blitzed, bombed, plastered,* and *hammered.* (These are mild ones; some others are unprintable.) In provoking laughter, dysphemisms offer a person an alternative way to deal with uncomfortable ideas.

Some euphemisms are necessary. Using offensive language would be foolish. Business communicators, however, must develop a sense of the appropriateness of euphemisms. Where ideas are oversoftened, people may regard the language used as prissy, cowardly, or evasive. When euphemisms go too far, they can make people suspicious, since writers and speakers sometimes use euphemisms on purpose to deceive. In extreme cases, euphemisms can draw ridicule. For instance, pundits have taken sniper-shots at congressional expense account padders by suggesting they are "ethically challenged."

Go easy with euphemisms. Readers and listeners aren't stupid. Their suspicions flare when they feel someone is avoiding the truth. Assess your audience. Don't offend, but don't say what is untrue.

Jargon

Jargon is the specialized language of a given occupational group. Accountants, lawyers, finance people, doctors, and telephone line repairers all have their specialized language. Here are some examples and the associated specialties:

sinking fund (finance)

connectivity (computer information systems)

OABs, for "opinions, attitudes, and beliefs" (marketing research)

SKUs, for stock-keeping units (inventory management)

animal-unit-month (range management)

redlining (insurance)

deadheading (transportation)

NIMBY, for "not in my back yard" (waste management)

Specialists need their jargon. Use jargon, however, only with others who understand the language of your specialty.

If you work in a specialized setting and use specialized terms, be sure your audience knows what they mean. When communicating with other specialists, feel free to use the jargon. It would be an error and a waste of time not to, for specialized terms are usually coined to shorten a long explanation or to name something new, something that had no name before.

When communicating with nonspecialists, use specialized terms *only* if the reader is familiar with them. If the reader is not, either (1) define the term before you use it or (2) find another way to say what you need to say.

Insecure writers sometimes try to impress a reader by using terms that are "above" that reader's comprehension. Business readers are seldom impressed by someone else's jargon. Instead, they get annoyed, suspicious, or sometimes even insulted.

New Language

All language changes, though slowly. Each time something is invented, it is named. Thirty years ago, the word *software* didn't exist. When it first appeared, it was considered jargon. Today, when even very young children use software to play video games and do homework, *software* can't be considered jargon any more.

New words enter the language constantly. Many, though not all, are useful to business-persons. Avoid using new words your readers or listeners do not know.

Many new words gain acceptance slowly. The useful word *Ms.* has had a hard struggle. The word *prioritize* still bothers some people, but the synonym, *rank according to priority,* is four words long.

We pick up new language from conversations with others and from the mass media. We casually speak of "the learning curve," "stonewalling" someone, and being "at the cutting edge." Many new terms begin as metaphors, then spread and develop until most businesspeople know what they mean. For instance, managers who have negotiated rich financial packages for leaving positions are said to have *golden parachutes.* Managers who are so well compensated in their present jobs that they cannot think of leaving have *golden handcuffs*. Managers who accept a sweet retirement deal take *the golden handshake*. Underlings who have only modest retirement deals have *tin parachutes*. The language of corporate takeovers generated a long list of metaphors, including *white knight, poison pill,* and *sharkproofing*.

In making your judgments on these judgment-call word choices, follow your audience's preferences. When in doubt, use familiar standard English.

THE GOAL: A MATURE BUSINESS-WRITING STYLE

The best business style contains varied sentence structure and vocabulary but remains readable. When writers can go beyond correctness and find the exact word needed and the best sentence and paragraph structure for the thought, they are mature stylists.

This skill does not develop by accident. Most writers build their vocabularies by *reading* attentively rather than by memorizing vocabulary lists. They build variation into their writing style by observing how other effective writers achieve their desired effects.

The more business writers read, the more they can observe and learn from professional writers whose efforts appear in the business press.

Reading also helps business writers stay abreast of the latest developments in business. The "what" to write is integral to the "how" of writing it. Reading makes business writers more knowledgeable and effective businesspeople.

"I've found my voice, Penny. It's deep, wise, and compassionate."

Drawing by Leo Cullum; © 1992 The New Yorker Magazine, Inc.

Whether you write with a keyboard or a pen, readers hear your words in their heads. Skilled writers create an excellent impression of themselves and their business units.

Good business writing appears in the many books published on business subjects, as well as in the business section of any metropolitan daily newspaper, in *The Wall Street Journal, Barron's, Fortune, Money, Entrepreneur, Business Week,* and many other business periodicals. Nearly everything this textbook says about good business writing characterizes the writing in those periodicals.

Business writers who make reading some of this material part of their daily routine profit in two ways. They enhance their mastery of the language, and they broaden their understanding of the business world. If you are taking other business courses besides communication, you will find that reading business periodicals makes the material in those courses easier to understand. In the business world, you will find that your reading will add to your effectiveness on the job.

When you read an issue of *The Wall Street Journal* or *Business Week* to develop your language power, notice *how* these professional business writers write. Note their word choice. (When you come across unfamiliar words, try to figure out their meanings from context first. If you cannot, then look them up, make a note of their meanings, and try to learn them.) Notice the ways professional writers avoid passive-voice verbs—how they keep the style lively, interesting, but in no way distracting. Try to incorporate in your own writing some of the things the pros do.

Keep on reading as much good writing as you can possibly find time for. Keep building your mental word bank. Make a good friend of your dictionary. The more words you know, the more varied the audiences you can write for and the better you can choose your words for each audience.

WRITING FOR READERS IN OTHER COUNTRIES

You may have read that Japanese writers and speakers use extraordinarily polite language, begin their letters with a pleasant reference to the season of the year, and favor indirection. If you have seen British business letters, you may have noticed many expressions termed "outdated" in this chapter. The tone of British business correspondence seems formal by our standards.

An American business writer who is likely to write for non-American readers should try to learn as much as possible about those readers' expectations. These two examples do call for some adjustment on the part of the writer. Though many Japanese readers diligently study the ways of other cultures, an effort to write using some of *their* conventions is likely to please. British business is more attentive to hierarchy and status than American business. Glenda Hudson, a British scholar teaching in the United States, has remarked that what we consider naturalness in writing can seem breezy and disrespectful to British business readers.[3] Our standards of courtesy may fall short.

Differences among languages may or may not affect the way we write for non-U.S. readers. For instance, you may know that German words and sentences tend to run long. The German language uses compound words where speakers of English would use phrases. German sentences can be exceedingly complex. This makes little difference, however, when German readers are reading English. They will prefer that we keep it simple.

Short, simple sentence structure and word choice are even more helpful to people whose first language is not English than they are to the rest of us.

[3]Glenda A. Hudson, *"Internationalizing College Business Communication Courses: Addressing the Expanding Outer World,"* paper presented at the meeting of the Association for Business Communication, San Antonio, Tex., November 1990.

Chapter Three

Metaphors and slang can baffle non-American readers, though some jargon may be quite familiar to them.

The newer versions of the major word processing programs offer computer-assisted spelling checkers, writing checkers, and thesauruses. These tools are often a great boon to business writers revising their messages.

COMPUTER AIDS TO REVISING

Spelling Checkers

Upon command, you can send a spelling checker through the document you have keyed in. Most spelling checkers work by comparing the words in your document with the words in their dictionaries. The spelling checker stops at any word it does not recognize, asks you onscreen whether the word is misspelled, and suggests corrections.

The program's dictionary does not contain all the words in the English language. Therefore, if you have used an unusual word, the spelling checker will highlight it as a potential misspelling. It will also highlight any customer's unusual name as a potential misspelling. However, the program will let you put the new word into its dictionary if you wish. Once you do, you need never accidentally misspell that word again.

The drawback of many spelling checkers is that they show you only the words they do not recognize. If you misspell one word and accidentally hit the spelling of another word, the program won't signal you. If you enter *you* for *your,* the program will accept the error because it recognizes *you* as an acceptable word.

Newer versions of spelling checkers help users check "suspicious" spellings. These checkers contain lists of frequently misspelled or easily confused words. If you confuse *accept* and *except,* the program may help you. Regardless of the program's capabilities, however, the responsibility for correct spelling lies with you.

Certain elements of good writing can be checked by a computer program. Many software companies offer packages to help a writer avoid specific writing weaknesses, including

Writing Checkers

- Excessive use of passive voice
- Overuse of *I, me, my*
- Clichés or inappropriate euphemisms
- Faulty parallel structure
- Vagueness and excessive abstraction
- Wordy phrases
- Subject-verb agreement errors
- Noun-pronoun agreement errors
- Some punctuation problems
- Some usage errors
- Incomplete word processing changes, such as *the the* or *this it.*

Typically, the program has in memory a list of things it has been told to recognize as problems. In your document, the program will pick out any element corresponding to its list, offer suggestions for revision, and ask you whether you want to make any changes. You would then key in what you want. Sometimes you would make the change. Sometimes you would not.

Language is complex, and a computer program knows only what a programmer can tell it. Because language includes many variables that require a writer's judgment call, many elements of good writing are beyond what a computer program can check—at least for now.

People with weak writing skills will find writing and spelling checkers helpful for solving some of their writing problems. People with good writing skills may find a writing checker an irritation. One writer commented that Lincoln's Gettysburg Address would have been severely criticized by a typical writing checker. It "offended" by repetition, abstractness, and "wordy" phrases such as *fourscore and seven years ago.* But few would suggest that Lincoln's famous speech contained weak writing.

Good business writers get more benefit from spelling checkers, writing checkers, and thesauruses than weak writers do. Writers need to know *when* and *when not* to take the computer's recommendation and where the computer is *not* helpful.

Thesauruses

Are you stumped for an elusive synonym? Do you know that the word you need exists, but you have been thinking for 10 minutes and it won't come to you? Use a computerized thesaurus to help you find it.

The newer versions of the best-known word processing programs offer a thesaurus. Usually all you have to do is press a key, enter or highlight the word you want to replace, and send the program searching.

Some thesauruses offer both synonyms and antonyms (words with meanings opposite to those of the given words). Some offer help in deciding which words belong in which contexts.

Some thesauruses merely offer lists of synonyms. If you are unfamiliar with many of the words on the lists, seeing the synonyms will not help you much, and you will need to consult your dictionary. The better your existing sense of language, the faster and more effectively you can use a computerized thesaurus. Often just seeing the synonym onscreen will let you say, "That's the one."

REVIEW

Analyzing readers' expectations permits writers to adapt their style to fit the task and the audience. In general, good business style is concise, clear, and inconspicuous. Style choices affect writers' credibility. Messages should be courteous, correct, suitable for the medium selected, natural, positive, interesting, and readable.

This chapter also covered means of achieving coherence and effective emphasis. Language choices must not convey bias, whether intended or unintended, against any group. In general, readers prefer short, plain, familiar, concrete word choices emphasizing lively verbs and nouns. For different readers and situations, however, writers must write at the level most acceptable to their readers.

As language changes, slowly but continuously, new words enter the language. Writers must make sensible word choices within the evolving categories of slang, euphemism, jargon, and new general business vocabulary.

Increasingly, communicators must interact with persons from other nations and cultures. Reading business news improves our understanding of non-U.S. communication audiences and also builds word power.

Computerized spelling and writing checkers can improve writers' ability to revise the messages they craft.

Analyze yourself as a business writer. Make a list of your strengths and weaknesses. Be as impartial as you can. Give yourself credit where you deserve it. Set some meaningful goals to improve your weaker areas. Start by marking the Business Writer's Self-Analysis.

Business Writer's Self-Analysis

Below are some fundamentals of good business writing. On a scale of 1 to 5
(1 = "needs attention"; 5 = "good habit formed"), mark the extent to which
you have formed good habits.

Do I

1 – 2 – 3 – 4 – 5	Have and *use* a good desk dictionary?
1 – 2 – 3 – 4 – 5	Have and *use* a grammar/usage handbook?
1 – 2 – 3 – 4 – 5	Read to increase my word power?
1 – 2 – 3 – 4 – 5	Understand my purpose clearly before beginning to write?
1 – 2 – 3 – 4 – 5	Remember that each message makes an impression of me and of the unit I represent?
1 – 2 – 3 – 4 – 5	Analyze my own intentions and motives?
1 – 2 – 3 – 4 – 5	Analyze the needs of my reader?
1 – 2 – 3 – 4 – 5	Choose my medium carefully?
1 – 2 – 3 – 4 – 5	Choose words carefully for denotation and connotation?
1 – 2 – 3 – 4 – 5	Strive for a sincere, courteous, businesslike tone?
1 – 2 – 3 – 4 – 5	Use a plain, clear, correct style?
1 – 2 – 3 – 4 – 5	Both write and revise?
1 – 2 – 3 – 4 – 5	Seek—and take constructively—the criticism of others?
1 – 2 – 3 – 4 – 5	Always write from a firm foundation of honesty and ethics?

APPLICATION EXERCISES

1. What elements of style interfere with readability?

2. What are the different denotations of these words: *state, stick, down, drag, draft, crash, bar, pick, pull, turn, out, jump, ice, gross, clip?*

3. What are the various means of emphasizing an idea?

4. Revise the following examples to improve conciseness.

   a. Oftentimes it was necessary for Rob to communicate both verbally and in writing with people quite a bit higher in the organization. His productivity reflected that he did this well because his tasks were accomplished in a timely manner.

   b. Our organization accepted and understood the fact that many of its recently hired employees were new and not yet fully or adequately trained. If Colin, a new mid-level employee, had admitted what he did not know and asked for help instead of guessing or trying to figure out what to do, he would have received help and it would not have been held against him. As it was, he completely destroyed the project.

   c. Our new work space was square in shape, surrounded on all sides by partitions. Each Monday at 9 A.M. in the morning our supervisor convened us all together in this common area and outlined the work for the week to come.

   d. When the delivery drivers returned back to the dock Friday afternoon, they received checks in the amount of their regular pay but also including a holiday bonus as well.

   e. Many sources agree that Peale's sets the standard for customer service, and their success in gaining new markets is attributed to their customer service. Peale's is an example of what customer service is all about. Their corporate legends, for example, put Peale's customer service on a pedestal. When it all boils down, the customer is what will determine the fate of any corporation.

5. Revise the following examples to improve credibility.

   a. We all want you to feel very, very welcome in this organization. It's one big happy family. My door is always open. Bring all your problems to me.

   b. This plan for tripling sales is awesome, and I just can't understand why no one has thought of it before. I'm positive the chief is going to love it.

   c. We'll have no problem improving efficiency. We're going to make productivity our middle name.

   d. This design is tremendously unique. We expect it to create a real sensation in the market and generate astronomical sales.

   e. Quality circles are the best trend in participatory management in years. Wherever they are implemented, productivity is going to rise.

6. Revise the following examples to make the language more positive.

   a. Your communication exceeds the boundary of your job classification. You are intruding on someone else's job, for which you have no authority.

   b. The sales department should not have told you we could make this component for what you are willing to pay.

   c. Stop trying to tell me how to do my work.

   d. Your work is never going to measure up. Start looking for another job.

   e. Your demands are unwarranted. You are asking for service that you have not paid for.

7. Rewrite the noun clumps in the following examples.

   a. Our production line job rotation policy requires management level employees to exchange places twice a year with ten-year veteran line workers.

   b. This consumer opinion marketing report discusses winter season outerwear buying trends.

   c. The inexperienced retail bank branch manager demanded that merchant customer service tellers perform loan office filing tasks as well.

   d. Ability to formulate adequate crisis situation control plans became one of the most important public affairs officer promotion criteria.

   e. The year 1979 was the earliest that detailed office absorption information statistics were tracked. No office space demand forecasting models were then available.

8. Rewrite the following examples using active voice.

   a. All his statements were communicated by memo and no opinions were ever given by phone.

   b. Organizational leaders need to be told when customers are disappointed by service representatives, so that corrective action can be taken.

   c. It has been made very clear by Ms. Allbright that turnaround time must be improved. If rebuilt machines are not returned to users by the promised date, penalties may be assessed.

d. Because fault was admitted, the clerk was felt to have obligated the firm. He was admonished and directed not to be misled into any similar error in the future.

e. Critical comments should not be made in public, especially when these remarks can be overheard by subordinates or customers.

9. Improve coherence and transition in the following paragraphs. You may need to reorder ideas, rewrite sentences, and add or change transitional words.

a. We cooperated on a project with a worker who was new to the department, who knew the company well, but did not adhere to its guidelines. This was Allen. The project was critical to a new-product offering. Management had promised delivery by June 1. Allen always said his part of the project was on schedule. Our department is frank. If something is not on schedule we are encouraged to say so. Allen's part was actually behind, and falling farther behind every week. We counted on Allen but he caused us all to miss the deadline and the whole department looked bad.

b. In interviews, applicants should display confidence. Applicants have only 20 or 30 minutes in which to present themselves. If they do not give full, developed responses to questions, the interviewer has no means of differentiating their skills from those of other applicants for the job. The initial impression sets the tone for the entire interview. If they walk, move, and shake hands timidly, they may be judged unable to hold their own with co-workers and clients.

c. One unethical behavior is knowingly withholding information another person has a right to have. Sometimes products are so shoddy that they harm others who rely on them. Recognizing the various kinds of unethical actions is the first step to applying pressure to stop them. Unethical people are ready to lie for the sake of gain. Still another unethical act is taking money for inferior goods or services.

d. Laptop and notebook computers are commonplace in the 1990s. Only 10 or 15 years ago a "portable" computer weighed 60 pounds or more. Now a seven-pound computer can hold many large application programs and still offer a user plenty of computing power for doing work. The old portables took up a great deal of desk space. Laptop computers can communicate via fax and modem with distant sites. Short battery life between charges is a drawback of many laptops.

e. Being overqualified for a job can lead to a number of problems. Being able to finish tasks early sometimes gives people time to disturb other workers and to arouse discontent. Often they hope to be promoted when no legitimate promotion path leads upward from the job they hold. Hiring the most talented person for a job is not always a good idea. Too low a level of challenge can make them discontented.

10. Eliminate the "isms" in the following examples.

a. Most of the engineers enjoy working with Marie. She's one of the guys. You never hear her whining about equal opportunity. She pulls her share of the load.

b. We're multicultural here. We have hardly any Caucasians, and we all get along just fine. Why, I'm even starting to like watermelon and tacos.

c. We all need to slow down and help Faye out now and then, right, Faye? When Faye and my mom were kids, nobody had ever heard of computers.

d. Kent, our auditor, an epilepsy victim, is no problem at all as long as he takes his medicine. Don't worry about Kent. In fact, he has an idea for automating one time-consuming step in the audit.

e. The vibrant Shelly Norcross, newly promoted marketing vice president, will improve the scenery around headquarters, and I'm not talking about landscaping.

f. Mark doesn't seem to understand that nurses avoid bragging about their own skills. He's always volunteering instead of rotating duty the way the rest of us do. He's just a typical self-promoting male.

g. That new division manager thinks she can get her program going just by asserting her shiny new authority. Pushy broad! There's a reason for the glass ceiling.

11. Make word choice in the following examples shorter, plainer, more familiar, and more concrete where needed.

a. Workers will please curb their loquacity during any hiatus in the workday. It is requisite that we apply ourselves with diligence in order to win through to our goal.

b. These reports are abysmal. Do not expect plaudits in return for this infelicitous compendium.

c. Despite expeditious and concerted application, we are not sanguine about our nascent organization's ability to overcome our larger and better funded adversaries.

d. Vis-à-vis your rather byzantine plan, surely you are cognizant that actual authority for carrying it out emanates from my office alone.

e. No one wishes to denigrate your intentions; yet the prodigality of these expenditures suggests that full understanding of your fiduciary responsibility may to some extent have eluded you.

12. In the following examples, make it easier for the reader to locate the subjects and verbs.

   a. One of the brokers who accepted an inappropriate offer and several others who knew about the case received formal warnings.

   b. An individual faced with a crisis and not knowing whether to consult management or act decided to act. Litigation, by the time she was able to convince management that the decision was correct, was in excess of $3 million.

   c. During one whole week in late January, while we were working hard on a proposal, at the worst possible time, the only area marketing sales rep, despite the looming deadline, decided to decrease the number of hours spent on site.

   d. Working all day Saturday and Sunday, coordinating with engineering, and calling in two temps to assist, the pricing department had the proposal ready Sunday night, though the program manager seemed neither to realize nor to appreciate the extra work done to bring his project in on time.

   e. The most important way people gain promotion in Bayard-Bookman, a multistate retail organization specializing in hard goods, especially audio equipment and household appliances, is through positive visibility.

13. In the following examples, identify and, if necessary, translate elements of slang. For each, discuss circumstances where the term would be appropriate or inappropriate.

   a. You think this was an epic sesh? Take a tall glass of reality. The big guys weren't even listening to you.

   b. I'm new here. Can you throw down the 411? Where's the supply room?

   c. You heard the CEO say bonuses are going to be paid even with the fourth-quarter losses? Get outa here!

   d. The new manager RIFd three assistants. Then Kay and David got bogus appraisals when they expected at least average ratings. You and I aren't hearing about all scheduled meetings. Go figure.

   e. You think Tom isn't playing with a full deck? You're clueless. Get a life.

14. Discuss the differences among the following sets of terms. Which are most euphemistic? Least euphemistic? What connotations distinguish them? Add to each set if you can.

   a. garbage, refuse, trash, landfill contents, waste, recyclables

   b. servants, staff, retainers, people, help, associates

   c. false teeth, dentures, bridgework, appliance

   d. arrest, detain, bust, apprehend, take into custody

   e. spy, secret agent, intelligence agent, investigator, private eye

   f. indoctrination, education, programming, brainwashing, orientation

   g. dying, "no codes," slipping away, terminal, going into the great sleep, going away

   h. cheap, reasonable, inexpensive, great value

   i. steal, liberate, pilfer, embezzle, rip off, snitch

   j. lie, prevaricate, stretch the truth, fabricate, tell a little white lie, falsify, embroider the truth

15. Rewrite the following examples using the *least* disturbing words. Consider connotations, and keep in mind that what you say must sound sincere and credible.

   a. You're wrong.

   b. You don't have a job any more.

   c. You are insubordinate.

   d. We don't have enough money.

   e. Your work is poor.

   f. We can't do what you want.

CASES

Discuss the problems of writing style in each of the following cases. What paper personality is established in each message? What style elements create it? What are its advantages and disadvantages?

As your instructor directs, rewrite one or more messages to correct the style and other problems.

1. Letter from a Word Processing Agency to a Prospective Customer

Dear Ms. Parsons:

I'd like to introduce you to the services of our agency, Blaze Word Processing. When you finish this letter I'll hope I've interested you enough to get in touch with us and send us some of your high volume word processing production work.

We pay exceedingly close attention to each and every client's particular and special needs. We do this whether we are retained on a temporary or permanent basis. We don't make erors. We absolutely always get it right the first time.

We serve law firms, general medical offices, out-patient surgery clinic facilities, other professionals, and lots of general business organizations. We can work 24 hours a day if extra effort is required by your time schedule. Pick-up and delivery can be arranged for a very slight extra charge usually in the neighborhood of 5 percent.

We would like to be considered the next time a new person is needed in your office or when your capabilities are exceeded by your work load. Tell me if I can give you any further information on your particular and unique needs. Remember, Blaze is hot!

Sincerely,

2. Letter from Property Tax Department of a Development Company to a Purchaser

Dear Mr. Eddings:

This will acknowledge receipt of your letter dated October 30, 1992, in re Account Number 13-07687, addressed to Mrs. B. Knabesvater.

Now that your property has been paid in full, the Warranty Deed was sent to the Recorders Office on October 22, 1992. Therefore your 1992 and subsequent tax invoices will be mailed to you directly by the Breen County Tax Office.

It is incumbent upon you to keep the Assessor's Office aware of any change in your address in the future.

Per the terms of your Real Estate Purchase agreement, the ownership records could not be recorded to your name from the Trustee name until such time as your contract was paid in full.

The questions relating to your for sale signs have been referred to the Architectural Committee and you will doubtless hear from them shortly.

We are desirous that the foregoing has been responsive to your inquiry and please do not hesitate to contact this office if we can be of additional assistance.

Sincerely yours,

3. Collection Letter

Ms. Chamblee:

This is to inform you that your account at our store is OVER DUE.

It is our policy to write an informational letter to all new patrons, like yourself, immediately if we do not receive a payment on time, by the first of the month. Recognizing that you may be used to more lenient credit policies and may not have read the credit agreement, we do this for your benefit, so that you are aware of our no-grace policy and can plan to make all future payments ON TIME.

If you neglected to read our contract, let me remind you that any LATE PAYMENTS, those received after the first of the month, are not credited to your account until the following month and thus incur extra interest. Unfortunately, we have been forced to adopt this policy for our own protection due

to an increased number of clients with unprofessional budgetary habits.

I hope this information will save you interest on your account in the future and look forward to doing more business with you.

P.S. We are also enclosing a lovely nature calendar as a personal gift to you.

4. Letter from an Insurance Agent to an Insured

Ms. Imelda Cronin:

Your claim for insurance to cover the repair of your car and your neighbor's was received in this office last Thursday. Thank you.

You claim that your car rolled out of the driveway and smashed into a neighbor's car across the street and now you want us to pay for the repair to her car and to yours as well. First let me tell you that your right, your covered for the damage to her's. I sent an adjuster to her house and all the necessary forms have been completed and her car is already in the shop being fixed to her satisfaction.

Now about your problem. I am sorry to tell you that there is nothing I can do for you. Even though you were not driving the car, we must assume that you neglected to set the brake or put it in park. So that leaves it up to you to fix.

You are eligible though to receive, under your auto insurance clause F, $15.00 a day of coverage to cover the rental of another car while your's is in the shop being repaired. I hope it doesn't cost too much. If you refuse to rent a car, we will still pay you $10.00 a day to cover the bus or whatever.

Also, since this claim did require a settlement on our part, we will be raising your insurance premiums. I can't tell you how much, but someone will be in contact with you soon about that.

Thank you for coming to us with your problems. We are here for you.

Sincerely,

5. Letter from a Real Estate Salesperson to a Prospect

Question: What is this message really saying? This writer is using euphemisms and "code words" to market in a way that is not permitted by law.

Mr. Blanc:

I'm contacting you about our new real estate listings because your name was given to me by a friend in common who appreciates your discriminating taste. We have some lovely homes—all exclusive listings—to offer for sale.

Considering your status in the community and your concerns for your family, I can assure you that each of these dwellings is in an environmentally secure neighborhood, with private security, schools, churches, and old-fashioned shopping centers close at hand.

Owing to your excellent credit rating and our private lending sources, we are also able to skip many of the tedious formalities so often required in a normal sale.

I do hope you give me a call, so I can discuss our area over the telephone.

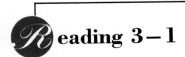

CHOOSING A STYLE

Reading 3–1

Arthur H. Bell and Roger Wyse

Is there one divine business style? Of course not. Even the advice in this book against a heavy, ambiguous style must sometimes give way to the situation at hand.

Consider the dilemma of a company executive, for example, who is asked by a reporter to comment on the company's liability in a recent chemical spill. A short, terse answer—"No comment"—may arouse hostility. Yet a frank, sincere answer—"We probably have a great deal of liability in the matter"—may be legally and professionally disastrous. What to do?

Learning to change styles to meet situations is an extremely valuable business skill. The executive faced with the dilemma described above chose to "fog" the question through somewhat obtuse, ambiguous language:

While it is impossible at this time to make a full assessment of the unfortunate incident to which you refer, I can say that the company has obtained the services of an independent review agency of the government to assist it in evaluating both the causes and the ramifications of the incident.

Is such guff successful? It depends upon the occasion. In this case, the obtuse statement bought time for the executive and the company. The real answer could come later in a carefully worded and legally reviewed press statement.

Remember that "good business style," like a "good personality," is really a bouquet of different styles, all ready to serve as the situation demands.

Source: Arthur H. Bell and Roger Wyse, *The One-Minute Business Writer* (Homewood, Ill.: Dow Jones–Irwin, 1987), p. 58.

MUTUAL FUNDS TRY SOMETHING NEW: PLAIN ENGLISH

Reading 3–2

Kathy M. Kristof

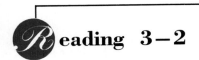

Key investment documents put out by mutual funds have always sounded something like the Coneheads from "Saturday Night Live." They were incomprehensibly technical. But now, a handful of investment companies are trying something novel—communicating in plain English.

- Fidelity Investments, the nation's biggest fund company, with $165 billion in assets, just finished a major overhaul of its prospectus—the legal document that spells out the strategies, risks, past performance and fees associated with an individual fund. The documents have been rewritten, reorganized, and redesigned to set off important sections, show more with graphics, and treat English like a first language. The result: They're actually fairly easy to comprehend.
- John Hancock, an insurance company that operates a family of 32 mutual funds, just issued new annual reports—the once-a-year updates that tell you how your fund has invested and performed.

    The new document contains frank commentary from fund managers, who talk about which investments soared and which ones bombed and why. They also discuss future strategies and clarify the points with graphs and pie charts.

- T. Rowe Price is also in the process of revamping its annual reports. The Baltimore-based fund company says it expects to have new annuals out by spring.

    "We are going to try to use the English language," vowed Ed Bernard, the company's vice president of marketing.

Although some talk about the revised materials is clearly tongue-in-cheek, the issue is not silly.

Over the last two decades, mutual funds have become one of the nation's most pervasive investment vehicles. Industry experts estimate that 36 million individuals own stocks or bonds through a mutual fund. Mutual fund managers now control more than $1.5 trillion in assets.

The most important documents put out by these funds—the annual reports and prospectuses—have been dull, dry, technical, colorless, poorly organized, and nearly impossible to read. As a result, some investors simply don't wade through all the jargon. And that can leave them woefully unprepared for the risks they're taking.

This problem is nearly as old as the industry itself. But fund managers have devoted new attention to it for a simple reason: Today's low interest rates have sent thousands of bank and thrift depositors scurrying for other opportunities.

These individuals, who are believed to be somewhat less sophisticated than the average mutual fund investor, have poured billions of dollars into mutual funds during the last several months.

Net sales into mutual funds totaled $132.8 billion during the first eight months of 1992 versus $65.9 billion during the same period a year ago. If this pace continues, 1992 will be a record year for the mutual fund industry.

Industry experts fear, however, that these newcomers don't fully understand mutual funds and are consequently somewhat uncomfortable with their investments.

If fund managers are not able to change that—and fairly quickly—the newcomers are likely to abandon the industry the moment interest rates rise. And they'll take their billions of dollars with them.

"There is an element of shareholder retention here," said J. William Benintende, a spokesman for John Hancock Mutual Funds. "If shareholders are comfortable with their investment and feel like the fund company is doing right by them, you are more likely to retain those assets even when the alternatives become more favorable."

The recent emphasis on clear communication may have other roots as well. Some experts suggest that investors are increasingly impatient. They want to be able to get the information they need by scanning investment documents instead of having to spend hours wading through legalese.

Statistics indicate that the bulk of American women are now working and trying to divvy up household chores. That leaves both parents with less time to relax, play with their kids, or consider their investment options. Some fear that these busy folks will only invest with mutual funds if they can do so with a minimum of time and effort.

"People have just so much time," said Ellen G. Hoffman, senior vice president at Fidelity Investments in Boston.

"Because we made it so difficult to invest, they had to spend more time than they wanted to. Some of them might just have decided to go elsewhere."

Kathy M. Kristof, "Mutual Funds Try Something New: Plain English," *Los Angeles Times,* November 1, 1992, p. D4.

Chapter Four

Short Reports and Proposals

Reports are more or less formal presentations of information, informed opinion, and analysis written to help people who must make plans or decisions. Typically, reports are prepared either on request or on a predetermined schedule.

Short reports—generally those shorter than 10 pages—tend to be informal, simply formatted documents that allow the recipient to understand a point quickly and with little effort. They may take the form of a letter or memo and are often addressed to a client, boss, associate, or several people.

Although less formal than long reports, short reports involve the same steps in preparation. You decide on the subject matter of the report (often called *defining the problem*), gather information about the subject, organize and analyze that information, and present it in a clear, understandable way.

The ability to write effective short reports will be a key to success in your business career. In business, you get rewarded for getting things done, and short reports will help you do that. Although some report assignments ask only for information, analysis of the information often helps the reader use it. By providing clear and logical analysis, you can help your company take effective action—and help you advance in your career.

In this chapter, we will look at the general structure of short reports and how to plan, organize, and write them. Then we will analyze some specific examples of the various kinds of short reports and show how to apply the general concepts in greater detail.

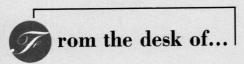

From the desk of...

Corporate Culture Clash

Laura Marks
Sales Representative

The memo upset all of us, but it just made Susan furious. We'd been able to do our jobs the way we saw fit as long as we accomplished our sales goals. Then Helen, the new manager, wrote us the memo explaining the new weekly reports—two of them, due every Friday. We used to be able to meet with the manager and discuss our projects, not have to write up all the details.

Susan feels the new manager is just a dictator! Helen doesn't believe in our company's open-door policy—she wants us to "observe proper channels" and go see our direct supervisor about problems. Susan sent problems straight to the manager and complained. Now she's considered a troublemaker and doesn't get assigned to special projects anymore.

I think the new reports are a pain, but they're not all bad. I still can do pretty much what I want, and I don't have to sit in boring meetings where everyone does their "show and tell."

Businesses require many reports, both oral and written, to keep internal and external audiences informed about proposals, projections, and progress. Reports also help you let your bosses know both what you are doing *and* how well you are communicating.

PLANNING THE SHORT REPORT

Before you begin to write your report, you must plan it. As discussed in Chapter 1, time spent planning will both save you time and make the report more effective.

Purpose of the Report

The form and content of the report will depend on the report's purpose. Are you trying to explain direct-mail advertising to a client? Persuade your boss to buy some new computer equipment? Describe the labor situation in a plant where a strike is threatened? Tell others in your company what you learned at a seminar? Describe to a client why he or she should use a particular kind of network software? Each of these purposes would lead to a completely different report, not only in content but also in the way that content is presented.

In each of the above cases, as in most business situations, the successful business communicator may be trying to sell with the report, even when the selling is neither direct nor obvious. People who succeed in business do more than describe situations; they also propose appropriate responses to those situations, and they get those responses implemented.

Such selling can be either direct or subtle. The selling aspect of persuading your boss to buy some computer equipment or a client to use particular software is obvious. The selling is subtler when, in explaining direct-mail advertising, you may also be suggesting how the client can use it. Likewise, in describing the labor situation, you may also be recommending a way to avoid the strike. Finally, in talking about the seminar, you may be recommending a change in your company's procedures.

Audience

You will write your reports differently for different audiences. Are you writing to your boss? A client? Your colleagues? The board of directors? Shareholders?

What combination of these audiences will read the report? How will that audience react to the report? Are you simply informing them about something they will probably agree with or persuading them to do something they may resist? As in all communication, the report should be written for those who will read it. (See Chapter 1 for more on audience analysis.)

Once you have decided on the purpose and audience of the report, you must plan how you will achieve that purpose with that audience. At this stage, your planning directly concerns the report, its form, and its content.

The short report may be a simple memo (appropriate for a short report to be distributed entirely within the company) or a letter (suitable for a report to be distributed to outsiders). Or it may have a somewhat more formal structure, as in a report to the board of directors.

Form of the Report

Sometimes when you are writing a short report, you already have all the information you need. More often, however, you will have to do at least some research to complete the report, gathering information from company records, the library, or an electronic database. Occasionally you will have to create new data from primary research. Chapters 5 and 6 describe how to complete the research you need.

Content of the Report

Once you have gathered your information, you must decide how much of it to include. To learn enough about a subject to write a report on it, you need to gather more information than the reader will need and select the details that are most important.

What you include in the report will depend on who your reader is and what you expect her or his reaction to be. Are you reporting on matters on which readers will accept what you say as fact, or must you have authorities to support you?

How much of what you know will help the reader reach a logical conclusion? The report should give the reader all the information he or she will need to reach a logical conclusion—and no more. Assume the reader is a busy person; do not include data that are not material to the matter at hand. Be sure, however, to include everything that could be important. It is not always clear what the reader will consider important, and it is better to err slightly on the side of inclusion. An informed reader who agrees with you will back you more strongly later; a reader who feels inadequately informed because you left out certain information may later turn against your recommendation.

If you have gathered information from a variety of sources and reached your own conclusions, you probably will want to report those conclusions as your own, without attribution. More often, though, you will report on what others have said or written. In those cases, you must always credit your sources, for two reasons. First, claiming others' works as your own is *plagiarism,* a subject covered fully in Chapter 5. Second, proper attribution will give the report greater credibility. Suppose you are recommending to the treasurer that she move the company's investments into shorter-term notes because interest rates will rise. A forecast of higher interest rates from the Chairman of the Board of Governors of the Federal Reserve is generally stronger support for this recommendation than an unsupported assertion that rates are likely to rise. Methods for attributing materials from outside sources also are described in Chapter 5, and examples appear in Appendix C.

Although the short report is less formal than the long report, proper headings can often help the reader understand what you are saying. Headings should be descriptive and tell what the reader should expect. While it is acceptable to use headings like "Statement of Problem" and "Recommendations," the reader will learn more from "Causes of Labor Unrest" and "How to Avoid a Strike." One conventional heading system is illustrated in Chapter 2.

Graphics, Tables, and Exhibits

If the report contains complicated statistical or financial information, a graph, table, or both may help the reader understand it. For example, in a quarterly report to shareholders you might say:

> The company had earnings of $7.5 million, or $.83 per share, on sales of $173.8 million in the quarter ending March 31, 1994, up from earnings of $6.9 million, or $.78 per share, on sales of $165.2 million in the comparable quarter the previous year.

Think how much clearer this explanation is if the sentence is accompanied by the following table:

	Three months ended March 31, 1994	Three months ended March 31, 1993
Sales	$173,800,000	$165,200,000
Earnings	$ 7,500,000	$ 6,900,000
Earnings per share	$.83	$.78

Most recent data in first column shows importance.

The following graphic presentation of the same information may also help the reader understand:

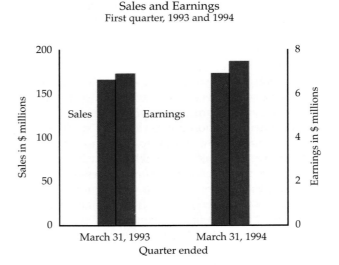

Sales and Earnings
First quarter, 1993 and 1994

Chronological order shows trend.

Note that the graph presents the data in chronological order, while the table is in reverse chronological order. In a table, you will often put the more important information (in this case, the results being announced) first, whereas the graphic presentation is clearer if the upward trend is shown. You will learn more about graphic presentation of materials in Chapter 7.

Even a report with only a few numbers can benefit from diagrams or pictures if they will help the reader understand a difficult concept. For example, one type of computer network has a central hub to which all the other computers are connected; in another type, every computer is connected to every other computer. Think how much more your readers will understand if they see this diagram:

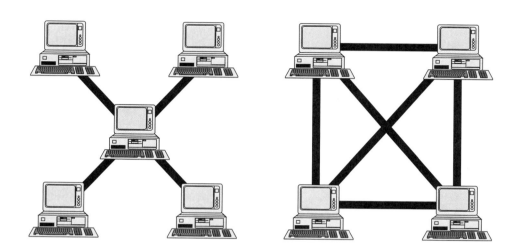

One error many communicators make is to use graphics just because technology allows them to. Unnecessary graphics do not add to understanding; they merely lengthen and clutter the report. Do not include a picture of the plant where the strike is threatened just because you are able to scan it into your computer. Use it only if it will truly help the reader understand the situation, for example, by showing where strikers might set up picket lines.

REPORT FORMATS

Short reports are usually formatted as memos, letters, or abbreviated forms of long reports. Most memo and letter reports do not have covers, letters of transmittal, appendixes, or other formal elements. However, you often can make such reports clearer by including subheads and graphics that would not ordinarily appear in a letter or memo.

Memo reports generally are used within a company. The first page includes the standard memo headings the company uses, showing the date, recipient, sender, and subject. You might use a memo report to tell your boss the status of a project (a status report), show management how a van pool system could help the company comply with environmental regulations (a feasibility report), request that a new job be created under you (a justification report), or give your assessment of the likelihood of a strike.

Letter reports are sent to people outside the company. Here again, the first page will look like a typical letter. A letter report might go to a client to propose changes in his accounting system to improve internal controls, to a customer to give the results of your analysis of her production line, or to a prospective customer to detail a proposed new system (a proposal).

REPORT-WRITING STYLE

The style of your report will depend on the report's purpose, audience, and message. In all cases, keep in mind the principles you learned in Chapters 1, 2, and 3. Write clearly and avoid using wordy expressions. Avoid jargon. Use language that is appropriate for the audience. Use standard formal business English. Avoid meaningless or condescending phrases.

Remember that in business, it is safe to assume that every reader is busy and has very little time to read your report. Make the reader's job as easy as possible. If you can, allow him or her to deal with the report without reading all of it. An executive summary that presents your conclusions or recommendations and briefly describes the logic behind them may be all some readers need. Often the report will go to people—usually higher-ranking people—who are not directly involved with the matter at hand. Save those people time, and they will find your report-writing style valuable. The first paragraphs in the reports in Exhibits 4–1, 4–2, and 4–3 are examples of such brief summary paragraphs.

If the report is simply factual and conveys no unpleasant surprises, use direct, active sentences. Tell the reader the conclusion early; then support it with facts, outside opinions, charts, and whatever else is appropriate. Repeat the conclusion at the end.

If the report reaches a conclusion that you expect the reader will contest, you may want to use a different order. In such a case, you may get better results by leading the reader to the conclusion, providing the evidence early, and getting the reader to nod his or her head in agreement, so that by the time you state the conclusion, the reader will have reached the same conclusion.

EXAMPLES OF SHORT REPORTS

Justification Reports and Feasibility Reports

Justification reports and feasibility reports are closely related. Both recommend action on some future activity, **justification reports** from the viewpoint of *should* we do it and **feasibility reports** from the viewpoint of *can* we do it. In each case, you develop much of the same information to support the recommended action.

These and other definitions of report types are the authors'; they are, as any classification system must be, somewhat arbitrary. When you get into the work world, you probably will find that your employer either doesn't talk about kinds of reports or has its own internal system of classification that differs from this one. It is less important for you to learn this system than to learn how to write these kinds of reports, regardless of what they are called.

For example, you could write either a justification report, as in Exhibit 4–1, or a feasibility report, as in Exhibit 4–2, on starting a van pool plan to reduce environmental effects of employee commuting. Each report might recommend implementing such a plan.

A **justification report** would focus on why the company should have van pooling. The report would support the plan on the basis of its benefits to employees and the community, how it would be administered to achieve the maximum benefit at the least cost, how the company could promote it to employees, and what it would cost. The report would contain enough detail to allow the reader to reach a reasoned conclusion about the desirability of such a program. Such a report might be prepared and submitted to management by the human resources department to suggest a new employee benefit.

A **feasibility report** would emphasize how the company could implement van pooling. The report might be written by the human resources department

Memorandum

To: James B. Irving

From: Walter Chang

Date: April 17, 1995

Subject: <u>Van pooling as an employee benefit</u>

<u>Van Pooling Is a Low-Cost, Desired Employee Benefit</u>

Why company
should have
van pooling

Van pooling is a way of reducing the load on our parking
facilities, offering a savings to participating employees, and
improving our position as an environmentally sensitive company.
The estimated cost of such a program is less than $2,000 per
month, and our employees want it.

<u>Description of Van Pooling</u>

In the proposed van pooling system, the company will lease 15-
passenger vans and provide them to groups of employees formed to
commute together. One employee volunteer is assigned as a
principal driver; that person drives most of the time and takes
care of routine maintenance of the van. Two other employees are
back-up drivers; one of them drives when the principal driver
cannot. Employees pay $60 per month to ride in the van, which is
significantly less than the cost of driving alone in one's car
and somewhat less than the total cost of the van program. The
primary driver would pay nothing; the two back-up drivers, $50
each.

Advantages to employees are:

>   It costs less than driving alone.

>   They can do other things, like read, while they are
>   commuting.

>   They are with other people during the commute.

>   The time on the freeway will be less because the vans can
>   use the car pool lanes.

>   They will be comfortable, with good seating and air
>   conditioning.

>   They won't have to worry about driving on slippery streets
>   in bad weather.

Advantages to the company are:

>   Employee socializing during commutes will help make them a
>   more cohesive group on the job.

James B. Irving   2   April 17, 1995

Adding the program will improve our position as an environmentally sensitive company, both in reality and as seen by the community.

Employees like the program; it will, therefore, help continue our strong relations with our employees.

Costs of Van Pooling

According to the city office of commuter assistance, the cost of a full maintenance lease of a 15-passenger van is $985 per month. Fuel costs for employees living in the areas where our employees live would be $238 per month. With an average of 11 persons per van, these costs would be offset by a total of $580 per month (8 persons at $60 each, 2 back-up drivers at $50, and the primary driver). Thus, the net cost per van would be $643. We estimate that we will need 3 vans to serve the major areas where our employees live, for a total cost of $1,929 per month.

You will see this table in feasibility report, too.

Van Pooling Monthly Costs

Costs:	
Lease cost	$ 985
Fuel cost	238
Total costs	$1,223
Receipts:	
Regular passengers (8 @ $60)	$ 480
Back up drivers (2 @ $50)	100
Total receipts	$ 580
Net cost per van	$ 643
Total net cost (3 vans @ $643)	$1,929

Employees Like Van Pooling

We held meetings at which we described van pooling to employees and asked them their thoughts. We gave them a survey that asked if they would use van pooling if it were available and what they thought were the most attractive and least attractive features of the program. We received 19 usable survey forms. The results of this survey are:

Employee Survey on Van Pooling

Would you use van pooling if it were available?

Yes	5	26%
No	7	37%
Don't know	7	37%

James B. Irving   3   April 17, 1995

Favorable comments from employees included:

    It would be great not to have to drive every day.

    I would get to work faster because I could use the car pool
    lanes.

    I'd love to be able to read in the van.

    You mean if I drove the van, it would cost me nothing?
    I'll drive!

Unfavorable comments included:

    I don't believe your cost figures. I drive an old car, and
    it just doesn't cost me that much.

    I don't want to have to depend on 10 other people to get to
    work every day.

    I like to be able to run errands on my way home from work.
    In the van, I can't.

    You base your costs on assuming that I own a car just to
    get to work. I'd keep the car anyway, so I won't save that
    much.

<u>Recommend Van Pooling as a New Employee Benefit</u>

We recommend that the company adopt a van pooling program as a
new employee benefit. This program will be relatively
inexpensive, costing less than $2,000 per month, and it will
improve our relations with both our employees and the community.

EXHIBIT 4–2   Feasibility Report

Memorandum

To: James B. Irving

From: Walter Chang

Date: April 17, 1995

Subject: <u>Van pooling to comply with Ordinance A403.5</u>

How company
can afford
van pooling

<u>Van Pooling Is the Lowest-Cost Way of Complying with New Law</u>

Offering and promoting van pooling will be our least expensive
way of complying with the new ordinance requiring us, as an
employer of 100 or more persons, to reduce the number of
employees who drive to work. Van pools have also proved to be
popular with employees of companies that have them.

<u>Requirements of the Ordinance</u>

Company
must do
something

The new law requires that all employers of 100 or more persons
put in place a plan to reduce the number of cars on the road for
employees commuting by 15%. The plan must be in place by January
1, 1995, and must have a reasonable chance of achieving the
reduction by January 1, 1996.

The law states that a plan will be viewed as in compliance if it
includes any one of the following three elements:

Van pooling
is allowed

1. A van pooling program promoted in ways that will attract
    large numbers of employees to participate.

2. Subsidized use of mass transit if mass transit is
    available to sufficient numbers of employees.

3. A program of compensation to employees who find alternate
    methods of commuting. Requirements include requiring
    parking permits for the use of the parking lot and
    restricting the availability of on-street parking.

<u>Description of Alternatives</u>

<u>Van pooling</u>: The company would provide 15-passenger vans for
each major commute area. A principal driver would be
designated for each van, along with two back-up drivers. The
principal driver would drive at all times except when he or
she is not working, when one of the back-up drivers would
drive. The principal driver would be responsible for keeping
the van in good running order, handling routine maintenance,
and filling it with gasoline. The company would pay all
expenses. Employees who are part of the van pool would be
charged $60 per month, except the drivers. The primary
driver would pay nothing, and the back-up drivers would pay
$50 per month.

James B. Irving   2   April 17, 1995

Subsidy for mass transit: Employees who choose to ride the
bus to work would be paid half of the cost of their monthly
ride tickets.

Payments for not driving: The company would issue permits to
all employees who choose to drive to work. The parking lot
would be marked with visitor spaces and employee spaces.
Security would check the lot daily to ensure that all cars
parked in employee spaces have appropriate permits.
Employees who do not get permits would be paid $30 per month.
All streets within two blocks of the plant would be marked
for two-hour parking (the city will do the marking and
enforcement).

Costs of alternative programs

Van pooling: According to the city office of commuter
assistance, the cost of a full maintenance lease of a 15-
passenger van is $985 per month. Fuel costs for employees
living in the areas where our employees live would be $238
per month. With an average of 11 persons per van, these
costs would be offset by a total of $580 per month (8 persons
at $60 each, 2 back-up drivers at $50, and the primary
driver). Thus, the net cost per van would be $643 per van.
To achieve our needed 15% reduction in driving, we would need
3 vans, for a total cost of $1,929 per month.

                    Van Pooling Monthly Costs

Costs:
     Lease cost $ 985
     Fuel cost   238
     Total costs $1,223
Receipts:
     Regular passengers (8 @ $60) $ 480
     Back-up drivers (2 @ $50)   100
     Total receipts $ 580
Net cost per van $ 643

Total net cost (3 vans @ $643) $1,929

Mass transit subsidies: Monthly passes average $57 on local
buses. Fourteen of our employees now take the bus. To
reduce auto commuting by 15%, 20 more employees would have to
take the bus. A subsidy to the 34 employees who would then
be taking the bus would cost $28.50 each, for a total of $969
per month.

One problem with this alterative is that the nearest bus stop
is at Fourth and Madison Streets, which is about one-half
mile from our facility. We do not expect that we can induce

EXHIBIT 4-2 continued

James B. Irving 3 April 17, 1995

20 more of our employees to ride the bus if they have to walk
that far, especially in the winter. In talks with the
Metropolitan Transit Authority, they have told us that they
will reroute buses for us if we will pay for the added costs.
They estimate the cost of rerouting a bus to our plant gates
from the nearest stop at $2 per bus per day. We would need
to reroute buses on three routes which each have buses every
half hour from 7 A. M. to 6 P. M. and every hour the rest of
the day. That is a total of 35 buses per route. Cost of the
rerouting would be $6,120 per month.

Mass Transit Subsidy Monthly Cost

Direct cost of subsidy (34 employees @ 28.50)	$ 969
Cost of rerouting buses (3 routes @ 35 buses per route per day for 30 days @ $2 per bus per day)	6,300
Total cost of mass transit subsidy	$7,269

<u>Payments for not driving</u>: At present, we have an average of
122 cars in our parking lot on each working day. We have no
way of identifying which are employee cars, although it is
likely that almost all are. To implement this alternative,
we will have to restripe the lot and add signs restricting
parking to cars with permits. The one-time cost of
restriping and signage is $6,400. The signs and striping
should last three years, which results in a cost of $231 per
month for depreciation and interest.

We estimate that the $30 monthly payment will attract 15
persons who regularly drive now. In addition, we will have
to pay those who do not now drive, another 33 persons. Total
cost for payments will be $1,440 per month.

Permits will have to be changed monthly to allow employees to
change and to account for new hires and terminations.
Permits will cost $.50 each, or a total of $60 per month.
Security estimates that it will take one hour each day to
patrol the lot, note licenses of parked cars without permits,
identify them as employee or other, and call the tow company,
if necessary. At $13.50 per hour, including fringes and
taxes, that costs $284 per month. Total costs would be
$2,015, including $231 for depreciation and interest, $1,440
for payments to employees, $60 for permits, and $284 for
security payroll.

```
              Payments for Not Driving Monthly Cost

    Depreciation and interest         $   231
    Payments to employees
      (48 persons @ $30)                 1,440
    Permits (120 @ $.50)                    60
    Security (1 hour per day for
      21 days per month @
      $13.50 per hour)                  ___284
    Total cost of payments for
      not driving                      $2,015
```

Employee Relations Aspects of Alternatives

We held departmental meetings, at which we described the new law
to employees and asked them their thoughts. We gave them a
survey which asked which method they would be most likely to use,
which method they would use if it were the only one available,
and what they thought were the most attractive and least
attractive features of each. We received 137 usable survey
forms. The results of this survey are:

Preference for Alternate Commuting Methods
Percent of Employees

Which method:	Van Pooling	Mass Transit	Pay for Not Driving	None
Would you prefer?	12.4%	5.1%	8.8%	73.7%
Would you use?	22.6%	13.9%	18.2%	70.9%

Van pooling is most acceptable to employees

Favorable comments from employees included:

For van pooling:

   It would be great not to have to drive every day.

   I would get to work faster because I could use the car pool
   lanes.

   I'd love to be able to read in the van.

   You mean if I drove the van, it would cost me nothing? I'll
   drive!

For mass transit subsidies:

   I take the bus already. I'd be happy if you helped pay for
   it.

James B. Irving   5   April 17, 1995

For payments for not driving:

> I'm sure I could find a ride if it were worth it to me.

> I'd take the bus and walk the half mile for the right price.

Unfavorable comments included:

Against van pooling:

> I don't believe your cost figures. I drive an old car, and it just doesn't cost me that much.

> I don't want to have to depend on 10 other people to get to work every day.

> I like to be able to run errands on my way home from work. In the van, I can't.

> You base your costs on assuming that I own a car just to get to work. I'd keep the car anyway, so I won't save that much.

Against mass transit subsidies:

> I can't take the bus--there's none in my neighborhood.

> The closest bus to the plant stops a half mile away. I can't walk through the rain and snow that far!

> I drive to work in 25 minutes, door to door. With transfers and waiting, it would take me nearly an hour on the bus.

> I know the bus is cheaper now and I don't take it. I wouldn't ride on that thing if it were free.

Against payments for not driving:

> I'd quit driving to work if I could figure out how. Paying me won't help--tell me how.

> If you paint all the curbs red, there will be a mess parking around here. It's already bad enough.

Recommend Van Pooling to Comply with New Law

Van pooling is best alternative We recommend that the company adopt a van pooling program as its way of complying with the new law. It is the least expensive alternative (although only slightly less expensive than payments for not driving), and it is the plan most liked by our employees.

to suggest a way to comply with a new ordinance requiring the company to reduce the number of cars its employees drive to work. It would focus on the costs of the program, on promoting the plan to employees to achieve the maximum reduction in driving, on other benefits of the program (including employee and community relations), and on structuring the program to meet the new requirements.

Note that each type of report would contain sections on (1) effects on employee and community relations, (2) cost data, and (3) internal promotion plans. The difference lies in the emphasis: The justification report concentrates on benefits, and the feasibility report focuses on costs. Note how Exhibit 4–1, the justification report, and Exhibit 4–2, the feasibility report, contain much of the same information but with a different emphasis.

Audit reports show the results of an analysis of a system and its output and may recommend changes to the system. A CPA might write an audit report about a company's accounting system, a computer analyst a report about a computerized inventory system, and a security manager a report about a system to prevent shoplifting.

In most audit reports, you will have to give the reader information he or she doesn't want to hear—that there are avoidable losses. In addition, you will make recommendations for changes to prevent future losses. You must be careful not to get the reader so angry from the first part that the second part is ignored or resisted.

One way to do this is to use passive, indirect phrasing. If a company has an inventory storage area that you found unattended and unlocked, you could include that information in your report in either of these sentences:

> The storekeeper left the inventory locker abandoned and unlocked on three occasions.

> Three times over the four-month period, the inventory locker was unattended and not properly secured.

If you were responsible for the storekeeper's activities, how would these sentences make you feel? The first sentence accuses one of your people of dereliction of duty, with direct phrasing and emotionally charged words like *abandoned.* The second sentence informs you about a relatively rare occurrence in which your employee was careless. The first sentence is short and direct; the second is a little longer and more passive and does not mention the storekeeper.

Another way to reduce the impact of the negative news is to bury it in the middle of the report. The first and last parts of any report have the most impact; use them for the points you want the reader to focus on. The middle part is less powerful and can be used for the material that needs to be in the report but is either less important or more likely to cause the reader to react negatively.

The audit report in Exhibit 4–3 is written to the person responsible for the preparation of the status report. The report is simple and brief, and the writer deemphasizes the negative findings and concentrates on the proposed change.

Progress reports keep someone informed on the status of a major project. The intended reader might be a customer, a client, a government agency, your

Memorandum

To: Rosa Fernandez

From: Arlene Williams

Date: July 22, 1994

Subject: Review of Weekly Status Report

To improve the usefulness of the Weekly Status Report, I
recommend that the average daily hours worked be taken from the
cash register sign-on and -off times, rather than the handwritten
sheets that are now submitted by each store. This change will
reduce the cost of preparing the report, as the store managers
will no longer be required to prepare the manual hours worked
sheets and at the same time improve the accuracy of the sales per
employee hour data that we use to evaluate store managers.

Passive voice—
no one blamed
In a review of the status reports for the fiscal quarter ended
April 30, hours worked were reported below hours that were
actually paid, as detailed in the payroll records, every week in
17 stores. In the other 15 stores, reported hours worked were
below hours paid between 5 and 10 weeks and above in the
remaining weeks. In no week did a store's reported hours worked
exactly match the hours paid.

The change can be accomplished by having the payroll department
give a copy of the one-page Payroll Summary by Store report,
which it already prepares, to the clerical employee who does the
Weekly Status Report.

boss, or corporate headquarters. In the report, you detail what has happened since the last progress report, including where each major phase of the project stands against its schedule.

The form of the progress report will depend on the following:

- How big is the project?
- When did you last report progress?
- How often do you report progress?
- How close is the reader to the project?
- Is the news good?

A very large project, like the construction of a dam, often has a formal progress report structure, with regular reports on each phase of the project. There may be PERT charts or Gantt charts, which help manage the progress of major projects, included in the report along with the status of each item in the chart.

A smaller project may require less formal reporting. Exhibit 4–4 is a progress report on the preparation of a business plan. Note that it gives details very simply and elaborates only on the parts of the project that involve current activities. Also note that in the next to last paragraph, the writer uses the status report to help keep things on track with the client. This simple progress report could also have been presented without the table, but the table makes it easier to keep everything clear.

Proposals are reports designed specifically to sell. A proposal can be as simple as a memo you write to your boss telling why you should be assigned a job or as complicated as a detailed description, running many thousands of pages, telling why an engineering firm should be chosen to design and build a hydroelectric dam.

Regardless of length, all proposals have the following in common:

- There is an identifiable project to be done.
- The writer of the proposal is trying to be the one chosen to do that project.

To get the assignment, the writer generally must show (1) an understanding of the project, (2) qualifications to get the project done, and (3) a reasonable cost.

Often, especially in government contracting, the proposal is written in response to a **request for proposal,** or **RFP,** which contains detailed information about what the buyer wants. The RFP also tells how the proposal should be written and when it is due. If you are writing a proposal in response to an RFP, your first step is to read the RFP carefully. Your proposal must meet its requirements. If it doesn't it will be "nonresponsive," and a nonresponsive proposal will not be considered, even if it is better than any responsive proposal made.

Exhibit 4–5 illustrates a brief proposal. The writer describes the nature of the work to be performed, the reasons the reader needs the work done, the writer's qualifications to do the work, and the cost of the work. It also outlines a business plan, which is a special kind of long report.

Planning Consultants, Inc.
4544 Opportunity Way
Albuquerque, NM 87443
(505)555-7834

June 17, 1994

Ms. Elizabeth T. Sheffield, President
Sidereal Software, Inc.
995 Fourteenth Street
Albuquerque, NM 87402

Dear Ms. Sheffield:

The business plan for your navigation software package is on
schedule for completion by July 22, as we agreed when we began to
write it. Status of each section is:

*Table gives all
information
clearly &
quickly*

Section	Due Date	Status
Executive Summary	7/15	
Product	6/10	Completed
Market	6/24	Research completed. You will have draft by 6/20.
Management	6/17	Have your comments, will complete changes by 6/22
Marketing	6/10	Completed
Operations	7/1	Writing begun 6/15. On schedule
Financial	7/8	Will begin 6/24
Printing and Binding	7/22	

Please let us know your schedule so we can meet to go over your
comments on the market section by the 22nd and get the changes
incorporated by the 24th. If you are going to be out of town
again, we will fax the market section to wherever you are and get
your comments by telephone.

Everything looks good for a completion before your presentation
to the venture capitalists on August 1.

Sincerely,

Darnell Washington

Darnell Washington

Alan R. Culpepper
Management Consulting
734 Third Avenue
New York, NY 10017

March 24, 1995

Mr. Harvey Wilson
Wilson Avionics Corporation
9779 82nd Street
Chicago, IL   60625

Dear Mr. Wilson:

To raise money for a company like Wilson Avionics, you need a
business plan that will convince investors that you have covered
all the issues that you will face in making it a profitable,
growing company. Your own business history, of course, will be
the most important single element in their considerations.

In addition, an investor group will want to know that your
plans for manufacturing and selling your test equipment,
developing new products, and controlling your costs are
reasonable--that you have a good chance of doing what you say you
are going to do. For that part, your plan should include
evidence showing details behind the moves you plan to make.

I propose to prepare a plan for you that will give those
details, a plan that will:

*Shows
understanding
of project*

- Show that the market for your kind of test equipment is
  large enough to support the volumes that you project.

- Show that your product is enough better than competitive
  products to gain a significant share of the market.

- Tell why your people will be able to turn the ideas for
  the business into a real business.

- Provide detailed expense plans, with an organization plan
  for support.

- Compare your operation with those of your competition,
  based on available competitive data.

- Give detailed financial plans that can be used for exit
  strategy valuations.

The plan will be your plan; it will incorporate your ideas,
strategies, and objectives. In preparing it, I will take your
input, test it for reasonableness and consistency (e.g., Can you
hire the people you need for the money you have budgeted? Can
you produce your instruments for the cost you have projected?
Are your marketing budgets enough to ensure the successful sale
of the product?), add a market analysis, determine the financial
implications of your plan, and present it professionally.

Wilson Avionics Corporation   Proposal

Specifically, the plan will include:

1. An executive summary.

2. A history of the company.

3. An analysis of the market for avionics test equipment.

4. A description of your products, both present and planned.

5. A management analysis that will include an organization chart and biographies of your key managers.

6. A description of your operating strategy.

7. A financial plan that will include a detailed budget for the first year (annual totals only) and a monthly summary plan of income statements, balance sheets, and cash flows for three years.

Shows qualification to do project

In preparing this plan, I will call upon the planning skills I have developed through 25 years of preparing long and short range plans and the information resources available to me.

The plan will be approximately 20 pages, exclusive of the financial schedules. It will be completed approximately 6 weeks from the time you and I meet to develop the plan outline. The timing will be, in part, dependent on the speed with which you can respond to requests for information about your strategies, products, expansion plans, etc., as they arise.

Clearly states cost

For this plan, my compensation will be:

1. $4,000 upon signing of this agreement.

2. $4,000 upon your receipt of a complete, acceptable plan (acceptance not to be unreasonably withheld).

To accept this proposal, please sign below and return one original to me with a check for $4,000. This offer is valid until April 1, 1995. I will begin working as soon as we can schedule a time to get together.

Accepted:
Wilson Avionics Corporation

Allen R. Culpepper   _____date_____
                          Harvey Wilson

In this chapter you learned that a short report, although less formal than a long report, generally requires the same steps in its preparation. First, you decide on the subject matter, gather information about the subject, organize and analyze the information, and present it clearly.

Planning is critical to the writing of a report. You have to decide on the purpose of the report and analyze the readership you expect. Then you must decide how to achieve your purpose with the report. You will

- Select a format.
- Choose the information you will present.
- Organize that information with appropriate headings.
- Decide what, if any, graphics or tables to use.

Short reports usually are formatted as either memos, letters, or abbreviated forms of long reports. Report style generally is good business style. Reports often begin with a brief summary of their logic and recommendations or conclusions to allow busy readers to use the reports without having to read them completely.

You saw examples of justification and feasibility reports, which approach the same issue but from different directions; an audit report, which makes a recommendation for change while deemphasizing bad news; a progress report, which informs readers about the status of a major project; and a proposal, which attempts to persuade the reader that certain work needs to be done, outlines the writer's qualifications to do the work, and details the costs involved.

APPLICATION EXERCISES

1. Think about your major and the career to which it may lead. What kinds of short reports are you likely to write? How will these reports affect your career?

2. When would you use a memo report? When would you write a letter report? Why?

3. Read the following first sentences from reports. Decide in what circumstances, if any, each is appropriate. Consider the audience and the purpose of the report. How can these sentences be improved?

    a. From a progress report:

       We are sorry to tell you that the project is three weeks behind plan and will not be completed until June 30.

    b. From an audit report sent to the company controller and to the manager of the accounts payable department:

       In the attached review of the accounts payable department, you will see that the department is on standard in six areas, above standard in five, and below standard in three.

    c. From a justification report for upgrading your department's computers sent to the director of information systems, who must approve such upgrades:

       We would like to upgrade the computers in the engineering department to UNIX workstations.

4. Each of the following sentences conveys the same information that might be found in an audit report. How do they differ? When might each be appropriate?

    The department is substandard in its processing of orders.

    Orders are being processed more slowly than corporate standards.

5. Describe the difference between a justification report and a feasibility report.

6. When might you use a table in your report? A graph? A photograph?

7. Look at the progress report in Exhibit 4–4. Assume the marketing section of the plan, due on June 10, was not completed on time, is not yet completed, and won't be completed until July 5. You still expect the plan to be printed and bound by July 22. How does that change your report? How would your report change if, due to the delay in the marketing section, you didn't expect to be able to deliver the plan until August 1?

CASES

1. **Proposal: Class Report.** You are assigned a major report for this class to be completed over the remainder of the term. Write a proposal to your instructor selling him or her on the concept for your report. Write your proposal as though you were in competition with other class members to do this particular report. Include a timetable, with specific checkpoints for completion of research, completion of first draft, and so on. While price is not an issue, you must show why you are qualified to report on your subject.

2. **Progress Report: Computer Software System Development.** As project manager for the development of a military computer software system, you are required to submit progress reports to the Department of Defense each quarter. The software will allow the U.S. Navy to track the locations of all its aircraft worldwide through satellite communications. The system is very complex, involving not only tracking but also encryption of the data so they are available only to navy personnel.

The software has four major modules—aircraft identification, tracking, communication, and encryption. It is now the end of June 1994, and your status report is due. The aircraft identification module was scheduled to be completely written by May 15; it was completed on May 10 and is now in testing, as planned. The tracking module is to be written by July 23 and is about a week behind schedule. The communication module uses programs that have been used for many years, so it is fully developed and tested. The encryption module, however, is behind schedule. Your company's mathematicians have been unable to make as much progress as expected in developing the mathematical model that is needed before the programmers can begin writing the program. The model was scheduled to be completed in April 1994; the expected completion date is now July 31. Although you can make up some of the development time, completion of the overall software system is expected to be three months behind the scheduled date of May 15, 1995.

Write a status report on this project to the Department of Defense.

		1994	1987	Change
Prices:	Senior monthly ticket (allows 21 weekday rounds of golf)	$38.00	$34.00	+12%
	Residents' round, City Course	12.50	8.25	+52%
	Residents' round, Ocean Course	14.50	9.25	+57%
Usage:	Average rounds per senior ticket = 11.5			
	Average cost per round = $3.30			
	City Course—48% of play is by seniors			
	Ocean Course—26% of play is by seniors			

3. **Short Memo Report: Raising Golf Prices for Senior Citizens.** As recreation department manager for your city, write a memo report to the city council asking for a rate increase for your two local public golf courses. The facts you have collected over the past few years are shown in the table above.

You think seniors should pay $45 for a monthly ticket good for a maximum of 15 weekday rounds. You have nothing against elderly people, but all costs are going up, and this increase would raise between $100,000 and $160,000 a year to use for scheduled maintenance and approved capital improvements at the two courses.

The Golf Division's Enterprise Fund gave $500,000 to the city's general fund in 1992, which leaves enough for maintenance and improvements. With the fee increase, your operation could improve the courses even more *and* give more money to the city for other areas with budget cuts, such as police and fire coverage.

You recognize that it's hard for the city council to vote for a rate increase for senior citizens, but you think you can give them enough facts to show why the increase is fair and would benefit the city as a whole.

Write a persuasive memo to convince the city council. Use graphics if possible.

4. **Justification Report: Expansion of Sales Force.** As national sales manager of Smoky Mountain Drapery Company, you see that your company is losing market share to competitors. In January 1993, Smoky Mountain introduced a new line of lower-priced curtains and drapes. It has not taken off as other companies' similar lines have. It is now November 1993, and you are analyzing the problem.

You see that your salespeople, who traditionally have sold to department stores, furniture stores, and interior designers, are unable to call on the offices of the new kinds of home stores, like Bed and Bath Boutique and Simpson's. You decide the answer is to create an entirely separate sales force to sell only to the home furnishings superstores.

Smoky Mountain's selling cost has averaged 14.2 percent of sales for the last seven years. Because of the lower prices and thinner margins on the new line, you think your selling cost should not exceed 10.5 percent if the line is to be profitable.

You plan to hire a sales manager and six direct salespeople. Their compensation and other costs will be as follows:

	Sales Manager	Salespeople
Salary	$75,000	—
Commission	1%	5%
Fringe benefits and taxes	$20,000	1%
Travel	$50,000	$30,000 each
Office support	$60,000	$ 5,000 each

Sales of the new draperies and curtains are expected to be $4 million for all of 1993, well short of the $10 million that is in the budget for the year. You expect that the new sales force will increase sales of the product line to $12 million in 1994 and $20 million in 1995.

Write a justification report to your boss, the vice president of sales and marketing, that she can use to persuade the president of the company to approve the expenditures for the new sales force. The vice president agrees with your proposal, but you don't yet know what the president will think.

5. **Memo Report: Biotech Manufacturing Space.** Your company, Bioclone, Inc., has developed a line of modular DNA that both commercial and university biotechnology labs can use as tools in their research. You are about to convert from a research to a manufacturing company, and you need more space. As facilities manager, you have been asked to survey the market and select a building for the additional facility.

You decide that your criteria for the new plant are its size, availability of future expansion space, cost, tenant improvement allowances, location, parking, and mass transit availability. After several weeks of reviewing properties, you have narrowed your list down to four.

Property 1, located near the university and most of the biotech labs, meets your minimum size of 100,000 square feet. There are another 100,000 square feet on which the landlord will give you first right of refusal, which will allow for future expansion. Rent is $12 per square foot, net (Bioclone has to pay real estate taxes, which for this property are estimated at $1.75 per square foot). The landlord will pay up to $15 per square foot in tenant improvements—the interior improvements needed to turn a building shell into a finished plant. You estimate that for a new building, the total cost of the work you will need will be $25 per square foot. The building has a parking lot with 300 spaces, but there is no bus or rail service near the building.

Property 2 also is near the university. It has a total of 125,000 square feet that will rent for $15 per square foot, gross (the landlord pays real estate taxes). This building is freestanding, with no adjacent expansion area. The tenant improvement allowance is $17 per square foot. There are 180 parking spaces, and the building is one block from a bus stop with buses from all over the city.

Property 3 is located in an older area downtown. It has 137,000 square feet on two floors. Rent is $6.50 per square foot. The interior is completely finished, with 30,000 square feet of office space, which will suit your needs. The manufacturing area will have to be completely redone, with new plumbing and air conditioning. The landlord has agreed to pay half the improvement cost, which you expect to be $28 per square foot for the 107,000 square feet of plant area. Parking is available near the building in commercial lots that charge $6 per day or $90 per month. Excellent public transportation serves the building.

Property 4 is in a suburban industrial park and recently was vacated by another biotech lab that wanted to be closer to the university. The improvements you will need are minimal—only about $5 per square foot—but the landlord will not contribute anything toward them. Rent is $11 per square foot for the 140,000-square-foot building, which has 210 parking spaces. There is bus service close by, but it serves only a relatively small residential area.

Write a report to management recommending one of these buildings and explaining your recommendation. Use tables to compare the buildings. Use a map of your city to show locations.

6. **Short Research Report: Financing Export Sales.** Alphomer Technologies, Inc., a manufacturer of telecommunications equipment, has started to receive many requests for bids from Mexican and Canadian companies since the signing of the North American Free Trade Agreement. As assistant treasurer, you have been assigned to find out how to get paid if you accept an order and ship it. You know it is difficult to collect a receivable from another country if the customer chooses not to pay. Your investigation tells you that in addition to selling on open account, you can accept cash in advance, insist on a letter of credit, or use export credit insurance.

Accepting cash in advance is, of course, the easiest option for you and the most secure. However, many of your potential customers are relatively small companies, and they are either unwilling or unable to give you the $50,000 to $100,000 that a system costs before it is even shipped.

Export credit insurance, which is offered by the Export-Import Bank of the United States, guarantees that you will get paid if the customer does not pay, whether for its own reasons or because of currency restrictions that prevent it from paying.

Under a letter of credit, a bank guarantees payment of your invoice. You need only provide proof of shipment.

After doing some library research to fill in the details on export finance procedures and policies, recommend a set of policies for Alphomer Technologies in a report of not more than five pages.

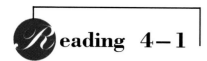

WINNING THE PAPER WARS

Reading 4—1 | *Don M. Ricks*

When the Readers of managers are in charge and talking with each other, Consultant asks them: What do you want me to tell the Writers in your people? What do you most want them to *do* when they write a memo or report for you? The *Readers within senior executives*—industry to industry, agency to agency, large organization and small, in North America and abroad—*have been giving the same five answers for 20 years.*

1. *Have them tell me, right at the beginning, why they are writing.* If they want me to approve an expenditure; if they want me to attend a meeting; if they want me to reverse a decision; if they want me to read their memo and offer my opinion; even if they just want me to note the thing and file it; I need to know that first. Then I can listen to what the document says. And the more negative or troublesome their news may be, the more I need them to announce it in the first paragraph. I don't want to read clear to the end and then have something sprung on me.

2. *Tell them to explain things to me.* They should especially explain what seems so "obvious." Making me aware of the obvious is probably the reason for writing the memo or report in the first place. I've got plenty of work of my own to keep track of; they should never expect me to be on top of the details of their operation. But when there is something I *should* know, their job is to make sure I find out. I'm never offended when someone makes my work easier by delivering up information in an explicit, interpreted form I can understand immediately and put to use.

3. *I want them to use words I can understand. In fact, they should make mental pictures for me.* I want them to keep their language simple and concrete. Instead of saying "Market trends for appliances appear to be improving," they should say "People have started buying more appliances." I

don't want to have to figure out what they mean by "An inclusive series of personal interviews was conducted at the management level in order to determine what should constitute the initial step." They should just say, "We asked all the managers what they thought we should do first." I have a mountain of reading every day. I don't have time for word puzzles.

4. *Tell them to give me all the information I need to do what they want, or to understand what they think I should know—and only that information.* A report should not read like a final examination in the subject. It's not a test of how much the writer knows. Nor should it be a collection of the odds and ends that happened to come to mind at the time of writing. Writers should plan each document by asking themselves, "If I had to make this decision, what would I want someone to tell me?" They then should select, from everything they might say, *only* the data that will help me; and then they should make sure I get *all* of it.

5. *Also remind them that I, too, am human.* I prefer to be addressed as a fellow member of the same species, not an automaton. Especially if the issue is troublesome, a constructive tone is important. When someone starts off with, "It has come to our attention . . .," I feel like kicking him in the teeth. But if he starts with, "I'm sorry to be the bearer of bad news, but you need to know that . . .," the disappointment is easier to swallow.

Consultant has been getting these five messages from people's Inner Readers, week in and week out, for years. The part of us that reads is straightforward. It just wants to get the desk cleared and go home feeling the day has been worth living.

Source: Don M. Ricks, *Winning the Paper Wars* (Homewood, Ill.: Dow Jones—Irwin, 1990), pp. 74—75.

Chapter Five

Secondary Research for Business Reporting

PREVIEW

This chapter stresses the practical value of reports to business organizations. You will develop skill in conducting secondary research, that is, locating business information already in print. You will read about computer-assisted searching tools in libraries and see how computers can help you locate resources much more easily than business students could only a few years ago. Many of the library resources will continue to be useful to you in your business career.

You will see how to handle secondary information with integrity while not letting the mechanics of documentation become obtrusive. ●

Eileen Klein
Internal Auditor

rom the desk of...

Our firm, Banyan Manufacturing, got hit with a $500,000 court judgment. What for? Sexual harassment. One guy, a mid-level manager, kept bothering one secretary. She told him she wasn't interested in him and finally complained to her supervisor and to human resources, but nobody took any action. He'd make some suggestive remark every time he saw her. He didn't care whether the rest of us heard. It was really unpleasant, but the rest of us couldn't do anything about it.

She finally consulted an attorney and filed suit. The higher-ups pled ignorance, but the judge didn't buy it. "Newspapers, the management literature, and trade journals in practically every occupation have covered this topic," he said. "You'll pay this judgment, and I strongly suggest you consult the literature, draw up a firm policy on the subject, and make sure this isn't repeated."

When the president of Banyan read the amounts of the judgments in other sexual harassment cases, he decided not to appeal. We've got training workshops and a strong policy now. The information was there for the reading in the library before any of this happened.

REPORTS AND RESEARCH

A business report is an organized presentation of information gathered for the purpose of solving a business problem.

In the vignette that opens this chapter, top management needed information about sexual harassment. The human resources manager could easily have headed off the problem by obtaining sound information on the subject and reporting on it (including its heavy dollar and human costs) either in writing or as a presentation to management.

A **business report** is an organized presentation of information gathered for the purpose of solving a business problem. Reports can be written, oral, or both. They differ in complexity, length, importance, audience, and many other ways. For instance, some proposals (discussed in Chapter Four) are only one or two pages long. The audience often consists of one person. However, proposals can be among the longest reports generated in business. When an aerospace firm prepares a proposal that competes for a billion-dollar government contract, the finished proposal with its supporting paperwork amounts to thousands of pounds. In Washington, thousands of people constitute the multiple audiences who will examine the proposal.

Because research and reporting demand thoroughness, a great deal of time, and meticulous attention to detail, businesspersons must plan carefully for efficiency and effectiveness. Research and reporting must be systematic.

Truth

Business research requires complete impartiality.

Research requires a completely dispassionate mindset. In everyday business life, we make many decisions based on inferences drawn from a few facts we perceive as relevant. We make many decisions based on our opinions, our limited experience, a few opinions asked of co-workers, and sometimes our "gut feeling." For many decisions, these sources suffice. When a problem needs research, however, we do not say, "Go with your feeling on this." Instead, we search for the truth and try our best to perceive it without the overlay of our opinions or wishes.

Laying aside predispositions is much harder than most people realize. We tend to perceive our biases as the truth. We perceive and remember selectively unless we force ourselves to do otherwise. We exclude whole avenues of inquiry if we think we know ahead of time what we will find.

Researchers cannot afford to do these things. Research costs a great deal in time, money, and resources. If we taint a research study with our biases, we not only lose all those costs but also run the additional risk of making a high-cost business decision based on findings that are wrong.

Researchers perform **secondary research** when they locate a variety of existing information and integrate it into a report that fills a given business need. They perform **primary research** when they generate the data themselves through observational, survey, or experimental research.

Secondary and Primary Research Differentiated

When we do secondary research, we obtain and use the published findings of other researchers. When we do primary research, we generate the data ourselves.

Sometimes a business problem requires only secondary research to solve it. The answer may already exist either in the company's own records or in a published article or book. That solution is usually the least costly. Most primary research takes more time, money, and resources than secondary.

Suppose an organization is interested in the morale and motivation advantages of employee suggestion systems. The literature in most university libraries offers many articles on this topic. From secondary research information alone, a businessperson could design and implement a good system.

Might primary research be needed? It is possible. For instance, if a management shakeup and layoffs have demoralized the firm's employees, simply *providing* a suggestion system might create a backlash along the lines of "I've got a suggestion for you: Hire back my friends!!!" It could worsen morale rather than improve it. An opinion survey, on the other hand, would tell top managers where the sensitive areas are and help them customize and implement the suggestion system to empower the employees and avoid triggering cynicism.

Secondary research will often suffice when the business problem is a qualitative or common one. If others have met and dealt with the problem, the answer may already exist in print or in the company's own files. Many business problems, however, are unique or specific to a given environment or situation. These are likely to need primary research. Many reports require both secondary and primary research, and most primary research is preceded by secondary.

Business reports originate from a need. Typically a manager perceives a question she cannot answer with existing information and delegates the problem to a subordinate. The subordinate, after conferring with the manager, systematically tackles the problem. Because research and reporting are costly, people in business usually do not undertake them without authorization from superiors.

Research Reports: Origin and Process

Usually a superior authorizes a subordinate to perform research and prepare a report.

Whether reports are primary or secondary, writers take the same steps:

- Recognizing and defining the research problem or question.
- Examining a variety of means of addressing it.
- Choosing the best means.
- Planning the research project.
- Implementing the plan to gather the data.
- Analyzing the findings.
- Presenting the answer to the problem in an oral or written report.

Suppose top managers of Dymo Manufacturing recognized that they need to purchase a computer-based network, or LAN (local area network), to link all

A Research Report Case

the firm's microcomputers and minicomputers. They have deferred the decision because of the bewildering array of products and the speed with which technology becomes obsolete. Finally, they ask their administrative office manager, John Ashe, to find out "what's out there" in LANs.

Ashe has basic knowledge about LANs because he reads several trade and professional journals. He can think of dozens of ways to phrase the **research question.** The question that may occur to you first—"Which LAN shall we buy?"— is not the first one to be answered. The question "What LANs exist?" is needlessly broad. Instead, he analyzes his audience, his firm's top management, and focuses first on the organization's needs. This approach permits him to exclude a great many products. Had he begun with "What products are in development?" or even "What products are for sale?" he would be tackling an unnecessarily large problem. He would spend much of his productive time merely trying to keep up with advances in network technology.

As Ashe narrows his focus and considers what he can do with available time and resources, he is working with scope and limitations. The **scope statement** says, "The report will cover a, b, d, and g, but not c and f," and demonstrates that this coverage will solve the problem. A **limitations statement** may be needed if broader coverage would be useful though perhaps not critical. The limitations statement tells what constraints, such as limits on the researcher's time, money, resources, mobility, or access to information, prevent broader coverage.

Ashe spends several hours in a nearby university library reading some trade journals and other technical publications on networks. He does not attempt to exhaust the topic; this early research is exploratory only. His aim is to satisfy himself that no major technological breakthrough is imminent and to gain more information with which he can help management direct him on how to proceed.

In a series of conferences with management, Ashe pins down his assignment further. From his reading, he knows the minimum amount they will have to spend. Is there a cost ceiling? Of course there is. Are there machines in the firm that don't have to be on the network? Probably. Will we expect the vendor to provide training? Negotiable. Which features are critical, and which are merely nice to have? And so on.

After Ashe has considered all these points, his research question emerges: "What LANs that will serve this firm's needs are available in the cost range of $45,000 to $55,000?"

Where will Ashe find the information to answer this question? The secondary information he used for background research fell into two categories: new-product information, written mainly by vendors and subtly competitive and sales oriented; and research studies, written primarily by scholars and theorists but addressing concerns unlike his own. The reading was helpful, but his answer does not lie there.

His knowledge enhanced by his recent reading, Ashe plans primary data gathering. He makes a list of features that management has agreed are critical and has ranked in importance. He adds some features that would be "nice to have" and assigns a weight to each. Then he sends a request for bid to each vendor likely to offer an appropriate product. His communication to them describes the features desired and contains questions about cost, training, service, capacity for upgrade, and other necessities. It also requests reliable cost figures and several other numbers.

When the bids come in, Ashe incorporates the rankings and weights decided on earlier. His results generate some new figures that clearly show him who the top four contenders are.

The report Ashe writes for his managers contains sufficient background information to prepare them for the business decision they will make. The main part of the report transmits and analyzes the data he generated. Ashe might have a vendor in mind that he hopes the managers will choose. Unless they have asked him for his recommendation, however, his job is to present the four choices impartially for management's decision. His report outline will look like this:

Introduction
    Background to the problem
    Statement of the problem
    Purpose of (need for) the research
    Scope and limitations
    Methods of gathering data
    Report preview
Comparison among LAN Vendors' Proposals
    Criteria for choice among vendors
    Analysis of data
    Reasons for excluding all except four
    Advantages and disadvantages of the four contenders
        Company 1
        Company 2
        Company 3
        Company 4
Conclusion
    Summary of findings
    Inferences drawn
    [Recommendation]

The word *Recommendation* is in brackets because its presence or absence depends on what management has asked for. If the managers have not requested a recommendation, Ashe would not presume to offer one.

Note that on this project Ashe spent a high proportion of his time in planning. This long planning time characterizes most business research reports. Before Ashe set out to obtain his data, he tried to foresee what might go wrong. He also prepared in advance the means by which he would analyze his data.

As researchers plan their projects—especially if they are writing a formal proposal—they are, in effect, already writing the introduction to the finished report. Before beginning to collect data, they must already know the exact statement of the problem or question, scope and limitations of the research, need for the research, and methods of gathering the data. These elements compose the most important part of a report's introduction. Often the general outline of the report body is implicit in the way researchers organize and divide up their data-gathering task.

Researchers also know from the outset whether they are to write an **informational** or an **analytical** report. Management tells them either simply to present the information, with a summary and the conclusions that can be

Foreseeing the Shape of the Finished Report

Introductory and concluding sections of business research reports tend to contain the same elements, but the bodies of different reports are organized differently.

drawn from it, or to analyze it and make a recommendation for management's decision. Thus, writers know from the beginning whether the report's ending section will have two elements—a summary and conclusions—or those elements plus a third, the recommendations.

Business Reports Contrasted with Other Research Reports

These problem-solving or question-answering reports differ in several ways from research reports you may have written in other classes. The business research report's introduction needs all the elements shown in the introduction section of John Ashe's outline: a precise statement of the problem or question, a statement of the need for the study, its exact scope, and so on. Recall that business readers work on many projects simultaneously, and the introduction must quickly revive their mental set for the report to come. Writers must resist offering excessive background detail. Rarely will readers be as fascinated by the background as the writers are. Readers have no time to read any more than they need to make a sound decision.

A business report writer who is asked to make a recommendation should recognize the task as a piece of soft, not hard, persuasion. If you have been asked to write persuasively in other classes, realize that readers of business reports will react negatively to emotional appeals or to the point-scoring, adversarial tactics of formal debate.

Even when writing reports leading to a recommendation, credible business report writers present findings in a fair and balanced way.

Presenting information for another person's decision calls upon a writer's integrity. Even if writers have been asked for a recommendation, they must present fairly the information leading up to the recommendation. The decision makers have placed their trust in the writer, and the writer must approach the task responsibly. The writer's credibility is important for all report writing, but especially for the kinds of reports that persuade, such as justification reports.

SECONDARY RESEARCH FOR BUSINESS REPORTING

Learning to use library resources can give a businessperson a lifetime edge over many competitors who may not even know such information exists.

Businesspeople with experience in using a college library have an immediate edge over those without it. People can gain access to an enormous volume of timely information if they know how to use the library. But most people, according to Lavin, do not.[1] Lavin says that managers routinely underutilize secondary research and often are put off by the sheer volume of information available. They skim a periodical or two, when and if they get around to it, but usually they get their business information haphazardly and passively, from business associates who know little more than they do. The vast amounts of available information languish unused, Lavin says, because managers do not know the information is there and, if they did, would have no clue how to find it.

Navigating the Library

Library research is detective work. Rarely do researchers begin a library task knowing exactly which few references they must find to support the academic paper or business report they must prepare. The person who thinks, "Well, I think I'll just read around in current periodicals until I find what I need" will flounder forever.

If you are not already familiar with the library, first familiarize yourself with the floor plan:

- Locate the library catalog.
- Find the reference desk.

[1]Michael R. Lavin, *Business Information: How to Find It, How to Use It,* 2nd ed. (Phoenix: Oryx Press, 1992), pp. 19–20.

- Look for the indexes to business periodicals (paper or hard-bound indexes, computer-assisted indexes).
- Explore possible use of other computer-assisted reference tools.
- Find out where current issues of periodicals are shelved and where older, bound issues are located.
- Learn whether government documents are shelved separately from other holdings.
- Locate microforms—microfilm, microfiche, and so on.

Next, plan your search strategy. Check the library catalog to find out what books are immediately available. (Most computerized catalogs tell users immediately whether a book is checked out or available on the shelf.) Find out which indexes will be most productive. (Few business researchers should spend much time using the *Reader's Guide to Periodical Literature.* It may be familiar to you, but it indexes everything from *Mademoiselle* to *Bicycling.* Conserve your time and move to the *Business Periodicals Index* instead.) Realize that each library tool is itself systematic, and spend a few minutes examining the directions for using the tool before you begin turning pages or pressing keys.

Starting a research project early is essential, for any challenging research is complex. Some researchers say that if you do not feel overwhelmed at some point in your research, you either don't understand the situation yet or are not working on a worthwhile project.

Most research projects require that you collect far more information than you can possibly provide to a reader and then select intelligently what is pertinent. What you omit and your reasons for omitting it are as important as what you include. Be ready to learn more than you will ultimately need to know. While you must stay on task in the library, you must also cultivate an open mind. If you enter the library with your mind made up about what you will learn, you do not have a researcher's attitude. Researchers must "watch the horizons" as well as pursue the topic.

Computer-assisted research tools are changing the methods of data gathering for business and academia. America's university and college libraries are in transition from the use of paper indexes to various automated indexes and information delivery formats. The change is still in progress. In this section, we will look at both manual and computer-aided library research.

Realize that you cannot learn and use dozens of library information-finding tools all at once. However, knowing your way around the library gives you "information power" to carry with you out into the competitive workplace. Our best advice is this:

- Make numerous visits to the library, using more than one reference tool each time and a new one on each visit.
- Proceed slowly.
- Avoid information overload.
- Start using the library instead of television as your business news source. When you read the library's copy of *The Wall Street Journal* or *Business Week,* use that library visit to examine one more reference tool.

Libraries are rich resources when you learn to use their orderly systems.

The Changing Face of the Business Library

Learn one new reference tool each time you visit the library. Be a "power user."

Look at *Value Line, Standard & Poor's Industry Surveys,* and so on. Examine the specialized periodical indexes for your business major: the *Accounting & Tax Index* or *Human Resource Abstracts.* Many experts refer to highly computer-literate people as "power users." Become a power user of the library and you will gain another equally important set of "power tools for the intellect."[2]

Library Catalog

Every library maintains a **catalog** of all its holdings. Contents of the catalog will vary from library to library. Even the types of contents might vary, since different libraries may support different special interests. The catalog lists all the books in the library's collection. Some catalogs also list all the government documents the library holds; others maintain a separate listing for these items. Some catalogs also list all the periodicals and other serial publications the library holds, whereas others list them separately.

Manual catalogs consist of banks of long drawers in large cabinets. The drawers, arranged alphabetically, contain alphabetically arranged cards (usually 3 by 5 inches), one card for each book. Most manual catalogs contain three sets of cards. The author catalog contains books arranged by the last name of the author. The title catalog contains the same books arranged by the first important word of the book's title. The subject catalog contains the same books arranged by the topic on which they are written. The subject catalog contains considerable, but not exhaustive, cross-referencing by subtopic.

Computerized, or online, catalogs are databases containing these same kinds of information. The user need not sort laboriously through trays of 3-by-5 cards and copy information from them. Instead, the user follows onscreen instructions to type in a request using the familiar author, title, or subject categories. The computer searches for the requested data and flashes the result on the screen. If the user is satisfied, she can hit a "print" key, and a printer will make a hard copy of the result.

Many libraries now have online computerized catalogs that cut your search time greatly.

Users of manual catalogs can often obtain fairly good information by less than systematic means. They can browse through card drawers, work by approximation, play hit-and-miss with subject categories, and hit often enough to get most of what they need.

Computerized catalogs are faster and more helpful than manual catalogs, provided the user's request is carefully made. They are, however, time consuming when the user makes an unspecific request. In a manual catalog, a user might look up the subject *personnel* and realize at once that she cannot use three whole drawers full of references. If she types *s-personnel* into a computer catalog, however, the computer will dutifully search out all 14,682 sources with *personnel* as one of their subject headings. It will take time. At the end of the computer search, the screen will say that 14,682 items were found and will invite her to inspect them one by one. In kindness, it will also suggest that she narrow her search by adding a subheading to *personnel.*

In searching a computer-assisted database, whether it is on a CD-ROM disk (see page 141) or an online network, you can narrow the search by typing in more keywords. If you enter one term, you will probably get more items than if you enter two. The computer, instructed to look for two terms, excludes all entries in which only one of the terms appears. If you enter three terms, the computer finds only the entries in which all three appear.

You may see the term **Boolean operator.** If the system is set up to use

<hr />

[2]Philip N. James, "What Is the User Interface?" *Journal of Information Systems Management* 3, no. 2 (Spring 1986), pp. 52–53.

Boolean (sometimes called **logical**) commands, you have considerable power to select exactly what you need and nothing more. If you supply two keywords, the command AND links those two terms, and the system finds all sources (and only those sources) in which both terms appear. The operator OR, however, allows you to use multiple synonyms for the same concept. OR finds for you all sources in which *one or the other* of your keywords appears. AND excludes titles not containing both keywords. The NOT operator lets you exclude whole areas of an inclusive topic. If you want readings on *business negotiation,* for example, you might enter those two keywords (the AND link is assumed unless you specify otherwise). Depending on the scope of your interest, you might want to link *sales* as an OR term. You may wish to exclude the area of *labor* negotiation with NOT *labor.*

Library of Congress and LC Subject Headings

Most manual and computerized catalogs use a classification system called the *Library of Congress Subject Headings (LCSH).* This system organizes the voluminous collection in the Library of Congress, the nation's premier library. Other libraries use the LC subject headings system, as do a number of periodical indexes. Two such indexes are the *Business Periodicals Index* and the *Public Affairs Information Service (PAIS) International in Print,* discussed a bit later.

In the LCSH system, each book bears a unique call number. The call numbers of books on a given subject all bear the same beginning; the rest of the number differentiates the books within the subject's subcategories. For instance, call numbers for most of a library's books on business begin with H. A book on managing and training older workers is numbered HD6279.07.

When using any computer-assisted search tool, more experienced users look at the **subject headings** (sometimes called **keywords, topic headings,** or **descriptors**) used in the LCSH system before they set the computer to work. They have to make sure that what they call their topic is the same thing the computer calls it. If it is not, the computer will say it has nothing on the topic.

Subject headings, the names under which information on given topics is filed, are sometimes called *keywords, topic headings,* or *descriptors.*

Most libraries have a reference work called the *Library of Congress Subject Headings.* Usually located at the reference desk, this work, the size of a three-volume, unabridged dictionary, lists out all the names of all the topics used by the Library of Congress system and cross-references them extensively. In the *LC Subject Headings* you will find what your topic is called; you may also find a list of names it is *not* called. Even if you have found some works on your topic, the *Library of Congress Subject Headings* will offer you a number of related topics to search.

A user familiar with the way the automated systems work gains a degree of speed, flexibility, and thoroughness unavailable through manual systems. Computerized catalogs let users combine requests, restrict or expand searches after they have started and generated too broad or too narrow an output, exclude certain subsets from the search, and examine lists of related topics and subtopics.

Periodicals and Other Serials

Besides books, libraries contain files of **periodicals:** scholarly and professional journals, popular magazines, newspapers, trade journals, yearbooks, and other periodicals published serially, that is, on a regular and continuing basis. Examples include *Harvard Business Review, ABA Banking Journal, Business Horizons, MIS Quarterly, Executive, Academy of Management Review,* and many hundreds of others. Libraries usually have the most recent year or two avail-

Serials, or periodicals, are publications issued on a regular basis: daily, weekly, monthly, quarterly, yearly, and so on.

able as loose issues. Older issues are available in bound volumes, in microform, or both.

No college library will have every periodical or even, necessarily, the whole lifetime run of any one periodical. Many libraries participate in Interlibrary Loan, a cooperative system in which libraries exchange issues or photocopies of articles upon the request of their patrons. Libraries also lend books through Interlibrary Loan.

Indexes to Periodicals

A library's catalog lists the holdings of that particular library. Indexes to periodical literature are not specific to one library. Instead, an **index** lists, by subject and sometimes by title and/or author, all the articles published in every issue of all the periodicals it covers.

There are many indexes to business literature. No two indexes to periodical literature cover exactly the same array of periodicals.

Consider an interlibrary loan— but allow plenty of time.

The indexes may list articles in periodicals to which your library does not subscribe. Typically the interlibrary loan department can obtain them for you, but you must begin your research early enough to give them lead time, usually ten days at minimum.

It was once possible to classify reference tools according to hard-copy or computer-assisted format. Some still exist only in hard copy. Increasingly, however, reference tools are computerized and searchable via CD-ROM or online; some are offered in multiple forms. Some, like *InfoTrac* (discussed next), may allow users to download information onto their own diskettes. It is also no longer easy to assign library reference works to clear-cut categories such as periodical indexes or corporate directories. Computers, bringing vast data storage potential and pinpoint random-access searching, let information providers offer combinations of sources.

InfoTrac.   *InfoTrac* is a CD-ROM-based index—actually, it is a family of indexes and services. If your school library has *InfoTrac,* you will need to check which of the component parts are offered on the system. In its most basic form, *InfoTrac* is a periodical index. Because it comes out very soon after the indexed serials are published, it may contain typographical errors. Use it, because it is fast, inclusive, friendly, and powerful. But double-check bibliographic and other data in the index entry with the serial article itself. A helpful feature of *InfoTrac* allows the local library to insert, at each index entry, a note telling whether the library has that periodical.

If your library's *InfoTrac* has additional parts, you may be able to obtain, on the same terminal, corporate directory information, brokerage house reports on publicly held firms, and many other kinds of information.

Business Periodicals Index.   The *Business Periodicals Index* covers about 350 of the most frequently used business serials published in the English language. This index is carefully prepared and very accurate. In its hard-bound book format, it has been the premier business periodical index in college libraries for decades. Now some online services, such as DIALOG, BRS, and BRS/After Dark, offer computerized access to *BPI.*

During the current year, soft-cover updates are issued; then the whole year's index issues are cumulated and hard bound. Many researchers find the *BPI* comfortable to use because it employs the same organization and abbreviations as the familiar *Reader's Guide to Periodical Literature.*

Note, however, that some of those abbreviations are nonstandard for the three recognized documentation styles. When you are using the indexes to gather your data, think ahead to the information you will need in preparing your documentation and bibliography. Find and record in full such things as volume numbers and page numbers. Your reader will be dissatisfied if you give page numbers as "38–39+" or a date as "Ap93."

Public Affairs Information Service (PAIS) International in Print. Business researchers are likely to locate useful materials through *PAIS*. It indexes periodicals, government documents, and some books on public policy, that is, laws, regulations, and related topics. Business and public policy affect one another in countless ways; thus, many business topics can be found through this index. Volumes are annual, with soft-bound quarterly issues.

Predicasts F&S indexes. *Predicasts F&S* indexes lead business researchers to periodical articles on industry, company, and product information. There are several: *F&S Index United States, F&S Index Europe,* and *F&S Index International* cover the respective areas of the world. These indexes are on CD as well as in paper format.

The F&S Indexes give extremely broad coverage—about 2,000 trade journals, newspapers, and other serials. *F&S Index United States* comes in two sections. If you know the company on which you need information, begin with Section 2, "Companies." If not, use Section 1, "Industries and Products." In Section 1, find the heading, arranged in order of SIC (Standard Industrial Classification) Code, for the industry or product on which your search centers.

Under that heading, you will find a number of citations of articles on that industry or product. In both Section 1 and Section 2, you will see a publication abbreviation, date, and page number for each article. The article is designated not by title but by a summarizing phrase. The publications range from business newspapers to financial publications, trade journals, and special reports. The *Europe* and the *International* indexes have a third volume, "Countries."

PROMT. *PROMT* stands for *Predicasts Overview of Markets and Technology.* It exists in both printed and online format, and it indexes about 1,000 serials. Its entries offer more substantial articles, on average, than do the Predicasts F&S Indexes. In addition, PROMT contains abstracts of articles. PROMT is a good source for statistical data.

The Wall Street Journal Index. *The Wall Street Journal Index* is a detailed index to the nation's oldest continuous financial-news daily, *The Wall Street Journal.* This index is divided into two sections, one organized by subject and the other by company name. Each citation includes a very short summary of the article; the letter *S, M,* or *L* for a short, medium, or long article; the date; section; page; and column.

Note that while indexes to magazines and journals use the actual title of an article in their citations, *The WSJ Index,* like many indexes to newspapers, uses instead a brief summary. Thus, when you move to the newspaper copy or microform copy to find the article, the citation you copy from *The WSJ Index* will correspond not to the newspaper headline but to the main idea in the article's lead paragraph.

Newspaper indexes offer a bonus. Because important news stories tend to develop day by day, you can read a minihistory of a news event right in the index, where each day's new development becomes the index entry for that day under that subject.

Many university libraries also carry indexes to other important newspapers. You are likely to find an index to *The New York Times,* the *Christian Science Monitor,* and the *Los Angeles Times;* and there may be others.

ABI/Inform.   *ABI/Inform* is a bibliographic database available online through DIALOG, BRS, and other systems but also purchased by some libraries in CD-ROM format. It offers abstracts as well as citations and is updated monthly. It does especially well covering academic and scholarly articles but also indexes numerous trade, practitioner, and general business periodicals.

Indexes to Government Documents

Government documents departments in libraries contain a wealth of information, with thousands of new titles every year. Your librarian can show you how to locate what you need.

The GPO, or Government Printing Office, issues some 50,000 titles from federal agencies every year.

Monthly Catalog.   The *Monthly Catalog,* from Congressional Information Service, indexes these titles, which include pamphlets, books, periodicals, special reports, and other formats. Paper, online, and CD-ROM versions of the "Mo-Cat" are offered. The classification system for government documents uses "SuDocs" (Superintendent of Documents) numbers.

Your library might index government documents in a separate catalog or database or in with its regular holdings. You will also need to find out whether your library sets apart a special section for documents or shelves them with its regular collection.

American Statistics Index.   To locate quickly the many statistical studies and statistical charts and maps published by the government, use the *American Statistics Index.* Besides index listings, it contains abstracts and actual tables and graphs. *ASI* is also available online through DIALOG.

Statistical Abstract of the United States.   The *Statistical Abstract of the United States* gathers, summarizes, and indexes statistical studies of social, political, and economic aspects of the United States. You can find year-to-year figures on average per capita income, prison population, numbers of credit card holders, numbers of self-employed workers, and thousands of other useful data categories.

Government documents are more useful than most businesspeople realize. They contain much excellent information that is available nowhere else.

Corporate Directories

By using corporate directories, you can find sales, lines of business, number of employees, names of top executives and managers of corporations—and much more.

Sometimes your research will require you to locate detailed information about specific organizations. Most college and university libraries have multiple corporate directories. A few are the *Million Dollar Directory; Dun's Business Rankings;* the *Directory of Corporate Affiliations; Standard and Poor's Register of Corporations, Directors and Executives; Moody's Manuals;* and *Value Line.*

Hard-Copy and Microform Resources

Microforms take up little library space and permit users immediate access to valuable information that most libraries could not offer in hard-copy form.

Most of us like the comfortable feel and convenience of a hard-copy book or journal issue. Most of us would rather not read an article or chapter on a microfilm or microfiche reader. Making copies of microform materials costs more and sometimes yields unattractive results—gray, crooked, oddly shaped copies, sometimes even partially cut off when we misalign the desired portion of a whole newspaper page on the microfilm platen. The future, however, probably contains more, not fewer, microforms. Library storage space is costly, and the information explosion, like the Big Bang, keeps expanding what libraries are expected to store. More information will be stored on the familiar microfilm and microfiche. Realizing that the alternative is not having the information at all, we adapt to microform use. The *Business Index, Magazine Index,* and *Newspaper Index* are three indexes that contain the actual pieces listed in their indexes. You look up the subject in the index, and it directs you to a microform containing the whole text of the article.

Unless you live in one of the country's largest cities, your local daily newspaper may not be indexed at all. This is frustrating when you read it daily, recall a pertinent piece from sometime during the last year, and have no way of locating it. *Business Newsbank* offers you some hope. *Business Newsbank* covers a portion of at least one major metropolitan daily in each state, usually the largest paper in the state's capital. Because it concentrates on business, economic, and political news, it helps you only if what you are looking for falls into one of those categories. If the piece is indexed in *Business Newsbank,* though, you know that you will find it there in your library on microfiche.

CD/ROM

CD/ROM stands for *Compact Disk Read-Only Memory.* Vendors began offering research tools in this format in the late 1980s. Enormous quantities of data are published on a compact disk looking exactly like the familiar music CDs. *Read-only memory* means that a user can read the information via a computer but cannot "write to memory," that is, cannot change the information on the CD in any way.

A typical CD holds at least 600 million bytes of memory. One CD offers as much memory as 500 of the familiar 3½-inch, high-density diskettes, which hold 1.2 million bytes each. In practical terms, this means that the text of a multivolume encyclopedia can be stored on one compact disk. Encyclopaedia Britannica, in fact, offers the 26-volume, 8.75-million-word, grade-school-level *Compton's Encyclopedia* on one compact disk.[3]

Most compact disk (CD/ROM) business resources are powerful, useful, convenient, and user friendly.

Several business indexes already are offered on CD/ROM, with more to come. Using them is much like using a library's online catalog. In both cases, you type in a request using the system's descriptors and symbols, wait while the computer processes the request, view the result onscreen, and print it out if you desire.

A sampling of research tools now on CD-ROM includes *ABI/Inform, Business Dateline* (with the full texts of business articles), *Moody's International, Compact D/SEC* (formerly *Compact Disclosure*), *General Business File,* the GPO *Monthly Catalog, PsycLIT, Social Sciences Index, EconLit,* and *Books in Print.*

A word of caution: Not all systems use the same instructions and descriptors. For best results, some learning time is necessary. With each new generation of these systems, however, they become friendlier; and they are developing fast.

Online Searches

Computer-assisted tools available to you, hands-on, in your university library only begin to show the possibilities computers offer researchers. Chances are that your library has at least one librarian who specializes in the use of computer databases and is familiar with the very complex "controlled vocabulary" many of them use. Your library can access numerous databases offered by various vendors.

[3]John Schwartz, "A Computer Encyclopedia," *Newsweek,* March 19, 1990, p. 45.

You will need to spend some time with the library specialist, possibly by appointment, to discuss your search strategy. Most online searches cost money, chargeable by the online minute, by the printed bibliographic entry or abstract, or by some other means of reckoning. You and the librarian must structure your search in advance to conserve time and money. With the librarian, you will select several keywords or descriptors to elicit all the bibliographic references you need and none that you do not need. The latter category is more worrisome. If your search is too narrow, you can search again. If your search is too broad, however, the computer will pull up hundreds of references that have nothing to do with your topic. You do not want to pay for all these!

QUOTING, PARAPHRASING, CITING, AND DOCUMENTING

Be a responsible researcher: Quote, cite, and document.

Given that you can photocopy a printed page exactly, can print out a bibliographic citation exactly from a database, and can even download a set of financial information from a compact disk onto your own disk, no errors should ever enter quoted material. They do, though. The computers and copiers do not make the errors—humans do. Every time a human researcher transfers a piece of information, error is possible. When the human researcher is juggling many other responsibilities and has not left enough time to do the research task carefully, errors are virtually certain.

A researcher's responsibility is to check, double-check, and triple-check his or her material for errors. Indeed, manuscripts for books like this one are checked many times for accuracy. Yet it's a rare book that contains no errors at all.

When you are using other writers' thoughts and words, your obligations become even more critical. Scholars—researchers and writers—have generated a set of rules for treating material by other authors. We must adhere to them; writers who do not do so gain a bad reputation. The correct practices are not difficult, but they require an attention to detail that does not appeal to people who are in a hurry.

Quoting

When you quote anything word for word, enclose the material within quotation marks. Quotations must be reproduced exactly, right down to the last comma and capital letter. Cite the source. Bibliographic data must be correct, complete, and properly formatted.

Paraphrasing means putting another person's idea in your own words. Most of the time, paraphrasing requires you to cite the source. You need not document the source under the following conditions:

- *The material is common to many different sources.* When *The New York Times* "breaks" a story, writers at first attribute the facts to that source. But after a story has developed and been carried by many other periodicals, the researcher need not trace it back to *The New York Times.* When you use this kind of material, it is considerate to offer your readers the source you used so that they can learn more about what you are telling them.

- *The material is basic information within a given discipline.* For instance, virtually all marketing textbooks refer to the marketing mix variables of product, promotion, price, and place. The first time a reader comes across these terms, he may think he needs to document them. However, researchers need to read enough to know what is and is not basic to the discipline in which they are working.

- *The material is a matter of public record.* You need not document, for instance, the president's birth date, the Dow Jones Industrial Average close on a given day, or the conviction record of Ivan Boesky.

When in doubt, *do* cite. If you have written well, you will often interest your readers in learning more about the topic, and they will appreciate your consideration in offering them your sources. In cases where citation is required, do it meticulously. Do not take chances on an issue so important to your integrity.

When in doubt, *do* cite your source.

An ugly word, plagiarism. Writers **plagiarize** when they quote word for word, or nearly so, and fail to give credit, or when they use the ideas of others and fail to give credit. They plagiarize when they take the thoughts, words, or ideas of another and pass them off as their own. Sometimes they do not understand good practice sufficiently. Sometimes they understand but are careless. Sometimes they intend fraud and believe their cheating will go undetected. In an imperfect world, sometimes it does.

Plagiarism

When plagiarism occurs, those who depend on researchers' honesty feel betrayed and outraged. Researchers build on the work of other researchers. They wonder, if they cannot trust scholars and researchers, whether they can trust anyone at all. When a case of scholarly dishonesty hits the mass media, the researcher's reputation is tainted for the rest of his or her life. The research itself becomes suspect, and the public views the researcher's institution in a bad light as well.

Plagiarism is a betrayal of trust.

The more prominent the cheater, the bigger the outcry. U.S. congressman Joe Biden borrowed from earlier famous speakers in his speeches without giving credit. Writer Gregg Easterbrook, in describing his own feelings about having his work plagiarized, offers a depressing series of comparable incidents. One involved a dean at a prominent eastern university who delivered a commencement address, chunks of which he appropriated from an essay by a film critic. The second concerned a professor at a western state university whose published textbook contained an entire chapter lifted from another person's book.[4] A former colleague of one of the authors of this text was appalled to find one of his own published articles republished with a stranger's name on it in another journal.

Plagiarism should not occur at all. The fact that some people whose conduct should be exemplary are guilty does not make plagiarism excusable.

Documenting meticulously is not hard. Keep a record of what you found and where you found it. As you take notes, mark all word-for-word material with quotation marks. Paraphrase liberally, but be sure to write down the source. On each photocopy write complete, accurate bibliographic information. As you gather information from a computer source, note its sources. If you forget and find yourself with a quotable paragraph whose source you have lost or forgotten, do not be tempted to skip documenting it. Retrace your library steps, relocate the material, and document it. If you cannot find the material again, do not use it.

Following Good Scholarly Practice

Let's examine paraphrasing more closely. Suppose you wish to use some material that is common knowledge within a given discipline. Just how much must you change the text before it is "in your own words"? The answer is, you must change it quite a bit. Inexperienced or disaster-prone writers may change

[4]Gregg Easterbrook, "The Sincerest Flattery," *Newsweek,* July 29, 1991, p. 45.

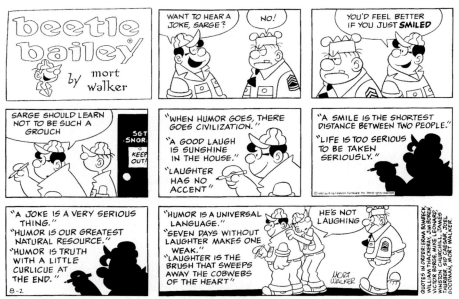

Cartoonist Mort Walker acknowledges the original source of each witty saying he uses in this strip.

just a few words, such as present-tense verbs to past-tense verbs, a couple of synonyms, and the introduction to a sentence. Does that make it their own words? It does not. The more appealing the wording is, the more tempted a writer might be to claim it as his or her own. However, distinctive writing tends to be memorable, and the plagiarizer is just that much more likely to be found out.

Let's say you want to paraphrase and give credit rather than quote a passage. How do you give credit when you use another source's paraphrased ideas within your own discussion? Where do you put the citation? How do you keep it from becoming awkward? The following example shows original text and a portion of a discussion that refers to and paraphrases it:

Original text:

> Employees and lower-level managers must not only see a reasonable relationship between pay and position; they must also see a relationship between effort and results. If the old adage "It doesn't matter how hard you work, everyone gets paid the same" is true, then naturally the workers wonder, why work hard? Incentives to encourage people to work more help hold down wages, benefits, and compensation costs. In Japan workers receive about 25 percent of their total pay in the form of flexible bonuses. In America, the average is still only 1 percent. . . . If nearly half our workers believe there is no relationship between pay and efforts, we have a serious credibility problem. (Denton, 1991, 46).

Paraphrased text in a discussion of motivation:

> Among those who disagree with Herzberg's insistence that money is not a positive motivator is D. K. Denton (1991), who sharply criticizes

American industry's neglect of flexible pay as an influence on productivity. He notes that Japanese workers realize about 25 percent of their total pay in performance-dependent bonuses, whereas in America the percentage of wages dependent upon performance averages only 1 percent. Denton argues that when workers see no link between performance and pay, management loses credibility. (p. 46)

Herzberg's work on motivators and dissatisfiers is basic to management theory, although good practice still usually attaches his name to these influential ideas. Denton's ideas are attributed carefully. At first mention of his name, the in-text date citation references his work, full bibliographic details of which are given in a reference list at the end of the user's paper on motivation. Wording ("He notes," "Denton argues") clarifies the continued dependence on Denton's work, and the page reference at the paragraph's end completes the reference. The writer cites Denton according to good practice but does not let the referencing task become distracting.

The parenthetical notes in both paragraphs refer to the full bibliographic entry that would be given in the alphabetized list of sources at the end of the paper. Using APA style (discussed shortly), the item would say,

Denton, D. K. (1991, September-October). What's wrong with these employees? *Business Horizons, 34*(5), 45–49.

Three Citation Systems

We document each source in a note (footnote, endnote, or in-text note) and again in a bibliographic reference at the end of the report.

Researchers use one of three common citation systems. Scholars in the humanities use MLA (Modern Language Association) style or University of Chicago style, sometimes called Turabian after the scholar who codified this style. Business and the social sciences more often use APA (American Psychological Association) style.

American Psychological Association. (1983). *Publication manual of the American Psychological Association* (3rd ed.). Washington, DC: American Psychological Association.

Turabian, K. L., and Honigsblum, B. B. (1987). *A manual for writers of term papers, theses, and dissertations.* (5th ed.). Chicago: University of Chicago Press.

Achtert, W. S., and Gibaldi, J. (1985). *The MLA style manual.* New York: Modern Language Association.

Parenthetical In-Text Referencing

In research papers for your other classes, your instructors may have asked you to use in-text reference notes, footnotes, or endnotes. An **in-text reference** appears in parentheses within the discussion. A **footnote** goes at the bottom of the page on which you reference a source. An **endnote** appears in a list with all other endnotes on a separate page or pages at the end of the document. Your instructor for this class will specify which form of source noting to use.

Because most business readers find formal footnotes distracting, we recommend in-text parenthetical referencing, which all three style manuals now endorse as an alternative to formal footnotes or endnotes. This time- and trouble-saving method frees you of the more burdensome aspects of source noting and creates little distraction for business readers. The source note itself is shortened, and you need not juggle space to place it at the bottom of a page or at the end of the report.

Instead, as you quote or paraphrase a secondary source in your text, you open a parenthesis and give very brief data that refers the reader to your alphabetized bibliographic list at the end of the document. Close the parenthesis and go right on with your discussion. Within the parentheses, depending on which style manual you are following, you will give some combination of the author's last name, the date of publication, and the page or pages where the referenced material can be found.

You are, of course, free to mention the author's name within your discussion. You can give any information that the reader will find useful. Any element mentioned in your text—the author's name, for example—need not appear in the parenthetical note. Your note (using APA style) could say, "(Mulholland, 1986, p. 302)" or, if you have named author and year in the text, the in-text reference note need say only "(p. 302)."

Ironically, just when footnotes gave way to in-text referencing, newer versions of major word processing programs incorporated easy footnoting functions. On each page where a source note is needed, the program "remembers" and allows space for the note. When you print the report, the word processor places each footnote at the bottom of the appropriate page.

The Bibliography

The **bibliography** is a list of all the sources you have used. It occupies a separate page or pages at the end of the paper. Alphabetize the list by last name of author (first author, if there are two or more). Items with no author listed are alphabetized by the first important word of the title.

In a bibliographic citation for a periodical article, give inclusive page numbers for the whole article. Where you cite and note the article in your discussion, reference only the page or pages you are citing.

You can choose one of three headings for the bibliography. *Works Cited* indicates that the list contains only the works you quoted or paraphrased in the paper. *Works Consulted* is more inclusive, containing all cited works and any sources you read and learned from but did not cite. For instance, if one or more sources provided you with background necessary for understanding your topic, you would list them in "Works Consulted." Your instructor may prefer that you use *Bibliography,* which can replace either of these headings.

Appendix C discusses and gives examples of bibliographic and reference note entries for all three bibliographic styles: APA, MLA, and University of Chicago. Your instructor will tell you which style to use.

Consistency in Documentation Style

If your instructor has no preference regarding citation style and you do the choosing, remember that you must be consistent. Consistency is not as automatic as it might seem. Many works you cite will follow one of the three styles and thus be inconsistent with the other two. Your library indexes or your source works might follow none of the three best-known styles. Abbreviations, for instance, might be nonstandard. Or titles that your style manual says must be "headline-style" (all important words in the title capitalized) may be "sentence-style" (only the first word of the title and the first word following an internal colon capitalized) in an index or published text.

Where your source uses a different documentation style, make the necessary changes in the citation and reference when you bring them into your bibliography. Your list must be internally consistent.

Do not mix styles within your paper. Make the necessary changes so that all your references and bibliographic entries follow the style that governs your paper.

In this or a similar class, your instructor is likely to ask you to research a problem and report on your findings. Some instructors assign a problem; others permit students to select their own.

Suppose you are asked to choose your own topic. Here are some factors to guide you toward selecting a researchable topic. The criteria may operate differently depending on whether your assignment involves secondary or primary research.

Your research topic must be

- Of appropriate size and complexity.
- Narrow but not trivial in scope.
- Original.
- Useful to business.
- Treatable by objective means rather than by value judgments.
- One for which you have sufficient time, money, mobility, and skill.
- One for which an answer can be found.
- One that you can approach objectively.

A newcomer to any field will need to do preliminary reading in the field's literature before choosing a topic. Zikmund mentions the Iceberg Principle of research: A typical research problem shows only a small portion of itself, with the main bulk of the problem, like 80 percent of an iceberg, hidden.[5] Most topics at first look smaller and more manageable than they really are. Answers to some questions are beyond the reach of students—and indeed of all but the most resource-rich researchers.

Nonbusiness questions are often fascinating but not worth enough to business or business researchers to justify investing resources in them. Topics like competitive diving, rockhounding, or figurine collecting may have business aspects, but those aspects are few and probably not well covered in business periodicals, if covered at all.

Objectivity characterizes good business research. Often a student researcher argues strenuously to be allowed to pursue a topic about which he or she cannot be objective. A student who volunteers weekends to work among the homeless probably should not investigate the attitudes of store owners on streets where the homeless congregate.

Your first choice of topic will almost certainly be too broad. Consider this first draft of a student's research problem:

> I propose to discuss entrepreneurship and all of its ramifications in the United States economy.

From further reading and discussion, this student learned how many subproblems this main problem would encompass.

Definition is the first difficulty. What is entrepreneurship? What kinds of activities does it include and exclude? Can entrepreneurship exist within a large corporation? A not-for-profit organization? Will the paper include the forms of entrepreneurship practiced in cultures very unlike that of mainstream

---

[5]William G. Zikmund, *Business Research Methods* (Hinsdale, Ill.: Dryden Press, 1984), p. 54.

America? Can barter systems support entrepreneurship? Do independent entrepreneurs face problems different from those of franchise holders? "All of its ramifications in the United States economy" contains a bewildering array of possibilities. Entrepreneurship has affected geographic population shifts, upward social mobility, prosperity cycles, federal monetary policy, bankruptcy practices, and the national debt, just to name a few.

Researchers must narrow their topics, stating explicitly what they will and will not cover.

A business researcher must explicitly say what she will cover. Whatever is not excluded must be covered in depth.

Small business is easier to define than *entrepreneurship.* The former term implies certain limits on size. Much research has been published on small business by both private and government researchers. Notably, because small businesses account for a large percentage of the gross national product, the government accumulates figures on small-business failures. Zeroing in on the narrower (but still broad) topic of small-business failures, a student researcher might draft this research problem:

> When small businesses fail, what are the main reasons? Which ones can the business person control? This paper will attempt to learn which factors, in the opinion of experts, can be influenced by the small-business person's own planning and information gathering.

The topic is probably still too broad. Further reading may concentrate the researcher's interest on just the problem of undercapitalization or just the problem of selecting a location for the business. Then the student's topic becomes:

> In what ways have the sources of capital for small-business start-ups changed between 1983 and 1993?

The researcher's extra reading on broader aspects of her topic, although not directly applicable to the paper she will write, will make her more confident and credible in writing about her narrowed topic.

REVIEW

This chapter discussed conducting secondary research leading to a long, formal report intended to solve a business problem. Persons doing secondary research systematically gather information collected and published by others. Primary researchers generate through their own efforts data that did not exist before. An impartial attitude must govern every phase of data gathering and report preparation.

The chapter explored a typical business research case and differentiated between business reports and reports done in other disciplines.

Most secondary research is performed in libraries, which offer a wide variety of information in both familiar and new forms. Library skills remain useful throughout a person's business career. To utilize libraries' considerable resources, researchers must learn what their libraries hold, tap into the manual and the computer-assisted information-finding tools, and plan and follow a thorough research strategy. Though not all college and university libraries have all the same reference tools, Chapter 5 covered resources typical of many.

Researchers must handle secondary information with integrity, quoting, citing, and documenting meticulously and using consistently a recognized documentation style. This chapter provided guidelines for paraphrasing.

Finally, the chapter discussed means of defining and narrowing a suitable secondary-research topic.

APPLICATION EXERCISES

1. What is the definition of a business report?

2. Why is objectivity important in business research, and why is it so difficult to achieve?

3. Explain the distinction between primary and secondary business research.

4. Explain this statement: "Library research conducted to solve a business problem must be systematic."

5. What resources fall into the category of "periodicals"?

6. Under what circumstances are you permitted to use information without citing the source from which you obtained it?

7. Carefully define *paraphrase* and *plagiarize.*

8. In the library, look in the catalog or serials list to find out what periodicals your library carries in your chosen major. Make a list.

   Examine current issues of each periodical you listed. Notice the difference between scholarly and practitioner, or trade, periodicals. Scholarly journals publish very narrowly focused and exhaustive academic research. Articles in these journals have dozens or even hundreds of bibliographic references each. Other periodicals, published for nonacademic business readers, typically take a practical approach in their articles. They often "translate" the latest in the highly specialized academic journals to make it accessible to less specialized readers.

   Revise your list, dividing the periodicals you examined into "scholarly" and "practitioner/trade." Bring the list to class for discussion or for handing in, as your instructor directs.

9. In the library, as you read current issues of the periodicals in your chosen major, make a list of "hot topics" in your business discipline. Which topics are new? Which are being explored most vigorously? Which are controversial? In which areas have genuinely new discoveries been made? Bring the list to class for discussion or for handing in, as your instructor directs.

10. Select a business topic that you are curious about and would like to research in the library. Try to narrow down your topic. Briefly write out your idea for your instructor. Based on his or her feedback, write a proposal to perform research.

CASES

1. **Explore a Report Topic: Health Care.** Even with the government's intention to require health-care coverage for all Americans, most workers will still have to make some decisions of their own about the type of health coverage to get. The broad choice is between a health maintenance organization (HMO) and an indemnity, or fee-for-service, plan. What kinds of workers (income, socioeconomic level, age, and so on) choose which kind of plan? What criteria govern their choice?

2. **Explore a Report Topic: Virtual Reality in Business.** Which applications of virtual reality are businesses most likely to use in the next decade? Investigate the meaning of this term, explore what this technology offers, and read the opinions of various experts on the feasibility of its various business applications.

3. **Explore a Report Topic: Family Leave Policies.** Family-leave policies are much in the news. Employees often have dependents, either children or elderly parents, who at times require employees to miss work to care for them. Many are calling on businesses to make provisions for family leave in these situations. However, many businesses believe such a policy will be all cost and no benefit. Is this a valid point? Explore experts' opinions on the probable costs and benefits to businesses of implementing a family-leave policy.

4. **Explore a Report Topic: Business Ethics Training.** What are businesses doing to promote ethical conduct among their managers and employees? Do they offer awareness training? Do they institute explicit policies with penalties? Do they rely on people's own decency? Have they found innovative ways to promote ethics? Do they do nothing at all? Examine the literature on this subject.

5. **Explore a Report Topic: Employing Persons with Disabilities.** Full employment is a goal of a productive nation, and great strides have been made in employing persons with disabilities. Examine the literature on the Americans with Disabilities Act. What additional information published recently by the government and in business periodicals can you locate about employing persons with disabilities?

6. **Explore a Report Topic: Operating a Pro Sports Team.** What has been written about the business of operating professional sports teams? Owners and managers must consider salary structure, sources of profit and loss, costs of

litigation, and other financial matters that create risks and benefits in the pro sports industry. Locate and read articles and books that have explored this subject.

7. **Explore a Report Topic: Controlling Employee Theft.** One of the greatest threats to businesses is employee theft. Businesses must pass on to legitimate customers the cost of "shrinkage," the amount of product that disappears and is never accounted for—and the amount is staggering. What means do businesses have to fight employee theft? Which are most effective? Gather and read periodical articles on this subject.

8. **Explore a Report Topic: Markets for Recycled Material.** Most people approve of recycling in principle, and most enthusiastically join in recycling efforts. Some studies, however, are now showing that a heavy proportion of recycled material has a limited market. Some recycled material costs more to gather, sort, and transport than it will sell for. Read periodical articles to learn about the dimensions of this problem and what solutions are being proposed.

9. **Explore a Report Topic: Labor-Management Cooperation in the Big Three.** What changes have occurred in the last 20 years in the way the Big Three U.S. automakers have dealt with unions? Faced with the threat of competition from abroad, in what ways have management and unions cooperated? In the literature you read about this subject, trace the evolution of the relationship between automaker unions and management.

10. **Explore a Report Topic: Business Support for Schools.** Businesses in the United States voluntarily help out educational institutions. They donate money or goods such as computers or furniture, and they institute cooperative training programs such as internships. Examine articles on this subject. In what other ways do businesses help educational institutions? What benefits do they gain by their efforts and contributions?

Chapter Six

Primary Research for Business Reporting

PREVIEW

This chapter describes two important means of gathering primary data: observational research and survey research. You will acquire a working knowledge of how to perform research using these two methods. Also, knowing the uses of these methods will make you a more knowledgeable *user* of research data generated by others. ●

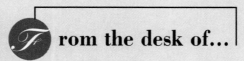

****

A Great Idea or an Expensive Mistake? Primary Research Will Test

**Boyd Malpezzi
Production Manager**

At Polyply Products we fabricate and wholesale plastic bags of assorted sizes, strengths, colors, and shapes to manufacturers, who package their products in them. I'm Boyd. Most of my responsibility is production, but we're a small business and we cooperate on the marketing function.

Each year we mail out our catalog to previous customers and to prospects on eight lists that we buy from a list broker. The prospect lists cost $95 per thousand names and, even using bulk mail, we spend a lot on postage. I know advertising is a legitimate expense, but I'd surely like to know whether we're getting more orders from repeat customers or from businesses on those expensive names lists.

What if we stopped binding the order blank into our catalog and instead used differently coded order blanks for existing customers and for prospects on each of the eight lists we buy? Colors wouldn't work, since so many people fax orders now. Codes would work. We could track the sources of our orders and maybe drop the less profitable lists and save a lot in mailing costs too. I think I'll propose the idea to my boss.

PRIMARY DATA GATHERING

Observational research obtains and analyzes data that can be perceived by the human senses or by devices that enhance perception.

Survey research obtains information using questionnaires or opinionnaires administered by mail, by phone, or in person.

While observational and survey research do not change anything in what they measure, experimental research changes something and then measures the effect of the change.

The problem solver in the opening profile is considering a simple observational research project. He will gather primary data. Researchers perform primary research when they generate data that did not exist in any published form before. Observational, survey, and experimental research, the three main forms of primary research, can all generate projects ranging from simple to very complex. Some research problems require a combination of these primary research methods.

Observational research consists of recording the data that researchers can perceive through their five senses or through a machine or device enhancing what those five senses can do. Researchers generally construct an instrument—a checklist or counting device—that permits them to conserve their available time, that is, to spend maximum time perceiving and minimum time recording. Researchers do not interact with those being observed. In fact, the more unobtrusive they are, the more likely they are to obtain undistorted data. They simply record what they are able to perceive from outside.

In **survey research,** sometimes called *normative research,* researchers interact with the persons about whom they are collecting data. Researchers construct a questionnaire or opinionnaire and administer it to their target audience. They take care not to influence or predispose the responses in any way.

In **experimental research,** researchers set up carefully controlled conditions in which they create one change and measure the effect of that change on someone or something else. (Experimental research is beyond this book's scope.)

On average, observational research is cheaper than survey research, and survey research is cheaper than experimental research. Common sense counsels researchers to use the least expensive means to gain the information needed. For instance, do not send out a questionnaire if you can get what you need from an observation or from secondary sources.

All primary research methods require systematic and meticulous planning. The most challenging part of the planning is figuring out what can go wrong and preventing it. "If anything can go wrong, it will go wrong, and at the worst possible time," says Murphy's Law. Successful primary researchers are on constant alert for Murphy's evil influence.

Designing any of the three types of research projects requires many steps. Each phase of the plan requires the researcher to consider what will happen in every other phase. For instance, a researcher must plan in detail how data will be treated even while designing a questionnaire. If the researcher does not plan, the data obtained may be wonderfully interesting but impossible to analyze statistically. In many cases of business research, statistical analysis is required to turn data into useful information.

All three research types use terms like *variable, valid,* and *reliable.* A **variable** is anything whose changes are of interest and can be measured and recorded. The volume of a chemical compound, the number of people who pass a given corner on a given day, and the speed of a racehorse could all be variables.

A variable is anything a researcher can measure and record.

The words **valid** and **reliable** carry particular meanings when researchers use them. We say data are valid when the researchers actually measure what they intend to measure. We say data are reliable when the results are accurate and would be reproducible if the data gathering were repeated using the same means.

VALIDITY AND RELIABILITY

Valid research measures what it sets out to measure.

Reliable research measures accurately and reproducibly.

In some research projects, validity might not present a problem. To take a simple example, suppose you want to know how much rain falls between midnight November 3 and midnight November 4. You would place a narrow, straight-sided container out in the open, away from trees, buildings, or other shelter. You would bar pranksters and thirsty creatures. If the rain gauge was empty at midnight November 3, it rained overnight, and you found an inch of rain at midnight November 4, you can validly say an inch of rain has fallen.

Sometimes researchers have to measure a variable that they can measure and use it as a fairly good reading on a similar variable that they cannot measure. Children's intelligence tests make a good example. Experts have worked for decades to perfect intelligence tests, but even the test makers acknowledge that these devices have had shortcomings. Intelligence is invisible, an internal, mental construct measurable only through what can be seen on the outside. To add to the problem, over a hundred different types of human ability compose what we call "intelligence," and the most familiar pencil-and-paper intelligence tests measure only a handful of those. How, for example, do we measure the component of intelligence called *intuition?* For the most part, we don't measure it. We don't even know exactly what it is.

To ensure or improve validity, researchers have to recognize where the problems may lie. For many years, intelligence tests were constructed using the background knowledge and vocabulary of the average middle-class Caucasian child. For all those years, the intelligence of children who did not fit this category was mismeasured. Their brains could perform the tasks just as well, on average, as those of the "average" children, but they lacked some of the verbal symbols needed to understand the question, problem, or task on the test and to formulate their response. The tests "showed" that they were less intelligent because bias was unintentionally built into the tests. The tests were thought to measure the ability to use verbal symbols, but they measured something else instead: the knowledge of a certain set of verbal symbols.

BENT OFFERINGS by Don Addis. By permission of Don Addis and Creators Syndicate.

This astronomer's conclusions are not valid. He is not measuring what he thinks he is measuring. Still, since his instrument is faulty, he will obtain the same results each time he tries.

Test developers gradually came to understand this error and have worked to improve the tests' validity, that is, their ability to measure in actuality what they set out to measure. Today's tests are much freer of bias, but we still have the problem of measuring an intangible using only what can be seen from the outside. The results of the tests are useful, but teachers and administrators use them with caution, remaining alert for signs of intellect and talent that the tests might fail to measure.

Now consider intelligence tests in the context of reliability. The tests are reliable in that the same test given to the same group of children will generate the same results. Insofar as they are able to measure, they measure accurately and reproducibly. Reliability is not enough, however, without validity.

Data become unreliable when the means of measurement are inconsistent from subject to subject. To use a simple example, suppose you had a 36-inch cloth measuring tape that became half an inch longer when the weather was humid and the fibers relaxed. Your results on a dry day would differ from those on a damp day. Imagine the difference two dozen of these faulty tapes would make to a small-business garment manufacturer. Garment pieces cut on one day could not be sewn to garment pieces cut on a different day, and thousands of dollars in material and labor would be lost.

As another example, suppose you hire survey personnel to interview people in a mall to measure preferences for and satisfaction with the kinds of fast food offered in the mall's food plaza. The majority of your interviewers are mothers of young school-age children interested in a few hours of part-time work during school hours.

Now think about what different groups of people spend money on in mall food plazas. What if, despite the training they received, the interviewers are hesitant to approach certain groups of shoppers? The junior-high kids who eat there during the school lunch break will be wearing whatever bizarre clothing and hairstyle is current, may talk too loudly on subjects the moms hope their children don't think about yet, and may in fact represent the moms' worst nightmares about what their kids will be like in four years.

Suppose the interviewers avoid approaching these youngsters or approach them timidly or in an authoritarian way ("I know what you're supposed to eat!"). If one or more of your interviewers avoid these young people, they will be underrepresented in your study. If the interviewers do not make it easy for the young people to talk to them, the youngsters' responses, and any resulting data on their preferences, may be distorted or lacking. The findings from your carefully structured questions may not be reliable, that is, not accurate or reproducible.

Questions about validity and reliability enter all kinds of research, but especially that done by primary research means. Let's look at those methods separately.

OBSERVATIONAL RESEARCH

Imagine for a moment that you are a marketer. What kinds of data about target markets might you want to observe? You would like to know which people buy what products in what quantities. You could, of course, send out a survey and ask them, but that would be costly and slow. Also, people tend to claim that they buy classier products than they actually do buy.

You could stand near the cash register with a long checklist and mark it each time a customer buys a product in which you are interested, but that is hopelessly inefficient. Consider, though, that many grocery chains now use optical scanners at the cash registers. Though we may not have thought about them in this way, creative thinkers have set those computer-linked scanners up to perform a systematic observation. The computer records the quantity of each product in inventory and, via scanner, records each item sold. As it counts items, it provides observational data in which marketers are keenly interested. They can compare data on products ordered and sold at stores in different neighborhoods, each of a known socioeconomic level, and draw inferences about which stock items are profitable in which neighborhoods.

The scanner is an enhancement of human beings' five senses. Some much simpler observations use only human eyes and ears. An observational researcher might stand near a new-product display in a video store, count the passersby who look at the display, and perhaps time the length of their gaze. Results could be compared with data from an observation incorporating a different type of display. Another project might require an observer to document walking patterns of shoppers in a large store's cosmetics department, to create a basis for rearranging counters in that department to slow the shoppers down and cause them to look directly at more products.

Not all observational research involves watching people. Much can be learned just by looking at places where people have been. For instance, the placement of chairs in a room after a meeting might suggest one kind of meeting if chairs were left in a rough circle and another kind if chairs were left in rows facing the front. Empty food containers people threw away tell us what

Observation can include seeing, hearing, smelling, touching, and tasting. Researchers can observe while something is happening or after it has occurred.

they consumed. Direct-mail pieces discarded unopened tell us what the people did not read.

Planning

Researchers don't just walk to a site and say, "I think I'll collect some data here." As in all other useful research, observational researchers decide on their objective and plan the observation to reach it. They find out what they are likely to see, what it means when they see it, how they will know for certain when they see it, and what counts and what does not.

They create an instrument—a checklist, for example—for recording what they observe. They test it extensively, because if the instrument is flawed, the data are unlikely to be useful.

Pilot Testing

You pilot-test an instrument by trying it out in an environment or with subjects *like* those you want to measure.

Researchers try out their instruments in a situation as similar as possible to the one in which they will actually gather their data. This process is called **pilot testing** the instrument. Most problems with the instrument will show up in this way. If problems are few and minor, the researchers revise the instrument and proceed with data gathering. If many and/or serious problems appear, the researchers revise extensively, repeat the pilot-testing step, and perhaps revise again before using the instrument in the actual research situation.

A Simple Observational Research Case

Sales are sharply down in one district of a medium-size software company. The six district sales reps have been complaining that their strategy meetings are a waste of time. Turnover has been high; four of the six reps have spent fewer than seven months in this job. Farley, their manager, who sits in on most meetings but does not run them, has given them positive pep talks and negative chewing-outs, but sales have improved only minimally. Each week Farley and one rep (reps chair the meetings on a revolving basis) make and distribute an agenda, but the meetings generate little in the way of either ideas or motivation.

Farley wishes the reps had all turned over. He believes the two longer-term reps, Ferraro and Teague, are troublemakers and hotshots. Farley's boss, Kupman, is not so sure. He thinks Farley is overvaluing the newcomers. With sales so poor, he feels they have yet to prove themselves, whereas the other two were contributing when sales were strong. He also thinks the dynamics of their meetings should be examined. Kupman and Farley finally agree that more information is needed and an impartial third party should gather it. The reps agree that the meetings need attention; everybody wants to see sales where they should be.

Kupman and Farley ask Morrisey, the human resources manager, to meet with the two of them. Morrisey does so, bringing along a number of articles on meetings. After discussing topics from the articles, they decide the research question is "What behaviors in these meetings are robbing the meetings of their productivity?"

Morrisey attends the sales reps' Monday strategy meeting as an observer, simply to see what there is to see. After being told that Morrisey is there to observe and "give us some tips," the reps welcome him. They feel a little self-conscious at first but then get down to business. Morrisey takes some semistructured notes and audiotapes the meeting. He studies the notes and tape and reviews the literature on meeting behavior. Then Kupman, Farley, and Morrisey meet to draft a grid-style checksheet with a variety of meeting be-

EXHIBIT 6–1   Sample Observation Instrument

Observation Instrument—Meeting Behaviors

Sales Strategy Meeting

Date _____

	Pennell	Schwartz	Ferraro	Lorimer	Teague	Chavez
Positive						
Initiate new idea						
Support previous						
Expand previous						
Critique previous						
Ask factual question						
Request clarification						
Inject positive humor						
Ask consensus						
Facilitate flow						
Unclassifiable positive						
Negative						
Move off subject						
Obstruct						
Inject negative humor						
Attack						

haviors down the left margin and the six reps' names at the heads of the columns across the top.

At the next Monday meeting, Morrisey sits in and makes a trial observation using the checksheet. By now the reps are used to having him there. After this meeting, Morrisey adds two categories to the checksheet and enlarges the boxes on the grid for the behaviors that might be expected to occur more frequently.

Having sat in on two meetings, Morrisey has decided how he will classify such things as one-syllable comments ("Yeah?" "Yeah!" or "We-e-e-ell"). Now he can begin the actual observation. The reps do not change their behavior; they thought he was doing the observation all along. Morrisey formally observes two of the strategy meetings. After doing so, he feels confident that he has good information. He examines his category counts for each of the six reps and draws some inferences.

When he meets with Kupman and Farley, he makes an oral report to them with several recommendations. The counts of his checkmarks show clearly that Farley is right about Teague but wrong about Ferraro. Teague's contributions to the meeting, though made in a kind, sincere tone, are negative four out of five times. His comments do not fit in the "attack" or "ridicule" categories, nor does he critique constructively. Instead, he obstructs. In one meeting, Morrisey documented eight ideas whose promise was never explored because Teague's "It won't work; trust me; I've been here longer" attitude discouraged the idea's author. Amid the other reps' comments, Teague's defeatist comments were not recognized for what they were. Neither Teague nor the other reps realized he was such a "wet blanket."

Morrisey makes some other suggestions. Three newcomers need encouragement; in contrast, Schwartz should be counseled to rein in her high spirits. A little positive humor goes a long way, but Schwartz should hone her comedy club skills on her own time. Finally, Morrisey recommends the use of a training video on facilitating meetings. The agendas are good, he says, and so is the practice of rotating the chair. He offers to repeat the observation in three months.

He might not need to do so. In general, organization members want to support the group's objectives. In this case, having an impartial outsider present the results of observational research might solve the problem.

SURVEY RESEARCH

Survey research moves beyond what the senses can perceive through observation. A **survey** is the process of systematically asking a limited group of persons to respond to the same set of questions or opinion items. The instrument used is called a *questionnaire* or *opinionnaire.* Typically researchers draft the instrument after careful study of their own topic and other survey instruments, revise it, subject it to one or more pilot tests, and revise it further before administering it to their target audience.

Sometimes researchers want to gather facts about a large group, called a **population.** When they obtain those facts from every member of that group, the work is called a **census.** Most often, however, their time and resources permit gathering the facts from only a percentage of a large group. When they proceed in this way, we say they use a **sample.**

A population is an entire large group in which a researcher is interested.

Like survey research, observational research and experimental research can employ random samples. Since survey research uses sampling most of the time, we'll focus on sampling here.

Sampling

Sampling is the process of selecting a few units from a large group, measuring or learning something about those units, and reasoning that what is true of those units may be true of the large group.

Samples may be random (probability) or nonrandom (nonprobability). Random samples permit researchers to generalize their findings with greater confidence to the whole of the large group sampled. Random samples also let researchers apply a much broader range of statistical measures to their data and draw many more inferences. We will discuss random sampling in detail shortly. First, let's look at some means of nonrandom sampling.

Nonrandom Samples

Two common means of **nonrandom sampling** are the convenience sample and the judgment sample.

A **convenience sample** is a smaller, accessible group of persons who resemble in important ways the larger population targeted. The researchers collect data from the smaller group and cautiously draw such inferences as they can. They can suggest that the findings probably apply to the larger population in some useful ways, but they cannot demonstrate that they do. When they report their findings, they do so with this disclaimer.

For instance, suppose a researcher wants to know how high school students who can input 50 words per minute on one word processor will respond to having to acquire the same level of word processing skill on a different computer with a different operating system and program. The researcher could argue that if he controlled for such demographics as socioeconomic level, results of research using students in one high school could represent sufficiently the results likely to be obtained if the research were repeated in other schools with the same demographics.

In using a **judgment sample,** researchers develop a list of test units using their best judgment that measurements made on those units will generate useful information about a subject they represent.

For instance, suppose a researcher wants to know CPAs' (certified public accountants') opinions about a federal tax regulation limiting deductions of business entertainment expenses. She might not need to make sure all cities and states are represented proportionally among her interviewees. She can put together a judgment sample of CPAs in several known locations that seem representative to her. Even allowing for some differences in CPAs' client entertaining from state to state or city to city, the law is likely to affect them all in much the same way. From interviewing a judgment sample of CPAs, the researcher can obtain meaningful information about the effect of the tax regulation on CPAs. The information will not, however, be statistically representative. When researchers using a judgment sample report their results, they specify the nature of the sample and draw their inferences cautiously.

The principle of **random sampling** is this:

> When a sample is drawn at random from a large number of test units, each test unit in the whole has an equal chance of being selected.

When the sample is truly random, whatever is true of the selected test units is true of the entire number of potential test units. To sample randomly, researchers must be able to reach every unit of a group. Any units that are unreachable will not have the necessary equal chance of being selected.

A researcher selects a *random sample* of a population and generalizes that what is true of the sample is likely to be true of the entire group from which the sample came.

Population. Much business research is performed using people as test units. However, many other things can also be sampled. Medics draw blood samples to test for antibodies, cholesterol, or drug residues. Grain buyers scoop out samples of wheat from a carload to test for moisture. Samples of swimming pool water are tested for acid and chlorine. Samples of garden soil are tested for nitrogen and other nutrients. In these random-sample cases, we infer that what is true of the test units is true of the whole. The medic treats the whole person, the grain buyer prices and purchases the carload, and so on.

A population can be a large number of people. It can be the population of a city, a nation, or a special-interest group. We can also speak of the total number of stray dogs in Cuming County as a population of stray dogs.

If the number of test units is small, researchers can choose to test them all, performing a census rather than taking a sample.

Typically, business researchers need to find out something about too many people to ask them all. In those cases, they opt for a random sample.

Sampling frame.   To sample a population randomly, researchers must know the identity of and be able to reach every member of the population. In practice, this is rarely possible. Researchers often use an existing list, available from an organization or a list broker, that approximates the desired population. This list is called a **sampling frame,** and a random sample is drawn from it.

For instance, researchers in business communication often wish to survey business communication teachers. No list contains all such teachers. The membership list of the Association for Business Communication, however, contains a substantial number of them. Let's say the researcher is interested in the teachers' attitudes toward tax-supported funding for education. The researcher must consider whether the pertinent attitudes of business communication teachers who are members of ABC are likely to differ from those of nonmembers. For the study on tax support for education, the groups are not likely to differ much. The ABC list is probably a good sampling frame.

Homogeneous or heterogeneous population.   If the population is **homogeneous,** that is, much the same in most important respects, a smaller sample can represent it well. If the population is **heterogeneous,** that is, full of variations, a larger sample is needed to assure representativeness. In the examples that follow, we'll assume a fairly homogeneous population.

Types of Random Samples

Researchers have developed many complex and highly effective types of random sampling. Let's look at some simple forms.

Simple random sample.   In a **simple random sample,** the name or identity of each member of the population is recorded on a slip of paper. All the slips are combined and scrambled thoroughly. If the researcher wants a 10 percent sample and there are 1,000 names, he draws 100 names. Statistically, whatever is discovered to be true of the 100 is very likely to be true of the 1,000.

Systematic random sample.   Most researchers do not use scrambled slips of papers in selecting their samples. Rather, they simply use an alphabetized list of the population from which they select a **systematic random sample.** Let's say the researcher has the same population as in the simple random example, 1,000. To obtain a 10 percent sample and ensure randomness, the researcher chooses at random a number between 1 and 10. (He could do this easily with a shuffled deck of cards or a pair of dice.) If he pulls or rolls a 4, 4 becomes his starting point. Starting with the fourth name on the list, he takes every 10th name: the 14th, the 24th, the 34th, and so on. Whatever is true of the sample drawn by this means is just as likely to be true of the 1,000 as was the sample drawn from the scrambled name slips.

Stratified random sample.   Sometimes researchers need to divide a population, and the sample they draw, into unequal-size portions. In such a case, they may use a **stratified random sample.** The work force of a medium-size business, for example, contains multiple internal classifications. For convenience, let's use a work force of 1,000 and suppose researchers need to divide it by length of time worked at this firm, by sex, and by salary level.

Personnel figures show the following breakdowns:

Length of Time Worked	Sex	Salary Level
10% 25 years and over	53% Male	8% $90,000 and above
11% 20–24 years	47% Female	10% $75,000–$89,999
12% 16–19 years		12% $60,000–$74,999
12% 10–15 years		30% $45,000–$59,999
30% 6–9 years		26% $30,000–$44,999
25% Under 5 years		12% $15,000–$29,999
		2% $14,999 and below

The researchers will draw a random 10 percent sample, making sure that the 100 names they draw represent the categories just listed. The resulting sample will contain 53 males and 47 females. Of the 100 people, 10 will have been with the company at least 25 years, 26 will earn between $30,000 and $44,999, and so on.

Researchers concern themselves with accurate sampling procedures to make sure their research results will enable good business decisions. Primary research has many steps, and an error at any step not only carries the error through the whole effort but also contaminates subsequent steps and thus multiplies the error. The correct business decision is supposed to recoup the costs of research. The incorrect business decision based on bad research, however, turns the investment in research into sunk costs, and the bad decision itself generally costs much more besides.

Because of its costs and the costs of the decisions it supports, business research must be carried out meticulously.

Questionnaire Construction

Most of us have responded to one or more questionnaires. Businesses use questionnaires extensively, from the brief, informal pick-up forms found in hotels ("How was our service? Please answer these few questions") to ambitious, multipage survey efforts. Thorough planning and development lead up to the printed questionnaire the respondent sees.

Survey instruments are either questionnaires or opinionnaires. A **questionnaire** contains mostly question-format items. An **opinionnaire** consists mainly of statements to which the respondent is invited to react. For example, opinionnaire items might say,

My supervisor offers me constructive criticism.	SA A N D SD

or

Others in my work group would say I am a cooperative person.	SA A N D SD

The respondent is instructed to mark agreement or disagreement on the SA (strongly agree) to SD (strongly disagree) scale.

Whether developing a questionnaire or an opinionnaire, researchers construct the survey instrument in steps. They decide what they want to know and from whom they can probably find it out. Then they draft a set of questions or opinion items to elicit the desired information. This task might sound easier than it is. In fact, most questionnaires require numerous drafts and tests before the researcher can be sure that the responses received will answer the research question validly and reliably.

Recall the communication model discussed in Chapter One. No two people have identical attitudes, reactions to words, or knowledge of a subject. Yet researchers have to ask all their research subjects the same questions in the same ways. Those questions have to mean the same things to all the people who will answer them.

The value of surveys lies in the researcher's ability to treat a large number of responses together. From doing so, the researcher infers something about a still larger number of respondents from whom she or he drew the sample actually surveyed. If the questions do not mean the same thing to all respondents, their answers will not be comparable. The researcher's efforts to tally and categorize these answers will therefore be meaningless.

Open-Ended and Closed-Ended Questionnaire Items

Questions can be open ended or closed ended. **Open-ended questions** permit the respondent to answer as he or she likes. **Closed-ended questions** restrict the respondent's choice to a set of answers to be treated in a specified way. An example of an open-ended question is

What general-studies courses do you think you will enjoy most during college?

An example of a closed-ended question is this rank-ordering item:

Rank the following general-studies courses in the order of your preference of them. Place a 10 next to the course you believe you would enjoy most, a 9 next to the one you would enjoy second best, an 8 next to the one you would enjoy third best, and so on, ending with a 1 for the one you would enjoy least.

_____ American history		_____ Music appreciation
_____ English literature		_____ Art and architecture survey
_____ Survey of philosophy		_____ American literature
_____ World history		_____ Introduction to geology
_____ Astronomy		_____ Fundamentals of psychology

The *rank-ordering* question is only one of numerous kinds of closed-ended questions, more of which we will discuss shortly. Whether you choose closed-ended or open-ended questions depends on your research goals and on what information you can reasonably expect your respondent to provide.

In the example just given, one influence on the choice of question format was the actual array of possible answers in which the researcher was interested. A researcher interested in the whole spectrum of general-studies courses could not ask the respondent to name *and* rank the 300 or more general-studies offerings. A respondent cannot easily rank order more than about 10 items.

The open-ended question given earlier will obtain many different course names. Some courses will be incorrectly named and will be hard or impossible to assign to categories. Some courses will be listed that are *not* general-studies courses. Some respondents will forget altogether one or more courses or subject matter areas in which they might actually be quite interested. They will tend to list courses they have heard others mention. Since even anonymous survey respondents like to idealize their own behavior, they may name courses that sound more learned or more prestigious than those they would really like to take.

Many other inaccuracies, both intentional and unintentional, will influence the validity and reliability of cumulated responses to this open-ended item. Yet if the researcher is at an exploratory stage of research, hard numbers may be less important than other considerations. For instance, from the tallied responses to this item, the researcher could certainly pick out the 10 courses that were named most frequently.

A closed-ended, rank-ordering question permits the researcher to weight responses. In asking this kind of question, the researcher has already narrowed down the array to 10 courses and is probably at a later stage of inquiry. Processing the responses to the question in the preceding example will tell the researcher with certainty how the response audience as a whole views these (and only these) 10 courses.

Open-ended questions are easy to write, but they allow a broad range of potential answers, some of which may not be easily categorized. Because open-ended questions usually take more of a respondent's time than closed-ended questions do, respondents are more likely to leave some or all of them unanswered.

Closed-ended questions must be written with great care. Whereas open-ended questions leave the field open for replies the researcher might not have foreseen, closed-ended questions prevent the respondent from giving any answer the researcher has not anticipated and built into the question.

In all types of questions, but particularly closed-ended questions, wording is crucial. Here are some principles to keep in mind when writing questionnaires:

Writing the Questions

- Word choice must be simple and familiar, not pretentious or stuffy.
- The language chosen must not convey any bias or contain any ambiguity.
- Where the researcher has a choice between a word with high connotation and a synonym with neutral connotation, the more neutral word should be used.
- The question should not threaten the respondent's ego.
- Each question should be easy to answer.
- Questions must not be complex. Each should ask only one thing.
- Every question must be worth asking. Respondents' time is hard to obtain and must not be wasted.
- Questions should be formulated with a view to the kind of data they will generate. The researcher must be able to code, classify, and cumulate them and, in many cases, subject them to statistical testing.

Typically, respondents are not at first interested in cooperating with a researcher. There is "nothing in it for them." Even after the researcher has persuaded them to respond, it takes very little to turn them off again. For instance, if the survey seems too long, they will throw it away. If a question seems hard or troublesome to answer, they will leave it blank or stop responding altogether. If the survey questions irritate them, they may quit responding. If they cannot figure out what they are supposed to do, they often decline to do anything.

Anything in a questionnaire that bothers the respondent might make that respondent decide not to cooperate.

With this in mind, the researcher tries to view the survey instrument as the reader will view it. The hardest part of this task is adjusting the mind so as to approach the questionnaire "cold," that is, without much interest, prior knowledge, or motivation to complete it.

Closed-ended questions, of which the rank-ordering question is one kind, take many other forms.

Types of Closed-Ended Questions

Multiple choice. In the **multiple-choice** format, the respondent marks only one choice. A multiple-choice item must exhaust all possible alternatives, and those alternatives must be mutually exclusive.

Multiple-choice items are easy to draft when the categories are familiar, clear, and well defined. For instance, questions like the following have two, and only two, answers:

Are you a U.S. citizen?

_____yes

_____no

Are you male or female?

_____male

_____female

For a question like

Have you been vaccinated for smallpox?

the respondent can answer *yes, no,* or *don't know.* There are no other possible responses.

With respect to marital status, one person might consider that an individual is either married, never married, separated, divorced, or widowed. But not everyone would agree. Some modern living arrangements confound traditional classifications. Individuals might respond that they are in a "common-law marriage," a "same-sex marriage," or a "long-term committed relationship" and insist that they are in none of the other categories.

Alternatives for a multiple-choice item must be exhaustive and mutually exclusive. If you believe they are but think occasional respondents may find your alternatives insufficient, list your standard categories and then offer a response category that says,

_____ other. (Please specify.)_____

In this way, you will obtain accurate counts in your standard categories and be able to account for respondents who did not mark one of those.

Checklist. A researcher uses a **checklist** when multiple responses are desired. The instruction to the respondent is usually "Mark all that apply." Here is an example:

Please mark all the kinds of luncheon food items you have purchased at Lunch Unlimited during the last 30 days.

_____ Pasta	_____ Quiche	_____ Pastries
_____ Hamburger	_____ Submarine sandwich	_____ Fried chicken
_____ Pizza	_____ Oriental food	_____ Philly steak
_____ Mexican food	_____ Soup or chili	_____ Salad bar

Rating scale. Researchers use several other types of questions when they foresee a range of opinion. One is the **rating scale.** The respondent is instructed to indicate an opinion by marking a letter, number, or other sequential symbol on a specified continuum. The following item uses a rating scale:

Please rate the service you have received during the last 30 days from Lunch Unlimited. Use a scale of 1 to 10, with 1 being the least favorable and 10 being the most favorable rating.

My rating of Lunch Unlimited's service during the last 30 days is _____.

Semantic differential. A **semantic-differential** item offers a pair of opposed descriptive words that can be applied to the topic under discussion. The researcher asks the respondent to mark his or her opinion on a continuum connecting the opposites. Here is an example:

Below are several pairs of opposed words that could describe the food at a restaurant. Between the pairs of words is a range in which respondents can mark their opinion. Consider that the middle of the scale, 4, is "neutral" or "no opinion." Please *circle the number* that represents your opinion about the food at Lunch Unlimited.

```
imaginative ------1---------2---------3---------4---------5---------6---------7---------------dull
stale -------------1---------2---------3---------4---------5---------6---------7--------------fresh
appetizing -------1---------2---------3---------4---------5---------6---------7-----unappetizing
ample -----------1---------2---------3---------4---------5---------6---------7------------skimpy
junk--------------1---------2---------3---------4---------5---------6---------7--------nutritious
messy -----------1---------2---------3---------4---------5---------6---------7---------------neat
```

Likert scale. A typical **Likert scale** item offers a statement and a series of response options indicating degree of agreement or disagreement. The following example is a Likert-type item, which would be one of a series of statements. The respondent would be directed to mark the box most nearly approximating his or her opinion about the statement.

College business juniors, in general, have a well-developed sense of ethical conduct.

Strongly Agree	Agree	Neutral, No opinion	Disagree	Strongly Disagree
☐	☐	☐	☐	☐

Ordering Items on Questionnaires

After writing and revising all the items for clarity, absence of bias, and all other possible flaws, the researcher puts the questions on the questionnaire in the most logical order. It is important that the order of the items make sense. If one question will not be understood until after another question has been asked and answered, be sure the two questions are in the correct sequence.

Also, try to move from easy to more difficult. If the more time-consuming or troublesome questions are asked first, the respondent might not bother continuing. If the respondent quits late in the questionnaire but mails it back having marked all but a couple of items, the questionnaire is probably usable for at least part of the researcher's purpose. If the respondent has marked only two items, the researcher will not have a usable response.

Although demographic items are easy to answer, they are generally placed last on an instrument because in most studies they are less crucial than the idea subject matter of the survey. Most respondents answer them no matter where they are placed.

Pilot Testing Questionnaires

As in any other kind of primary research, researchers using questionnaires test their instruments and procedures. Even after several iterations of a questionnaire, problems may persist unknown to the researchers. In a pilot test, they try out the questionnaire and administration procedure on a test audience, ideally one similar to the audience actually targeted but *not* the same one.

Sometimes the questionnaire and procedure will work perfectly. Other times minimal problems can be discovered and corrected easily. Still other times a major problem emerges, one that would destroy the project if undetected.

A student of one of the authors set out to test senior citizens' satisfaction with the services offered at a community senior center. The student carefully drafted a short questionnaire and tried it out successfully on her classmates. She wanted more evidence, however, that the questionnaire would work on the intended audience. She asked the director of the senior center in a different community to allow her to test the questionnaire with its members. Permission granted, she went there, introduced herself and her purpose briefly, found the members receptive, and handed out the forms.

The respondents marked the forms and handed them back—rather soon, she thought. Then she noticed that most of them were not turning to the second page. She began pointing out the second page to the rest of the respondents. With this reminder, some filled out the second page (though not enthusiastically), but several said something like "No, dear, I'm finished," or "I have to play bridge now."

Enough people filled out the second page that she was able to spot the couple of remaining problems with the instrument's wording. The problem of the disregarded second page, however, would never have emerged had she ceased pilot testing after the in-class trial of the questionnaire. Fully half of her questions, answered by relatively few members of her ultimate target audience, might have generated unreliable data.

Her solution was to reformat the questionnaire to fit all the items on one side of one 8.5″ × 14″ page. From that point on, her project was problem free.

Administering the Survey

Researchers' ideal goal, to get 100 percent of the target respondents to answer, is virtually never met. Realistically, they shoot for the highest possible response rate and do everything they can to prevent nonresponse.

A number of techniques appear to increase response rate. For instance, more people will respond if they can do so anonymously. Also, more people will respond if the questionnaire package looks attractive and professional.

What percentage response rate is high enough? Putting down a single percentage would be meaningless. If the population and the sample are fairly homogeneous, you need a lower percentage response to be confident that the respondents represent the sample, just as a smaller sample can represent a homogeneous population well. If the population is full of variations, a larger sample is needed to represent it, and a larger percentage of the sample must respond before you can assume representativeness.

> Whether a given response rate is sufficient depends on how homogeneous a population is.

Researchers survey their target respondents by mail, by telephone, or in person. Each method has advantages and disadvantages. For instance, in-person and telephone interviewers find it harder than mail survey researchers do to ensure that all respondents are asked the same questions in the same ways. A question on paper is the same question on every questionnaire mailed. A question read or spoken aloud might carry differences in tone of voice, degree of hesitancy, and other vocal signals. In-person interviewers have even broader scope for unintentional change. Nonverbal signals can distort or confuse meaning even more than auditory signals, which also exist in in-person situations.

Open-ended responses, whether obtained in writing by mail or orally by phone or in person, are subject to interpretation by the person who takes them down, codes them, or categorizes them. Not all respondents will have good communication skills, and even good communicators can miscommunicate if they are in a hurry or under stress. Both sender error and receiver error create more problems in open-ended than in closed-ended items.

Mail surveys work well if you have several weeks. The mailing must be prepared meticulously. Because you won't be there in person to explain anything ambiguous, lack of clarity can be fatal. You must foresee any possible problems and solve them in advance.

Mail Surveys

You must prepare a list of recipients and extra labels for all of them so that you can send a reminder. Send the reminder about 10 days after the initial mailing. Some researchers use multiple reminders; each one adds about 10 days.

Whereas a phone or in-person questionnaire can consist of just the questionnaire and a brief script, the mailed questionnaire is more of a package. You will have, at minimum, the questionnaire, a cover letter, and a return envelope. Other enclosures might be needed. The package cannot become too large, or respondents will be discouraged from completing it.

The persuasive cover letter should explain the subject without prejudicing the response. Because you cannot stand over your recipients and make them respond, your letter must also motivate them to complete and return the form. Usually you do this by showing how the study will benefit the reader or a cause the reader will find important.

Once the mailing has been sent, most of the administering work is done. Mailed questionnaires are relatively inexpensive when you consider the cost of the many hours spent in telephone and in-person interviews. Another cost advantage is that you can often use bulk-mail postage rates for the outward mailings.

Mailed questionnaires have another advantage in that every respondent receives the same thing in the same form. Consistency of administration is built in. When administering telephone and in-person questionnaires, in contrast, researchers have to be on their guard against inconsistency of administration.

Because a person's tone of voice, pauses, and other signals can convey approval, disapproval, and many other attitudes, researchers giving a questionnaire orally must be extra careful not to lead the interviewee in any way. They must not convey, or even hint at, their own opinions. They must encourage the respondent to complete the interview without prejudicing his or her response.

Telephone Surveys

The respondent's hanging up too soon is a continual danger. Telephone respondents, weary of phone solicitations, sales, and other "junk messages," are often unwilling even to begin the interview. Researchers must combat the automatic assumption that they are "selling something." Some researchers notify respondents by letter several days before the interview and reassure them that the call is legitimate research and not a sales pitch. Those who call "cold," that is, with no advance notice, must usually convince an unwilling person to allow the interruption and expend some time.

Researchers must take down respondents' answers without bias. This is easy for yes-no questions or multiple-choice items. Many phone interview questions, however, are open ended. The ability to obtain rich data is an advantage of phone and in-person interviewing, but, as you read in previous chapters, people sometimes choose and understand words quite differently. Bypassing, in which neither sender nor receiver realizes that misunderstanding has occurred, can lead to bias. Bias can also intrude when respondents are long-winded and the researcher must condense an answer, or when respondents' language skills are weak and the researcher must determine what they actually mean.

Researchers can probe ("Could you explain what you mean by that?" "Can you comment about why you feel as you do?"), but they must word the probe carefully. For instance, "What do you mean by that?" or "Why?" could be understood as disapproval.

Not everyone can be reached by telephone. Some people lack phones. Some have unlisted numbers. Some are gone a great deal. When researchers have to try many times to reach a given respondent, the cost of the research rises.

Both telephone and in-person interviewers must present the questions in exactly the same way to each respondent. If the questions are worded differently, or if the meaning is obscured by gestures or tone of voice, the answers will not be comparable and cannot be treated in the same category.

In-Person Surveys

Surveying respondents in person brings its own problems. If reaching people by phone is difficult, reaching them in person is harder. Factors such as geographic distances and work schedules make it hard for interviewer and interviewee to meet. Some desirable respondents have little discretionary time and resist using it to talk with a researcher. The researcher should say how long the questionnaire will take and keep rigidly within that time.

As with phone questionnaires, interviewers must take care not to lead, must not approve, disapprove, or hint at their own opinion, and must take down information without bias. In person, interviewers can read a wider range of nonverbal signals than are available to mail or phone interviewers. They can see when respondents need encouragement. They can deal more effectively with respondents who do not express themselves well. Finally, it is harder for respondents to get away once the in-person interview has begun; they cannot just hang up the phone or throw away the written questionnaire.

TREATING DATA

What have you counted or measured, what can you do with it, and what does it mean? Once you have gathered your primary research data, your next step is to select, process, and organize it so that it is meaningful to the business reader.

For each question, you add up numbers of responses in different categories. This yields a **frequency distribution.** Different research objectives call for different kinds of treatment. Among the simpler calculations you might need to run are **percentages, cross-tabulations, mean, median, mode,** and **standard deviation.**

Suppose you had 492 respondents to a survey. One item on the survey was the following statement, on which respondents marked a five-point agreement-disagreement scale:

Percentages

The organization where I work is supportive of the needs of employees' families.

You tabulated responses and obtained these figures:

SA: 15   A: 46   N: 112   D: 255   SD: 64

Dividing each figure by the total, 492, yields these percentages:

3.1 percent   9.3 percent   22.7 percent   51.8 percent   13.1 percent

A likely conclusion is that most employees do not find the organization supportive of families.

In the preceding example, do the female employees feel the same way, on average, as the male employees? Using **cross-tabulation,** you can show the relationship between sex and degree of agreement and disagreement. You have 198 female (40.3 percent) and 294 (59.7 percent) male respondents. Lay out a chart and insert your counts to see how the categories form:

Cross-tabulation

	SA	A	N	D	SD	Total
Male	12	32	66	165	19	294
Female	3	14	46	90	45	198
Total	15	46	112	255	64	492

You can easily calculate percentages using these figures. Divide the number in each category for males by the total number of males. Then do the same for females:

	SA	A	N	D	SD	Total
Male	4.1	10.9	22.4	56.1	6.5	100
Female	1.5	7.1	23.2	45.5	22.7	100

These percentages seem to indicate that females believe the organization is less supportive of families than males do, although the differences are not pronounced except at the extremes.

When we talk about measures of central tendency and measures of dispersion, we are making statements about the way all our numbers, considered together, tend to group toward a middle point or to spread away from the middle point. The **mean,** the **median,** and the **mode** are called **measures of central tendency.** This means that all three of these figures are different ways of thinking about the *middle* of a distribution of data.

Mean, Median, and Mode

To illustrate, think about the following set of test scores. In a mythical university, 100 first-year business students take an objective-format final exam in principles of management.

Distribution of 100 Exam Scores		
Score	Number of Students Earning This Score	
98	x	(1 × 98 = 98)
97	x	(1 × 97 = 97)
94	x	(1 × 94 = 94)
92	xxx	(3 × 92 = 276)
91	xx	(2 × 91 = 182)
88	xxxxx	(5 × 88 = 440)
87	xxx	(3 × 87 = 261)
85	xxxxx	(5 × 85 = 425)
84	xxxxxx	(6 × 84 = 504)
83	xxxx	(4 × 83 = 332)
82	xxxxxxx	(7 × 82 = 574)
81	xxxxxxxx	(8 × 81 = 648)
76	xxxxxxxxxxxxx	(13 × 76 = 988)
75	xxxxxxxxx	(9 × 75 = 675)
74	xxxxxxxxxxxxx	(13 × 74 = 962)
70	xxxxx	(5 × 70 = 350)
69	xxxx	(4 × 69 = 276)
66	xx	(2 × 66 = 132)
65	xx	(2 × 65 = 130)
61	x	(1 × 61 = 61)
59	xx	(2 × 59 = 118)
49	x	(1 × 49 = 49)
45	x	(1 × 45 = 45)
35	x	(1 × 35 = 35)

The mean is the familiar arithmetic average.

To find the **mean** (arithmetic average), total the *scores* received by all students (7,752). Then divide by the *number of students* (7,752 /100). The mean is 77.52.

In an array arranged from lowest to highest, the median is the middle value.

To find the **median** (or midpoint), count from either end of the distribution to the middle (50th) score. The median is 76.

The **mode** is the most frequently occurring score. This distribution has two scores with the same and highest number of occurrences. This distribution is bimodal; the modes in our example are 76 and 74.

In a normal distribution, values tend to cluster around the middle of the distribution and taper off toward the ends.

In this example, the distribution is close to what statisticians call a **normal distribution:** Scores tend to group around the middle and tail off at the ends. The normal distribution is sometimes called a **bell-shaped curve.** If you turn the diagram on its side, you will note that the rise and fall of the curve roughly resembles a short, wide bell. In a graphic, however, as you'll learn in Chapter 7, you would leave spaces for scores that no student earned.

In a normal distribution, all three measures of central tendency are close together. Where the distribution has very high or very low values, the mean and the median can be quite different. For instance, if the hypothetical class diagrammed had half a dozen students who received a score of zero, the mean would be pulled lower and the median would stay approximately where it is.

Standard Deviation

The **standard deviation** is the most frequently used of the **measures of dispersion,** that is, of the figures used to describe the tendency of an array of data in a distribution to move away from the center of the distribution.

If a population is very homogeneous, the measurements will tend to cluster around the middle, and the standard deviation will be small and might even approach zero. If the population is heterogeneous, the measurements will spread away from the middle, and the standard deviation will be large.

The formula for standard deviation is the *square root* of the quantity

$$\frac{\Sigma x^2}{N}$$

Don't be alarmed; this notation simply represents a six-step calculation. Most people use a calculator or, better still, a computer program such as SPSS to run the calculations, because the numbers tend to become large. The six steps are as follows:

1. Compute the mean.
2. Subtract the mean from each value in the distribution.
3. Square (multiply by itself) each of the differences.
4. Add the squared differences. (The symbol Σ means "sum." The x^2 stands for the squared differences.)
5. Divide that total by the number (N) of values in the distribution.
6. Take the square root of what you get from step 5.

That number is the standard deviation

Like the measures of central tendency, the standard deviation is a summary statistic. It tells something about the way the distribution looks as a whole.

Like the mean, the standard deviation can be affected heavily if there are extreme values.

Data considered one by one can be interesting, but the real interest lies in the data considered as a whole. These simple statistics help us understand and describe sets of data.

INTERPRETING DATA AND DRAWING CONCLUSIONS

From numerical research data, you will carefully draw the inferences your numbers and statistics permit. If you have been able to use random sampling and to ensure that your returns represent fairly the population from which your sample was drawn, you can use much more complex and powerful data treatments than fall within the scope of this book. The more rigorous your statistical treatment, the greater the certainty with which you can draw your conclusions.

From qualitative data—that is, from answers to non-numeric or to open-ended questions—you will be able to do simple kinds of categorizing and counting. While the data tend to be highly interesting, no impressive statistical operations can be done, and conclusions should be drawn with caution.

DEFINING *YOUR* PRIMARY RESEARCH PROBLEM

Ashe's case in Chapter Five and Morrisey's case earlier in this chapter exemplify the way business researchers refine research questions and plan the research. If you are to do primary research within a business, you will discuss it thoroughly with the person who has authorized it. You will define the problem together with great care: The way you ask the question determines the kind of answer you will get. If you get a good answer to the wrong question, your own and your business's time, resources, and effort will have been wasted.

If you design your own primary research project, you will narrow and focus the research question yourself. The problem selection criteria given at the end of Chapter Five apply here as well. In primary research, however, you must be even more careful to keep the project within the limits of your time, money, mobility, and access to information.

For instance, you might be deeply interested in learning the extent of embezzlement in the largest corporations in your state. Do not imagine, however, that you will be able to distribute a questionnaire and elicit this information. You will not be able to find out things that people are motivated to hide.

Allow plenty of time. Start everything early, because Murphy's Law governs the universe. Primary research is linear: Each stage sets up the next stage and those after it. A problem you have not foreseen can derail your project. You have only this school term for the project, so think through every step of your project in advance to head off problems.

Take on a small project, and do it thoroughly. If you perform an observation, be meticulous. If you do a questionnaire, keep its focus tight. You will probably care a great deal about your subject and be curious about it. But remember that your respondents do not want to spend a lot of time, so do not let your curiosity lead you into asking more than is absolutely necessary.

REVIEW

In contrast to secondary researchers, who gather information published by others, primary researchers generate new data. Primary research must be systematically planned and carried out, and impartiality is essential. *Valid* research measures what it sets out to measure. *Reliable* research is accurate and reproducible.

Observational research gathers data perceivable by the senses or through mechanical means of enhancing sensory ability. Researchers develop and pilot test a checksheet or other means of recording observations in a systematic way.

Survey research consists of administering a questionnaire or an opinionnaire to selected respondents. The means of selecting respondents determines how generalizable the findings are. A random sample permits generalizing statistical findings to the entire larger group from which it was selected. A nonrandom sample, such as a convenience or judgment sample, may be very useful but cannot safely be said to represent an entire population.

Questionnaires may contain open-ended or closed-ended questions. Data from open-ended questions can be interesting and useful but are less easy to interpret and categorize. Closed-ended questions include rank-ordering items, checklists, multiple-choice items, rating scales, semantic-differential items, and Likert scale items. Wording and ordering questionnaire items are critical, and this chapter offered guidelines. Pilot testing the survey instrument is essential. Means of administering surveys include mail, phone, and in-person interview.

Researchers analyze their data to give it meaning. This chapter described basic and familiar statistics, including frequency counts, mean, median, and mode, percentages, cross-tabulations, and standard deviation. Examining these and other aspects of the research findings permit the drawing of careful conclusions.

APPLICATION EXERCISES

1. What kinds of data might a supervisor collect using observational research in the administrative office of a business? What kinds of observational data might an inspector collect while monitoring safety at a construction site?

2. What distinguishes observational research from survey research?

3. Discuss the shortcomings of each of the following as possible questionnaire items.
   a. How old are you?
   b. Have you ever cheated on your income tax?
   c. In your career thus far, what do you most wish you had done differently?
   d. Was math the subject you hated most in school?

      _____ yes _____ no
   e. How often did your parents leave you at home alone before you were 10 years old?
   f. Where do the funds come from that are used to operate your school? Please answer in percentages.
   g. Which of the following factors will most ameliorate the recessionary conditions in this county? Please rank order them, assigning a 5 to the most influential factor, a 4 to the next most influential factor, and so on down to 1 for the least influential factor.

      _____ passing Senate Bill 101b
      _____ levying a 1.5 percent Value-Added Tax
      _____ seeking a federal grant under the LTMP program
      _____ creating county liaisons with businesses to encourage training programs
      _____ electing Bill Tubbs to the legislature
   h. Do you understand and approve of the initiative requiring law enforcement officials to furlough juvenile criminals after they serve three months of their sentence?
   i. What is your political party registration?

      _____ Democrat
      _____ Republican
   j. Television is responsible for today's low moral climate.

Strongly agree	Agree	Neutral, no opinion	Disagree	Strongly disagree
☐	☐	☐	☐	☐

4. Use your creativity and think of types of observational data you might usefully collect. What purposes might they serve? What kind of instrument (checksheet or other means of recording data) would you need to construct?

How important would it be to pilot test the instrument?

5. Grades on objective (multiple-choice and true-false) exams are widely used to measure actual learning. Such tests are used to assign course grades. Also, results of standardized tests such as the SAT and the GMAT determine which students may enter which programs and (arguably) how they will spend the rest of their lives. To what extent are these practices valid? What factors might diminish their validity? Discuss.

6. With the public library system's permission, you are collecting interview data in branch libraries on whether parents of young children would buy their youngsters controversial books such as those narrating folktales from diverse cultures or those in which the main-character child's caregivers are two unmarried males. You are one interviewer; you have trained others and stationed them in three other branch libraries. One is a young Caucasian male with a bushy red beard and an earring. Another is a young man who looks a lot like Bob Keeshan (Captain Kangaroo on children's TV). The third is a 55-year-old African-American woman. Discuss whether you think the differences in appearance among the interviewers will affect the reliability of the interview data.

7. You work a 40+-hour week and are enrolled in a night business communication class. Your school collects student activity fees from all its enrollees, whether or not they participate in activities. You disagree with some of the ways this money is used, and you believe at least 75 percent of the other students in the school feel the same way. You survey the other members of your evening business communication class to discover their opinions on the subject. What kind of sample do you have? How much can you generalize your findings? Defend your answer.

8. In your city of about 2 million people, an active local chapter of the American Marketing Association (AMA) has been supportive of the student Marketing Club at your school. You wonder what the local chapter could tell you about job satisfaction in marketing careers. You request and receive the membership list for the local 314-member AMA chapter. To get a 20 percent sample, you start with the third name on the alphabetically arranged list and select every fifth name after that. You mail a short, well-tested questionnaire to the 62 people whose names were selected. Forty-five answer your survey. Can you generalize your findings fairly safely to the whole 314-member group? Discuss.

9. By what means can survey researchers increase the willingness of mail questionnaire respondents to respond? Telephone survey respondents? In-person interview respondents?

10. Alpha-Betics has 26 employees who have been with the company at least five years. Human resources has tabulated several statistics on these long-term employees. The number for sick days represents a five-year total. Salary is for the current year.

Name	Sick Days	Salary	Years with Company	Top Educational Grade Level	Age
Abel	8	32,600	6	16	30
Beatrice	7	19,500	8	13	32
Carrie	3	35,400	10	16	35
Dietrich	11	31,800	8	14	40
Evan	15	17,500	5	10	32
Fern	8	18,800	11	12	47
Gordon	0	95,000	25	18	55
Hoang	2	28,500	13	16	40
Inez	11	19,400	8	12	35
Joan	0	18,300	5	12	25
Kamal	9	22,800	5	13	27
Leon	4	32,900	7	16	27
Mort	32	30,100	14	15	36
Nathan	21	18,500	5	12	26
Oliver	3	19,400	14	12	35
Patty	15	28,800	6	14	27
Quintano	12	29,400	9	14	37
Rose	2	85,900	22	16	49
Saburo	4	25,700	6	12	27
Tim	7	38,800	15	16	35
Urbano	10	22,400	5	12	29
Velia	0	28,900	11	14	33
Wanda	5	39,400	10	14	28
Xica	16	24,800	9	12	32
Yolanda	6	45,900	8	18	30
Zebulon	2	48,200	12	16	46

a. Why is the average (mean) salary for these employees higher than the median salary?

b. For number of sick days, what is the median? The mode? Do you think the mode in the sick-day distribution is very useful as a measure of central tendency? Why or why not?

c. What is the median age of these personnel? What is the average educational level of these personnel?

d. Which column contains the closest approximation to a "normal distribution?"

e. Among these employees, what is the average number of years worked for this firm?

f. What percentage of these employees earn more than $40,000? What percentage earn less than $30,000?

CASES

The following questions could be investigated using primary research methods. As your instructor directs, plan and carry out a small-scale primary research project on one of these or on a question of your own or your instructor's choice. These investigations require a completely impartial attitude at every stage of the research. Many of them require further narrowing and refining. Also, remember that with limited time and resources, most findings would be preliminary and not widely generalizable.

1. **Women's Opportunities in Previously Male-Dominated Professions.** Women have moved into professions formerly dominated by men. In their own views, do they have comparable opportunities for pay and advancement? Some examples of such professions are engineering, chemistry, law, and accountancy. (You will be able to think of others.) Within a profession, identify 20 women and develop a questionnaire which you administer by phone or mail to gather preliminary findings on the question. One avenue for identifying respondents: Through the student affiliate of the professional organization in your major, get in touch with the leaders of the local chapter of the professional organization and request their cooperation.

2. **Means of Decreasing Commuter Traffic.**
Possibility A: What businesses in your locality foster means of cutting down on commuter traffic? If you can find 10 such businesses, ask them what means they support and what the costs and benefits are. Do they reward people who live close to one another if those people car-pool? Do they subsidize vans? Do they support telecommuting?
Possibility B: At a busy intersection in your city during rush hour, observe one lane of traffic. Count the number of cars with only one person inside. Do this for half an hour on five different days. Analyze what you see. What in-depth study could you design to follow up and build on your observation?
Possibility C: If most people in your vicinity drive alone to work, survey a convenience sample of 30 people to determine (1) how feasible car-pooling would be and (2) what the minimum incentive would be that would get them to car-pool. You will need a number of different questions to obtain useful, reliable, valid information.

3. **Gathering Data for Your Employer.** Where you work, is your company considering any equipment purchase or upgrade? Computers? A copier? A truck or van? Interview the appropriate person to learn what the firm's needs are. Offer to gather systematic information for them on what is available for what price and whether to buy or lease.

4. **Anti-Male Bias in Advertising?** What is the incidence of "male bashing" in print advertising? Set up and conduct an observation. Select one or two mass-audience magazines that carry heavy consumer advertising. Devise a checksheet with appropriate categories. For people portrayed in ads, make categories for *type of ad, number of persons* (one? two? a group?) and *sex* (male[s] only? female[s] only? male[s] and female[s]?). Then set up a systematic means of deciding how the persons are being presented—for instance, as intelligent and competent or as unintelligent and foolish. (These are not necessarily ideal categories; you will develop your categories as you plan the research.) You may or may not wish to add other categories (age, race, and so on). Scan several issues before you try to design your checksheet. Then select the two most recent years for which your library has current issues. If the magazine is a weekly, analyze one issue every other month; if monthly, analyze every other month. Tally your results and draw inferences.

5. **Gathering Data for an "Adopted" Small Business.** Many small businesses operate in your area. Because most maintain only enough personnel to deliver their main product or service, many lack information that would help them either increase sales or cut costs. For instance, suppose a restaurant advertises in the Yellow Pages, in the weekly free shopper newspaper, and via flyers placed on auto windshields in parking lots, but does not know which medium actually brings in most of its new customers. Gathering and analyzing this information systematically would help them a great deal. Look for a small business you can "adopt" for six weeks or so. Ask them what information they need. Offer to solve a modest primary information-gathering task for them in return for their letting you use the research for your project for this class.

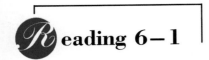

CONSUMER GROUPS WORRIED BY TREND TO USE SURVEYS IN ADS

by Denise Gellene

First Interstate Bank's customer service is tops. You can count on USAir to be on time. Arm & Hammer's toothpaste is good for your teeth.

That, at least, is what the companies maintain, based on a variety of surveys.

People who follow advertising trends say the recession has led to a proliferation of surveys that gauge a product's popularity or performance. With money tight, consumers need a good reason to buy—and surveys seem to provide that.

"Consumers look for something to hang their hat on," said William Young, president of Market Trends, a Bellevue, Wash., market research firm. "If a company has something that says it is best, it makes sense to let people know."

But critics say surveys rarely tell consumers anything useful and often appear slanted to favor a product. In a few recent cases, government officials have told advertisers to stop using certain unscientific surveys.

In California, the Department of Consumer Affairs forced a Bay Area thrift, California Savings & Loan, to drop radio ads that boasted "superior . . . helpfulness and customer service." A state investigation revealed that the claim was based on a survey of just 16 of the S&L's customers.

"Deceptive advertising is rampant," said Jim Conran, director of the Consumer Affairs Department. He is setting up volunteer "truth squads" of retired people to investigate product claims and do comparison shopping.

Some surveys appear valid. For example, First Interstate hired an outside firm, Market Trends, to send a "mystery shopper" to every branch and to most branches of 18 competitors. Its ads are careful to point out that the confidential survey did not rate products, such as checking accounts, a bank spokeswoman said. First Interstate said it took pains to make certain it was statistically accurate, and no one has challenged it. . . .

Other claims are harder for consumers to assess. In an ad for Arm & Hammer's Dental Care, a toothpaste that contains baking soda, the company states that "two out of three dentists recommend baking soda for healthier teeth and gums."

What the ads don't say is that many of the dentists surveyed also endorsed fluoride toothpaste, dental floss and mouthwashes. What's more, Arm & Hammer talked to 300 dentists—a group that UC Riverside statistics professor James Press says is "too small to tell you anything reliable."

Arm & Hammer defended its survey, but refused to answer questions about it, saying it was confidential.

As a marketing device, surveys aren't new. Car makers have long touted good grades on surveys conducted by automotive consultants and industry publications. Supermarket chains regularly churn out "low price" surveys.

The survey is undergoing something of a renaissance lately as companies try to persuade recession-weary consumers to buy. "It is no longer enough to be useful," said Ronald H. Smithies, vice president of the Washington-based Better Business Bureau. "Companies feel they've got to claim their product is better. It is part of the urgency of today."

Smithies heads a bureau division that investigates advertising claims. With Harvard Business School marketing professor Bruce Buchanan, Smithies analyzed 119 taste claims made by manufacturers since 1974. The analysis, published in the *Journal of Advertising Research* in June, found that only 43% of taste claims were substantiated. Among the brands whose claims were based on faulty research, according to Smithies and Buchanan, were Comet Rice, Tropicana, Crisco and Bumble Bee. . . .

Statisticians say it is easy to slant a survey by asking leading questions and leaving out certain demographic groups. "I could do it—no problem," said Frederick Wiseman, a marketing professor at Northeastern University in Boston.

Wiseman helped take the fizz out of diet cola claims in Massachusetts two years ago. Reviewing survey data for the Massachusetts Department of Consumer Affairs, Wiseman found that neither Diet Coke nor Diet Pepsi was "preferred by consumers," as claimed.

The cola companies withdrew their boasts after Wiseman found that Diet Coke had ignored the western half of the country and that Diet Pepsi had only questioned people who lived within 100 miles of four bottling plants.

"The quality of the research was not very good," Wiseman said.

Several statisticians interviewed said they generally don't believe marketing claims. Unless an ad explains its methodology, "I ignore it," UC Riverside's Press said.

Increasingly, companies are borrowing the research of others—consumer groups, government agencies and market research companies. Tylenol Gelcaps relied on confidential A. C. Nielsen survey data to buttress its claim that "more people switched" to it last year "than any other pain reliever." A spokesman for Tylenol maker Johnson & Johnson said the Nielsen survey showed that Gelcaps had the highest sales growth of all pain relievers—results that no one in the industry disputes.

What brands did the new Gelcaps users switch from? Johnson & Johnson isn't exactly sure. The spokesman said it looks as if some competitors lost out—and, possibly Tylenol tablets and caplets.

Source: Denise Gellene, *Los Angeles Times,* September 4, 1991, pp. D1, D3.

Even when outside research is used, an advertiser's claim isn't necessarily reliable. The survey that got California Savings into trouble was done by Consumer Checkbook, a Bay Area consumer organization. Consumer Checkbook President Robert M. Krughoff said the survey wasn't scientific. "It was intended as a guide for consumers," he said. "Not proof."

And Consumer Action of San Francisco got into a dispute last spring with a firm that used the consumer group's survey to tout its long-distance service as a "best buy."

"It was a complete distortion," said Ken McEldowney, president of Consumer Action. "We never called anything a best buy." He declined to identify the company, which withdrew the ad. Burned by the experience, Consumer Action no longer lets companies use its surveys in advertisements.

Then there is the case of USAir. Citing a government survey, USAir claimed in splashy ads last month that it had the best on-time record of "any of the seven largest airlines."

It didn't appear in the fine print, but there was a good reason why USAir compared itself to the industry's top seven. Government statistics showed that the eighth-largest airline, Pan Am, had the best on-time record. USAir was really No. 2.

USAir defended its decision to omit Pan Am. "It's too small to consider a competitor," spokeswoman Agnes Huff said. The Department of Transportation had no comment on how its statistics were used.

Executives at Pan Am "had a good chuckle over that ad," spokesman Alan Loflin said. "It shows how you can use surveys to say anything."

Graphics

PREVIEW

Today's business readers are receiving more and more of their information in visual form. Although visuals accompany long reports more often than short ones, short reports can often use one or more exhibits to excellent effect. This chapter presents manual and computer-assisted means of creating a variety of exhibit types, including tables, pie charts, bar charts, line charts, and maps.

Visuals for oral presentations differ in important ways from those for written presentations. For talks, visuals must be even simpler and clearer than those for written documents. Examples of title slides, outline slides, and others will be shown and discussed.

Much business information, particularly instructional information, travels by computer screen. The design of that screen affects the receiver's ability to make use of the information. This chapter examines numerous computer screen design principles. ●

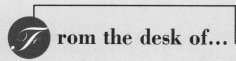

**Alicia Moss
Budget Analyst**

I work in accounting at a midwestern manufacturer. One of my duties is to prepare monthly production cost analyses, and the figures for the swing shift didn't seem quite right.

I showed some figures to Sami, my supervisor. She just nodded and said, "Don't worry, Alicia; nothing here is too far off." But I did worry. Why were the swing shift's unit costs higher? My real problem was that my boss had told me to ignore the matter; I couldn't spend more time investigating. How could I get her attention?

I made a series of multiple line charts showing the differences among the three shifts. There it was at a glance. Sami saw at once that the swing shift was out of line in material overruns, employee turnover, unaccounted-for tools, accidents, absenteeism, and units produced.

Sami immediately took my charts to the vice president, who traced the situation back to a shift supervisor who routinely yelled at the majority of his subordinates, showed favoritism to others, and turned a blind eye to waste and theft. A conservative estimate showed that we had been losing about $17,500 per month for at least three months.

An effective graphic device can be the "picture worth a thousand words." Until Sami saw Alicia's exhibit, she was not perceiving the problem. This chapter discusses and illustrates many kinds of graphics for use in written and oral presentations.

ANOTHER WAY TO LOOK AT AND THINK ABOUT INFORMATION

Audience and situation analysis affects graphics as well as written communication.

Thus far, we have discussed communication using primarily the written word. Within written messages, especially longer ones such as formal reports, one or more effective graphic devices will often clarify the written content. Sometimes graphics let the writer write less and still inform the reader fully.

As in all other essentials of business communication, preparing good graphics requires analysis of the receiver and the situation. Many factors affect the kinds of graphics a writer prepares. For instance, high-level and specialized business readers can deal with more complexity in visuals than those with less background. Engineers, on the average, expect more use of tables in place of graphs and greater complexity in graphs than most mainstream business readers do. Receivers listening to a presentation require simpler, higher-impact graphics than do receivers reading a report.

Data to be presented graphically can come from secondary sources or from primary research. We use graphics to clarify points that would be harder to comprehend in writing alone. One graphic, for instance, can show readers the pattern, idea, or trend in a large set of numeric data. Readers would have to study much longer to derive the same information from the data presented in paragraph, or even table, form. Graphics *supplement* written material, however. They help improve communication within the text but do not substitute for clear discussion.

A person who has always spoken a European language tends to read a graphic representation the way English reads: horizontally, left to right, top to

Chapter Seven

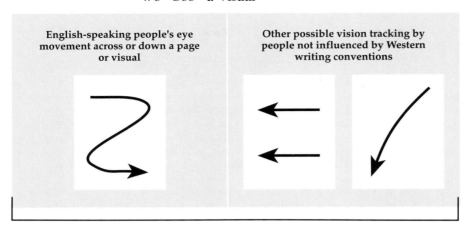

EXHIBIT 7–1   How Language Conventions Influence the Way We "See" a Visual

English-speaking people's eye movement across or down a page or visual

Other possible vision tracking by people not influenced by Western writing conventions

bottom. Arabic is read horizontally from right to left. Chinese is read vertically from top to bottom and right to left. A Chinese book printed in classical style is read from back to front. American businesspeople sometimes make presentations to business groups from non-Western nations. Even if the presenters arrange for a translator, visuals prepared without regard for this simple but important difference might baffle the audience. (See Exhibit 7–1.)

For example, a presentation promoting a children's cough syrup might show three pictures in a row across a slide: first, the child miserable and coughing; next, the child accepting a spoonful of cough syrup from an adult's hand; last, a smiling or sleeping child. To an audience not used to processing information from left to right, the cough medicine appears to make a healthy child sick.

DESIGNING VISUALS FOR WRITTEN AND ORAL COMMUNICATIONS

Presentation visuals must be simple. The audience must be able to listen and see at the same time.

Exhibits conveying business information must display simplicity, clarity, impact, and truthfulness. Written messages put different constraints on the communicator than do oral messages. Take simplicity. A visual used in a talk cannot be as complex as one used in a report. A listener must process speech at the same time he or she studies the visual, whereas a reader can study a visual with undivided attention. Similarly, visuals prepared for a speech need greater impact than those prepared for a report. Many attention-getting devices—a picture of a pointing hand, a stop sign, or a shooting star containing an important word—might please listeners but annoy readers.

Simplicity

A visual "tells a story."

The brain processes images differently than it does text. The purpose of many visuals is to show readers a pattern, a whole, or a set of relationships. Because the brain takes in the image as a unit, the graphic should be no more complex than is necessary. If one line on a line graph will tell the writer's story, two lines are too many. If you find yourself tempted to graph more than three or four lines on one line graph, you should consider creating multiple graphs with fewer lines or ask yourself whether the reader really needs that much detail.

If you are a specialist, you will often prepare reports for receivers outside your specialty. Keep in mind that what you view as simple might not be so simple for nonspecialist receivers.

Clarity

A visual is clear when the reader can understand its main message quickly and with very little effort. If the reader has to spend time deciphering a puzzling visual or correcting an initial misunderstanding, the writer has not achieved clarity.

Impact

Impact goes hand in hand with simplicity and clarity; yet a visual can be simple and clear without having much impact. A visual has impact when it quickly attracts favorable attention. It does this through appropriate, bold, clean, sharp, pleasing design and balance of its components. A visual intended for oral presentation must be bolder than one to be used in a written report.

Truthfulness

The visual message must be true to fact and to the surrounding text.

It is possible—and unethical—to label everything carefully in a graphic but still, by distorting the impression made by the visual element, imply something untrue. For example, suppose a marketer responsible for weak sales of a given product wants to evade blame. In making a line graph of a very small rise in sales, he might stretch the vertical axis to give the impression that the small rise was steep.

Remember: In visuals, the image *is* the idea. The initial meaning a receiver derives from a glance at a visual must be the same as the meaning she or he would obtain from a longer, more penetrating study of the visual and accompanying text. If the *quick* picture is half true or not true, the visual must be revised.

Critics of television news and of some newspapers say that these media often sacrifice truthfulness for impact. For instance, the pie chart in Exhibit 7–2 shows what seems a wasteful division of an animal charity's budget. Along

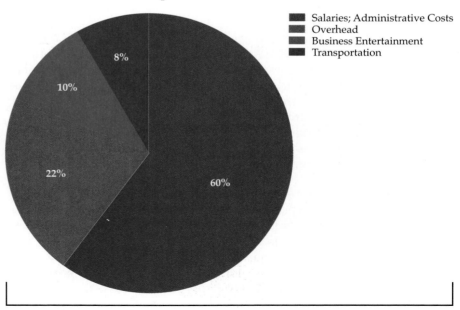

EXHIBIT 7–2   A Potentially Misleading Visual

Figure 1
Expenses of Critter Conservation

- Salaries; Administrative Costs
- Overhead
- Business Entertainment
- Transportation

8%
10%
22%
60%

This visual could mislead. It tells a different "story" than the text surrounding it tells.

with other information, the accompanying news story says that this 100-percent pie chart shows the division of one 25-percent *segment* of a budget, the rest of which (the other 75 percent) is paid out in direct support of the cause served by the charity. A potential contributor who is merely skimming the newspaper, however, receives an untrue visual message that angers him or her.

To meet the expectations of business readers, the report writer must label the visual, title it, size it appropriately, introduce it, place it, frame it with white space, document it, and interpret it.

The label identifies the kind of graphic and a number. Many report writers divide their visuals into **tables** (information presented in rows and columns) and **figures** (other kinds of visuals, including graphs, charts, maps, scattergrams, pictograms, and the like). If you have one figure, label it "Figure 1." If you have one figure and one table, the figure is "Figure 1" and the table is "Table 1." Some report writers with only one or two of each type combine them into one series and label them "Exhibit 1," "Exhibit 2," and "Exhibit 3."

In your report's table of contents, the visuals and their page numbers should appear in a separate list below the text headings and their page numbers.

Labeling the Visual

Title your exhibit specifically and concretely. Remember the who-what-when-where-why-how, and decide which of these elements are most informative. The title should tell your reader exactly what to look for in your visual. Here are two examples:

Titling the Visual

Rising Cost of Overtime

Third-Quarter Profits by Region

Two factors influence size: importance and complexity. A relatively minor and simple visual should not take up an entire page when you have only 12 pages of space. If an exhibit is important and complex, however, it may require a page. In general, exhibits smaller than a quarter of a page are hard to read.

Sizing the Visual

A full-page exhibit might be vertical ("tall" or "portrait" format) or horizontal ("wide" or "landscape" format). If it is horizontal and must be turned 90 degrees for placement, be sure to place it so that its top is at the paper's left margin and the bottom is at the right.

If you have photocopied your exhibit, or if the computer program in which you create your graph gives no sizing options, you may still need to change its size. You can do so if you use a photocopier with enlarging and reducing capability.

If you have access to a scanner, you can digitize any image. In fact, the newest and most expensive scanners will digitize three-dimensional items in full color. New-generation cameras record snapshots digitally and store them on floppy disks instead of film. A frame of videotape or television can be "grabbed" as an image. Any exhibit you can obtain as a digitized image you can probably enlarge or reduce by using a painting, drawing, graphics, or desktop publishing program.

Mention the graphic in the text before you show it. The wording can vary, as these three examples show:

Introducing the Visual

QualiCare Inc. has paid out 37 percent more in overtime this year than in 1992 and 44 percent more than in 1991, as shown in Figure 1.

QualiCare Inc. has paid 37 percent more in overtime than in 1992 and 44 percent more than in 1991. (See Figure 1 on page 12.)

Figure 1 (see page 12) shows the increasing amounts of overtime QualiCare Inc. has paid in 1991, 1992, and 1993.

Placing the Visual

Business readers expect a visual to appear soon after it is mentioned in the text. If you have room on the same page where you introduce it, place it right after you mention it. If you are too near the bottom of a page to do that, reword your introducing statement to say "as shown in Figure 1 on page 4" or "See Figure 1 on page 4."

Do not put visuals at the end of the report unless you are sure your reader or your organization prefers them there. Appendixes are intended for material that is useful but not integral to your discussion. (Examples might be background correspondence or tables of raw data.) In general, readers like to see visuals integrated within the report body.

Framing the Visual

Allow enough **white space** (text-free space) not only for the visual but also for any labels that are to go outside the square or oblong shape of the visual. For example, the labels for vertical and horizontal axes of graphs require space. Allow room for your visual's label and title if they do not fall within the graphic itself. Allow space for a source note, if needed. Finally, allow a little more empty space between visual and report text to achieve clear separation and an uncrowded, pleasing appearance.

Documenting the Visual

Did you generate the data yourself or obtain the material from another source? If your data are primary, you do not need a source note. If you believe your reader might not understand that you generated the data yourself, use wording like this just underneath your exhibit:

Source: Primary.

If you created the exhibit from data you found in a secondary source, you must document the source. If, for example, you drew a line graph using data you obtained from public records or from tables or discussion in a published article, you would state your source briefly or more fully, as appropriate:

Source: U.S. Department of Agriculture, 1993.

Source: Marbury, J. M. (1991, Nov. 16). Undercount of census data in four Colorado counties. *Denver Herald,* A3, A22.

Sometimes you will locate a visual so precisely suited to your needs that you reproduce it word for word. You might even cut and paste a clean photocopy of an exhibit from a secondary source and make it part of your report. (See Exhibit 7–26 on page 205 for instructions.) Give full bibliographic data so the reader will understand your use of the exhibit:

Source: Beltran, E. (1990, Aug. 3). Ridership of commuter rail picking up speed after slow start. *Los Angeles Times,* B1.

Interpreting the Visual

Sometimes you will discuss the visual as you introduce it. For a relatively simple graphic, this may suffice. Other visuals will require more commentary. Exhibit 7–3 shows a graphic that has been labeled, titled, sized, introduced, placed, framed, documented, and interpreted.

EXHIBIT 7–3   Report Page Showing Correctly Treated Graphic

14

While early proponents of job-sharing viewed it as a solution to workers' problems such as continuing their education, providing for child- and elder-care, and filling other scheduling needs, not all high-tech firms have reported the expected rise in usage. (See Table 3.) In fact, two of the four firms represented in the table saw initial enthusiasm wane after two promising years.

Introduction

Interpretation

White space

Table 3					*Label*

Incidence of Job-Sharing in Workforce of Four Aerospace Firms, 1989 - 1992   *Descriptive title*

Corporation	1989	1990	1991	1992
Specific Dynamics	0.5%	0.7%	1.1%	4.1%
Tallis Industries	0.2%	0.9%	2.8%	2.0%
Jetways Inc.	1.1%	3.3%	3.1%	2.9%
Stratospherics	3.0%	4.1%	3.0%	2.6%

Source: Porter, M.L. (1992, Oct. 16) Innovative work-sharing programs show mixed trends. Financial Journal, B1, B12.   *Documentation*

White space

The decrease in job-sharing may result more from the recession's disastrous effect on the aerospace industry than from disenchantment with job-sharing. In recessionary times, two-earner families in an unstable job market may not wish to trade away half a job when a fully employed spouse may face layoff.

TYPES OF REPORT GRAPHICS

What do you want to say with your graphic? What main point must it carry? What are you comparing with what? Answers to these questions will guide your selection among the types of graphics to use in reports.

Reports may contain tables, bar graphs, line graphs, pie charts, maps, pictographs, photographs, diagrams, line drawings, and specialized types of bar graphs and line graphs. (The words **graph** and **chart** are often used interchangeably.) We will cover those you are most likely to need in preparing your business reports and discuss which ones are appropriate for which kind of information.

Tables

Tables present numbers and sometimes words in columns and rows. Readers grasp series of numbers in table form more easily than they do the same numbers represented in paragraph form.

Tables have more impact than text but less impact than figures.

The visual impact of tables is lower than that of figures. Graphs, for instance, show proportions and relative sizes, which tables cannot do. However, readers can handle *more* numbers in table form than in graph form. Readers have no problem understanding a table containing ten rows and seven columns. A line graph containing ten lines, each with seven plot points, might look so busy and complicated that readers would skip it. If your reader needs all those numbers to understand your point, a table is the way to go.

Formal Tables

Formal tables are usually boxed, ruled, or both. (See Exhibit 7−4.) A formally treated table says to the reader, "This is important. Study it." The content should be important enough to warrant this level of attention. Theoretically, writers can show many more rows, columns, and numbers than Exhibit 7−4 contains. Tables, however, like all other elements in reports, must be concise, showing only as much as the reader needs and no more.

Informal Tables

Informal tables, sometimes called *spot tables,* need not receive the full treatment accorded formal ones. Most informal tables are, in essence, lists with items in columns. They are not boxed, labeled, or titled, but merely indented.

ⒺXHIBIT 7−4   Formal Table

Table 2

Second Quarter, Rolled Metal Division, In-State

In tables, the columns and rows require labels.

AGENT	TERRITORY	GROSS ($)	NET ($)
Bailey	Northeast	36,837	18,362
Kuraoka	Central	31,371	18,482
Kahn	West	27,260	16,159
Boudin	Southwest	29,772	14,651
Essinger	Southeast	19,816	10,118
TOTAL		145,056	77,772

For the .25 oz. Sextant cologne brand, advertising expenses over the last four years divided as follows:

MEDIUM	1989	1990	1991	1992
fashion magazine	95,000	100,000	98,500	108,000
television, network	150,000	135,000	140,000	125,000
television, cable	100,000	116,000	250,000	280,000
point-of-purchase	35,000	38,000	42,000	60,000
TOTAL	380,000	389,000	530,500	573,000

Advertising less on network and more on cable television and increasing promotions using the much less expensive point-of-purchase medium have generated increased sales, which section 2.2 on Revenue will cover.

White space is important around informal tables.

This textbook contains a number of informal tables. Exhibit 7−5 is an example of an informal table as it occurs within a report text.

Informal tables appear more often in short reports but are not restricted to them. Sometimes long, formal reports use formally treated tables *and* several spot tables.

Visuals that are more picture than words are generally classified as **figures.** Depending on what story your graphic must tell, you can choose from among pie charts, several kinds of bar graphs, several types of line graphs, diagrams, maps, and still other options. Figures may be offered as "spot" or informal exhibits, but their use in this way is less frequent than that of informal tables.

Figures

Figures, which are usually presented formally, require the same careful labeling and treatment that formal tables do. Figures may need a **legend** as well. Many kinds of figures—maps and component bar graphs, for example— use several colors or cross-hatch patterns to distinguish their parts. The legend, or key, is a minichart within the figure telling what each color or pattern means. Sometimes the legend's labels are all together. Sometimes the labels are separated and placed near the components they identify.

The legend identifies elements within a figure.

Let's look at the most frequently used types of figures.

Choose a **pie chart** when you need to zero in on the parts of a whole. As you draw a pie chart,

Pie Charts

A pie chart graphs the divisions of a whole.

- Arrange the slices in the order of largest to smallest.
- Start the largest slice at 12 noon on the pie and proceed clockwise.
- Do not try to graph more than about eight segments.

Exhibit 7−6 shows a pie chart. Though most exhibits in this textbook use color, this one shows differentiation among parts using only black and white. You—and most computer graphics packages—can differentiate using direc-

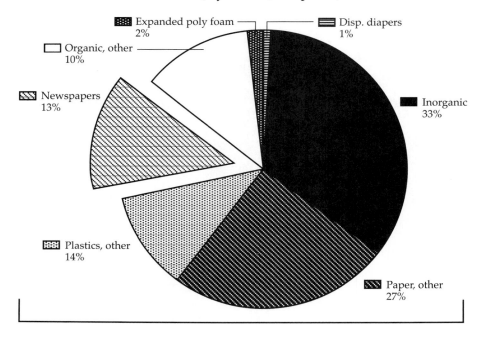

Figure 3
Landfill Contents, by Volume, Compacted, 1972–1992

tional stripes, thick or thin stripes, solid black, solid white, a pattern of tiny dots, cross-hatching, and many other patterns. Be sure the legend matches the patterns.

Pie charts can be used in pairs. For example, competitors selling a similar product or service compete for market share, that is, for the largest share of a finite number of customers. Using one pie for the whole market share for each year, we can graph each vendor's success in marketing. In Exhibit 7–7, a reader can quickly grasp the division of this camping goods market. Note that the two pies for the two years do not depict any change in overall market *size* over those years. This is appropriate if increase in market size is irrelevant to the main point, which is market share.

A reader can quickly comprehend comparisons between two pies. Three or more pies, however, are less easy to understand than a segmented 100 percent bar graph (see page 193). Bar charts come in many forms, as we will see next.

Bar Charts

Bar charts permit comparison of two or more items by showing amount or distance along a scale.

Bar charts show amount or distance along a scale.

Simple bar chart.   **Bar graphs** have a horizontal axis and a vertical axis; each must be labeled clearly. (Vertical bar charts are sometimes called **column charts.**) At least one axis on a bar graph will be numerical; the other may be numerical or it may be a series of labeled items. Numerical scales must start at zero, and intervals marked along the scale must be equal.

Whether in vertical or horizontal format, the bars should be of equal width. Each bar should be identified. Shadings, cross-hatchings, or colors can be used to distinguish among the bars.

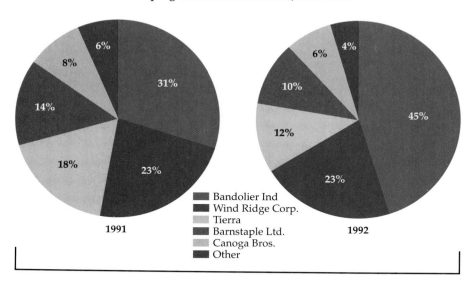

Figure 6
Bandolier's Growth
Camping Goods Market Share, 1991–1992

Legend:
- Bandolier Ind
- Wind Ridge Corp.
- Tierra
- Barnstaple Ltd.
- Canoga Bros.
- Other

1991: 31%, 23%, 18%, 14%, 8%, 6%

1992: 45%, 23%, 12%, 10%, 6%, 4%

The simple horizontal bar chart in Exhibit 7−8 lists 10 oil and utility stocks and shows them all within a safe and respectable range for the early 1990s. The bars are labeled, and the numerical axis, labeled as representing percentages, starts at zero, which is standard for all bar charts.

Grouped bar graphs.   Suppose you want to graph quantities for a series of years but also show some important subdivisions of the quantities. You might choose a *grouped bar graph* to do so.

Exhibit 7−9 shows sales volume for six successive years on a bar chart and also shows how the subdivisions of a sales region compared with one another. Note the labels on the axes and the use of a legend to identify the area subdivisions. Exhibit 7−9 also shows numerical value labels with the bars; these are optional.

Exhibit 7−10 shows a vertical bar graph comparing math and verbal scores among a group of students. The information you want to show determines the arrangement of the labeled bars. You can order them by school grade as in Exhibit 7−10, chronologically as in Exhibit 7−9, geographically, from lowest to highest scores, or in any other way your reader will find logical. The "story" this graph tells is that math scores outpace verbal scores until grade 9, after which verbal scores rise past math scores and remain consistently high while math scores trail off.

Scale breaks.   Although numerical scales must start at zero, sometimes the "story" is relevant to only a segment of the scale between zero and the scale's top mark. Under these circumstances you introduce a **scale break,** as shown in Exhibit 7−11.

When using a scale break, take care that the visual element still tells the story fairly and truthfully. What readers see must reflect faithfully any worded message on which the visual is based.

EXHIBIT 7–8   Simple Bar Chart

Figure 3
Recommended List of Ten Successful Oil and Gas Stocks

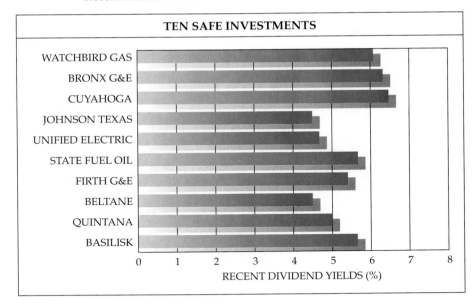

TEN SAFE INVESTMENTS

EXHIBIT 7–9   Vertical and Horizontal Grouped Bar Charts

Figure 1
ANNUAL AREA SALES DATA

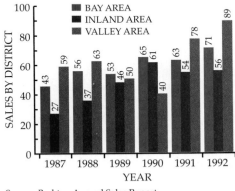

Source: Brekton Annual Sales Report
Los Angeles Area

Figure 1
ANNUAL AREA SALES DATA

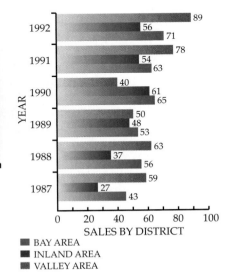

Source: Brekton Annual Sales Report
Los Angeles Area

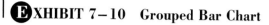

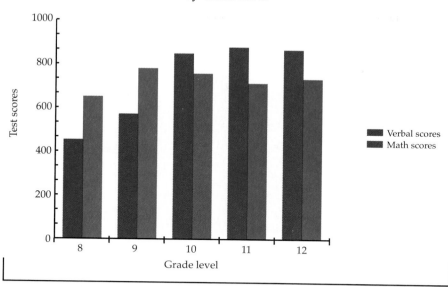

Figure 5
Comparison of Math and Verbal Scores
by Grade Level

EXHIBIT 7-11   **Bar Graph with Scale Break, Vertical Format
(Left) and Horizontal Format (Right)**

Figure 7
Change in Electricians'
Compensation 1980–1990

Figure 7
Change in Electricians'
Compensation 1980–1990

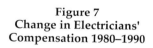

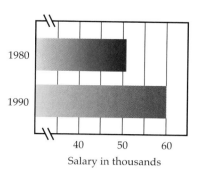

Source: National Survey of Senior
Electricians Wages and Benefits

Source: National Survey of Senior
Electricians Wages and Benefits

Segmented 100 percent bar graph.   When differences both within and among
several wholes are important, the **segmented 100 percent bar chart** rather
than the pie chart is the correct format to use. (See Exhibit 7–12). Readers can
compare two pies, but they perceive differences among three or more pies less
readily. All the bars are the same height because the "story" emphasizes the

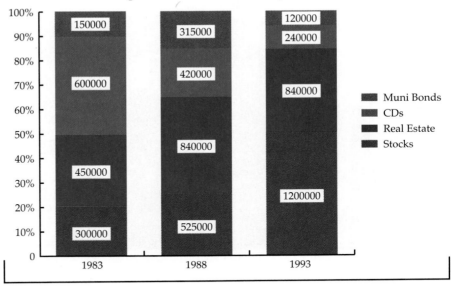

EXHIBIT 7–12   Segmented 100 Percent Bar Chart

Figure 7
Change in One Portfolio over 10-year Period

percentage makeup of each bar relative to that of the other bars. In the example shown, although the portfolio grows between 1983 and 1993, this graphic treatment emphasizes the division of its total value as investment conditions change.

Component bar graphs.   The **component bar graph** (see Exhibit 7–13) can compare multiple different-size wholes and at the same time show the components of those wholes. This graph's basic "story" is a rapid rise in the number of installed fax machines, but the use of components shows that the increase in use in government and business is more dramatic than that in homes. Glance back at Exhibit 7–12 to see a different story: There the emphasis is on the division of the whole rather than on the overall rise in portfolio value.

Positive-negative bar graphs.   As Exhibit 7–14 shows, a bar graph can show positive and negative values by placing the zero point in the middle of the scale instead of at the bottom.

Line Charts

Bar graphs and line graphs serve some, but not all, of the same purposes.

Line charts show change over time (time series) and frequency distribution. The vertical axis is usually used for amount and the horizontal axis for time.

Line charts cover some of the same territory as bar charts in that both can be used to display change over time and both can show frequency distribution. Bar charts, however, emphasize *amounts* at specific sequential times or for specific entities, while line charts emphasize *changes in amount through time or distribution*—that is, trends.

Simple line charts.   Exhibit 7–15 presents a simple line chart showing number of deliveries per month made by a small transportation company. The story shows considerable seasonal fluctuation but a gradual rise in traffic.

EXHIBIT 7-13 Component Bar Graph

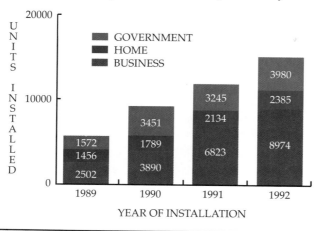

Figure 2
Increased FAX Machine Installations in Chicago
by Sector as Reported in Recent Buyer's Survey

EXHIBIT 7-14 Positive-Negative Bar Graph

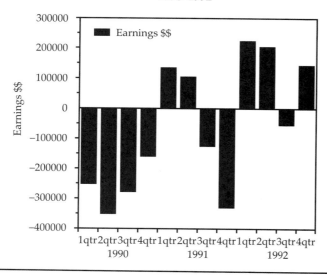

Figure 9
Barchester Inc. Earnings
1990–1992

Multiple-line charts. **Multiple-line charts** show comparisons among series of items. These graphs should show no more than three or four lines. More than that would make the graph confusing. Exhibit 7– 16 shows a multiple-line graph.

You need to distinguish among the multiple lines so that the reader can easily link them with a legend or key. You can use color to differentiate the

By permission of Johnny Hart and Creators Syndicate, Inc.

Whether the line means stock price or heart rate, the news looks bad.

Ⓔ XHIBIT 7–15   Line Chart

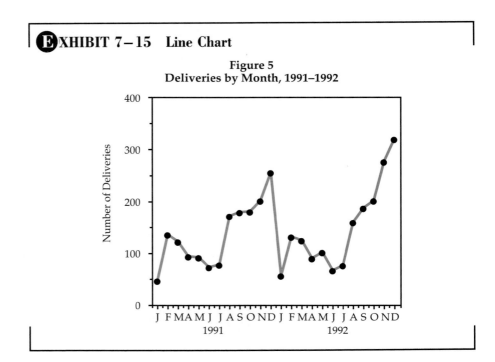

Figure 5
Deliveries by Month, 1991–1992

lines. You can also use different kinds of lines, such as dotted, dashed, unbroken, and thick. You can even use use different small shapes to mark the graph points connected by the lines, as in Exhibit 7–16. One line might have square bullets, another round bullets, another diamonds, and so on.

Cumulative line charts.   Sometimes called **area charts** or **surface charts, cumulative line charts** stack quantities of the same kind on top of one another so that the reader can see both the totals and the components. Exhibit 7–17 shows a simple cumulative line chart. The visual point of this graph is that while revenues rise rapidly, expenses also rise, so that the business's net shows only a modest rise.

Exhibits 7–18 and 7–19 show the same data, a frequency distribution, presented as a component bar chart and a cumulative line chart, respectively. Both charts show each department's expenditures for out-of-house services for a six-month period.

Figure 12
Per Capita Consumption of Meat Reflecting
Dietary Changes in U.S. Eating Habits

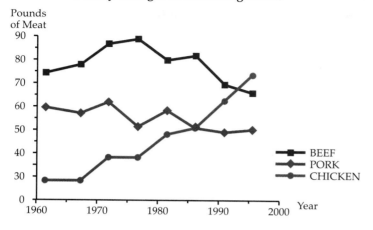

Source: U.S. Department of Agriculture

Figure 4
Revenue, Showing Expenses and Net
1985–1993

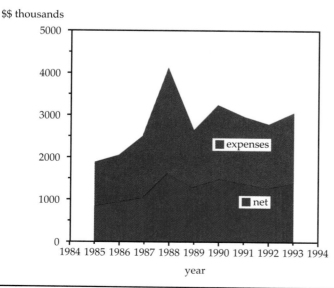

EXHIBIT 7–18   Component Bar Chart Showing Same Data as
Cumulative Line Chart in Exhibit 7–19

Figure 7
Externally Purchased Services by Department

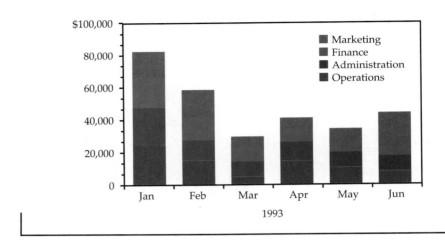

EXHIBIT 7–19   Cumulative Line Chart

Figure 7
Externally Purchased Services by Department

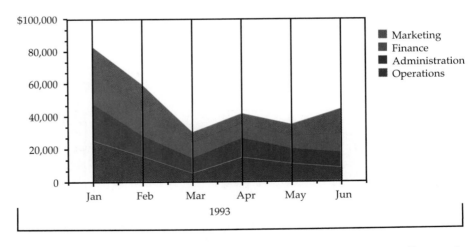

Positive-negative line charts.   Line graphs can show negative as well as positive values. The zero point is in the middle of the numeric axis. A horizontal line at the zero point, as in Exhibit 7–20, helps the reader quickly see which points show positive and which show negative values.

You may have found yourself describing a mental image to another person and thinking, "If only I had a picture of this!" In a report, do not devote paragraph after paragraph to description when you can obtain or produce an image. To

*Drawings, Diagrams, and
Photographs*

Chapter Seven

EXHIBIT 7–20   Positive-Negative Line Chart

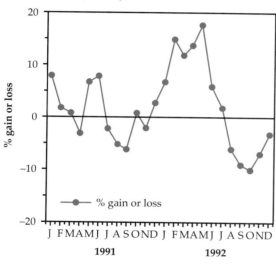

Figure 6
Rehling & Sons Fund
January 1991–December 1992

see the benefit of using a drawing or a diagram, examine the cutaway drawing in Exhibit 7–21.

The drawing shows the familiar washing machine, but with a difference: Two sensors read information and send it to a microprocessor able to deal with imprecise categories. The microprocessor treats the information using "fuzzy rules," that is, rules with ranges and combinations, which output signals regulating the washer settings to yield optimal cleaning results. With the diagram, a nonspecialist reader understands clearly. Without the diagram, most of us would probably still be wondering what it means.

A photograph may provide more detail than a drawing. This richness of detail may or may not be desirable. For example, a photo of a person's face is useful if subtlety of expression is important to the story. A photo instead of the exploded, cut-away, x-ray drawing of the washing machine in Exhibit 7–21, however, would have less detail. The reader would be less able to spot the sensors and the microprocessor among the familiar washing machine parts.

The choice between a diagram and a photo depends on how much visual detail is relevant.

Graphics   199

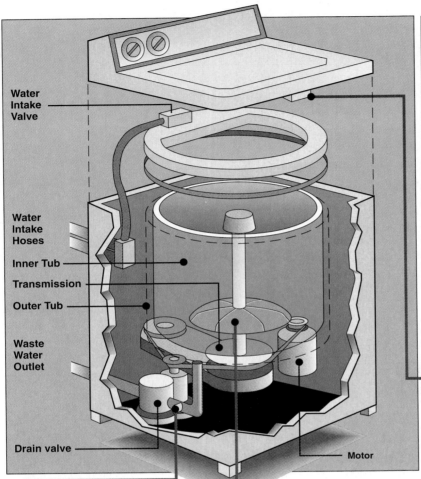

Water Intake Valve

Water Intake Hoses

Inner Tub

Transmission

Outer Tub

Waste Water Outlet

Drain valve

Motor

How Fuzzy Logic Works

Fuzzy logic is an attempt to make machines reason more like humans—taking into account a number of factors that are not precise to make a common-sense judgment. When fuzzy theory is applied to control systems in machines, a number of variables are represented in mathematical terms that are analyzed simultaneously to make operational decisions. The following illustrates how fuzzy logic is used in a washing machine manufactured by Matsushita Electric Industrial Co.:

3 **The microprocessor** receives this information in imprecise categories. For example: The optical sensor says the water is clean, somewhat dirty or very dirty and the agitator says the load is small, medium or very large. The microprocessor contains "fuzzy rules" that help it to interpret this general information and choose one of about 600 combinations. Each choice contains a set of orders telling the machine how much water to let in and how much time to allow for the wash, rinse, and spin cycles (or whether to repeat any, or all, of the cycles). One result after the fuzzy rules are applied might be an order for the machine to use lots of water, multiple rinse cycles and to extend the spin time if the load is large and the clothing very dirty.

1 **The optical sensor** in the waste water pipe sends a beam of light through the water. The way in which this beam is distorted determines how much dirt or oil there is in the water as well as whether powder or liquid detergent is being used. This information is sent to the microprocessor.

2 **The agitator** turns the clothes in the washing machine to remove the dirt. The agitator motor measures the resistance it feels as it turns back and forth to help determine the size of the load and roughly what type of material is in the clothing. The larger the load and more absorbent the cloth, the greater the resistance is likely to be. The motor sends the information to the microprocessor.

Source: *Los Angeles Times,* February 17, 1992, pp. D1, D4.

Pictograms

Pictograms are an eye-catching variant of bar charts. Like bar charts, they can be vertical or horizontal. Magazines and newspapers use them because they seize attention at the same time they inform.

In a pictogram, a small image or symbol represents a given quantity, such as a sum of money or a number of units. If one dollar sign ($) image represents $1,000, a stack or row of six of them represents $6,000. The image used should

EXHIBIT 7–22 Pictogram

Figure 8
Imported Vehicles Triple 1989–1993

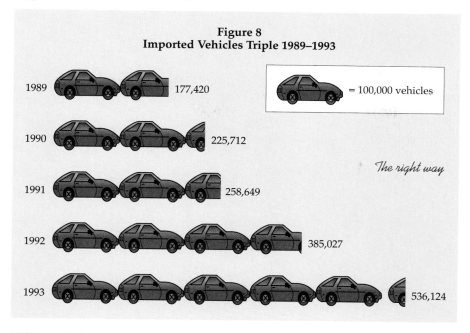

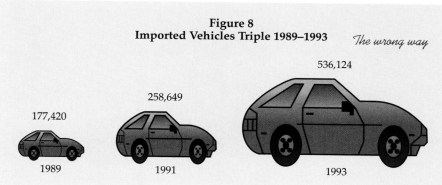

Top example gives correct visual impression; bottom example is visually misleading.

suggest the idea content of the graphic. For instance, flour production could be graphed using small images of bags of flour. On the pictogram bars, an increase in quantity is shown by an increase in the number of whatever symbol is chosen. You could show 6 million tons of flour with a row of six bags and show part of a bag to represent a fraction of a seventh million.

The essential point in pictogram construction is to *keep the image the same size* as you replicate it to increase the quantity represented. Sometimes you will see *inappropriate* examples that compare quantities by showing one little symbol and one or more progressively larger versions of the same symbol. The visual image is misleading (see Exhibit 7–22). Images should show growth in a quantity by expanding along one dimension. If, as in the second example in

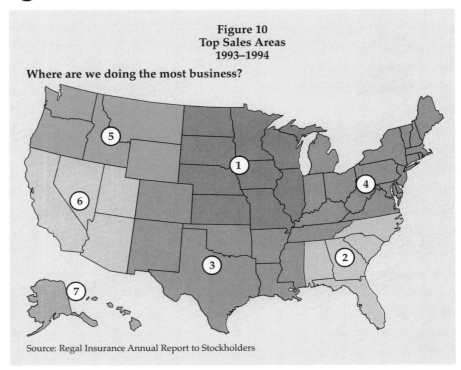

Figure 10
Top Sales Areas
1993–1994

Where are we doing the most business?

Source: Regal Insurance Annual Report to Stockholders

In a pictogram, show increase along one dimension, not two.

Exhibit 7–22, the image grows along two dimensions, the human eye "reads" a much greater quantity from the much larger bulk of the image. This visual impression is false.

Maps

Choose a map when you need to present a geographic distribution visually. For instance, you can show average income, life span, or education level by district, city, county, state, area of a country, or country.

Among low-tech options, atlases and road maps are readily available for you to trace. (Use an enlarging and reducing photocopier as needed.) You can add data and other identification with neat hand lettering or typewriting. If you have a computer graphics package, maps are almost certainly one of your options. Follow the easy directions to produce a professional-looking map exhibit.

Exhibit 7–23 is a simple map illustrating rank order in sales by region.

COMPUTER OPTIONS

Avoid "chart junk" in computer-drawn graphics.

Computer graphics packages such as Harvard Graphics, along with drawing and painting programs and image scanners, offer a business writer many options. The newest versions of widely used spreadsheet programs such as Lotus 1-2-3 and Excel also offer flexible graphing capability. Presentation programs, such as Microsoft Powerpoint and Aldus Persuasion, offer ease and flexibility in creating graphics for use in talks.

The same principles of simplicity, clarity, impact, and truthfulness should guide your use of computer packages. Beginning users sometimes put too much information and format variation into visuals simply because such options are available. They should not do so: High-tech junk is just as bad as low-tech junk.

Not all visuals depend on expensive equipment and know-how to achieve high quality. Following are some low-tech alternatives that can produce equally effective results.

A meticulous person can produce an attractive graphic using only drawing and cutting tools, a copy machine, whiting-out fluid, and a typewriter or word processor.

Sometimes a source will provide you with an excellent set of figures in paragraph or table form from which you can draw your own graph. Use grid-ruled graph paper or plain paper that you have carefully ruled lightly in pencil. Exhibit 7–24 shows a hand-drawn graphic.

Alternatively, if you rule your paper using the same intervals that separate lines on a typewriter or printer (usually six single-spaced lines per vertical inch), you can typewrite or computer print all the identifying material, including exhibit number and title, labels for vertical and horizontal axes as needed, and source note. Exhibit 7–25 combines typing and drawing.

Whether you type or hand print, remember that all the labels must fit within normal margins. Do not let them bulge out into margins, and use plenty of white space to separate them from the text of your report.

ATTRACTIVE LOW-TECH OPTIONS

Cutting and Pasting

Drawing Your Own Exhibit

EXHIBIT 7–24   **Hand-Drawn Graph on Graph Paper**

FIGURE 4

Pantown Residents Use of Community Recreation Center

Response Category	Percent responding
Daily	11%
At least once a week	13%
Several times a month	6%
About once a month	9%
Once every few months	5%
A few times a year	10%
Once a year	3%
Less than once a year	13%
Never been there	30%

Source: Ivy, L.M. (1993, June 6). Community services investigated as waste of tax dollars. *Pantown Press*, p. A1.

ⒺXHIBIT 7–25   **Typed and Hand-Drawn Graphic**

FIGURE 4
Pantown Residents Use of Community Recreation Center

Response Category	Percent responding
Daily	☐ 11%
At least once a week	☐ 13%
Several times a month	☐ 6%
About once a month	☐ 9%
Once every few months	☐ 5%
A few times a year	☐ 10%
Once a year	☐ 3%
Less than once a year	☐ 13%
Never been there	☐ 30%

Source: Ivy, L.M. (1993, June 6). Community services
    investigated as waste of tax dollars. Pantown Press, p. A1.

Using a Photocopied Visual

Sometimes one of your reference sources will contain a visual, such as a **graph**, table, or drawing, perfectly suited to your purpose. To use it, make a clean photocopy. For best results, use a copier that can enlarge or diminish an image so that you can size the visual attractively and legibly for your report. Draft a source note to include below the visual.

Putting It Together

Type or print the page on which you intend to use the visual, leaving space not only for the square or oblong graphic you drew or photocopied but also for elements you are adding, such as your exhibit number, exhibit title, identification of components, and source note. Leave enough additional white space to separate all these elements from the report text in an attractive way. With a ruler, make light pencil guide lines to ensure exact vertical and horizontal alignment. (Erase the lines later.) Make sure the left and right margins are exactly those you will use in the report itself. Then paste up your elements and photocopy the result. Use opaque whiting-out fluid to remove any traces of lines. Then photocopy the page again to obtain your finished product.

Exhibit 7–26 shows the steps in preparing a report page with a cut-and-pasted graphic. Plan all these steps carefully. You do not want to do any of them a second time.

Clip Art

Clip art refers to collections of pictures, usually line drawings or engravings. Many such items are in the public domain, which means you can copy and use them without obtaining permission. Check for a copyright before you copy a visual. If the image is under copyright, use it only as permitted.

Software vendors have accumulated some of the pictures, created many others, and offered "clip art libraries" on disk. Some are available as "shareware"; that is, you examine them and send a small fee to the maker if you intend to use them. Books of clip art have been available for a long time. Printshops often have clip art, as might your college library.

EXHIBIT 7-26   Steps in Cut-and-Paste Insertion of Graphic in Report

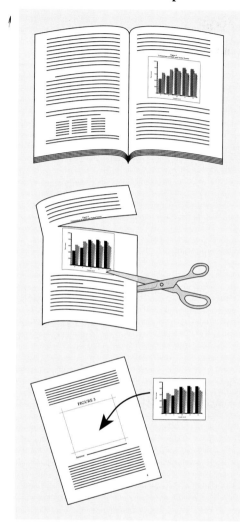

Step 1: You have found a useful graphic in a journal article. Photocopy the page.

If the exhibit's size is appropriate for its importance in your report, photocopy it as is. If not, find a copier that enlarges and reduces. Modify size as needed.

Make sure copy is clear and free of unwanted specks or lines. Use whiting-out fluid as needed.

Step 2: Trim away elements you don't need. For instance, you'll use *your* exhibit number, not theirs.

Step 3: On the report page you have prepared with exhibit number and title, source note, ample space, and penciled guide lines, tape or paste your photocopy in place.

Photocopy your page. Use whiting-out fluid to clean it up. Photocopy page again. This page becomes part of your finished report.

Many of the pictures exist for fun or for nonbusiness uses. Some of the most beautiful clip art is suitable for illustrating fantasy, science fiction, or adventure fiction.

Clip art you might find useful includes small images of business-related objects. For instance, in a vertical bar graph comparing amounts of cheese produced by different states, you could use a small drawing of a wedge of Swiss cheese. You could make many copies of the wedge, let each wedge stand for 1,000 tons of product, and stack them neatly one on top of another in a bar to show the total amount produced by a state. If the amounts do not round out to neat thousands of tons, you can cut the topmost wedge to show a fraction of 1,000 tons. (See Exhibit 7-27.)

You can also find small pictures of arrows, faces, computers, buildings, human figures, stars, flags, sunbursts, foods, vehicles, checkmarks, animals,

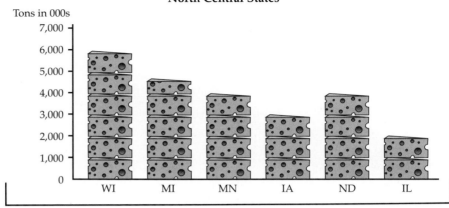

Figure 8
Cheese Production, 1992
North Central States

Tons in 000s

geometric shapes, borders, and so on. If an image is useful as a symbol, you will find it in clip art libraries.

You can use the low-tech copy, cut, and paste method, or you can import computerized clip art into one of the many computer drawing, graphing, or word processing programs available.

With a computer drawing or painting program, you can copy an image hundreds of times if you choose, expand it or reduce it, rotate it in space, invert it vertically or horizontally, and stretch it vertically or horizontally, among many other things.

Be aware that not all images are equally acceptable to all cultures. For example, certain animals (serpent, rat, cricket) carry different symbolism in different countries. An icon (a small, simplified image) of a woman might work well in the United States but offend sensibilities in some other nations. A plain white cross, sometimes used in the United States to symbolize mortality figures, would make little sense in an area where Christianity is not a major influence and crosses are not used as grave markers.

PRESENTATION VISUALS

Presentation visuals should be "twice as simple and four times as bold" as visuals used in written reports.

According to Zelazny,

> A chart used in a visual presentation must be at least twice as simple and four times as bold as one used in a report. It's the same as the distinction between a billboard that must be read and understood in the time you drive past it and a magazine advertisement that you can study in detail.[1]

Why use graphics in an oral presentation at all? Isn't standing up there and giving a good presentation enough? Aren't graphics just frills and extra work? Not really. To appreciate the importance of using visuals to accompany oral messages, imagine someone explaining how to use a computer software pro-

[1]Gene Zelazny, *Say It with Charts: The Executive's Guide to Successful Presentations,* 2nd ed. (Homewood, Ill.: Business One Irwin, 1991), p. 5.

gram to you over the telephone. Even if the speaker is skilled and knowledge-able, words are not enough. *Seeing* what the speaker is describing makes a significant difference.

In business communicators' talks, presentation graphics

- Introduce the speaker and topic.
- Present an overview of organization.
- Emphasize important points.
- Clarify difficult concepts.
- Reemphasize the purpose of the presentation.

Visuals are valuable in written reports because they put complex information into a more understandable form. Similarly, in oral presentations, graphs and illustrations aid understanding. Diagrams can reduce complex ideas into their essential components. An appropriate picture or drawing helps people see what they are hearing.

A second value of presentation visuals is that they solve a problem inherent in listening to talks. Your receivers listen at your pace, not theirs. They can't pause to think about something or turn back to earlier information. Because of this essential difference between written and oral communication, good speakers learn to keep their listeners with them. The basic structure of oral reports (discussed in Chapter Nine) helps, but worded structure alone is not enough. Visuals help listeners stay with the speaker.

Chapter Nine covers many more types of visuals than we will discuss here. In this section we will focus on overhead transparencies or 35mm slides (we will refer to both types simply as *slides*). However, the same content and much the same format could be offered in other forms, such as a prepared flipchart exhibit, a deskchart exhibit, part of a computer show, or various other media.

Examine Exhibit 7–28 to see the various purposes different slides serve. The opening slide (Slide 1) is simple but important. It answers the audience's first questions: who you are and what you are going to speak about. Using such a slide shows your listeners that you are professional and organized. Conveying this image enhances your personal confidence: You know you are getting off to a good start.

Project this opening slide behind you as you begin to speak. This will reinforce and strengthen your opening remarks. Use this introductory slide only once, briefly, at the start of the talk.

Slide 2 is an example of an organizer. It tells the audience three things in advance:

- The extent or coverage of the presentation.
- The basic components of the topic.
- The order in which they will be discussed.

This slide is a simplified version of the outline for your presentation. When you share it with the audience beforehand, they can follow you easily as you continue. In other words, everyone is "on the same page."

The other forms of graphics discussed in this section are normally used only once during a presentation, but you can use your organizational slide several times. You can use it once at the beginning of your talk and then put it away or refer to it several times during the presentation to refresh listeners' mem-

Presentation visuals should help the audience understand purpose, structure, and emphasis.

Introducing the Speaker and the Topic

Presenting an Overview of the Talk's Organization

EXHIBIT 7–28   Examples from a Set of Presentation Graphics

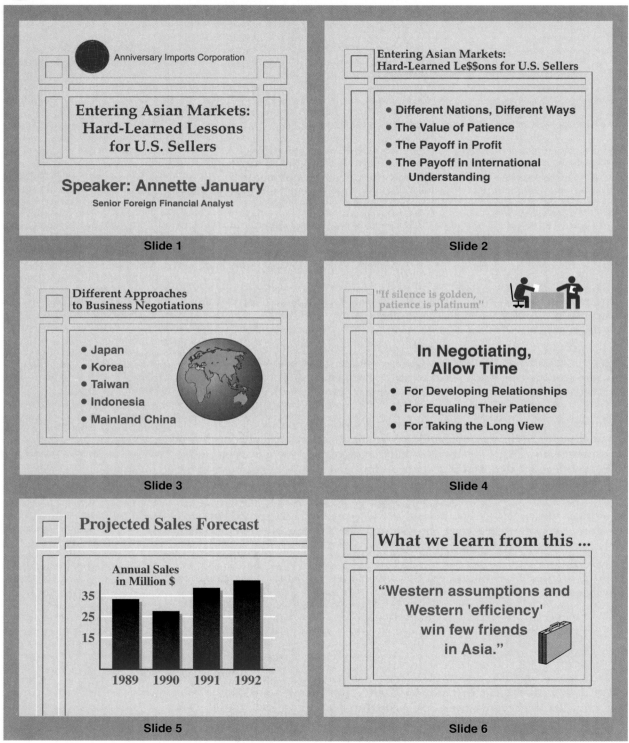

ories. If appropriate, you can use it again at the conclusion to reinforce what you have covered.

Slides 3 and 4 are expansions of main topics shown in Slide 2. Showing the listeners more about these items underscores the ideas' importance. Presenters do not have to have a slide to illustrate every item they discuss, but using these graphics adds visual emphasis to important points.

Emphasizing Important Points

Concepts, whether theoretical ideas or conclusions drawn from numerical data, can confuse or even elude listeners if they are presented without sufficient explanation and graphic support. Slide 5 is a simple picture of the "payoff" for understanding different cultural values. In this form, "the numbers" can become a motivating device.

Clarifying Concepts

This example illustrates a valuable tip in working with graphics: Ask yourself whether you, sitting in the audience, would follow a given point more easily if it were accompanied by a visual. Don't overload your presentations with slides, but don't hesitate to include one when it will make something easier to understand or remember.

The introductory slide is memorable because of its place in the presentation. What the audience sees first has a strong psychological impact. Likewise, the graphic they see last makes a strong impression because it *is* last. They will also expect you to tell them what is most important at the end of your presentation. Don't let them down. For example, you might say as you show a visual like Slide 6, "If there's one thing I want you to remember from our meeting today, it's this: . . ." If you bring back your organizational slide (Slide 2) to summarize at the end of your presentation, make it precede your final-message slide.

Reemphasizing the Purpose of the Presentation

You may be asked to instruct others using computer screens instead of either paper documents or oral presentations. For instance, the procedure report, a common type of short report, may slowly be giving way to onscreen instruction (*computer-aided instruction,* or *CAI*). Other kinds of communication via computer screens exist as well.

COMPUTER SCREEN DESIGN

Computer screen design shares some features with printed-page design but offers some very different features you can use to add value. Conciseness, clarity, consistency, familiar language, short sentences and paragraphs, itemized lists, headings, and white space are as desirable in screen design as they are in all business communication. Some elements that differ include color use, scrolling and other movement, sound, and automatic pacing. This section presents a quick overview of some principles to keep in mind. The screens shown in Exhibit 7–29 are modest, showing only a few of a virtually unlimited array of possibilities.

Control time.   Onscreen information can appear slowly or quickly. The difficulty of the information and your users' reading speed and experience should govern how rapidly information appears.

Use space inventively and effectively.   A screen can start anywhere, not just at top left. An image can start in the middle and spread outward to fill the screen. For images, these unusual origin points can be memorable and effective. For text, however, users should be able to look in the same place every time for such things as menu prompts, screen numbers, response areas, and information areas. Consistency is essential.

EXHIBIT 7–29   Four Sample Screens for Computer-Aided Instruction

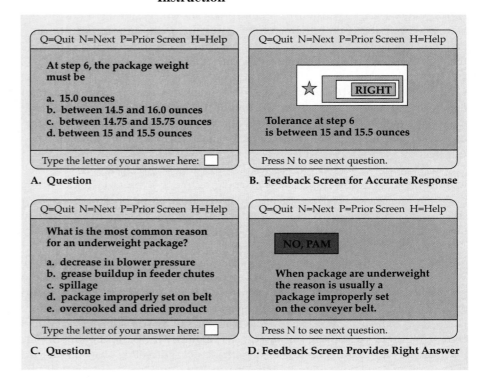

A. Question

B. Feedback Screen for Accurate Response

C. Question

D. Feedback Screen Provides Right Answer

Use plenty of white space. This term still applies to space with nothing in it, even though you may see every color *except* white on a screen.

Keep screens readable.   Sequence words from left to right, not from top to bottom. Stay with familiar words and abbreviations (omit periods in abbreviations). Use short sentences and short lines. Be predictable. Use familiar emphasis principles.

Emphasis principles are important in every communication medium.

Use options judiciously.   A designer has a wealth of options, including boldface, color, moving graphics, underlining, sound, reverse video, and flashing. Using too many of these devices too frequently, however, violates principles of good design and interferes with their ability to emphasize. (Remember that if everything is emphasized, nothing is.) To help users get the most out of your screens, make some basic design choices and use them consistently.

Make sure each screen is complete and self-contained.   Because flipping back and forth among different screens is awkward, each screen should be self-contained. Everything needed for one task should appear on a single screen.

Use strong colors that are pleasing onscreen.   Using too many colors will distract users from your messages. Strong colors—red, green, yellow, blue, white—are best. Use intelligently the colors associated with symbolic meanings, such as green for *go* and red for *stop*. Color well used adds interest to screens, but black-and-white screens are preferable to screens that overuse color.

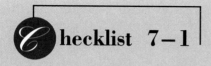

Checklist 7–1

Graphics

1. Is a graphic the best way to communicate the message?
2. Is the graphic appropriate for readers' knowledge, background, and preferences?
3. Is the graphic as simple as it can be while still telling its story?
4. Is the graphic clear?
5. Does the graphic possess visual impact?
6. Is the graphic truthful?
7. Is the treatment of the graphic complete? Have you provided

   - An exhibit type and numeric or alphabetic label?
   - A descriptive title?
   - Appropriate size?
   - An introduction in the text?
   - Placement soon after the introduction?

   - Appropriate framing with white space?
   - Accurate documentation?
   - Interpretation?

8. Is your selected format appropriate for the story?
9. Are all labels, such as column and row headings, axis labels, and legend, present and clear?
10. Is emphasis appropriate?
11. If hand drawn, is the graphic carefully prepared and sized to fit, complete with all needed labels, axes, legends, and white space, within a page's margins?
12. If presentation visuals, are they sufficiently bold, simple, and clear to communicate quickly while you are speaking?

Reinforce color use with narrative. Make sure the message is complete irrespective of the color. Use blue or green for text and hotter colors (which tend to "pulse" too much for text) for graphics. Because paper *reflects* colors and screens *produce* light, colors on paper look different than the same colors do on a screen. Also, color combinations that work well on paper do not necessarily work onscreen.

Hold down the amount of text. Text lines should not exceed about eight to ten words. Shorter lines permit the use of accompanying small graphics. Sometimes text lines can be superimposed on a photographic visual.

As you prepare and revise graphics for assignments or business use, refer to Checklist 7–1.

REVIEW

Graphics—tables, charts, maps, and other kinds of visuals—supplement and clarify written text. Visuals require simplicity, clarity, impact, and truthfulness. Visuals that accompany oral presentations should be simpler than those used in written communications.

Visuals in written reports must be labeled with a number, titled descriptively, sized appropriately, introduced and interpreted in the text, placed as close as possible to the introduction, and documented correctly.

Types of visuals include tables and figures. Tables may be informal ("spot") or formal. Figures include pie charts, simple bar charts, segmented 100 percent bar graphs, grouped bar graphs, component bar graphs, positive-negative bar graphs, simple line charts, multiple line charts, cumulative line charts, positive-negative line charts, drawings and diagrams, and maps. Although many visuals are created using a computer, graphics programs, and clip art, manually prepared cut-and-paste graphics sometimes serve the purpose.

Presentation visuals should be simple and bold. They serve to introduce speaker and topic, present an overview of the speaker's organization, emphasize important points, clarify difficult concepts, and reemphasize the purpose of the presentation.

When developing a communication consisting of a series of computer screens, follow good screen design principles.

APPLICATION EXERCISES

1. Why should graphics designed for oral presentations be simpler and bolder than those intended for written reports?

2. Writers who need to display the components of one or more wholes can choose between two kinds of figures. What kinds of figures are these, and what factors govern the choice?

3. Consider this statement: "If a graphic is good enough, a report writer need not cover its material in the report text at all." Is this statement true or untrue? Discuss.

4. If you had to graph monthly fuel usage over a period of 48 months, would you use a bar chart or a line chart? Why?

5. What are some ways a visual can lie or distort the facts?

6. What is the proper treatment of visuals in written reports, according to the expectations of most business readers?

7. Distinguish between a table and a figure.

8. In a graphic, what is a legend?

9. What are the guidelines for drawing pie charts?

10. What are the various kinds of bar charts? For what purpose is each type used?

11. Although bar charts and line charts serve some of the same purposes, under what circumstances would a line chart be the only correct choice?

12. When is a diagram of an object more informative than a photograph of the object?

13. Have you used a computerized graphics package? What are its advantages? Does it have any disadvantages?

14. In what ways do presentation visuals differ from those prepared for written reports? In what ways are they similar?

15. What are some guidelines for designing computer screens to be used in computer-aided instruction?

CASES

1. **Interpreting a Map Graphic.** The accompanying map shows percentages of problem real estate loans, by state, for the second quarter of 1992. What "story" does this map tell?

2. **Comparing Two Newspapers' Use of Graphics.** From the daily newspaper that serves your area, find one or more business-related news stories containing graphs or charts that you

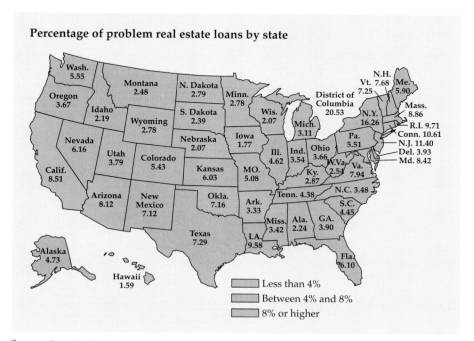

Source: *Los Angeles Times*, September 10, 1992, p. D-1.

Graphics 213

consider clear and effective. Obtain a recent copy of *USA Today.* Bring to class the business section of *USA Today* and either hard copies or photocopies of the news stories you located in your area daily newspaper. Be ready to discuss how the two newspapers approach the use of business graphics. Are they similar or dissimilar? How? Which has more impact? Which is clearer? Which is simpler? Are both truthful? Defend your opinions.

3. **A Table: Organizing Your Budget.** What are your personal expenses for a typical month? Create a table showing expenses in each of five to seven budget categories. Label everything clearly.

4. **A Bar Graph: Comparing Profits.** You have been asked to track the profits of seven of the largest U.S. public companies. For the third quarter of 1992, profits for the companies were as follows: Bank America, $476,000,000; Coca-Cola, $541,000,000; Merck, $644,000,000; AT&T, $963,000,000; General Electric, $1,110,000,000; Exxon, $1,135,000,000; and Philip Morris, $1,291,000,000. Prepare a bar graph showing these profits. Be sure all necessary components are present. Consider using the wording "in millions" or "$ millions" to avoid long rows of zeros.

5. **Line Charts: Tracking Advertising and Volume.** Budweiser's advertising expenditures and volume of beer sold from 1982–1992 were as follows:

Year	Adv. Exp.	Vol. Sold
1982	$ 48 m	41.0 m barrels
1983	$ 70 m	43.4 m barrels
1984	$ 72 m	44.3 m barrels
1985	$ 76 m	46.2 m barrels
1986	$113 m	48.2 m barrels
1987	$113 m	49.7 m barrels
1988	$137 m	50.3 m barrels
1989	$116 m	50.0 m barrels
1990	$ 77 m	49.0 m barrels
1991	$ 88 m	46.2 m barrels
1992	$123 m	46.3 m barrels

Create two line charts that give this information. Write a short paragraph explaining the main idea a reader should derive from looking at the two charts as a pair.

6. **Pies or Segmented Bars? Showing Division of CEO Pay.** The Hay Group's Executive Compensation Database contains figures on the components of a chief executive officer's compensation package as they changed between 1985 and 1991. In 1985 a CEO's base salary accounted for 52 percent, annual bonus for 22 percent, long-term award for 8 percent, benefits for 16 percent, and perks (perquisites) for 2 percent. In 1991 CEO base salary accounted for 35 percent of total compensation, annual bonus for 22 percent, long-term award for 31 percent, benefits for 11 percent, and perks for 1 percent. Prepare a graphic showing this "story." Be sure to include all the necessary components.

7. **A Positive-Negative Bar Chart: Showing Average Returns.** Following are the percentage returns on the average general stock mutual fund, 1975–1992. Make a positive-negative bar chart showing these data graphically. After labeling everything appropriately, write a statement interpreting the graph.

Year	Percent	Year	Percent	Year	Percent
1975	35	1981	−1	1987	1
1976	27	1982	26	1988	15
1977	6	1983	21	1989	24
1978	12	1984	−2	1990	−7
1979	29	1985	28	1991	36
1980	34	1986	14	1992	9

8. **Converting a Table to a Graph.** From your daily newspaper's business section, find a *table* containing figures about any element of business that interests you. Photocopy the table, being sure to collect the information you would need to document it. Then decide how some or all of the information could be presented graphically. Create your graph. Make it complete.

9. **A Bar Chart: Graphing Sales Totals.** Use your library skills to find the answer to this question: For the most recent year for which statistics are complete, what are the top 10 selling cars and trucks in the United States? Make a bar graph showing total units sold for these models.

10. **A Pair of Pies: Showing Where the Money Isn't.** As you examine operating costs for your department in March, the end of the first quarter of your budget year, you learn that telephone charges have risen dramatically while your operating budget has not risen at all. You are planning a memo asking your people to control their phone use closely. Here are the figures: For both last year and this year, $54,000 was budgeted for total operating costs, which comprise office supplies, photocopying, insurance and machine repair, mail costs, and telephone.

Last year, supplies cost $21,600 (40 percent), photocopying $12,960 (24 percent), insurance and machine repair $5,400 (10 percent), mail expenses $8,640 (16 percent), and phone charges $5,400 (10 percent).

As of March of this year, you have already paid for unforeseen and uninsured repairs that will elevate this category of expense to $7,560, or 14 percent, for the year *if* nothing more goes wrong. Mail expenses, supplies, and photocopying look likely to stay within—but just barely within—

budget for the year. Phone charges, if employees continue as they have begun, will rise to $9,720.

You need a pair of pie charts to clarify the problem for them. Graph last year's expenses. Then show in the second pie that phone charges are soaking up an unplanned 18 percent of your total overhead. The supplies budget is virtually the only one you can tap. This pie chart's message is that your company's supplies budget will be out of funds by October unless phone use is sharply curbed.

*R*eading 7.1

WORDS ON THE WALL

Audrey Thompson

Here you are, again. Seated in a darkened conference room in an office or hotel, straining an ear to the drone of a presenter, distracted too often by a cough, the creak of a chair, and the fact that your buns are going slowly numb. Your eyes glaze at flash after flash of illegible, dull, and ineffectual slides. Your comprehension is now as dim as the hall, and you yearn for the final slide that will be titled, inevitably, "Conclusion."

We've all had to endure this slide-induced torpor. Why, then, do we so quickly forget the ordeal when it's time to project our own words on the wall?

Slides and overheads are as pervasive in business as campaign promises in an election year—and, alas, often as empty. Yet presentation visuals, like their printed cousins letters and reports, must have a clear purpose and message if they are to be worthwhile.

I'm not talking about how pretty a slide looks here. I'm talking about content. About the *communication* part of business communication.

Persuasion's outliner is a great tool for getting your thoughts organized enough to present them. But don't fall into the trap of stopping there. Visuals belong to your audience. They exist to synthesize your main points and to give your listeners a road map of where you're going. In many ways, they do for the spoken word what headlines and subheads do for a printed piece. Anything else is a waste of your audience's time.

Ten Percent Is All You Get

Statistics have long shown that audiences recall only 10 percent of most oral presentations. Your job is to put that 10 percent on the slides. A good way to accomplish this is to subject each visual to a four-pass edit, revising it with your reader in mind. The four steps are:

- *The content edit.* Verify that each slide adds something the audience needs to know. Delete anything that isn't unique, specific, and relevant to

comprehension. Streamline, rearrange, and split up content, so that each visual covers only one concept.

- *The conciseness edit.* If an audience can't grasp the main message in 5 to 10 seconds, the slide's not working. Watch the length of phrasing. Break sentences into bulleted lists, giving only their main points. Pare out any extraneous or redundant words, numbers, and labels.

- *The copyedit.* Make bulleted lists parallel in construction (e.g., all noun phrases or all verb phrases). Establish and follow a consistent style of capitalization and labeling. Fix grammar. Vary your use of language.

- *The proofread.* Verify all spelling, especially of people's names. Double-check numbers and data.

For every visual, ask yourself: If this were a handout, would a reader be able to recall the gist of what I said by reading it a week from now?

Make the Most of Your Medium

Like any communication medium, slide shows have advantages and limitations that dictate their best content and usage.

Have an agenda slide. The old presenter's adage is "Tell 'em what you're going to tell 'em, tell 'em, then tell 'em what you told 'em." You're up there to communicate, so tell your audience up front what to expect from you. Leave the mystery to Agatha Christie.

Never read your slides verbatim. It insults your audience, and it makes you superfluous. The visuals are there to convey the 10 percent you want your group to recall; *you're* there to convey the 90 percent that supports and explains those points.

Source: Audrey Thompson, "Words on the Wall," *Aldus Magazine,* September/October 1992, pp. 39–42.

Allow only one minute per slide, so the audience stays attentive. Slide builds can be a valuable pacing tool, but don't overdo it—you don't want the audience fidgeting over how many more bullets they have yet to sit through.

Vary the kinds of slides in your show. A parade of pie charts is just as wearying as slide after slide of text.

Know when *not* to use a slide. If you simply can't compress a concept enough to fit it legibly on one or more visuals, *you're using the wrong medium for that particular message.* By all means, stop the show to hold a discussion, direct attention to a handout, provide an ancillary report, or give a demonstration.

When you go the extra step of assessing what you want your listeners to understand from each visual, you'll never hear it said, "Gee, the slides were beautiful. Too bad they didn't say anything."

Nine Common Faults and Their Cures

1. *Too many words.* Having over 35 words on a slide undermines your delivery, forcing your audience to choose between attending to you and reading the visual. At worst, it reduces *you* to reading the slide verbatim, damaging your credibility as a speaker.

   Cut to the chase, but don't be concise at the expense of comprehension. Reduce the text down to your essentials. Use brief phrases, broken into bulleted points where appropriate. Then your audience can quickly grasp your direction, leaving them free to listen to your more engaging speech.

2. *Too many bulleted points.* Too many points are impossible to absorb at once. They also force a slide to be on screen too long, draining energy from your presentation and your listeners.

   Keep to a maximum of five bullets or eight lines per slide, and confine each slide to one concept. Expand a lengthy subject to two slides, or reorganize the bullets by topic, each with its own slide. Avoid subbullets unless your audience needs them; often, they represent a level of detail better left to speaker notes.

3. *Too much information.* Information overload is particularly easy with data. When you let yourself get caught up in statistics and labels, viewers will lose sight of the main point—or may miss it entirely. . . .

   Choose the one point you want the audience to get, . . . *and delete all other material as irrelevant.* Juggle information into smaller pieces. . . . You can fill in supporting statistics orally. (And round the figures when you speak: "over a third" is much easier to grasp than "37 percent.")

4. *Slides that say nothing to the audience.* If a slide about the hotel industry has bulleted points reading "Food," "Rooms," "Services," and "Rates,"

it's just acting as a speaker prompt. Honor your audience's time and intelligence: if you have something to say, expand the copy to summarize it; if not, delete the slide.

5. *Long or meaningless titles.* In the real world, it's inevitable that some slide titles will be uninspiring, but they should never be vague, cryptic, pointless, or so heavy that they outweigh the 10 percent you want the audience to grasp.

   Make titles *say* something, whether to encapsulate your point or titillate interest. Vary the style with topic titles ("Bonus Plan"), thematic titles ("Bonus Plan Increasing Productivity"), and assertive titles ("We Must Implement Bonus Plan Now"). Put in verbs. Edit down to the important words. Use subheads to carry text that's repeated from slide to slide. And don't be afraid to get a little creative—standbys like "Conclusion," "Summary," and "Agenda" work in a pinch but get old quickly. (On the other hand, don't sacrifice comprehension for cleverness.)

6. *Cryptic phrases, abbreviations, and jargon.* Buzz words, acronyms, and abbreviations can belittle or baffle an audience. Don't use them unless you're absolutely sure that *all* your listeners are familiar with the terms. A slide that talks about "Mfg reqs," "JITs," and "BOMs" might make sense to members of the manufacturing department, but not to their colleagues in marketing.

7. *Nonparallel construction of text.* Bullet points that don't sound similar grate on the sensibilities and mar quick comprehension. Here's a typical example:

The Cinder-Cone Volcano

- Composed of congealed lava
- Lava cinders form round cone
- Usually leave a bowl-shaped crater
- Can find them throughout western North America

Strive instead for the rhythm and logic of like-sounding phrases—start all bullets with a verb, for example, or with an adjective or noun phrase. The example above would be much easier to take in if the last three bulleted points followed the form of the first, like this:

- Composed of congealed laval
- Has round cone of lava cinders
- Characterized by bowl-shaped crater
- Found throughout western North America

(Note that the verbs "is" and "are" can often be treated as understood.)

Such parallelism enhances understanding and doesn't ring awkwardly on the ear. It's important to set up subheads, labels, and titles consistently among similar slides, as well.

8. *Conspicuous punctuation and capitalization.* Avoid the salt-shaker approach to punctuation and capitalization. In slides above all other formats, every extra jot and tittle inhibits quick understanding. Similarly, too many capitals dilute a message by making *everything* seem important.

Punctuate only enough to clarify your points. Omit colons and periods at ends of titles, phrases, and bullet entries. Capitalize consistently within the same show. Usually, you're safe to capitalize all important words in titles, the first word of a bulleted point, and the first word in labels and subheads.

9. *Spelling errors.* There's nothing like a two-foot-tall typo to upstage you. Proofread your text. Run the spelling checker. Have a co-worker read the slides *before* you commit them to film. It's better to catch a howler now than to be one later.

Chapter Eight

Report Organization and Format

PREVIEW

During your career, you may be called on to write, or participate in the writing of, a longer, formal report. Such a project can be a major step forward for you, especially if you are the person who is primarily responsible for the report.

In this chapter, you will learn how to write a formal report. You will see how to outline your report considering its audience, purpose, and schedule. Many long reports are written by groups of people; you will learn how to coordinate such a group. You will also learn about report organization and style and how that style can vary depending on the purpose and type of report.

Next, you will go through all of the parts of a report, seeing how they fit together and why. Finally, you will see an example of a long report, with notes that will help you when writing your own report.   ●

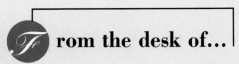

From the desk of...

Report Writing Opportunity

Ken Dixon
Assistant Product Manager

I can't believe it! Two months ago, I was just another analyst. I'd finished the market study of the new ice cream flavors; the focus group seemed to like the ones with cookie dough in them. Sarah, my boss, asked me to take the results and write a report proposing a new line based on that study. She said it needed to cover how we would manufacture and market it as well as costs, prices, labeling—in short, everything.

I haven't worked so hard in all my life! I had to learn about our costs and profit margins. The lawyers covered the labeling issues. Jim in the plant wrote the section on what we would need for manufacturing. I had to edit it so that everyone could understand both the legalese and the technical jargon, and that made me learn a lot about labeling rules and manufacturing. But it was worth it. Sarah liked my report; she sent it upstairs. They must have liked it there, too. They decided to start a new line, and I'm the assistant product manager!

A long report is a significant investment for a business. When you are given the chance to write one, you have an opportunity to reveal your talents to key people in the company. If you do a good job on the report, that exposure can lead to a faster promotion. This chapter will help you learn to write the kind of report that will impress those key people.

PRACTICAL OUTLINING OF A LONGER PROJECT

When working on a report that may be 15 to 150 or more pages long, you have to take care to structure it so it does not end up choppy and disconnected. This book, for example, has two authors, 16 chapters, and many contributions from outside sources. If we had just sat down and started writing, we might have covered all the topics we wanted to, but you would have had a hard time figuring out how the parts of business communication fit together.

To avoid this kind of problem, we sat down early, decided what the book needed to cover and what kind of tone we wanted, prepared a detailed outline based on a consistent structure for each chapter—preview, body, review, exercises, cases, and readings—and decided who would write each chapter based on our individual skills and preferences. If we have done our job well, the book should work as a unified whole, and you should learn how to communicate effectively in business.

Writing a long report starts with the same kind of process. Specifically, the people who will write the report should

1. *Identify the audience, purpose, and due date.* Is the purpose of the report to get the board of directors to select a health plan at the next board meeting? To recommend a new advertising campaign to the director of marketing at a meeting next week? To outline the capital budget for the coming year?

2. *Decide what the report will cover.* If the report is to propose an action based on research yet to be done, you must determine what the possible decisions are. If you have already made a decision based on facts you now have, you need to decide how to present that recommendation most effectively.

Working on a report as part of a team involves both individual and group effort. Often, team members meet about report content and revisions—either face to face or via a computer network.

3. *Write an outline of the report.* This outline can be brief, but it should include all the essential parts of the report in enough detail to give both a guide to use while writing the report and a feel for how much work will be involved in each part of the report.

4. *Determine how long each part of the report will take to prepare and in what order you must complete the parts.* For example, in writing a business plan, completed market research is essential for generating an estimate of the total market for the product. The total market size, in turn, is needed before you can estimate product sales. And you have to know the sales estimates before you can prepare financial statements.

   At this stage, look at the time allocations to see whether they are consistent with the deadlines you face. If you need three weeks to complete a report for the board meeting a week from Wednesday, you'd better start planning over again.

   Remember too that once the report is written, it must be produced. It takes time—more time than many people realize— to run a word-processed manuscript through desktop publishing, turn it into a finished product, and get it reproduced and bound. You may find, for example, that it will take two or three days to physically produce 15 copies of a 20-page report.

5. *Decide who will write each part of the report.* Usually you will also want to have some other part of the writing team read each report part.

6. *Decide on the report style.* How many levels of headings will you have? How will you identify each level? How will you identify exhibits and tables, and where will they appear? How will you cite sources? If all members of the writing team use the same style, the report will

PEANUTS reprinted by permission of UFS, Inc.

A long report is a big project, so allow yourself enough time.

look like a unified whole. If not, it will look like a combination of individual reports that do not fit together well.

After you have decided on these preliminaries, you will all be writing with a common purpose and style. Later, after each section is completed, you will need only to add transitional language to lead the reader from one section to the next and complete the production of the report.

Organizing by Structure

Organizing a multipage report is easier if you divide the work into sections. Use the organizing principles you learned in Chapter 1 to see what kind of organization your topic and audience seem to call for (analysis, cause-effect, chronological, spatial, decision criteria).

Another decision you will need to make is whether to use direct or indirect structure. Will your report message generally meet with reader approval, disappointment, or resistance? When a report includes an executive summary near the beginning, readers will know your conclusions right away—and if you *don't* include a summary, readers may turn to the conclusion section and read that first. As a result, you can't really use a completely inductive structure in which you hold your main points until you have presented your evidence that those points are true. However, you can certainly present parts of the report inductively, building up an argument before you reveal your conclusion. You can use passive voice for ideas the reader would find negative and show reader benefit for ideas the reader may resist.

Report Organization in Other Cultures

People in other cultures have strong ideas about how reports should be organized. Therefore, if you are writing a report for non-U.S. readers, or reading a report from another country, you will need to keep their preferences in mind. Here are some examples from Iris Varner, who has studied international communication in great detail:

- Japanese reports tend to present information in chronological order.
- Germans include a detailed discussion of background material whether or not the reader needs it; they think that all reports need a thorough introductory section on the topic.
- French reports move from abstract to concrete, first discussing the theory behind the problem and then the history of the problem.
- Reports in Latin countries sometimes omit bad news altogether because employees don't want to mention negative findings, or present

Dagwood needs to analyze the audience *first*, not *last*.

bad news in a misleading way rather than as a problem area to be discussed.[1]

Report Process Checklist

Planning your report writing even before you begin your research can save you time, because you will already have focused on why and how you will prepare the report later. Checklist 8–1 outlines the steps to take when preparing your long report. As with all messages, first consider your audience to avoid problems later.

REPORT STYLE

Report style includes two facets: how the report looks and how it sounds to the reader. The *look* is determined by the use of type fonts, graphics, levels of headings, and the like. The *sound* is the result of the way you write the report. You will use different styles for different levels of reports.

The Look of the Report

To get an idea of a report with a consistent look, consider the look of this book (which is really a long instructional report):

- The binding is attractive and tells you immediately what is inside.
- The type is easy to read. It is a serif face, which is easier to read than a sans serif face because you learned to read in books with this kind of type. Also, the type is large enough to read easily. Most readers of this book are under 40. Especially when writing for an audience that is over 40, remember that many people may have difficulty reading small print. Therefore, select a relatively large type size for your report.
- The headings are consistent. The chapter titles are all in 89 point Bodoni Condensed (the initial letter is Kuenstler Script Medium). Main headings within chapters are in all capital letters, bold, and 14-point size. Secondary headings are upper- and lowercase, bold, and 12-point size. When you look at any heading in this book, you can tell from its style how important it is—whether it starts a completely new topic or continues by developing an existing one.
- Figures, sidebars, and tables are each presented in a consistent way. As with headings, when you see one, you know immediately what it is.

[1]Iris I. Varner, *Contemporary Business Writing* (Hinsdale, Ill.: Dryden Press, 1987), p. 398.

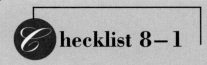

Checklist 8–1

The Report Process

- Identify the audience, purpose, and due date.
- Decide what the report will cover (decision? recommendations?).
- Determine how long each part of the report will take to prepare and in what order the parts must be completed.
- Decide who will write each part of the report, if it is a team effort.
- Decide on the report style (layout *and* writing style). You will choose a writing style based on your audience, the level of formality of the report, and the report's purpose, among other things.
- Begin your research and collect your source list for the final report.

- Organize your findings and write your report introduction.
- Write up your results into the body of your report.
- Form conclusions (and recommendations, if appropriate).
- Enhance your report with graphics.
- Write the preliminary pages of your report (summary, transmittal, table of contents, title page).
- Revise for most effective layout design and writing style.

The Sound of the Report

This book also provides a good example of writing style. It is clear, direct writing. In your report writing, you, too, should strive for clarity and directness. Compare the following two paragraphs:

> In most cases, the sound of a report should be like the sound of this book. Write short, direct sentences. Include examples to help the audience visualize your points.

> When you are preparing a report, it should be done such that its tone is similar to that of this textbook. If your sentences are shorter and written in active voice, it may be less difficult for the reader to gain a full understanding of them. In addition, it may be more apparent to the reader what you mean if you include examples of the application of the principles you espouse, as he or she may be able thereby to form a mental image of said principle.

Both paragraphs say the same thing, but the second is about three times as long and is full of awkward phrases. Both paragraphs, however, give good advice: Keep your writing clear and simple.

The style of this book is not the only good report style. For your report, you may want to use some other style that is more consistent with the report's purpose. A report on fashion trends may be attention getting and breezy:

> Soft is in. We saw soft fabrics, soft lace, soft colors. Skirts are long and flowing—full, not tailored. Sleeves are puffy, often sheer.

An annual report to the shareholders of a bank would be far more conservative:

> Interest rates last year remained firm. Your company was able to maintain an average spread between interest earned on invested funds and interest paid on deposits of 3.3 percent, up .1 percent from the previous year.

In the paragraph from the fashion report, you can almost picture the dresses. The paragraph from the bank report gives a sense of solidity and conservatism. In each case, the style should be consistent throughout the report.

When you have bad news to give or expect someone to contest the report's conclusions, you may want to consider a less direct writing style. In such cases, consider using passive voice and the other techniques described in Chapter 10 to soften the impact so that it will be better received.

Just as you would in a letter or memo, show the reader what you are talking about by using examples, specific details, and graphics. Using these methods of adding concreteness to your writing will make it both clearer and more interesting to readers—and also more likely to produce the results you want.

Show Your Reader—Don't Just Tell

The following examples help illustrate the difference between merely *telling*—giving just a bare recitation of simple facts—and *showing*—giving details that create a much stronger image in the reader's mind:

Don't Tell	Do Show
Some other film processors have experienced significant film sales increases by using this display.	Tuskeegee Photo doubled film sales with this display.
A shakeout in the industry is occurring as smaller firms are either being bought out or run out of business by larger firms.	Small companies have suffered in the market. Exotek went bankrupt; Wayco Systems merged into Huge Conglomerate.
Japan is very crowded.	Japan is very crowded. When you want to ride the subway during rush hours, you may find yourself pushed onto your train by a transit employee; it's the only way they can fill the cars tightly enough.

Note that adding details does not necessarily result in more words. In the second example above, both versions are about the same length, while in the first, the improved version is actually shorter.

Report Style Checklist

How you write your report can affect your reader's understanding and acceptance of it, so be sure to revise your draft for appropriate style for your audience and your topic. Be objective: Don't allow your personal opinions to

FRANK AND ERNEST by Bob Thaves

FRANK & ERNEST reprinted by permission of NEA, Inc.

Reports use objective style.

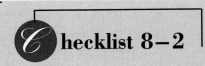

Report Style

Word Choice

- Can your words be understood by your audience? What if laypeople need to understand your report? Check for pompous language and technical jargon.
- Have you chosen specific words that convey your ideas clearly? Check for vagueness and wordiness.
- Have you involved the reader through use of active voice rather than passive voice when discussing important positive points? Passive voice is appropriate for downplaying or subordinating ideas, but active voice lets you focus on who is taking the action.

Sentences and Paragraphs

- Are your sentences short enough (averaging 16–18 words) to need little internal punctuation? Of course, you will have some very short sentences (for emphasis) and some long ones (including a list, for example), but write so that the structure of your sentences enhances rather than hinders understanding.

- Are your paragraphs relatively short (about eight typed lines)? Short paragraphs will seem easier to your reader and thus encourage reading of your material. A large block of type looks intimidating and may hinder understanding as a result. Also, short paragraphs require fewer transitions to guide the reader through the ideas presented.

Organizing Structure

- Did you use several levels of headings to guide the reader by showing the relative importance of parts?
- Did you use topic sentences, summarizing sentences, and transitions to show how ideas relate to one another?
- Did you itemize (list) particularly important points for emphasis? Did you *number* one list only, using bullets or dashes to highlight the rest of the lists?

Graphics

- Did you help the reader understand your ideas though graphics that add value to your words? Graphics help make your report clearer and more interesting.

affect your writing or conclusions. Write so that you sound like a thoughtful person, but keep *personality* out of the report. Checklist 8–2 summarizes the main points of report style.

CONVENTIONAL PAGES IN FORMAL REPORTS

Once you have completed your research, organized and written the report, added graphics, and done all the revision needed on the body of the report, you still have a few pages left to write. At this point, you will write an executive summary of your investigation and findings, a letter or memo of transmittal to the reader, and a table of contents (and possibly a table of illustrations) to help guide the reader through the report. Unlike the body of the report, which may be single- or double-spaced, the transmittal and the summary should be single-spaced. You will also need to lay out the title page and choose a cover for the report. *Don't* expect to write the pages in the order the reader will see them. Even the preliminary pages can take a lot of time if you *design* too much before writing the body of the report. Exhibit 8–1 on page 228 shows you how the pages fit together.

FoxTrot

by Bill Amend

Write first; *then* design your report.

Cover Choices

Your employer may stock certain cover types or colors for specific kinds of reports. Some firms coordinate printing so that business cards, promotional material, and report covers all carry the same logo and are on similar paper.

In many small companies, the report writer has to decide on the cover. The reader will want a report that lies flat for reading ease. Thus, you should use a cover or binding method that allows the report to open and lie flat easily. A comb binding works well, as does the kind of purchased cover that has prongs in the binding to insert in punched holes. Perfect binding, such as used by *Reader's Digest,* can be folded flat with little difficulty. Both comb and perfect bindings are available at many large copy centers.

One kind of cover we do *not* recommend is the clear, colored plastic kind with the plastic spine; the spine can fall off thin papers and squeeze off thick papers and often slips off when the reader tries to fold the pages flat for ease of reading. Because many people need to read business reports with a pen in hand, they don't have a free hand to hold the pages down to keep the report open.

When setting the margins of the report, be sure to leave a little extra room on the left side to allow for the binding. Top, bottom, and right margins can be 1 inch (as in a memo or letter); however, the left margin should be 1¼ or 1½ inches or the reader may have trouble reading the print that's squeezed into the binding. WordPerfect®, for example, leaves a 1¼-inch margin for binding and can place the binding alternately on the left and right sides of the page if you plan to print the report with double-sided pages.

Always put the title of the report on the cover. The reader shouldn't have to open the report and look at the title page to see what the report is about. If the cover has a small window toward the top, place the title on the page underneath—called the *title fly*—so that it shows through. You can put a short title on the cover as long as it identifies the report. Most consultants also put the client's name and their firm's name. Doing so both identifies the report as written specifically for that client and gives the consultant some publicity.

Even if you are writing a report within your firm (and will use a memo of transmittal rather than a letter of transmittal), you need to identify the report topic on the cover. Imagine how much trouble it would be to find a specific report in a firm's library if all the reports had the same cover and no title!

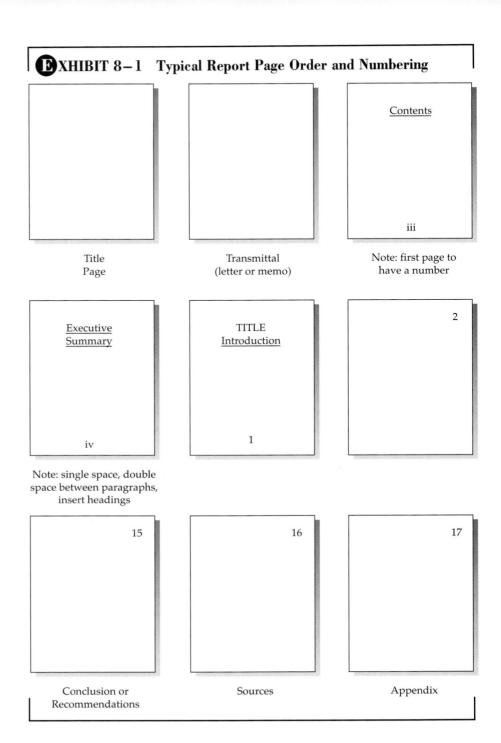

EXHIBIT 8–1   Typical Report Page Order and Numbering

Title Page

Transmittal (letter or memo)

Contents

iii

Note: first page to have a number

Executive Summary

iv

Note: single space, double space between paragraphs, insert headings

TITLE
Introduction

1

2

15

Conclusion or Recommendations

16

Sources

17

Appendix

Title Page

The first page of the report—the *title page*—should include the name of the report, the name of the authorizer (and usually this person's title), your name (and the firm's name if you are an outside consultant, or your title if you are writing for your own company), and the date of the report. In Exhibit 8–2, these items are centered and spaced so that the page looks balanced. If you are writing a group report, you usually put all the writers' names on the title page.

EXHIBIT 8–2 Sample Title Page

Emphasis on title of report

PLANNING A SUCCESSFUL
INCENTIVE PROGRAM

Tells who asked for the report

Prepared For

Roger L. Smith

Science Applications International Corporation

Gives names of writers

by

Successful Incentives Group

Contributing Authors:
Janice Monday
Eddie Clancy
Rose Wong

Date report was written

April 21, 1994

Letters of Authorization or Acceptance (Optional)

In formal reports, you may sometimes bind in the *letters of authorization or acceptance* from the authorizer. These are most common in reports written in response to a government request for proposal. The letter of acceptance is a type of contract certifying what has been agreed on by the authorizer and the writer. You will probably not write one of these letters for a class report.

Letter or Memo of Transmittal

Next is a *letter* or *memo of transmittal* (see Exhibits 8–3 and 8–4). Here you usually mention in the first paragraph that this is the complete report (and remind the reader of the topic in case he or she has assigned more than one report recently). Then you add one or more paragraphs giving some details about the report or the investigation, add a paragraph thanking the other people who helped on the report, and close with an offer to do more reporting projects in the future. Like a regular letter or memo, the transmittal is single-spaced.

Table of Contents

To give the reader a quick overview of the report, insert a *table of contents* listing headings from the finished report (see Exhibit 8–5). Be sure to list them exactly as they appear in the report. If you have room on the page, it's very helpful to include all the headings from the report. If the reader does not need every subheading, use the headings from every section down through the lowest level you want to include. In the complete report included at the end of this chapter, for example, if you include all the subheads under "Corporate Benefits of Employee Fitness Program," you cannot omit the same-level sub-heads under "Motivation." You may include Roman or decimal outline symbols in the table of contents or omit them altogether, especially if the heading positions show the relative importance of each heading.

Title this page simply *Contents,* since it's obviously a table. List only the beginning page numbers of each section (inclusive pages, such as "11–14," go only in an index, which the report will not include). Use leader dots to guide the reader's eye to the page number where the listed material appears; be sure to space the dots evenly so that they all line up. Right-justify the page numbers so that the last digits of all page numbers are aligned vertically as in Exhibit 8–5.

This:

Introduction	1
Body Text	2
Appendix	13

Not this (no spaces between dots):

Introduction	1
Body Text..	2
Appendix	13

And not this (dots not lined up vertically):

Introduction	1
Body text.	2
Appendix	13

And not this (right margin not aligned):

Introduction	1
Body Text	2
Appendix	13

TECHNOLOGIES, Inc.

Date: April 21, 1994

To: Ms. Howell, V.P. Human Resouces

From: Ad Hoc Committee on Newsletter Development

Subject: DEVELOPMENT OF A COMPANY NEWSLETTER

*Opens with
purpose of
report*
Here is the information on how to compile a company
newsletter.

*Explains plan
and coverage of
report*
This report summarizes the various aspects of a successful
newsletter. The details covered include not only the
content, but design, layout, and various computer programs
that are available to companies wishing to produce their own
newsletters.

*Ends with
future action*
When we make our presentation to the board of directors on
May 5, 1994, we will be able to answer any further questions
that may arise.

12511 Hightech Drive
Oakland, CA 74619
415 532 6439

R hodes
Engineering
Consortium

April 21, 1994

Ms. Judith Foster
Widgets International
1562 W. Palm Beach Lane
San Diego, CA 92105–7768

Dear Ms. Foster:

Opens with
purpose of
report

Here is the report you requested providing information on
initiating a successful joint venture in Japan.

Explains plan
of report

This report discusses cultural and social factors you will
face along with important aspects of the Japanese work
environment and job training.

Ends with
future action

We look forward to our presentation to your board of
directors on April 28, 1994.

Sincerely,

Brian Penzes

Brian Penzes
Project Manager

■ **2000 North Parkway**
Eugene, OR 97401
(503) 346-3461

CONTENTS

Preliminary section title not indented

Numbers flush right (tens columns lined up)

Section titles after body of report not indented

Table of Illustrations (Optional)

Because you are writing a problem-solving technical report, you will doubtless include some graphics to help the reader see your points more easily. Because these illustrations are important to the reader's understanding of the report, you may want to list them (1) in a separate *table of illustrations,* (2) at the end of the table of contents, or (3) in the table of contents within the sections where they appear.

Report graphics, which you learned how to design and prepare in Chapter 7, are often something the reader will want to look up quickly. Listing them in one of the three ways just given helps the reader use the information you have so carefully prepared. Exhibit 8–6 lists illustrations at the end of the table of contents; Exhibit 8–7 integrates them within the contents list.

Preface to Readers (Optional)

Sometimes one person will authorize you to write a report even though the report is to be written to other readers. Suppose the dean of your school asked you, one of last year's graduates who has landed a great job, to write a report for this year's seniors explaining how to succeed at job interviews. You would write the transmittal letter to the dean but could add a preface to the readers, the graduating seniors, explaining what the report will help them do. Writing a *preface* to readers gives you a chance to talk to the readers and prepare them for the information you have organized for them.

Executive Summary

The *executive summary* is a very important part of the report, because it presents your investigation and findings in an abbreviated form that can be sent, say, to all the branch offices of the company. Because many offices save paper by not printing multiple copies of reports, the summary serves almost as an advertisement for the entire report. After reading the summary, someone in another office might ask for the complete report. If he or she needed only the overview of the report, the summary alone could provide it.

To prepare the executive summary, put the title of the report at the top of the page (in case copies of the summary are sent out separately from the rest of the report). Then write a paragraph summarizing your investigation, conclusions, and recommendations. Follow with a paragraph or two on each major section of the report, using the same major headings used in the report. If you have written the report as part of a writing team, each member can summarize his or her section. Remember, though, that someone has to write the first paragraph that contains the overall summary. The executive summary, like the letter or memo of transmittal, is single-spaced. Exhibit 8–9 shows an executive summary.

Body of the Report

Numbering the Pages

All the preceding pages—the preliminaries to the body of the report—are numbered with small Roman numerals at the center bottom of each page, beginning with the table of contents, usually as page iii. The first page of the body of the report should have an Arabic numeral at the center bottom; successive pages are conventionally numbered in the upper right corner. All remaining pages have Arabic numerals, even those that follow the body of the report.

Introduction

The most important thing to remember about the introduction to the report is that it needs to introduce the report itself rather than the topic. As a result,

CONTENTS

FIGURES

VI. Telecommunication for the International Branches

    A. Private Lines vs. Frame Relay

    B. The X.25 Option

Illustrations listed in sections of report where they appear

        Figure 2: Comparison of X.25 Packet Switching and Frame Relay

        Figure 3: Comparison of Leased Lines and Frame Relay Services

    C. T1 Networks

        Figure 4: The New International Frame Relay Services

        Figure 5: Costs of Equipment Using Public Frame Relay

PREFACE

As a graduating senior in the College of Business Administration, you are entering a final phase of your education: finding an appropriate job in which you can apply your training and experience. An important part of this job search process is interviewing successfully.

This report, written by last year's graduates, will give you practical advice on how to interview well. The topics discussed are:

—preparing for your on-campus interview,

—writing thank-you notes to interviewers,

—planning for your second interview,

—choosing which offer to accept, and

—acceptance and rejection letters.

Title of report repeated so page could be separately reproduced

IMPROVE INTERNAL COMMUNICATION WITH A CORPORATE NEWSLETTER

Executive Summary

Publishing a newsletter will give Amalgamated Manufacturing many benefits. It is an excellent medium for communication between management and employees and also an excellent way to improve employee morale.

Conclusion given in first paragraph

In a large company like Amalgamated, the Human Resources Department is the most logical publisher of the newsletter. Because it will be an internal newsletter, we won't have to use the mail for distribution. Distributing the newsletter with employee paychecks is the most efficient and cost effective means of distribution.

The frequency of our newsletter is also very important. Sending a newsletter out once every quarter is probably the minimum we should consider.

Headings included to guide reader

Content

The content of a newsletter can either improve or damage internal relations with employees. People are more concerned with stories affecting their jobs than stories of personal news. A variety and balance of stories and their themes will maintain reader interest.

Management must ensure that the tone of the newsletter makes the readers feel that they are getting complete and honest information. Management must not use the newsletter in a condescending manner to employees; this will only succeed in damaging internal relations.

The name of the newsletter needs to relate to all employees in the organization. A survey of employees before starting the newsletter helps to determine what they want to see in it.

Design and Layout

A two-column, four-page newsletter works best. The newsletter should have a well-chosen title, with conservative application of color, white space, and art.

Details

The software package used to produce the newsletter will be the deciding factor of many of the details of the newsletter. Type fonts and sizes, spacing between columns and sentences are all details that are controlled by the software package that we choose.

the introduction will practically write itself. You don't need to be clever or creative—just tell the reader

- What the report is about.
- What kind of investigating you did (briefly).
- Any limitations that arose (not just time and money, which affect nearly every report).
- (Optional) Some background on why the topic is important to the company.
- The plan of the report.

A typical introduction is between a half-page and a full page long. Remember, you don't need to tell much about the topic itself. The purpose of the introduction is to set up the report for the reader. Then you can talk about the topic and how you went about solving the assigned problem.

You can add some background about the problem and research method. However, such information should not take more than one paragraph, or at most two. If the background is so important that it would require one or more pages, make it the next section of the report. If the research method needs to be described so that someone else could replicate your work (perform the same experiment following your instructions), put the entire detailed description in an appendix and briefly summarize it in the introduction.

Keep remembering audience analysis: Don't tell the readers more than they need to know to understand your findings. In particular, don't give more background than necessary just because it is easy information to gather. If you are writing the report as an outside consultant, for example, you certainly don't need to tell readers the history of their own company! In dividing material for a classroom team report, plan to put background material in an appendix so that everyone in the group can participate in analysis of your findings rather than having one person do only information gathering.

Exhibits 8–10 through 8–12 illustrate several ways to set up the introduction. Exhibit 8–13 shows an introduction with some pitfalls to avoid.

As in longer letters and memos, use descriptive headings to guide the reader. Avoid generic headings such as "Findings" that give the reader little or no information.

Choosing Effective Headings

Use headings like those in the sample report at the end of the chapter:

- Costs of Employee Fitness Program.
- Corporate Benefits of Employee Fitness Program.
- Employee Benefits of Employee Fitness Program.

Repeating words in parallel headings (such as "Employee Fitness Program" in the sample report) helps the reader see the flow of information from one area to another.

Use several levels of headings, as described in Chapter 2. You want the reader to be able to see that a major heading is coming up or that the new material is a subpart of the section he or she just finished reading.

Be sure to underline or boldface all the headings so they stand out from the double-spaced text. You can leave an extra space before the major (second-level) headings to set these main sections off even more. *Don't* start each main section on a new page. Many books start a new page for each chapter, but reports, being shorter, don't need the extra space.

I.   EMPLOYEE TURNOVER

Opens with
purpose

This report presents information to help you retain current and
future employees.

Covers
method of
investigation

We have gathered our information from current literature on the
topic of reducing employee turnover. Because biotechnology is a
relatively new field, little specific, industry-related data
exists. We have included both this specific information and more
general information about reducing employee turnover as it
relates to biotechnology.

Ends with
plan of
report

We have included statistics that illustrate the importance of
retaining employees; how to hire the "right" employee for the
job; how to specifically and cost-effectively train new
employees; how to make them feel a part of your company's
culture; and how to reward them for a job well done.

1.0   INTRODUCTION

Covers
purpose and
plan in one
paragraph

This report will help you decide whether to design new automobile
insurance forms. We discuss why having efficient, easy-to-use
forms is important for your business. We include a list of basic
elements found in good forms design and apply these elements in
designing specific automobile insurance documents for you. We
then show how to adapt these documents to your computer system.

Arriving at Recommendations   If you are writing an analytical report, you will provide the reader(s) with
recommendations. Although recommendations usually propose a course of
action, occasionally you might tell the reader *not* to take the course of action
you have investigated. For example, if you were investigating whether a company should computerize a part of its operation, you might conclude that the
cost is too high at this time. This gives the company officers useful information
as well as background material when they look at the issue again in a few years,
when the company is larger.

INTRODUCTION

Opens with
purpose

In this report I have gathered information about interactive videodisc (IVD) training, a new form of training on the cutting edge of technology. Report sections cover:

Itemizes the
plan of the
report

        --what IVD is
        --how IVD works
        --advantages of videodisc training
        --cost analysis
        --effects of videodisc instruction

Ends with
action (leaves
decision up to
reader)

After reading this report, you will be able to decide to what extent videodisc training can help FIG Manufacturing.

EXHIBIT 8–13   **A Vague Introduction**

INTRODUCTION

Introduction
on topic, not
report

According to Joseph Duffus in <u>Consumers' Research Magazine</u> (October 1991), until recently, Electronic Information Services could only be accessed in the closed world of corporations and universities. As more and more Americans are acquiring personal computers and modems, online services have proliferated. These services are being used for a variety of purposes at home and in businesses.

Plan is
vague and
costs are
unclear

This report presents detailed analysis of available electronic information services and gives examples of applications in key areas as defined by your clients' specific needs. As costs of using online services vary considerably, we briefly summarize startup costs and usage rates for each of the services we recommend.

TABLE OF CONTENTS

Appendices are listed at the end of the report contents so reader knows where they are if needed

iii

If you are writing an informational report, you provide a summary and conclusions, even though you do not recommend a course of action to readers.

Many reports have *appendices* or *exhibits* to enable readers (or sometimes secondary readers, to whom the report is passed on) to see additional information that isn't necessary to support the conclusions but is nevertheless useful. For example, if your report compared several software packages to help a client decide which one to use, you would discuss the comparison and the client's criteria in the body of the report and attach as appendices vendor brochures on the software features, software reviews, and so on.

Appendices or Exhibits

In our sample report, the appendices include fitness center schedules, newsletters, and the questionnaires used to help define the employees' needs in a fitness program. The contents of these items are discussed in the body of the report, but the reader need not see them to make a decision. We omitted them from the report to save space, but you can see the complete listing in the table of contents.

If you have a number of appendices, you might want to label each item so the reader can find different pieces easily, especially if they include items that do not fit the $8\frac{1}{2}'' \times 11''$ format, like brochures. You can put on tabs or cover sheets, or list the appendices in the table of contents and then number the pages for easy reference. Exhibit 8–14 shows a contents page that lists the appendices at the end. If you are using the kind of technical topic outline described later in this chapter, the exhibits, which will be short reports in themselves, will need titles and consecutive page numbers and should be listed in the table of contents.

For your *source list,* use a title like "References Cited," "References Consulted," "Source List," "List of Sources Consulted," "Helpful Sources," or "Bibliography." Use whichever documentation method your instructor recommends (we describe and give examples of MLA, APA, and Chicago *Manual of Style* in Appendix C). The sample report at the end of this chapter contains APA-style source notations.

Source List

Checklist 8–3 lists potential problem areas—use it as you begin to revise your report.

Report Revision Checklist

The outlines shown in Exhibits 8–5, 8–6, and 8–7 are common ways of organizing a formal report. Here is another method, often used in technical fields such as engineering:

A CONVENTIONAL TECHNICAL TOPIC OUTLINE

Title page
Letter of transmittal
Table of contents
Table of illustrations
Executive summary
Body of report
   Introduction
   Discussion and evaluation of exhibits
   Conclusion
   Exhibits (entire subreports, such as environmental impact reports)
Source list

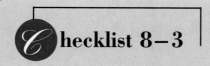

Checklist 8–3

Report Revision

Cover

- Will the cover lie flat when opened?
- Does the title show on the cover?
- Is the cover attractive?

Title Page

Does the title page include the following information?

- Descriptive title of report
- Specific audience for report
- Name(s) of writer(s)
- Date of report

Table of Contents

- Are page numbers flush right?
- Are only first pages of sections given? (Inclusive pages are for indexes.)
- Are leader dots every other space (not every space)?
- Are consistent levels of headings shown?
- Is the page titled *Contents?*
- Is the page the first numbered page and given page number iii?

Executive Summary

- Does it begin with a summary paragraph?
- Does it include the major report headings?
- Is each section summarized in a meaningful paragraph or two?
- Are pages numbered with small Roman numerals?

Body of Report

- Are headings other than *Introduction, Conclusion,* and *Recommendations* descriptive and helpful to the reader?
- Do main headings (second and third level) have spaces above and below them?
- Are the headings in predictable places to help guide the reader?
- Does the *introduction* describe the report content and plan rather than the topic itself?
- Does the *conclusion* tie main points together?
- Are the *recommendations* (if any) a specific list of actions to take next?

Graphics

- Is each graphic numbered and labeled (*Table* for tables, *Figure* or *Exhibit* for all other graphics)?
- Is each graphic placed as close as possible to its discussion?
- Is each graphic introduced, integrated into the text, and then discussed to put it in context for the reader?
- Is each graphic the appropriate size for the information it presents?
- Are labels on the graphics readable?
- Is color used well?
- If a graphic is not original, is the source given?

Sources

- Are sources given in a consistent format (MLA, APA, etc.)?

Appendices

- Do appendices (if any) contain information readers would like to see but do not have to see?
- Are they listed either on the contents page or on a separate cover sheet?

SAMPLE REPORT   The sample report on pages 245–263 will give you an idea of what a completed report looks like. We adapted it from a real-life student report to serve as a model for you to follow when setting up your report. We added annotations and comments to help you see how the authors investigated, organized, and wrote up their findings.

DEVELOPING A FITNESS COMPONENT OF
OUR WELLNESS PROGRAM

Prepared for:
Jim Johnson, HR Director

by
Catherine Morgan & Linda Mason
April 23, 1994

```
To:    Jim Johnson, Human Resources Director
From:  Catherine Morgan and Linda Mason
Subj:  Proposed Physical Fitness Program
Date:  April 23, 1994
```

Following our March 19 schedule, here is our report, Developing a
Fitness Component of Our Wellness Program.

After researching the benefits of an employee fitness program and
developing selection criteria from an employee survey, we
interviewed representatives of three local fitness facilities --
Family Fitness Centers, Gold's Gym, and Holiday Spa. We recommend
Family Fitness, and our report details a two-step plan of action
consisting of implementation and fitness program evaluation.

If you have any questions or would like us to prepare the visuals
for next week's presentation at the Board of Directors' meeting,
please let us know.

TABLE OF CONTENTS

iv

EXECUTIVE SUMMARY

FITNESS FACILITY RECOMMENDATION

To begin the fitness component of our wellness program, we recommend subsidizing employees' memberships at Family Fitness Centers. Based on a comparison of three San Diego fitness facilities, Family Fitness provides multiple locations and flexible child care services at a comparatively reasonable cost. The staff is CPR-certified, and the center reinforces wellness values, a necessary complement to our existing program.

We recommend that the corporation pay the $90 initiation fee and half of the $14 monthly dues for each employee. Based on a 60 percent participation rate, the total corporate costs are $1,890.00 for the initiation fee plus $2,268.00 in annual dues.

Implementation will be accomplished in two stages, pre-enrollment and enrollment. We recommend an evaluation of the fitness program at six months from implementation to measure its impact upon: absenteeism and productivity, turnover, job satisfaction, and health care costs.

BACKGROUND

The fitness facility location decision involves choosing between an on-site or off-site facility. Because of low financial commitment, limited employer liability, and minimal participation requirements, we chose an off-site program with corporate sponsorship. Operating costs include health screening, programs, and incentives.

Studies have demonstrated that exercise results in many corporate benefits, such as: reduced absenteeism, improved job satisfaction, reduced turnover, improved productivity, and reduced health care costs. Employee benefits include improved morale, reduced stress, and improved self-image.

To bolster participation, we need to use motivation techniques, which can be voluntary, mandatory, and/or incentive-based.

FITNESS FACILITY SELECTION CRITERIA

Upon completion of an employee survey, we developed seven fitness facility criteria: accessibility, variety of exercise options, child care, cost, safety, extensive hours of operation, and wellness values.

v

<u>FITNESS FACILITY COMPARISON</u>

We conducted personal interviews with representatives of Family Fitness, Gold's Gym, and Holiday Spa. Although similar with regard to exercise options and hours of operation, they differed primarily in accessibility, availability of child care, and cost.

vi

This report will describe a recommended solution to our employee problems of increased absenteeism, reduced job satisfaction, increased turnover, reduced productivity, and increased health care costs. We believe that an employee fitness program is our answer and would reflect the company's concern for the well-being of its workers. This report will provide information on corporate physical fitness research, various fitness facility location options and our recommendation, fitness facility selection criteria, fitness facility comparison, our recommendation, and a plan of action.

We reviewed the literature on employee fitness programs and interviewed managers at appropriate fitness centers. We restricted the analysis to three major chains because these offered the greatest the greatest range of opportunities for our widespread local employee base.

Recent employee statistics indicate concerns in the areas of absenteeism, job satisfaction, turnover, productivity, and health care costs. Although we currently have a "wellness" program, we do not have a physical fitness component. After extensive research, we have found studies that show exercise has a positive effect on addressing these five problems.

COSTS AND BENEFITS OF FITNESS

According to the National Association of Governors' Council on Physical Fitness in Business, "employees in fitness programs have lower turnover rates; lower absenteeism--one to four fewer sick days a year; lower health care costs--saving $100 to $1,000 per year, per employee; and fewer hospital and rehabilitation days after injury" (Adler, 1990, p. 14).

Based on our research, numerous studies substantiate the positive effects of physical fitness for both the employer and employee. We will discuss both corporate and employee costs and benefits of the employee fitness program. We will conclude with employee motivation techniques.

COSTS OF EMPLOYEE FITNESS PROGRAM

The Fitness Facility Location Decision Companies that offer an exercise program to their employees must decide upon an off-site or on-site location for the fitness facility. Hoffman and Hobson suggest that there are essentially three location alternatives:

1. Off-site Program with Corporate Sponsorship
   Employees join an off-site fitness facility and

1

participate in facility developed programs with membership fees subsidized by the employer;

2. <u>Off-site Facility with Corporate Sponsorship and Organization</u> The employer negotiates with an off-site facility to make it available to employees during certain hours and assumes a greater responsibility for fitness program development; and

3. <u>On-site Program with Total Corporate Involvement</u> The employer develops an employee fitness center and comprehensive program at the workplace (1984, pp. 101-102).

Table 1 compares the decision criteria with the type of program.

Criterion		Off-Site Program	Off-Site Facility	On-Site Program	
Cost & Corporate Commitment	+	Low	Medium	High	−
Employer Liability	+	Low	Medium	High	−
Control of Participation & Progress	−	Low	Medium	High	+
Participation Minimum	+	Low	Medium	High	−

Table 1: Off-Site vs. On-Site Decision Criteria.

As you can see, each choice has advantages and disadvantages. The off-site program with corporate sponsorship has the lowest financial commitment, minimizes employer liability for employee injuries, and does not require a minimum number of participants to be economically feasible. However, the employer has the least control over employee participation and progress. In contrast, the on-site program with total corporate involvement maximizes an employer's ability to monitor employee participation and progress, but it requires the greatest financial and participation commitments and exposes the employer to the greatest potential liability. The off-site facility with corporate sponsorship and organization occupies a moderate position with respect to cost, liability, control, and participation.

<u>Location Recommendation</u> Corporate fitness programs range from reimbursement for off-site fitness memberships to on-site construction of elaborate million-dollar fitness facilities. For example, UNUM Life Insurance offers its field employees a $250

reimbursement when they participate in exercise classes at the fitness facility of their choice (Maxey, 1991, p. 11C). At the other extreme, Tenneco built a two-story, 100,000-square-foot fitness facility for $11 million, and PepsiCo Inc. created a N.Y. health complex at a cost of $2 million (Gatty, 1985, p. 19).

Since we are just beginning the fitness phase of our current wellness program and are unable to provide the funding necessary for the development of an on-site fitness center, we recommend an off-site fitness program with corporate sponsorship. This would limit our financial commitment and potential liability while providing an opportunity to assess the impact of exercise upon our workforce. Although tracking employee participation will be more difficult, we can develop a questionnaire to adequately monitor employee progress. In addition, our mobile sales force would receive greater benefit from using multiple off-site facilities than using one on-site center.

Operating Costs Health screening, programs, and incentives are the primary operating costs for an employee fitness program (Chang & Boyle, 1989, p. 46). We will discuss these three areas later in the report.

CORPORATE BENEFITS OF EMPLOYEE FITNESS PROGRAM

Reduced Absenteeism According to Employee Benefit Plan Review (Fitness, 1989, pp. 38-39), General Electric (GE) Company, Cincinnati, Ohio, performed a study on employees who participate in fitness or recreation programs. It randomly selected 900 employees who were divided into four groups: fitness center members; recreation program members; members of both; and nonmembers. GE defined absenteeism to include both sick days and personal days (other than vacation) and used personnel files to measure it. The results demonstrated that nonmembers missed an average of nine days per year while members--of either or both programs--missed an average of about five days per year.

In support of the findings of the GE study, the results of the 1983 and 1985 National Health Interview Surveys revealed that "physical activity is one of a few factors that have a statistically significant effect on absenteeism" (p. 40). And, as a result of this study, General Electric cites estimated annual savings in excess of $2.8 million due to reduced absenteeism (p. 40).

Another example of reduced absenteeism is Johnson & Johnson's "Live for Life" program. According to Shenk (1989, p. 37), employees at locations with the program experienced 18 percent lower absenteeism rates than employees at locations without the program.

Improved Job Satisfaction To determine job satisfaction,

GE, described in the above section, distributed questionnaires to the 900 employees. According to Employee Benefit Plan Review (Fitness, p. 40), dissatisfaction measures centered on the job environment and "examined salary, working conditions, company policies and administration, and interpersonal relations." Job satisfaction was based on "motivation factors that influence a positive job attitude, such as achievement, recognition, responsibility, and advancement." The results of this study revealed that nonmembers measured significantly less job satisfaction than members in either or both programs.

Reduced Turnover. Fitness programs also pay off in the intangible areas of retention and recruiting since a perceived pleasant working environment can retain as well as recruit employees (Chang & Boyle, p. 47).

- According to Lockheed, its turnover rate is 13% lower among regular exercisers (Chang & Boyle, p. 47).

- The GE study, cited above, concluded that satisfied employees are likely to have lower turnover rates (Fitness, p. 40).

Improved Productivity. Based on research conducted at Tenneco, Inc., William B. Baun, manager of health and fitness, states, "in a corporation with a health and fitness program, a positive association exists between above-average job performance and exercise adherence, and a negative association exists between poor job performance and [poor] exercise adherence" (Gatty, p. 19). The reason for this is that fitness requires discipline.

A 1986 study of Mesa Petroleum's company-sponsored fitness program supports these findings (Keaton & Semb, 1990, p. 81). In 1982 and 1983, the estimated productivity difference between participants and nonparticipants totaled $700,000 and $1.3 million, respectively. "These figures represent company gains in net income due to increased productivity resulting from less absenteeism and a more positive mental attitude among the employees who participated" (p. 81).

Reduced Health Care Costs. Many companies are finding that it makes more sense to prevent illness rather than spend money on health care bills (Adler, p. 14).

- "AT&T's health care costs are $3 million a day for employees, dependents, and retirees" (Adler, p. 14)

- According to Chang and Boyle, "When each of the Fortune 500 companies are losing an average of $88 million a year to employee illness and more than $100 million a year for employee medical coverage, health and fitness promotion becomes a wise investment" (p. 46).

- Johnson & Johnson reported that employees who had access to its "Live for Life" program for two-and-a-half years had 40 percent lower hospitalization costs than employees at sites without the program (Trenk, p. 37).

- In 1984, Mesa Petroleum's management estimated that nonparticipants in its fitness program averaged $434 per person in medical costs. Participants averaged only $173 each--a savings of approximately $200,000 in company-wide medical expenses (Keaton & Semb, p. 81).

EMPLOYEE BENEFITS OF EMPLOYEE FITNESS PROGRAM

The SHRM Foundation conducted a study of employees in a fitness program with Industrial Products Producer and Financial Institution Processing Center (Parett & Whitney, 1990, p. 81). In response to a questionnaire, employees from both companies reported benefits, displayed in Figure 1, attained through their programs.

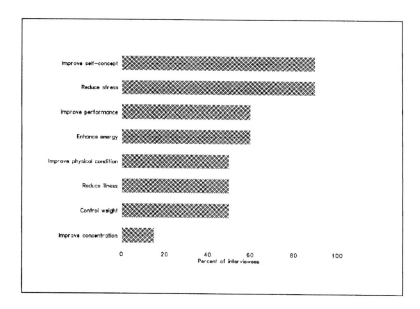

Figure 1: Benefits Reported by Those Who Exercise.

According to Parett and Whitney, a company must consider not only directly measurable financial payback but also indirect measurement and judgment to decide about fitness programs (p. 84).

Table 2 incorporates both employer and employee benefits by time frame.

Time Frame		Benefits	Accrue to:
Short term	3-4 months	--Improved physical fitness --Reduced health risks	Employee
Intermediate term	1 year	--Reduced absenteeism --Improved employee morale	Employer
		--Developed and improved self-image and self-confidence	Employee
Long term	>3-5 years	--Increased productivity and overall organizational effectiveness --Decreased health care costs	Employer

Table 2: Employer and Employee Fitness Benefits by Time Frame

Fitness programs also pay off in intangible ways such as increasing employee morale. As you can see in Table 2, it is only in the long term (three to five years minimum) that the corporation truly receives the benefits of sponsoring a fitness program (Hoffman & Hobson, p. 110).

MOTIVATION

According to Hoffman and Hobson (pp. 103-104), we can motivate employees to join fitness programs in three ways:

Voluntary This method is optimal because it is the simplest and least costly. Employees participate because they want to participate out of self-interest. The employees' primary motivating force is personal rather than organizational benefit.

Mandatory Although controversial, this method is used widely in Japan. Employees participate in daily calisthenics sessions to promote fitness.

Incentives Employers can use financial rewards to stimulate and encourage participation. They pay bonuses for achieving and/or maintaining a desired level of fitness. In some companies, employees are paid for their time spent working out. Also, some employers pay workers on a piece-meal rate--a predetermined fee for each mile run, each push-up, and/or each pound lost. This method encourages not only participation but also achievement.

Table 3 is an employee action and maximum monetary incentive schedule used at Mesa Limited Partnership. In 1986, it paid $115,000 in physical fitness bonuses to its employees (Keaton & Semb, p. 83).

Employee Action	Cash Incentive (Maximum)
Complete written test and submit to glucose, cholesterol, and blood pressure checks.	$240
A spouse who participates in the major medical program and fulfills all requirements.	216
Exercise three times per week (as verified by attendance records).	36
A full year without absenteeism.	72
Bonus for full year without absenteeism.	36
A full year without a major medical claim.	72
Nonsmoker.	36
Meeting established fitness goals.	220
TOTAL	$928

Table 3: Mesa Limited Partnership Employee Physical Fitness Actions and Cash Incentives

Other examples of incentives include:

- Employees of Townsend Engineering, a designer and manufacturer of meat processing equipment, earn points toward winning a $200 credit toward items purchased from a sporting goods store or services provided by a travel agency (Maxey, p. 11C).

- Kurt Malicki, President of Pegasus Personal Fitness Centers, Dallas, asks his employees to make a list of rewards ranging from $25 to $200 that they'd like to receive for reaching weekly and monthly goals. Some of these rewards are concert tickets, limousine rentals, and half days off. These customized incentives have resulted in its sales doubling since 1985. "They know what motivates them better than I do, so I just ask!" (Tailor-made, 1991, p. 76).

FITNESS FACILITY SELECTION CRITERIA

In a recent survey, employees were asked to indicate the most important features of a fitness facility. From their responses, we developed the following criteria for selecting an off-site center:

1. <u>Accessibility</u> The center(s) must be conveniently located with respect to the office, their homes, and field sales call locations. Employees stated that easy accessibility would increase their participation and motivation.

2. <u>Variety of Exercise Options</u> The facility should offer our employees exercise options ranging from aerobics and racquetball to weight machines and free weight training.

3. <u>Child Care</u> Over half the employees ranked babysitting services as an important feature. Both working couples and single parents felt that the availability of child care would increase their participation in an exercise program.

4. <u>Cost</u> The fitness facility must be reasonably priced. Most respondents indicated that the fitness membership would be a useful employee benefit only if the employer paid the initiation fee and a portion of the monthly dues.

5. <u>Safety</u> Since some employees will be starting exercise programs after a long period of inactivity, they are concerned about the initial health assessment and fitness staff training qualifications.

6. <u>Extensive Hours of Operation</u> The facility should have early morning, late night, and weekend hours to accommodate the various work schedules.

7. <u>Wellness Values</u> Employees expressed an interest in a fitness facility that focuses upon wellness rather than hard-core training.

FITNESS FACILITY COMPARISON

We visited three of the well-known fitness facilities in San Diego County and conducted personal interviews to gather information on features and services. Each fitness facility was judged according to the criteria developed from our employee survey.

Family Fitness, Gold's Gym, and Holiday Spa all provide a wide variety of exercise options including cardiovascular and weight training exercises. The aerobics classes cater to all ability levels, and their free weights are comprehensive. All three offer extensive hours of operation seven days a week with early morning, late night, and weekend hours. Appendix A provides a detailed description of the three facilities' programs and services, and Appendix B provides their aerobics schedules. Appendix C is a Holiday Spa brochure.

Table 4 highlights the differentiating features of the three fitness centers based on our criteria (Archuleta, 1992; Marmet, 1992; Moore, 1992; Slancik, 1992).

Criterion	Family Fitness	Gold's Gym	Holiday Spa
Accessibility			
Closest Club	El Cajon	El Cajon	Mission Valley
San Diego Clubs	10 Family Fitness	Must use only club of enrollment	2 Holiday Clubs
Affiliated Clubs	IPFA & APFC	IPFA	APFC
Child Care			
Hours	Every day	Every day except Sunday	None
Rates	$1.50 per hour	$1.50 per hour $1.00/hour additional child Monthly child care passes	
Cost per Employee	$90 initiation fee (waived every 4th member) + $14/month dues	$149 initiation fee (5 or more members) + $19/month dues	$359 for first year. Following years $2/month dues
Safety			
Certification	CPR, in house training	National certification	In-house training
Health Assessment	Self-reported, counseling	Exercise physiologist	Self-reported, counseling
Wellness Values	Newsletter, nutrition seminars	Nutritional analysis	None

Table 4: Fitness Center Comparison.

Accessibility is limited for both Gold's Gym and Holiday Spa. Gold's Gym requires that members exercise only in the club of enrollment when they are within San Diego County but allows them to use any of the numerous International Physical Fitness

Association (IPFA) health clubs when traveling. Although Holiday allows you to use any of its fitness facilities, it has only two locations in San Diego County. The closest facility to our El Cajon office is located in Mission Valley, while the other is in National City. When traveling, Holiday Spa members can use any clubs affiliated through the Association of Physical Fitness Centers (APFC). In contrast, the Family Fitness membership entitles the employee to use any of the ten facilities in San Diego County and both IPFA and APFC health clubs when traveling. Appendix D provides the local sites of the fitness centers.

The availability of child care is an important consideration for our employees. Although Holiday Spa does not provide this service, both Family Fitness and Gold's Gym offer a variety of hours at reasonable prices. Notice that only Family Fitness provides Sunday hours, and only Gold's Gym offers reduced rates for additional children and monthly child care passes.

With respect to cost, Family Fitness and Holiday Spa offer the most affordable exercise memberships. Total first-year costs at Family Fitness are $258.00 per employee ($90.00 initiation fee plus $14 monthly dues), and the initiation fee is waived for every fourth corporate member. The annual cost for subsequent years is $168.00 per employee. Holiday Spa offers a special membership with first-year costs of $359.00 and annual renewals of just $24.00 per employee. In contrast, Gold's Gym offers the most expensive membership with first-year costs of $377.00 ($149.00 initiation plus $19 monthly dues) and subsequent annual costs of $228.00 per employee. (Note: These fees would be our programs and health screening operating costs.)

Safety is a concern of currently inactive employees. Holiday Spa staff reviews a preexercise health questionnaire with each new member, and staff members must complete an in-house training program. Although this is adequate, we were more impressed with Family Fitness and Gold's Gym requirements. In addition to the health questionnaire and in-house training, each employee at Family Fitness must be certified in CPR. At Gold's Gym, new members meet with an exercise physiologist to determine heart rate, blood pressure, body measurements, flexibility, and lung capacity.

The reinforcement of wellness values links the fitness component to our current wellness program. While Holiday Spa focuses mainly upon exercise, Family Fitness and Gold's Gym stress the total wellness of its members. Family Fitness produces a monthly newsletter with health promotion articles, offers periodic nutrition seminars, and is presently constructing a wellness center within the El Cajon fitness center. Appendix E is a sample newsletter. Gold's Gym provides personalized nutrition counseling to complement its personalized exercise program. Appendix F describes its nutritional analysis.

FITNESS FACILITY RECOMMENDATION

Based upon the comparison of fitness facility features and services, we recommend offering our employees memberships at Family Fitness Centers. This facility offers our employees maximum flexibility in selecting an exercise location and the convenience of child care seven days a week. The Family Fitness staff is CPR-certified, and the center reinforces wellness values through its monthly newsletter and nutrition seminars.

These benefits can be offered to our employees at a comparatively reasonable cost. We recommend that our company pay the $90 initiation fee and half of the $14 monthly dues. Family Fitness waives the initiation fee for every fourth corporate membership. Table 5 shows the cost to our company with various levels of employee participation.

Employee Participation	Number of Members	Total Initiation Cost	Corporate Share of Monthly Dues
40%	18	$1,260	$126
50%	23	$1,620	$161
60%	**27**	**$1,890**	**$189**
70%	32	$2,160	$224
80%	36	$2,430	$252
90%	41	$2,790	$287
100%	45	$3,060	$315

Table 5: Corporate Cost Depends Upon Employee Participation

Based upon our estimate that 60% of our 45 employees will be interested in joining, the total corporate cost will be $1,890 for the initiation fee plus $2,268 in annual dues.

PLAN OF ACTION

Implementation   The fitness component of our wellness program will be implemented in two stages:

1. Pre-enrollment
   - Develop an incentive system to encourage ongoing participation
   - Conduct introductory employee meetings to announce the fitness program

- Publicize the fitness component in company correspondences
- Meet with employees to discuss the benefits of exercise and exercise safety
- Compile past data on employee absenteeism, turnover, and health care costs
- Conduct a pre-test measurement of employee job satisfaction

2. <u>Enrollment</u>
   - Arrange group enrollment times with Family Fitness
   - Arrange group tours of the facility with Family Fitness
   - Ensure that each employee has completed a health questionnaire and is receiving personalized exercise programming

<u>Fitness Program Evaluation</u> We recommend an evaluation of the fitness program at six months from implementation to measure its impact upon the following employee variables:

- <u>Absenteeism and Productivity</u>
  Check employee time cards, and use salary information to assess productivity changes.

- <u>Turnover</u>
  Examine employment records.

- <u>Employee Job Satisfaction and Perceived Benefits from Exercise</u>
  Use questionnaires in Appendices G and H.

- <u>Health Care Costs</u>
  Compare health care claim costs with previous time periods.

A complete analysis after six months should give us an initial indication of the viability of this program. To accomplish this, we will use Appendix G, a pre- and post-exercise job satisfaction questionnaire, to measure employees' job satisfaction. Also, to see how often employees are using Family Fitness and gather their perceptions of exercise benefits, we will use the questionnaire in Appendix H.

As described in Table 2, we should be aware of the short-, intermediate-, and long- term benefits from an employee fitness program. Although the six-month evaluation will serve as a benchmark for progress, a true cost/benefit analysis is not possible unless the corporation takes a long-term perspective.

SOURCE LIST

Adler, S. (1990, May 21). Employers celebrate employee fitness. <u>Business Insurance</u>, p. 14.

Archuleta, G. Membership Counselor, Gold's Gym, El Cajon, CA. (1992, March 28). Personal interview.

Chang, O. H., & Boyle, C. (1989, January). Fitness programs: Hefty expense or wise investment? <u>Management Accounting</u>, p. 45-50.

Fitness programs can reduce employer costs. (1989). <u>Employee Benefit Plan Review</u> (5), 38-44.

Gatty, B. (1985). How fitness works out. <u>Nation's Business</u>, <u>73</u>, 18-24.

Hoffman, J. J., Jr., & Hobson, C. J. (1984). Physical fitness and employee effectiveness. <u>Personnel Administrator</u>, <u>29</u>, 101-113.

Keaton, P. N., & Semb, M. J. (1990, September). Shaping up the bottom line. <u>HR Magazine</u>, pp. 81-86.

Marmet, D., Assistant Manager, Family Fitness Centers, El Cajon, CA. (1992, March 23). Personal interview.

Maxey, B. (1991, April 29). Employer, employees gain in wellness program. <u>Journal of Commerce</u>, p. 11C.

Moore, D., Manager, Holiday Spa, Mission Valley, San Diego, CA. (1992, March 26). Personal interview.

Parett, C. M., & Whitney, G. G. (1990, December). Exercise makes employees work better. <u>HR Magazine</u>, pp. 81-84.

Physical fitness & employee effectiveness. (1984). <u>Personnel Administrator</u>, <u>29</u>, 101-113.

Slancik, K., Corporate Accounts Manager, Holiday Spa, Huntington Beach, CA. (1992, April 3). Telephone interview.

Tailor-made rewards. (1991, February). <u>Inc.</u>, p. 76.

Trenk, B. S. (1989, August). Corporate fitness programs become hearty investments. <u>Management Review</u>, pp. 33-37.

Writing a long report requires more organization because you have more material to work with. However, you use the same good writing skills you have developed in writing shorter messages.

REVIEW

First, plan your report:

- Identify the audience, purpose, and due date.
- Decide what the report will cover.

- Determine how long the report will take to prepare and in what order the parts must be completed.
- Decide who will write each part of the report, if it is a team project.
- Determine the report style (layout, writing style).

Then start the report-writing process:

- Begin your research and collect your source list for the final report.
- Organize your findings and write the report introduction.
- Write up your results into the body of the report.
- Form conclusions and recommendations, if appropriate.
- Enhance your report with graphics.
- Write the preliminary pages of the report (summary, transmittal, table of contents, title page).
- Revise for most effective layout design and writing style.

Use the writing style most effective for the reader and circumstances of this particular report.

The best look for the report will include:

- A cover with the report title.
- Easy-to-read type.
- Consistent headings.
- Appropriate graphics elements.

The best sound for the report will include:

- Specific, clear, active words.
- Words the reader will understand.
- Active voice.
- Relatively short sentences and paragraphs.
- Topic sentences, summarizing sentences, and transitions.
- Itemizing of important points.
- Graphic elements that will help the reader understand the report.

Your report should include these elements:

- Title page, with name of authorizer, author(s), and date.
- Letter of authorization or acceptance (optional).
- Letter or memo of transmittal.
- Table of contents.
- Table of illustrations (optional).
- Preface to readers (optional).
- Executive summary.
- Body of report
- Introduction.
- Data, findings, and discussion.
- Conclusion and recommendations (if any).
- Appendices or exhibits.
- Source list.

APPLICATION EXERCISES

1. Using the Report Process checklist on page 224, write out the first five steps for the topic you have chosen for the class report. How does your audience affect the style you will use?

2. Put the following headings in logical order. Then place them on a page so that the reader can see which are second-, third-, and fourth-level headings.

   Form Number

   Logical Grouping of Data

   Instructions for Using the Form

   Technical Functions

   Procedural Functions

   Establishing a Forms Program

   Documenting Information Flows

   Forms Design and Layout

   Forms Control Group

   Administrative Functions

   Name of Form

   Proper Use of Graphics

3. Find examples of two different styles of business writing. Explain how the styles differ. Then tell why the styles fit their respective audiences.

4. Name the four pieces of information that appear on a properly prepared title page.

5. Explain when you will use a letter of transmittal and when you will use a memo of transmittal. What is the primary difference between them?

6. Investigate your word processing program's features. How will you make the numbers on your contents page flush right?

7. Explain when you would use a preface in your report.

8. Which three parts of your report will tell the reader the purpose of the report? Why is this information repeated?

9. Explain the difference between conclusions and recommendations.

10. If your class report will have an appendix, where will you put it? Can you number its pages?

CASES

1. **Choosing Your Own Topic.** If your instructor allows you to develop your own topic for a long analytical report, use the following guidelines. (You can also use them to further develop other topics.)

   Good topics usually focus on solving a problem. The problem may be one faced by a business, nonprofit organization, or small government entity. The following are examples of topics that have worked well for three former students.

   How Can Kelly Quick Printing Attract More Business Customers? (Problem analysis includes designing a marketing plan to attract the target market.)

   What Fund-Raising Projects Could Raise $50,000 for the Bristol Court Theatre? (Problem analysis includes identifying projects, finding out what fund-raisers have already been used in the theater area, planning theater-related fund-raiser.)

   Which Computer Is Best for Special Education Classes at Hoover Elementary School? (Problem analysis includes finding out needs of special education students, and identifying which computers have these characteristics.)

   Notice that *these topics are also specific* (dealing with a specific firm or entity), *narrow* (defined to

   cover only one problem), and, at this point, *stated as a question* (because you do not have an answer yet).

   Potential readers of the report should be a very small group or, better yet, one person. If you try to write to a larger audience, several things happen. You can't write directly to a decision maker. You can't aim the report at a certain person whose opinions and background on the topic you can at least partially identify. You may lose focus because you provide information for a wide audience rather than just the information needed to make a decision.

   The audiences for the topics listed above were given specific names: Christine Kelly, president, Kelly Printing; Ralph Brennan, business manager, Bristol Court Theatre; and Donald Varcoe, principal, Hoover Elementary School.

   You sometimes need to write to the board of directors of a company, but you should direct the transmittal letter to the chair of the board (by name) to keep the report focused on the decision maker.

   Difficult audiences include large groups such as state legislatures, anyone who might want to rent a car, or people who want to learn about computers. The last two groups are perfect audiences for magazines or specialized newspapers and journals. The first group might get position papers from corporations or other groups, but those aren't necessarily analytical reports.

Analysis versus Information: Because this will be an analytical report, you will need to gather information on your topic as described in Chapters 5 and 6 and then sort it out and interpret it. For example, if you find out the technical specifications for three fax/modem boards for a computer, that's information. If you show which product your client should buy based on client needs, price, features, and other criteria, that's analysis. Think *show* rather than *tell.* Give information that applies to your reader's needs, not just "generic" information.

A good class topic should send you to the library to obtain secondary information and give you an opportunity to gather some primary information through surveys, interviews, or observation. The library research will show you what has previously been done on this topic on related companies, and the primary research will give you current opinions and facts on the topic. Your instructor may assign you a completely primary or completely secondary research report.

When you have chosen and developed your topic, submit a proposal to your instructor for approval. Write a memo that includes the following:

DATE:
TO: Your Instructor
FROM: Your Name (or Group Name for a team report)
SUBJECT: TOPIC FOR ANALYTICAL REPORT

Paragraph 1: Tell what your topic is and why it is important for you to solve this particular problem.

Paragraph 2: Explain who your audience is and how this will affect your report (audience analysis).

Paragraph 3: List the main parts of your report between the introduction and conclusion. If this is a team report, tell who will write each section.

Paragraph 4: Describe the sources you will use to get relevant information for your report.

Paragraph 5: Give your time line for completing this report.

A less academic way to do this proposal is to write a letter to your client or a memo to your boss covering this material so they will know how you plan to proceed with the project.

If you need to change your outline later, add sources, or otherwise alter your plan, get your instructor's approval. Once you have chosen an approved topic, try to stay with it to avoid having to start your research over.

2. **Comparison Report Case.** Genetic Technologies has just received approval from the Food and Drug Administration to begin manufacturing Menorem, a new drug to treat Hodgkin's disease patients. As operations manager of the company, you have been asked to write a report recommending a location for the manufacturing plant.

Your company headquarters and research facility are located in San Mateo, California, close to the research labs at Stanford and the financial center of San Francisco. You would like to locate the manufacturing close by if feasible, because there are many costs associated with a remote location—executive travel (air fares, travel time), telephone and courier, and other coordination costs. Also, the Bay Area has a heavy concentration of biotech companies, so you will be able to hire the skilled work force you need for manufacturing.

However, you know that locating in the Bay Area has its own costs. Labor rates and living costs are high. California environmental regulations will make your plant cost more and take longer to complete. Water, a key factor in your manufacturing process, is both scarce and expensive.

The state of Colorado has been trying to develop the area around the University of Colorado in Boulder as a center for biotech manufacturing. It offers tax incentives for new facilities, a reliable, skilled labor force at relatively low costs, and help in getting the environmental and other permits necessary to build a new plant. Water is readily available and inexpensive.

Write a report recommending a site either near your headquarters or in Boulder. Make your decision based on labor costs and availability, water cost and availability, coordination costs, living costs and conditions, plant construction costs and timing, and taxes.

3. **Report Topics.** With guidance from your instructor, select one of the following topics for your long analytical report. Choose a topic that hasn't been used too often recently so that people you will want to talk to for your research will be willing to talk to college students. Locate the business or institution in either your college town or your home town. Make sure your information is up to date. Write the report to the person indicated.

 a. To Mayor Jane Corbin: Should the city begin a curbside recycling program?

b. To personnel manager LaVon Williams: Should Watertown Manufacturing start a child-care center for its 225-person work force?

c. To owner Walter Bates: Should Bates Appliances advertise on the radio, in the newspaper, or by direct mail?

d. To branch executive vice president Edna Sims: At which of two locations should United National Bank open its new college-area branch?

e. To director of information systems Earl Chan: Which of two local area network software systems should the company use for its networked DOS-based computers?

f. To president Lyn Baswell: What incentives should be adopted for the sales force of Premium Copier Company?

g. To executive director Robin Wallison: Should the Chamber of Commerce offer its members a group health insurance program?

h. To owner Tim Carter: Should Carter Machining own or lease its new numerically controlled milling machine?

i. To business manager Carl Masters: Should the Symphony Orchestra begin a summer pops concert series?

j. To city manager James Kawanaga: Should the city offer tax incentives to entice manufacturing companies to locate there?

k. To transit director Wayne Northrop: Should the transit system buy and use minibuses for low-ridership routes?

l. To marketing director Maria Gomez: How should United States Foods promote its new sports drink, Refresh?

m. To investor Janos Pulaski: What is the best way to get real-time stock quotations into his office?

4. **Corporate Travel Policy.** Using business periodicals, travel industry publications, and interviews as your sources, write a report to the controller of a mid-size company recommending a corporate travel policy. Look at airline, hotel, and rental car rates; tax treatment of employee expenses; and other issues you think should affect the firm's policy.

Alternate assignment: Write this report for the director of a nonprofit organization.

5. **Short Comparison Reports.** If your instructor assigns a less extensive report (about 10 pages), the following topics may give you some ideas from which you can develop a topic.

a. Which mountain bike should University Bike Shop carry to increase sales to students?

b. Which economy car is the best choice for a paralegal who drives 300 business miles a

week and is reimbursed for her expenses?

c. Which postal service provides the best service and price for a small business that sends 10 time-sensitive packages weighing under three pounds per week to clients in large cities? What if the clients are in small towns? What if business increases to 20 packages a week? What if some packages weigh only one pound?

d. Which method of desalinization would be most cost effective for a beach city on the West Coast? For Saudi Arabia?

6. **Major Event Report.** Your city will be hosting a major event (the Super Bowl, a World Cup Soccer match, a world's fair, or some other one-time event that will draw over 100,000 people) in about a year. If you are in a small city or town, pick a city with facilities that could support such an event. You are a consultant hired by one of these kinds of business: (a) limousine service, (b) restaurant, (c) jazz club, (d) small hotel, (e) taxi company, (f) car rental company, or (g) business services company (secretarial, fax, etc.). Your client has asked you how best to take advantage of this opportunity for additional business.

In your report, tell how to package services, how to promote them, and how best to prepare for the temporary influx of business. Remember: This is a one-time event, so you can't expand the restaurant or buy a lot of new limousines just for it. You probably can hire some temporary people and may be able to add some temporary facilities. Advise your client how to finance any such additional people or facilities. You can get information on the impact of events like this from the Chamber of Commerce in a city that has hosted such an event in the past.

7. **Pacific Rim Office.** You work for a Big Six accounting firm in management advisory services (MAS). Your boss tells you the firm is going to open a Pacific Rim office. He asks you to write a report detailing what the firm needs to know to have a successful office in the chosen location. Specifically cover the following:

a. How do the country's customs differ from American customs, particularly with respect to business practice? Look for things like the significance of colors, the concept of personal space, the way business is conducted, taboos about body parts, and anything else an American would need to know to avoid looking foolish.

b. What industries should the firm concentrate on serving? Look not only at the businesses that are important now but also at which part of the economy is growing fastest.

c. How do the laws of the country differ for business? For example, what are the legal forms of companies (partnerships, proprietorships, corporations)? What kinds of taxes are there? How do contract laws differ? What about patents and local ownership laws? You won't be able to cover this completely, so try to find out just the major differences.

d. Who are the major trading partners? How is trade conducted, and how does that differ from the way trade is conducted in the United States? What is U.S. tariff policy for this country?

e. What is the available labor pool? Will the firm be able to hire most of the people locally, or will it have to be staffed with Americans? Look at all levels of employees.

Prepare your report for one of these countries:

Singapore	China
Hong Kong	South Korea
Malaysia	Philippines
Taiwan	

Sources include the following:

Price Waterhouse. *Doing Business in ____* series.

Culturegrams: *The Nations Around Us,* David M. Kennedy Center for International Studies, Brigham Young University, Provo, Utah.

Robert Grosse and Duane Kujawa, *International Business,* 2nd ed. (Homewood, Ill.: Richard D. Irwin, 1992).

U.S. Department of Commerce and the consular office of the country you choose.

8. **Marketing Strategy Report.** Plumbing Computer Company has developed a system that allows plumbing companies to dispatch their servicepeople to customers via radio communications to hand-held computers in the trucks. The home office sends a message telling the serviceperson who and where the next customer is and what needs to be done. The message also gives any special instructions.

When the technician arrives at the job, he or she enters that information in the hand-held computer, and the clock starts. Any supplies or materials used on the job are logged by passing a bar code reader across a label on the materials. When the job is completed, the technician enters that information into the hand-held computer, and the job clock stops. The computer calculates an invoice, which is printed in the truck and given to the customer. Then the technician attaches the computer to the radio and sends all of the information to the central office, which starts the process over again.

The information from the truck's radio transmission is used to update inventory and accounting records in the central office, with no further manual input. When the technician returns to the shop at the end of the day, the truck is restocked based on the computer reports sent in during the day telling what materials were used.

The Plumbing Computer Company system ties in to the accounting software the company already uses. There are six major software packages used by plumbing companies, with installed bases of from 500 to 5,000 companies. The plumbing companies using these packages have an average of 25 trucks each. Plumbing Computer systems cost about $5,000 per truck.

As marketing director of Plumbing Computer, write a report to Edward Schwartz, president, telling him how best to sell his systems to the plumbing contractors. Should he make an exclusive arrangement with the largest plumbing software company or try to work with all of them? (Because each software package is different, Schwartz will have to modify *his* software slightly to make it work properly with each package.) Should he have his own sales force, use representatives, or pay the software company salespeople to sell the systems? Should he advertise? If so, how? Direct mail? Trade magazines?

9. **Wireless Communication.** You run a regional sales office, and it's important to give your clients up-to-date information. In an NCR white paper, *Mobile Network Computing,* you read about wireless computers that can give your salespeople up-to-the-minute information on prices, technical data, and availability of products.

Do some research and write a report to your boss, Sylvia Shepard, about how this technology can help you. Can you identify a product that would enable you to send a note to a colleague during a meeting? Could a secretary compare a team's calendars electronically and schedule a meeting?

You don't necessarily have to decide what products to buy right now, but sell Shepard on the idea so she can approve mobile offices for your people at about $5,000 each.

To get an idea of how the technology can help improve an office, try to find out about products by IBM (PCRadio 9075), Apple (Newton's personal Digital Assistant), Motorola (RPM405i modem and EMBARC wireless information service), and others. Look for newer equipment, too; this list was current at this writing, but technology changes very quickly.[2]

10. **Health-Care Cost Containment.** You work for Sellers and Son, a large advertising agency, as director of employee benefits. Your boss, Carlos Romero, director of human resources, has just seen an article about the health-care system that *Forbes* magazine implemented in 1992. He has asked you to report back on how the Forbes system is working and whether it would reduce health care costs for Sellers and Son.

If a Forbes employee has health insurance claims of less than $500 in a year, the company pays that employee twice the difference, plus all applicable taxes. For example, if Susan Barnes has claims of only $400, the difference is $500 −

$400 = $100. Forbes pays her twice the $100, or $200, plus taxes.

Employees "quickly realized that each dollar of claims costs them $2 and that they win if total submissions are under $1,000 (if your expenses are $800 and you don't submit them to the insurer, you will receive that $1,000 and come out ahead by $200)." Routine claims and paperwork are cut down. Health insurance premiums dropped by 10 percent the first year, while average premiums were rising by 20 percent and more.

Write your report to Romero with a recommendation about the Forbes health-care policy.[3]

---

[2]Based on Jesse Cole, "It's in the Pocket," *Sky,* December 1992, pp. 82–89.

[3]Based on Malcolm S. Forbes, Jr., "How Forbes Cured Spiraling Health Care Costs," *Forbes,* January 19, 1993, p. 25.

Chapter Nine

Oral Presentations

PREVIEW

Nearly all businesspeople make oral reports and presentations in the course of their work. They speak to convey needed information economically and memorably. If you understand the basics of oral business presentations (and do not hold yourself up to the inapplicable standards of network television), your anxiety about speaking will diminish and your chances of success will greatly increase.

In this chapter, we will discuss self-analysis and audience analysis, the parts of a talk, different modes of delivery, ways to control nonverbals, and ways to organize both informative and persuasive talks. Presentation visuals will be discussed and compared. You will also read about several kinds of video presentations. ●

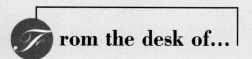

From the desk of...

Just an Everyday Business Presentation? Help!

Julian Parks
Account Executive

Vince, who has worked with me at Secrist and Associates for five weeks, wasn't eating his lunch. "What's wrong?" I asked him. "I'm presenting our proposal to the management team at Boulez Inc. Thursday," he said. "Actually, I'm thinking just how long till I get fired after I blow the presentation. I've never done this before, and $20,000 worth of business is riding on it. Julian, I don't think I can do this at all."

"Try to move away from how *you* feel," I said. "Put yourself inside the audience's heads. What's in it for them to choose us? You know their problem and our corresponding services down to the finest detail. This proposal will succeed when you show them how ideally those two things match."

"They'll see I'm petrified and write me off," Vince said.

"No, they won't, Vince. To audiences, confidence is just a set of behaviors. Act out the behaviors and they won't even suspect you're scared. Now go organize what you already know. Come and practice the talk on me this afternoon. We'll spend some time on it tomorrow, too."

THE SELF AND THE AUDIENCE

In this chapter, we assume you have done relatively little speaking in front of groups. A few lucky people seem to be "born speakers," and a few more gain experience early. Many, however, have avoided giving presentations entirely or have given just a few talks, fearing and hating every moment.

Many businesspeople give talks regularly. If your mind resists the idea of making presentations, you may be imagining yourself in front of certain past audiences you will never deal with. Maybe in high school the class clown sat in the back of the room staring at you and wiggling his eyebrows to make you laugh and ruin your speech. Maybe you've seen a street-corner radical being heckled by the passers-by he insults. Business audiences, unlike these, consist of rational and generally well-intentioned adults. As you read this chapter, then, keep these points in mind:

- Working in business, you will be giving talks.
- Practice will make you a more effective speaker.
- Audiences generally want speakers to succeed.
- Audiences have a surprisingly wide tolerance for individual speakers' differences.

Good speakers gain favorable visibility.

As you move through the steps in preparing to speak before a group, you will lay some of the groundwork for all the talks you will give in your career. Your ability to give a good oral presentation will bear strongly on your promotability.

Speakers need to cause audiences to view them as (1) knowledgeable and (2) likable. To achieve these two goals, speakers learn their material thoroughly—not memorizing it, but instead becoming completely familiar with it. Then they practice giving their talk until it is fluent and natural.

Good Speakers Know Themselves

A newcomer to speaking sometimes "knows" things that simply aren't true. For instance, people tell themselves, "I'll be boring." "I'll make stupid mistakes."

"I'll forget everything." These attitudes create negative behaviors, and sure enough, the speaker causes the outcomes he or she wants so much to avoid.

Speech coaches know that belief follows behavior. To an audience, speaker confidence is simply a set of behaviors, which we will take up in this chapter. If you exhibit these behaviors despite any fears you may have, the audience will perceive you as confident. When you behave confidently and see people responding as you wish, you will feel genuine confidence. Continued speaking experiences will reinforce that confidence.

Acting confident leads to being confident.

Many seasoned speakers admit that as beginners they were almost paralyzed with fear. Many good speakers still feel "butterflies in the stomach" just before giving a talk. This minor nervousness, however, is rarely harmful. In fact, it gives most speakers an important surge of energy as they begin speaking, just when they need it most.

Nothing can substitute for experience in giving talks. Seek out opportunities to practice. In particular, check out Toastmasters. Most localities have one or more chapters of this organization. Check your local phone book, or call the Chamber of Commerce to obtain the numbers of contact persons. Larger corporations have their own chapters. Your school may have one. You can attend as an observer as many times as you wish. Participating in Toastmasters is inexpensive and has changed many fearful speakers into highly effective and comfortable presenters.

The most important self-truth a speaker knows is "I can give this audience something they will value." As you go through the self-analysis task, ask yourself:

- What do I already know about this topic?
- What do I still need to learn?
- What are my useful attitudes and feelings about this topic?
- What are my biases, and how can I minimize their influence as I gather and present information?

Whatever your subject, the way you present it will depend on the people to whom you will speak. Different audiences bring different sets of information needs and different levels of ability, attention, and receptiveness. Although audiences differ, they all bring one question to a presentation: "What's in it for me?" (the WIIFM factor). As you move through the audience evaluation list that follows, resolve to answer this question for them early in your talk and keep the question in your mind as you continue to speak. If you do, you will retain their attention and never waste their time.

Good Speakers Know Their Audiences

Respond to your audience's WIIFM.

Often you will already know your audience well. For instance, if you supervise a small group of employees, you will have conversed with them frequently and will know a great deal about them. For less familiar audiences, learn ahead of time at least these facts:

1. *Their level of knowledge about your topic.* If they know very little, you will spend much of your speaking time conveying basic information. If they are well grounded in the topic, you can talk about finer details.

2. *Their level of academic preparation.* Have most members of your audience graduated from or at least attended college? Or will you be speaking mainly to people who completed only high school and perhaps even considered dropping out at one time?

Oral Presentation

3. *Their level of receptiveness.* Will they welcome the material, or will they resist certain parts?

4. *Their approximate average age.* Are they established and long-term members of the work force, or are they younger people without extensive experience?

5. *Their socioeconomic level.* People's underlying assumptions about many things change as they advance in earning power.

6. *Their number.* With a group of 50, you will interact differently than you will with a group of 10.

You will have to research some audiences. If, for instance, you will be explaining a new plant-security policy to a community group outside your organization, go to the person with whom you arranged the speech and ask your questions. Be particularly alert for information on how this audience already feels about the new policy. If, on the other hand, you will be giving a new-product briefing to top management, ask their staffers your questions. For instance, you will need to know how detailed their knowledge is on the existing product line and whether they feel especially committed to the product the new one will replace.

The nature of your audience determines the length, the level of formality, and the degree of sophistication in what you present. As with any other message, your audience also determines word choice and the many other basic language choices. You will be considering your audience's needs from the moment you begin gathering your content.

As you plan and organize your information, remember that listeners have certain limitations that readers do not have. Listeners cannot move back and forth in the information stream the way readers can. They receive each word only once. Speakers help their listeners by using a simple, familiar, understandable plan for the talk, explicitly stating that plan in their introduction, sticking to the plan and referring to it, point by point, in the body of the talk, and recapping the plan in the conclusion. Presentation visuals, covered in Chapter Seven, help the audience follow the talk's organization.

About Audiences in General

Audiences are usually receptive. Typically, listeners want speakers to look good and do well. An audience will not be against the speaker unless he or she offends them in some way or the situation is tense and they somehow feel the speaker is to blame. Such cases are rare and almost never occur unforeseen.

Audiences want speakers to succeed.

Remember that your audience wants to help you. If you look at your audience, they will look at you, and their attentiveness will encourage you. If your face looks friendly (even if you're scared stiff), *their* faces will look friendly. You have to help them, though. They don't want you to exclaim, "Oh, I'm so nervous!" They don't want you to apologize profusely if you have to pause to recollect a word or reinsert an idea you omitted earlier. You are only human, and so is your audience. A completely flawless presentation is unrealistic and probably not even desirable. If you look too slick or sound too "canned," you will risk sounding insincere.

You must breathe. Tense people breathe shallowly or forget to pause for breath. You are allowed to pause. You may occasionally use an incomplete sentence if the context is clear. If you say "um" twice in the talk, no one will notice it. If you say "um" every fourth word, of course, this nonword will drive your audience crazy. The principle here is that your audience will happily tolerate your individuality, within fairly broad limits. Different speakers, even

GARFIELD reprinted by permission of UFS, Inc.

Positive imaging works for speakers. Garfield needs to be more audience centered.

the top speakers on the lecture circuit, have different styles. Preparing thoroughly, however, will help you stay within your audience's tolerance limits.

Just before beginning your presentation, prepare your mind by **positive imaging.** Create positive mental pictures of yourself and your audience. Remind yourself that you are fully prepared and eager to tell your audience something they really need. Tell yourself, "I like these people. They are going to like what I have to say." Think, "I feel tall. I'm a strong, energetic person. This is going to go well." Thinking these positive thoughts helps turn nervousness into energy. When you think tall, you will stand erect. When you think energy, you can project it. When you think "friendly," your face becomes pleasant. Its muscles unfreeze and become ready to add expressiveness to your words and voice.

Use positive imaging.

BEGINNING, MIDDLE, AND END

In many business presentations, your audience will be ready to hear you. Like written reports, most business presentations fill receivers' need for information. Your business presentations will not be expected to entertain.

Thus, for many presentations, some of the "attention grabbers" you may have heard about might be undesirable. Engage the audience's attention and involve their interest early in your talk, but don't waste their costly time. Don't bother opening with a personal anecdote. Who cares what your Uncle Joe used to say? Don't open with a joke. Either everyone has already heard it, or it's not relevant to your subject, or it's in bad taste. The only humor that nearly always works in a business presentation is a little mild kidding of oneself. Don't open with a definition. "*Webster* says, . . ." sounds juvenile. Open with a shocking statement? Business audiences are tolerant, but they're not tolerant of baloney.

Within the first few sentences, the audience needs to know exactly what you will do and what use it will be to them. Time-honored advice says, "Tell them what you will tell them, tell them, then tell them what you have told them." Your introduction needs to accomplish the first of those tasks. If you have an opener that is witty, engaging, relevant to the subject, and not trite, use it. But the opener is an integral part of the speech. It is not its own reason for being. What the audience really wants in the introduction is WIIFM: "What's in it for me?"

Project energy as you speak. It sustains audience interest because it conveys *your* interest. You are the expert on the subject. Your enthusiasm and knowledge will bring the material home to your audience.

The body of your talk should have a fairly simple structure. You will have communicated it to your audience in your introduction, and the audience should be able to follow that plan easily as you speak. We will cover some options for organizing a talk later in this chapter.

Your talk also needs a clear ending. Beginning speakers often end their talks abruptly, sometimes leaving their own voices at middle-of-the-sentence pitch. The audience has no idea they have finished. Or the beginner finishes with "blah-blah-blah-blah-blah-blah-thank you" or "blah-blah-blah-blah-blah-blah-any questions?" Or "That's about all I have to say" or "Well, that's it." Do not end your talks so weakly and unmemorably.

Plan a solid conclusion. After completing the last main point in the body of your talk, pause briefly, then verbally signal your move to your conclusion section. Some people say, "In summary, . . ." or "In conclusion, . . . ," but try to do better than that. For instance, you can say, "You've heard three cases showing the need for improved interagency exchange. The plan I've outlined will provide for it." Then tell them again what you have told them.

With your last few words, give your voice the sound of an ending: Use a downward vocal intonation. Then stop, wait a couple of seconds, and then ask for questions if you have planned time for them. If not, wait a second or two, then leave the podium. Leaving that brief silence doesn't come to most people naturally, but it is the way professionals end a talk.

DELIVERY STYLES AND TECHNIQUES

Speech teachers and trainers recognize four styles of speeches. Some speeches are read word for word from a prepared manuscript. Some are committed to memory and spoken word for word. Some, called **extemporaneous** speeches, are given using only a prepared outline or set of notes. Others, called **impromptu** speeches, are given with no preparation at all. Extemporaneous and impromptu talks are by far the most common in business.

Manuscript Speeches, Read or Memorized

Manuscript speeches are infrequent in business.

In everyday business you are unlikely to give a memorized speech. Your instructor is unlikely to assign or permit you to give one. Still, because you have probably seen important speakers use a manuscript, we will discuss them briefly.

A speaker reads a prepared manuscript when the wording of the material is critical. Reading a speech well requires as much preparation as giving one extemporaneously. People who will read a prepared manuscript have the speech typed in large type, triple-spaced, on one side of the paper. They mark the text for pauses, gestures, and even facial expressions. Then they rehearse it many times, making sure that it sounds like talk rather than like reading, that the phrasing sounds natural, that the wording is characteristic of them and not someone else, and that they can actually bring the sounds out of their mouths without tripping over words.

To a beginning speaker, reading a talk looks like the easy way. She might not believe she can give a speech without reading it. She also might not understand about the extensive preparation needed for reading from a manuscript. Consequently, audiences suffer as she rapidly reads in a singsong voice stilted material from a notebook-paper scrawl, stumbling over words. This is not speaking.

Occasionally a person might commit a whole speech to memory. A memorized speech might be appropriate, for instance, when the speaker will give it again and again to different audiences. These speakers, too, prepare exhaustively. The talk should sound like "talk," not a recital. This kind of clean delivery doesn't just happen.

In general, business audiences tolerate a well-read or memorized speech but prefer an extemporaneous one. They like to feel that the speaker is interacting with them, looking at them, almost conversing with them. In fact, the best presenters of read or memorized speeches simulate this manner. Extemporaneous delivery is also by far the most foolproof. Because it is also the most frequent delivery style in business, we will cover it more extensively than the other styles.

Most business presentations are extemporaneous.

Extemporaneous Speaking

An extemporaneous speaker talks from a few notes, an outline, a few visual aids, or a combination of these cues. In most cases, the talk never exists in written form.

Beginning speakers resist the idea of just *speaking* to an audience. Often they clutch pages of writing the way infants clutch their blankets. The sooner a beginning speaker breaks loose from a written-out text, the sooner he begins to develop as a speaker. Underprepared beginners' eyes "default" to the typewritten, printed out, or penned pages. Their voices develop the repetitive singsong of unpracticed reading or reciting. Their audiences' minds drift off to the golf course or the lake.

Should a speaker never write out a speech he intends to give extemporaneously? Some speakers like to write out the talk in order to time it carefully. Some think better on paper and like to see, study, and revise their thoughts in that form. Sometimes the material will be distributed to the audience as a handout after the talk is over. Whatever the reasons for committing a talk to paper, before beginning to rehearse the talk a speaker must break free of all those words on all that paper.

Speakers must speak, not read.

Written material a speaker carries to the front for an extemporaneous talk should include no more than an outline and a few notes. Outline and notes should be on a *few* cards, which the speaker numbers in order, refers to sparingly, and uses in a natural and nondistracting way.

The speaker must use these notes in his rehearsals. It is essential to actually *talk* the talk—the whole talk—a number of times. The ideas need not always be worded exactly the same way. In fact, if the wording varies, the speaker has more options (synonyms, for instance, or spare examples to illustrate main points) than if he stays slavishly with uniform wording. He also sounds more spontaneous. Another important part of rehearsing is actually working with the note cards and audiovisual aids. Rehearsal will show where a transparency is unwieldy, a chart is unclear, the cues on the cards need modification, the order can be improved, a memory lapse is possible, and so on.

Audiences like spontaneity.

Many speech trainers urge speakers to memorize openings and closings. They correctly believe that a speaker's first and last words must be meticulously chosen because their position makes them most memorable to the audience. If you are in serious danger of "drawing a blank," prepare two special cue cards, one for the opener and one for the close, containing *minimal* cues to make your memory foolproof. Practice the opener and the close until you don't need those two cards at all. Then take them with you to the talk and don't refer to them unless your mind goes blank (which will be exceedingly unlikely). In the middle of a talk, forgetting something is relatively unimportant. At the beginning and end, however, a speaker cannot take that chance.

Impromptu Speaking

A businessperson gives an impromptu speech when he is asked, without any chance to prepare, to respond to a question or to "say a few words." Impromptu speeches may sound risky and potentially humiliating, but they need not be.

Rarely are people given absolutely no inkling that they might be called on. If you work in a group where people are sometimes asked to respond impromptu, chances are excellent that one day soon your turn will come. Just from observing, you will have a pretty good advance idea about what kinds of questions are asked, how long a respectable response lasts, and what degree of awkwardness is within tolerance, just to name a few variables.

You *can* prepare, actually. In your projects at work, what might others ask about? Formulate some likely questions and mentally rough out responses. In fact, you already handle many impromptu questions in meetings and on the telephone. You exercise impromptu skills when you get someone's answering machine instead of the human being you expected. Reducing your thoughts to a short message is one of the most important impromptu skills.

Think of an impromptu talk in this way: Your job is to operate your mouth for X time and sound intelligent. If you have X time, you will be able to cover a given and limited number of main ideas. Because businesspeople rarely waste time by asking someone to speak in an area where he or she lacks expertise, you will have something, probably plenty, to say.

Asked for impromptu remarks, a speaker should pause to organize before answering.

You can and should take a few seconds to marshal your thoughts before beginning to speak. Think about what ideas you want to cover, and think of a simple organizational scheme for covering them. Do not begin to speak before you have done so. Remember, you need to sound knowledgeable. You might begin by restating the question or request, even rewording it if doing so permits you to give a better or more useful response. Then, just as in the other delivery styles, tell your audience what you intend to tell them, tell them, and then tell them what you just said.

In one minute, for instance, you might be able to give two pros and two cons of a new plan just proposed and under discussion. In five minutes, you might have time to make an assertion and illustrate it with several examples. In eight minutes, you can probably give a capsule comparison of sales in regions A, B, and C. Note that each of these examples uses a different organizing scheme: pros and cons, illustration by example, and coverage by geographical region.

Impromptu talks are not expected to be flawless. Rather than striving for perfection, work to convey interest in your subject matter and respect for your listeners. Look at them; their faces will be responding to you. Good talks are interactions rather than performances.

Think of your content, organize it, and talk. You will sound knowledgeable.

CONTROLLING NONVERBALS AND PARAVERBALS

Nonverbals and paraverbals can drown out words.

Some of the strongest influences on an audience's response are **nonverbal signals** (unworded messages such as posture, position, movement, and facial expression) and **paraverbal signals** (noncontent elements of a worded message such as tone of voice, pitch, and intensity). In this section, we will examine some of the appropriate signals for speakers to send nonverbally and paraverbally.

Before we begin, remember that although audiences are fairly tolerant of speakers' individual differences, they have expectations about speaker behavior. As you read, consider how you will meet your audience's expectations and find a natural-feeling place within their range of tolerance.

Speakers send a message by the way they walk to the front of the room and say their first few words. They should walk to the front with a confident, deliberate stride, maintain erect posture once they arrive, and spend a second or two of silence giving the audience a friendly look.

Most of us have seen beginners who creep or shuffle to the front like a condemned prisoner approaching the gallows. They consult their notes worriedly, sigh, and eye the exit sign with longing. Then they suddenly brighten up, smile radiantly down at their notecards, and read "Good morning." Obviously, this is the wrong approach. Speakers need to be "in character" from the moment their audience begins looking in their direction.

Good grooming is essential and must be complete *before* the speaker enters the room. Nervous beginners sometimes finish grooming or undo perfectly good grooming while in front of the audience. We've seen speakers tidy up hair, check to see that all eight earrings are accounted for, and tighten or loosen the necktie knot—unaware that they were doing so.

Speakers need to dress to meet the audience's expectations. For business presentations, that means professional-looking business clothing. One expert suggests that to make the best impression, a speaker should dress a fraction more conservatively than the people he or she will address. In most business presentations, both women and men are advised to wear good-quality, dark-colored suits and attractive, good-quality, but low-key accessories. The idea is that a speaker's job is not only to convey content but also to inspire confidence. Anything that looks flashy to an audience can undermine the speaker's credibility.[1]

Audiences prefer open, interested facial expressions that change as the ideas change. Individuals (and cultures) vary widely in degree of expressiveness. One person's rubber-faced expressiveness makes a more staid person think of monkeys. Another person's immovable face makes a more expressive person think of tombstone carvings. Here too, be aware of an acceptable range of audience tolerance and avoid the extremes. If you are too near the extremes, becoming aware will help you begin to modify a habit that might get in the way of your advancement.

An occasional smile is a positive nonverbal signal. Constant smiling, however, is a negative nonverbal, conveying nervousness or insincerity to many people. Women tend to smile more than they should, as speakers. If speakers maintain a friendly expression around the eyes, a smile can be just one among many lively and communicative expressions.

Practiced speakers control their hands but gesture for appropriate emphasis at the right points in the talk. Unpracticed speakers may find that their mouths are saying one thing and their hands another. For instance, a hand might be tapping on the lectern, clenching and unclenching, diving in and out and in and out of a pocket, hiding behind the speaker's back, clicking a pen, twirling a curl of hair, and so on. Hands must not be allowed to go their own way during a talk.

Students often ask, "Then what am I supposed to do with my hands?" The answer is: Make your hands work for you. As you rehearse your speech, re-

Posture

Grooming

Dress

Face

Becoming aware of nonverbals precedes improving them.

Hands

Hands should support a speaker's message, not put on a show all their own.

[1]Richard J. Kulda, "Dressing to Win," *Professional Eloquence Letter,* June 1, 1977.

hearse your gestures as well. When you are not gesturing, your hands should be at rest. Where? They can be at your sides, or they can rest lightly on (but not clutch) the lectern. One hand, but not both, can be in a pocket (but don't trap it there). One hand can hold a pointer. One hand can hold your few notecards (but should keep them inconspicuous). However, keep your hands available so that you can move them deliberately when you want to.

Gestures emphasize words or phrases, and the principle of emphasis is *differentness*. For instance, underlining emphasizes because it contrasts with nonunderlined material. If everything were underlined, nothing would be emphasized. The same holds true with gestures. If hand movements are virtually constant, they cease to have meaning and instead distract.

Feet

Keeping the weight evenly distributed on both feet achieves two ends. First, the speaker looks stable rather than off balance or jittery. He isn't tempted to lean on or clutch the lectern. Also to be avoided are slumping to one side, frequent shifting weight from one foot to another, turning a foot to one side, attempting to wrap one ankle around the other, and excessive walking around. Speakers can walk and change position, but they should do so deliberately rather than to work off adrenalin.

Eye Contact

Keep a high level of eye contact with the audience.

While going through a presentation, speakers move their eyes from one audience member's face to another, lingering a few seconds before moving on. Speakers don't look at every single face in the audience. Rather, they find a receptive face in each *section* of the audience: front left, front right, center, back left, and back right. In this way, the whole audience feels included.

Eyes must not *avoid* the audience. Unpracticed speakers' eyes tend to "default" to the notes or to the floor, ceiling, or back wall. Speakers' eye contact helps the audience pay attention. Furthermore, speakers need to read audience nonverbals. If audience members do not understand something or become distracted or inattentive, the speaker can modify the talk to get them back on track.

Poise

Speakers must stay "in character" while walking confidently back to sit down. We have heard a speaker mutter, "That was gross!" as he slunk away from the lectern. We have heard "Whew!!" and "Thank God that's over." To undercut effectiveness and behave unprofessionally at the end, after all that work, is foolish.

The right signals come much more easily to the speaker who has prepared thoroughly than to the one who has avoided preparing and rehearsing. People who say they loathe speaking have the most to gain by good preparation.

Voice and Paraverbals

Audiences will tolerate a wide range of voice traits. However, speakers should avoid the limits of audience tolerance and cultivate those voice attributes that project energy and enthusiasm.

Voices vary in a number of characteristics. Some paraverbals are **pitch** (high, medium, or low tones), **range** (variability from highest to lowest pitch), **speed** (the rate at which the presenter speaks), and **volume** (loudness or projection). Other variables include **articulation** (ability to enunciate clearly) and **fluency.**

If you naturally have an excellent speaking voice, you probably have few problems. Not all potential speakers are thus gifted, and certain voice characteristics can work against speaking effectiveness. From vocal differences in factors like loudness and speed, audiences infer a positive or negative *para-verbal* message, an added message accompanying the worded message.

- *Pitch.* A high voice may seem to lack authority. A high-pitched voice is a disadvantage for both women and men. Many business speakers work to develop a deeper-toned voice.

- *Range.* A voice with very limited range bores an audience. Although a speaker may feel enthusiastic about his or her subject, a one-note delivery communicates the opposite. Media announcers deliberately use a wide vocal range. Effective business presenters can do just as well.

- *Speed.* A too-rapid delivery interferes with the audience's ability to keep up; too slow a pace invites them to daydream. Audiences sometimes suspect a fast talker of insincerity or uncontrolled nerves and a slow speaker of slow-wittedness or lack of interest. Audiences welcome purposeful variations in speed just as they do variety in pitch and volume. Also, they know the speaker has to pause for breath now and then.

- *Volume.* A small, soft voice undermines a speaker's authoritative presence and in some cases prevents all or part of the audience from hearing. Too loud a voice is irritating. Speakers need to be able to project their voices enough to fill the room comfortably.

- *Articulation.* Clear, distinct, but natural enunciation projects intelligence and credibility. Mumbling has the opposite effect. Exaggerated enunciation can make an audience feel patronized.

- *Fluency.* Practiced speakers rarely have to grope for a word. Still, the normal stream of speech contains pauses. Effective speakers control their pauses, sometimes using them to add emphasis or to signal a transition. Pauses should not be filled with intrusive sounds such as "you know" or "I mean." If you have an "um" habit, now is the time to break it.

Whether audiences' negative reactions to some paraverbals are fair is beside the point. If speakers can minimize the negatives by developing their voices, they will reach their goals more easily. Most people can learn to project their voices and to communicate energy. Most can develop their voices' range, whether to lower the overall range or simply to increase variation. Many can and should improve their articulation.

Pleasant, low-pitched, easily heard voices project authority and credibility.

DRABBLE reprinted by permission of UFS, Inc.

Norman has to articulate much more clearly to become an effective business presenter.

Most students can improve the "listenability" of their voices just by becoming aware of what they need to change. In unusual cases, a student may want to pay a voice coach for some lessons. Ask your instructor to videotape one or more of your presentations. You won't fully understand what you need to work on until you see yourself on tape. As you watch the tape, you will see many things you are doing well. Give yourself credit. Doing so will give you more incentive to work on what does need improvement.

Nonverbals and paraverbals exert a strong influence on the audience's reception of a talk's content. Human beings are loaded with biases that operate full time without their owners' even being aware of them. If you can control some of the elements that precondition the audience's evaluation of what you say, you will meet the goals of your presentation much more effectively.

Thus far, we have been discussing the *how* of presentations. Next, we will focus on the *what.*

INFORMING AND PERSUADING

Informing and persuading are not two separate things. Most messages do some of both but intend mainly to do one or the other.

Speakers who set out to persuade must usually provide information to support what they want their hearers to think, feel, or do. Speakers informing audiences who do not know them may have to persuade their hearers to view *them* as credible before the *information* will be accepted. In an example of the way informing and persuading often mix, an upper-level manager's talk describes two cost-cutting measures. He tells his subordinates that the measures will initially be uncomfortable but will lead to long-term benefits. The talk mainly informs them what will be done, but the subtext persuades: "We need your cooperation. Opposing the measures will hurt everybody."

The material to follow shows how to plan and organize talks when the content is mainly informational, then how to plan and organize talks when the content is mainly persuasive. Chapter Eleven discusses informing and persuading in more detail.

Informative Presentations

Every day, businesspersons convey information orally. When several people need the information, a business presentation is often the most efficient medium. The more important the information, the audience, and the business need served by the talk, the more carefully the speaker prepares.

The organizational plans for informative talks are familiar.

Between your carefully constructed beginning and ending, you can organize the body of your talk using one or a combination of these familiar patterns, which you learned about in Chapter One:

Chronological	Geographic
Description	Analysis
Cause and effect	Definition
Classification	Illustration by examples
Narration	Process
Problem-solution	Comparison and contrast

Speakers and audiences use these patterns daily as ways of thinking about experience. All can be used alone or in combinations. Let's take one example, analysis. An introduction could say:

The market for luxury skin-care products has five main segments. I'll outline these and then show you, on the basis of our research, the two segments where our competitors are strong, the two where they are most vulnerable, and the three where our line can best be promoted.

The audience, now knowing that the body of the talk will be arranged according to division of a whole into its parts, will easily follow the speaker's organization. In the body of the talk, the speaker must let the audience know, both verbally and nonverbally, when he moves from one point to the next. In his concluding section, he must summarize according to this same plan.

Persuasive Presentations

The persuasive speaking we do in business tends not to be fancy, catchy, or shocking. It tends to be workaday and low key. Persuasive speaking in business is rarely debatelike, performancelike, or confrontational. It is more like an outgrowth of persuading interpersonally, which we do constantly. Much of what we learn in life about successful and unsuccessful persuasion will carry over into persuading in business. For instance, in business persuasive talks, just as in our daily living, we call as *little attention to our differences with our audience* as we can and still accomplish all or part of our persuasive goal.

In business, persuasion builds common ground and deemphasizes differences between speaker and audience.

Stated abstractly, our persuasive goal is to modify our audience's opinions, attitudes, beliefs, or behaviors. Stated concretely, our goal in a persuasive talk might be to get a fragmented work group back on track, to get the firm's executives to endorse a capital expenditure, to open the minds of 30 first-line supervisors to the idea of quality circles, or to replace with the truth a rumor flourishing in the grapevine. The list could go on and on.

Informative speaking usually reaches its goal: It informs. In contrast, even the best persuasive presentations sometimes fail to persuade. Persuasion is harder. Emotions, ego involvement, elements of the business situation, and even personal history can create obstacles.

Objective and Audience

Suppose we take on the task of getting the first-line supervisors to consider quality circles. Already you can see that the persuasive goal and the audience are closely connected. Audience analysis is critical and can be complicated. If the supervisors are neutral but uninformed, the task is relatively easy. But what if Roth, the most influential supervisor, has seen quality circles not only fail but also create a sour working environment in her last job? She has talked about the experience, and the supervisors are very dubious of QCs. Your persuasive goal changes.

In the first case, where the audience is neutral, you present the benefits a well-managed QC program can bring. In the second case, you do not yet try to influence the group until you have conversed extensively with Roth to learn what her experiences were, why the other QC program failed, how much she has generalized her opinion of QCs, how much influence she has with the other supervisors, and whether she is open to revising her opinion.

Degree of Opposition: Multiple Messages

If an audience is strongly opposed to your position, you will rarely change their minds with one message and usually should not try. Instead, think in terms of multiple messages. A more modest goal is not to change them but to ask them to try to understand some of the reasons why others feel differently than they do. This you can do, and, more important, they will let you do it. They will hear you. If they think, however, that you want them to change from "Absolutely not!" to "Yes, of course we will," they will not listen to you at all.

The usual result of this less assertive talk is some actual softening of their opposition. (Not all audience members will change, and those who do will not all change to the same degree.) Your next message can take your persuasion one or two steps further. If you have enough time and opportunity, you can eventually win many of them to your way of thinking.

Organizational Patterns for Persuading

If your persuasive task is to develop the reasons why an opposing idea is wrong, the following structure might work well. It arranges arguments (reasons, pieces of evidence) according to their relative strength:

- Introduce the subject, developing common ground, that is, ideas that both you and your audience know and agree on.
- Discuss one or more strong pro arguments.
- Mention one or more weaker pro arguments.
- Cite and refute one or more opposing arguments.
- Return to strong pro arguments; discuss at least one more.
- Summarize the main points.
- Say confidently what you would like the audience to do or believe.

Primacy and recency govern placement of the strongest arguments.

The placement of the strongest arguments first and last makes use of the principles of **primacy** and **recency.** Audiences remember best what they hear or read first (prime position) and what they hear or read last (most recently). The less important ideas are placed in the middle, where audiences' attention tends to lessen.

Some of the opposing arguments need to be mentioned and refuted. Choose opposing arguments you can deal with and show as well as possible how they are weaker or less important than the audience might think. Sometimes the arguments against can be turned into (weak) arguments for.

The ideal counterarguments to bring up are those that permit you to refute them strongly and convincingly. If the audience has an opportunity for questions afterward, you might be asked about some of the others. If you can, offer some evidence against the counterargument. If you cannot, one strategy is to acknowledge that no solution is perfect and then add a restatement of one of your stronger arguments.

For sections within your talk, any of the patterns listed on page 282 for informative speaking might suit your persuasive task as well. For example, you might use a comparison-and-contrast pattern for one of your arguments and the process pattern for another.

The motivated sequence can lead an audience from initial uninvolvement to action.

If your persuasive task is to motivate, unify a group, or sell an idea in some other way, the AIDA (attention-interest-desire-action) pattern might work well. A more common name for this arrangement is the **motivated sequence.** It's useful for a persuasive effort in which the receiver is initially uninterested in the subject, the speaker, or any part of the situation. Business speakers must sometimes persuade people just to listen before they can persuade them to do anything else.

The motivated sequence has five steps—attention, need, satisfaction, visualization, and action:

1. Use an attention-getting opener to grab the audience's attention.
2. Establish and develop the audience's need for your plan or idea.
3. Demonstrate that your plan or idea will satisfy the need.
4. Encourage listeners to visualize themselves having solved the problem, enjoying the result of the new idea.

5. Move the audience to whatever action you have in mind: increasing their sense of team spirit, re-igniting their enthusiasm for a project, or conveying warmth and welcome to customers.

How might this sequence work? Suppose a speaker has to give a pep talk about workplace safety to a group of employees who have grown lax. The opener might describe a workplace accident, with clear examples of its pain and cost (step 1). Then the speaker might say, "You know we have a gain-sharing plan in place here. In the next few minutes, I'll show you three cases where increased attention to safety on the job yielded employee bonuses of 4.3 percent, 6 percent, and 18 percent, respectively." The audience now has in mind the speaker's plan (step 2).

Three detailed examples would follow, each showing a cause-and-effect pattern. The examples would talk about cost savings and pain avoidance—about the accidents that *didn't* happen (step 3). The speaker would then ask listeners to think about how they might spend or invest their share of the gain (step 4).

An ending might be: "We can all make this work. We just need to be a little sharper and a little more alert, to clean up the work area, to get rid of the hazards. It'll be fun to spend that percentage we save—and you won't have to go visit an accident victim in the hospital, or be that victim yourself" (step 5).

As in other forms of business communication, your task is to analyze the source (yourself), analyze the communication situation (including the problem), analyze the receiver, and craft the message. The message grows out of all the other elements.

PRESENTATION VISUALS AND AUDIOVISUALS

Increasingly, business speakers add interest, value, and impact to their oral presentations by using audiovisual aids. Studies have shown that presentations using well-prepared and appropriate visuals are more convincing and more memorable than presentations without them. Vendors continue to offer speakers better means of preparing these aids. Because striking, high-tech, simple-to-prepare audiovisuals have become common, business audiences' expectations have risen. While low-tech, simple aids are still useful, more speakers are reaping the rewards of learning to use higher-tech AV, such as multimedia, which we will describe later in this section. Table 9–1 shows the strengths and drawbacks of the various kinds of audiovisuals to be treated in the section to follow.

Take great care in preparing all types of audiovisuals. Since they are likely to contain the elements you want to emphasize, the impression they make tends to be a lasting one. Your visuals need an attractive appearance, perfect spelling, adequate size and readability, a logical order, and strong impact. The impression they make, positive or negative, will represent you memorably.

Presentation visuals make a strong impression. Make sure it's a good impression.

Practice using your visuals as you rehearse your talk. Here are some guidelines for handling your audiovisuals smoothly and effectively:

- Keep them simple.
- Have them in the correct order and ready to use. For instance, peeling sticky paper backing off transparencies can be noisy and awkward, so do this before you need them.
- Use visuals smoothly, without fumbling.
- Give the audience enough time to read each visual.

TABLE 9–1 Audiovisual Options: Advantages and Disadvantages

	Handouts	Chalkboards, Whiteboards	Flipcharts	Posters	Deskcharts	Overheads	35 mm Slides	Audiotape	Videotape	Computer Shows	Multimedia
Use in normal light?	+	+	+	+	+	+	−	+	+	+	+
Professional-looking?	+	−	?	+	+	?	+	?	?	+	+
Reusable?	+	−	?	?	+	+	+	+	+	+	+
Versatile?	+	?	−	−	?	+	+	?	+	+	+
Equipment easy to get?	+	+	+	+	+	+	+	+	+	−	−
Inexpensive?	+	+	+	+	+	+	?	?	?	?	−
Change easily?	+	+	+	−	+	+	?	?	?	+	?

+ a strength of this medium
− a weakness of this medium
? it depends

John Maher/Stock Boston

Oral presentations, especially when accompanied by visuals, present business information powerfully. This speaker is projecting actual computer-screen images, which she can change using a computer keyboard as she speaks.

- Remove a visual when you are finished using it.
- Don't simply read a visual to your audience. Discuss it.
- Avoid letting your body block the audience's view of any audiovisual.

An oral report based on the written report illustrated in Chapter 8 generated a set of nine visuals. The slides shown in Exhibit 9–1 would be most suitable for overhead transparencies or 35mm slides. They could, however, assume the form of handouts, flipcharts, posters, or deskcharts as well, and could be incorporated into any of the more complex media, such as videotape. As sequenced, the nine slides illustrate the oral report's "story."

Next, we'll examine the different kinds of AV available.

Handouts

Virtually anything you can replicate can become a handout. Most handouts are printed on ordinary paper, but even these can be impressive. One handout we saw recently boasted a cover page containing a picture of a compact disk, made out of shiny compact-disk material, but flat and flexible as the paper on which it was mounted. It was made of iron-on material the speaker had found at an art supply store. Handouts can be inexpensive or they can be slick and costly, as are the four-color, card-stock pocket folders containing multiple color-printed pages in different sizes and formats.

A handout might be an outline of the talk, a paper copy of all transparencies used in the talk, a bibliography, a diagram, a copy of a written report related to the oral report, or a combination of all these. Many other options exist.

When should handouts be distributed? Something short and basic, like an outline, can be passed out at the beginning. A longer handout, however, such as a copy of the complete report, will draw audience members' attention away

Long handout? Do not give it out till the talk is over.

Slide 1

Slide 2

Slide 3

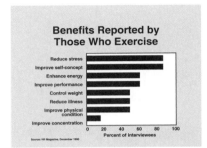

Slide 4

Slide 5

Slide 6

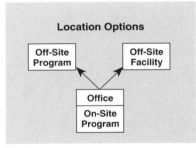

Slide 7

Slide 8

Slide 9

The nine slides serve different purposes:

Slide 1 introduces the speakers and the topic.
Slide 2 presents the talk's organization.
Slide 3 presents one of the important points, Corporate Benefits.
Slide 4 presents and elaborates with a bar graph the important section Employee Benefits.
Slide 5 presents an important point, Motivation.
Slide 6 details a subsection of Motivation, Incentives.
Slide 7 introduces the section of the talk on Facility Location.
Slide 8 shows the decision matrix for Facility Location.
Slide 9 sums up the main benefits leading organizations to consider employee fitness programs.

from the speaker as they scan ahead of where the speaker wants them to be. Many speakers tell an audience what the handout will contain and then pass it out at the end. This information permits audience members to limit notetaking to only those notes the handout does not offer. Thus, their attention remains on the speaker.

Most other audiovisual aids occupy a place near the speaker. Since they must be large enough for a group to see, they are often sizable and sometimes distract the audience's attention from the speaker. Speakers have to (1) keep the audience's attention where it should be and (2) avoid blocking the visual with their bodies while using it.

Chalkboards or Whiteboards

If you will be demonstrating a process, such as the calculation of a formula or a multistep problem and solution, a chalkboard or whiteboard might be best for your purpose. These aids are versatile, common, and low in cost. However, the speaker cannot write on the board while facing the audience. Eye contact is lost during that time, and the audience has nothing to do until the speaker turns back to them. Attention can wander. In addition, some speakers write so rapidly on the board that the result is illegible.

Flipcharts

Flipcharts are inexpensive and versatile but, like chalkboards, they require the user to turn away from the audience unless they have been prepared in advance. Turning the large, unwieldy, crackly pages creates a minor distraction. The easels for flipcharts are often wobbly, but can be moved around easily.

A speaker can draw or write each page's exhibit in advance. Best practice recommends leaving a blank page at the beginning and every other page blank. Thus, an exhibit remains covered until needed. The speaker can turn a blank page after finishing with each exhibit and can direct the audience's attention as desired. Many speakers trace lightly in pencil what they will write boldly in marking-pen strokes during the talk. Doing so yields a neat result, especially if the user is ordinarily a hasty scribbler.

Some speakers begin with a completely blank tablet, develop the entire talk as they write phrases on the flipchart, and tear off each sheet and tape it to the wall in sequence. This technique makes for a vigorous, dynamic talk. A second advantage—especially if the material is complex, as in engineering or the sciences—is that the audience can view the entire presentation as a whole. The disadvantage is the visual chaos this method can create.

Posters

The stiff cardboard used for posters gives speakers more options for charts, illustrations, lists, photographs, and other graphics. Because posters are already prepared, the speaker retains eye contact with the audience. They are inexpensive but somewhat unwieldy, and they require an easel or hooks on the front wall to hold them. Posterboard comes in many weights and sizes. Choose board heavy enough to stand sturdily on the easel without curling or falling over. Use large, dark, clear lettering on a white or yellow background so that even those sitting in the back can read the poster easily.

Deskcharts

For a small audience—say, five or six people—deskcharts combine the advantages of flipcharts and posters. Deskcharts are small, prepared posters, usually in landscape format. If you turn your notebook so that the spiral is at the top, you are looking at the basic size and shape of a deck of deskcharts. Because deskcharts are loosebound, you can stand them on a desk and turn them like the pages of a flipchart.

Overhead Transparencies

Transparencies may offer the fewest disadvantages and the most advantages. Overhead projectors are readily obtainable and transparencies are inexpensive and easy to make. Unlike 35 mm slides and motion picture film, overheads do not require turning all the lights off.

Overhead transparencies are inexpensive and versatile.

With transparency marking pens, you can draw or hand-letter a transparency in advance or develop an exhibit on a transparency as you speak. You can draw, type, or print out a good, clear paper original and make an excellent transparency on a photocopier. Color transparencies have been available at a reasonable price since about 1989.

Computer programs and output devices offer speakers great variety. Increasingly, schools and organizations are making these computer tools available to their members. Transparencies made on a color printer or plotter can add great vividness and impact to a talk.

35 mm Slides

Slide shows, especially when accompanied by sound, look very sharp and professional. They also fall into a different cost category. Yes, an amateur can make a series of good slides inexpensively. When audiences see a slide projector, though, they tend to expect a "dog-and-pony show"—something with variety, pizzazz, imagination, and often music or sound effects.

A business or educational speaker may have access to an in-house production department. Speakers can also locate many small-business vendors of AV production services. These services offer advice, guidance, and many additional options.

The more a speaker spends on a given slide show (or any other audiovisual) the more he expects to get out of it. Costly AV should either serve a very important one-time purpose or have good capacity for multiple use. Slides alone are easy to change. Slides with audio are less adaptable.

Even the best slide shows are limited to two-dimensional color images that audiences view in a darkened room. Live narration, if provided, seems to come from a disembodied voice. If the narration is recorded, the speaker essentially disappears until the slide show is finished, when he must regain the audience's attention.

Audiotape Recordings

Audiotape recordings are useful for illustrating some brief segments of a talk. For example, a speaker could play a recording of the reactions of people in a target market to a new product or idea. A taped comment from an expert on the given topic might make a piece of evidence particularly convincing. A speaker could use a short bit of music to set a mood. But a business presentation accents the visual and should not rely too heavily on audio effects.

Videotapes

Camcorders, which dropped in price to about $700 in 1991, are now within many speakers' personal budgets. Most camcorder owners, however, lack the production skills needed to create a videotape of sufficient quality to enhance an important business presentation. For a relatively informal talk, a homemade videotape can work for you. For a full-fledged business presentation, you will do best to hire professionals.

Videotape opens enormous possibilities to presenters. Anything you can show by any other medium you can show on videotape—and much more. You can tape a skit, a "talking head," a mood piece, a demonstration, a segment of a focus group, or the steps in solving a problem, just to name a few possibilities. You can add music and other sound effects. You can use stills like photographs, diagrams, and models. Voiceover is easy, you can retape any number of times, and editing the tape is not difficult.

Playback equipment is easy to find and lets you show the tape in ordinary room light. The video screen is large enough for viewers to see clearly, but not so large that you have to compete with it.

EXHIBIT 9–2 Four Examples of Computer-Drawn Stills

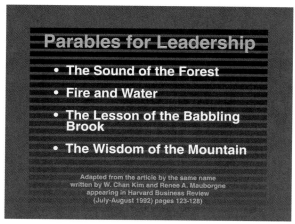

(a) an outline

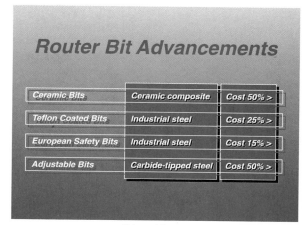

(b) a table

(c) a listing

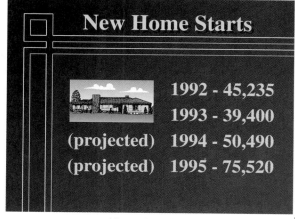

(d) trend numbers

Several computer application packages permit the user to build onscreen color presentation exhibits quickly and easily. The four examples shown in Exhibit 9–2 were built using one such package, Microsoft Powerpoint™.

Most of your images will be stills or will use very limited animation, but they are versatile and can be revised with a few keystrokes. Also, any image you can digitize can be inserted into a computer presentation. If you do not wish to show your images on a computer screen, you can print them out on a color printer or output them as 35mm color slides.

Computer "Shows"

Multimedia combines existing audiovisual options and permits a user to move back and forth among them. This new computer-based approach to audiovisuals is poised to develop rapidly for business use.

Most multimedia systems employ a compact disk. This super-high digital storage medium can hold, for instance, a 24-volume encyclopedia on one disk and permit the user to access it at random. Besides text, it can store audio signals and visual images in both still and full-motion form.

Multimedia

Oral Presentation

The possibilities of this medium go far beyond those of videotape (which it can incorporate). For instance, suppose a corporate trainer is addressing a group of 30 insurance adjuster trainees. She gives her introduction, then switches on the video playback screens from her keyboard. Trainees see and hear a typical and relatively trouble-free meeting between an adjuster and a claimant. The trainer then shows the text of the policies in small or large segments. She can highlight a word and call up more detailed information about it. She can also call up case law pertaining to similar claims.

In addition, the trainer can show comparable encounters between an adjuster and insured parties, including encounters that caused problems because of tactless word choice, unclear terminology or jargon, inattention, or misdirection. She can zero in on any part of the video, pausing for discussion at any time. She can play tapes of angry encounters backed by harsh music and sound to simulate the stress levels trainees must learn to deal with. She can teach one or two coping mechanisms, showing, telling, and referencing psychology literature—all onscreen from her keyboard. She can play telephone scripts that lead to a satisfactory outcome for both parties and telephone scripts that do not. This array only begins to tap the potential applications of multimedia technology in business presentations.

Ensuring Your Visuals' Success

Clearly, business presenters have many choices in audiovisual aids, ranging from simple and inexpensive to elaborate and costly. The topic, the audience, and the business need will determine your choices among these options. In all cases, however, you must prepare AV materials meticulously and use them with grace, skill, and smoothness. As with all other aspects of presentations, practice is critical to success.

Well ahead of your talk, check out the place where you will be speaking. How does the room look? Are there power outlets for your projector(s)? Will you need one or more extension cords? If you need to darken or partially darken the room, can you do so easily? Is there a lectern? A microphone?

PRESENTING ON VIDEO

When business presentations are recorded on video, a few elements assume particular importance. These elements differ depending on whether the person is speaking for the media, for in-house use, or for a videoconference.

Presenting for the Media

When we discuss presenting on video for the media, we do not mean in a time of crisis. In the case of a crisis or emergency on company premises (a fire, a robbery, an accidental death, or other catastrophic occurrence), most organizations' communication policies refer members of the media to designated spokespersons. If you are approached by a reporter or editor, politely refer inquiries to those designated persons. Only these people should give media representatives any information at all.

You might receive an inquiry, however, about a topic of public interest that happens to be in your area of expertise. You might be asked to speak about the topic, either in front of a group or in an interview. *Always* ask your organization's public affairs or public relations representative to check for authorization. Sometimes, for legal or public image reasons, offering your expertise could harm your firm. Keep in mind that businesses operate in a litigious and volatile environment.

Suppose your superiors authorize you to give an interview or that you run a small business and are the only spokesperson. Brainstorm all the questions you might be asked and prepare short, concise, informative answers to all of them. Keep word choice positive.

Remember that interviewees are often quoted in "sound bites" (15- to 45-second clips). Leading with your key points, prepare answers in that manner, so that you are easy and interesting to quote. Use language that will be familiar to the audience, and keep their WIIFM ("What's in it for me?") in mind.

Be sure to find out exactly how much time you will have, where the tape will be recorded, who will be present, what kind of AV you should prepare, and what the format should be. Find out exactly who the intended media viewers are. (Time of day makes a difference. Cable or network channel makes a difference.) Visualize these viewers' backgrounds and interests. Then plan fascinating material designed not only for this audience but also for the reporter and the editor.

As you plan your speech, resolve not to use it as a forum for applauding your organization or unit. The mass media are especially sensitive to puffery. They will resent it, will almost certainly cut it, and may treat your whole talk less respectfully than they would if you had kept it straight.

Then practice. Get a critique. Practice on videotape, and practice again.

Dress professionally and conservatively. Many, though not all, television people still recommend avoiding white and black. Avoid flash of any kind. Any jewelry should be conservative; remember that strong lights sometimes accompany cameras. If a tie bar or other flat, shiny surface reflects a high-wattage beam back into the camera lens, the effect will be distracting.

Probably the most important difference between a media presentation and other types of presentations is this: Only the people physically sitting there in the room with you are sure to hear all of what you say. Once you are on videotape, the media staff can do what they like with the tape. They are ethical, yet they are still selling a product. They will not drastically alter what you have said, but they will cut out whatever is not extremely interesting. Your opinions may differ from theirs in that what you consider to be essential explanation may be to them just so much wind.

As you speak, then, keep in mind that you are likely to be edited. Make your most interesting statements so clear that they will make sense even if the material developing them is cut. Make the explanation useful but not crucial. Entirely avoid irony (saying one thing and implying, usually nonverbally, the opposite). Irony can be humorous, but an astonishing number of people misunderstand it. Educate and inform. Stay away from anything controversial. Show your most professional, approachable, authoritative, and credible manner. Be pleasant and positive. When you finish an answer, stop. The interviewer may continue to look at you expectantly, but don't fill the pause; wait for the next question.

If unexpected questions come, remember your impromptu skills, and pause to think and organize an answer before you reply. If a question is phrased inappropriately, rephrase it before you respond. If you are asked an unfair "either-or question" or a question with an untrue or misleading lead-in, correct the wording (do not repeat the untrue wording as you do so), rephrase the question, and respond with one of the points you prepared. You, not they, decide what you will answer. Stay pleasant.

Keep your eye contact open and sincere. Make sure nonverbals do not convey anything negative.

Never say anything "off the record." Consider that everything you say can be quoted and that the microphone is always on. Roger Ailes, author of *You*

What speakers say to the media must retain its intended meaning even if it is cut drastically and quoted out of context.

Cover yourself, but do not sound hostile or defensive.

Oral Presentation   **293**

Are the Message, tells of an experience he had while being interviewed for the television program "60 Minutes":

> The person interviewing me was either trying to relax me or thought he'd get me to open up in some way in an unguarded moment. He ordered his crew to take a break. But I noticed that, while the crew locked their recording gear in place and drifted away, the camera lenses were uncapped and pointed at me. I heard the faint whir of the camera motor and I knew it was still on. The trick didn't work, so they officially continued the interview.[2]

If you are asked questions that you cannot or must not answer, avoid the phrase, "No comment." Instead, say, "I don't know, but I will find out and have the answer for you at 10 A.M. tomorrow." Or "The person to ask about that is Marcia Kepperly." Or "I'm sorry, but that information is proprietary." *Never* say anything that is untrue.

Finally, be sure to make your own recording of the interview session.

Presenting for In-house Uses

Videotaped presentations for in-house uses permit you more control over the preparation and editing than do those for the mass media. They are also more likely to be retained for repeated use. You, your unit, and the AV production workers, whether they are in-house or from an outside agency, typically will share the goal of making the videotaped presentation excellent. Tap the experience of others who have made presentations. Listen to advice. Find out what didn't work.

Audience analysis will be straightforward. If, for example, your firm puts out a video newsletter for employees every 90 days, your audience is the whole organization, all levels. Suppose you are asked to talk about bringing a new and newsworthy development online. You will need to convey not only information about the project but also your enthusiasm toward it. Your persuasive subtext, expressed nonverbally, paraverbally, and sincerely, will be: "This is an interesting job. This is a good place to work."

As another example, suppose you are asked to make a training film on a basic procedure for new hires in your department. Your audience has no knowledge of your organization beyond first-week orientation. The basic tasks are performed by people with little technical knowledge; thus, your presentation must be elementary without being condescending. As you can see, your agenda is very different from that in the first example.

In essence, you will present a procedure report in video form. You will move step by step through a process. Clarity will be greatly enhanced, however, because at every step you can show as well as tell. Present the steps in the order that makes sense to the new employees, not to you. Omit nothing, but do not bring up anything they don't need to know. Think of all possible questions a newcomer might have, and make sure the presentation answers them at the time they would arise. Your purpose is mainly informative. The only persuasive element is the confidence you convey that your audience will be able to do this task well.

For in-house videos, presenters wear what they would wear under ordinary, on-the-job circumstances, such as shirtsleeves or labcoats. Usually dress becomes formal only when the representative of the firm is shown meeting people from the outside. Even top management, although they may appear in coat

[2]Roger Ailes, *You Are the Message* (Homewood, Ill.: Dow Jones–Irwin, 1988), p. 164.

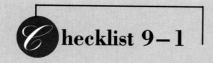

Checklist 9–1

Extemporaneous Presentation

As you rehearse your presentation—and again if you are able to view it on videotape—ask yourself these questions:

- What initial impression do I make?
- Is my introduction interesting? Does it tell what I'll say, develop WIIFM, and lay out a plan my audience can follow easily?
- Am I standing erect but comfortably?
- Am I maintaining eye contact with my audience nearly 100 percent of the time?
- Am I including my whole audience?
- Am I keeping my eyes off my notecards except for brief, necessary referral?
- Is my face lively and communicative?
- Is my voice appropriate in pitch?
  - Does it vary within a broad and pleasant range?
  - Is my volume right? Does it vary appropriately?
  - Am I too fast? Too slow?
  - Am I enunciating clearly?
  - Do I have control over sounds like *um*?

- Am I helping my audience follow my organization?
- Am I using my audiovisual exhibits effectively?
- If I were an audience member, would I find the content valuable?
- Do I sound credible?
- Am I projecting a fairly high level of comfort?
- Are my hands controlled, either working for me or at rest?
- Am I staying within my allotted time?
- Do I provide clear transition to my concluding section?
- Do I summarize?
  - Do I recap my main purpose?
  - Do I reinforce the WIIFM?
  - If a persuasive talk, do I ask the audience to take needed action?
- Do I end confidently, with a final-sounding downward intonation and good eye contact?

and tie at the beginning of an in-house video, often opt for less formality when they move to nuts-and-bolts matters. A possible exception: Women managers often prefer to be videotaped wearing the suit jacket or blazer. Viewers are still too likely to assume they are not in positions of authority otherwise.

For all in-house video presentations, especially if they will be used often, practice—and practice again.

Videoconferenced presentations usually occur within the context of a meeting. Like in-person meetings, videoconferenced meetings fill a one-time need, with a different agenda each time. Most of the material on meetings in this text (see Chapter 15) applies to meetings by videoconference. A presenter might be a main event and speak for 15 minutes or more, or one of several contributors, speaking for just a few minutes.

Presenting for Videoconferences

Because videoconference time is expensive (though less expensive than the travel it replaces), speakers must condense. They analyze carefully the level of existing knowledge of the videoconference participants to learn what not to spend time on. Then they plan and organize a succinct talk.

A videoconference must use meeting time economically to meet the participants' goal.

A videoconference presenter faces one challenge peculiar to the medium. When people meet for the first time by videoconference, the level of trust and liking is lower than it is when they meet in person. The medium does not make this difference when participants already know each other. As you can infer, an informational speaker must take extra care in establishing credibility. In addition to credibility, a speaker with a persuasive goal needs to work harder to establish common ground with those on the other end of the conference.

REVIEW

Oral business presentations or reports give audiences material that they need. Speakers must analyze audiences with respect to background and knowledge; receptiveness; education, age, and other demographics; and size of audience. Business audiences generally support speakers; they expect competence but not perfection. Speakers need to know themselves well, work to project confidence, plan talks carefully, practice thoroughly, and prepare their own minds by positive imaging before beginning to speak.

Business presentations need a strong opening and close and an organized body. Speakers need to give plenty of "direction signals" to help the audience follow the talk's structure. Most business presentations are extemporaneous; other forms are manuscript and impromptu speaking.

Effective speakers control nonverbal and paraverbal signals to project competence, energy, and enthusiasm. Nonverbals include erect posture and stable stance, careful grooming, appropriate dress, communicative facial expression, deliberate use of gesture, and full eye contact that takes in all parts of the audience. Paraverbals—variations in voice accompanying words—include pitch, range, speed, volume, articulation, and fluency.

Informational presentations follow familiar, logical patterns. Persuasive presentations, which make use of psychology and indirection, follow different patterns.

Business presenters use visuals such as handouts, chalkboards, flipcharts, posters, deskcharts, transparencies, 35mm slides, and audio- or videotapes. Communications technology offers new computer-assisted media. Video presentations include those for mass media, for in-house purposes, and for video-conferencing.

APPLICATION EXERCISES

1. Describe a typical business audience's attitude toward, and expectations of, a business speaker.

2. Does a speaker's nervousness always show? Explain.

3. Explain positive imaging, and give examples of helpful ways to visualize oneself and one's audience.

4. What audience analysis must business speakers perform?

5. What are some ways business presentations differ from other kinds of speeches, such as after-dinner speeches, political speeches, and speech class assignments?

6. Give several reasons typical business presentations are seldom memorized or read from a manuscript.

7. Differentiate between extemporaneous and impromptu speaking.

8. In your experience, what nonverbals are hardest for beginning speakers to control? Why? What suggestions can you make to help control them?

9. "Business audiences are unfair when they react negatively to a speaker's high or soft voice, monotone delivery, or 'um' intrusions." Do you agree or disagree? Discuss your reasons.

10. Distinguish between speaking to inform and speaking to persuade. Is there always a firm dividing line between the two kinds of talks?

11. How are persuasive talks organized? Why are they organized in those ways?

12. Discuss the advantages and disadvantages of handouts, chalkboards, flipcharts, posters, transparencies, and 35mm slides.

13. Would you attempt to make a videotape to use as a visual in a presentation? What would you have to do to make it effective?

14. "The mass media have a grudge against business. Reporters are always trying to embarrass businesspeople in interviews." Do you agree or disagree? Discuss your reasons.

15. What precautions does a business interviewee need to take with respect to a video interview intended for the media?

CASES

1. **Critiquing a Pro.**   Watch a professional give a speech. For instance, you might choose an on-campus guest speaker or an influential person speaking on a cable or network channel. In writing, analyze and evaluate the effectiveness of what you saw and heard. Specify whether the speaker read the speech or spoke extemporaneously. In either case, did it sound natural and professional? Evaluate the speaker and the speech in terms of the aspects of presentation covered in this chapter. Include suggestions for improvement.

2. **Generating Interest and Informing.**   Based on your present knowledge and interests, fill in the blank in this sentence: "As future businesspersons, my classmates should be aware of_____ ." Virtually any business-related topic could fill the blank. Examples—just to get you started thinking—include GATT (General Agreement on Tariffs and Trade), disposable cameras, hurricane warning systems, time management, the North American Free Trade Agreement, the under-12 market for compact disks, business and political slogans. Choose your own topic. You don't have to know or learn everything about a topic to introduce it and show that it is important to business. *In a three-minute presentation, show your class why your topic is important to them.* Inform and interest them.

3. **Summarizing a News Story.**   Your library subscribes to one or more daily newspapers. Read the business section of several recent issues. *Select a news feature of importance to students preparing to work in business.* The article could be about politics, economics, influential individuals, scientific breakthroughs, military issues, or virtually anything else likely to influence what happens in business. *Study the article and prepare a three-minute summary to present orally to your class.* Tell them why the content is important; tell them the content; then tell them what you have told them. Inform and interest them. Develop WIIFM.

4. **Suggesting a Way to Solve a Problem.**   *In a five-minute presentation, present a well-developed idea for improving a function, service, or facility on your campus.* Campuses and students' perceptions differ, but possibilities might include bike parking, use of student fees, bookstore practices at opening of term, pedestrian safety, a cumbersome procedure, recreational facilities, campus elections, or appearance of the campus. You will think of dozens of others.

5. **Presenting Your Research.** *Present extemporaneously to your class the most important material from your written report.* Keep in mind the differences between oral and written reports. You will not be presenting everything you wrote. Select content to suit your audience's needs. Make your talk interesting. Build a strong structure with excellent introduction and conclusion and an easy-to-follow body. Prepare one or more visuals. Practice with your notes and visuals until you sound like a professional. Aim at giving your audience 100 percent eye contact. Your instructor will set time limits and other specifics of the assignment.

6. **Increasing Intercultural Awareness.** Interview a non-U.S.-born student on your campus. *Ask your subject to describe the aspects of daily living and interpersonal communication that seem most different from those of his or her home country.* (If you were born in another country, interview a non-U.S.-born student whose home country is different from yours.) What experiences were most startling when the person first arrived? Try hard to see through this international student's eyes and to understand the different assumptions and reasons underlying the different practices. Then, *in an oral presentation, tell your classmates what you learned.* Make certain they know why this information is useful and important.

7. **Presenting a Feasibility Report: What Options at What Costs?** Your organization will hold a retirement dinner party for seven 30-year members, two of whom are vice presidents. You are asked by the planning committee to price musical entertainment for the occasion. The four-hour Friday evening party, to be attended by 150 guests of all ages, will include dancing. What does a five-person combo cost, and what kinds of music can they offer? How about a DJ who plays recorded music on state-of-the-art equipment? Are there other alternatives? *Report orally on the committee's options.*

8. **Reporting on Development of New Service Businesses.** What small service businesses did not exist 15 or 20 years ago? An example might be the plant-care services that supply, care for, and replace the growing plants that adorn many offices. *Find out about another relatively new small service business. Report on it orally to your class.*

9. **Presenting Results of Comparative Pricing Study.** The vice president of administration is reviewing suppliers. Your firm's office manager has assigned you this task: Make a list of 25 common office supplies, including a 10-ream case of copy paper, a box of 100 $9'' \times 12''$ clasp envelopes, a box of 100 letter-size manila folders, and 22 other items of your choice. Price your choices at two office supply vendors. Compare prices. If one vendor is higher, are additional advantages offered that justify the price differential? Are the two vendors about the same? *Present your findings orally, along with a recommendation, to the vice president and the seven managers she supervises (the office manager is one).*

10. **Presenting Results of a Site Selection Study.** Your employer owns several photocopying stores and is considering expansion. You are asked to *gather cost figures on 1,200 square feet of office space in two different sections of your town.* The decision maker has in mind locating in a strip shopping center or a downtown building. Up to 15 parking spaces are desirable. Visit the two sites. *Present orally what you learn; include visuals.*

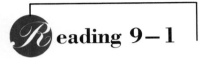

GUIDELINES FOR BETTER VISUALS

Reading 9–1 | *Marian K. Woodall*

1. Aim for cleanness and clarity. Resist the impulse to be too fancy; even though your computer system enables you to mix six different type faces, don't. Don't let the art overwhelm the message.

2. Aim for simplicity. When using a drawing of a mechanism, for example, resist the temptation to fill in or label all the fields or parts. Include enough detail for authenticity. Label those parts necessary to make the point that that specific graphic is supporting, plus one or two major items for perspective.

3. When developing word visuals, be brief. Use words or short phrases, not sentences. Use single-syllable words whenever possible. Use common

Source: Marian K. Woodall, *Speaking to a Group* (Lake Oswego, Ore.: Professional Business Communications, 1990), pp. 112–13.

abbreviations (you can explain them as you debrief the slide).

4. Use capitals and lower case lettering rather than all caps. People read more quickly by scanning the ascenders and descenders (the parts of letters which come above and below the regular line of type). Use bold when you want extra emphasis, instead of capital letters.

5. Use color. Remember what your audience sees on television. But resist the opportunity to be gaudy.

6. Headings or titles should usually be in large type. Subheads should be in the same font (type style), with smaller type than the headings. Consider bold or some other special treatment for emphasis of a key word or phrase.

7. For bold visual impact on short lists, use bullets, closed boxes, or closed circles rather than asterisks or open characters.

8. If you have more than three items in a subhead consider numbering or lettering them. If the items must be taken in order—if they are steps in a process, for example—it is important to number them. You remind the audience of the importance of keeping them in order.

NOTE—If the material requires more depth than subheads, print that extra material only on the paper copy of the handouts that you give the audience. An overhead or slide should generally have only the title and the briefly phrased, bulleted subheads.

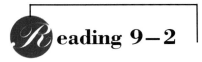

THE NOT-SO-HIDDEN BENEFITS OF POWERFUL SPEAKING

Dorothy Leeds

I have seen what a newfound speaking ability can do for a person. Being a good presenter makes you visible, and in corporations, money, resources, and power flow to the visible high achiever. The visibility that speaking abilities give you becomes part of your overall professional growth. A colleague of mine at a large Fortune 500 company moved through the ranks with startling speed and ease. Many of his peers were just as competent, but he was a very good public speaker; his presentations were effective, persuasive events. He had an undeniable edge.

I also watched the careers of two executives at a large manufacturing firm. She was a highly persuasive speaker who had studied public speaking and ran dynamic meetings. She really knew how to inform and persuade. He, on the other hand, was a dull speaker. After five years, she was vice-president of their division, and he was still a manager. Needless to say, the executives may well have been equally competent. If you don't use public speaking to your advantage, someone else will use it to his.

There is just so much spotlight to go around, and it's a given that speakers occupy it regularly. Presenting in public is advertising with subtlety: You are displaying your abilities without touting them. As the old rhyme reminds us:

The codfish lays ten thousand eggs, the homely hen lays one.
The codfish never cackles to tell us what she's done; and so we scorn the codfish while the homely hen we prize.
It only goes to show you that it pays to advertise.

Source: from POWERSPEAK: The Complete Guide to Persuasive Public Speaking and Presenting by Dorothy Leeds. New York: Berkley Books (originally published by Prentice-Hall, 1988).

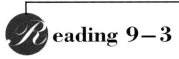

THE ORIGINS OF PUBLIC-SPEAKING PANIC

Dorothy Leeds

As a speaker, you're a person apart from the crowd. People are more comfortable in groups than leading them; that way, no one is on the spot, and others can carry the conversation if you run out of ideas. Speaking isolates you; it removes you from your peers and designates you different from everyone else—you're the one who has something worthwhile to say. Some people relish this attention; others, understandably, find the sudden spotlight daunting. The trick is to accept your being singled out; it's temporary, and it's probably an honor, too. So try to see it as an honor, since your perception of the event will be crucial to your success.

Source: from POWERSPEAK: The Complete Guide to Persuasive Public Speaking and Presenting by Dorothy Leeds. New York: Berkley Books (originally published by Prentice-Hall, 1988).

It also helps if you don't let the spotlight become a barrier. Many novice speakers blow up their isolation in their own mind, until it takes on exaggerated importance. Think less about yourself and more about your audience and some of the fear will leave, as you perceive yourself not as isolated but as part of the group you're addressing—a group that *wants* to hear what you have to say.

Except for optional question-and-answer sessions, speaking is a one-way street. You don't get the direct feedback conversation provides. You're not sure if people are really following you. You can see their eyes—though not very well—but you don't know what they're thinking. A person may leave the room, and you feel personally rejected, even though he is only stepping outside to make a phone call. A joke you've told many times with great success may not get a laugh.

What's missing is swift feedback and knowledge of where you stand, and the absence of this throws you off. Everyone, not just speakers, needs feedback. To prove this point, a man in a pub took bets from people in the pub and challenged one of England's champion dart throwers that he could make the expert falter in less than four throws—and without interfering with the throw itself. The challenger held up a piece of paper in front of the champion just after he released the dart—so the champion could not see how he did—and then removed the dart before the next throw. Sure enough, the champion's game went to pieces in three throws. Without seeing—instantly—the results of each throw, he missed the next shots.

People do get reactions to their speeches—afterward. Knowing that during the speech you will plunge ahead like the dart thrower, without feedback, accounts for much of the nervousness speakers feel. But forewarned is indeed forearmed. Expect the pauses, the small silences, and they won't seem strange. Different audiences will also react differently; don't expect the same noises from both a general audience and one with a very technical bent. And don't misread reactions out of sheer nervousness. Silence can indicate deep thought and agreement as much as it can alert you to boredom.

I once saw a speaker address a small group in a U-shaped seating arrangement. At the back of the room, a man seemed to be paying no attention; he spent the entire speech scribbling and gazing into space. During the break, other people in the audience asked the speaker how he could tolerate the noticeably rude man. The speaker was relaxed; he said he just focused on the rest of the seemingly more interested audience. But after the session was over, the scribbler came up to the speaker, identified himself as a reporter, said he was particularly fascinated by the presentation and would be writing an article on it, and thanked the speaker. Moral: Don't guess at what your audience's reactions mean. It detracts from your effectiveness to worry about those who don't seem to be listening, since they may be listening the hardest, anyway.

When I tell someone they can learn to be a commanding speaker, I usually get a swift, standard protest: "But you can't learn it; public speaking is a talent you are either born with or not." Not so. Public speaking is not an innate skill; good speakers are *made*—not born—through hard work and practice. As with any learned skill, some people are better than others, but everyone can work at it successfully.

If someone had told me twenty years ago that I, with my wispy voice and fear of crowds, would really enjoy public speaking, I would not have believed a word. But it's true; and one of the most important kinds of power speaking brings you is the power to change your own perception of yourself—not to mention other people's perceptions of you.

Giving a speech is not a natural, ordinary event. Speakers who expect to feel at ease are kidding themselves. It may seem hard to believe that even the most polished, experienced speakers get nervous, but they do. So don't expect, or long for, relaxation; expect the nervous excitement and energy that come from the task at hand. In other words, use fear to your advantage; charisma and adrenaline are closely linked.

Chapter Ten

Indirect Messages: Handling Negative and Sensitive Information

PREVIEW

In this chapter, you will learn more about indirect messages and how to send tactful and effective messages containing negative or sensitive information. When sending information directly to a reading or listening audience, you can begin with the most important piece of information, because that is what the audience is waiting for. An indirect message, on the other hand, can begin with a number of different ideas, but not with the most important piece of information, because the audience hopes to read or hear something else.

Usually you will choose to be indirect when refusing to do something; when making adjustments that will only partially satisfy the customer's concerns; when dealing with mail-order problems such as incomplete information, back orders, and substitute orders; and when handling personnel problems. Being indirect means handling a potentially negative situation with tact and extra attention to audience reaction.

A number of negative or disappointing messages are handled by phone or fax if the problem can be fixed more quickly that way (order problems, for example). Regardless of the medium used, you should prepare the message with attention to the "you attitude" and audience analysis so that you do not run the risk of unintentionally alienating a customer.

Using passive voice, emphasizing positive over negative, and avoiding negative words are three techniques for conveying disappointing information while taking the reader's or listener's feelings into consideration. ●

Scott Carlyle
Department Manager

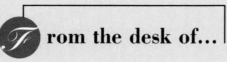

rom the desk of... | Customer-Friendly Operations?

In retail, you've got to remember that the customer is always right—if you "win" an argument, you're likely to *lose* the customer! I had to let go a clerk who explained "policy" in depth to a customer asking why one size of a product was on sale in one department and the other size wasn't on sale in another department.

Instead of making the customer angry with all the explanation (and refusal to do what she asked), the clerk should just have given the customer the $5 difference as a credit or refund—it was really just a pricing mistake, and he made us look unfriendly and rigid in his attempt to make us look right. We're supposed to be a customer-friendly company, after all. Instead of gaining $5, he lost us a long-time customer who used to spend over $1,000 a year here!

Not all business messages should be direct. If you need to tell your reader or listener something negative, it is often best to do so indirectly. This softens the blow and can prepare your audience for your explanation. You *don't* want to argue with a customer over who is right!

PSYCHOLOGICAL REASONS FOR INDIRECTNESS

In most cases, when people ask for something, they think there is a chance they will get what they want. As a result, when you refuse someone's request, you need to consider the human interaction that's taking place. You need to say no tactfully so the reader or listener doesn't feel foolish for having asked in the first place.

To convey negative information successfully, you should give priority to the human considerations of the situation. If you can give the negative message without blaming the reader (by using passive voice, for example), your reader will probably accept it more easily.

Think about a time when you had to give someone bad news over the phone, such as your decision to break up with the person you had been dating for months. Surely you didn't call the person and say, "Roger, I don't want to see you any more." More likely, you began, "Roger, there's something we need to talk about." However, while we tend to use indirectness in *speaking* of bad news, when we convey bad news in *writing,* we are often more blunt and less attentive to the reader's feelings. In organizing a negative message, we need to be concerned with both the negative part (you didn't get the job, we don't give out samples) *and* getting the reader to listen to our explanation.

One objection to the negative phrases many business writers used in the past is that they sound so insincere that the reader loses interest in the explanation. If you don't treat the reader as a thinking human being in the beginning of the letter, he or she will not expect you to be truthful later. Phrases such as "we would like to thank you for considering us," "we regret to inform you that . . . " or "I'm really sorry that . . . " don't sound like the writer *means* them. Save apologies for really extreme situations; don't apologize for simple business decisions and other daily occurrences. When you do apologize, do so convincingly.

Audience analysis is very important in planning negative messages. If you think first how your reader or listener might react to your message, you will be on your way to writing a more successful message, whether a letter, memo, voice or E-mail message, or report.

Remember the audience analysis checklist from Chapter 1. The last question is "What action do you want your audience to take as a result of your message?" In direct messages, you can get action quickly by getting right to the point, because the audience agrees with your point of view or expects your information. In indirect messages, you need to prove your case before offering your conclusion or action to allow the reader time to accept your point of view.

In a direct message, the most important piece of information is the news you convey. In an indirect message, the most important thing is the fact that you have listened to the reader's request or concern. By being indirect, you can be diplomatic *and* keep the customer. For the same reason, as you will see in Chapter 11, in persuading you think first of reader benefit and then of your gain from the granted request.

A conventional outline for an indirect message appeared in Chapter 1:

STEPS IN WRITING INDIRECT NEGATIVE OR SENSITIVE MESSAGES

- Begin with a buffer to set up the situation.
- Explain the problem.
- Imply or embed the negative.
- Get the necessary action.
- End on a positive note.

Notice how the steps in this process differ from those for direct business messages discussed in Chapter 2.

Because the reader needs to be prepared for the negative or sensitive information, begin with a **buffer,** an opening statement that shows agreement with something the reader said (but *not* with the request, for example, if you are turning down a request.) A buffer needs to be *agreeable, noncommital* (not saying that the request will be granted), *relevant* (not coming out of left field and unrelated to later information), *concise,* and *transitional.* In the later examples of refused requests for donations, for example, note how the buffers set the stage for an agreeable discussion with the reader but do not promise fulfillment of the request.

Begin with a Buffer to Set Up the Situation

Consider the opening of the Beatse Confection letter that appears in full later in Exhibit 10–1 (page 307):

> Your Shakespeare Birthday Festival sounds like a wonderful addition to the schedule of family-oriented outdoor events here in San Clemente.

This opening is friendly and agreeable. It acknowledges that the festival is a worthy project, but it stops short of offering to support the event. The writer has added enough detail to sound well informed; the opening isn't just an empty cliché.

Make the explanation logical and as specific as is reasonable, remembering that specifics are more credible that generalities. Here is the explanation from the Beatse Confection letter:

Explain the Problem

> As you can imagine, Beatse Confection International is approached by a large number of charities, social groups, foundations, and organizations from all of our marketing

areas in the Southwest. While we would like to help all of these worthwhile efforts, we have found that the most efficient and equitable approach is to extend a "helping hand" through our corporate donations to United Way.

This explanation is logical, relatively specific, and friendly but businesslike. It stresses *fairness*—a positive value—rather than mentioning limited resources or the reader's having an unworthy cause—both negatives.

Imply or Embed the Negative

Notice how the preceding excerpt says *no* without actually using the word. By telling the reader what the company *can* do (donate through United Way), the letter eliminates other options, such as donating directly to the reader's event. An even stronger way to do this would be to reword the last part of the sentence:

extend a "helping hand" exclusively through our corporate donations to United Way.

Using a word like *exclusively, solely,* or *only* makes it clear to the reader that the writer will not do what the reader asked because the requested action is not included in this limited group of acceptable actions. The writer has clearly said *no* without saying so directly.

If a stronger refusal seems in order, *embed* the negative material by placing it in the middle of a paragraph rather than implying the action as the preceding example does. This subordinates the negative information to the explanation and helps retain the reader's goodwill.

Get the Necessary Action

Some negative messages require no further action on the part of the reader (and the writer doesn't want the reader to reply or to continue the process any longer). Take care of any necessary action toward the end of the letter or memo.

End on a Positive Note

The final idea to present to the reader is a positive one (*don't* refer again to the negative part of the message). Here is how the Beatse Confection letter ends:

We wish your festival every success.

This positive ending is friendly, but it promises nothing. Further, it doesn't refer to the request again or use negative language such as "we regret we cannot fulfill your request at this time." The writer has listened to the reader's request and said *no,* rejecting the request idea but *not* the reader.

NEGATIVE BUSINESS SITUATIONS

Some common negative or sensitive situations that occur in business are (1) refusals, (2) adjustments and claims, (3) order problems, and (4) personnel problems.

Refusals

Tactful rejection letters such as those in Exhibits 10–1 through 10–3 give reasonable explanations and let the reader down gently. Exhibit 10–1 gives the full version of the letter whose parts we examined earlier. Exhibit 10–2 is another refusal for a similar fund-raising cause. Notice how the explanation and implied refusal in the second paragraph limit Adrian Arcades' donations to "children and teenagers in need." Since the USO is not primarily a children's organization, it will not receive a donation. Here again, the writer has said *no* without actually *saying* so.

Your initial reaction may be "Why on earth are these people bothering us for a donation?" But remember that all of those fund-raising organizations are

"Our Business is Sweet"

Beatse Confection International
8215 Industrial Park Plaza - Suite 1207
West Covina, CA 91790

January 6, 1994

Ms. Elizabeth Villarosa
Shakespeare's Birthday Festival
1515 Prado Drive
West Covina, CA 92672

Dear Ms. Villarosa:

Friendly, agreeable buffer

Your Shakespeare Birthday Festival sounds like a wonderful addition to the schedule of family-oriented outdoor events here in West Covina.

Reasonable explanation

Implied refusal

As you can imagine, Beatse Confection International is approached by a large number of charities, social groups, foundations and organizations from all of our marketing areas in the Southwest. While we would like to help all of these worthwhile efforts, we have found that the most efficient and equitable approach is to extend a "helping hand" through our corporate donations to United Way.

Positive ending

We wish your festival every success.

Sincerely,

James C. Beatse
President/CEO

Adrian Arcades
Amusements
83 Edison Lane
Jersey City, NJ 07306

June 24, 1994

Ms. Ruth Duncan
USO Annual Dinner
59 Rosewood Parkway
Long Island, NY 11245

Dear Ms. Duncan:

Friendly, opening

Thank you very much for inviting Adrian Arcades to be a part of your USO Annual Dinner.

Reasonable explanation with implied refusal

Adrian Arcades receives contribution requests from numerous organizations almost on a daily basis and it would be wonderful if we could help each one. Adrian Arcades believes in strong community involvement. However, since we are a video game company, we think our contributions should be directed towards groups aiding children and teenagers in need.

Positive ending

Good luck and best wishes for a successful event!

Sincerely,

Albert Adrian

Albert Adrian
Promotions Director

PIEDRAS NOVELTY COMPANY

JOSE AGUADILLA - PROPRIETOR   BOX 28115 UPR STATION   RIO PIEDRAS, PR 00931-8115   (809) 578-3544

June 24, 1994

Mr. Robert Stewart
Bass Fishing Boosters
1207 River Drive
Melbourne, FL 21901

Dear Mr. Stewart:

Establishes the procedure for judging donation requests

As is the case for all contribution requests, your recent inquiry was presented to Piedras Novelty Company's Contributions Committee for consideration.

Refuses politely, leaving the door open for further requests

While the committee is unable to honor the request of your organization at this time, we appreciate your thinking of Piedras Novelty. We invite you to contact us regarding similar endeavors in the future.

Sincerely,

Jose Aguadilla

Jose Aguadilla, Proprietor

filled with potential customers for your business. A tactful turndown (sometimes called a TNT, or "thanks, but no thanks" letter) may build you some goodwill. In Exhibit 10–1, the *no* was the only reply received from three similar companies approached. Of course, Beatse Confection looks better than the others because of its courtesy, even though none donated to the cause.

Exhibit 10–3 gives another potential reason for saying *no* to a request. The stilted language ("for consideration") and the unnecessary passive voice ("was presented," "is unable to") make this message distant, but the letter leaves the door open for future inquiries and leaves the reader believing that the writer seriously considered the request.

Now consider Exhibit 10–4, a refusal that concentrates on saying *no* rather than on the reader's reaction to the message. This tritely worded message does have a few positive points: The company *is* replying to the request (many firms lose the opportunity to create goodwill by at least answering letters asking for contributions); the letter speaks of assisting as an opportunity rather than something negative; and the letter wishes the boutique good luck in its event.

However, the negative aspects more than offset these positive points. The letter contains trite phrasing ("Thank you for your interest," "we regret that we must decline"). It includes little explanation—why might the boutique give to others and not to us? Overall, the letter sounds condescending. The writer has failed to realize that the organization's members are potential customers for his store!

Of course, not all refusals involve fund-raising efforts. You might refuse to present a talk at an organization's meeting, refuse to give an information interview to a job seeker who wants contacts in your field, or refuse to sell your product at wholesale to a potential customer trying to avoid retail prices.

Adjustments and Compromises on Complaints

Sometimes you will have to tell a customer that you cannot grant a requested refund or adjustment. When replying to a customer who had a concern about your product or service, you need to acknowledge the problem yet leave a positive impression rather than dwelling on the negative occurrence. You may tactfully refuse to take the reader's desired action entirely or partially. You can refuse an adjustment and carefully explain why (as in Exhibit 10–5) or offer the reader an action other than the one requested (see Exhibits 10–7 and 10–8 on pages 312 and 314).

In essence, a customer who complains regrets having done business with you—and you need to change that opinion. To regain the customer's goodwill, you need to explain the situation *and* remind the customer that the product or service in question is a good one. Of course, you don't begin directly with this *resale*—an effort to reinforce the customer's purchase decision—in a way that sounds like you are arguing with the reader about the value of the product.

Adjustments

In another example (Exhibit 10–5), an orthodontist is rejecting a request from a parent to fill her child's cavities for free. This businesslike refusal maintains client goodwill. It tactfully reminds the parent of the signed care agreement, and solves the problem (the child's cavities) by providing an answer (go to your regular dentist)—but it does *not* give the parent the free work requested.

The form letter from Ford Motor Company (Exhibit 10–6) rejects a customer's request politely but firmly. It attempts to close the issue while encouraging possible future interaction on other matters. The indirectly

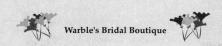

Warble's Bridal Boutique

November 15, 1993

Ms. Olita Carmichael
3921 Cashell Drive
Syracuse, NY 13220

Dear Ms. Carmichael:

Trite opening   Thank you for your interest in Warble's Bridal
Boutique.

Vague and   As you can imagine, we receive many requests from
negative   worthy organizations seeking assistance in their fund-
raising efforts. Unfortunately, it is not feasible for
us to assist every organization.

Refuses directly   With this in mind, we regret that we must decline the
opportunity to assist your organization at this time.

Sounds less   Please accept our best wishes for a successful event.
than sincere

Sincerely,

Craig Warble
Events Co-ordinator

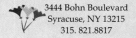

3444 Bohn Boulevard
Syracuse, NY 13215
315. 821.8817

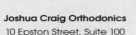

Joshua Craig Orthodonics
10 Epston Street, Suite 100
Canton, OH 44720

December 15, 1994

Mrs. James Smith
4711 South Evans Street
Canton, OH 44735

Dear Mrs. Smith:

Buffer is agreeable but equivocal

Like you, we are concerned about the condition of your son, Jim's, teeth. We care about teeth; that's why we try to give each patient the best, straightest teeth. Always first in our minds in our practice of orthodontistry is avoiding damage to the teeth we are straightening.

Negative information is embedded

Despite the most careful attention to sound and hygienic dental practice by both our patients and our staff, however, cavities do occasionally occur. As explained in the videotapes you were shown and the care agreement you signed, we suggest that you have Dr. Waymond, your family dentist, fill any cavities that may occur during the orthodontia process, as she is a specialist in that kind of care.

Ending looks positively to the future

Jim is making good progress in his treatment. We currently project that his braces will come off in about three months, to be replaced by a retainer.

Sincerely,

Raymond Gutierrez, D.D.S.

Ford Motor Company

The American Road
Dearborn, Michigan 48121

Dear Mr. Sample:

We have received the information necessary to respond fully to your inquiry concerning service problems with your (vehicle model).

Although the joint efforts of your dealer and our representative have not met with your expectations, we feel that every consideration has been given to the matter and the decision reached was correct.

If you have concerns other than those we have already reviewed, please contact the service manager of your dealership.

Thank you for contacting us.

National Conservatory Theatre

April 7, 1994

Mr. Randy Moore
5552 Golden Gate Avenue
Oakland, CA 94618

Dear Mr. Moore:

Buffer finds a topic reader can agree with

I appreciate your note about your experience at last week's performance of Redwood Curtain.

Explanation is specific and honest

Our somewhat antiquated air conditioning system was indeed caught unready by the extremely hot weather on Thursday. The ventilation system is certainly one of the features we intend to modernize in our Theatre Drive '95 Campaign. I can assure you that we appreciate your patronage of the National Conservatory Theatre, and, had there been any possible repair of the system, we would have made it.

Mentions future improvements

As you may be aware, the NCT has proudly joined the American Association of Regional Theatres as of April 1, and we shall be implementing new subscriber programs so that our service is all that you expect from a major regional theatre.

Gives reader some compensation for the negative experience

Please use the enclosed two for one ticket voucher to attend another performance this season (or invite friends to join you on your regular evening). Just call the box office at 459-5507 to choose your performance date. I look forward to seeing you at NCT this season.

Sincerely,

Dave Clapper
Managing Director

50 LIDA STREET   SAN FRANCISCO, CA 94102   (415) 877-3130

presented message is that Ford has considered and investigated the customer's request or concern and does not think the company is at fault. The first paragraph introduces the idea that the inquiry about service problems has been fully investigated. The second paragraph says *no* politely and firmly. The third paragraph tells how to deal with other, future concerns. The letter ends on a friendly note. This type of form response may still not satisfy the reader, but is a reasonable form response to a recurring problem.

In replying to a customer's complaint or concern letter, you can sometimes give the customer something that is easy for you to give and often costs you less than the value to the customer. Examples of such a "free" gift would be a complimentary hotel stay from a hotel (subject to availability so that you don't lose a paying customer), a free drink in the bar from a restaurant (only your cost is involved), or free theater tickets from a theater (again, subject to availability).

The letter in Exhibit 10–7 does a reasonable job of pacifying a customer who attended a performance during an unseasonal heat wave in an older theater with a broken air conditioning system. The reader gets two theater tickets for his inconvenience, and—equally important—the writer makes an effort to sound helpful and concerned. If the reader had asked for his money back, the example would show a compromise adjustment, one in which the reader receives an action other than that requested, but a logical action (discussed in the next section).

It is impossible to satisfy every customer concern through compensation that would be cost effective for a business. However, a service-oriented business at least attempts to make the customer feel listened to and understood. The explanation part of a negative message often can help convey this expression of helpfulness by discussing changes in procedure that the reader's complaint helped institute or future changes that will improve the situation. Don't go so far as to promise that something "will never happen again" unless you are *very* sure you can fulfill that promise. Of course, some customers will be impossible to satisfy despite your best efforts.

Another type of adjustment letter involves a compromise: giving something logical, but not what the reader asked for. The bookseller in Exhibit 10–8 not only provides the customer with new binders but also transfers the reference series into them. Clearly a business will choose this action only when an

Compromise Adjustments

Calvin and Hobbes   by Bill Watterson

Calvin has an objection to every one of Hobbes' ideas.

Indirect Messages: Handling Negative and Sensitive Information |

◆ ◆ ◆
B e a m i s h
booksellers, ltd.

July 17, 1993

Mr. Pradip Singh
4314 Windsor Court
North York, Ontario

Dear Mr. Singh:

Positive buffer with resale on the product

The Walpole Optics Reference series, with its monthly updates, is one of the most widely used and highly respected references in current developments in optics. You must have referred to yours many times to have worn out its binders in only a year.

Compromise adjustment (a new type of binder rather than a complete replacement or cancelled order)

So you won't have to do without this valuable reference in your business, we will upgrade your binders to the Library version, which is designed to withstand frequent use, at no charge.

Action sounds easy and helpful

Final sentence stresses satisfaction and resale

Just give us a call; we will come out to your office and transfer your existing issues to the new binders. Then, you can continue to get the regular updates you have found so valuable in the past.

Sincerely,

Lucinda Beamish

Lucinda Beamish

48-113 International Court
London, Ontario
CANADA N6A 5K4
(519) 671-3732

expensive product is involved (here, an ongoing monthly series) and it wants to satisfy—and keep—the customer.

After refusals and adjustments, order problems are the largest category of negative business messages. The key goal in all order problem letters is *keeping the order.* In handling the potential negatives of a delay or a substitution, emphasize positives (when the products will arrive, what a good choice the purchase was) over negatives (how long the delay will be, what information the customer forgot to give you).

Order Problems

Resale—reminding a customer about the good features of a product—can help keep a customer from canceling an order due to a delay or reinforce a customer's positive feelings about an order. Resale differs from sales promotion in that it refers to products the customer has already ordered or expressed an interest in, whereas sales promotion refers to new or related products.

Using Resale to Keep Orders

If an order will be delayed because of production problems or because the buyer omitted a piece of information, resale can help you keep the order. Specific, audience-centered resale reminds the reader why the product choice was a good one in the first place. The paragraphs from order problem letters in this chapter show some good examples of product resale.

Even if you *can* send something right away, resale can help you make the customer feel glad about ordering the product:

> The personally autographed Michael Jordan wall poster is a collector's item. Framed in a solid oak frame with gold accents, this poster is sure to be cherished for years to come. It is on its way now, soon to be enjoyed by your grandson.

Resale to a single customer emphasizes different features than those used in resale to a dealer of a product. If the wall poster in the preceding example is being sent in quantity to a dealer, a more appropriate resale strategy would be to mention how quickly the product sells, what the markup is, and whether national advertising for the product exists.

Order problems fall into three main groups:

- Back orders (you cannot ship the goods right away).
- Missing information (the customer didn't give you all the information about size, color, etc. that you need before shipping the product).
- Substitutions (you don't carry the product ordered, but you carry another product that serves the same purpose).

Often not all items ordered by mail are available to send at once. In Chapter 2, you saw a postcard used by one company to tell a customer that an item is out of stock (see page 33):

Back Orders

> The product(s) noted below is out of stock. Because our supplier is not able to tell us when we may expect shipment, it is necessary to cancel this order. Your account will not be billed for this merchandise.
>
> We are sorry to disappoint you, and wish to apologize for any inconvenience this may cause. We hope that we may be of service at some future time.

In Chapter 2, we looked at this message as an example of a possibly misused form—if only one item is out of stock, the whole order doesn't need to be cancelled. Now let's consider it as a negative message. The explanation is that the supplier can't give a delivery date close enough to reasonably expect the customer to wait for the item or items. However, this situation is probably not enough of a crisis to warrant all the apologizing in the second paragraph.

Exhibit 10–9 shows how another mail-order company handled a similar situation. This letter is a good example of adaptation to the customer (it mentions specifics from the customer's order letter). It also includes major parts of an indirect message involving negative material:

- It begins indirectly, with information showing interest in the customer rather than a direct notification of the delay.
- The writer explains the delay in terms specific enough to sound believable and stresses when the down jacket *will* arrive rather than how much later than it was expected.
- Mail-order requirements follow, allowing the reader to take further action if necessary.
- The letter ends on a positive, helpful note.

If the letter writer had added information about insulated hiking boots, he would have made a *sales promotion.* In contrast, the information in the letter is *resale,* because the customer had already ordered the jacket.

Mail-order regulations.   Because the Federal Trade Commission regulates selling by mail, mail-order letters contain some standard information. The letter in Exhibit 10–9 shows that you can present legal information and still sound like a friendly, helpful person. Here are the standards mail order companies must follow:

- Goods need to be shipped within 30 days if your ad didn't state another time frame (often six to eight weeks for things like premiums, items for which you send in proofs of purchase and often a small amount of money). The 30 days begin when you have all the necessary order information and have received the customer's check or credit card authorization.
- If you won't be able to meet this deadline, you need to notify the customer and offer a refund if the customer doesn't want to wait until the new delivery date.
- The FTC says that if you can't ship when scheduled and *don't* notify the customer, you must cancel the order and refund the customer's money. Refunds must be given within seven business days after you receive the refund request; credit card refunds, however, can be issued within one billing cycle.

The best explanation for a back order (an order you can't send when expected) is a legitimate production problem (preferably one that shows good sales and quality product rather than inept management, of course.) Remember to stress the positive (better goods, arrival date) rather than the negative (production problem, delay in arrival).

More back-order problems.   The next example, two paragraphs from a back-order response, fits the product in its informal tone and uses enough specific detail to sound reasonable. The resale makes the volleyball sound official and special.

Resale on the product.

> Your water-resistant leather volleyball by Sideout is used worldwide. It is the official ball for the PVA (Pro Volleyball Association). Sinjun Smith, the #1-ranked beach volleyball player, says it's the best ball on the market.

Explorer's
Outerwear

Clothing for the Adventurous

October 30, 1994

Mr. Richard Wilson
2425 29th Street West
Seattle, CA 98199

Dear Mr. Wilson:

Specific buffer sounds interested in customer's needs

Your upcoming trip to Greenland to inspect a research project for the University of Washington sounds like a great opportunity and we're pleased you relied on us for expedition gear.

Back order stresses satisfaction and resale

Because our supplier has been unable to receive down and feathers from China because of the political unrest, your down jacket will be shipped on November 7.

Resale reminds reader of jacket's good features

This 100% goose down jacket is rated at 500 fill power to keep you comfortable at temperatures down to 20 below zero, and its teal green Gore-Tex (TM) fabric is both waterproof and breathable to keep you dry in all climates.

Mail-order legal requirements are included

We're doing everything we can to speed it along to you. If, however, you do not want to wait, give us a toll-free call at 1-800-729-4593.

1. Request a substitute color, style, or size of your choice, or
2. Cancel your order. Prepaid orders will be refunded immediately. Credit card orders are not billed until shipped, so if we cancel your charge order-- your account will remain untouched.

Pleasant personalized ending

We look forward to serving you again and are proud to be a part of your research effort.

Sincerely yours,

Carlson Imo
Order Fulfillment Manager

17775   Bear Avenue   Bellevue, WA   98008

Our last shipment of leather was not cured correctly, meaning it wouldn't repel water the way it should. We did not accept this shipment, nor would we substitute lesser leathers, so we shut down production. A large stock of quality leather is on its way. As soon as we receive it, you can bet your ball will be on its way, to arrive by November 1.

Notice that the explanation is positive and businesslike: Production of the product was delayed to improve the good's quality (a good *reader benefit* reason for the delay).

You don't have to explain every delay in great detail, especially if you can tell the customer when the goods will arrive. The emphasis in a back order should always be on when the goods will arrive rather than on how long the delay will be.

The following back-order paragraph stresses resale on the product to reinforce the reader's desire for the article even if it will arrive a little later than expected. Notice how the technical language assumes the reader already understands the product:

Specific resale.

The increase in demand for this VCR is due to the high quality, namely the high-tech tracking system, the post–same day recording system, and the multipurpose remote control. Along with the high quality, the special holiday price cannot be beat. As you are reading this, production is moving rapidly so that your VCR will be at your door by December 17.

Missing Information (Incomplete Order)

If the delay is the customer's fault—missing information, payment not included, ordered from a catalog with former pricing—you need to get the information tactfully and quickly. Remind the customer of the product's good features through resale, and downplay any delay as much as you can. It speeds up the process to give the customer enough information in the letter so that he or she doesn't have to find the catalog to make the missing choice.

The letter in Exhibit 10–10 uses resale to remind the reader what a good choice the product was and gives the choices omitted in the order so the reader can provide the missing information easily and quickly. The product comes alive for the reader because the writer uses *psychological description,* which portrays the reader actually using the product. Contrast this approach with technical specifications such as "The wall hanging measures 22 inches by 36 inches." Clearly, the psychological description makes the product sound more interesting and helps the reader picture herself using it.

Notice how the action paragraph at the end makes the action sound easy ("just check") and stresses the product's arrival rather than its delay. The *action* part of an effective message makes the action clear, makes it sound easy, and motivates the reader to take the action right way.

Here is another example using good resale and psychological description to encourage the reader to send in missing information quickly.

Emphasis on satisfying reader rather than on missing information.

The little Tommy Toy Train you have ordered for your nephew comes in many eye-catching colors. The red, blue, or green trains are just the right size for small hands to play with. So that we may send the correct train that you've so carefully chosen, will you please circle the color of your choice on the enclosed reply card?

This letter included the missing information choices as an enclosure rather than as part of the letter.

The next example takes care of the order problem (missing size) but doesn't include resale to remind the customer what a good product it is.

Owensboro
Manufacturing,
Inc.

January 17, 1994

Ms. Hillary Marks
1168 Tamarack Lane
Libertyville, IL 60048

Dear Ms. Marks:

Positive opening sends available products

A Barn Raising quilt and Country Kitchen tablecloth are on their way to you; UPS should deliver them by January 24 so that you can continue your decorating project.

Psychological description of product

To help transform your home into a relaxing country cabin, the Lakes and Streams wall hanging that you've ordered comes in colors that coordinate with your Barn Raising quilt and Country Kitchen tablecloth. To guarantee your satisfaction, will you please specify your color choice?

Specific choices listed

_____earthy browns
_____foresty greens
_____sunset pinks
_____snowy white and blue

Action sounds easy

Just check the color you prefer and return this form to us; your wall hanging will be shipped as soon as we hear from you.

Sincerely,

Annie Petersen

Annie Petersen
Customer Service

2000 Selwyn Avenue
Charlotte, NC 28274
704 377 2500

Because this writer misses the opportunity to help the reader really picture the product, this letter is less effective than the other examples. The writer is also unnecessarily vague, for example, using the word *options* to mean *sizes* and *accommodate* instead of *fit.*

Makes action easy and positive.

> Your fresh-cut holly wreath is an excellent gift selection for your in-laws. We offer many options, which are sure to accommodate any space. Just circle your desired size on the enclosed return card, and the holly wreath will be delivered to Boston on the date you requested.

The last incomplete-order letter, Exhibit 10–11, shows recognition that this is a repeat customer (and also a large customer). The incomplete information is taken care of smoothly even though it is complicated by two possible choices of action *and* two choices of packaging. (The customer might have meant to send just one choice to all her customers, or she might want to choose different gift packaging for different customers.) Notice how in the last paragraph the writer sends this good customer a free gift of crackers. This gift doubles as a sales promotion on a new product that could be added to each order, but the writer does not come across as pushy. The gift will at the least please the customer and at the most lead to future orders.

Substitutions

A third type of order problem arises when you no longer carry the item ordered. In this case, if you carry no reasonable substitute item, you may be able to retain the customer's goodwill by referring him or her to a dealer who *does* carry the item.

If you carry a product that will serve the customer's purpose, you should try to sell that item as a *substitute.* If you remember that the key to order problem letters is keeping the order, you can see how to proceed here. Selling a substitute poses a few points of concern for a business writer:

- *Substitute* is a negative word; it sounds like something not as good as the original. Therefore, don't refer to the new item a substitute.
- If the substitute is costlier than the original, you may seem greedy.
- If the price of the substitute is higher than that of the original item, stress its additional or superior features. If the price is lower, emphasize the item's good performance.
- You need to decide whether to send the new item(s) automatically or wait until the customer actually orders it.

The last point requires some thought. Theoretically, if you ship unordered goods, the customer can keep them without paying. Since this is a possibility, however remote, you may choose to send only relatively low-priced items in a substitution.

When asking for a specific order for the new item, be sure to sound positive even though you will probably remind the reader that he or she can return the item if not pleased with it. Also include this reminder if you send the substitute on a trial basis.

Once you have established that you stock product B rather than product A, the order problem letter becomes a sales letter on product B. To encourage the customer to prefer product B, use its specific name often and the name of product A as little as possible.

EXHIBIT 10–11   Incomplete-Order Letter with Sales Promotion

KAISER
CHEESE
PRODUCTS, INC.

October 24, 1995

Ms. Adele Guidoni
Adams Office Equipment
411 North Adams Avenue
Chicago, IL 60601

Dear Ms. Guidoni:

Recognizes repeat customer (which keeps "thank you" opening from being a cliche)

  Thank you for your order again this year for Christmas gift cheese packages. Hearing from old friends like you is what makes our holiday season such fun every year.

Positive news about delivery news

  We will ship your order of 50 four-pound cheese and sausage packages on November 30, as you have instructed. These packages are sent in either

Clear choices

  ____ a basket (gift #4024 at $17.55 plus shipping) or

  ____ a walnut bowl (gift #3771 at 21.45 plus shipping).

Action simplified

  So we can get these to your customers promptly, just check which item you want on a copy of this letter and return it. Or, if you wish to send baskets to some customers and walnut bowls to others, send us another copy of your list, indicating on it which gift each is to receive. We will be able to meet your mailing date if you have the information to us by November 20.

Customer gift (sales promotion on a new product)

  You will receive by express mail a box of our wonderful new water crackers with a pound each of the gouda cheese and salami that you have chosen. For only $2.50 more per gift, you can add one of these boxes to your gifts. Let us know if you'd like to add this for your customers.

Sincerely,

Larry R. Kaiser

Larry R. Kaiser

5800 BLUE LINE ROAD
LA CROSSE, WI 54603
(608) 758-2200

LOWELL
BUSINESS CENTER

"Specializing in Business and Office Supplies"

July 23, 1994

Ms. Ann Huss
Huss Manufacturing, Inc.
800 Farmington Avenue
West Hartford, CT 60125

Dear Ms. Huss:

Buffer sells value and services

    As a business owner, you know how important it is to control your costs. We at Lowell Business Centers know that, too, and are always on the alert for ways to help you. One way is to stock the best value merchandise for you.

Mention substitute first

Sell substitute's features

    The Yoshida model 34 electric stapler you ordered on July 15 is a good example. We have found that Walker staplers are, item-for-item, of better quality at lower prices--and they are American-made. They are now the only brand we stock. The Walker Power+ model, equivalent to the model 34, has been shown in independent tests to last longer and jam less than the Yoshida. And it's only $27.88, about $3 less than the Yoshida 34.

Ask for order
Last line reminds of positive features of substitute

    Just fax or call us, and we'll fill your order for 12 Walker Power+ staplers; they will work better for you and save you money. And, as always, you can get a full refund if you are not satisfied. But we think you'll find the Walker Power+ to be long-lasting, easy to use, and a great buy.

Sincerely,

Lars G. Clavick

Lars G. Clavick

867 Mount Carmel Avenue
West Hartford, CT 06117

The last paragraph of the letter in Exhibit 10–12 would be different if Mr. Clavick decided to fill the order. In that case, it would read:

> We're shipping you 12 Walker Power+ staplers; they will work better for you and save you money. And, as always, you can get a full refund if you are not satisfied. But we think you'll find the Walker Power+ to be long-lasting, easy to use, and a great buy.

Orders with More Than One Problem

Many order problems actually involve combination orders, or orders with more than one problem. In such a case, take a logical approach to the problems. First, find out whether any products can be sent right away. If so, this news becomes your opening, and you don't need to write a buffer. Then discuss the other products in whatever order seems most logical—connect related products, perhaps, or group products that need further information.

Be sure to sum up any action at the end: A refund? More money owed? Charge to account? How much? Does the reader have to return anything, such as an order form, information about which product is desired, a broken item, a misprinted item, or an agreement to substitute a product? Check the letter for transitions that make the information flow smoothly from product to product.

Personnel Problems

In most indirect negative messages, a writer needs to be most concerned with the reader's feelings about the negative response. That is why you should speak as positively as you can and explain rather than give excuses. When the negative information involves people rather than things, this reader-centered attitude is all the more important. While in many cases you need to leave a paper trail in the event the person will be fired later, it's important to remain objective and tactful.

Remember our E-mail stories from Chapter 2? Clearly E-mail or voice mail is *not* the best method to use to fire employees or give other people-related bad news. People don't react well to negative information about themselves, so avoid being blunt.

If you had applied for a job, would you rather hear that "we had many highly qualified candidates this year" (as in Exhibit 10–13) or that "you were less qualified than other candidates"? This conventional turndown ends with a commonly made promise to keep a résumé on file. This is probably the business version of a social lie ("we must get together sometime" instead of "let's have lunch on Friday"). Most likely, the résumé will remain on file without being matched to new openings. Even though the reader probably knows that the chances of being considered for a future position are slim to none,

Ms. Trellis' blunt approach will probably backfire.

Indirect Messages: Handling Negative and Sensitive Information

CRIMSON
STEEL
COMPANY

"Forging ahead since 1923 "

May 10, 1994

Mr. Charles Ogino
2340 South Cedar Crest Boulevard
Allentown, PA 18120

*Cliche beginning,
but next sentence
establishes large
number of
candidates for the
job*

Dear Mr. Ogino:

Thank you for your interest in Crimson Steel Company.
Yours was one of 100 responses to our advertisement for
a plant human resources assistant.

*Does not put
down candidate
in explaining
that he was not
chosen*

*Offers possible
future help (so
candidate doesn't
feel completely
rejected)*

While your credentials are impressive, there were a
number of candidates whose backgrounds more nearly
match our needs for this position. With your
permission, we will keep your resume on file for other
openings for which you might be better suited.

Sincerely,

Helen Aguon
Helen Aguon
Director of Human Resources

3218 Germantown Avenue
Bethlehem, PA 108015
(215) 758-3000

including a statement about putting the résumé on file is a gentler way to turn down a job applicant.

When writing about current employees, be careful to be objective and specific. Randi Toler Sachs, author of *Productive Performance Appraisals,* recommends keeping a performance journal to help you remember details at performance review time and writing objective, specific comments both for employee feedback and for legal protection (a "paper trail") in cases where employees must be disciplined or let go. Here are some examples from this helpful book:

Specifics

You're not living up to your potential. (vague cliché)

versus

I was sure you had enough experience in this area to handle this assignment. Why do you think you've had trouble getting the work done correctly?[1]

Positive Tone

It's too bad you'll never succeed with your attitude. (negative)

versus

You have the ability to do well and succeed. You need to change the behaviors that are standing in the way of your success. (Cite specific examples.)[2]

Focusing on Positive Future Rather Than Past Problems

After mentioning the employee's low rating: "Let's not dwell on the past except to identify the problems and see how we can correct them. From today on, we have a new goal to reach."[3]

Dealing with personnel problems requires the same tact and audience awareness needed in handling product and service problems, with additional emphasis on people skills and potential legal pitfalls. In Chapter 16, "Communication in Managing and Supervising," we discuss this topic in detail.

The words you choose affect how your reader or listener will feel about your information. This aspect of business *tone* can help you convey negative information more successfully by avoiding blame, downplaying the negative, and choosing positive ways to state ideas.

As we discussed in Chapter 1, one way to avoid sounding unnecessarily negative is to use passive voice to describe problem areas rather than active voice, which places responsibility more firmly. Look at the following pairs of examples:

The guest checks have not been tallied weekly.

versus

Miss Smith, the bookkeeper, has not tallied the guest checks every week.

HOW TO CONVEY NEGATIVE INFORMATION

Passive versus Active Voice

---

[1] Randi Toler Sachs, *Productive Performance Appraisals* (New York: American Management Association, 1992), p. 25.

[2] Sachs, p. 77.

[3] Sachs, p. 73.

Sales goals for the first and third quarters were not met.

versus

Ms. Campbell did not meet her sales goals for the first and third quarters.

The second version of each example places blame so strongly that it seems almost mean spirited. The passive version, in contrast, states the problem clearly without placing blame. You may have to use the active-voice version in some cases, but consider whether you can use passive voice to soften the blame somewhat.

Subordination versus Emphasis: Emphasize the Positive

Another way to downplay negative information is to emphasize the positive side of things. Remember your tools of emphasis and subordination:

Emphasis	Subordination
More words on the subject	Fewer words
Active-voice verbs	Passive voice
Specific nouns	General nouns
Includes pronouns, people	Mentions things, ideas
Bold print, lists, headings	Straight narrative

Be optimistic: Tell when the goods (*not* the order) will be delivered rather than how long the delay will be; explain how much value there is for the price instead of the fact that the price has gone up; and describe how the problem can be solved instead of discussing the problem itself. For example, if you were asked to discuss course registration at your crowded college, you would receive a better response if you outlined the problem and then discussed solutions instead of going into great detail about how inconvenient and time consuming the current procedure is.

Avoiding Negative Language

In Chapter 11, "Writing to Persuade," we discuss word choice at length. Using words such as *mistake, problem, error, mess, refuse, fault, reject, unfortunately,* or *guilt* will make the reader react negatively. Using positive language, in contrast, should make the reader react positively, as you learned in Chapter 3. Think of times when someone said to you, "You always forget to. . . ."or "You never remember to. . . . " People rise to our expectations (or lower themselves to the low level we assign them to).

Using positive words where possible makes a message more open to acceptance than using negative words. Be especially wary about words such as *claim* ("You claim that your automobile was damaged in a collision on March 23"). This may convey one idea to you ("you state that these are the facts") and another to your reader ("but I don't believe you"). *Denotation* (the dictionary definition) of *claim* is "to state as a fact or as one's belief; assert."[4] But the *connotation* (emotional associations a person brings to the word) often adds a feeling that the facts are one-sided, that the speaker has exaggerated or slanted them.

[4]*Webster's New World Dictionary,* Third College Edition (New York: Simon & Schuster, 1988).

Other seemingly harmless words include *but, you,* and *me.* According to negotiation expert William Ury, say *yes, and* rather than *but,* especially when negotiating or trying to convince someone.[5] That way you can acknowledge the other point of view and then add your ideas. (*But* sounds as though you are disagreeing—which you are—and may make the other person think of counterarguments rather than considering your idea.)

As in personnel problems, use *we* to show common corporate goals rather than *you.* ("How can *we* save money on the company utility bill?" versus "*You* always forget to turn the lights off"). *We* expresses teamwork better than does *you and I,* which implies two opposing points of view.

HANDLING MIXED MESSAGES: SOME POSITIVE AND SOME NEGATIVE INFORMATION

Frequently you will need to send a message that combines positive and negative material. Mention the positive items first rather than using a buffer. For example, in the case of an order response, first mention the items you *can* send and then discuss the problem (in positive words, of course). Your underlying rule is to think of your reader: How can you best explain the potential or real problem to him or her and get agreement, even if tacit, that you are doing the right thing?

Because few business messages are entirely positive or negative, use common sense and apply sound communication principles to decide on a logical and effective order for your material.

DIRECT NEGATIVE MESSAGES

Some negative messages can be direct rather than indirect. We do not recommend that you apologize in detail for daily business problems, for the most effective responses to those kinds of problems are the positive, problem-solving, and audience-centered responses discussed so far. However, some larger business problems require a more direct response.

According to one expert, Clare Ansberry, *The Wall Street Journal* ("Forgive or Forget: Firms Face Decision Whether to Apologize for Their Mistakes," November 24, 1987), companies with a strong interest in communications may apologize directly to boost their credibility and show their concern for customer service. Some notable examples include Lee Iacocca's apology after Chrysler executives disengaged odometers (1986), Coca-Cola's confession that removing the original Coke had been a mistake (1985), and Continental Airlines' apology for poor service following its rapid expansion in 1987.

In the case of a serious problem, like the Union Carbide plant gas leak in Bhopal, India, the company established a relief fund for victims and sent the CEO to India within days to express the firm's concern. However, it did not issue a public apology because of the enormity of the incident. A more recent case occurred in 1993, when a number of people became ill and one child died after eating Jack in the Box hamburgers contaminated with bacteria. Foodmaker, the parent company, established a relief fund; changed its buying, cooking, and testing procedures; and published a public message that directly addressed, but did not apologize for, the problem. Without a direct response to this negative situation, media speculation would have made it hard for Foodmaker to assure customers that this type of incident would not happen again.

[5]William Ury, *Getting Past No: Negotiating with Difficult People* (New York: Bantam Books, 1991).

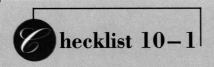

Checklist 10-1

Negative Message

Does the opening use positive information (if any) or a buffer to show agreement with the reader on some point but *not* on the request?

- Does the message sound sincere and believable?
- Does resale on the product or "on the house" (services of the business generally) help convince the reader that the product was a good choice originally?
- Is the negative embedded or implied so that the positive explanation is emphasized?
- Is the explanation positive and reasonable?
  - Don't hide behind "policy."
  - Use reader's problem to improve operations.
- Is the compromise (if any) reasonable and cost effective?

- In a substitution, does the sales language on the new product use psychological description to encourage the reader to see himself or herself using it?
- Are action details summed up at the end?
  - Money?
  - Returns?
  - Reader action?
- Is the ending friendly and positively forward looking?
- Is the tone reasonable and helpful but firm?
- Is the language more positive than negative?
- Is audience reaction sufficiently taken into account?
- Will the reader be satisfied with the explanation and response?

Direct negative messages are uncommon, but they can be valuable in defusing serious situations. Note that such messages still go on to explain, just as indirect ones do.

The Heinz Company example in Exhibit 10–14 shows how a company can explain a negative situation to employees so they have ammunition when friends and neighbors ask why Heinz didn't cooperate with the movie company filming *Hoffa* by allowing the producer to build a set on a parking lot for 2½ months. The Pittsburgh company otherwise bore the brunt of an angry press conference when the movie director of the film claimed Heinz was uncooperative. According to the Heinz Public Communications office, this memo was widely circulated and greatly appreciated by employees for explaining *positively* why the decision was made.

Checklist 10–1 lists reminders for creating effective negative messages.

Heinz U.S.A.

Heinz

Division of H. J. Heinz Company

P.O. Box 57
Pittsburgh, Pennsylvania 15230-0057

Employee Communication
March 10, 1992

TO: HEINZ U.S.A. PITTSBURGH EMPLOYEES

FROM: BETH ADAMS

SUBJECT: **FILMING OF "HOFFA"**

You may have heard or read recently that Heinz U.S.A. turned down a request to be used as a site for the filming of a scene in the upcoming "Hoffa" movie that is being shot in Pittsburgh.

Our decision was not made casually. In fact, management, representatives from Pittsburgh Factory and the HeinzSite project, Local 325, Factory Personnel, Employee Services, Engineering and Communications met with the location manager, the Pittsburgh Film Office, the producers and set designers several times over the past 6 weeks in order to fully consider their request from every possible angle.

The bottom line, however, was that the producer's needs, spanning a period of 2 to 2-1/2 months, would have jeopardized our tight schedule for completing the factory restructuring project.

Included in the producer's proposal were the following (commencing in February and continuing through the first week of April):

- taking over and converting to a railroad yard about 150 parking spaces in the lots adjacent to and in front of the Western Electric Building

- constructing an elevator at street level to access the roof of the Cereal Building on which would be built Jimmy Hoffa's office and from which shooting of the "mob" scene would take place

- traffic and truck congestion from 18-wheelers and trailers for the equipment, staff and personnel

- bringing in 1000 "extras" for the nights of shooting

- using space in Western Electric for storage and construction

It was with regret that we turned down this opportunity, particularly because it would have been an interesting and fun experience for employees to observe and perhaps participate in.

Nevertheless, on-time, on-budget completion of the Pittsburgh Factory restructuring is of greater long-term value to our employees and to the city of Pittsburgh than the shooting of this film.

Hopefully, this information will help employees understand our reasoning and provide background and answers for questions from friends and neighbors.

Giving someone bad news may not be pleasant, but often it calls for giving just another objective message. Don't be any more negative than you have to be, and remember that this kind of message may create stronger feelings in your reader than any other type. Do not apologize, but *do* explain. Handled correctly, negative business situations can be changed from problems into opportunities to create customer goodwill.

Do:

Have empathy for your reader.

Look for what you *can* do for the reader.

Emphasize the positive.

Deemphasize or subordinate the negative.

Explain fully.

Treat the reader as an individual.

Use resale to reinforce the original purchase decision.

Keep your temper even if the customer is angry.

Be sincere; avoid clichés.

Don't:

Condescend to your reader.

Use negative language.

Emphasize the bad news.

Blame or argue with the reader.

Hide behind "policy."

Ignore the individual behind the request.

Handling negative information indirectly is a useful skill for showing customers and employees that their concerns are being considered even if the matters are not being solved in the way they requested originally.

APPLICATION EXERCISES

1. From your experience as a consumer, describe one or two examples of good or poor customer service you have received from a company. How can a company satisfy a customer at little or no cost?

2. Discuss how a buffer beginning to an indirect negative message can be agreeable, noncommital, relevant, concise, and transitional. Use buffers from the examples in this chapter to prove your point.

3. How can you say *no* without really saying the word? Use the examples in the chapter to back up your points.

4. Discuss the differences among an adjustment, an adjustment refusal, and an adjustment compromise. Rewrite the Beamish Booksellers letter (Exhibit 10−8) as an adjustment approval *or* as an adjustment refusal.

5. Using the Explorer's Outerwear letter (Exhibit 10−9), develop a form letter that could serve as a customer reply instead. Be sure to avoid the pitfalls shown in the poor form postcard that appears in the back-order section on page 317.

6. Evaluate the following back-order explanation:

   Our hand-carved back scratchers have been a hot-selling item all over the world. This item relieves the itching sensation while giving you a deep massage. We have just hired 25 new wood carvers with 10 years' or more experience each to ensure quality products. With this extra help for the season we are sure you will receive your back scratcher by the end of November.

7. Add psychological description to the order problem example about the wreath on page 322 to help the reader picture the product.

8. Using Exhibit 10−11 (Kaiser Cheese letter), explain the difference between *resale* and *sales promotion* material.

9. Using Exhibit 10−12 (Lowell Business Center letter), explain the different ways to handle the action part of a substitute order problem.

10. Find and discuss several examples of active voice and negative language to describe a problem. Rewrite the examples using passive voice and positive language to describe the problem more effectively. (Example: "You forgot to turn off the lights" versus "The office lights were left on.")

CASES

1. **Unwelcome News: Telling a Parent Her Child Can't Participate.** Your church or other group is sponsoring a children's musical this season (give it a name and a theme). You are director of youth activities. You notified parents that you would like children in grades 1−6 to participate in the musical. At the first scheduled practice, a kindergartner attended. You have talked it over with the other directors, and all agree that you can't allow this child to participate without allowing others in her age group to participate also. Write a letter to the child's mother explaining why her child can't participate in this year's musical.

2. **Refusal: Convincing an Insurance Company You Are Right.** You are the owner of a small office building and have been insured by the same company for the past 15 years. Last month, a new underwriting inspector visited your building. Following the visit, you received a letter from your insurance company telling you to make the following changes *within 60 days* or it will discontinue your policy.

- The spring latch locks on the upstairs exit and basement office must be upgraded to at least a single-cylinder deadbolt to reduce the potential for loss by theft.

- At least one 10-pound, ABC-type fire extinguisher must be obtained and mounted on each occupied floor. This will reduce the potential for property damage by fire.

You are really amazed by this report, since the 6-pound ABC category fire extinguishers on each floor (including a new one on the lower level) have been adequate since you have owned the building; you have proof that they have been serviced as required each year. You also wonder about the new lock requirement. You sarcastically think that you could hire a full-time security guard, put barbed wire around the building, or require each tenant and client to go through a metal detector. Since tenants are legally responsible for their own "loss by theft" and knew the level of security in the building when they signed their leases, you can't see how this new requirement applies to your building. If you added the security measures, you would probably have to raise the rent. In a way, you are grateful for having possible deficiencies pointed out, but fulfilling these new requirements would mean extra work and expense that don't seem justified.

Write a letter to your insurance agent, Ms. Christina Reynolds, pointing out why you should not have to make the changes. You have always had a good business relationship with her and her agency and would rather not have to change insurers at this point.

3. **Customer Refund Denial.** As customer service manager for a major widget manufacturer, you receive this letter from one of your best customers:

> Major Widget Users, Inc.
> 800 North Michigan Avenue
> Chicago, Illinois 60601
>
> June 17, 1994
>
> Wild Widget Corporation
> 1234 Main Street
> Cleveland, Ohio
>
> Gentlemen:
>
> You guys have done it now. We have been using Antic Federal widgets for years, and you have never failed us like you did this time.
>
> The last batch of widgets we got from you were all bad. We tried to feed these things into our new automatic inserters, but they just wouldn't go. Our engineers spent hours trying to figure out what was wrong and came up empty. It can't be the inserters—they are state-of-the art, high-speed German Schnell inserters.
>
> We want our money back. And you had better pay for the 43 hours our engineers spent trying to make your widgets work, or you'll hear from our lawyers. Plus, there's a little matter of a week's downtime on the equipment. Altogether, this adds up to $40,786.52. We expect to see your check by return mail.
>
> Sincerely,
>
> M. M. Major

You investigate and find out they were trying to insert ⅜″ widgets and the Schnell inserters are calibrated only for metric sizes. Thus, the fault is theirs. Write a letter to Ms. Major denying the claim. Offer to air freight new widgets in the right size and to take back any remaining ⅜″ widgets for credit. Your company is willing to pay freight both ways.

4. **Compromise Adjustment: Telling a Customer No While Offering a Solution.** You own and manage Prestige Printing Company, a medium-size printing business. Two weeks ago, your firm printed 5,000 copies of a sales brochure for Equilibration, Inc., a manufacturer of weighing and measuring devices and supplies. You dealt with Mark Krautner, sales vice president. For the

cover and for 25 percent of the inside pages, Krautner specified that you use some coated paper he had purchased from another vendor. (Coated paper is necessary for printing in the handsome, dark-red, glossy ink that Equilibration uses for its raised logo and for the color portions of the brochure.) He said, "I've had years of experience designing sales materials and working with printers. I know paper, and I know prices. You know, you should think about getting your paper from this supplier too."

Although you had not seen this brand of paper before, you agreed to use it. However, Krautner did not receive as large a price break from you as he expected. Although you discounted your price because he was supplying the paper, you explained that extra handling of the nonroutine supply added to your costs. The two of you agreed on a price of $2.82 per copy for 5,000 copies. He sent you the cover stock and text-weight paper. You printed and delivered the brochures and billed Equilibration for $14,100.

A week later, you received a letter from the president of Equilibration, Lawrence M. Irving, telling you that Equilibration was not going to pay for the brochure: "We have no intention of sending these brochures to our clients. Your work is completely unacceptable. Our logo and our glossy ruby-red color is part of our firm's image. You've made the raised logo look like dried blood—it's a dull, disgusting brown—and on the brochure pages, not only is the ink this repulsive color, but the ink has also spread. We can't sell precision instruments out of a brochure printed by obvious amateurs. We expect you to reprint the 5,000 brochures, at no cost to us, to our satisfaction. Thanks to your incompetence, we are dangerously close to our mail-out date. Have the brochures on our dock within five working days."

You phone Equilibration's sales department, but Mark Krautner is out of town and has been for eight days. You phone the receiving department and learn that although a signature showed on-time delivery, no one from sales picked up the brochures for a week. The cartons sat on the dock (roofed and chain-link fenced) during the hottest week of the summer before anyone opened or inspected them. You know your own paper and ink, and your work was not at fault.

You would like to keep Equilibration as a client, which requires the goodwill of both Krautner and Irving. You might consider offering to redo the job at cost, since you still have the master pages and cover for the job, but *you would specify using your own paper.* (If

Equilibration goes elsewhere, the pages will have to be reshot; that cost, as well as the company's tight schedule, is on your side.) On the job for them you made $.38 per copy, but you won't collect it if the bill isn't paid.

5. **Response to Rental Car Overcharge Complaint.** You are vice president for customer service at We're Number 1 Car Rental Company. The president of your company has sent you an angry letter he received from a customer who claimed to have been overcharged. The customer, Barbara Bendella, said, "Surely your company is tired of having employees ask for stress-related disability because of all the customers screaming at them at the rental counter!" Ms. Bendella attached the following New York State consumer fraud complaint to her letter:

I am the editor of a major travel publication, and needed to rent a car in New York City. I called We're Number 1 Car Rental, a major car rental firm, and was quoted a $43.99 guaranteed corporate rate—and given a confirmation number. When I received my rental contract at the airport counter, I found the rate tucked into the top of the right hand corner with a lot of other numbers—$77. Upon questioning the clerk, I got one of those "I'm just doing my job" replies; New York City has special "residential rates" to compensate for higher New York State liability requirements for rental firms.

I am very angry—a confirmed rate shouldn't change at the counter! The clerk didn't tell me about the new rate, but just handed me a contract to sign! After a discussion that grew louder and louder, I got to speak to the supervisor, who said, "Those are the rules. There's nothing we can do. There's no one else you can speak to."

Because I didn't get the name of the 800-number clerk who processed my reservation, I have no proof that I wasn't told about the higher resident rate. After 90 minutes of arguing with the supervisor and the clerk, I missed my appointment, had a headache, and promised never to rent from that firm again. I even told the supervisor that I wrote for a travel publication, and the response was: "I don't care if you write about it, those are the rules. We can't expect our 800-number operators to know every rule for every state."

I'd like to forget this incident as a one-time episode, but heard from one of my department heads that the same company pulled something similar when the department head went to Albuquerque to a professional meeting. The car rental reservation was made six months in advance by the company's travel department.

At the counter, the contract had a price twice as high as the confirmed rate. This time, the reason was that the travel agent had not reconfirmed within 30 days of the trip and had not prepaid with a credit card. The department head argued at the time that the rate was confirmed, and furthermore that

the travel department had a credit card number to charge it to. The response: "A lot of travel agents make that mistake. There's nothing I can do. There's no one else you can talk to. Those are the rules."

Clearly this rental company has a problem communicating its "rules" to the employees and agents it works with! It makes a lot of money on these "mistakes," raising my—and everyone's—cost of doing business. I know that some forward-thinking travel industry leaders such as National Car Rental and the Ritz-Carlton Hotels empower their employees to make decisions costing a certain amount on the spot. This total quality management (TQM) technique seems to be an especially good one for a service business such as the travel industry, where satisfying customers means return business.[1]

Write a letter to Barbara Bendella telling her that you are not going to give her a refund of the claimed overcharge. Remember, she is the travel editor for a major travel magazine, so you must maintain her goodwill. Although you cannot offer her a refund, you can give her a 10 percent discount on her next rental.

6. **Combination Order Letter.** As a salesperson for Data Processing Distribution, Inc., you have received an order from Data Depot, one of your retailer customers, for a variety of products. They ordered 10 cases of 5¼″ high-density diskettes at $166.45 per case; 24 copies of Microware Planner, a spreadsheet program, at $124 each; 12 toner cartridges for the Printomatic 4 laser printer at $62.34 each; and 18 Digitronics model A7 left-handed, three-button mice at $16.22 each. You can ship only the diskettes within 24 hours, your normal turnaround time. The Microware Planner software comes with either 3½″ or 5¼″ diskettes; you need to know how many of each the customer needs. You are out of stock of the toner cartridges but expect them to be back in stock on June 27, four weeks from today. You do not carry the Digitronics mice and never have. However, you do carry the competitive Electromouse line; its left-handed three-button mouse sells at wholesale for $17.35 each.

Write a letter to Winston Whitehead, owner of Data Depot, explaining the problems with the order. Persuade him to switch to the Electromouse. (Remember that he may be able to charge a higher price for the Electromouse than the Digitronics mouse, thus making a higher profit.)

7. **Unwelcome News: Changing the Parking System.** Bellavista, Inc., plans to change its parking arrangements. (Be aware that parking, or

---

[1]Partly based on Laurie Berger, "Empowerment? Hah!" *Corporate Travel,* January 1993, p. 4.

the lack of it, is a sore point with employees all over the country, so *any* change will be looked at as a potentially negative one.) Parking has become a problem as the firm has grown. A second lot is to be opened, but it will be a two-block walk from the plant. The old lot next to the building will remain, but the 10 executives get the best spots; 30 spaces will be reserved for visitors; and 12 spaces will be for meritorious employees (employee-of-the-month in 12 departments). There weren't nearly enough spaces to start with. Some people have parked on the streets, but nearby residents have been complaining. The new lot is greatly needed.

Your job is to convey the news that most employees will be walking two blocks, but at least there will *be* parking spaces for them. Help them deal with this change. Tell them what to do, how it will work, what the deal will be on employee-of-the-month, and so on. This memo should probably run about one single-spaced page. The TO line should say, TO: Employees of Bellavista

Note: As in many of the cases in this book, the information in this case sketches the scene to give you, the writer, a feel for the situation. *Don't* give the employees all this information (they know it), and *do* explain clearly and positively. Think what the company can do: Shuttle bus? A different parking place after dark? What about in bad weather?

8. **Unwelcome News: Canceling the Company Picnic.** You work in employee relations. Until three years ago, your company sponsored an annual picnic, with cookout food and games for employees and families. Three years ago, two new competitors within the industry and a recession in the overall economy pinched the company's budget so hard that it had to eliminate the picnic. The situation was as bad, or worse, the following two years. However, although no one in authority actually said so, the informal communication network spread the word that there might be a picnic this year.

But it can't happen. The finance department and the president have been trying to avoid a 5 percent layoff, and have succeeded thus far, but the problems persist.

You have the task of drafting (probably for the president's eventual signature) a memo explaining tactfully why there won't be a picnic again this year. You will need to create a realistic rationale for the decision *and* take into account the disappointment employees will feel. Don't make anyone mad. Don't make the situation sound any worse than it already is, but don't sound like a wimp either. You can't offer employees anything

tangible to make them feel better, but perhaps you can talk about intangible benefits of working for this firm.

9. **Unwelcome News: Convincing Employees Change Is Good.** Bellavista, Inc., has had to trim expenses. It has spun off one of its former units, which is now an independently run small organization called NewDay Services. The new organization will provide some services to Bellavista as well as to other client organizations and will lease 25 percent of Bellavista's building as part of the arrangement. Jobs have not been lost; NewDay was receptive to retaining Bellavista's workers.

NewDay is well capitalized and intends to expand rather aggressively. NewDay and Bellavista are discussing the possibility of NewDay's leasing more of Bellavista's physical plant. Of the original 100,000 square feet, NewDay uses 25,000, but Bellavista's remaining employees have not had to move.

Now they probably will, however. Bellavista has decided to lease another 10,000 square feet to NewDay Services. Draft a memo to all employees conveying the fact that Bellavista will be operating in 10,000 fewer square feet. Think about the personnel issues involved here (you may want to do some reading on office arrangement, modern filing methods, and employee motivation). How can space be used more efficiently with the least loss of convenience and prestige (people expect a certain amount and kind of workspace)? Increase use of electronic over paper files? Create an open office concept, with cubicles instead of private offices? Which people, and how many, will have to move and/or give up some of their space? How will this be decided? Will the decision be perceived as fair? What else will employees dislike about the news?

Try to present this news in the least negative way possible. Can you "sweeten" the news at all? Are there any ways the firm can give employees something to compensate them (that won't cost much)?

10. **Memo to the File on Employee Tardiness.** Fred Williams, supervisor of the loading dock, comes to you, the human resources manager, and tells you that Tom Fender, one of the employees there, has been late for work "almost every day for the past month." Williams wants you to reprimand Fender. You talk to the payroll department, which confirms that Fender was late by 15 to 45 minutes on 14 of the 22 working days last month. Company policy requires that you give the employee a written reprimand for tardiness during a private meeting with him or

her and that a copy of the reprimand go into the employee's file.

Write a memo reprimanding Tom Fender. Remember: You want to cure the tardiness problem, leave a record in the file that will provide support for a termination for cause should that become necessary, and, at the same time, encourage Fender to continue his otherwise good job performance.

SERVICE WITHOUT A SMILE CAN BE DEADLY

Reading 10—1 *Jane Applegate*

When a salesclerk ignores you or refuses to accept a return of merchandise, how many people do you tell?

Customer service experts say the average unhappy customer complains to about half a dozen friends, neighbors and colleagues about poor service. Imagine the impact that 10 unhappy customers could have on your earnings.

"For a small business that can't afford other kinds of promotion, word of mouth is a life and death factor," said William Davidow, co-author of "Total Customer Service," published by Harper & Row.

Davidow, a Menlo Park, Calif., venture capitalist, said small-business owners should ask their best customers to describe exactly what kind of service they expect. Then ask the customers if they recommend your firm to others. And, if not, why not?

In recent years, too many companies have focused on profit and competition, leaving customers to fend for themselves. But American consumers, impressed by the high quality and good service provided by many Japanese and European companies, are demanding better service today.

Even such giants as IBM are paying heed: To provide greater convenience for his rural customers, an IBM sales representative in North Carolina created a portable showroom—the "Solution Mobile"—by filling a mobile home with computer equipment and visiting customers at their homes and businesses.

But no matter what size your business is, you should take a close look at how you treat customers and clients.

"Customer service expectations have to be set by the top management of a company," said Ellen Forman, president of Courtesy Counts. Her Potomac, Md., company reports on employee performance and attitude by sending representatives to visit stores across the country.

Forman, who founded the company 10 years ago, said the message from the business owner has to be loud, clear and consistent.

"The president might say, 'Customer service is the most important thing for us, so do it,' " said Forman. "But the next person down the line might say, 'Count the inventory' and the next, 'Clean up the store.' "

Elaine Locksley, founder of the Locksley Group in Pacific Palisades, said customer service gives companies a measurable edge over the competition. Locksley sends shoppers into large and small businesses to monitor their service and provide customer service training programs, if necessary.

Locksley developed her customer service techniques while working for 20 years in the savings and loan industry. After hiring mystery shoppers of all ages to visit stores, banks and other businesses, she presents the owners with a detailed report. She says she expects the information to be shared with employees.

Kay Hollenbeck, a "mystery shopper" and manager at the Locksley Group, said one of the fastest ways to lose business is for a salesclerk to be talking on the telephone, see a customer standing there and then turn his or her back on the customer. Another sure turnoff is for a salesperson to start helping a customer and then get distracted and never return.

Even the best training programs and promises of cash rewards won't be effective unless your employees feel a sense of ownership and pride in the business, according to Locksley. Everyone who works for you should be given the power to make decisions needed to please your customers.

"We were concerned that even with all the thousands of dollars spent on our training program, when the boss is gone, the standards drop," said Jack Ryan, whose parents Bob and Jean Ryan opened their first women's apparel store in 1954. Today, there are three Jean Ryan stores employing about 30 full- and part-time workers in Orange County.

"We are living in a service-oriented society," said Ryan. "With too many competitors you have to offer better service."

Locksley's shoppers visit Ryan's stores at different times of the day and week. Frequently, they make a purchase or return an item.

"We try to use her service as a positive tool," said Ryan. He said if an employee is presented with a negative report, they usually attribute it to being too busy with other customers.

John Irving, senior vice president at Premier Bank in Northridge, pays about $450 a month for Locksley's services. For that fee, Locksley reports on three visits and three phone calls to Premier's three bank branches. Irving said it is money well spent because "an outside opinion has a tremendous value."

Once you figure out what customers expect and where you are falling short, quickly establish ways to improve

Source: Jane Applegate, "Service Without a Smile Can Be Deadly," *Los Angeles Times,* June 15, 1990, pp. D3, D7.

your service. But Davidow said written policies and programs won't work if you don't have the infrastructure in place to help your employees. For example, having legions of employees trained to answer the phone properly won't matter if you don't have enough phone lines to serve customers.

If you can't afford to pay professional shoppers to monitor the service you provide, ask a few friends or relatives who are not known to your employees to check on the service. Knowing what goes on when you are not around is vital to the success of your business. Especially since customer service experts estimate that it costs about 10 times more to bring in one new customer than to keep an old one.

Improving Customer Service

- Ask your best customers to honestly tell you what kind of service they expect from your company.

- Establish clear and simple service policies to match customers' expectations.
- Give authority to people at every level so they feel empowered to provide good service.
- Eliminate all red tape involved in merchandise returns.
- Set clear customer service goals for your employees and make sure that everyone understands them.
- Provide specific training and information so employees know exactly what to do in every situation.
- Make employees accountable for their actions.
- Write specific job descriptions for every employee and offer incentives for promotion so people don't feel stuck in a dead-end job.
- Publicly reward and recognize good service.
- If you can't hire an outside firm, ask your friends or neighbors to visit your business and report on the service they received.

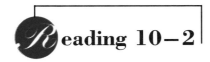 eading 10–2

DO YOU HAVE THE RIGHT ATTITUDE TOWARDS CLIENTS?

David W. Cottle

Most people are persuaded more by attitude than by logic. This is because most people are strongly influenced by their emotions, and emotions are contagious. Complainers will tend to adopt the same emotional attitude that you have. If you get angry, they'll get angry. If they're angry when they call but you are friendly, they'll tend to get friendly, too.

Let's look at the difference a negative or positive attitude can make. Specifically, let's look at the difference as perceived by the client between willingness to solve a problem and ability to solve a problem.

1. Willing and Able
Clients obviously like to deal with people who are both willing and able to solve their problem. You handle any complaint or client request with speed and care. No problem.

When handling a complaint, assure clients you are helping them willingly, not grudgingly. Say things like: "Thanks for calling this to my attention," or "I'm glad I found out about this situation; this way I can take steps to make sure it doesn't happen to other clients, too. Thanks for telling me."

2. Willing and Unable
But what happens when you get a request for something you cannot do? You simply cannot deliver what the client wants.

Examples:
- A client asks you to come to a meeting on short notice when you have another appointment.
- A client has an emergency, and your secretary doesn't know where you are to get a message to you.
- An insolvent client wants a business loan; you're willing to help but unable to do so.

From the client's viewpoint, the next best thing to "willing and able" is to be at least willing to help even if you are unable. Having "your heart in the right place" is worth points, even if you can't perform. This is an example of the manner in which you deliver a service overcoming temporary lapses in your ability to provide a satisfactory service outcome.

Source: David W. Cottle, "How to Turn Complaints into Increased Client Loyalty," *The Practical Accountant* 25, no. 6 (June 1992), p. 29.

In such cases, all you can do is sympathize. But don't underestimate the value of sympathy to a client. I once had a client who sold a partnership interest with a negative tax basis. The client almost gave it away and had to pay tax on the negative basis. He complained loud and long about the unfairness of his having to pay tax on a phantom gain when he had not received any money. I couldn't help him, so I sympathized. Once he grasped the situation and felt my sympathy, he became a loyal client again.

Note: Don't tell clients what you cannot do; tell them what you can do. If they want you to do something beyond your power, don't let their attention remain on your failure to help. If there is anything, no matter how small, you can do, offer to do it. For example: "Sally, I'm sorry I can't meet with you at 2:00 this afternoon. How about 5:30? Or we could meet at 7:00 tomorrow morning for breakfast."

3. Able but Unwilling

People are extremely frustrated by service people who are able to help (or who seem to be able to help) but are unwilling. For example: A major corporation employee who was leaving town on business got his paycheck ahead of time. He asked his bank to cash the postdated payroll check. Legally, the bank couldn't do it, but the teller—instead of explaining the legal restrictions—merely refused to cash the check. The customer had the check; the bank had the money. The customer perceived that the bank was able but unwilling to help him when in fact the bank was unable to solve his problem. What could have been a positive experience with the bank (or at least a neutral one) turned into a negative experience. The bank got a failing grade on the customer's "invisible report card" on the quality of their service.

Have you ever taken a telephone call from a second client when you were still in a meeting with the first client? Doing this is like letting the client who telephoned "cut in line" in front of the client who is in your office. Has your receptionist kept a client waiting to be announced while the receptionist finished what was obviously a personal telephone call?

The only hope people have when confronted by an "able but unwilling" situation is if they can just convince the service provider to be willing to help, then they will be serviced.

You may believe that your clients would never run into an "able but unwilling" situation in your firm. You may believe that your clients would never perceive you as being unwilling to help them. But let's look back at my client who sold the partnership interest and owed tax on the negative basis. At first, he thought I was able to report no gain on the sale but was unwilling to do so. This also affected his evaluation of my competence as an accountant. First, I had to carefully explain the "why" so the client could see that both he and I had no choice. In other words, I had to convince the client of my inability to report the sale at no gain. Then the client could accept that I was willing to help but unable to do so.

4. Unwilling and Unable

The least desirable accountant is perceived as both unwilling and unable to provide a service to the client. The attitude seems to say, "I can't help you, but even if I could, I wouldn't." Diligently avoid hiring such employees, and if you find one, rapidly ensure that they become a former employee. Make sure your clients understand that you are always willing to help them, even when you are unable to do so.

Chapter Eleven

Writing to Persuade

PREVIEW

This chapter covers perhaps the most challenging types of business messages, those that must influence or change what the receiver thinks or does. Business makes heavy use of persuasion. Individuals, departments, and organizations are interdependent. They need to get one another to take actions, make changes, and cooperate.

Both inside and outside organizations, businesspeople frequently need to influence others. For instance, a project manager might tell a team member, "Purchasing has been sitting on our proposal since March 2. Call them and get some action out of them without making them mad." Or a manager might have the task of showing the city council why a rezoning that her company wants is also good for the city.

Whether you need to persuade people on an idea like teamwork or cooperation or on a product or service, you will consider ways in which what you offer will benefit your recipients—and you will "sell" those benefits. People take action because they believe it will be in their best interest to do so. They consider the "what's-in-it-for-me" factor (WIIFM). ●

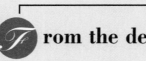

From the desk of... | What's in It for Eve to Help Me?

Vic Osmond
Project Support Planner

In project organizations, work teams form to do a job and disperse when it's finished. Sometimes a new project begins before a prior one is completely cleaned up. This week I have to get Eve Benedetti, a talented engineer whose time is in heavy demand, to put in about a day's documentation time on a job she considers done. She's already on another project.

I'll write a memo and follow up with E-mail. Just in case she hears other "squeaky wheels," I want her to agree in writing. I'll need to head off her initial objection that some other engineer can document this work. She doesn't have to help, strictly speaking, but no one else would do this work as well.

I can appeal to an important belief of hers: Eve understands the value of documentation in generating repeat business and good word of mouth. I've heard her say that after our salespeople all go home, the documentation is what stays with the client and represents this company. Maybe I can find her some extra resources and sweeten the offer for her a little.

PERSUASION DEFINED

Most business messages are mainly informative or mainly persuasive, but few are *only* one or the other.

Persuasion is a conscious effort by an individual to modify or change the opinions, attitudes, beliefs, or behaviors of another individual or group through the transmission of a message. No distinct line separates informational messages from persuasive ones, however. Many messages do both. To illustrate, we might place individual examples of different message types on a continuum, as shown in Exhibit 11–1.

To persuade or inform effectively, business communicators must monitor their intentions and purposes regarding the reader. They must not accidentally persuade when the task is to inform. When other businesspeople need objective facts, communicators must be able to provide them free of personal bias.

Yet few human communications are entirely free of all persuasiveness. For instance, when the writer of an informative report works to demonstrate his credibility, he is influencing an opinion of the reader. Nearly all informational messages contain at least minimal persuasion. Conversely, most persuasive messages contain a great deal of information.

Elements of Persuasion

Persuaders must consider their receivers, themselves as senders, the situation, the ethics involved, specific strategies and techniques, and the structure of the message.

When attempting to persuade in business communication, writers analyze their audience closely. Then they select, order, and word the elements of their message to encourage the desired responses from that audience. On the basis of this analysis, they appeal to the audience's *reason* and *feelings.* They say nothing untrue. They begin with familiar statements the audience agrees with and gradually add new material that will move the audience toward the "new" agreement. Exhibit 11–2 is a fairly simple persuasive memo. Marginal notes direct your attention to several persuasive elements.

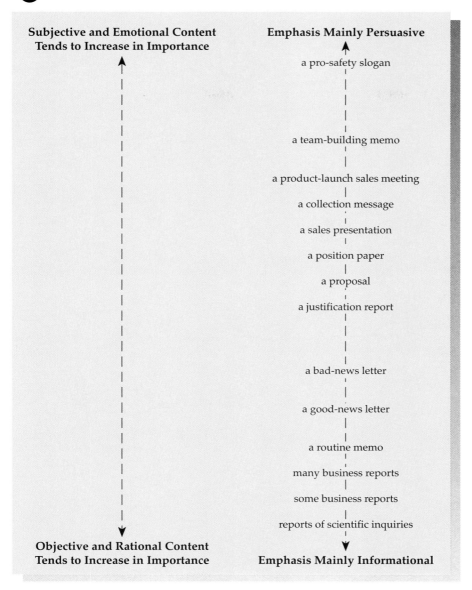

ⒺXHIBIT 11–1   Information-Persuasion Continuum

Subjective and Emotional Content
Tends to Increase in Importance

Emphasis Mainly Persuasive

a pro-safety slogan

a team-building memo

a product-launch sales meeting

a collection message

a sales presentation

a position paper

a proposal

a justification report

a bad-news letter

a good-news letter

a routine memo

many business reports

some business reports

reports of scientific inquiries

Objective and Rational Content
Tends to Increase in Importance

Emphasis Mainly Informational

Human nature gives rise to some characteristics of particular interest to those who study persuasion. Receivers of messages

- Are influenced by emotion and reason.
- Judge the reliability of the sender.
- Dislike dissonance (mixed feelings, ambivalence).
- Are persuaded to varying degrees.
- Respond to reinforcement.

Receivers of Persuasive Messages

Val-U Capital Warehouse, Inc.

Memorandum

To: Courtney Moto, Store Manager

From: Will North, Asst. Operations Manager

Date: March 3, 19xx

Subject: Security of Fine Jewelry Bay

North establishes common ground by recalling for Moto the problem and two proposed solutions.

Language such as "a concern" is rational and cool; when emotion attaches to words like "break into," the danger does not seem overstated.

Along with rational proof, fear appeal is used. Word choice includes "in less than a minute" and "complete burglary...before an armed response could arrive."

"Vulnerable" re-introduces the fear appeal; "eliminating that risk" offers to relieve the fear.

During our current remodel we have seen two major proposals on how best to secure the Fine Jewelry bay. One idea is to place contacts on reinforced doors and the other is to place safes under the selling counters.

The Fine Jewelry bay, in its free-standing form, is a concern because of both our employees' safety and the security of the merchandise. By placing safes under the counter, we do a better job of ensuring both. The safes, as opposed to the contacts and reinforced doors, are much more difficult to break into and thus more cost effective.

North argues for greater human safety and more secure merchandise. Both are based on Moto's WIIFM.

According to the security manager's proposal, contacts have not proven very effective in other stores. The contacts and reinforced doors can be broken into in less than a minute, and a complete burglary could be carried out before an armed response could even arrive. Safes, in contrast, while about 22 percent more costly initially, have proven to be considerably more effective in deterring theft. Adding safes to our existing security would make a potential burglary much more time consuming and thus less appealing.

North justifies the higher price of safes by demonstrating much greater benefits. Word choice like "deterring theft" is reassuring.

Having to carry the jewelry to and from the main safe at opening and closing leaves our associates very vulnerable. With safes under the counters, we will be able to store the merchandise in the bay overnight, thereby eliminating that risk.

Since we must take action on this matter by fiscal year end, I would appreciate your approval for the purchase of the safes, both for the security of our merchandise and, more important, for the safety of our associates.

Linking the benefits to the requested action, North asks for Moto's approval of his recommended solution.

- Dislike holding opinions different from those of others whom they hold in esteem.
- Operate within a specific frame of reference.

Let's examine these characteristics one at a time. As you read, look at Exhibit 11–3, a request for a favor, to see how the writer has carefully considered his reader.

People are influenced by emotion as well as by reason. Everyone is influenced by feelings to some extent, and some are influenced heavily. Consider this list of emotional "sets" a persuader might key into:

Emotion and Reason

Self-esteem	Feelings of inadequacy
Shyness	Irritation
Love of risk	Sense of duty
Fear of loss	Protectiveness toward others
Uneasiness	Boredom
Love of excitement	Vanity
Hero worship	Envy
Greed	Commitment to principles
Personal responsibility	Fear of looking foolish
Feeling virtuous	Feeling generous
Enjoyment of winning	

Hundreds of other kinds of emotions move people.

In appealing to these and other emotions, a persuasive writer should usually do so subtly. A shade of difference in a word's connotation may tap into an emotion successfully where a blatant appeal to that emotion would fail.

Most emotional appeals in business persuasion should be subtle.

A successful persuader is careful not to underestimate the complexities of the receiver's attitudes and beliefs. Both communicator and receiver generally have more than one reason for feeling the way they do. Some of the reasons are consciously known; some are dim and sometimes distorted memories, often deeply rooted in the past and built up from many different experiences. In some cases, a person has forgotten the reasons behind his or her beliefs or attitudes, but those reasons are influential just the same.

Receivers judge the reliability of senders. They might doubt even a true message if it comes from someone with low credibility. Business communicators must take care that no aspect of their communication suggests they are not believable. For instance, bad appearance of a written communication, exaggeration, lack of evidence, or lack of organization can suggest unreliability. How communicators behave day to day also affects their credibility in an organization and makes what they say and write more believable or less so.

Sender Reliability

People dislike being undecided or confused about events they perceive as meaningful to them. This ambivalent state is called **dissonance** or **lack of closure.** People are eager to resolve problems and make decisions, proceeding on the basis of the best information they have available to them. Both emotion and reason enter into their decisions.

Dissonance

Dissonance means having mixed or unresolved thoughts or feelings about a matter of importance.

EXHIBIT 11–3   Request for a Favor

Associated Student Organizations
College of Business, Wichita State University, Wichita, KS 67208

May 3, 19xx

Ms. Patricia A. Shesky
Vice President, Personnel and Administration
Otoe Manufacturing Corporation
11400 Plains Parkway
Wichita, KS   67211

Dear Ms. Shesky:

Opener offers optimistic frame of reference.

With the manufacturing sector clearly reviving, you may be interested in an idea regarding the supply of trained staff.

Other important firms use WSU's interns. Refers to WIIFM.

The business college at State has placed interns with four other large Wichita firms (Barnes & Baxter, Columbine Chemical, T&I Inc., and Farbenroth) since 1986.   The opportunity to create an internship program at Otoe would strengthen our program and offer Otoe many benefits.

Specifies WIIFM. Word choice summons positive emotions.

Interns are an excellent source of committed workers.   Grateful for the chance to gain career experience and exposure to knowledgeable individuals, they are eager to perform well for you. For minimum wage, employer organizations receive informed problem-solvers with fresh skills to put to work. The interns know that a desirable grade in finance or marketing depends on their ability to fulfill your expectations.   You will see an intense motivation to learn, absorb, and contribute.

Heads off possible concern about quality.

Because students pass a rigorous screening to qualify for internships, you will see only strong applicants.

Offers evidence to appeal to reason.

Statistics show that 87 percent of the firms with internships hire some of their interns as regular employees upon graduation. The turnover rate of employees who are former interns is substantially lower than of other employees, as shown in several studies I'd be glad to send you. In addition, training costs when interns are hired are much less.

If Shesky pencils in costs or merely makes checkmarks alongside named tasks, she will reinforce her interest.

The left column of the enclosed sheet lists 36 important tasks other firms have assigned to interns.   The middle column shows cost savings achieved. Why not check which tasks your staffers might be able to assign to interns? The right-hand column has space for you to estimate your cost savings.

Patricia A. Shesky   May 3, 19xx

The College of Business publishes a quarterly newsletter with space devoted regularly to the firms that support us. This positive exposure could only add to your strong reputation for community citizenship.

Would you consider creating three to five internships at OMC for top business finance and marketing majors, Ms. Shesky? We have developed materials that will greatly reduce the paperwork for you.

If you would like the research studies I mentioned, please call 316-461-7731.   I will follow up next week to answer any questions you may have.   Thank you for considering internships, a genuine win-win arrangement.

Sincerely,

Val Mykenos

Val Mykenos
President, Associated Student Organizations

Enclosure

pc: M. P. Katz, III, Faculty Advisor

Degrees of Persuasion

People are persuaded to varying degrees. A communication might make a great deal of difference to one person but much less difference to another. The communication might be more or less effective for the *same* person on different days, depending on the person's outlook, mood, and other experiences each day. A person might be strongly persuaded the first day she or he hears a message but forget and slip back to the original opinion later. If a receiver's original opinion is firmly set, little persuasion, or none at all, may result.

A sender needs to know the degree of agreement needed. For example, persuasion can achieve a person's silent internal agreement more easily than the person's spoken or written support in front of other people. Similarly, such verbal support is easier to achieve than action (hence the popular phrase "Put your money where your mouth is"). Once a person has openly committed himself before others, however, he is less likely to revert to his original opinion than if his agreement is unspoken. A person who has committed herself by action as well as by speech or writing is still less likely to revert.

Reinforcement

Reinforcement makes newly acquired attitudes or beliefs firmer.

Typically a person's words or actions **reinforce** his or her agreement with a persuasive message. People do not like to appear inconsistent. Reinforcement makes the change in a person firmer and more permanent. Once people have made a decision, they tend to notice or create more reasons why it was a good decision and to ignore reasons that do not confirm their decision.

Persuasive writers use reinforcement in many ways. For one, they try to emphasize facts and messages they want readers to agree with and to minimize facts and messages they want readers to ignore. They also try to move their readers toward a decision and to confirm the decision once the readers have made it.

Forms of reward and punishment can move a person toward agreement and reinforce her agreement once she has given it. The persuader can tell the receiver "what's in it for her" if she decides rightly and the negative consequences likely if she does not. "When you agree to help out at the Special Olympics, you're buying into a special kind of warmth" offers an intangible but valuable reward. Consider the opposite message: "For a day these kids' disabilities disappear. For a day they're just kids having fun. They're counting on you. Are you going to let them down?" This message promises a psychic punishment for the receiver: The children's disappointment won't feel good to the person who let them down. Maybe the receiver will agree to help and thus avoid this guilty feeling.

Finally, a persuader can praise a receiver for having the right attitude. A persuader can sometimes even offer some tangible reward.

Reference Groups

Reference groups or persons are others whom an individual holds in esteem, wishes to resemble, and tends to imitate.

Human beings often share opinions, attitudes, and beliefs with **reference groups,** that is, with others whom they admire or respect and wish to resemble. For example, many people who belong to fitness clubs emphasize looking good and following fashion. A new member might rely heavily on longer-term members' opinions about what is and is not fashionable. He will probably be open to persuasive messages about clothing, hair care, entertainment, and even politics if the messages come from sources associated with or resembling fitness buffs.

Frame of Reference

The success of a persuasive message may depend on the receiver's **frame of reference,** that is, on the receiver's mood, state of mind, and mental associations with the subject. It's helpful to a business writer to know the frame of reference in which the message will be received.

A person might have different frames of reference prevailing at different times and in different situations. For example, consider the work force in a high-tech industry where decreased demand has led to layoffs. Suppose a recruiter for a job retraining program phones an employee of Megabyte Inc. just after Megabyte's quarterly report has shown a 1.8 percent rise in orders. The worker might not show much interest. Suppose, however, that the same recruiter calls the employee after the morning paper has announced more layoffs at Megabyte. Under these bad-news circumstances, the worker might be open to a job retraining pitch.

Often a receiver's frame of reference can be adjusted by a message. A sender can word a message to suggest a given frame of reference to a receiver. Words can create a mood, recall memories, or put a message in a different perspective.

Knowing the receiver's frame of reference can sometimes tell a writer what to stress and what to avoid. For instance, the banking and savings and loan industries have been hard-pressed recently. To increase market share, managers of Commercial Federal Bank might launch a campaign to increase customers' perceptions of ComFed's friendliness. Tellers and other public-contact employees will carry out the campaign. How might they best be motivated? Where many banks are merging or failing, employees would probably respond less favorably to persuasion based on bonuses or awards than they would to persuasion based on saving their jobs.

These examples show that in persuasion, readers' perceptions of facts determine their decisions. When facts cannot be changed, problems can sometimes be solved by changing people's attitudes toward the facts.

Senders of Persuasive Messages

Like the receiver, the sender of every persuasive message is a rational and emotional human being with many different, and sometimes conflicting, motivations. To persuade effectively, a sender must be self-aware but receiver oriented.

The best advice to all business communicators is *know yourself.* Preparing either to inform or to persuade, you analyze your intended receiver's frame of reference. Be aware of your own frame of reference as well so you can make your own emotions work for you—suggesting the right word connotation, for example—rather than against you.

The best persuaders see and understand clearly all the facts and arguments—those that support their position and those that oppose it. If they lack objectivity, they may treat both kinds of facts inappropriately. They might, for instance, assume that what seems true to them will also seem true to the audience and underdevelop the arguments that support their position. Or they might assume that the ideas opposing their position will seem no more important to the audience than to themselves and thus ignore or argue insufficiently against those ideas.

The successful persuasive writer states things as they will be meaningful to the receiver, not as they are meaningful to the sender. A person unaware of his own feelings on a subject will have difficulty getting far enough outside those feelings to influence another person.

The next piece of advice is *know your task.* Deliberately inform or deliberately persuade, but do not intend to do one and accidentally do the other.

The sender of a message must *be perceived as credible* by the receiver, or the message will be rejected. First, the writer needs to *be* credible in his or her organization. *Control of a message's tone* also affects credibility, particularly when writers address persons who do not know them. If a persuasive letter strikes receivers as sly, evasive, exaggerated, crafty, or secretive, for example, they are unlikely to believe the writer. Therefore, the tone must be courteous, sincere, and businesslike.

The "you" attitude is especially important in persuasion.

Keeping the "you" attitude at the mind's forefront helps a writer maintain an appropriate tone. The writer constantly needs to ask, "How would this sentence strike me if I were in the reader's place?" A persuasive message must never seem to scold, preach, push, lecture, beg, threaten, whine, or flatter. Rather, it should invite the reader to think along with the writer as the writer pursues a reasonable, easy-to-follow, reader-centered discourse.

To be perceived as credible, the sender must *meet the receiver's expectations.* As you already learned, businesspeople expect good standard English, correct spelling, professional appearance, clarity, courtesy, conciseness, and good organization. They also expect the writer's words and actions to be consistent. They do not want to be set up for one kind of message and given another.

Persuasion stresses commonality between sender and receiver.

Reader analysis should suggest similarities between writer and reader. When the writer can create the impression that they are much alike or have a common interest, an underlying message can be "I'm like you. I understand what you need." Readers who believe the writer thinks the way they think will be more likely to follow the writer's leads and arguments than will readers who believe they are very different.

The Situation Surrounding the Persuasion

Situations requiring persuasion are nearly always complex. Most issues have many sides, and, as you have learned, communicators have many reasons for feeling as they do. Several situational factors can help communicators frame persuasion well.

The Issue Itself

Sometimes the nature of the issue you are writing about will let you infer the reader's state of mind. For example, if the reader recently had a bad experience with your firm, you may have to work with her residual anger as well as your persuasive goal. If the reader is a lending officer at a commercial bank, your business proposal is not the only one he has to consider. If this lender likes your proposal but controls only limited funds and stands to make more money from several other contenders, his dissonance level is probably high.

Power and Status Levels of Sender and Receiver

Senders must take power and status differences into account.

Status and power levels regulate persuaders' word choice as well as choice of strategies and techniques. Writers persuading people of higher rank take a deferential tone and emphasize strong reader benefits. Persuading people on the same level, writers treat their readers as equals and might refer to mutual benefits as well as strong reader benefits.

When writers have higher status and more power than their receivers, they often simply *direct* receivers' activities. Influencing the routine work behavior of subordinates, for instance, is straightforward. Organizations run on an underlying assumption that subordinates agree to do their work as superiors direct (within reason) or else leave the organization. Few managers want subordinates to leave; rather, they want them to stay and do their jobs well.

The kinds of persuasion that accompany direct orders, however, will differ greatly from those used on audiences who have no obligation to listen. A deferential tone could cause subordinates to view superiors as weak. Still, even when people know they have to follow orders, productivity is generally higher when they *want* to do what they have to do. Thus, managers do well to be courteous and businesslike about directing, use appropriate motivation techniques, and use negative message content only when necessary.

In unequal power relationships, of course, the power and status differential is only one variable in choosing persuasive techniques.

Another situational element the writer needs to consider is the circumstances in which the reader will receive the message. Will she be alone or among other people? In a pleasant or an unpleasant environment? Under high stress or low stress? In a distracting or a distraction-free environment?

The Receiver's Immediate Environment

These factors determine the amount and kind of attention a reader can give a message, as well as the reader's attitude in approaching it. If the message will be read during the busiest time of the reader's day, many interruptions may prevent the reader's giving it more than brief and partial attention. Such circumstances present the writer with special problems and increase the chance that the communication will fail. To minimize such problems, you can sometimes

Time is a constant pressure for both persuaders and their receivers.

- Time the arrival of a communication so that it will be given sufficient attention. For example, public relations writers customarily time press releases to arrive at newspapers at low-pressure times of the week.
- Suggest that the recipient read your message not the moment it arrives but when he has a quiet minute or two.
- Word the message compellingly to hold the reader's attention despite other distractions.

But you must hold the receiver's attention. As you will see later in this chapter, a persuasive message depends on order and completeness more than many informational messages do. A persuasive message with parts missing may lose its effectiveness, whether the gaps are due to the writer's carelessness or to the reader's inattention.

Time constraints create pressure and problems for all business writers, but especially for persuasive writers. How long can you take to analyze, write, and revise? The boss asks you for a thorough treatment, and he wants it yesterday! How long will the busy reader keep reading? You must keep the reader's attention all the way down to the move to action, or the persuasion will have little effect.

Skilled persuaders possess considerable power over others. They can win trust and move others to do as they wish. Probably no message is free of the potential for abuse. Still, persuasive messages raise questions about ethics sooner than informational messages do because, on the average, persuasive messages ask for more, on a less full and rational basis, than do informational messages. To what extent may people manipulate others within the bounds of ethics? The answer is not simple.

Ethics and Persuasion

Recall the discussion of truth in Chapter Five and of the filter in Chapter One. Truth is hard to find, and most of the time people act on their own or others' filtered perceptions and interpretations. People are sometimes scared, sometimes angry, sometimes playful. They exaggerate. They stretch the truth. Sometimes their listeners recognize this, and sometimes they do not. The point

No one is a completely objective perceiver.

is that people deal fairly comfortably with versions of reality that vary from one person to another.

"Do no harm" is one good guiding phrase, but neither it nor any other maxim will cover all situations. Each persuader must examine his or her own ethical standards and locate the line that he or she will not cross. Law, morality, and social pressure help establish ethical boundaries, but individuals find themselves working with issues and in situations where these forces are insufficient guides. Several ideas, discussed here, can help you formulate your own ethical "measuring sticks" for the complexities of business persuasion.

Different Activities Have Different Rules That Persuaders Must Learn and Play By

Persuaders must recognize the rules of a situation or activity and adhere to them.

Many business activities have their own sets of rules, and persuasion proceeds in these various contexts. Negotiating, for instance, is gamelike, whether two workers are angling for the desk nearer the window or two conglomerates are bargaining over the sale of a subsidiary. In recreation, we are used to game strategies that involve purposeful misleading and bluffing, as negotiating sometimes does. For instance, we applaud team athletes who fake one move to distract the opponents from the move they really intend to make.

Negotiators, like athletes and their fans, understand that the rules of the activity involve risk. Ethical negotiators play by the rules but build their skills. A beginner might do poorly against even an ethical opponent because the beginner has not yet mastered the tactics. In the nature of negotiations, win-win outcomes are ideal but not usual. Usually one party gets the better of the other. Sometimes one party gets everything. People enter these negotiations willingly, however, and agree to the rules of the activity in the hope of gaining from the exchange.

Another important example of a gamelike business activity with well-understood rules is the employment interview. No one should lie in an interview, but only a fool would list all his or her weaknesses when asked. The interviewer would deem such an applicant hopelessly naive and unlikely to represent the organization well. The implicit rules say that both parties will represent their positive points strongly and conceal or deemphasize their negative ones.

Most everyday buying and selling is simple: "I give you this if you pay me that." If people do not want to buy, they do not have to. Some high-pressure selling, however, uses tactics that are ethically questionable. Consider also the sales pitches that are carefully scripted to

- Conceal the nature and degree of the indebtedness.
- Conceal the fact that a sale is being made and money will be owed.
- Pretend to cure terminal illness or hopeless loneliness.
- Sell something worthless by playing on ignorance, guilt, or fear for one's loved ones.

We will always have such persuaders as the telephone boiler room scammers who trap the elderly into buying useless "commemorative coins" as investments; the door-to-door, no-name-encyclopedia sellers who sell a $500 time contract to welfare recipients with no food in the cupboard; the fakes who sell "cures" to AIDS patients; and countless others. These "games" are *not* understood or agreed to by those who are victimized. They are unethical.

All Messages Are Selective

Chapter One reminded you that no message ever says everything about anything. Communicators encode messages by selecting and combining symbols from a limitless array of possibilities.

We need to select and encode fairly, given the situation. To inform ethically, we convey as much information as is needed for specific receivers' understanding. When we persuade ethically, being careful to do no harm, we create our messages using selected true information and emotional appeals that will be meaningful to specific receivers.

Lying is wrong. Having said that, we acknowledge that "Tell him I'm not home" is not the same size wrong as the lie that destroys a person's life. Also relevant are the differences in perception from one person to another. Two people often report quite differently an incident that both witnessed, but both are telling truth as they see it.

Persuaders Should Not Falsify

Lying is one means of persuading unethically. The cleverest unethical persuaders, however, manage to avoid outright lies but still cause their victims to believe something untrue. If you have studied critical thinking, you have encountered terms like *cardstacking, leading questions,* and *guilt by association*—all different techniques for conveying untruth without saying it.

Remember too that after reading a persuasive message, the recipient still makes a free choice. A persuader can only persuade. If a persuader is able to control, then coercion, not persuasion, is occurring.

Receiver Has Free Choice

We have an "open system." Every day we are exposed to conflicting opinions and to many sides of issues. Every person is free to disagree with other people, with the government, and with any institution. Receivers of persuasive communications are used to hearing persuasion and evaluating it for themselves.

Finally, receivers accept a persuasive message when and if they see the message as meeting a need. If it does not meet their need, they reject it. Persuasion is universally useful. We are all consumers as well as providers of persuasion. We need others' arguments and evidence because we are all busy. We cannot—and do not want to—discover and reason out everything for ourselves. We look for helpful shortcuts in making up our minds.

Effective Persuasion Fulfills Receiver's Need

Every day receivers evaluate many competing—even conflicting—persuasive messages and judge their worth and ability to fulfill receivers' WIIFM.

People who read persuasive messages read them because they see the topic made meaningful for them. If the message offers them something they want (WIIFM), they are willing to listen or to read. If they can infer a trustworthy sender who meets a need, they tend to accept the message.

A strong motive for persuading ethically is our need for the ethical persuasive messages of others. No reader wants to be abused. Persuasion is a powerful set of skills, to be handled, like all power, responsibly.

Persuaders learn various techniques and strategies. In this section we will mention and give examples of several of these. You will be able to relate some of the techniques and strategies to what we have said about the receiver, the sender, and the situation.

Strategies and Techniques

Liking. The use of **liking** is also called the use of **ingratiation** or **friendship.** Persuaders might communicate in their most pleasant, charming way, sometimes referring outright to their feelings of affinity. For instance:

> We've been friends a long time. We've gone through a lot and seen each other through the tough times. That's why I'm coming to you first with this idea.

Approached in this winsome way, the recipient might be moved to be a "nice guy" in return.

Altruism.   An appeal to **altruism** is an appeal to people's generosity. People are capable of behaving selflessly if their basic decency and warmheartedness are tapped. Some charitable appeals are based on this aspect alone. Unless an individual is angry or turned off, sometimes an appeal to altruism can suffice. This example shows an appeal to altruism:

> I'm sorry you're leaving us, but I'm really glad you have such a good opportunity. You've done a great job for us, especially considering the chaos you inherited from the last supervisor. You don't have to do this, but I wonder if you'd consider writing up the four most important procedures you devised. You've said you wanted to make lasting improvements where you work. If you'd write those procedures, the difference you've made would continue for years to come.

Scarcity.   Dandelions are beautiful if you really look at them. If they were hard to grow we would be nurturing them, not attacking them with trowel and herbicide. People desire what is hard to get. Marketers know that if they price certain products too low—even if costs permit a low price—people will refuse to buy them. Thus, persuaders often use the reality or the appearance of **scarcity** to motivate. Here are examples:

> This model will be unavailable after the first of the year.

> We have just four of these left.

> Orders have been high. You don't want to risk stockouts.

> We're not even offering the SX16 to most of our clients.

The fewer people who can afford (earn, win, find) something, the more we want to have it ourselves.

Positive and negative altercasting.   **Altercasting** means inviting individuals to perceive themselves differently in a particular way, either better than they are (positive altercasting) or worse than they are (negative altercasting). The first example here shows positive altercasting, the second negative:

> You're an unassuming kind of person, Leon. Maybe you don't think of yourself as a person who can make or break a program. You are, though. Your help on this project. . . .

> Sara, the people in your work group don't seem to be doing their share. This group's productivity is at the bottom of our ranking. I've about given up on the rest of them—I don't have any functional authority over them. But you know, most of us don't want to think you're the same as they are.

If the persuader can get these people to cast themselves in a role he or she likes better than what they are at present, they might change their behavior.

Positive and negative esteem.   All people care, to varying degrees, what others think of them. If a persuader can make us believe that doing as she or he wants will gain us the favorable attention of others, we just might do it. Wording in the first example suggests **positive esteem;** in the second, **negative esteem:**

> Your friends will be impressed when you. . . .

> Wearing a cheap watch is going to lose you some sales appointments. This is an important purchase you're making.

Even artificially created scarcity can motivate people to want what is scarce.

Altercasting gets individuals to see themselves playing roles they admire and wish to resemble or dislike and try to avoid.

Selling makes heavy use of people's anxiety about the opinions of others. So does team building.

Positive and negative expertise. Offering the educated opinion of selected experts is often persuasive. The first example uses **positive expertise** and the second **negative expertise:**

> Eight of the top ten stock-watch newsletters say that Brindisi stock mutual fund is likely to earn an annual average of 19 percent from 1993 to 1998.

> Six thousand research scientists support this position paper saying CFCs harm the ozone layer. Our firm must install this device to filter and convert fumes, and we need to change our manufacturing process as soon as is feasible.

True, experts often disagree violently with other experts, but persuaders do not have to represent all sides *if the sources they select are indeed competent and credible.* Years ago, some advertisers came under federal scrutiny for using "experts" who were really actors dressed as doctors, researchers, and other specialists and for showing fake testing evidence. This practice was unethical, and the government now prohibits this kind of advertising.

Reward and punishment, promise and threat. People can be rewarded or punished for behaving in a given way. Some rewards, like raises and job perks, are tangible. Persuaders can also give praise, compliments, public recognition, and more interesting work to do. Persuaders can punish with embarrassment, loss, dislike, and many other negatives, and they can threaten these things as well.

Some threats and promises can be shown to grow out of a situation. If persuaders can show the persuadee how to change the situation, the individual can avoid the threat and obtain the benefit:

> I know we have to push our delivery drivers hard to generate fast service. It's our competitive edge. Still, it's pure luck that we haven't had any worse problems than a couple of fender-benders. We should seriously consider airbags in the vans before we get hit with a workers' comp claim—or worse. Maybe a disability lawsuit.

Using "the situation" as the aversive element can keep the persuader from seeming to be the "bad guy": "It's out of my hands. It's up to you now."

Learning. People like to learn. They often respond favorably to approaches like "Did you know. . . ?" All messages are partial and selective. "Did you know" messages can be selected as well to inform and educate hearers about the aspects of a subject that work to the persuader's benefit. For instance, when businesses recruit applicants for a job, they offer selected information. They talk about opportunity for advancement but omit mention of the co-worker who annoyed the last jobholder into quitting. (The new hire might get along fine with this co-worker.)

Persuaders must not say things that are false. But they can select and emphasize statements in favor of their position and downplay statements against their position.

Reciprocity and indebtedness. People remember debts, and they want to be

> Remember last month when I stayed late to help you get that 500-piece mailing out? You could sure help me out now if you'd. . . .

Reciprocity is a powerful technique because it appeals to people's need to feel fair and balanced.

Several years ago, members of a donation-seeking organization stationed themselves in airports and pressed a very small gift, a flower, upon each passerby. Then they followed the person and talked about donations to their cause. When the person tried to leave, they pursued. If the person tried to give back the flower, they said, "No, it's a present—really!" and continued to press for a contribution. Often people made a donation. Even though they did not want the flower and did not support the cause, they *had* the flower and felt bound to pay something back. The force of indebtedness is very strong.

This is an extreme and possibly unethical example. Still, people do favors for others who have done them favors or given them something. Until the debt is paid, people feel dissonance.

Consistency.   Although we all defend our right to change our minds, persuaders can still make us feel stupid by implying that we are inconsistent. This persuader is using the **consistency** technique:

> Ms. Gillespie, you've been a strong supporter of the firm's investing in job training all along; and this seminar in Aspen is an excellent opportunity for me to hone sales and presentation skills.

Ralph Waldo Emerson said, "A foolish consistency is the hobgoblin of little minds," but persuaders can often lead people even to a foolish consistency. Once people "buy into" an idea, they will sometimes let others lead them where they should not rationally go:

> Remember we talked about your working on Christmas if I could get you Thanksgiving, New Year's Eve, and New Year's Day off?
>
> Yes, I remember.
>
> Remember you said Christmas wasn't going to be a big deal this year because all your family is going to be away?
>
> Yeah, really, it's no big deal.
>
> I'm really sorry, but I can't get you those days off. You'll still work on Christmas, though, won't you? Because after all, your family still isn't going to be here. And you can take some other days off. . . .

The persuader gives the consistency technique a try. The other person can always say no.

Easy compliance.   Receivers of persuasive messages often cite reasons why they cannot comply. Persuaders should create ways to make the desired action easy. Often they can neutralize excuses and remove obstacles. For instance, "Call 1-818-JAY-CEEE for free transportation to this important community event" might greatly increase customer turnout for a merchants' street fair.

Relative size of request.   Persuaders sometimes make an extreme opening request, intending to make concessions. The persuadee, who may not have intended to spend anything at all, feels relief from the initial shock when the cost comes down. He might feel like paying the lowered price. The technique is exemplified in this dialog:

> Can we buy this designer wall covering for the reception area?
>
> Of course not!
>
> Well, can we at least paint in there? It would cost much less.
>
> Oh, I guess so.

Although persuasive techniques and strategies are well known even to the very young, this cartoon reminds us that they don't always work.

Persuaders can also add small things to big things. If a persuadee already agrees to a large request, the persuader can sometimes attach one or more smaller requests because they seem minor alongside the big one:

> We're getting the new metal desks, credenzas, and horizontal files. Could we consider getting new wastebaskets and desk sets too?

Word choice. In strictly informational writing and speaking, you generally stay with low-connotation words—words without strong emotional associations. In persuasive writing and speaking, because people generally make a decision based at least in part on how they feel, sometimes words with strong connotations work better than the other kind.

However, while highly flavored words will move people more, *it is harder to control the direction and distance they go.* Using emotion-laden words can work for you, but analyze your reader with great care before choosing the words. Too emotional a word or the wrong kind of word can misfire and move a reader a great deal—in a direction you don't want. For example, many businesspeople respond better to a request for "an early response" than to a request for "a quick decision." *Quick* seems to suggest that the response is to be made without a chance to think things over. *Early* has no such connotation. If people sense that they are being rushed into something, they won't do it.

As a second example, look at two versions of part of an adverse personnel evaluation, given orally and in private:

> Jeff, we expect you to seek psychiatric treatment immediately. Your behavior lately is pushy and belligerent. If you don't knuckle under, you know, we can fire you.

> Jeff, we strongly advise you to obtain some counseling soon. Your behavior lately seems too assertive. If we can't help you to improve your attitude, you might have to be let go.

Both versions contain words with some emotional connotation. The second version, although milder in emotional connotation, will have a more predictable effect. The first one will either persuade thoroughly or backfire altogether. The hearer might hurry out and get the counseling, or he might start a lawsuit against the company.

Offering alternatives. People will often go along with you when you *assume* they will do what you want and you give them a choice of ways to do it. For example, a persuader might spend 10 minutes explaining to the receiver why her help is needed on a new project and then say, "Would you rather work

Rereading the coverage of word choice in Chapter Three can help you in word choice decisions in persuasive messages. Connotation is especially relevant.

Writing to Persuade | 359

THE FAR SIDE By GARY LARSON

Still no money, huh?... Well, let's see if Rudy and his <u>wiffle bat</u> can help encourage you.

Ineffective tools of persuasion

Reciprocity would work better: "In return for our not killing you, you give us all your money. Deal?" (It wouldn't be funny, but it would work.)

with Carter on program planning or with Lauren on documentation?" The receiver is fairly likely to choose one of these responsibilities, either of which the persuader likes, rather than choose the unspoken and very real third option: "No, I don't want to help on this project."

Here is part of a recruitment letter from a vocational tech school to graduating high school seniors:

> You're just out of school and looking at your options. You've probably seen the limited choices available to people without postsecondary education. The military is downsizing; the job market is depressed. XYZ Technical College is here to help. Choose computer programming. Or dental hygiene. Consider being a medical assistant. XYZ has nearly 50 other programs that will offer you comfortable earnings.

Another way a persuader can use alternatives is by setting up a good one and one or more bad ones. From the receiver's point of view, they may be about equally attractive. The persuader, though, presents attractively the one he wants chosen and presents unattractively the ones he doesn't want chosen. For example:

> Under present circumstances, we lose every way. Employees call in sick to stay home with a sick family member. Or employees leave the sick person alone and sit here in the office distracted with worry and do substandard work. We lose talent if we fire

people with dependents; we lose talent if we avoid hiring people with dependents. If we subsidize dependent care, we can hire people for their talent and count on getting the benefit of that talent.

Participation and visualization.   Sometimes persuasive writers can get readers to perform an activity or at least to think through a process with them. When readers do this, especially if it involves actual motion, they become more absorbed in the activity than if it were merely described to them. Participation reinforces whatever enjoyment or interest they feel.

Have you noticed how often sales letters include an order card requiring activity on the reader's part? Sometimes, for instance, the reader has to punch out a round cardboard token that says *yes* and put it into a slot on the order card. Sellers use these devices because they reinforce the appeal.

In an issue of *Digest Week* is a loose cardstock ad. A thoughtful-looking spokeswoman asks, "Is your relationship in trouble? Take this simple 10-point quiz." The reader can mark *yes* or *no* boxes to questions about typical disagreements dating couples have. After the quiz, designed to make the reader a little uneasy, comes a bold-type paragraph:

> How does your relationship compare to the average American's? In the May issue, psychologist Dr. June Jacobs discusses three magic ways to keep the glow alive. Subscribe now to make sure you don't miss her fascinating analysis of romance in the USA.

Easy subscription instructions follow, with option to pay later. The card folds shut; the opposite side is addressed to *Digest Week*'s subscription office; and return postage is paid. The reader of the February issue marked the quiz, became interested, had a pen in hand, filled in her name and address, and became a subscriber.

Senders of other persuasive messages can use the same principles. Let's say a business writer has to persuade a group of executives to modify a business's building entrance to improve access for people using wheelchairs. The writer might urge the executives to imagine themselves on the sidewalk looking up the three steps to the building's front door—and realize that, because they can't get up those steps, they can't even apply for a job they could perform competently.

"Yes."   The "yes" technique is related to audience participation. If the persuader has been doing a good job, and if the reader has been going along agreeably, sometimes the persuader will use a series of questions he's pretty sure the reader will answer with *yes*. The last of the four or five questions is the point on which the persuader wants agreement.

Here is an example. A foundation for providing care to homeless small children sends a letter asking for donations. Near the end is this sequence:

> Daily, we see hunger and pain looking at us from a child's eyes. Can you imagine these tiny children and their great need? Can you envision the pain of parents when we have to tell them we just can't care for any more? Don't you think a child ought to have a real chance? Then won't you help us today? Even if you contribute only what you'd spend dining out, you can save a child's future—maybe even a life.

Use this technique sparingly and cautiously. A series of questions like these tends to carry high emotion. And as we've mentioned before, high emotion can backfire.

Persuaders choose carefully among these techniques as they structure and develop persuasive messages. Receivers will not be persuaded solely on the

Participation and visualization involve the reader more closely in the ideas and behaviors the persuader is urging.

basis of participation, altruism, reciprocity, or scarcity. Other content elements, both rational and emotional, will fill out a structural plan selected to suit the need. The next section discusses structural options.

Structuring a Written Persuasive Message

Having analyzed the sender (himself), the communication situation, and the receiver, the persuader structures the message. The message grows out of all the other elements.

Most of our discussion here will concern *written* and *single-effort* or *"one-shot"* persuasive communications, since they are common in everyday business communication. Note, though, that many persuasive efforts are done over time—months or even years—and involve many separate communications in succession.

Persuasive Structure Based on Rational Arguments

Where a persuader has to build a case, the most common structure arranges arguments (reasons, pieces of evidence) according to how strong they are. Although the many different strategies and techniques just covered do find place in such messages, building a sound rational basis is essential.

The following outline shows an effective sequence. The opener introduces the subject, using ideas that both reader and writer know and agree on and establishing common ground.

- Opener
- Strong "pro" argument(s)
- Weaker "pro" argument(s)
- Citing and refuting one or more opposing arguments
- Strong "pro" argument(s)
- Summary
- Move to action

Primacy emphasizes because an idea is placed first. Recency emphasizes because an idea is the last one a reader encounters.

The number of arguments in each division can vary, but their placement should not vary much. The placement of the strongest arguments first and last makes use of the principles of **primacy** and **recency.** Audience members remember best what they hear or read first (prime position) and what they hear or read last (most recently). The less important ideas are placed in the middle, where an audience's attention tends to lessen.

The deemphasized middle section is also the place for mentioning and refuting some of the opposing arguments. The ideal counterarguments to bring up are those that permit strong and convincing refutation. The persuader chooses several such arguments and shows as clearly as possible how they are weaker or less important than the reader might think. Sometimes the arguments "against" can be turned into (weak) arguments "for."

A sound refutation of *any* arguments will demonstrate that the opposing position has its weaknesses. Very strong arguments against the persuader's position, however, are best omitted. If the persuader brings up a strong opposing argument but does not attack it effectively, he or she will do the opposition a favor.

Exhibit 11–4 shows an example of a memo report that must build a case. Marginal notes point to the structural elements of this memo, as well as to other elements of persuasion.

The Motivated Sequence

Many persuasive messages—which are usually shorter than the memorandum in Exhibit 11–4—emphasize case building less and emotional needs more. A

MEMORANDUM

To: Basil Cairn, Vice President, Chair, Strategic Planning Committee

From: Louis Bellinger, Vice President, Production

Date: October 20, 19xx

Subject: Meeting Expected Production Needs

Bellinger lays common ground with a pleasing reference to a rise in sales they both expect.

The anticipated 35 percent increase in sales over the next two years will indeed be an impressive accomplishment from our sales staff. To fill the orders they take, we will of course have to increase production and increase it beyond our present capacity. The company's historical production rates and capabilities, coupled with an in-depth analysis, show a need for capital outlay. Modifying some of our current machinery and purchasing some new equipment will enable production to meet the increased demand that our sales force will generate.

This sentence states the preferred solution - a capital outlay - to a problem - production's foreseen inability to meet sales demand.

Referring to the rational bases for the case to be built helps establish credible tone.

Data-based proofs support the preferred solution.

The numbers do not support the disliked solution.

A drawback of the preferred solution is minimized.

Option: Purchase and Upgrade of Equipment

As you can see from the enclosed report from Amato Equipment Co., by buying upgrades to our existing molding machines and three new molding machines, we will increase our capacity by about 75 percent and at the same time reduce our cost per unit by 5.7 percent. Our internal analysis, also enclosed, shows that the alternative of adding a third shift will increase production by only 36 percent, owing to the lower productivity we have historically obtained on graveyard shifts. With shift premiums our cost per unit is actually higher for the night shift despite not having to charge any additional fixed equipment costs to the shift.

The molders that we are now running were purchased in 1984. While the basic machines are still sound, they need to be rebuilt to bring them back to original specs and to have modern controls added to them. This rebuilding will reduce maintenance costs and down time, which, as you can see from the maintenance log summary that is enclosed, have been rising over the last three years.

Option: Adding a Third Shift

While adding a third shift would cover our capacity needs if our equipment stays in working order, our costs would be higher than with the new equipment for several reasons.

First, with shift premiums, lower productivity, and higher accident rates, our burdened unit labor cost would rise by over 60 percent. Since labor is 43 percent of our total variable cost, this means an increase of 26 percent in total unit variable costs. There is no way that spreading the fixed costs of the equipment over the additional production of the third shift can compensate for this.

Second, we now use the time that a third shift would operate for maintenance on the machinery. Because it is so old, we need this down time to keep the machines running during the working shifts. If we go to a third shift, we will have to try to keep the equipment running all the time. When the machines do go down, we will have to deal not only with repair costs, but also with the cost of lost production and idle workers.

This message devotes four paragraphs to refuting the opposite position and shows that choosing wrongly will bring several negative consequences

Third, the existing equipment is difficult to keep on spec because of its age and the quality of the controls available when it was installed. We are losing a substantial amount of material to scrap because of defective output. This problem will worsen if we can't use the third shift time for maintenance.

Cost Analysis

New machinery:

Cost of rebuilding current equipment	$275,400
Purchase of 3 new molders	552,500
Stock of parts for new molders	47,000
Total	874,900

Annual labor cost reduction from new equipment	228,000

Third shift:

Annual labor cost, burdened	417,000

The preferred solution's initial higher costs are shown to be lower over a longer term.

Two "sweeteners" help to motivate the desired choice.

The move to action is implied but clear: Decide in favor. Call me.

Thus, by an investment of $874,900, we will generate a net savings in labor alone of $417,000 plus $228,000, or $645,000. This gives us a payback period of about 16 months, well within our standard of 24 months. In addition, we will be well positioned to handle even larger increases in sales.

We have a fixed bid from Amato for the modifications. P.J. Jackson in purchasing has gone over the contracts and is satisfied that they are in line with our purchasing standards. Amato has tentatively agreed to oversee the adjustment, installation, and initial operation of added parts and equipment at no charge. Amato has also offered to provide us with training technicians for 30 days at no charge.

Many implementation elements are already arranged. Barriers to the decision are diminished.

This is a key project to put into our capital budget for next year. I'll be happy to meet with the Strategic Planning Committee to discuss the opportunities offered by this plan and to answer any questions anyone may have.

plan for such messages is often called the **motivated sequence.** It's especially useful in persuading a reader initially uninterested in the subject, the writer, or any part of the situation. This sequence also works when the reader is aware of the situation but not expecting messages about it. The motivated sequence has five steps: **attention, need, satisfaction, visualization,** and **action:**

- *Attention:* An attention-getting opener hooks the receiver's interest and gets her to start to read.
- *Need:* The writer works to establish and develop the reader's need for his plan, idea, service, or product.
- *Satisfaction:* The writer demonstrates that his plan, idea, service, or product will satisfy the receiver's need.
- *Visualization:* the writer encourages the reader to visualize herself having solved the problem, enjoying the product, or putting the service to use.
- *Action:* The writer moves the reader to whatever action he has in mind—authorizing an action, for example, or placing an order.

Exhibit 11–5, a memo that offers a staffing suggestion, uses the motivated sequence. Examine the other persuasive elements in this memo too.

Checklist 11–1 for persuasive messages is found on page 372.

The AIDA Sequence

The **AIDA** pattern (*a*ttention, *i*nterest, *d*esire, *a*ction) resembles the motivated sequence in several ways. AIDA underlies the sales letters you will look at next.

Specialized Persuasive Writing: Selling by Mail

Working for or perhaps owning a small business, you may need to write specialized persuasive letters promoting direct-mail sales. Mail-order firms' sales are in the billions annually. Effective letters drive many of these sales.

Specialized Prospect Lists

You have probably given your name, address, and other useful information to many potential sellers without knowing it. Whenever you send in a refund coupon, order from a catalog, sign up for a drawing, drop your business card in a jar for a premium, or even enroll in school, your name goes on a list with others who have done the same thing. These lists are bought and sold.

Computer capabilities permit list brokers to perform specialized sorting and accurate updating. Lists can be sorted for almost any variable: age, income, address, educational level, and sometimes even religion, approximate net worth, and other information about which people feel somewhat sensitive.[1]

Direct-mail selling costs per prospect contacted are relatively high. Therefore, sales letters must generate enough orders to justify their expense. Sales letters sent to an undifferentiated audience (the "shotgun" approach) will get few sales. Thus, sellers of goods and services eagerly buy sorted lists from list brokers, which they can find in the yellow pages of the business-to-business telephone book. With an accurate list tailored to their product or service (the "rifle" approach) sellers can harvest a profitable percentage of orders. For most products and services, an order rate of about 10 percent is profitable.

However, 10 percent is hard to get. Recipients often discard sales messages unread. As recipients, we find ourselves resistant: "More junk mail. What a

Sales letters go to carefully selected categories of recipients.

---

[1]Some people believe computerized accumulation, storage, sorting, and exchange of such data amounts to a systematic, nationwide invasion of privacy. They are also concerned about possible misuse of this information.

MEMORANDUM

To: Ms. Nancy Soames, Vice President, Branch Manager
From: Steven Sixtus, Customer Service Representative
Date: April 27, 19xx
Subject: Internal Hiring of Employees

The stark, specific language seizes attention.

One heart bypass case, one transferred spouse, and one retirement have left our branch short three staff, with only the retirement vacancy foreseen.

The second paragraph outlines the need.

I can see the added burden on you to find new employees quickly; you've had to delegate and oversee the work formerly done by the new-accounts people and the secretary. This extra work has added a lot of pressure to your job.

Paragraphs three, four, and five offer satisfaction of the need.

I noticed external ads for these positions in this morning's <u>Courier</u>. I'd like to strongly suggest moving some already qualified and deserving employees in our own branch into these positions, instead of hiring from outside our branch or company.

Many Qualified Employees

Rational appeals include
• known resources as opposed to more risky unknown ones
• opportunity because of competitor's layoffs
• saving recruitment and benefit costs
• saving scarce time

There are at least four employees in our branch who are already qualified for these positions. All are bilingual, all can type at least 40 wpm, and all are excellent salespeople. Some of them even have had previous new-accounts and secretarial experience. They all work hard, are energetic, exhibit skill with customers, and have been with our branch for more than two years. Their previous work reviews, which you have on file, would show you good evidence of their strengths. Given the chance, they'd do well, and it's a chance I know they'd appreciate.

Emotional appeals include
• increased motivation from promoted employees
• lowered stress
• gratitude

Lower Cost to Find Tellers

Since we hired two new tellers, we wouldn't be understaffed if we filled from the teller staff. Teller positions are also easier to staff than new accounts and the secretarial position, so it wouldn't take long to find new tellers. I know that a competitor, Merchants Bank, is currently trying to eliminate full-time teller positions. Their cuts offer us the perfect chance to move two full-time tellers to the open positions and hire part-time staff in their place. This step would reduce benefit costs.

The second last paragraph invites the reader to visualize the stress relief the recommended solution would bring.

With the $um-$um-$ummertime promotion coming, consider the relief you'd feel at having this unplanned personnel shortage solved. Your time and energy could be freed up for the manifold and demanding work of managing a branch in this competitive industry.

The ending paragraph specifies and recommends action.

We're having a hard time filling these open new-accounts and secretarial positions. Good workers are hard to find. Why not fill these open jobs with people you already know to be capable, hard workers?

drag." "Don't waste my time." "If I wanted it, I'd go buy it." "Now what are you trying to get from me?" "What's the catch?"

For this reason, every aspect of a sales letter, from the exterior of the envelope all the way to the end of the letter and its enclosures, must be tailored to the reader. To succeed, the persuasion must meet and fulfill the receiver's need.

As we discuss the persuasive sales letter medium, we will sometimes refer to an effective sales letter package from *Highlights for Children,* shown in Exhibits 11−6 and 11−7 (pages 369 and 371).

Once in a while, a seller writes a sales letter for one single reader with a lot of money to invest or spend. In most cases, though, the same sales letter is written to many people, all the people on one of the lists just discussed. Their being on this list means that they are alike in one or more ways important to the seller. The seller prepares a mailing tailored to people *with the characteristics that put them on that particular list.*

Analyzing the Intended Reader

For example, the sales staff of the educational periodical *Highlights for Children* can easily locate and buy a list of moderate-to-high-income grandparents under 60. The sellers can assume that these people are fairly likely to

- Possess disposable income.
- Have one or more grandchildren of an age appropriate to the product.
- Want their grandchildren to "have advantages."
- Be more interested in childhood learning than they had time to be when their own children were small.
- Feel some guilt about not spending more time on their own children's childhood learning.
- Wish to seem thoughtful and deliberate about gift giving.
- Want their grandchildren to love them.

Besides these "grandparental" factors, people on this list share other characteristics a persuader can appeal to. For instance, like most other consumers, they probably respond to rational proofs as well as to emotional tugs, enjoy a bargain, understand a problem-and-solution presentation, choose an easy over a hard solution, feel indebtedness, and enjoy a colorful and attractive presentation.

Sellers must know everything about what they sell. They cannot say everything about it to any one audience, but they must be able to select material intelligently for a given prospect. They must believe in their product or service and consider it a good value to sell it convincingly. To sell its strengths, they must know its strengths; to compensate for its weaknesses (nothing can be all things to all people), they must know how it stacks up against its competition. They must foresee and answer questions and objections.

Understanding the Product or Service

Readers of sales letters could spend their money on thousands of other purchases. A successful sales letter makes readers want *this* product or service more—and order it.

The seller of *Highlights* can offer many attractive reasons why grandparents should subscribe for their grandkids. We will give examples in the section "An Effective Sales Letter Package" on pages 369−371.

Other possible purchases compete for a prospect's attention and money. Clearly sellers cannot compare and contrast their wares with all those possibilities. Buyers' attention, always short, will evaporate if a sales letter grows overlong without motivating them to continue.

Differentiating the Product or Service

In the time they have, sellers must show their product to be the most desirable of its kind for these readers. Usually they choose and fully develop a **central selling point**—a single main differentiating advantage—and summarize other advantages.

Organizing the Letter

On page 365, we mentioned the AIDA pattern. *A*ttention, *i*nterest, *d*esire, and *a*ction are the four main parts of a sales letter. The **attention** step must "hook" the readers' attention; the rest of the letter must maintain it. Attention must proceed to **interest** and then to a **desire** to buy. The seller attempts to be simultaneously brief and thorough as he or she builds readers' conviction that they want the benefits offered. The **action** step occurs at or near the ending. Here the seller invites the readers to order the product or service. The action should be easy—as nearly effortless as possible.

Readers have to part with some money, and most will not be eager to do so. In mentioning price, sellers emphasize the benefits and deemphasize the cost, often using one or more of these means:

- Put the price in an enclosure rather than in the letter itself.
- If you put the price in the letter, "bury" it in a relatively long paragraph about 80 percent of the way through the letter.
- Give the price only in small weekly or monthly units, not as a lump sum.
- Show the price to be less than the price of something else the prospect would buy without thinking much about it.

If the price is the main selling point, of course, the seller features it prominently.

At the action step, sometimes sellers offer an extra benefit for ordering immediately or by a certain date. After the signature block, a "P.S." can contain still another inducement to purchase. In fact, although a P.S. is supposedly an afterthought, its final position emphasizes its content.

Choosing Language

Sellers can use all their creativity in choosing language. Although sales letters should sound businesslike, their language can also be personal, sensory, vivid, imaginative, clever, memorable, and witty, in any combination.

Are you selling an additive that helps clean an automobile engine? Learning all about your product will let you talk about whatever benefits your data will support: smooth operation, perhaps, or clean combustion, freedom from wear, pollution abatement, engine efficiency, and faster pickup.

Are you selling soft-soled knit slippers to wear around the house? Create warm and cold word pictures: nippy mornings, hot coffee, the newspaper, and the warm slippers. Use language to sell comfort. Getting readers to imagine themselves already enjoying the product can be very effective. It feels good, and people like to buy a good feeling.

Be careful not to overstate. Do not try to move readers farther than they are willing to go. Describe the product or service in terms readers will respond to.

Don't be afraid to key into positive emotions. Similarly, do not overlook negative emotions such as anxiety, worry, or guilt. The *Highlights* letter uses these negative emotions subtly and effectively. All these emotions are natural, and people buy many things to meet emotional needs. As you address emotions, bear your ethical responsibility in mind: Do no harm, and offer value for value.

To sell a product or service, an effective sales letter sells benefits and feelings of satisfaction.

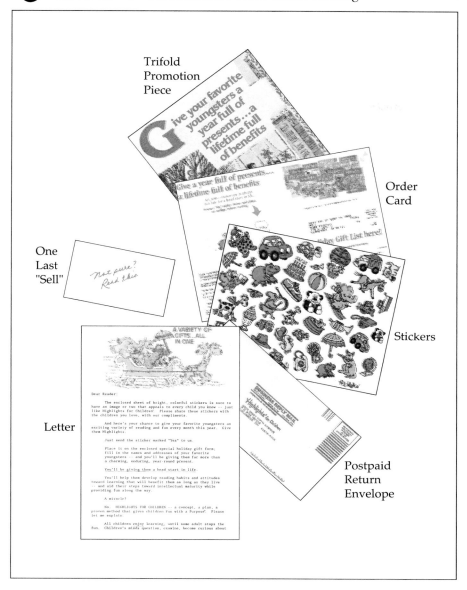

Ordering must seem virtually effortless. The less action the writer must obtain, the better. A simple, friendly-looking order card is easy to mark. Multiple options for payment (check, credit card number, bill later) allow buyers to put off thinking about payment. A postpaid return envelope saves them the time and expense of finding an envelope and sticking on first-class postage. Often sellers restate the main benefits again as they are moving the buyers to action.

Highlights for Children has been published for decades. Part of its success is due to product quality. Another part is due to effective sales messages. Exhibit 11-6 gives the complete *Highlights* sales package.

Ease of Ordering

If ordering takes much effort, readers won't do it. Make ordering easy.

AN EFFECTIVE SALES LETTER PACKAGE

The mailing was sent in early fall for holiday season sales. On the reverse side of the envelope is a sleigh in green and red against a deep blue sky. In the sleigh is a large, transparent, gift box shape through which you can see attractive pictures. An instruction says, "Pull open here," and the top of the envelope zips off cleanly. Inside the envelope are

- The promised 40 stickers (basic cute stuff—hippo, teddy bear, ball, birthday cake). Of course, you want to give them to a child—what a shame to waste them! This "freebie" makes you feel just slightly indebted.
- A color trifold showing typical art from the magazine and some lengthy promotional copy.
- An order blank with a sticker that you have to move from one place to another (it makes you want to play with it).
- A postpaid return envelope.
- A very effective sales letter.
- A small additional letter folded shut and saying on the outside, "Not sure? Read this."

The letter is shown in Exhibit 11–7. The opener says to give the free stickers to a child, then moves immediately to another present readers might want to give that child—*Highlights*.

The letter develops numerous benefits: learning advantages, good reading habits, and 11 issues for 11 separate fun occasions so that the child will be reminded of the giver 11 times a year. The central selling point, however, offers the magazine as a means of encouraging curiosity and creative learning. *You* want to be the enabler for this child. *You* don't want to be the one who has stifled a child's curiosity, as words like these remind you:

> All of a sudden, children are grown. And then what? Where have they gone, what's happened to the lost opportunities to help make minds more attuned to intellectual achievement and awareness of lasting values? The direction children take is determined very early in life—and you have the privilege of helping to forge mature, responsible citizens.

Emotional appeal does not edge out rational appeal. Five national civic organizations have endorsed the magazine. Three million parents and teachers have subscribed. And the "Not sure? Read this" enclosure contains more rational content.

Price is given not in the letter but in an enclosure. Also, the total subscription price is not given; rather, the enclosure gives the price per issue, which is just under $2. Finally, the P.S. says to remember those nice stickers—no obligation, of course (but you *do* have them, and you have *not* paid anything . . .).

The letter's length, at four pages, is not rare for sales messages, which are longer, on the average, than other kinds of business letters. If those grandparents on the prospect list are also subscribers to one or more magazines—which is something the sellers can specify when they order their names list—they are presumably willing to read a long letter if its content interests them.

The *Highlights* letter was written by highly skilled sales writers, but everything in it reflects the same principles covered in this chapter. It persuades

A VARIETY OF GIFTS...ALL IN ONE

Dear Reader:

The enclosed sheet of bright, colorful stickers is sure to have an image or two that appeals to every child you know -- just like Highlights for Children. Please share these stickers with the children you love, with our compliments.

And here's your chance to give your favorite youngsters an exciting variety of reading and fun every month this year. Give them Highlights.

Just send the sticker marked "Yes" to us.

Place it on the enclosed special holiday gift form; fill in the names and addresses of your favorite youngsters -- and you'll be giving them far more than a charming, enduring, year-round present.

You'll be giving them a head start in life.

You'll help them develop reading habits and attitudes toward learning that will benefit them as long as they live -- and aid their steps toward intellectual maturity while providing fun along the way.

A miracle?

No. HIGHLIGHTS FOR CHILDREN -- a concept, a plan, a proven method that gives children Fun with a Purpose. Please let me explain:

All children enjoy learning, until some adult stops the fun. Children's minds question, examine, become curious about

everything they do not know or understand. Even babies want to learn by touching everything. And you must say "NO!" to a hot stove, of course. With the pressures of today's fast-paced world, even some well-meaning adults say "NO!" to a child's curiosity.

"Why?" children ask. Perhaps over and over again.

But they really want to know. And Highlights can help ...

Help you provide your favorite youngsters with active, constructive learning, prepared by deeply concerned and experienced teachers and child psychologists ...

Help you solve the annual holiday problem, in a day of transitory values, by giving the fun-filled gift that lasts all year long ...

Help you prove -- even to preschoolers -- that reading is fun and worthwhile, too ...

Help you teach the values you yourself hold dear: self-confidence, manners, thoughtfulness ...

All of a sudden, children are grown.

And then what? Where have they gone, what's happened to the lost opportunities to help make minds more attuned to intellectual achievement and awareness of lasting values? The direction children take is determined very early in life -- and you have the privilege of helping to forge mature, responsible citizens.

Perhaps it's best said in the words of Highlights' Chairman (a former school principal, by the way):

"Having done one thing well, children do all things better."

You know it's true, because you've probably lived through the experience yourself. The problem, often, is to get children to do a thing well, to appreciate that they have, and then to want to repeat the experience.

As the enclosed brochure shows, fun-filled issues of Highlights can help -- regardless of a child's age, from preschool to preteen.

*   *   *

If you believe your favorite youngsters deserve Highlights' helping hand, the enclosed shopping list provides the answer.

Say "Yes" (by sticking the proper sticker into place) and you'll be activating a series of happy surprises:

1. A gift announcement that you can sign as you wish will be provided with each subscription you order -- if you order early. (We will send you an acknowledgment/invoice confirming your order.) If your order is not received early enough, we'll send an announcement to the children in your name.

2. The first issue of HIGHLIGHTS FOR CHILDREN will follow shortly, jammed with fun and learning for all children -- interesting, fun-to-know, useful information.

3. Then, throughout the whole year, your favorite children will be reminded of you as a fresh, new issue of Highlights arrives -- addressed to each child, given by you.

*   *   *

Some additional facts about the magazine may provide reasonable reassurance, and they're contained in the accompanying brochure. You may wish to look it over now.

As far as I know, there's no better gift for the price. Frankly, I don't believe we could have achieved 3,000,000 enthusiastic parent and teacher subscribers if there were.

You need not pay for your gift subscriptions until after the holiday season, if you prefer. Remember, too, that one

gift of Highlights takes care of a whole family of children. A bargain by any standard.

Think about it now, won't you? So many gifts are given to children in haste or last-minute desperation. So few last beyond the moment, much less the season.

You have the chance to do better. Just think about your favorite youngsters, then say YES to Highlights.

They ... and you ... will be glad you did.

Sincerely yours,

Elmer C. Meider, Jr.
President

ECM:ls

P.S. The charming collection of stickers represents the fun, variety, and value you'll find in every issue of Highlights. There is, of course, no obligation on your part. It's our gift to you, in hope that you'll decide to say YES and give Highlights to a young friend or two.

ethically and effectively. It targets the right audience, shows full understanding of the product's merits, differentiates its product from competition for the prospect's gift-giving dollars, uses typical inductive structure, uses vivid, motivating, commonsense language, rationally demonstrates value, and makes the action simple and fun to take.

A checklist for sales letters is found on page 372.

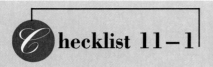

Checklist 11–1

Persuasive Message

- Does the opener arouse interest and establish common ground?
- Does the message sound reliable and credible?
- Is the tone appropriate, consistent, and carefully controlled?
- Are all aspects of the message appropriate for this sender, this reader, and this situation?
- Does the message sound reasonable?
- Are emotional appeals tailored to the specific reader's wants and needs (WIIFM)?
- Does the message consider this reader's frame of reference?

- Is the message appropriate to the sender's and receiver's respective power and status levels?
- Does the message persuade fairly and ethically?
- Are persuasive strategies and techniques carefully chosen for this reader and this situation?
- Is the right persuasive structure used?
- Does the message specify clearly what action or change is desired?
- Are barriers to action effectively reduced?
- Does the ending strongly motivate action?

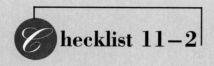

Checklist 11–2

Sales Letter

- Is the sales letter package attractive and professional looking?
- Does the letter's opener seize favorable *attention?*
- Is the product or service introduced in a way that turns attention to *interest?*
- Do structure and order encourage the readers to keep reading?
- Does a central selling point or theme unify the letter?

- Will reader benefits (WIIFM) create strong *desire* for the product or service in the minds of these readers?
- Is the language vivid and attractive?
- Are persuasive strategies carefully chosen for these readers?
- Is value clearly shown to outweigh price?
- Is the desired *action* clear?
- Is the action easy to take?

REVIEW

Persuasion is a conscious effort by one individual to modify or change the opinions, attitudes, beliefs, or behaviors of another individual or group through the transmission of a message. Although messages are mainly informative or mainly persuasive, many messages contain some combination of these two purposes. Psychological characteristics of both sender and receiver require special consideration in persuasion. Emotion and reason must be carefully balanced for receiver, sender, and situation.

Because persuasive messages are selective and (carefully) emotional, senders must persuade ethically. Senders must also select intelligently from among the many available persuasive techniques and strategies to create the desired response in readers.

Because structure is indirect, all message elements must keep the reader reading all the way to the move to action.

Sales messages, a subset of persuasive communication, move billions of dollars' worth of goods and services yearly. Most sales letters go to persons on specialized lists that permit writers to tailor sales appeals closely to groups of similar recipients. Most sales letters are structured using the AIDA formula (attention, desire, interest, and action), with price generally deemphasized in favor of reader benefits.

APPLICATION EXERCISES

1. Explain this statement: "Many business messages both inform and persuade." Give and discuss an example of a message that does both.

2. Define *dissonance.* Think of an example of a message that created a state of dissonance in you.

3. Give a business example in which the appeal to *consistency* would be persuasive.

4. Give business examples in which reinforcement is used to make persuasion more permanent.

5. What are your *reference groups?* What are those of your parents? Of your supervisor at work?

6. Think of a subject of continuing concern to you. (Examples might be grades, bills, your health or diet, the scarcity of discretionary money, taxes— whatever you have to think about over the long term.) Probably you do not always have the same frame of reference for this subject. What kinds of events or situations would change your frame of reference? How could a persuader use or modify that frame of reference to prepare you for a message about this subject?

7. Discuss, in terms of power and status levels of sender and receiver, the following message (body only) written from a teller to a branch manager. How would you improve it?

   It is no secret that superior customer service is the backbone of a financially secure and successfully operated branch. My philosophy is that success is not built upon the size of the account or the number of accounts, but on the strength of the relationship. We can open a record number of accounts in one day, but the next day an equal number may close their accounts.

   We can capture an entire segment of market share if we just remember to keep the customers' best interests in mind. If we, the staff members of Barker Hills Branch, pursue and preserve the fundamental principle of offering courteous and respectable service to our customers, the rewards are limitless. What are we waiting for? Let's implement a new customer service program for our staff members and let them understand the scope we stand to achieve.

   I propose a sales generator table, with information on home equity loans, consumer investment opportunities, business cards of all platform representatives, and suggestion box. We need posters in the break room to ensure that no one forgets our objectives in this campaign. An employee-of-the-month program will provide incentive for modeling and exemplifying superior customer service.

   I assure you that by spearheading this program, our branch will gain a higher volume of business. Good customer service creates positive visibility before our customers, "survey" shoppers, and upper management. High ratings from these people will translate into higher rankings in our division. We have everything to gain and nothing to lose in

   becoming number one. Remember, the dollar bills the customers get from tellers in banks are the same. What will differ are the tellers.

   Marty, I look forward to serving you and our branch customers. I believe we have a very optimistic future.

8. Comment on language and reader's WIIFM in the following message, written by a different teller to a different manager. How would you improve the message? Are there more positive ways to make some of the same points?

   As you know, our bank is in trouble. As customer service manager, I know you will be concerned with the recent customer service surveys. Based on these surveys, I have found that our customer service rating has declined steadily since the removal of the tellers' chairs. Because most of our tellers work eight-hour shifts on their feet, they can become grouchy toward the end of the day. Having the chance to rest their feet during the day, our tellers would convey a friendlier attitude toward our customers. As a result, your branch goal of a higher customer service rating would be met and surpassed.

   We both understand the original recommendation to remove the chairs. The reason, of course, was to discourage unproductive behavior on the part of the tellers. Alternatively, happier tellers would boost their productivity level. So I'm sure you can see the benefit of a higher productivity level; higher productivity means faster lines and satisfied customers.

   Mr. DeVille, I know bringing back the chairs will have only positive results on our customer service performance rating. After all, providing superior customer service is our job. Please endorse this proposal.

9. What examples of unethical persuasion have you observed? Be prepared to discuss these examples in class.

10. Refer to the section of the chapter on strategies and techniques beginning on page 355. Look at sales messages and letters to the editor in your newspaper and see how many examples of these different techniques and strategies you can find. Bring them to discuss in class.

11. Some editorial writers and political columnists in newspapers and news magazines may structure their pieces as described on page 362. Try to find one that follows this structure reasonably closely (it won't be perfect). Clip or photocopy the piece, mark the various sections (strong "pro" arguments, refutation, and so on) and hand it in to your instructor.

12. If you or members of your family receive sales messages in the mail, consider where the sender probably obtained your names and addresses. What other lists are you or they on? Church membership? *Business Week* subscribers? For any

one such list, write out the characteristics a seller could infer that people on that list probably share.

13. Brainstorm on paper all the vivid, sensory language that might help you sell *(a)* a vibrantly colored, sueded (sometimes called "sand-washed") silk shirt; *(b)* a set of speakers that would give maximum purity of sound for a CD player; *(c)* a one-pound box of the finest-quality chocolates.

14. Buyers of goods and services naturally respond to rational appeals such as good value for price. What other kinds of sales appeals have you seen your friends or family respond to? Be as specific as you can. Why do you think those particular appeals work for these individuals?

15. Read all the sales letter cases beginning on page 376. For each letter, develop a strong attention-getting first sentence. Be creative.

CASES

Cases for Persuasive Writing

Integrate selected content from this chapter as you write persuasive messages in response to these cases. Different techniques will be appropriate for different cases. Carefully analyze the reader (his or her position, interests, status, and needs), the persuasive situation, and your own position, interests, status, and needs.

1. **A Drive-up Window for Captain Kidder's.** You are a shift manager for Captain Kidder's, a fast-food restaurant specializing in fish and seafood sandwiches and dinners. You have strongly supported the efforts of Hank Kiddermeister, the owner-manager, to deliver first-rate food, service, and friendliness. You wish to sustain these features, but you believe market share won't increase any further until Kidder's installs a drive-through lane and offers window service. You believe many customers pass you by because, unlike some of your competitors, you do not offer this extra convenience.

    Write a persuasive memo to Kiddermeister. Build a case. In preparing, explore in your own mind what advantages a drive-in window offers besides convenience and fast service. What *disadvantages* would a drive-up window *avoid* for both customers and your restaurant?

2. **Lambkin's: Day Care for Kids with Disabilities.** You are a teacher-caregiver at Lambkin's, one of several competing day-care centers in a fairly affluent suburb. You know of several families with kids who have disabilities. These families can afford child care but cannot find providers able to give access to their special-needs children. The Americans with Disabilities Act will eventually require all day-care centers to adapt their premises to offer access to those with disabilities. Compliance will be slow for most centers, though, and enforcement will lag. You see an opportunity here. If Lambkin's takes the lead in adapting its premises and publicizes its readiness to serve families with special needs, it could gain some loyal long-term customers.

Lambkin's is laid out fairly spaciously and is all on one level; thus, modifications will cost Lambkin's less than most of its competitors.

   Do you think the mass media would consider a feature on the first day-care center to adapt? Think of other reasons that would help you sell this idea in *a memo to your boss, David Williford.*

3. **A Business Student Organization That Needs a Break.** You and three friends saved a virtually defunct student organization in your business major. You are president, and they are officers too. All four of you have slaved to bring the club back to life. Last May you obtained $250 in seed money from Student Governance (SG), an elected board responsible for allocating funds from student fees. All but $50 is scheduled to be repaid in October, after fall membership dues come in. Now, in October, you want to postpone repaying it until you get your membership up to a point where it supports the group's activities. You began with 4 members and now have 40; you believe you will break 100 if you can keep the activities going and publicize them. To do this you need to keep all your money until March.

   Estimate your cost figures. Then build your case in *a persuasive message to Mary Clare Macias, President of SG.* Develop SG's and Macias's WIIFM. Consider the purposes of student organizations.

4. **A Demo to Promote Service.** You are an assistant manager at All-Terrain Sports, a sporting goods store preparing for ski season. You believe setting up a demo of the expensive ski-tuning machine your store bought during the summer will draw heavy service business and hasten payback on the cost of the machine. You will need to field objections. The demo area reduces sales floor space. New carpeting has just been purchased. The machine runs on 220 volts; you would have to extend 220 service from the floor above through the ceiling down to this area.

Will the demo increase sales as well as service revenue? How and why? Write *a memo to persuade Helen Schussboom, the store owner.* You will need facts, figures, appeals, and rational arguments.

5. **The First Message in a Multimessage Series.** Is there a cause in which you strongly believe? Consider the people who dislike the cause. *Write a message in which you ask them* not to change their minds but merely *to understand why some people do believe in the cause.* Your message would be the first step in a series of possible messages, the last of which might actually induce them to change their minds. Think in terms of that ultimate goal, but do not attempt to reach it in your message. Your job is to create dissonance and to generate some empathy. Be sure to move outside your own feelings in writing this message.

6. **Help Yourself!** Develop your own problem for a persuasive message. Think of someone in your business or professional life whose support would help you solve a particular business or professional problem. *Write a persuasive letter or memo* in which you work to get that person's support. Analyze the person's needs and attitudes carefully. With tact and subtlety, structure the message to make the person receptive to your request. Use (selectively) some of the persuasive strategies discussed in this chapter. Do not be obvious about it, and be sure the strategies serve your persuasive goal—you are *not* being asked to use the strategies for their own sake.

Cases for Written Sales Messages

From your own or your instructor's choice among the following cases, create a hard-to-resist sales letter. Invent a name for each product or service (the case title is not necessarily a suitable name). Decide on a target audience, unless one is specified. For products, think about how you will treat and charge for shipping and handling. What questions will you have to answer? What barriers must be overcome? What will gain attention, interest, desire, and action? Sell benefits. Probe the audience's WIIFM. Make action easy to take.

7. **A Hands-Free Flashlight.** Sell a flashlight with a magnetic, adjustable swivel holder. People using flashlights usually need both hands for the task but have to use one to hold the light. Think about different tasks in which a nearby metal surface would hold the light and for which the user would need both hands. Sell benefits, using, for instance, visualization and participation. You can retail the holder and a good-quality flashlight for $15.99. Think about flashlight details: battery size, dimensions, materials.

8. **No Streaks, No Fooling.** Sell a window-cleaning service emphasizing quality. Competitors have undercut your price, but they have not obtained the market share they hoped for because of few repeat customers. Their mistake is an opportunity for you. Find out the price of such services in your area before you begin. When defining quality, consider neat employees, prompt service, reliability, special scheduling, and other expectations in addition to clean windows.

9. **A Foolproof Tire Gauge.** Sell a tire gauge with a lighted, digital readout. The product might be especially attractive to people who know car maintenance is essential but have little mechanical ability or tolerance for grime. The price is $22.

10. **Everything But the Food and the Ants.** Sell a picnic basket and utensil set. You have bought plain wicker clasp baskets and sturdy, brightly colored plates and glasses at an import store. Your employees have lined the baskets and hemmed matching fabric to make a picnic tablecloth and napkins. Through your writing, help the prospects see how exciting and fun the whole picnic layout looks. Do they have a choice of color or fabric pattern? At $29.95, the set is a great value. Sell the *fun* of a picnic.

11. **An Expandable Tote Bag.** Sell an expandable tote bag for traveling, priced at $34.99. The material is the supertough, woven, taffetalike vinyl fabric that bookbags and knapsacks are made of. At its smallest, the bag is about 10 inches high, 16 inches long, and 7 inches deep. Unzipping one zipper adds 7 inches of height. Unzipping the other zipper adds another 7 inches. Fully expanded, the bag is 24 inches high. Design in more features as desired: Type of closure? Wheels? Handle? Detachable shoulder strap? Describe all features. Decide on colors. If you emphasize convenience, explain exactly what that means in terms of this product.

12. **Honey, I Blew Up the New VCR.** You have never met a videocassette recorder (VCR) you couldn't program. Sell your services. Assume you have obtained a list of purchasers of top-of-the-line VCRs—the ones with dozens of features, 35-page owner's manuals full of small print and complex diagrams, and the capacity for reducing their new owners to gibbering idiots, especially if the owners also have cable TV and three remote-control handsets. Decide what you will charge, and whether by the hour or by the job. Sell peace of mind, troublefree use of the new gadget, and enjoyment of all the TV programs the users want to record. Don't make users feel stupid. Consider offering low-cost add-ons: (1) one free callback visit to reset the device after a power outage

wipes out all the programming and (2) a customized, one-page list of instructions so that owners can reset it themselves. Eventually you can probably sell both.

13. **Burglars Are Rarely Bookworms.** Starting with assorted new books you found marked down to a couple of dollars apiece, you and your hobby shop have made a very useful product for next to nothing. You have hollowed out the inside of each book and, using a lightweight and environmentally safe glue, produced a hiding place for valuables that a burglar will overlook. Depending on what you found marked down, your customers might select a type of book to blend in with their other books—a textbook, a novel, a cookbook, and so on. They can stow the Rolex inside *Radiccio World*, pearls inside the Plato. Sell this handsome, hardbound hidey-hole for at least $12.99. Figure in your labor, materials, overhead, and selling costs.

14. **Better Vision for When Your Eyes Are Barely Open.** Sell a magnifying mirror for applying makeup or shaving. At $15, the mirror has suction cups on the back to attach it to a tile wall or a standard mirror, leaving both hands free. For travel, the user can detach the suction cups and carry the mirror in a soft cloth slipcase.

15. **A Teardrop Full of Light.** You and your partner have a small business that produces glass ornaments, mouthblown and decorated by hand. Until now you have sold from temporary booths in shopping malls where, at $6.99, the ornaments practically sell themselves. Now sell them by mail. Your first offering is a four-inch glass teardrop in green, amber, blue, red, violet, or clear. It looks beautiful hanging in windows and, in season, on a Christmas tree. The clear ornaments can be custom decorated with hand-stained flowers or stars or personalized with hand-lettered gold inscriptions. The customer can order two phrases of up to 24 letters each: a name, *Happy Holidays, Baby's First Christmas,* and so on. Sell the ornaments in sets of four for $27.99 or singly at $7.99. Let the customer specify clear or color, which color(s), lettering, and so on. Sell light and color. Think of gift occasions. Use fresh, visual, appealing language.

Chapter Twelve

Job Search

PREVIEW

Selling yourself, your education, and your experience are valuable skills to learn and practice while you are still in school. In this chapter, you will learn how to apply the research, organizing, and persuading strategies discussed so far to help you get a job based on your education and experience. These strategies apply whether you are currently employed, attending school full time, or in a two- or four-year school.

We will cover how to gather information on prospective employers and on yourself, how to organize details on your background into an effective résumé, and how to create an accompanying cover letter or application letter to sell your skills to an employer and land an interview. We will also discuss how to keep a record of job contacts and results of interviews. Because keeping records is easiest if started early, we will suggest some organizing methods and forms for structuring and remembering the mass of information you will collect. ●

rom the desk of...

Getting a Job Is a Job in Itself!

Sue Williams
Assistant Loan Officer

I don't know what I must have been thinking. Here I was, finishing my senior year, getting a degree in finance, but I didn't have a job yet. My grades were good, so I figured it would be easy.

Graduation came and went, and still no job—or at least no job in finance. I kept my part-time job at the restaurant and went to full time, but that's not what I got the degree for. I wanted to get into banking. I answered ads, but nothing—not even any interviews.

After about six months, I decided something had to change. So I reexamined my job search to see what I could do differently. I began by looking at my résumé—there didn't seem to be anything wrong with it (but boy, was I wrong!). Then I looked at the market for my services. I checked on the banks in town and decided I wanted to work for one of the big ones, and there are only five of them. I analyzed each to see what I could do that it needed, who could hire me, and all the rest. Then I looked at myself. I saw that I had some skills that were useful to a banker. Finally, I looked again at my résumé, and I saw that it talked all about what *I* wanted, without focusing on what a bank wants.

I rewrote the résumé, concentrating on my courses in banking and finance, my year as treasurer of the student newspaper, and the personal service I had learned as a waitress. I made sure it looked good, with all of the typos from the old résumé gone. Then I sent it, with a good ''you'' attitude cover letter, to the senior lender at each of the banks. I got two interviews and a job offer.

Now I'm using what I learned and loving it. Why didn't I do it right the first time? I could have saved myself nine months of grief—and made twice as much money during that time.

Your job search will be much more effective if you do it correctly from the start. In this chapter and the next, you will learn how to have the best chance of getting the job you want.

ORGANIZING YOUR JOB SEARCH

To find a job that suits your qualifications, you'll first need to collect information on yourself, on companies, and on jobs. As you begin to go to interviews, you will need to keep records of whom you met, what you were asked, and what action will come next. To help you, all this information must be organized in a logical way.

As a starting point in your job search, you need to decide whether to assemble the information you will collect on your background, on industries and companies, and on specific jobs in a looseleaf notebook with dividers, a set of file folders, or on your computer. (At some point you will need to store prospective employers' names and addresses on your computer, but many people begin with written notes to sort through the information first.)

One way to organize the information you collect is in a notebook with five sections to cover your research from self-assessment through interviews. The headings for the sections might be as follows: (1) Skills/Interests, (2) Working Résumé, (3) Career Information, (4) Company Research, and (5) Interviews/

Job fairs are a good way to look over a number of companies quickly, gather information on prospective employers, and get cards of people you wish to contact later.

Company Visits.[1] However you choose to organize your information, experts from outplacement services (which help former employees find new jobs when a company downsizes, among other services) agree that you need to assemble information both on yourself and your qualifications *and* on prospective employers. Once you have listed skills, accomplishments, goals, and interests, you have the raw material with which to create an effective résumé and prepare for a strong interview performance.

In your notebook section or computer file on skills and interests, make lists of what you can do. Following are some category ideas to get you started, but you will probably think of more. Think of what you have learned in school, in volunteer work, in your jobs, and through personal interests. Then list your skills.

One way to list your skills is in terms of organizational functions, as in the following:

- **Technical skills** (computer programming, engineering drafting, communicating, financial analysis, writing, speaking): skills used alone in which you have developed proficiency.
- **Managerial skills** (organizing a team project, planning a budget, convincing others to take action, helping others learn how to work together on a project): skills used to manage other people or projects.
- **Marketing skills** (advertising, promotional writing and speaking, customer service, selling, market research, pricing): skills used to sell products and services.

DECIDING ON A CAREER: SELF-ANALYSIS

List 1: Skills

[1]Daryl L. Kerr, "A Resource Tool for Improving the Effectiveness of the Job Search: The Job Strategy Notebook," *The ABC Bulletin* 54, no. 3 (September 1991), pp. 4–14.

- **Information systems skills** (telecommunication networks, office automation, E-mail systems, information management): skills used to organize and transmit information.

You can see how to make similar lists of your skills in accounting and finance, human resources, and production and operations.

List 2: Abilities

Different people use their skills in different ways. Think of five or ten adjectives that describe you, then think of an example that *shows* the adjective is accurate. These examples can show positive or negative traits. Following is a list to get you started. List other adjectives that apply to you, and write examples that show the adjectives describe you accurately.

Adjective	Example
Energetic	I find time to finish my schoolwork, hold a part-time job, and exercise every day.
Accurate	
Good sense of humor	
Good with figures	
Good with my hands	
Careful	
Aggressive	
Extroverted	
Introverted	
Responsible	
Persevering	
Prompt	
Cooperative	
Imaginative	
Self-disciplined	
Competitive	

List 3: Accomplishments

Now begin putting your skills and abilities together to make a list of accomplishments you can draw from when you create your résumé and prepare for your interviews. Think of *results,* and use strong action verbs:

- Trained new staff.
- Increased sales by 8 percent.
- Planned computer changeover to local area network.

This exercise will help you write a strong résumé that emphasizes what you can do for an employer.

List 4: Ideal Job

Before you begin looking at prospective employers, consider your ideal job. What characteristics would it have? Do you prefer outdoor or indoor work? Would you be doing physical work, mental work, or both? Would you be working alone or as part of a team? Would you rather work with people or with ideas? Would you rather work independently or be supervised? What kind of boss do you want? What size of town would you like to live in? Would you rather have regular or flexible hours?

Although you may not land your dream job right away, you are ahead of the game if you know what you want. Sarah Caldwell, one of the first renowned female orchestra conductors, has said, "The best thing in life is to find a job you

"It's the old story. I was in the middle of a successful acting career when I was bitten by the accounting bug."

Drawing by Leo Cullom; © 1992 The New Yorker Magazine, Inc.

Most people don't make as dramatic a switch in careers as this man.

love and get someone to pay you to do it." You may change your mind over your working lifetime, but both you and your employer will be happier if you find work you enjoy doing.

Find out about prospective employers while you are still in school—don't wait until the semester in which you actually start interviewing. As you decide on your major and on the work you would like to do, think about what kind of company you want to work for and begin to learn about how companies in your chosen field differ.

John LaFevre, corporate recruiter and author of an excellent job search guide, defines *vocational maturity* as "having clearly defined goals, realistic expectations, and a specific idea of how you can contribute to a company's profitability."[2] To achieve vocational maturity, gather information on industries and specific companies' needs as well as on your skills and preferences. Then find out where these two sets of information overlap.

One of your first stops when gathering information about companies should be your on-campus placement office or career-planning center. This office can provide information such as majors that the company hires, number of employees, work locations, products, and so on. *The College Placement Annual,* published by the College Placement Council, organizes this information by major or discipline and also by geographic region.

Many companies that are recruiting leave brochures and sometimes videotapes describing the company to supplement the published annual placement

GATHERING INFORMATION ON PROSPECTIVE EMPLOYERS

Your Campus Career-Planning Office

[2]John LaFevre, *How You Really Get Hired,* 3rd ed. (Englewood Cliffs, N.J.: ARCO/Prentice-Hall, 1992), p. 61.

guides. For example, Andersen Consulting's videotape, *Transitions,* shows a number of recently hired employees discussing what working for a large consulting firm is like: the challenge, variety, and travel; how training and evaluation are done; the importance of teamwork; and how the firm fosters an individual's ability to succeed.

Usually placement offices also have a library of career-planning sources, offer interest tests such as the Strong Interest Inventory and the Myers-Briggs Type Indicator, and may have computerized career-choosing software to match your interests to possible jobs, as well as résumé preparation software. Placement offices also can provide help through internships and cooperative education programs. Become acquainted with this office early in your college years so that you can take full advantage of its services.

As you get closer to graduation, the placement office will probably offer you workshops in interviewing (some offer videotaping to help improve interviewing skills), help you prepare your résumé, and make your prepared file available to prospective employers in areas such as education. Also, this office usually has lists of job openings in adjacent states as well as in the local area. If you wish to move to another city, you can do some research on the area's employers at the placement office. Most placement offices provide a file service (for a fee) to send your résumé and letters of reference to requesting firms.

Of course, you can find most of the information available from the placement office from other sources—but remember that the services of your school's placement office are included in your student fees. We discuss career planning and placement office services in more detail in Chapter Thirteen.

Library Sources

Just as you can find library information on companies for school reports, you can do library research on companies as prospective employers and on cities where you might like to work. Your college library will have company listings, annual reports, and analyses in publications such as *Standard and Poor's Register of Corporations, Directors, and Executives; Corporate Technology Directory; Dun and Bradstreet Reference Book of Corporate Managements; Moody's Industry Review;* and yellow pages for other cities. You can also find current information in the business press, including *Business Week, Forbes, Fortune, Barron's,* and *The Wall Street Journal.* These sources are a good beginning for your industry and company profile research. For an industry, find out the following:

- Is the industry growing or maturing?
- Are sales increasing or decreasing?
- Who are the major competitors?
- Where are the main firms within the industry located?
- Are the companies generally expanding or downsizing?
- What is the future of this industry?

For a company you might like to work for, research the following:

- Company address and phone number.
- Who is in charge of the company?
- Who heads the functional area where you would work?
- What does the company produce, and what is its share of the industry's market?
- Who are the company's customers?

- In what cities is the company located?
- Who are the company's competitors?
- What were last year's sales?
- What is the trend of the last five years' sales?
- What is the trend of the last five years' profits?
- What is the return on investment (ROI) for the past five years?
- How many employees does the company have?

Do more thorough research on companies you would really like to work for, because knowing about the firm's past and future will help you develop an effective résumé, letter, and interview plan for that company.

Spend some time looking at the classified ads in a big-city Sunday newspaper. Don't limit yourself to the ones you are qualified for; also look for jobs that sound interesting to you. Keep a file of these companies for a while and see if some common themes emerge. You will at least become more familiar with kinds of jobs available, what they are called, and what education and experience they require. As interview time gets closer, scan at least two daily or weekly business sources for up-to-the-minute information about the companies with which you will interview.

Information from Recruiters

Career fairs offer opportunities to talk informally with college recruiters, schedule interviews, and get names of people to contact about jobs later. Even if you are not yet ready to interview, stop by and talk to recruiters about what their companies are seeking. You may find out about summer work opportunities or other ways to get your foot in the door at a company that interests you.

Many large companies offer summer internships to give students hands-on experience in their technical fields. These internships are usually advertised through the placement office and department chairs, among other places. Summer work such as this gives a student a chance to try out a work environment *and* gives a company an opportunity to look over the student as a prospective employee.

Professional Associations

Learn about the student organizations in your field, especially those that have a parent chapter of working professionals with whom you can meet for dinner sometime during the term. Professional organizations such as the American Marketing Association, the Data Processing Management Association, and others (there is one for nearly every major) will help you learn about the field and the people in it. They are also a good source of job leads.

Some professional associations also have career nights for students, practice interview sessions, and résumé workshops. Take advantage of this assistance, because it will make you a better job prospect. The practicing professionals you will meet in these organizations are one source of networking contacts who can help you with career information.

Networking

According to author Geraldine Henze, *networking* means "letting everyone you can think of know that you are looking for a job."[3] Henze suggests listing all contacts you can think of and then systematically contacting them. List fellow students; faculty; friends, relatives, and neighbors; business associates;

[3]Geraldine Henze, *Winning Career Moves,* (Homewood, Ill.: Business One Irwin), p. 99.

and professionals such as lawyers, doctors, and accountants. As you talk to your contacts, you can find out whether they know of jobs that match your qualifications, as well as other jobs that might interest you.

Information Interviews

Information interviews are one way to use networking contacts. When you establish contact with someone, make it clear whether you are seeking information *or* a job interview. As a student, the purpose of much of your networking will be to gather information about companies, employment trends, and what people do at their jobs. Don't presume that a conversation will lead to a job; your contact is doing you a favor just by spending time with you. Find out the following:

- What training is necessary for the job?
- What are the job responsibilities?
- What career advancement opportunities are available?
- What is the salary range?
- If the person had to do it over, what would he or she do the same? Differently?
- Whom else do you suggest I talk to about this kind of job?

Write a thank-you note to the person you interviewed for information just as you will to persons who grant you job interviews.

The Hidden Job Market

Networking is an important means of finding out about job availability because many jobs exist in the **hidden job market,** which consists of unadvertised and as yet unannounced jobs. Drake Beam Morin, one of the largest outplacement firms, tracks jobs found by its clients: 50 to 80 percent of jobs are found by targeting appropriate firms through research or by networking. Simply mailing standard letters to a list of firms nets 5 to 20 percent of jobs, whereas answering ads nets only 5 to 10 percent. In other words, the hidden job market is much larger than the advertised job market.

In your business reading or while watching business news on television, be alert for promotions (can you replace this person? be on the promoted person's new staff?), business openings or expansions, new products that might need support staff, new buildings, and increased advertising. These business change indicators may provide an employment idea on which you can follow up.

ASSEMBLING INFORMATION ON YOURSELF

Nearly every time you meet someone who could offer you a job or knows of a job available at his or her firm or elsewhere, one of the first things you will be asked for is your résumé. A good résumé—one that reflects your strengths and minimizes your potential weaknesses—will help you get the interview and thus improve your chances of getting the job. Because a résumé is a screening device, develop one that screens you *in,* not *out.*

Deciding what to put in your résumé and how to lay it out will be easier if you have a lifetime record already prepared—and keep it updated. This database will also come in handy when you fill out applications for jobs, graduate school, awards, and so on. Collect the information in a way that is easy to update, beginning a new page for each new category.

Maintaining Your Database

No matter what information you need about yourself for a résumé or job application, you will be able to assemble it, given enough time. If you keep track of names, places, dates, courses, and so on *now*, you will be able to assemble it more quickly. Then you can spend the extra time preparing for the interview, writing the admissions office essay about why you should get into a particular graduate school, or writing to obtain official transcripts.

Always have one copy of your official transcript on hand to verify details of your education. Because having a transcript sent takes time, especially around graduation (many students need one then, and the admissions and records office may become overloaded), having one copy of your own allows you to make copies to give to prospective employers if they need a temporary copy right away.

Different kinds of jobs will require different personal information. Some government jobs, for example, use a 171, a form that asks you to list all employers and instructors and then asks for references "who do not appear elsewhere on this form" — people who do not know you on a professional or school basis. Think about people you could use for such a reference.

If you go to law school or try to get a security clearance, you may be asked to list "all addresses at which you have ever received mail." If you are a typical student, who changes dorms and apartments at least once a year, this can present a problem. If your family has moved often because of military or other job requirements, you will have quite a list of addresses. So start *now* if you haven't done so already, and keep track of your addresses and other details in case you need them later.

One way to collect this personal information is in a looseleaf notebook. You can have a section for personal data such as addresses and other sections for job experience, education, activities, honors, and references. If you start a new page for each category, you can keep updating the information as you add to your life experiences. In a file or envelope at the back of your notebook (or separately, if you keep most of the records in a computer file), keep copies of academic transcripts, awards, letters of recommendation, old résumés, and copies of applications.

You can also store all your information in your computer, but be sure to keep backup copies in case you lose the data somehow. A number of software programs can help you collect the information you need. Some of these programs can also help you prepare your résumé. We discuss these programs more fully in Chapter Thirteen.

Experience and Past Successes

Jobs

Of course, you will want to keep a complete record of your job experiences. Write down (or enter into your computer file) the title of the job, company's name, address, and phone number, name of your supervisor, job duties you performed, salary at the beginning and the end of the job, why you changed jobs, and anything else you need to remember.

Only some of this information will appear on your résumé, but a job application may ask for additional information. The most important reason to write everything down, however, is that no matter what you think now, you won't remember all these details later. Any time you have to spend looking for this information later is time you could spend preparing for your interview.

Keep track annually of the percentage of college expenses that you earned. Employers often assume that a working student understands the value of education better than a student whose parents paid all college expenses. To earn this respect, keep track of earnings, scholarships won, and loans or grants obtained to finance your education. List volunteer work and internships in this section if you learned business skills such as organizing projects, giving and receiving instructions, meeting deadlines, and fund-raising.

Past Successes

In a separate section, keep track of your work successes. Why did you like a particular job? Did you win any awards? Were you left in charge when the supervisor was absent? Did you train other employees? Were you promoted? As you add material here, you may begin to see a pattern among these job attributes. You will also feel more positive about your experience. Even a low-level job teaches you responsibility, and you can see from your experience what you have learned along the way. Collecting such information will remind you of past successes and help you focus on your strong points—and you can take this renewed self-esteem with you to your interviews.

Richard Nelson Bolles' *What Color Is Your Parachute?* has useful exercises to help you pinpoint the kinds of things you like to do.[4] If you make lists of positive projects in which you have been involved, a pattern may emerge that will help you choose a job that matches your skills and life values. Your self-assessment lists of skills, attributes, and accomplishments can help you find successful projects to add to this section of your file.

Your career-planning office may have some exercises to help you identify your life values and match them to jobs that would interest you. *Skill Sorts and Value Sorts* (Career Research and Testing, 2005 Hamilton Avenue, Suite 250, San Jose, CA 95125, 408-559-4945) and *Deal Me In* (Career Systems, Inc., 1000 Vermont Avenue NW, Suite 1000, P.O. Box 34744, Washington, DC 20043, 1-800-283-8839) give you a chance to find out what you *like* to do (over what you *can* do) and what industries will best allow you to apply this knowledge.[5]

Educational Highlights

Your basic education section should list the schools you have attended (including grade school, if possible; you might need this information for a detailed application later). Give the name, address, and phone number of each school and dates attended.

Schools and Courses

In this section, list courses you took at each school attended, beginning with high school if you wish. At least list the unusual courses you took in high school (the courses other than those everyone getting a diploma had to take) and any courses that apply to your career plans (Math? Communication? Graphic design?). Be sure to list course number, title, and instructor as well as units of credit and grade, because you may need this level of detail when filling out an application later. Don't use just course numbers to identify courses, as you'll need a course title for the numbers to make sense if you need to use them on an application or in your cover letter. You can insert a copy of your transcript here if it contains complete information. Also list short courses, certificates received for training completed, and other education and training. Keep this section up to date, since later on it may be hard to remember when you took a course or what your score or rating was.

[4]Richard N. Bolles, *What Color Is Your Parachute?* (Berkeley: Ten Speed Press, 1991).

[5]For more information on these board games, see Maureen McNulty, "Getting to Know You," *Business Edge,* October 1992, p. 12, or the *Stanford Business School Magazine,* 1991.

Next, in a new section, list your favorite courses (and why they were favorites, as though an interviewer were asking you), the titles of your best papers (with dates), and any academic awards you received (with dates). Again you may begin to see a pattern that pinpoints your strengths.

Favorite Subjects, Best Papers, and Awards

In this section of the database, keep track of activities in which you have engaged in school, in church or temple, or in civic organizations. List dates, offices held, projects supervised, and awards won. Not all this information will necessarily appear in your résumé, but it *will* give you thorough personal information to choose from when preparing your résumé and may help you see patterns among your strengths.

Activities and Honors

Keep an ongoing list of references to choose from when constructing your résumé and preparing for interviews. Write down the name, title, address (including ZIP code), and phone number of each reference. Try to accumulate several job references, some professors (at least one in your major field), and a personal friend or a friend's parent who can give you a businesslike reference. Choose references who

References

- Have high personal credibility.
- Know you and your abilities well.
- Are willing to write a letter on your behalf or to refer you through a phone call.

If former employers or other persons or organizations give you letters of reference, keep them in the file. Most employment experts recommend inviting employers to contact references, rather than taking your letters to an interview or mailing them with your résumé.

Since job applicants have a legal right to inspect any records gathered and kept about them, few letters of reference say anything negative. Therefore, employers do not expect to find out a candidate's weaknesses through letters. Although employers place less importance on letters of reference than they used to, references are still a useful category of information to collect in your job portfolio or notebook. When asked for references, having the information already collected will give you time to concentrate on research about the job in question.

You will be able to prepare an effective résumé if you think of it as a sales brochure on yourself rather than a list of dates and jobs. A résumé needs to be truthful (both for ethical reasons and because many companies check up on information), but it is usually *not* a complete record of everything you have ever done. Save the complete lists for your applications.

PREPARING A RÉSUMÉ TO SELL YOURSELF

One form of résumé is called a *data sheet;* it includes only lists of dates, names of schools, jobs, and employers, with no descriptions. Since this is not a selling document, use it *only* if a prospective employer limits you to lists. This type of document might be helpful when filling out applications. If you mail it to someone, add details about your qualifications and other strong points in your application letter.

Once you have collected all the information about yourself to date (and resolved to *keep* it up to date so you won't have to scramble at the last minute to collect information when an ideal job comes up), you are ready to begin sorting out the information you want to use in your résumé. Remember: This is your sales brochure on yourself, so *you* can choose what appears on it.

Emphasize your strengths and downplay your weaker areas. Résumés are screened to sort out the best candidates (and remove as many less qualified ones as possible), so you want yours to stand out. But do it truthfully.

Résumé Ethics

When the economy is poor, some people inflate accomplishments on a résumé in the hope of gaining an interview. As a result, more companies are checking up on information such as degrees and companies worked for. People have been caught putting down Harvard Business School with no dates, hoping the recruiter will assume a Harvard degree, when in fact the person merely attended an executive education seminar for a few weeks.

Companies that might accept your being a few credits short of a degree even if college graduates are preferred will refuse to hire you if you lie on your application. Most applications contain a statement you must sign that swears the information on the application is correct. If an employer finds out later that certain information is not true, even if the information itself is not damaging, you can be fired. In 1992, the superintendent of the San Jose Unified School District was forced to resign because he had claimed a fake Ph.D. from Stanford years before.

Be aware that interviewers often ask detailed questions to verify statements on résumés about projects worked on and other claims. Certainly your résumé is a picture of your accomplishments rather than your weaknesses, but make it a picture you can support easily if questioned.

Résumé Emphasis

Using the principles of emphasis you learned in earlier chapters, highlight key points on your résumé so that the interviewer will easily see your strongest qualifications for the job available. Plan your résumé information as you sort it out so that you don't include inconsistencies that you will have to explain in the interview. And remember to present all of your positive points truthfully.

Word processing programs allow you to create different versions of your résumé for different jobs. For example, you may want to emphasize your background in finance in one résumé and your publishing experience in another. Try out different layouts of your material, evaluating which version best uses the available space. Exhibits 12–1, 12–2, and 12–3 present different versions of the same résumé. As you study them, note how emphasis on information varies according to how the material is laid out:

- Headings placed at the left give emphasis.
- Centered headings may take up more space.
- Dates placed at the left are emphasized.
- Dates placed at the end of a line are subordinated.
- Bold print emphasizes, as do capital letters.
- Bullets emphasize accomplishments.
- White space is important for reading ease.

The first version (Exhibit 12–1) puts headings at the left and does not emphasize with bold type. The second version (Exhibit 12–2) centers headings and the name and address block, giving greater visual emphasis and more internal white space (because of the narrower left margin on lines). The third version (Exhibit 12–3) shows varied type sizes and a "typeset" as opposed to

Emphasize name with caps

Headings placed at left give emphasis

Left dates are emphasized

J. J. ELMORE
650 East Denny Way
Seattle, Washington   98122
(206)555-7734

OBJECTIVE   To work as a broker, leading to a management
                   position.

EDUCATION
9/88-present   University of Washington
                   B. S. in Business Finance, August, 1993
                   Minor in English composition
                   Significant course work in banking, securities,
                   and corporate finance

WORK EXPERIENCE
4/90-present   <u>Analyst</u>, Academic Resources, University of
                   Washington
                   • Enter faculty budget information via computer
                     terminal
                   • Generate budget and accounting reports
                   • Research, organize, and create statistical reports
                   • Prepare and review special projects for the
                     Associate Vice President

8/89-4/90   <u>Student Analyst</u>, Academic Resources, University of
                   Washington
                   • Enter faculty budget information via computer
                     terminal
                   • Review and complete budget and personnel forms

Bullets emphasize accomplishments

ADDITIONAL SKILLS
                   • Experienced user of on-line database systems and
                     personal computers, including Macintosh, DOS, and
                     Windows environments.
                   • Expert user of spreadsheet software, including
                     Excel, 1-2-3, and Quattro Pro. Have developed
                     models for statistical analysis, present value
                     forecasting, and securities pricing.

PROFESSIONAL ACTIVITIES
Fall 92   <u>Secretary</u>, Finance & Investment Society (F & I).
                   • Managed monthly luncheons
                   • Arranged guest speakers
                   • Represented F & I at Financial Analyst luncheon

Fall 91   <u>Social Director</u>, F & I
                   • Organized annual awards banquet
                   • Supervised committee chairs for marketing,
                     reservations, and financing

White space is important for reading ease

Bold print emphasizes

Name is in all caps

Centered headings give visual space

J. J. ELMORE
650 East Denny Way
Seattle, Washington   98122
(206)555-7734

OBJECTIVE

To work as a broker, leading to a management position.

EDUCATION

Left dates emphasized

9/88–
Present

University of Washington
B. S. in Business Finance, August, 1993
Minor in English composition
Significant course work in banking, securities, and
corporate finance

WORK EXPERIENCE

8/89–
Present

Academic Resources, University of Washington

4/90–
Present

Bullets emphasize accomplishments

Analyst
- Enter faculty budget information via computer terminal
- Generate budget and accounting reports
- Research, organize, and create statistical reports
- Prepare and review special projects for the Associate
  Vice President

8/89–4/90

Student Analyst
- Enter faculty budget information via computer terminal
- Review and complete budget and personnel forms

ADDITIONAL SKILLS

- Experienced user of on-line database systems and
  personal computers, including Macintosh, DOS, and
  Windows environments.
- Expert user of spreadsheet software, including Excel,
  1-2-3, and Quattro Pro. Have developed models for
  statistical analysis, present value forecasting, and
  securities pricing.

PROFESSIONAL ACTIVITIES

Fall 92

Secretary, Finance & Investment Society (F & I)
- Managed monthly luncheons
- Arranged guest speakers
- Represented F & I at Financial Analyst luncheon

Fall 91

More internal white space

Social Director, F & I
- Organized annual awards banquet
- Supervised committee chairs for marketing, reservations,
  and financing

Typeset look is professional

Centered headings give visual space

J. J. Elmore
650 East Denny Way
Seattle, Washington   98122
(206)555-7734

OBJECTIVE

To work as a broker, leading to a management position.

EDUCATION

Smaller type gives layout space if needed

9/88-present   University of Washington
B. S. in Business Finance, August, 1993
Minor in English composition
Significant course work in banking, securities, and corporate finance

WORK EXPERIENCE

8/89-present   Academic Resources, University of Washington

4/90-present   Analyst
- Enter faculty budget information via computer terminal
- Generate budget and accounting reports
- Research, organize, and create statistical reports
- Prepare and review special projects for the Associate Vice President

8/89-4/90   Student Analyst
- Enter faculty budget information via computer terminal
- Review and complete budget and personnel forms

ADDITIONAL SKILLS

- Experienced user of on-line database systems and personal computers, including Macintosh, DOS, and Windows environments.

Internal white space may be too extensive

- Expert user of spreadsheet software, including Excel, 1-2-3, and Quattro Pro. Have developed models for statistical analysis, present value forecasting, and securities pricing.

PROFESSIONAL ACTIVITIES

Fall 92   Secretary, Finance & Investment Society (F & I)
- Managed monthly luncheons
- Arranged guest speakers
- Represented F & I at Financial Analyst luncheon

Fall 91   Social Director, F & I
- Organized annual awards banquet
- Supervised committee chairs for marketing, reservations, and financing

a typewritten layout for a very professional look. The ability to use smaller type (available in computer software) gives you more white space and additional layout flexibility.

All three versions of this résumé stress education and related work experience. The writer also gives helpful details about computer experience and professional activities in a finance organization.

Conventional Information Categories

The usual categories found in résumés are (1) job objective, (2) education, (3) experience, (4) activities, and (5) references. However, you need not present these categories in the order given here. If your experience will sell your skills to an employer better than your degree will, put experience before education on your résumé.

If you have a great deal of experience to report, you may run out of room on the page for references, omitting them altogether. Many interviewers will ask for references, however, so take a page of references to the interview, on the same letterhead used for your résumé. References are expected from a recent graduate. Résumés of more experienced persons often omit references, but an applicant provides them before a job offer is made.

Try for a full, well-laid-out, one-page résumé. If you have a great deal of important information, use two full pages, perhaps printed back to back. If you staple or clip two pages together, use a second page heading (shown below) in case the pages are accidentally separated.

Gregory J. Iverson

Page 2

Plan a good sales brochure on yourself—emphasize positive points, make layout effective, and proofread so it looks professional.

Present items using parallel construction. For example, use all noun phrases or all verb phrases in a section; don't use full sentences or periods at the ends of lines. You may need periods in some sections to divide ideas, however, or at the end of your objective.

You may prefer to get your résumé typeset rather than produce it yourself. The most effective way to do this is to produce an original containing the information, with some suggestions on layout; take it to a résumé service for suggestions and typesetting; and then proofread the final version before making copies. Be aware that some résumé services produce résumés that *look* alike regardless of differences in experience and education; this cookie-cutter look may not convey the impression you desire, of an employee who can do original work.

A résumé service can charge you up to $300, which may include revisions later as you add information. Richard K. Irish, author of *Go Hire Yourself an Employer,* points out a potential drawback of this type of résumé: An employer can tell when a résumé service has put your information into its mold. "A résumé is a personal reflection, a self-portrait. Hiring a stranger to write up your biography guarantees a loss of personality."[6]

Some items traditionally included in résumés are now out of favor. Pictures used to be included, sometimes even printed on the résumé. Today, due to equal opportunity regulations, companies no longer include pictures even in current employee files. Including a picture might get your résumé rejected on

---

[6]Robert McGarvey, "Search and Employ," *US Air,* November 24, 1989, p. 28.

that ground alone, since the employer is not supposed to choose candidates based on race. Personal information such as height, weight, marital status, and number of children is no longer included, because it is not relevant to the job. Willingness to relocate might still be mentioned, although most firms assume this.

A wealth of information on résumés exists. Read all you can, and then produce the best résumé for *you*. We will give you some common alternatives in our examples, but only you can choose the best approach for your own life material.

Most experts on job search recommend that, after putting your name, address(es) and phone number(s) at the top of the page, with your name in all caps or bolder print to stand out from everything else on the page, you begin your résumé with a *job objective*. This brief statement—usually not a complete sentence—emphasizes what you can do for the company. Instead of giving an objective, you could title this section *Qualifications* and include a two- or three-sentence summary of how you qualify for the position.

Job Objective

In writing your job objective, your goal is to narrow down what you want to do (to help the recruiter) but keep enough options open to show what you *can* do (to help yourself). Describe some combination of what you are looking for and what the company needs. Here are a few examples:

From a person looking for a job several years after his first college job:

> Purchasing or contract management position in a growing organization with opportunity for advancement.

From a person looking for a job as soon as she receives her degree:

> Staff accountant within a CPA firm that offers opportunity for continued career growth, including qualification for CPA licensing.

From a person looking for a less specific job in his field:

> The accounting profession, with an emphasis in tax or auditing.

From a person wishing to move up in her field once she gets her degree:

> Managing Court Reporter, in charge of administrative and personnel duties related to court reporters.

From a marketing major with lots of related experience:

> Member of a growing sales force, leading to a management-trainee position.

From a finance major looking for a summer job in his field:

> Intern/trainee for a marketable securities brokerage firm.

From an experienced manager who just received her MBA:

> Communication and public relations program management offering consulting projects for the Pacific Rim.

Finding the right balance between narrow but not too limited is the key to writing an effective job objective. Remember that a résumé is a screening device: Don't write such a limited objective that it screens you out of other jobs for which you are qualified. Write a narrow objective showing vocational maturity (you know what you want to do) *and* knowledge of company needs.

Emphasize what you can do for the company. Avoid self-centered-sounding clichés about "challenging and fulfilling" work that make the reader guess which job you might be able to fill.

Here are some tips on writing your job objective:

- It should *not* be a complete sentence, but you can add summarizing sentences about your background.
- It *should* include a key word about your area, such as marketing, management, accounting, communication, etc.
- It *should* be short and somewhat specific. (You may need more than one résumé to apply for different types of jobs, as we mentioned earlier.)
- It *should* emphasize what you can do for the company.

As you look for more advanced jobs later, you may wish to include the objective in your cover letter and begin your résumé with a *qualifications summary*. This approach allows you to tailor the objective to the specific job opening and use the résumé for factual support. A summary can be five or six lines long and should briefly list specialty area(s), type of business, years of experience, and relevant business characteristics. For example, suppose your objective is

Purchasing or contract management position in a growing organization.

Then your summary can read as follows:

Hard-working, professional purchasing and contract manager, with particular skills in construction, government, and retail purchasing. Creativity and ingenuity have won local and national recognition for my organization.

Since this type of summary emphasizes experience, it may be less appropriate for a recent graduate's use than for later career job searches.

Education

In the education section, put the name of your *school, major,* and *graduation date.* You can also put in your minor, mention special courses you took (but don't list *all* the courses that everyone with that major takes), mention your GPA if it is 3.0 or higher (discussed shortly), and list your community college or other schools attended.

Choose your material wisely here; you may need the extra space for your experience section. Remember to include material that will "sell" you, such as a degree in an appropriate field, academic awards that show your promise, or work with notable professors in your field. For example, if you want to go into circuit design, you won't mention your standard electrical engineering courses. But you *will* cite your VLSI and circuit logic courses, which apply more closely to the job you seek. Similarly, if you are a finance major, mention *specialized courses* such as financial institution management, investments, and portfolio management rather than basic finance courses. Show how you are especially qualified and thus stand out from the other finance majors in your graduating class.

As mentioned earlier, list your GPA if it is 3.0 or higher, but omit it if lower. If your field *requires* a listed GPA (as accounting does), list the best one of your overall, upper division, or major GPAs and label the GPA if it is not your overall GPA. If your school does not use a 4.0 scale, explain the GPA system it uses.

If you will receive a four-year degree, you might list your associate of arts (AA) degree to show the area you have studied if you plan to apply for jobs in that field. If you went to a renowned high school or prep school, you might mention that fact, again to show prior ties to the area in which you wish to work. Awards listed should show academic or leadership skills and should be as current as possible. For example, being a senior academic star is more important than having been homecoming princess your freshman year.

In addition to your degree(s), you can mention additional training that makes you an attractive job candidate, such as a real estate license, computer training, or language fluency and training. For jobs in conservative fields, you might *not* want to mention your private pilot's license or scuba-diving certificates. Save such details for more relevant jobs, or put them in the Activities section if you are sure that these somewhat risky activities won't screen you out of an interview invitation.

Decide whether you want to emphasize dates (you have no significant gaps in your educational history) or subordinate dates (the degree is more important than when you received it). Placing dates (month and year) in the left margin emphasizes them; placing dates at the end of a line subordinates them. Here is one way to present educational information (emphasizing dates):

EDUCATION

May 1993	Bachelor of Arts Recreational Therapy University of North Carolina–Chapel Hill
May 1991	Associate Degree Liberal Arts St. Mary's Junior College, Raleigh, NC

Here is another way that takes up three fewer lines and subordinates the dates:

EDUCATION   B.A. in Recreational Therapy, May 1993
University of North Carolina–Chapel Hill
A.A. in Liberal Arts, May 1991
St. Mary's Junior College, Raleigh, NC

If you need to show extra training in this section, here is one approach (make sure the course titles are self-explanatory):

EDUCATION
B.S.B.A., National College, Rapid City, SD, 1983
   Management of Defense Acquisition Contracts, 1987
      In the top 5 in a class of 40
   Quantitative Techniques of Cost and
      Price Analysis, 1990

Here is another:

Leith's School of Food and Wine, London, England
   Graduate of Introductory Course, 1992

Alternatively, you can put dates in the margin to emphasize them (inclusive dates are more specific and preferred by many recruiters, but they do take up more space). Emphasize that you have received a degree in four or five years. If you have had gaps in your education or experience, subordinate that fact.

1/82–6/84   Latin American Institute, New York City
            Bilingual Secretarial Program
            in Spanish and English

If you list your GPA, remember to mention which system your school uses if not a 4.0 system. Also mention which courses the GPA is for, if not *all* your courses. Do not be too narrow here, though "GPA in Upper Division Accounting Courses" may imply that you had to search for good grades to mention. Here is one way to list a GPA:

Accounting and Business GPA   3.7

Experience

For a traditional résumé, your experience section will list your *work experience* in reverse chronological order (most recent first). Once again, you may put dates in the margin area or with the job description. You will need to make a design-related decision about whether to emphasize the job titles *or* the companies you worked for and list them accordingly. In describing your job duties, think in terms of *doing*. Use strong action verbs such as *designed, developed, oversaw, operated,* or *supplied* rather than *worked as* or *responsible for.*

Here is a partial list of action words:

administered	developed	introduced	ran
advanced	directed	invented	recruited
analyzed	discovered	judged	regulated
applied	employed	launched	reshaped
approved	enlarged	led	resolved
arranged	established	managed	restored
assigned	evaluated	negotiated	revised
awarded	executed	opened	scheduled
began	expanded	operated	served
commanded	extended	ordered	settled
conceived	governed	organized	shaped
conducted	guided	originated	solved
controlled	handled	oversaw	stabilized
coordinated	headed	planned	started
corrected	implemented	prepared	steered
created	improved	presented	straightened (out)
decided	inaugurated	produced	superintended
delegated	increased	progressed	supervised
designed	initiated	published	systematized
determined	installed	raised	trained

Following are some examples of Experience sections that worked for their candidates. The first is for a sales position:

FOOD SERVER, Fish Merchant, Edmond, Washington 8-90/6-93
Promoted food and wine specialties in a top-rated, high-volume seafood restaurant that emphasizes customer service and employee teamwork. Oriented and trained new employees.

The people skills learned in restaurant and bar work are useful ones to mention for many jobs, whether or not in sales, as nearly all jobs involve getting along with a variety of people.

The next example is for a brokerage job:

LOGISTICS/ MATERIEL MANAGEMENT Managed logistics and materiel functions for work center of large responsibility under extremely stressful situations. Coordinated logistics requirements with high-level personnel from other facilities. Controlled calibration requirements for life support systems equipment and maintained quality assurance control. U. S. Navy 1986-93

Here is an example for a marketing job:

July 1991/June 1993 **GTE EDUCATION SERVICES, INC.**   Irving, TX
Marketing Manager

Marketed online information services in consumer education. Coordinated and implemented advertising, public relations, direct marketing, telemarketing and trade show functions for start-up company. Supervised two employees. Reported to general manager.

- Developed national print campaign that generated over 1,000 qualified leads over three months.

- Assisted director of marketing in developing and implementing cross-product marketing plans.

- Supervised the development of all sales collateral.

- Developed free online database that increased network use by 6% over five months.

- Created new identity for existing trade show booth and collateral materials that established a stronger "call-to-action."

Notice how this example very specifically measures and quantifies the applicant's performance. This is a technique to consider to emphasize those jobs in which you had greatest responsibility.

Here is a description of an early job with fewer responsibilities (or one less relevant to the job being applied for):

9-87/9-90 **Optometric Assistant**
North Raleigh Eye Care Associates
Raleigh, NC

Reception, sales, eyeglasses fitting, patient testing for glaucoma, blood pressure.

The following example describes someone who owned his own business:

EXPERIENCE **Owner/Operator,** Sign Masters, Milwaukee, WI
Sold after three years
- Established successful small business still in operation
- Devised and maintained accounting system
- Negotiated contracts with commercial and governmental entities
- Prepared plans/drawings and obtained permits from City Planning Commission
- Generated sales
- Hired and supervised personnel

Here are two examples of volunteer experience showing responsibility:

1989 **Food Bank of Northwest North Carolina**
Junior League of Winston-Salem
Monitored agencies handling and distributing excess commodities to impoverished.

<pre>
1992-93   ADMINISTRATIVE ASSISTANT FOR COMMUNICATION
           Associated Students/UCLA
</pre>

Developed, coordinated, and implemented banquets, reunions, political forums, committees for a $5 million student corporation.

Now let's look at a couple of less effective experience sections. In the first example, the person has had experience but doesn't give enough details to allow the employer to evaluate the jobs:

Work Experience:
<pre>
    1990 to present   staff accountant, American First Bank
    1989-90   teller, Home Savings and Loan
    1988-89   waiter, Bahia Hotel
</pre>

In the next example, the applicant tells too much—by including current salary—to be able to negotiate later:

Professional Asset Securities, Inc.

Operations/Money Desk: 1-87 to 5-91
Maintaining business relations with financial institutions issuing CD rates through our firm. Quoting rate surveys and summing up current market trends. Transacting daily brokering operations. Maintaining account histories. Matching needs of clients and institutions. Reviving business with institutions that have been inactive. *Ending pay:* $2,500/month.

Don't include salary in a résumé! Save that kind of negotiating information for the interview.

Activities and Honors

You may fill the remainder of your résumé page (or second page, if you have a long work history) with an account of your activities and club work. Sometimes activities are a deciding factor in a hiring decision.

When evaluating the summary of activities you compiled earlier, look particularly for times when you held office, organized projects, or otherwise learned how to manage people. Some interviewers look for a history of leadership skills or for experience working in teams. You could mention group class projects in your education section if you don't have enough team experiences to warrant listing them in a separate activities section.

The amount of space to use here depends on how important the activity was *and* on how much space you have available. Add action verbs, and explain projects completed and offices held. Make whatever activities you use carry significant impact, but don't overstate your case.

FRANK & ERNEST® by Bob Thaves

FRANK & ERNEST reprinted by permission of NEA, Inc.

Do be positive, but *don't* exaggerate on your résumé.

Here is an activity section for an active person who had little space left on the résumé:

ACTIVITIES AND ORGANIZATIONS	President, University Honors Program, 1990
	Vice President, Business Student Council, 1991
	Member, Finance and Investment Society 1988–92
	Board Member, Finance Board, Associated Students
	Student Representative, Parents' Advisory Board

The following applicant had fewer activities but more space to fill:

ACTIVITIES AND ORGANIZATIONS	**Beta Alpha Psi,** Active member, 1993
	Nominated Director of Special Events, 1993
	National Association of Accountants
	Active member, 1993
	Toastmasters, Active member, 1993
	Tutor, Introductory and intermediate accounting, 1992–1993

Here is someone who had only limited space left but used it well:

AFFILIATIONS AND ACTIVITIES

Member: American Marketing Association, Computer Graphics User Group, Corpus Christi Toastmasters

Working knowledge of Lotus 1-2-3, WordPerfect, and Harvard Graphics

Avoid mentioning activities not relevant to your job objective. Mentioning religious or social organizations is risky. Although you can give information about ethnicity or religion that interviewers are not allowed to ask, you may inadvertently give a reason for screening you out of an interview. Instead, emphasize what you can do for the company through what you have learned from your activities, such as public speaking and group leadership.

References

If you have room, add references at the end of your résumé, at least when applying for your first job. However, experts advise omitting references altogether if you are applying for a job while still employed. In this case, of course, the reason for omitting references is to prevent the possibility that your current employer will be notified that you are looking for a job before you *want* him or her to be notified.

If you have enough space, you can put two references at the bottom of the page in mailing address form:

REFERENCES

Ms. Connie Rogers, Vice President
University Savings Association
1160 Dairy Ashford
Houston, TX 77079
(713) 596-4911

Mr. Bill Goldsmith,
President
Horizon Financial
4928 Rancho Grande
Olney, TX 76374
(817) 564-5033

You should also prepare a separate reference page to take to interviews. A full page will give you room for both work and school references in case the interviewer asks for them. Include work and school references rather than personal references, since the employers who contact them will usually do so to verify your work experience or classroom preparation for the job you seek.

If you have to choose between including references, which are a neutral form of job information, and stretching your activities to fill space, use the references. No one ever looked at a résumé and said, "How unusual, there are references here." Fill a few inches with references rather than listing activities and personal data unrelated to your job objective.

Because you will naturally choose references who will speak well of you, the prospective employer may not contact them because he or she expects a positive report. However, if any question about your qualifications arises, a reference may be able to clear it up easily. Federal government recruiters may be most likely to check references; they often use a mailed form to do so. However, always give a phone number for a reference if you can, since many prospective employers who use the references will call rather than write.

In selecting your references, choose people who know your qualifications well, ask permission to use their names, and send each person a copy of your résumé, preferably with a cover letter outlining the types of jobs you are applying for and the skills you have to offer companies. Rather than choosing a well-known professor who taught you in a large-section class, choose a professor who can comment specifically on your work.

As mentioned earlier, when you apply for jobs after your first job out of college, you will often choose not to use references. First, you don't want your current employer contacted until you are sure you have a better offer. Second, by then you will have more interesting and relevant material to fill the page on your résumé without including references.

Importance of Layout and Appearance

More than any other piece of business correspondence, a résumé needs to *look* good. This is your sales brochure on yourself, and you want those prospective employers to buy your skills. Try different layouts to make your information fit the available space attractively. Emphasize your strong points through appropriate headings, itemizing, and use of bold and capital letters. Finally, *proofread* for a perfect final copy.

You can center your headings on the page or put them at the left margin. Centered headings may take up a little more space, so that's a good choice if you think you may not have enough to fill the page. Headings at the left margin may leave you more room for job details, but you will need to consider where to put dates of past activities.

To save space, use phrases rather than whole sentences. Avoid periods at the ends of lines if the information makes sense without them. An obvious exception would be lists of work accomplishments for which you are not using bullets and separate lines to set off each listed item. In this situation, use periods to separate the items.

Look again at the earlier examples for a variety of layouts and ways to use emphasis.

Sample Formats

The résumé in Exhibit 12–4 stresses the writer's education and honors over her work experience, but it details with bullets the aspects of her experience most clearly related to her job objective in accounting. Her experience in supervision, inventory, and communication will be useful in her chosen field.

The two-page résumé in Exhibit 12–5 emphasizes excellent related job experience (note how the writer details changing responsibilities over five years with one company) and downplays the fact that the applicant changed colleges and has some gaps in his work/school history. Here is someone who took awhile to find himself but knows how to present his current strengths

Emphasizes name

KAREN LOHMILLER
7200 Saranac Court
Columbus, Ohio   43217
(614)555-9117

OBJECTIVE
Position in a public accounting firm involving auditing and tax work, with potential for advancement into management position.

EDUCATION
Ohio State University, Columbus, Ohio
Three semesters with major in accounting; graduation in December 1994; current GPA of 3.61.

Emphasizes education and honors

Lake County College, Mundelein, Illinois
Two years of general education courses with emphasis in mathematics.

HONORS
Ohio State University Dean's List, College of Business (Spring '93, Fall '93)

BankOhio Award in Mathematics

Life Member, Ohio Scholarship Federation

OUTSIDE ACTIVITIES
Member, National Association of Accountants, Ohio State University Chapter

WORK EXPERIENCE

Month and date emphasize actual work record

7/82-1/83   Lazarus Department Store, Columbus, Ohio
Assistant Manager, China and, subsequently, Fashion Accessories
- Supervise sales staff of up to 17 persons
- Communicate with buyers
- Resolve customer service issues
- Manage inventory controls

3/89-5/92   Marshall Field, Lake Forest, Illinois
Promoted from part-time sales to full-time assistant Department Manager, Housewares
- Supervise and schedule sales staff of 12 persons
- Conduct departmental physical inventory
- Implement price revisions

9/88-5/82   Network Planning, North Chicago, Illinois
Part-time office manager
- Manage accounts receivable and payable

GREGORY J. IVERSON
6675 Norman Boulevard
Park Ridge, Illinois   60068
(708)555-6382

OBJECTIVE   Management position in operations, inventory control, or
data processing.

Emphasizes
work   **EXPERIENCE**
experience

1988-1993   **MARSHALL FIELD & COMPANY**
             Woodfield Store, Schaumburg, Illinois

1992-93   Merchandise Handling Manager

Details   ● Supervised loading dock and six customer
increased   service/gift wrap stations
responsibility   ● Scheduled 40 employees
over five   ● Managed all shipping and receiving, return to vendor
years   claims, special event setups, department floor
                     moves, and home deliveries

1990-92   Inventory Control Auditor

             ● Originated position of branch inventory control
               auditor for entire chain
             ● Reviewed all paperwork for incoming or outgoing
               merchandise
             ● Conducted monthly inventories in high shortage
               departments
             ● Audited transaction documents, filing systems, POS
               till audits, and inventory taking procedures
             ● Taught journal procedures to Assistant Department
               Managers and new Area Managers
             ● Developed practice sample set of transaction
               documents for training classes
             ● Chaired Inventory Shortage Control and Safety
               committees
             ● Served on corporate Shortage Steering Committee

1988-90   Sales Associate

             ● Sold men's wear and fine jewelry

EXHIBIT 12-5   continued

Gregory J. Iverson   Page 2

1988   **THOMAS TEMPORARIES**
                  Chicago, Illinois

                  • Inspected and packaged on assembly lines for Baxter
                    Travenol and Xerox
                  • Prepared inventory reports for a retail candy
                    warehouse and a large women's apparel store
                  • Set up merchandise for sales and displays and
                    organized the stockroom merchandise in women's shoes
                    for Carson's

1988   **ADAMS OFFICE SUPPLY, INC.**
                  Elk Grove Village, Illinois

*Work gap
downplayed*   • Prepared merchandise for shipping
                  • Supervised use and refueling of forklifts

1985-1987   **JOSE KELLY'S IRISH MEXICAN RESTAURANT**
                  Schaumburg, Illinois

                  • As senior busboy, simplified the busing system,
                    reducing the number of busboys required on a shift

EDUCATION

1993   **NORTHWESTERN UNIVERSITY**
                  Evanston, Illinois

                  COBOL programming course

*Downplays
five-year
school record*   1986-1988   **UNIVERSITY OF ILLINOIS, CHICAGO**

                  B.S.B.A., major in accounting

1983-1985   **NORTHWESTERN UNIVERSITY**
                  Evanston, Illinois

                  95 quarter credits completed in mathematics,
                  chemistry, psychology, economics and general
                  education requirements

REFERENCES

*Uses
references to
have two
full pages*   James P. Finch   Ellen Carmichael
                  President   Associate Professor
                  Thomas Temporaries   Northwestern University
                  442 West Adams Avenue   2000 Sherman Street
                  Chicago, IL 60645   Evanston, IL 60202
                  (312)555-7834   (708)555-4000

well. The description of the busboy job shows excellent organizing ability. Not all of your previous jobs will lend themselves to this kind of positive detail, but include it if you can.

Chronological versus Functional Approach

For many years, résumés followed the reverse chronological format outlined so far in this chapter. An alternative format, devised in the 1970s, is one to consider if your experience and education do not fit the "usual" 22-year-old graduate model. This *functional* résumé enables you to highlight your skills rather than where and when you acquired them.

An advantage of the functional résumé is that time is downplayed. This is useful if you are older or are returning to the job market after some time off for raising a family or running your own business. Also, a functional résumé subordinates gaps in education or employment to the emphasized information on skills learned and projects completed.

A disadvantage of the functional résumé for fields in which age can be a problem, such as accounting, is that merely by using this type of résumé, you appear to be announcing "I'm older than your average student." If age is not a decision factor in your field, a functional résumé may present your qualifications very strongly.

As you progress in your field, you may find that a functional résumé shows your strengths more effectively than a chronological résumé would. Here again you want to gather all possible résumé information and then use it to present your qualifications in the strongest way you can. If you choose a functional résumé, do so because it presents your unusual background and qualifications more strongly than a more traditional résumé would.

The résumé in Exhibit 12−6, from an experienced employee receiving her MBA, highlights skills over dates. For example, only years appear, not months. Because she is moving from language training to business management, she needed to emphasize what she had learned over the years in jobs and at school rather than past job titles and dates of employment.

The résumé in Exhibit 12−7 uses a functional arrangement to highlight the skills learned in three years of restaurant work. The writer is able to emphasize her international and language experience, include some references, and mention her athletic experience (which shows teamwork) and college earnings— all one concise, well-planned page.

Stationery Choices

Whether you get your résumé copied or laid out and printed, the facility will offer you some paper choices. Unless you are in a creative field, choose a businesslike paper: color—white, cream, or grey; weight—at least 20-pound bond; size—8½″ × 11″. Buy extra paper to use for your application letters, and buy matching envelopes. If you prepare your own letterhead and envelope address copy on a laser printer, you can even have stationery and envelopes printed fairly inexpensively.

Remember **paper personality:** You want your job search package to *look* good and create a favorable first impression of your qualifications for the job. Some job seekers send their résumé and cover letter in a large envelope with interesting commemorative stamps; the advantage is that the résumé is unfolded and thus may stand out in a pile of résumés. Bear in mind, however, that much business mail is opened by someone other than the decision maker who reads it, so an attention-getting envelope may not achieve your desired effect. Checklist 12−1 sums up items to remember when preparing your résumé.

Anna Stepanovitch
4473 West Adams Avenue
San Diego, CA 92116
(619) 555-0691

OBJECTIVE	Communications and public relations program management offering consulting projects for Pacific Rim

DEGREES

San Diego State University
1990 MBA International Business
1983 MA Linguistics
1974 BA Russian *(Phi Beta Kappa)*

Foreign Languages
Japanese
Russian
Ukrainian

Emphasizes skills for new job

PROFESSIONAL SKILLS

Cross-Cultural Communication
- Assessed management training and staff needs
- Persuaded management to systematize placement
- Educated management on business practices
- Negotiated contract work for Tokyo office
- Implemented language training programs
- Translated academic and industrial literature

HR Development
- Assessed skills for promotion and placement
- Counseled clients on search strategies and training needs
- Developed placement evaluation materials

Management & Planning
- Supervised completion of 36 apartment units
- Negotiated purchase and financing of office interior
- Set up accounting, banking, and insurance services
- Advertised and sold educational programs

Market Research & Product Development
- Researched and analyzed hiring needs for office personnel
- Systematized skills and requirements database
- Wrote, translated and published program descriptions, promotional materials, and training manuals

WORK EXPERIENCE

Downplays jobs by giving less detail

1985-1989	**The WINS Consulting Group, Inc.** District Manager-Operations Communications Consultant	San Francisco Tokyo
1984-1985	**Mobil Oil** Skills and Communication Consultant	Tokyo Hiroshima
1977-1982	**Hiroshima University** Communications Lecturer and Consultant	Hiroshima
1973-1977	**San Diego State University** Instructor of Testing, Russian, and English	San Diego
1973-1977	**LATSEC, Inc.**	La Jolla

GERALDINE SCOTT
7546 Parkway Drive, Apartment 1C
Saint Louis, MO 63131
(314)555-5432

CAREER GOAL

A challenging position as a management trainee leading toward
marketing management in a multinational firm.

EDUCATION

Dec. 1993   Washington University, St. Louis
                 B. S., Business Administration
                 Concentration in international management and French

Highlights
management
and   RELATED SKILLS
marketing
skills from   Training   Currently train all new hostesses at Waldo's
restaurant   restaurant in Frontenac. Created a hostess guide
work   and test which is used widely throughout the
                               company.

                 Managing   Now supervise, schedule, and evaluate the progress
                               of ten hostesses. Interview prospective hostesses.

                 Accounting   Audit waiters, cocktail waitresses, and bartenders.

                                    EMPLOYMENT

Emphasizes   Waldo's, Frontenac, MO   August 1990-present
international   Waldo's, Belleville, IL   March 1990-August 1990
and
language   ACCOMPLISHMENTS
experience
                 ● Speak, read, and write French fluently
Shows   ● Familiar with Japanese
teamwork   ● Active member of AIESEC (International Association of Students
                   in Economics and Business Management)
Mentions   ● Successfully competed in swimming and track
college   ● Earned 90% of college expenses
earnings
                                    REFERENCES

                 Mr. Albert Sailer   Ms. Susan Armstrong
                 Instructor at Washington U.   General Manager
                 Marketing Consultant   Waldo's
                 11885 Olive Street   5024 Baltimore Drive
                 Creve Coeur, MO   63145   Frontenac, MO   63119
                 (314)555-6634   (314)555-8211

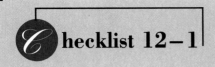

Checklist 12–1

Top of Page

- Name (in boldest or largest type on page)
- Address, phone number
- Alternate address or phone, if necessary

Job Objective

- Tells what you are looking for that the company needs
- Narrow but not too limited
- Shows vocational maturity
- Includes key word on functional area or major
- Emphasizes what you can do for the company

Education

- Minimum: school, major, graduation date
- GPA if 3.0 or higher (or required)
- Mentions *specialized* courses, if space is available

Experience

- Reverse chronological order
- Emphasizes either name of job *or* name of company
- Gives month and year for emphasis
- Lists accomplishments with bullets
- Uses strong verbs, quantifies accomplishments where possible
- Emphasizes skills the company needs

Activities

- Emphasizes leadership, teamwork, accomplishments
- Gives month and year for emphasis

References

- Includes name, title, address, town, state, ZIP code, and phone number for each
- May omit "furnished on request" if space is short
- Separate reference page prepared for interviews

Appearance

- Overall layout balanced
- Headings stand out, organize information
- Emphasizes strengths for employer
- Parallel construction within sections
- Uses only necessary periods and other punctuation
- Contains enough white space, large enough type for reading ease
- Doesn't overuse bold type, underlining, varied fonts, capitals
- *Thorough* Proofreading

Omissions

- Doesn't lie or exaggerate
- Doesn't abbreviate or use jargon that a reader may not understand
- Doesn't include age, race, marital status, religion, photograph
- Doesn't include salaries of past jobs or salary requirements
- Doesn't look as though it was written by another person

The purpose of the cover letter sent with a résumé is to gain an interview. This two-part package is a sales presentation on your qualifications for the job. Think of the cover letter as an application letter rather than merely a transmittal for the résumé. It should add information on where you learned of the job opening, expand on your qualifications, and ask for an interview.

Suppose you attend a meeting of the parent chapter of your major club, like the American Marketing Association, the Finance and Investment Society, or

CREATING A COVER LETTER THAT SELLS

the Data Processing Management Association. There you meet someone who says, "You sound like someone we might be able to hire; please send me one of your résumés." Do you put one of your résumés in an envelope, address it to the name on the person's card, and send it off? *No.* First, write a short cover letter, such as the one shown in Exhibit 12–8, in which you mention meeting the person, remind him or her of your qualifications, and refer to your enclosed résumé. Then mention that you look forward to your next contact (possibly an interview). Your goal is to sound enthusiastic and professional. Then mail the letter and résumé right away. You will effectively have used your opportunity to sell yourself. That is how you will get a job: by selling your attributes to a person who needs someone like you.

You can use the same persuasive approach to convince an employer to create an opening for you. Look at the two very specific cover letters in Exhibits 12–9 and 12–10 and see how they incorporate the features discussed in the following sections. Because canned letters won't create interest among professional human resources people, we will give fewer examples of complete letters than we did of résumés. Think hard about how your qualifications meet an employer's needs. Then *adapt* these suggestions and examples to fit your material.

Get Attention Right Away

As in any persuasive message, you need to start with something that will gain favorable attention. Rather than ask for an application or say you are looking for a job, talk about the work the firm needs done and why you are the person to do it.

Mention Contact, If Any

If you have heard about a job opening from a professor, career counselor, or personal contact, you might mention this person in your opening paragraph, especially if he or she is well known to your prospective employer. Indicating an association with the company (referral by an employee or an executive, a shareholder, or a local community leader) will help gain your letter a more thoughtful reading by a prospective employer.[7]

Mention the Job You Can Do

The most important thing to do in your first paragraph is to talk about *work.* You can get attention by mentioning strong qualifications, such as work experience, or talking about the job for which you are applying. Be sure to make it clear that you are applying for a job, but do it in a way that will gain you favorable attention.

Stress the Employer's Needs, Not Yours

Especially if the job for which you are applying seems like your dream job, be careful to emphasize how well you can meet the employer's needs rather than how well the job suits *your* needs. The tone you want to achieve is "Here is what I can do for you" rather than "This is a perfect job for me."

Here are two openings that have worked for our students:

Because of my college education in finance and my work experience as an electrical engineer, I could do an outstanding job for Air Products and Chemicals, Inc., in the Corporate Treasury Department.

As a college graduate with the background you are seeking, I believe I am a strong candidate for the available financial analyst position. The combination of a challenging undergraduate program at State University and work experience will enable me to work effectively and be productive immediately.

[7]Richard H. Beatty, *The Perfect Cover Letter* (New York: Wiley, 1989), Chapter 3.

7546 Parkway Drive, Apartment 1C
St. Louis, MO 63131
(314) 555-5432

March 17, 1994

Mr. Daniel Hebert
International Sales Manager
Ralston Purina, Inc.
1 Checkerboard Square
St. Louis, MO 63111

Dear Mr. Hebert:

Reminds reader of meeting

   Here is the resume you asked for at last night's AMA banquet. As we discussed, I speak French fluently and am interested in working for an international company such as Ralston Purina.

Mentions strong qualifications

   As you can see from the enclosed resume, Waldo's has entrusted me with helping to hire and train new hostesses. The interpersonal skills this has taught me will serve me well in my career.

Enthusiastic action ending

   I look forward to talking to you soon about the international marketing opportunities at Ralston Purina.

Sincerely,

Geraldine Scott

Geraldine Scott

Diane Alvarez
5335 Ridge Road
Albuquerque, NM   88534

April 2, 1995

Mr. William Washington
Marketing Manager
Southwestern Medical Corporation
2333 Lomas Street
Albuquerque, NM   88501

Dear Mr. Washington:

Gets attention and interest   As a marketer of medical services, could Southwestern Medical use a person with a marketing degree and five years of experience selling to adult consumers?

Relates skills to job needs   My market research courses, especially, have provided me with skills that can help you learn more about your customers. These skills are combined with experience as an assistant manager of a clothing store, selling primarily to persons over 30, persons who are major users of health care.

Action at end has final reminder of job skills   Please call me to arrange a convenient time for us to discuss my qualifications for work as a market researcher for you.

Sincerely,

Diane Alvarez

Diane Alvarez

Charles L. Mackey
4518 Maxwell Street
Chicago, IL   60644
(312) 555-6024

June 15, 1994

Ms. Beryl F. Newman
Executive Vice President
Ward & Bonner Property Management Co.
115 South LaSalle Street
Chicago, IL   60601

Dear Ms. Newman:

Gets attention with skills

Mentions ad

With a B. B. A. in real estate and practical experience in property management, I can help you and your clients as an entry level property manager, in the position you advertised in the April issue of <u>The Journal of Property Management</u>.

Emphasizes qualifications

Makes a potential negative positive

As you can see from the enclosed resume, my practical experience as a management intern has allowed me to assume the responsibility for client affairs. The work demanded an attention to detail and an ability to work directly with people. I am able to adapt quickly due to my years of detail-oriented work in the clerical field. I have practical experience with several word-processing programs and software such as "Property Management Plus."

Mentions related computer skills

Through a course in real estate investment analysis, I was able to learn the various aspects from the investor's perspective. I discovered the ease with which investment analysis and value determination techniques can be simulated on computer. I should be able to learn your treatment of these problems quickly.

Action stresses reader's needs

The skills I have gained on the job and in the classroom could be applied, under your guidance, to your clients. At a time convenient to you, I would be happy to meet you to discuss the ways in which I could best serve Ward & Bonner and its clients.

Sincerely,

Charles L. Mackey

Charles L. Mackey

Convince with Details

After an initial paragraph that gets the reader's attention and interest, use a paragraph or two to highlight your strong points for this job, using material from your enclosed résumé. Again, stress what specific skills you can offer the employer.

Expand on and Highlight the Résumé

Because one résumé can serve you in applying for a number of jobs, your cover letter is the differentiating factor. In your letter, you can add information about a previous job that fits well with the job you seek. Or you can point out the qualifications that make you particularly suited to this job.

Apply Information Rather than Listing It

Since your résumé already lists details, expand on this information in your letter. *Show* that you can do the job; don't just *tell.* Instead of saying, "I received my degree from . . . ," tell what you learned in getting that degree:

> My marketing courses taught me how to . . .

Tailor Letter to Job Description Where Possible

If the job applied for is from an ad or you are lucky enough to have a more complete job description, make sure your letter ties your qualifications to this specific job as much as you can. Analyze the advertisement for requirements, and match your qualifications to those requirements. Then write a letter that emphasizes how you are qualified to do the job specified.

Listing your qualifications in the same order mentioned in the ad is more effective than repeating the requirement and then stating that you meet it. In other words, you might list your qualifications as follows:

> Could your organization use a financial executive who
> - Grew up in the publishing industry,
> - Installed a computerized budgeting system for a publisher,
> - Supervised an accounting staff of 35, and
> - Cut operating backlogs and potential write-offs?

Since this advertisement was for a magazine publisher that needed a financial officer knowledgeable about publishing *and* experienced in financial matters, this list was an effective opening for a reply. If you must echo the wording of the advertisement in your letter, do so in a way that makes you sound knowledgeable about the job and its requirements rather than merely copying the ad.

Notice how the writer in Exhibit 12–9 (page 412) compares her retail experience in dealing with older customers to selling medical services to similar clients of Southwestern Medical Corporation.

Deal Positively with Negative Information

If you lack some qualification noted in the ad or your experience is in a different area, address the situation positively. Note how the writer in Exhibit 12–10 does this:

> I am able to adapt quickly due to my years of detail-oriented work in the clerical field.

One student who returned to graduate school after being laid off from two consecutive jobs during the 1992 recession put it this way:

> Because of the sluggish economy in San Diego, I was able to go back to school last year.

Mention Résumé Near the End

Mention your résumé near the end of your letter so that the reader will not put the letter down too soon. Point out some qualification as you refer to the résumé, as the writer in Exhibit 12–10 does:

As you can see from the enclosed résumé, my practical experience as a management intern has allowed me to assume the responsibility for client affairs.

Note also how the use of *enclosed* as an adjective forces him to describe the enclosure rather than just mention the fact that it is there.

Ask for an Interview and Remind Reader about Your Qualifications

Since your purpose in writing the cover letter is to be granted an interview, be sure to *ask* for an interview at the end of the letter. Mention some qualifications to remind the reader about the skills you have to offer the company. Be positive but not pushy. Note that recruiters are divided as to whether you should say that you will call at a certain time to set up the interview. The negative side: It sounds as though the interviewer has no choice. The positive side: It gives you some control over the process, especially if you are hard to reach by phone.

According to a poll in *Working Woman*,[8] writing "I will telephone your office to arrange an appointment" is considered by human resources professionals as too aggressive. A less pushy approach is: "I will telephone your secretary next week regarding your availability." Another writer-oriented way to mention calling is: "I will call you next week to ensure that you have received my résumé and perhaps to discuss briefly how my background can contribute to . . . "; then mention a positive point about the firm that your research has uncovered.

Make Sure the Reader Knows Where to Reach You

Of course, your letter and résumé will have your current address and phone number. Let the reader know if you will be available in his or her city at some future time, as this information might help you get an interview.

If you have an answering machine, make sure the message you leave is businesslike *and* that your roommates know how to take messages professionally. You can use a standard message like this:

You have reached 555-1234. Please leave your name and phone number, and Nancy or Rachel will call you back as soon as possible.

If you live in a setting where many people share one phone (like a dormitory), try to organize your group so that members take messages for one another in a way that sounds businesslike—and make sure the phone has a pen and pad of paper close by *at all times*. Your well-planned résumé and cover letters will begin to produce action, so be prepared to receive messages about interviews.

KEEP RECORDS OF JOB CONTACTS

Keep track of where you send and to whom you give your résumé. You might use company note cards, a separate section of your computer, or a form like the following:

RÉSUMÉ DISTRIBUTION RECORD

Company Name	Sent to	Date Sent	Follow-Up	Results	Further Action

In the follow-up column, note calls or further letters to remind the company of your interest. Also note here, or in another record on the company, details such as the secretary's name and the name of the person who referred you to the company. Later you will keep similar records of your interviews.

---

[8]"Letters Column," *Working Woman,* August 1989, p. 4.

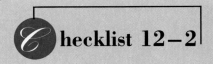

Checklist 12-2

Job Application Letter

Secures Favorable Attention

- Identifies central selling point: education, experience, combination
- Emphasizes serving the reader
- Mentions advertisement or contact for job
- Uses personal contact where appropriate
- Uses a personal compliment *if sincere*

Convinces Reader of Performance Ability

- Highlights most relevant résumé points
- Supplies evidence of accomplishments
- Emphasizes work the reader needs done
- Uses specific company knowledge
- Demonstrates ability to add value to the company
- Focused and organized
- Reader centered rather than writer centered

Asks for Appropriate Action

- Refers to résumé for details
- Asks for interview

- Is neither too pushy nor too weak: asks for appointment
- Expresses appreciation
- Reminds reader of positive skills brought to the job

Appearance

- Centered layout on page
- Full block, block, or modified block style
- Includes reader's name, title, company address
- Salutation includes reader's name
- Complimentary closing is *Sincerely* or *Sincerely yours*
- Letter includes three to five paragraphs
- *Thorough* proofreading

Adaptation

- Letters individualized for each reader
- Reflects personality and style, not canned presentation
- Uses *I* for naturalness, but doesn't overuse

REVIEW

A job search is real work in itself if you include all the steps in the process:

- Organize your information-collecting efforts into a notebook, a set of files, or a computer.
- Analyze yourself, your skills, abilities, and accomplishments, and your ideal job.
- Gather information on prospective employers.
- Investigate services your placement office provides.
- Check library sources, bookstores, and newspapers.
- Get information from recruiters.
- Network through professional and personal contacts.
- Set up some information interviews.
- Explore the hidden job market.
- Assemble a database on your addresses, education, job successes, activities, and references.
- Prepare a résumé to sell your skills.
- Write a variety of cover letters to package your résumé for different employers.
- Keep records of your job contacts so that you can follow up later.

Collect as much information as you can on yourself and on résumé layout. Then construct your résumé so that it presents a positive picture of you and your background. You may want to write different résumés for different jobs.

Write a specific cover letter for each job, tailoring your information to the job description as much as you can. Even if you have only one résumé, at least some parts of your letter should vary from company to company.

Armed with your effective résumé and letter, you will be invited to interviews, which we discuss in the next chapter.

APPLICATION EXERCISES

1. Write out a *skills list* like the one on pages 381–382. Try to come up with at least 20 skills in five or more different areas from your education, volunteer work, jobs, and personal interests.

2. Write out an *abilities* list like the one on page 382. List examples for at least 10 abilities (revise the sample list of abilities to fit your situation).

3. List five *accomplishments* (using a strong verb plus results) that you might use in a résumé, an application to graduate school, or a job interview.

4. Write a one-page memo to yourself describing your *ideal job.* Give enough detail so that a reader can see what the job entails and why you are well suited for it. Keep this memo in your job file so that you can look at it in five years and see how many of your goals you have met.

5. Write a one-page memo to your instructor outlining the services available at your school's placement office. Attach brochures. Discuss the three services that appear to be of most value to you.

6. List the names, addresses, and phone numbers of 10 companies for which you would like to work. Give the name and title of a decision maker who might hire someone with your qualifications. Write one or two summarizing paragraphs about *where* you found this information and *how* you

chose those companies. If some information is missing, how could you find it?

7. Begin your networking list by listing family friends, neighbors, social acquaintances, fellow workers, and club members who could tell you about their jobs, their companies, and potential jobs for you. Try to include between 15 and 30 people as your core list.

8. Choose one person from your networking list and arrange an information interview. Using the questions in the chapter on page 386 and adding some of your own, find out about that person's job and about the job market in that field. Write a memo to your instructor summarizing your information interview. Use headings to organize the information. **Do not** organize chronologically.

9. Arrange an interview with a human resources director or other decision maker at a firm in which you are interested. Interview this person to find out what the firm wants to see in and wants left out of a résumé and an application letter. You might take examples to be evaluated. Write a memo to your instructor summarizing your findings.

10. Give an oral presentation to the class on your findings from Application Exercise 5, 8, or 9.

CASES

1. **Compiling a Job Portfolio.** Compile your own job portfolio so that you will have a complete record of your background to use in filling out applications and developing a résumé. Include sections on your addresses, education, activities, work experience, and references as described in the chapter. Be sure to leave spaces for future additions so that you can keep the portfolio up to date.

2. **Writing a Self-Assessment Essay.** Write a self-assessment to use as an application essay for graduate school. Identify three accomplishments of which you are proud. Discuss them so that the reader sees their meaning and importance.

3. **Gathering Career Information.** Gather information about three possible careers suited to your interests and qualifications. Include the following: What skills are required? Does the job involve work with people? How closely will you be supervised? Where are jobs located? Is it a 9-to-5 workweek, or are hours flexible or unusual? What combination of physical and mental work is

involved? What happens as one advances in this company?

4. **Researching a Company.** Research a company that interests you and write a profile of it. Find out the following: What is the company's industry position (leader, founder, follower)? What does the company produce? What market share does this product have? Who are the company's major competitors? Who are the company's customers? What profits did the company earn over the last five or ten years? What sales figure did the company attain? What is the company's ROI? If you can, evaluate the company's culture: What is the management style? What is the work environment like? How does company management make decisions?

Begin your profile with information about the company: name, address, phone number, names and titles of people who could provide information to or hire people with your credentials. Then list the facts and opinions you have gathered about the company. You might use headings such as the following: Major Products and Services, Competitive Analysis, Major Locations, Organizational Culture and Structure, Employment Opportunities for New Graduates.

5. **Presenting a Picture of a Company.** Prepare an oral presentation on the company you selected in Case 4. This time analyze the company and give a picture of what it would be like to work there.

6. **Writing Two Contrasting Résumés.** Write a résumé for yourself to apply for a job in the Peace Corps or another social service or nonprofit agency. Next, revise the résumé to apply for a job with Procter & Gamble or another large corporation. What are the differences between the résumés?

7. **Answering a Want Ad.** Find a want ad from a newspaper, association journal, placement office, or other source for a job in the field you hope to enter upon graduation. Assuming you are graduating at the end of this semester, write a résumé and letter showing how you are qualified for this job. You may need to forecast your courses completed and future jobs if you are not yet actually ready to graduate.

8. **Applying for an Internship.** Find an internship, cooperative education, or work-study program with work related to the field you hope to enter upon graduation. Write a résumé and letter showing how you are qualified for this job based on your work to date.

9. **Applying for a Summer Job.** Answer the following ad for a summer job. Aim for work that will produce some strong accomplishments for your résumé when you graduate.

CRUISE JOBS

Earn $2,000+ per month working for Cruise Ships and Tour Companies. Holiday, Summer, and Full-Time employment available. Cruise staff, Tour guides, Waitpersons, Bartenders, Musicians, Counselors, etc. Cruise Employment Services, P.O. Box 1357, Miami, FL 33166.

10. **Applying for a Job While in School.** Find a job description at your school's placement or employment office for work you could do *now*. Write a résumé and letter to apply for that job.

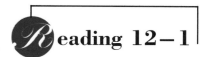

CREATING AN INVENTORY OF VOCATIONAL ASSETS

eading 12–1 | *Geraldine Henze*

Your in-depth descriptions of accomplishments furnish a wealth of information about your skills, personal characteristics, and preferences in terms of rewards and interpersonal contact. Using Table 1 (page 420) as a guide, organize this information and express it in terms of transferable assets—qualities meaningful in almost any position in almost any organization.

Source: Geraldine Henze, *Winning Career Moves* (Homewood, Ill.: Business One Irwin, 1992), pp. 75–76.

TABLE 1   Transferable Skills

Analytical Ability

Ability to:

Concentrate	Form and test	Draw conclusions	Reason logically
Perceive relationships	hypotheses	Define objectives	Identify assumptions
Grasp concepts quickly	Gather information	Solve problems	

Communication Skills

Ability to:

Listen well	Write clearly	Adapt messages to	Inspire confidence
Follow instructions	Give instructions	different audiences	Work well with a variety
Speak foreign languages	Work in groups	Read and retain	of people
Conduct meetings	Speak confidently	information	

Quantitative Ability

Ability to:

Work with numbers	Interpret numerical	Read and design graphs	Prepare forecasts
Explain calculations	results	Identify miscalculation	Work with a variety of
Develop financial plans	Perform calculations	Prepare budgets	software and
Keep accounting records	accurately		hardware

Technical Knowledge

Ability to:

Read technical reports,	Follow regulatory	Understand technical	Read blueprints
manuals, and journals	guidelines	terms and principles	Explain technical
			concepts

Decision-Making Ability

Ability to:

See and evaluate	Make decisions	Explain decisions	Anticipate impact of
alternatives	consistent with	Gather relevant	decisions
Consult others	organizational goals	information	

Organizational Skills

Ability to:

Plan activities	Manage own time	Set priorities	Co-ordinate activities of
Set and meet deadlines	Define goals	Tolerate interruptions	others
			Adjust to changes

Maturity and Initiative

Ability to:

Work independently	Innovate	Maintain composure	Take responsibility for
Encourage participation	Recognize need for help	Tolerate frustrations	decisions and results

Potential for Growth

Ability to:

Take reasonable risks	Learn from mistakes	Apply classroom	Set appropriate goals for
Persist at tough tasks	Recover from setbacks	learning to work	own development
Recognize strengths	Identify weaknesses		

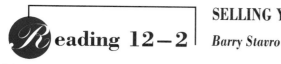
SELLING YOURSELF IN 30 SECONDS

Barry Stavro

It's taken years of schooling and experience on the job to build up the credentials listed on your résumé. But a personnel manager needs only 20 to 30 seconds to scan your résumé before deciding not to hire you, or to put your résumé in the pile of serious candidates.

Someone who has read thousands of résumés is Richard Andre, vice president of human resources at 20th Century Industries, a Woodland Hills-based auto insurance company. To pass the 30-second résumé test, he said, candidates must be concise. "We're looking for brief résumés, not five-pagers," he said. "They should be a page, or two at the most."

Another mistake, Andre said, is making a mistake. "Résumés should be grammatically correct. Nothing turns you off like typos or misspellings."

Tom Washington, author of the book *Résumé Power, Selling Yourself on Paper,* said another blunder is sending a résumé on yellow, orange or blue paper, instead of using white or off-white paper. "There are better ways to get people's attention than neon-colored paper," Washington said.

No matter how neat a résumé is, the real key is whether it is well-organized and written smartly enough to grab the attention of someone you have never met. As Washington put it: "Does the résumé sell this person? Or is the résumé just dates and a laundry list of titles and duties."

To develop the best résumé, Washington suggests writing notes on everything that comes to mind about past jobs, schooling, volunteer activities and any other special skills that you have. Write several rough drafts, then pare the information.

As you write, he said, don't just list what kind of job you had; give some examples that show results or goals you achieved at work. Washington includes in his book the résumé of someone who started as a waitress. Her résumé said she was very professional, got along well with customers and regularly took home the highest tips at the restaurant. "You should make the most out of whatever experience you have," Washington said. "Anything that demonstrates you were good at what you did."

The top of a résumé should list your name, address and phone number. If you have different day and nighttime phone numbers, list both—a missed call can cost you an interview. Keep your résumé up to date; don't just dust off an old copy.

Underneath your name, you can write a brief Qualifications section, in effect summarizing your skills. If you have worked at an office, and you want to find another office job and know how to operate personal computers and fax machines, mention those skills here.

Most résumés, however, are built around two essential sections: employment and education history. If you have stumbled through a lot of jobs, though, don't list them all.

Instead, list the most interesting ones and those where you worked the longest.

For women who are trying to find a job after taking time off to raise children, Washington urges them to list their past jobs, "even if it was five or 10 years ago." But they also should list any other recent activities in a separate section called Projects or Activities. "Whether it's the PTA, Cub Scouts or any organizational things, it shows a person is still active and able to organize," he said.

Education is the next section. Those who are college graduates should list their school and the degree they earned. If you went to college but did not graduate, you can still turn that into a plus. Write down the schools you attended and how many credits you earned. If any classes you took may relate to jobs you are applying for, list some course work.

And if you have taken some vocational training courses, list those as well. "It shows an employer they are serious and willing to take whatever preparation is needed," Washington said.

Other skills such as typing, personal-computer experience or speaking a foreign language should be listed at the bottom of a résumé. "Any bilingual capabilities these days are a plus to any business in southern California," Andre said.

After writing your résumé, ask a friend to check it for grammatical mistakes and to offer any suggestions on how to improve the content. If you are still unhappy with your résumé, try one of the scores of résumé services listed in the Yellow Pages.

For about $25 for a one-page résumé, these companies will make sure that everything is spelled right and will lay out your résumé in a computerized format and print it on fancy paper. The résumé services will also write your résumé from scratch. In effect, they will interview you, then compose a new résumé. But expect to pay $45 to $80 per page.

Once you have a résumé, send it out with a cover letter. Your letter should be brief—three or four paragraphs. Mention the job you are applying for, perhaps highlight something from your résumé and mention something about the company you are applying to.

Andre, for instance, is impressed when people know that 20th Century only sells auto and home insurance, not life insurance.

What he doesn't like are gimmicky letters. "Occasionally, people write a poem as part of a cover letter to be cute," Andre said. Insurance companies, he said, don't need any poets on the payroll.

Source: Barry Stavro, "Selling Yourself in 30 Seconds," *Los Angeles Times,* February 3, 1992, pp. 9–11.

Chapter Thirteen

Job Interviews

PREVIEW

You will learn many on-the-job skills in school and at your part-time and full-time jobs while in school. One of the most important skills for getting a job after you graduate is handling an interview successfully—a skill in which you won't get much practice while in school. This chapter will give you a preview of what to expect at your job interviews and how you can prepare for and succeed in them. Because company recruiters interview on many college campuses, we discuss how the typical on-campus recruiting system works.

In Chapter Twelve, you learned how to schedule interviews through networking and application letters. In this chapter we also discuss videotape and computer interviews, relatively new ways to evaluate job candidates. We discuss what happens in a typical 30-minute interview, explain how to succeed in your nonverbal interviews, and include many sample interview questions and techniques. We also discuss what may happen at a second, on-site interview at the company and how to approach this kind of interview, company tours, and lunches. We conclude with a discussion of thank-you letters, one of the final steps in the interview process, and explain how to negotiate salary once you receive a job offer. ●

**Margaret Arsland
College Recruiting
Manager**

rom the desk of...

I love to interview on campuses. Talking to the students is always so refreshing, even after 15 years of it.

The job market is tougher these days than when I started in the late sixties. The kids are more sophisticated now—and some of them aren't kids, either. The schools have gotten better about telling them what to expect in an interview, too.

Oh, there are always the applicants who show up in jeans, or with too much makeup, or wearing clothes that look like they've been slept in. That hasn't changed, although it happens less often. And there are the ones who haven't done their homework, so they don't know what Western Forest Products does. And the ones who have memorized answers to some of the stock interview questions, repeating their answers even when the question is a little different, showing that they can't think on their feet.

But it's a real pleasure to listen to the ones who can think and who can make me think. They can give answers to "What is your greatest accomplishment?" that frighten me, they are so good. For example, I had a 27-year-old economics major who said getting his degree involved not just working his way through school but breaking away from the gang in his old neighborhood, kicking his drug habit, and learning to read.

I love to interview on campus.

THE COLLEGE RECRUITING SYSTEM

As you discovered in Chapter Twelve, your college career-planning and placement office can be a valuable resource in your job hunt. In addition to providing a library of company information and career-planning testing and counseling, this office will typically offer workshops on résumé writing, interviewing, and job search techniques.

Workshops

Use campus resources as a starting point for your search.

Here are some sample titles of workshops offered by the placement office on one large campus: Orientation to On-Campus Interviewing; How to Write a Résumé; How to Interview Effectively; How to Find a Job; Business Etiquette; Tips for Getting That Job in Accounting/Marketing/Social Work/Recreation (different workshops for different majors, sometimes taught by practicing professionals in the field). Take advantage of workshops such as these so that you will be as well prepared as possible when interview time comes around.

Computerized Guidance

In addition to workshops and appointments with counselors, some placement offices offer computerized career-planning help. One sophisticated program is called SIGI PLUS (System of Interactive Guidance and Information PLUS). This program asks you self-assessment questions; then it matches your values to various occupations and provides some information about those occupations. The program takes three or four hours to complete.

Other, shorter programs include

- Please Understand Me (one hour).
- The Personal Assessment/Career System (45 minutes).

- Vocational Research Interest Inventory (VRII) (one hour).
- Major/Minor Finder (30–45 minutes).

A computer program is no substitute for a trained career counselor, of course, but these programs can help you find out how your skills match various occupations quickly and relatively inexpensively.

You can also find software that will help you write a résumé (Job Hunter's Survival Kit, Résumé Maker, Résumé Kit), prepare for and practice interviewing (The Winning Approach to Interviewing, Interview Scenarios, Successful Job Interviewing), identify occupations requiring similar skills (Dictionary of Occupational Titles), and see current nationwide job openings (Joblink and NEWS). Check to see what programs your career-planning and placement office has to offer. They are valuable aids for helping you choose and find a job.

Before your senior year, find out what information you will need to have on file to qualify for interviews and when the interview schedule begins. Also find out what information on students recruiters seek (Résumé only? Transcripts? Placement file?). Placement processes vary among schools and majors.

Some schools allow you to sign up with any companies of interest to you. Others, like the University of Virginia, use a bid system, in which you have a total number of points and interviews go to people who bid the most on a company. You may also be able to submit résumés—sometimes online—and companies interested in *you* will invite you to an interview.

The Placement Process

Find out what system your school uses to assign on-campus interviews.

Before you go to an interview, find out where the company is located, what its products are, who its competitors are, how it ranks in its industry, and any other information you can. Read career center brochures and library reports on companies, and keep up with the business press about developments in companies that interest you. Find out the organizational structure of a firm so that you can get a feel for how important the company thinks your department is.

Look at a directory of job titles to find out what the company calls the job you want to get. The *Occupational Outlook Handbook* also lists general salary information, at least for entry-level jobs. The U.S. Bureau of Labor Statistics publishes an annual *National Survey of Professional, Administrative, Technical, and Clerical Pay*. Business periodicals sometimes publish salary surveys, as does *Working Woman* magazine.

Your professional association should have salary figures. Read its publications or call the national headquarters to find out. You will be better prepared for interview questions if you have a clear picture of the industry from your research in the library and from interviews with professionals in the field.

PREPARING FOR AN INTERVIEW

Preliminary Company Research

Research companies *before* you meet representatives.

Of course, you won't limit your job search to campus interviews. As you learned in Chapter Twelve, contacts set up within a network can help you discover jobs in the hidden job market. Newspaper and professional journal ads target people trained in every specialty. Application letters sent with a résumé or phone calls to company decision makers can introduce you to potential employers.

In addition to a network information record (described in Chapter Twelve), keep a telephone log of your potential job contacts (See Exhibit 13–1). This record will help you stay on top of the details of your job search so that you

Networking, Applying to Companies Directly, and Answering Ads

Keep track of all job contacts.

Telephone Log   Page _____

Date	Name Phone#	Result (referrals, appointments, information, etc.)

can follow up. A similar record of where you have sent and handed out résumés is also useful as your circle of contacts widens.

Once you have identified through your research companies that can potentially use your services, contact company representatives to sell your skills and qualifications. Write a cover letter adapted to the company's needs that you have identified. In your letter, remember to

Contacting by Letter and by Telephone

1. Gain attention and interest by talking about what you can do for the company.
2. Convince the reader of your qualifications by using specific details.
3. Ask for an interview, adding a final reminder about the skills you can offer the company.

When you telephone a company in which you are interested, be as assertive as you can politely be; otherwise, you will be unable to speak to a decision maker whom you can convince about your qualifications. If you have already sent a letter and résumé, you can follow up with a phone call asking about a meeting to discuss future possibilities.

If the person is difficult to reach by phone, find out when the best time to call would be. If you can find out the person's work schedule, you can at least call at a convenient time for him or her. Plan what you will say to the assistant who answers the phone (if you say merely that you are looking for a job, your call will probably not get put through). Mention your network contact's name, and say that this contact suggested you call. Mention your letter and ask whether the person you are trying to reach has received it yet.

Newspaper advertisements, as well as ads in professional journals, are read by many candidates. For this reason, companies use such ads to demonstrate an effort to attract a broad pool of applicants and meet affirmative action requirements. When responding to such an ad, make sure that your cover letter clearly shows how you fit the job requirements. Your reader may be a human resources department screener who will send your letter on to a hiring manager. Each of these people needs to be able to see from your letter the value you can add to the company.

Answering Ads

Write a strong letter when answering ads.

Do *not* mention a specific salary, even if the ad says you must. At this point, simply give a range. Also, recognize that not all advertised jobs may actually be available. Perhaps an inside candidate is a strong contender, or the firm is trying to collect a file of nationally available candidates to meet Equal Employment Opportunity Act requirements. For these reasons, answering ads may give you only about a 10 percent response rate as you move into higher-level jobs. Even so, answering ads should be one part of your campaign to gain job interviews.

Employers hire *people,* not general qualifications, and an interview's purpose is to evaluate the candidate from the company's point of view. As the candidate has been invited based on paper qualifications, the interviewer will evaluate the person and how good his or her *fit* with the company is.

INTERVIEW FUNDAMENTALS

Interview questions can be closed, open-ended, probing, or a combination of these types.

Types of Questions

Closed. Answer **closed questions** with the requested factual data in a conversational format. Don't ramble, but don't *just* give your phone number, major, GPA, and so on.[1]

Open-Ended. Use **open-ended questions** to illustrate a strength. State your strength, give details to illustrate or prove your point, and tell the interviewer what you have just proven.

Probing. Answer **probing questions** with more detail about the topic you have been discussing.

Types of Interviewers

The person who interviews you may be a screener, a professional recruiter, a recent graduate or peer recruiter, or a hiring manager.

Screener. A **screener** is usually a human resources employee who verifies factual information on a résumé. The screener may be an expert at evaluating candidates; she screens for required qualifications.

Professional Recruiter. A **professional recruiter** may prefer the structured-interview format. This person is well trained and knows what a good candidate for the job will look like on paper and in personality. The professional recruiter also screens for required qualifications. He or she is comfortable with interviewing, makes eye contact, and asks legal questions.

Recent Graduate or Peer Recruiter. This type of interviewer may rely on conversation more than on a structured interview. This recruiter is most interested in how well you would fit in with the company.

Hiring Manager. A **hiring manager** knows the technical field intimately. Show him or her that *you* know the field. This person may not be trained to interview and generally uses the unstructured type of interview.

Types of Interviews

Three basic types of interview are the structured, unstructured, and stress interview.

Structured. The **structured interview** uses closed and open-ended questions. The candidate does most of the talking.

Unstructured. The **unstructured interview** is more casual. It may use probing and follow-up questions. This type of interview may seem more like a conversation, but remember that it is still an interview.

Stress. The **stress interview** uses *what-if* questions. Often the interviewer is a decision maker rather than a trained interviewer. This person is looking to see whether you can handle stress.

ELECTRONIC MEDIA IN INTERVIEWS

Technological advances have added to the types of interviews students may encounter. Interviews may be conducted by a computer, be videotaped, or be broadcast by satellite.

[1] John LaFevre, *How You Really Get Hired,* 3rd. ed. (New York: Prentice-Hall), p. 75.

Julie Houck/Tony Stone Images

In addition to selling your technical skills, in a successful job interview you also sell your enthusiasm and energy by *looking* interested and alert.

Computer Interviews

While not really suitable for executive jobs, computerized interviews are currently being used to evaluate candidates for lower-level positions.

Some advantages of computerized interviewing are time savings for interviewers, consistency of questions (since the program is the same for everyone), and elimination of possible interviewer bias. Art Bell reports that people seem to give more accurate information to a computer "even with questions about theft, drug abuse, and likeliness to quit."[2]

Experienced interviewers can develop for each job a set of basic, multiple-choice questions covering requirements (full time/part time, days of work, related experience) and expectations (good technical skills, success in working with difficult people). The basic program can be more helpful if it branches to more specific questions about answers, just as instructional software branches a student from easier questions into areas where the student's answers reveal he or she needs more work. Some programs insert the interviewee's name and ask more conversational questions, similar to those in the career-planning programs at a placement office.

With its built-in recordkeeping capabilities, the program can track how long it took an applicant to complete the interview, how long he or she paused before answering questions, and whether the applicant changed any answers. As is true with many tests, the computer can also quickly "score" the interview, taking answers that contradict other answers into account.[3]

Because these programs evaluate candidates at a basic level, they make it easier for the human resources office to compare candidates. First, each can-

Computer interviews have the advantage of an impersonal machine.

[2] Arthur H. Bell, *Extraviewing: Innovative Ways to Hire the Best* (Homewood, Ill.: Business One Irwin, 1992), p. 65.

[3] Bell, p. 66.

didate is scored on fundamental requirements and expectations. Second, each candidate has answered the same set of questions, varying only in details related to later answers. Third, all candidates are seen equally, since the computer doesn't recognize race, age, gender, appearance, or other factors that could cause initial bias.

These advantages of computer interviewing make it a workable idea at least for initial screening. If you must take such an interview, regard it as a relatively painless way to give and get factual information. And, as with all interviews, try not to screen yourself out of consideration for the job by giving answers that create an unfavorable impression. Remember that you may be videotaped while answering questions, so your body language is important. Try to appear pleasant and enthusiastic in the face of this faceless machine interview.

Videotaped Résumés

As we discussed in Chapter Twelve, career-planning and placement offices have for some time received videotaped presentations on companies that recruit on campus. The other half of the interview conversation—the candidate—is now also producing videos in one of two ways: as an animated résumé or as an interview performed by a neutral representative of a videotaping firm hired by the company attempting to fill a job.

A videotaped résumé isn't appropriate for all jobs.

If you are applying for a job in a conservative field such as accounting, engineering, or banking, a video résumé is probably not for you. Neither your lack of inclination toward an acting career nor the corporate culture at your prospective employer supports this type of presentation. In some personnel circles, a video résumé is regarded as a gimmick that detracts from an applicant's image.

However, in fields in which people skills are especially important, such as marketing, a video résumé might serve to show your personality much as an audition tape showcases an actor's talents. Of course, if you choose this option, you will have to produce a professional-looking video *and* back it up with a written résumé. As you would with all paid services, make sure the company producing your videotape has a sound business reputation.

Videotaped Interviews

A videotaped interview can be seen more than once and at different locations.

Videotaped interviews, arranged in professional studios, cover questions written by the prospective employer. As in all structured interviews, the same questions are asked of all candidates. An advantage for the interviewing company is that the interview can be shown a number of times and to a number of decision makers. According to Art Bell, unless later research finds that some groups are adversely affected by being videotaped, this type of interview is considered acceptable by the Equal Employment Opportunity Commission (EEOC).[4]

An advantage to candidates is the opportunity to be interviewed for jobs in distant cities or by companies that do not send recruiters to your area. Meeting prospective employers in person is preferable, if possible, but a video interview can showcase your personality better than a letter and résumé or a computerized interview would.

Satellite Interviews

Another electronic type of interview is the satellite interview, an "individualized videoconference" used as an extension of in-person interviews on campus. Unlike in a videotaped interview, in a live videoconference a candidate

[4]Bell, pp. 62–64.

can answer follow-up questions and elaborate on responses if the company representative wishes.[5]

Some organizations use group interviews. Two types of group interviews exist: one in which you are part of a group of candidates being interviewed at the same time or one in which you face a panel of interviewers. Each type requires a shift in your interviewing strategy.

If you are one of a group of interviewees, you need to come across as assertive without being aggressive. You want to be remembered positively as a leader, but you don't want to be seen as overbearing. You want to get some answers in early so that you are not always the last to respond. Try to convey some of your personality in addition to your factual answers so that the interviewer(s) will remember you as a person.

The panel type of group interview often occurs at on-site interviews, where a team of employees meets with the candidate at one time. If you are being interviewed by a panel, try to jot down all the interviewers' names so that you can refer to people by name at least some of the time. Just as though you had a small client audience around a conference table, try to make eye contact with various panel members as you give your answers. Again, convey some personality to avoid appearing stiff; try to project yourself as an interesting person rather than just another candidate.

Interviewers from certain fields, such as banking and consulting, use group interviews to evaluate how a candidate reacts under pressure and interacts with new people. Nonprofit groups may use a panel of interviewers because the panel as a whole is the decision maker.

Because the members of the group will formulate questions while you are answering one question, you will usually have less "breathing space" in a group interview. Ask for a moment to consider an answer if you need it. A group interview can be highly *structured*, with each member asking certain questions of every candidate, or highly *unstructured*, with interviewers interrupting the candidate and one another. Your goal in a group interview is to project the impression that you can do the job. Being strong enough to stand up to a group will help you showcase this quality.

Group interviews give you a chance to show your social skills.

THE TYPICAL 30-MINUTE INTERVIEW TIME FRAME

Most interviews with recruiters last just 30 minutes and follow a fairly conventional format. Thus, we will discuss this kind of interview in detail.

Of course, you will plan your interview clothes to create an attractive, professional impression. Arrive a few minutes early at the campus interview site. Take a minute to get yourself into a positive frame of mind. You want to impress the interviewers, but you also want to find out whether you would like to work with *them*.

Even if you were not impressed with the company in your information sessions, go into the interview with a positive attitude. Be objective. Focus on presenting positive information about your personality and your communication skills; interviewers hope to learn more than just about your technical knowledge. When you walk into the interview room, try to project enthusiasm, positiveness, and friendliness.

Convey enthusiasm and confidence.

The following sections will give you a breakdown of what is likely to happen during each stage of your interview.

[5]David R. Eyler, *Job Interviews that Mean Business* (New York: Random House, 1992), pp. 136–37.

Small Talk: 5 Minutes

Remember that first impressions are formed within the first two minutes, whether you are meeting a potential new friend or talking to an interviewer. The way you walk into the room, the way you shake hands, and the way you sit in a chair all convey an impression about you. Make sure it's a strong one.

To make you as comfortable as possible in a naturally stressful situation, your interviewer will usually begin with conversational comments about the campus, local sports, the weather, or your leisure activities. These conversational comments may grow from something you mentioned in your résumé. While this *is* part of the interview, try to relax and talk about these everyday subjects a little. Sound positive and upbeat, like the kind of person *you* would like to work with.

If your major is a technical one, and especially if your school is well known for turning out successful graduates in that major, you may find that your interviewer extends the "small talk" part of the interview. This is probably because the interviewer knows you are competent in the technical aspects of the field and is trying to find out about some of your other qualifications and how you will fit in with other employees.

Asking and Answering Questions: 15 Minutes

In this part of the interview, the interviewer gathers information about you. (We have included a number of sample questions later in the chapter.) Make your answers sound professional: thoughtful, developed, and confident. Be positive about your accomplishments without bragging. Add enough details to give the interviewer a picture of what you are discussing.

Adapt your answers to each company's needs.

The interviewer's questions, often derived from the material in your résumé, are aimed at getting a picture of your education and experience as they relate to the job. If you have done your homework on the company, you will know how to fit your qualifications to the job. Your goal here is to create the impression of someone who would both be able to do the job and fit into the company's culture.

"VERY IMPRESSIVE...A HUNTING MAJOR WITH A GATHERING MINOR."

© *1993; reprinted courtesy of Bunny Hoest and Parade Magazine.*

An interviewer will often derive questions from the material in your résumé.

When the interviewer has finished with his or her questions, you will probably be asked if *you* have any questions. Of course you do! Ask something job related or something current from your reading about the company in the business press. Do *not* ask about benefits, salary, or vacation. Remember that the company wants to hire you to *work*. You can negotiate salary when you are called with a job offer.

Candidate Questions: 5 Minutes

If you have read up on the company, you can develop several questions to ask the interviewer. You can even ask these questions earlier if there seems to be a lull in the interview; it will give you another chance to look prepared and interested.

You might ask what path the interviewer took to arrive at his or her own job, about what preparation would be best for the job, or with whom you would work. A possible final question is "When might I expect to hear from you?" Be sure to ask for the interviewer's card so that you can write a personal thank-you note.

Interview Write-Up: 5 Minutes

After you leave, the interviewer will take some notes to remember you by in a day filled with half-hour interviews. Following this model, you should make some notes of your own when you get home. What did you do well? What answers might you have improved? What questions were a surprise? Did you communicate your strong points regarding this job? Did you convey enthusiasm about the job and the company? A form such as Exhibit 13–2 will help you keep these records. Use each interview as a learning experience, and try to improve some aspect of your interviewing skills at every subsequent interview.

Evaluate each interview—do you still want to work for this company?

Now that you met with a company representative, do you still feel strongly that you want to work for this company? Is the job as good a fit for you as you anticipated? Do you think the company representative was impressed with you? Make a few notes in your file about these reactions.

In addition, make a computer entry or a file card for each interview listing the interviewer's name, address, and phone number, the date of the interview, and any follow-up activity. Keep a log such as that in Exhibit 13–3 in the front of your interview paper file to keep up with necessary action. For more detailed information on interview planning and follow-up, see Geraldine Henze's informative book *Winning Career Moves* (Homewood, Ill.: Business One Irwin, 1992).

THE NONVERBAL INTERVIEW

Some researchers say that only 10 percent of communication is in your words; the rest is in how you look and act. In addition to preparing for the content of your interview by researching the company and developing answers to potential interview questions, you will plan what to wear and consider situations that might arise so you can deal with them comfortably.

What You Wear

John Molloy's books *Dress for Success, Women's Dress for Success,* and *Live for Success* can give you some tips about how to look as though you fit the job for which you will interview.[6] Even though Molloy's books are a number of years old, he describes the business uniform most men still wear. Women's clothing standards have relaxed somewhat, but they still include a conservative inter-

---

[6]John T. Malloy, *Dress for Success* (New York: Warner Books, 1988); John T. Malloy, *Women's Dress for Success* (New York: Warner Books, 1987); John T. Malloy, *Live for Success* (New York: Bantam Books, 1985).

Interview Report

Date: _____

Interviewer: _____

Name, Title _____

Company _____

Address _____

Purpose of interview:
    ☐ Information   ☐ Job

    ☐ Networking   ☐ Other

Comments on my:
Preparation

Enthusiasm

Ability to respond to questions

Anxiety

What I learned from interview:
New questions I was asked

Good answers I gave

Answers I need to improve

Follow up:
    ☐ Thank-you letter   ☐ Follow-up call (date_____)

    ☐ Calls to referrals

Expected action from interviewer:
    Job offer (by date_____)

    Other_____

Interview Log   Page _____

Date	Name, Title Phone#	Result (referrals, appointments, information, offers, etc.)

view suit and appropriate blouse. Newer books such as Pamela Satran's *Dressing Smart: The Thinking Woman's Guide to Style* give more detail about what successful women wear to work today.[7]

What you look like is as important as what you say.

Anthony Medley's *Sweaty Palms* is another good source of information on interview dress and behavior.[8] Since the subject of this book is interviewing, Medley includes such details as remembering to wash your hands after you put on aftershave so that it won't get on the interviewer's hand when you shake hands.

Molloy found that actors who were pretending to be job candidates could be hired for completely inappropriate jobs because they were able to convey strength, confidence, and energy; move, talk, and dress correctly; and convince interviewers that they were capable of doing the job.

To be taken seriously in an interview, be conservative rather than memorable. (You can vary your clothing *later* when you get the job and see what other employees wear.) Both men and women often interview wearing navy blue or dark-gray suits. If yours is a field in which people don't wear suits, wear something a level above what people would wear to work on a typical day. One clue is to check out the interviewer, if you can, the semester before you have to interview to see what he or she is wearing.

Dress for the job you would like to have.

Wear something you feel comfortable in that suits the job for which you are applying. For example, retail merchandising jobs require some flair, so you might not have to wear a dark suit. One rule that still stands is "dress for the job you would like to have."

A successful interview look includes

- Well-polished shoes, recently heeled if necessary.
- An ironed shirt or blouse, even if permanent press.
- A good belt that looks new.
- Simple jewelry such as a watch, one ring per hand.

  For women: simple earrings and a pin *or* a necklace.
- Clean, trimmed nails.

  For women: clear or light-colored nail polish.
- Up-to-date eyeglass frames.
- A simple, conservative hairstyle.
- *No* frayed cuffs, missing buttons, worn belt marks from losing or gaining weight.

How Professional You Look and Act

Plan what to bring to the interview. Women should bring a purse *or* a briefcase, but not both. If you have a coat, a briefcase, a purse, and an umbrella, it will take you awhile to get organized to sit down. Consolidate so that you can concentrate on the task at hand—impressing the interviewer enough to get the job. At least keep your right hand free to shake hands. Arriving at the interview site five to ten minutes early will give you a chance to get mentally and physically prepared for the interview.

Walk into the room with confidence, holding your head high. A professional, confident look means business to interviewers. Shake hands when the inter-

---

[7]Pamela Satran, *Dressing Smart: The Thinking Woman's Guide to Style* (New York: Doubleday, 1992).

[8]H. Anthony Medley, *Sweaty Palms: The Neglected Art of Being Interviewed,* rev. ed. (Berkeley: Ten Speed Press, 1992).

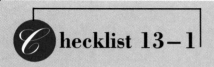

Checklist 13–1

The Nonverbal Interview

Some Do's

- Be on time for the interview. Even better, plan to arrive about five to ten minutes early.
- Look pleasant, but don't smile *all* the time.
- Take occasional, inconspicuous deep breaths to help you keep calm.
- Make your nonverbals match your words: *Look* eager, capable, sure of yourself.
- Stand and sit with good (but not stiff) posture.
- Lean forward slightly when sitting, with squared but not raised shoulders.
- Use slow movements rather than rushed ones that make you look nervous.
- Make eye contact as you would in an everyday conversation.
- Watch the interviewer's reactions for cues about loudness or the amount of information being given.
- Dress so that you feel confident in your appearance. Try on your outfit, including shoes, ahead of time. How does the suit *sit* as well as *fit?*
- Take a small notepad and pen to take any necessary notes during the interview.

Some Don'ts

- Don't chew gum.
- Don't drink coffee—you might spill it.
- Don't fidget—don't play with your hair, clothes, or something on the interviewer's desk, or things in your pockets.
- Don't smoke. (One in four companies will reject a candidate on the grounds of smoking alone.)
- Don't wear strong perfume or aftershave.
- Don't eat anything with a strong smell before the interview.
- Don't stare at the interviewer.
- Don't interrupt the interviewer.
- Don't think about anything but this interview.

---

viewer offers a handshake; don't initiate the handshake yourself. (Practice shaking hands beforehand if handshaking is new to you. You need to appear confident, but neither weak nor bone-crushingly strong.) When offered a chair, sit up and look alert; slouching will make you look tired or bored. Checklist 13–1 offers some do's and don'ts.

First impressions are very important.

According to Charissa Dunn, an important interview habit is to *sit still,* because nervous tension makes a person want to fidget.[9]

Another good source of business behavior tips is *Letitia Baldrige's Complete Guide to Executive Manners* (New York: Rawson Associates, 1985).

Don't worry about an occasional short period of silence during the interview. Interviewers often appreciate a candidate who really *thinks* about how to answer a question instead of having a pat, planned answer.

How You React to Silence

Nevertheless, silence can make a candidate nervous—and a nervous interviewee may try to fill the silence with words, any words, to dispel his or her discomfort. The best way to handle silence is to pause, then ask, "Would you like me to expand on my experience?" or whatever topic you have just been discussing. In fact, if the interviewer is making eye contact with you, he or she might be waiting for you to expand on your answer without intervening, a

Silence can be quite unnerving.

[9]Charissa Dunn, "Actions Speak Louder Than Words in Job Interview," *Business Education Forum,* November 1985, p. 15.

technique Art Bell calls a "silent inquiry."[10] An inexperienced interviewer, however, could merely be trying to think of another question.

Some experienced interviewers use silence as a stress technique, apparently hoping the interviewee will blurt out some negative information just to fill the silence. If you suspect this is the case, remain calm—and silent—looking at the interviewer as though you are waiting for him or her to ask the next question. Unless the interviewer wants to dispel the natural, conversational tone of the interview, a new question will soon follow.

SAMPLE INTERVIEW QUESTIONS AND ANSWERING TIPS

In preparing for your interviews, read all the lists of questions available at the placement office, since they are compiled by people in charge of interviewing college students. Ask other students what questions they have been asked. Read articles about current interview techniques, because trends develop over time. The following sections describe the categories of questions most commonly used for interviews.

Education Questions

Interviewers may ask factual questions about your school, major, or individual courses. They may also ask evaluative questions about *why* you took a certain course or which course(s) you preferred and why. Sample questions are:

- What elective courses did you take?
- If you could take more courses, what would you take? Why?
- Which marketing course did you like best?
- What are your plans for graduate study?
- What motivated you to seek a college degree?
- Tell me about the best and worst course you've ever taken.
- Why did you choose your elective courses?
- How was your education financed?
- What was there about the courses in your major that appealed to you?

Most questions about education can be answered with the relevant facts, but remember to illustrate your particular strengths that suit you for work with this company. Questions that ask about best and worst courses, jobs, or experiences tend to elicit answers revealing your *strengths* and *weaknesses* even if those two words are not used.

Experience Questions

In addition to the factual questions about jobs and volunteer experience, the interviewer might ask about what qualities you think make a good supervisor or how you know you have completed a project successfully. Adapt your actual work experience to the job for which you are applying as much as you can, just as you did in your application letter. Even if your work was in financial services, you can show skills you learned that can help you in a marketing job.

If a company requires experience, in addition to paid jobs you can talk about internships or cooperative education programs you arranged through school, about summer jobs related to your career, or even about volunteer work. Use this experience to show your managerial, financial, or marketing skills. Give specific examples of how you learned skills that will be useful on the job you seek.

---

[10]Arthur H. Bell, *The Complete Manager's Guide to Interviewing: How to Hire the Best* (Homewood, Ill.: Business One Irwin, 1989), p. 59.

If an interviewer tells you he or she thinks you do not have enough experience for the job, ask what challenges the job offers and use your experience to show how you can handle those problems.

Sample questions include:

- Tell me about your previous jobs.
- Is your work progress representative of your ability?
- What was your most disappointing work experience?
- How do you know if you've done a good job?
- How can a manager help you function better as an employee?
- Describe the situation at work you liked least.
- Describe a situation where you handled a problem with a coworker.
- What experience do you have that is relevant to this job?
- Tell me about your most challenging and least challenging jobs. (Illustrate strengths that apply to the job for which you are interviewing.)
- What was the main thing you learned on your last job?
- What changes have you made in your approach to others to become better accepted at work?
- What do you think are the drawbacks to pursuing as a career the kind of work you had in your last job?
- What work achievements have been recognized by your supervisors?
- What kind of people do you like to work with?
- In what ways has your job developed you to take on greater responsibilities?
- What are some things about which you and your supervisor might disagree?
- Can you describe for me a typical day in your job?
- Have you had a mentor?

Most questions about experience are best answered by telling what you know and have done in previous jobs that will be most useful in doing the job for which you are interviewing. Again, emphasize your strengths for this job based on your company and job research.

To get a feel for what kind of person you are, interviewers may ask about activities outside of classes and work. Do you volunteer? Have you been elected to office? Can you persuade people to work on a task together? Do you have good people skills?

Sample questions include:

- What do you get out of your activities outside of class?
- What do you do in your spare time?
- What kind of projects have you been involved in for X organization?
- Have you been in charge of a fund-raising project?
- What has your volunteer work taught you?
- What do you do for fun?
- How did you get team members on a project to do their share of the work?

Activities and Honors Questions

- What is your chief contribution to any group with which you have been involved?

Most questions about activities are best answered by mentioning those that would add to your value to the company. Fitness is a positive activity for any job; volunteer work with nonprofit agencies may help you interact with a company's future customers; club work has taught you to work effectively with diverse people. This is not the time to bring up activities that might be risky and thus raise the company's health benefit costs or activities that could screen you out from further consideration, such as political or religious affiliations.

Personal Qualities Questions

Interviewers try to find out whether you can lead people, are good at following directions, or are very conscientious. Formerly, a conventional way to elicit these and other pieces of information was to ask "What are your strengths?" Because so many candidates have given pat answers to this question, interviewers today are more apt to ask something like "What things about yourself wouldn't you change?" You might be asked what percentage of the funds for your college education you earned yourself, or what accomplishment you are most proud of.

Convey dependability in your answers.

If you have worked on team projects, usually try to find other things to do when your own work is done, make friends easily, or are accurate with details, make sure to mention these positive attributes.

As companies downsized during the recession of the early 1990s, they needed their remaining employees to work longer hours to get the job done. Here is a chance to illustrate how hard-working you are. Can you mention extra work, willingness to work long hours, or additional job responsibilities? If you have worked while attending school, you probably can offer a number of examples. The Bureau of Labor Statistics reports that 25 percent of U.S. workers work 49 or more hours per week.

Sample questions about personal qualities include:

- What things frustrate you the most? How do you deal with them?
- Tell me all about yourself.
- Tell me about a risk you have taken.
- Have you done anything to improve yourself in the past year?
- What motivates you?
- What accomplishment makes you most proud?
- Describe a decision you made in the last six months.
- What are your short-term and long-term goals?
- What difficulties did you encounter in the X leadership position?
- In what respects do you think you have improved in your decision making? (This positive-sounding question might lead you to tell about a mistake you made; be sure to give a positive answer instead.)
- What are your hopes for the future?
- Tell me about your long-term career objectives and what you feel you need to develop in yourself to be ready for such a job.
- Describe a cause you regard as important.
- Who or what in your life has influenced you most with regard to your career objectives?
- What kind of criticism do you get from your family?

- What do you do when you're having trouble solving a problem?
- Everyone says they want to work with people. Tell me *why*.
- What is the difference between your greatest success and your greatest failure?
- What things about yourself wouldn't you change? (This is another chance to immediately mention your strengths for this job.)
- Where would you live if you could choose anywhere?

Most questions about personal qualities are best answered by showing how you will be able to handle job problems when they arise. Be as specific as you can. Use a real-life account to illustrate your strengths for the job. Show how you will fit in with the existing corporate culture. Do not blame others; instead show what you have learned from your experiences.

If you mention an accomplishment, an interviewer may follow up by asking you to be more specific with questions like the following:

Follow-up Questions

- How many dollars did that suggestion save the company?
- What amount of that product did you sell in a month?
- How successful was that project?

Other follow-up questions allow the interviewer to probe your responses:

- Why?
- What was the most challenging aspect of . . . ?
- Who helped you the most in that situation?
- How did you feel about . . . ?
- In your role as leader, what was the most difficult interpersonal conflict you encountered? What did you do about it?

Most follow-up questions give you a chance to expand on your answers. In elaborating on a positive experience, be specific and quantify, if possible. For a negative experience, show what you learned that will help you succeed on the job you now seek.

To find out more about how a candidate will fit with a job, interviewers are beginning to ask what are called *critical incident skills* or *situational* questions. This type of question asks you to describe how you would handle a work problem. Instead of asking "Can you motivate others to do a good job?" the interviewer might say, "Give me an example of a situation where you needed to motivate others to finish a project." If you are asked a question like this, think of the skill needed to perform the task and answer accordingly. Be sure to *show* your skills through example rather than just state that you have those skills.

Critical-Incident Skills or Situational Questions

Show how your experience will serve the company.

Sample critical-incident skills questions are:

- Do your talents lean toward being analytical or creative?
- Give me an example of a time your work was criticized.
- Can you tell me about a project where you had to meet a difficult deadline? How did you finish on time?
- Tell me about a task you took on in a previous job or in a class that prepares you to handle the requirements we've been talking about.
- Show me how you solve a problem.

- Tell me about a time when you tried to help someone change. How did you go about it? How did it work?
- Tell me about an obstacle you had to overcome.
- If you had a problem with a subordinate's need to take off work often to help an aging parent, how would you handle it?
- What risks did you take in your last few jobs, and what was the result of those risks?

Interviewers usually arrive at these questions by considering the requirements of the job (Long hours? Lots of conflict? People skills?). You will be able to answer such questions successfully if you have done your job analysis homework.

Consider telling a "story" to answer a question of this type. Rather than just stating the percentage of college funds you earned, tell what you *learned* in doing so. Instead of merely describing the ideal job in abstract terms, tell about a job you actually had that helped you see the attributes of a good job. Reading 13–1 (page 455) on intercultural interviews has some good story-telling examples.

In the case of technical questions, try to describe how you arrived at the solution rather than just saying, "The answer is 27." Interviewers are interested in *how* you solve problems as well as in whether you can arrive at the answers. The ability to explain technical material clearly to nonexperts is a job skill much in demand, so answering such a question well will also illustrate your communication skills.

Atypical Questions

Stress Questions

As in many other aspects of the workplace, trends in interviews come and go. Stress interviews were common at one time, with interviewers doing things like nailing windows shut and asking candidates to open them, arguing with candidates' answers to questions, and generally belittling and trying to unnerve candidates. Fortunately, such extreme tactics are becoming increasingly rare.

Talk to your classmates about questions they have been asked in interviews. Most people like to talk about their "off-the-wall" experiences. At one time Merrill Lynch asked, "What would your obituary say if it were written tomorrow?" This kind of question forces you to think about what your accomplishments have been so far rather than what you plan to do later. Today some accounting firms are asking, "What would you like written on your tombstone?" This gives you a chance to talk either about your accomplishments so far *or* about your future goals. If you can translate such a question into a more recognizable form—into what the question seems to be getting at—you will have less trouble answering it.

Candidates for recreation jobs in Southern California were asked, "What would you do if you came to work and found your supervisor dead at her desk?" The question was supposed to elicit knowledge of the chain of command ("I'd call her immediate boss and notify him or her"), but probably more than one startled candidate blurted out, "I'd tell my friends there was a job open!" Interviewers at Microsoft ask questions such as "How many gas stations are in the United States?" The interviewer doesn't expect you to know the exact answer but wants you to show how you might arrive at an answer. (Procedure: Estimate the number of cars per gas station, assume the total number of cars in the United States, and divide the second figure by the first to find the possible number of stations.)

Find out what questions your classmates are being asked.

Here are some typical stress questions asked by some companies:

- What is the worst thing you've heard about our company?
- Wouldn't you really be happier in another job?
- Everybody has pet peeves. What are yours?
- Everybody likes to criticize. What do people criticize about you?
- The last person we hired lacked a good work ethic. How will you be different? (Ask what the person failed to do; it may give you a good picture of the corporate culture.)
- Will you stay with us long enough to make our training costs a good investment?
- How would you solve our marketing problem?

Recognize that you need not begin your answer instantly. Take time to think; then consider saying, "One approach that might work is to . . ." Your answer needs to be thoughtful, but it can allow for alternative ways to handle the problem.

Questions about weaknesses are somewhat unnerving, because a candidate wants to describe qualifications for the job, not reasons for *dis*qualification. The traditional advice is to mention

Questions About Weak Points

- A weakness that is really a strength ("I expect everyone to work as hard as I do").
- A weakness you have corrected ("I used to have trouble delegating work, but learned I can't do everything myself").
- A weakness that existed in the past but is really no longer relevant to this job.

You *must* be prepared for "weakness" questions to be able to turn your answers into strengths. If you must describe a potential weakness, make sure it is clearly job related and go on to discuss how you have compensated for it.[11] Because many people are so prepared that they almost seem to have canned answers for the strength and weakness questions, be aware that many versions of these questions exist.

Be prepared to speak positively of your weaknesses.

Possible weakness questions include:

- What would your parents/roommate/supervisor/faculty advisor/etc. say is your greatest weakness?
- What skills do you need to develop to progress in your career?

As with all your answers, return the subject to your strengths for this job and to your enthusiasm for positive ideas such as more responsibility.

Job seekers are not the only people who network. Employers also use networking to find out about job candidates. Since written references are seldom used today, interviewers may ask for *negative* references—people with whom you have had problems in earlier jobs. Consider who might be on that list; let those people know they might be getting a call. This kind of *damage control* may improve your image when the reference check occurs. A more positive

Networking by Employers

Prepare negative references for possible contacts.

[11]Geraldine Henze, *Winning Career Moves* (Homewood, Ill.: Business One Irwin, 1992), p. 150.

approach, however, is to contact ahead of time a few people with whom you have had honest differences but who would respond that you were a bright, fair-minded person who just happened to see things differently than they did.[12]

Some state agencies ask very specific job-related questions, such as "If you had X and Y happen on an audit of ABC company, what would you do?" Answering this kind of question gives you a chance to use your technical knowledge gained from school or from work experience.

Interviewers may also try to get a feel for how much you know about their companies and how well you would fit in. If you have done your company research, you can tailor your answers to allay these concerns by showing that you are enthusiastic about the company's location, know about its products, and understand at least something about the company's corporate culture.

Sample questions include:

- Why do you want to work for this company?
- What do you know about this business?
- We have many qualified applicants. Why should we hire *you* for this job? (This is your chance to list your qualifications and the several ways you match what the company needs in the person who fills the job.)
- How would you install a standard cost-accounting system?
- How long would it take you to make a contribution here?

Questions of this type give you an opportunity to show your technical knowledge and once again emphasize your strong points for this job.

Questions that Discriminate

In job interviews or on applications, employers are prohibited from asking questions that would elicit information prompting them to discriminate against ethnic or racial minorities, women, older workers, disabled persons, and a number of other classes protected under the equal employment opportunity laws. Nevertheless, the world is not a perfect place, and discrimination still exists. Companies, and even industries, may discriminate against women, homosexuals, African-Americans, white males (so-called reverse discrimination), or other groups. If you can prove that you did not get a job because of overt discrimination, you might get a cash award or even get the job in question. Consider, however, that first, discrimination is hard to prove, and second, that such a company might be an undesirable place to work. You may have run into either a bad interviewer or a symbol of the corporate culture.

As we discuss in Chapter 16, employers can ask job-related questions as long as they ask them of all applicants. If night work or travel is required, you need to be able to show that you can do it. (The days of asking women, "Will your husband allow you to travel?" are thankfully over.) Apparently, some companies actually used to ask, "What kind of birth control do you use?" Presumably the object of the question was to find out if having children would interfere with the person's work. When asked something so personal, one suggested response was "What an unusual question! What kind does your company recommend?"

Defusing an uncomfortable situation is better than confronting an interviewer outright. True, you can say, "That's an illegal question," but a more

Illegal questions are not about job requirements.

[12]Eyler, *Job Interviews that Mean Business*, pp. 19, 55.

low-key way of handling it—and difficult interview questions in general—is to think of what the interviewer is really asking and then answer *that* question.

An interviewer who asks a woman about plans for marriage and family, for example, could be trying to find out how career oriented she is. An appropriate response would be "If what you're asking is whether I'm committed to a career with this company, the answer is definitely 'Yes.' I stayed with my last job for three years and missed barely a week of work for health or personal reasons. I want to grow, and I finish what I start."[13]

Suppose the interviewer asks, "What kind of personal crises have forced you to miss work days?" Mention a one-time crisis, not your broken-down car or your children's accident-prone behavior. Emphasize that you will be at work every day, doing an effective job for the company.

In other words, you can handle touchy questions in one of three ways: You can collect enough information to file a complaint about the company, refusing to answer the question; you can answer the underlying question being asked; or you can answer the question directly.

Three articles in the September 1991 *Bulletin of the Association for Business Communication* discuss answering illegal interview questions. In one article, the authors explain that the appropriate way to respond depends on how concerned the candidate is about the impression being made (*not answering* meaning a lack of concern and *answering* meaning a desire to make a favorable impression).[14]

If you want to make a favorable impression, David Eyler recommends that you

> Answer a question that won't do you harm;
>
> Make an inoffensive aside that you had the impression such questions were illegal; and
>
> Avoid threatening the interviewer or labeling yourself litigious.[15]

Keeping the interviewer's goodwill while letting him or her know that you are aware of your rights is one positive way to handle discrimination questions.

You can assert yourself in an interview and still retain goodwill.

Discrimination on the basis of ethnic background, age, or sex has not disappeared from job interviews. Plan ahead of time what answers you can give to potentially discriminatory questions, if you can answer them at all.

Cultural bias is certainly never deliberately built into an interview, but interviewers tend to look for candidates who look and act as they themselves do. Thus, be sure to look and act self-confident, professional, and enthusiastic—like the kind of person they want to hire. Recruiters like to meet interesting people with a sense of individuality, just as you do. In an article on minority business students (Reading 13–1 in this chapter), Eileen Mahoney says, "You could be the only spot of color (literally and figuratively) on a recruiter's interview schedule—make it work to your advantage!"[16]

The article tells about three minority candidates who could have used stories about their backgrounds to emphasize how they were suited for the job. For example, a person from a culture that shows respect by limiting eye contact and giving a gentle handshake may appear too weak. When asked to

[13]Elizabeth Tener, "The New 'Guerilla Interview,'" *Self,* November 1987, p. 199.

[14]Jeff Springston and Joann Keyton, "Interview Response Training," *Bulletin of the Association for Business Communication,* September 1991, p. 29.

[15]Eyler, *Job Interviews That Mean Business,* p. 149.

[16]F. Eileen Mahoney, "The No Clash Interview," *Minority MBA* (1992–1993), p. 19.

"tell me about yourself," it might be a good idea to mention that you come from a more diffident culture and describe how that will help you deal with employees or customers. On the other hand, if you are naturally enthusiastic and talkative, make sure you act professional in the interview. Don't put off the interviewer by acting as though you are talking to one of your friends.

If you are the first person in your family to graduate from college and plan to help your younger brothers and sisters go to college, mention this in the light of wanting to succeed at your career to help others rather than of someone who expects to put family ahead of career.

Questions Asked by the Candidate

Remember that an interview is a directed conversation between at least two people. In addition to giving your answers, ask some questions as part of your side of the conversation. This is one chance to find out whether you would like to work for this company, as well as for the company to find out whether you are someone who would fit in there.

Questions at the End of the Interview

In the latter part of the interview, the interviewer will ask whether you have questions about the company. Your research will have given you some ideas, and some answers to the 20 questions in Table 13–1, listed by recruiters as the best ones students asked them in interviews.

Plan useful questions for each company.

Other questions to ask are those that relate to the literature the company provides about itself and its jobs. If the recruiting brochure describes a promotion path, you might ask how trainees are evaluated or what differentiates those who are promoted from those who are not. For example:

- How many people go through the training program in a year?
- How often do you give performance reviews?
- How much travel is involved?
- How frequently are employees relocated?
- Is there anything else I can tell you about my qualifications?
- What objectives would you like accomplished in this job in the next three months?

Find out what the job is really like.

Be certain to ask what action will come after the interview: "When might I expect to hear from you?"

Earlier in the Interview

One good time to ask questions is between the small talk and the time the interviewer begins his or her questions. If you are able to work in some questions early in the interview, ask what the interviewer is looking for and where the company is headed. Using this information, you can show how you are the person to do the job:

- What do you consider ideal experience for this job?
- What are the primary results you would like to see me produce?
- What personal qualities are needed to succeed in this job?
- Is this a new position?

SECOND INTERVIEWS

After your on-campus interview, you will likely be invited for a second interview by companies interested in hiring you. You have made the cut. Now take advantage of the extra knowledge you can gain from this interview to help you make your job decision.

TABLE 13–1 Questions to Ask about the Company in an Interview

1. What future changes do you see for the company?

2. Who are your competitors?

3. What makes your company different from others?

4. How does my job fit with the mission of the organization?

5. What will I be contributing to the organization?

6. What do you wish you had known about the company before you started?

7. How would top management describe the corporate culture, and how does this compare with things in the organization as they really are at the lower levels?

8. What are the ethical and environmental philosophies of your company?

9. What is this company's philosophy toward its employees?

10. What values are sacred to the company?

11. What do you see as the biggest areas of needed improvement within the company?

12. What are the short- and long-term strategic directions of the company?

13. What is the greatest challenge, from your perspective, that the organization faces during the next year?

14. Can I expect opportunities for advancement with the company if I work hard to prove myself?

15. Where would my career progress from my first assignment?

16. What was your career path within the company?

17. What makes your association with this company enjoyable?

18. What are the company's goals for the future?

19. If I do well, what will I be doing in five years?

20. What programs for minorities does your firm have?

Jack Falvey, "In the Real World," *Business Edge,* October 1992, p. 9.

Second interviews can take place in person or over the phone. The interview can be at the downtown office of a company located in the same town as your school, in another city nearby where you have expressed an interest in working, or in the corporate headquarters clear across the country. In all these cases (except a phone interview), you will have an opportunity to actually *see* the company at work in a way you could not at an interview with an on-campus recruiter.

This second, on-site interview, of course, helps you gather more information about the company and its location and culture. But don't let the excitement of an on-site visit make you forget that the company will also learn a lot about *you* at this interview.

The second interview can consist of another hour or so at the company's office, but it often includes lunch and perhaps even an entire day, especially if you are coming in from out of town. You will be introduced to a number of people, some of whom you will have time to talk to at some length. Whether it seems like a conversation or an interview, remember that it is still an interview. People will continue to try to find out how well you would fit into the company. They will also try to impress you so that you will accept their offer later.

An on-site interview gives you and the company a chance to look each other over.

You will need to use some business social skills as well as your technical skills to succeed at these interviews. You need to know how to travel efficiently, what receipts to save, what kinds of foods to order when your mind is on more than eating, and how to pack for a two-day trip.

Someone will probably meet your plane or at least arrange for you to be taken to your hotel, where your schedule of appointments will be waiting for you. Plan to wear appropriate business travel and interview clothing. Also plan to keep up your regular fitness routine while you are away; this will reduce stress and help you look energetic during what will probably be a long day or more of interviewing a number of new people. In addition to impressing these people, you want to be alert enough to be able to evaluate the company as an employer for you.

Here are some tips for preparing for on-site interviews:

- Find out whom you will see and what your schedule will be. Technical people will interview you for qualities other than those the screening recruiter did. Who is the decision maker?

- If it's an out-of-town meeting, establish who will arrange for travel, hotel, and meals. Find out when you will be reimbursed and what receipts to save.

- Plan business clothing for the entire time you will be with company representatives—from the time you arrive to the time you leave.

- Eat moderately and get enough sleep. Keep your energy high so that you look like an attractive candidate.

COMPANY TOURS AND LUNCHES

Prior to graduation, you may have an opportunity to tour companies in which you are interested, especially if your school is located in a larger city. These opportunities could come from student organizations like the Society for the Advancement of Management, the Finance and Investment Society, or AIESEC (a French acronym for the International Association of Economics and Management Students or Association Internationale des Étudiants en Sciences Économiques et Commercials). Your career-planning and placement office may set up tours of local companies, or you may know someone who offers you a personal tour.

Take these offers—you may find a company you would like to work for or find out that a company that interested you is not as you expected. You will get a chance not only to see the physical plant but also to meet people who work for the company. You will probably have a chance to ask questions and find out what it is like to work there.

Ask professionals questions about working in your field.

Observe the following signs of corporate culture:

- Are working conditions equal for all ranks of employees?
- Are employees polite and considerate, welcoming guests and appearing on time for appointments?
- Do people act friendly or cool toward the boss?
- What official communication publication do employees have?
- What is the company's tone and look?
- Are awards and signs of group activities evident?[17]

When you talk to company employees and contacts, ask

- What are the company goals?
- How long have most employees been there?
- Do employees get a lot of satisfaction working at the company?

The answers will tell you a great deal about the corporate culture, employee turnover, and work atmosphere.[18]

You will probably meet some people who are less interesting than others. Act attentive and interested with *all* company representatives; this is business, not a social visit with friends. Try to find out who your boss would be. Do you like this person? Will you learn something from him or her? Personal chemistry isn't everything, but having a good boss will really help you on the job, no matter how thorough your technical knowledge.

You may have read books about how to dress and other points about business etiquette. The hardest thing about a business lunch may be remembering that it *is* business, not a social occasion. Although it provides an opportunity for you to get to know company members better, it also gives them more time to look *you* over. Table 13–2 (page 450) offers some guidelines for handling a business lunch successfully.

Remember that lunch is still business.

Just as you try to dress professionally but inconspicuously, try to orchestrate your interview lunch so that people remember your interesting conversation rather than what or how much you ate or drank.

When you get home from a lunch, a tour, or an interview, you should write a thank-you note. This will help create a good impression of yourself *and* remind people you met who you are.

THANK-YOU LETTERS

At the end of the interview or tour, be sure to get a business card from your interviewer or host. That way you will be able to spell even unusual names correctly and learn the proper mailing address (which may well differ from the street address).

The Importance of Promptness and Accuracy

[17]Dan Moreau, "Take Charge of Your Career," *Changing Times,* October 1990, pp. 93–95.

[18]Marilyn Moats Kennedy, "The Workplace from Hell: How to Spot It Before You Sign On," *Glamour,* April 1992, p. 139.

TABLE 13–2 Guidelines for Handling a Business Lunch

1. Order food that is easy to eat. Avoid food that gets your hands or clothing dirty (this is not the time for fried chicken or spaghetti).
2. Avoid alcohol. Just as you wouldn't smoke in an interview (which this lunch is), don't do anything that might spoil your concentration. Remember, this is *work*.
3. Remember your manners: cut up your food, take small bites, chew with your mouth closed, tear your bread into pieces before buttering it, and do not talk with your mouth full. These "rules" sound elementary, but breaking any of them can create a poor enough impression to cost you a job offer.
4. Don't order more food or more expensive items than anyone else. Ask your interviewers for recommendations, since they probably know the restaurant well. It may be a treat for them to go to an expensive place with you, so let them set the tone. The general rule is to order something in the middle range of the menu, unless your host encourages you to order something more expensive.
5. If you are being interviewed by a company with plans to send you to one of its international offices, do research beforehand about the other country's eating customs. For example, Europeans use a knife and fork differently than you may be used to. For an Asian company, you should learn to use chopsticks and chopstick etiquette, such as not using your chopsticks to take food from the common serving dish. In Japan, if you clean your plate, it is assumed you want more food, so leave a little food on your plate. In Holland, a business colleague may offer you a small drink at any time of the day as part of Dutch hospitality. Take the drink, and at least *pretend* to drink it.

Letitia Baldrige, *Letitia Baldrige's Complete Guide to Business Manners* (New York: Rawson Associates, 1985), p. 170.

Thank-you notes *must* be written promptly.

Just as with personal thank-you notes such as those for birthday gifts, business thank-you notes are most appreciated when they are *prompt.* Try to get yours written the day after the interview or tour, if at all possible. If as much as a week passes, you will almost have to mention the reason for the delay in writing.

What if you were interviewed by a number of people during a company visit? Unless you can take the time to compose different notes to each person you met, write one good letter to the person who set up the interview and ask this person to thank the other people for spending time with you. If you write to each interviewer, do not send personalized form letters; they may show their letters to one another.

You may need to write more than one thank-you letter.

Another thank-you note that will gain you goodwill is one to the person who arranged the interview for you. Do *not* ask for another favor in this letter; if you have other topics to discuss, do so in another letter. The sole purpose of a thank-you letter is to thank someone.

General Outline

While it is important to personalize your note as much as possible—mentioning specifics from the interview, the tour, or your qualifications—most such thank-you notes are just a few paragraphs long and follow the same general pattern.

In the first paragraph, thank the interviewer or your tour host. You might say, *Thank the Recipient*

> I appreciate your spending time yesterday discussing the sales position ABC Corporation is filling. Hearing that you plan to open a new territory in New Mexico made me even more eager to begin my career with ABC.

In the second paragraph, talk about something that will help the interviewer remember you. It could be something you discussed, additional information you promised to get, or something you have learned about the company. As this is the most original paragraph of the letter, try to make it especially interesting: *Expand on Some Individualized Detail*

> Your recent purchase of notebook computers for sales staff will certainly help them keep up to the minute on prices and availability. The enclosed copy of the article we discussed shows how insurance salespeople can use notebook computers to give potential customers instant price quotes.

The third or last paragraph of the thank-you letter should end pleasantly with a forward look at your next contact with this person. Be positive and businesslike: *End with a Forward Look*

> I look forward to hearing from you about the contribution I can make to increasing sales at ABC Corporation.

To help make your thank-you letter gain you goodwill, *Gaining Goodwill with Thank-you Letters*

- Be prompt (within 24 hours of the interview).
- Be accurate (spell names correctly).
- Be brief (say thank you only once).
- Be specific (so you are memorable).
- Be positive (make them choose you).
- Be available for further interviews.

NEGOTIATING YOUR JOB OFFER

Salary

To successfully negotiate salary, you need to know two figures: the *minimum* you will accept and the *maximum* you think the company will offer. Your acceptable minimum should take into account how much money you need to live on, how much your specialty is worth in the current market, and how much money you think you should earn. Your personal feelings about where the job is located and what your promotion path is will also affect the price you set on your services.

To get an idea of the maximum the company might offer, collect available information so you can make an educated guess. Ask professional contacts what the *range* for someone like you is in their organizations. Ask executive recruiters, trade association members, and placement office personnel who perform salary surveys of positions offered to graduates.[19] *Plan your salary negotiation ahead of time.*

Employment experts agree that you should wait to discuss salary until the company makes you a job offer. Delay stating a figure until the employer has named one. Here are some suggested delaying statements: *Don't be the first to mention a salary figure.*

- I'm open and negotiable.
- I need to hear more about the position.

[19]Paul Hellman, *Ready, Aim, You're Hired* (New York: AMACON, 1986). Published in *Savvy,* March 1986, pp. 50–52.

- I'm sure that, should we come to an agreement about the position, we'll be able to work out the salary.
- It would be presumptuous of me to tell you what the job is worth. What did you have in mind?

If you follow one of these delaying statements with "What would be a starting salary for someone with my qualifications?" or "What kind of range have you allocated to this position?" you are likely to receive the specific answer you are after.

When the interviewer names a salary, *do not say anything.* Try to remain silent for up to 30 seconds. The first offer is usually near the bottom of the range for the job, and the interviewer will probably raise that number if you remain silent. If the amount is too low, you may be able to get a promise to have your salary reviewed in three months based on your performance, even if the company gives only annual reviews. All future raises are based on your initial salary, however, so don't sell yourself short. When a company is making you an offer, you are in your strongest bargaining position.

When the interviewer names a range or a specific number, wait, then make a counteroffer—perhaps 20 percent higher or 10 percent under the maximum you have figured the company will offer if the offer seems low.

When comparing two offers, include benefits: What is a company car, paid parking, or other benefits worth to you?

From your research, you should be aware of benefits offered to employees in your field. Standard benefits include personal holidays, paid vacation, different types of insurance, educational programs, and possibly financial incentives such as stock options. Some larger companies pay for company cars, relocation costs, spouse relocation, and club membership.

Don't accept an offer too quickly—sleep on it.

Whether the issue is salary, benefits, or some other aspect of the job offer, *delay* your employment decision at least overnight to feel sure that it is the best decision for you and to make the employer want you more. Once you have the offer, clarify details about your future, such as timing of performance and salary reviews, relocation and benefit policies, and available resources for accomplishing your job.

REVIEW

Job interviews give you an opportunity to present yourself well for available jobs. You can succeed at interviewing by doing your company homework, finding out what questions might be asked, and preparing for the interview as though it were a research and speaking assignment. This chapter presented a number of guidelines for preparing for interviews, answering the various types of interview questions, handling second interviews, and negotiating job offers:

- Use campus resources for company research and recruiter contact.
- Practice interviewing by role-playing, if possible.
- Learn about kinds of interview questions (open, closed, probing).
- Learn about kinds of interviewers (screener, professional, peer, hiring manager).
- Learn about kinds of interviews (structured, unstructured, stress, group).
- Prepare for possible computer and video interviews.
- Plan your interview clothing to convey a positive impression.

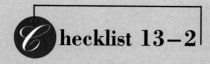

Checklist 13-2

Know Yourself

Research:

- Assets, skills, abilities.
- Preferred corporate culture.
- Preferred geographic location.
- Preferred work type
  With people?
  With machines?
  With information?
  Indoors or outdoors?
  Scheduled or flexible hours?

Know the Jobs

Research:

- Company background, strengths, products, future plans.
- Companies that are hiring people with your background.
- Companies that sound interesting but are not hiring.
- Contacts who know about the hidden job market.

- Descriptions of jobs and required qualifications.

Plan the Search

- Develop a résumé.
- Plan an adaptable cover letter.
- Alert references about possible contacts, current résumé, job qualifications.
- Schedule on-campus interviews.
- Identify and contact other prospective employers.

Prepare for Interview

- Study company literature for each employer.
- Plan questions to ask representatives of each company.
- Consider salary requirements.
- Gather salary data.
- Practice answering common questions.

- Study nonverbal behavior and uses of silence.
- Study interview questions and possible answers (education, experience, activities and honors, personal qualities).
- Learn how to deal with situational, job-related, and discriminatory questions.
- Plan some questions to ask in the interview.
- Review your skills and abilities lists to go into an interview feeling positive about yourself and your skills.
- Prepare for on-site interviews and company tours.
- Write thank-you letters to enhance your candidacy for the job.
- Successfully negotiate salary and benefits once you receive an offer.

APPLICATION EXERCISES

1. List three sources you will use to identify prospective employers. How will you find more information on the companies than these sources can make available to you?

2. Based on a typical thirty-minute interview, what do you plan to accomplish in the first five minutes?

3. How do you plan to emphasize your education *or* your experience (whichever qualifies you more for the job applied for)?

4. List several questions you should *not* ask an interviewer.

5. What do you plan to wear to your interviews? Why did you choose this specific outfit? What nonverbal impression are you trying to convey?

6. Imagine you are going to a group interview to choose candidates for an exchange program with another university or in another country. How can you make yourself memorable in a positive way?

7. Write a summary of what you expect to happen on a second interview with a company that takes place at the company's headquarters. What two aspects of the interview worry you the most? Why? What can you do to better prepare for them?

8. An interviewer asks, "Show me how you solve a problem." Write out your answer.

9. What are your action choices if an interviewer asks you an illegal question?

10. How can you deal with silence in an interview?

CASES

1. **Researching Jobs.** Using the *Occupational Outlook Handbook,* find five jobs that interest you. List these jobs and the entry-level salary for each. Write a paragraph explaining why you are suited to each of these jobs.

2. **Researching a Company.** Research a company that plans to send recruiters to your campus to interview potential job candidates. Find out as much of the following information as you can. Then write up a company profile to prepare yourself for an interview.
   a. Name of recruiter
   b. Size of organization in industry
   c. Potential growth and competition
   d. Annual sales growth over past five years
   e. Complete product line or services, including new products
   f. Age of top managers and their backgrounds
   g. Corporate culture
   h. Type of training program
   i. Promotional path and relocation policies

3. **Questioning a Recruiter.** Based on your company research in Case 2, write out 10 questions to ask this recruiter. Think of questions that show that you already have some knowledge of the company.

4. **Explaining your Interest.** The interviewer of the company in Case 2 asks, "Why are you interested in our company?" Write out your answer.

5. **Selling your Qualifications.** Write a list of three main points about yourself that you want to

communicate in an interview. What stories could you tell to briefly illustrate these points? Write out one of these stories.

6. **Role-playing an Interview.** With two classmates, role-play part of an interview involving at least four interview questions. One student should act as an observer and take notes. Then each of you reports to the class what went well and what you would like to have changed about the interview.

7. **Writing a Memo on Interviewing.** Find two or three recent articles on interviewing. Write a memo to your placement office telling how to prepare students for current interview styles (cite your sources).

8. **Writing a Follow-up Letter.** Write a follow-up letter to a recruiter with whom you had an on-campus interview. Mention some aspect of your education or experience that will further qualify you for the job. Three weeks have passed since your interview.

9. **Writing a Thank-You Letter.** Write a thank-you letter to your interviewers at an on-site interview with a company in which you are very interested. You just flew home from the headquarters city. Do you have any receipts that were not already reimbursed?

10. **Accepting a Job Offer.** Write a letter accepting a job offer. Be sure to clarify any necessary details, such as when you can begin work, and to convey enthusiasm about your new job.

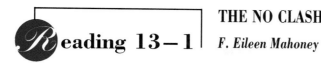

THE NO CLASH INTERVIEW

Reading 13—1 | *F. Eileen Mahoney*

Everett Begay was getting worried. He'd been through five interviews and had no job offers. He was careful to be on his best behavior and to be especially polite to the employment recruiters. His grades were high and his skills were good, but something was obviously wrong.

Ana Gonzales thought her first interview was going well. She was answering the questions honestly and openly like her career counselor had advised. When asked about her five-year goals, she told the recruiter she wanted to earn enough money to put her younger sister through school and then start her own family, providing them with opportunities she hadn't had. The interview went downhill from there.

Dwight Williams was excited about his interview. He put forth an extra effort to be friendly and relaxed with the corporate recruiter. When the recruiter asked Dwight what he had to offer the company, Dwight tried to rely on his energy and enthusiasm because he had no previous related work experience. The more zealous he became in his efforts to convince the recruiter how much he wanted the job, the more the recruiter seemed to withdraw.

The corporate interview can be a nerve-wracking ordeal. You can go into an interview feeling confident and excited and come out feeling deflated and dazed. When an interview doesn't go well it is sometimes difficult to determine exactly what went wrong.

Corporations, like any other group of people, have their own identity consisting of cultural norms, appropriate behaviors and unspoken expectations. Research has shown that interviewers unconsciously like candidates who look, act and think as they do, demonstrating characteristics similar to those of the corporate culture. In fact, this "likability factor" is often unintentionally given more weight in hiring decisions than an applicant's specific abilities, resulting in culturally biased interviews.

This puts women and people of color at a distinct disadvantage because they are still underrepresented in the corporate environment. Not only are covert corporate codes of behavior unknown to minority candidates, but they often run counter to their personal beliefs and cultural values. However, this does not have to interfere with a successful job hunt. Women and people of color can circumvent any subtle discrimination they encounter in the interview process by using the following tips.

Know the Interviewer's Expectations

Most recruiters have a conscious or unconscious picture of the "ideal candidate" in the interview process. Following are some characteristics that employers typically respond to favorably:

- Self-confidence: demonstrated by a strong handshake, ready smile and good eye contact.

- Leadership: ability to cite specific examples of personal achievements and strengths.
- Goal Orientation: the ability to express short- and long-term goals as they pertain to the job.
- Professionalism: indicated through the use of grammatically correct English with no slang or "peer" words.
- Composure: remaining calm under pressure and handling stress questions comfortably.
- Enthusiasm: excitement about the job and a sincere desire to become a part of the organization and industry.
- Authenticity: capable of portraying a sense of individuality that is interesting and sincere.

These characteristics may strike a chord of discomfort for some people because they inherently clash with personal and/or cultural values. Rather than try to change your entire value system or just fake it in the interview process, it is better to find a way to express yourself in ways that not only feel right for you but are comfortable for the recruiter as well. The first step in being able to do this requires some self analysis and reflection.

Clarify What You Want and What You Have to Offer

Before you try to compete in a culturally biased interview, you must have a clear understanding of your values, cultural heritage, and personal strengths. Too often people approach the job hunt with a one-down attitude of "I hope they like me." Remember, you will be spending the majority of your wakeful state on the job, and thus should be interviewing with an attitude of "I hope I like them." Ideally, you want to land a job that is enjoyable as well as compatible with your value system.

In order to do this, you need to develop a set of criteria by which to evaluate potential organizations. These criteria should not be limited to salary and other benefits—these are poor compensation for a boring job that requires you to sell out your personal beliefs. Instead, consider what tasks you have found interesting and enjoyable in the past. Also, think about what values have impacted your life decisions. The most rewarding jobs are ones that are compatible with these criteria.

As important as clarifying what you want is knowing what you can do. The recruiter's job is to predict your future performance in the company based on your previous performance in academics, work, and other activities. You can make this task easier by having several ready examples of activities that clearly demonstrate your most marketable skills.

Research the Company

Once you have a solid picture of who you are and what you want, you need to get a clearer picture of each company that seriously interests you. This requires extensive research. Don't rely solely on your campus placement office. Instead, utilize the campus and public libraries to search for articles about the organization or its employees. Talk to customers or clients who use the services or products of the organization and ask them for their impressions. Talk to employees of the organization and find out how they feel about working there. Contact the public relations department of the corporation and ask them to send you any information that will give insight into the values of the organization and its leaders. Talk to members of professional organizations who might be able to tell you how the company rates in the industry. Talk to teachers, advisors, placement center staff and the alumni office for names of previous graduates who may know something about the specific organization or the industry as a whole.

Company research is key in surviving the culturally biased interview. Gathering information about the company increases the opportunity for you to examine their corporate culture, learning what they value in employees. Compare this to what you have determined to be personally important to you; then decide if the company will be a good match. You can also go to the interview better prepared to impress the recruiter.

Making Cultural Differences Work for You

If you find yourself in a situation where your personal values and style are at odds with the recruiter's, this doesn't mean you are destined to fail in the interview. Authenticity was mentioned as a positive quality in candidates by many recruiters. In conjunction with this they have reported they enjoy interviewing "interesting" students. You could be the only spot of color (literally and figuratively) on a recruiter's interview schedule—make it work to your advantage!

Remember, cultural bias in an interview is usually not intentional. Interviewers evaluate you with a certain perspective they may not even be aware is discriminatory. Use the interview as an opportunity to share insights about your cultural norms and values. Change the recruiter's perspective! Be careful, however, to weave relevance into your information—what you share should be pertinent to the type of employee you would make. To exemplify how this could be done, consider the plight of the three candidates mentioned in the beginning of this article.

In the case of Everett Begay, in the tradition of his Navajo culture, he was showing the recruiter great respect by offering a gentle handshake and limiting direct eye contact. In addition, leadership among his people is demonstrated in deeds, not words, and cooperation for the good of the group is highly valued. Thus, he was not inclined to talk about his individual accomplishments. Unfortunately, most recruiters would interpret these behaviors as indicating that Everett was a shy underachiever. Everett could have corrected this misinterpretation by explaining his behavior during the course of the interview. For example, if asked "Tell me about yourself" he could have replied, "In order to tell you about myself, I need first to tell you a little about my culture. Are you very familiar with Native American traditions?" He could go on from there to clue in the recruiter.

For Ana Gonzales to talk about her family in relation to her long-term goals was natural. Growing up in the barrios, family had always been a major focus of her life. Thanks to their love and encouragement, she was the first child in her family to graduate from college. But the recruiter could misconstrue her emphasis to mean that career would not be as important as family and her job performance would suffer as a result.

Ana could have improved her answer by sharing with the recruiter what it was like growing up in the barrios and the important role family played in her graduation from college. This could shed light on why financing her sister's education was so important, and leave the recruiter with the impression that Ana is a person of integrity and determination. Ana could have strengthened her answer by combining personal and professional goals.

Unfortunately, there is still a strong misconception that women who have children are going to be less productive than male co-workers, so women should avoid mentioning plans to start a family no matter how distant those plans might be.

Dwight Williams was known among his peers for his friendly, outgoing personality. In his efforts to ingratiate the recruiter, Dwight was talking to him as he would a peer. The recruiter misinterpreted this friendly attitude and assumed Dwight lacked professionalism. A more formal communication style coupled with his exuberant enthusiasm would have probably scored more points.

When the recruiter pressed Dwight about what he could offer the company, Dwight fell prey to the common assumption that paid work experience is the only way to demonstrate relevant skills. He could have emphasized transferable skills developed through participation in areas such as athletics, academics, church and community events. Some of the most marketable skills are those developed through non-paid activities. The recruiter needs to be convinced that not only do you want the job, but you have the skills necessary to do the job.

The Benefits of a Culturally Biased Interview

Culturally biased interviews can act as a screening tool for you to eliminate organizations. You should prepare for an interview, express your strengths in a context the recruiter understands, and attempt to share insights into your cultural heritage. If you do this and still come away feeling the interview was a bomb, maybe that particular company was not a good match for you. After all, would you really want to work for an organization that could not appreciate your cultural heritage?

If you suspect the interview went poorly because of personal discrimination on the part of the recruiter, being screened out can help you decide how much you really want to work for that organization. If, based on your company research, you feel the company is still the best match for you, write to someone else in the company. Get the name of someone in the specific department where you want to work, explain why you want to work for them and what you have to offer. Mention that you had the opportunity to interview with one representative of the organization, but felt you would like to talk with an additional person. This extra effort and persistence often impresses employers and results in a second interview and an eventual job offer.

Some Final Comments

Remember that enthusiasm doesn't have to be portrayed through high energy and a "cheerleading" demeanor. Quiet people can convey enthusiasm by indicating their desire to work in the industry and by asking informed questions about the company.

If you find yourself stumped by a question you don't know how to answer, don't fake it. Instead of trying to tell the recruiter what you think he or she wants to hear, answer truthfully. A simple "I'm not sure" or a request for clarification is appropriate. Your honesty will make a better impression than a fumbled attempt to bluff. Recruiters realize that we are all human; to retain your composure through a nerve-wracking interview is admirable in itself.

Many people feel insecure about interviewing when they have a low GPA. Though repeated studies have shown that college GPA is not a good indicator of future job performance, some recruiters still ask about it. If your GPA is not high, admit it but let the recruiter know it is not a good indicator of your abilities. Then, go on to talk about what you can do and offer specific examples of past performance to back up your statements.

For many college students, the formal corporate interview process is unfamiliar and frightening. To get over any fear and improve your performance, go through a practice or mock interview.

If you follow these general interviewing tips, you will perform better in any interview situation regardless of the recruiter's gender or color. You will also be better able to assess each organization's corporate culture and make a solid decision which company is the best for you.

Storytelling as an Interviewing Art Form

Successful interviewees are those that can give enough vivid, unique information in their responses to capture the recruiter's attention. Not only do the recruiters find their responses interesting but also memorable.

For example, when doing a practice interview with a student, I asked him "What qualities do you look for in a good supervisor?"

He paused for a short while and then said, "I think a good supervisor is one who is hard-working, willing to help out when needed, can give clear direction and develop teamwork."

That was an okay answer, but not great. Later, when going over his performance I asked the student if there were any questions he found particularly difficult. He smiled and said, "Oh yeah. That one about a good supervisor. All I could think of was my old captain on the fishing boat I worked on during the summer in Alaska. Eddie was this big, burly guy with a long, white beard. I always admired him because he was super hard working and would get down and dirty with the rest of us. He didn't act superior. And our boat had the highest safety record in the harbor because he was able to tell us exactly who should be doing what and where. We never got in each other's way and functioned as a team on dangerous high seas. But I didn't think I should mention him because he wasn't a professional or anything."

His second answer said essentially the same thing as the first, but in a much more colorful manner. When you answer questions, give a slice of life in your response when possible. Paint a thumbnail sketch for the recruiter that can give insight into your personality and make you a memorable candidate.

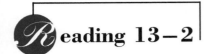
HOW TO PROVE YOUR WAY TO A JOB OFFER

We have looked at each of the three steps required to prove a strength:

Step I: State the strength you will prove.

Step II: Experience episode.

Step III: Tell what has just been proven.

Putting the three steps together in a concise mini-presentation (SET) will dramatically improve interviewing success. Examine our three examples with all three steps put together in a SET (note the transition through each step).

Example A: SET to Prove Leadership. "My greatest strength is motivating and leading others to achieve a defined goal. I have always had a high degree of energy and impatience to get things done. For example, I was elected chairman of the Homecoming Float Committee for three years in a row. I had the real challenge of supervising and coordinating the efforts of as many as fifty high school students to get the floats done on time. We received the first-place trophy for each of the three years—a record that still stands at the school. I continued gaining successful leadership experience during my college years as a class officer and as a project leader for our senior project. In that project I managed a team of eight engineering students whose prescribed goal was to design and build a concrete boat. I think I played a key role in building a great team spirit, and a little bit of each of us went down when she was sunk to become a fish haven. To summarize, I believe that these examples show that my greatest strength is leadership to motivate others to achieve prescribed goals."

Example B: SET to Prove Social Poise Necessary to Entertain Customers. "I believe that being close to customers is a critically important aspect of sales. I enjoy the company of a wide variety of personality types and a broad spectrum of activities from golf to opera. Personally, I think the requirement to entertain customers in various cultural and social settings adds real excitement to the sales process. A nice restaurant can certainly offer a complementary atmosphere in which to conduct business, and I appreciate a fine wine and excellent food presentation, but a pleasant round of golf or an evening of theater can be equally effective. The real purpose of entertainment is to leave the guest with a good feeling about the salesperson, the company, and the time spent together sharing a social experience. With a 12 handicap, I can offer a good round of golf to any caliber player without risking embarrassment to a guest or myself. Also, as indicated on my resume, I enjoy a wide variety of interests; the entertainment function would just enhance my own quality of life. The entertainment function of the sales position would be a real pleasure, not a chore."

Example C: SET to Prove Competence in Field. "I believe that grades do have a reasonable amount of validity in predicting ability and competence, but I also feel that experience carries equal value. As you can see from my resume, I have a 3.1 grade point average. The grades demonstrate an achieved level of technical understanding in marketing, but I believe the real strength I have to offer is the ability to take the theory and book learning and apply the knowledge in a business environment. Last summer I worked as an intern at Ajax Company—they manufacture more than fifty different kinds of kitchen utensils. I was assigned to the advertising/brand management division to assist in the release of a new product. The marketing study I completed was used to determine the testing area demographics. I received an outstanding rating at the end of the summer and in fact have received an offer from Ajax to enter their training program. By the way, the product has been very successful and is projected to represent 2 percent of sales by the third quarter of next year. I feel confident that my formal training and the solid field experience I have discussed prove my technical competence to achieve results."

Conclusion

Using SETS to substantiate and prove that you offer certain strengths is a powerful tool that clearly separates you from the competition. Have you ever been interviewed for a position that you knew you could handle and would enjoy and yet still received a turndown? Have you ever wondered why you received a turndown from an interview that went well? *Unless required strengths are proven, the interviewer will never extend an offer.*

You should develop and practice several SETS that prove the strengths you offer. They should not be memorized, but rather should flow naturally in a conversational manner during the interview. A SET can often be modified slightly to prove many different strengths. For example, the job candidate who used the float-building experience episode could slightly modify the SET and use it to prove ability to work as a team player.

SETS should be brief, concise, and focused to ensure that the interviewer is convinced that you do, in fact, offer that strength. Few candidates realize the importance of proving *required* strengths. You are now one of the few—congratulations.

Source: John LaFevre, *How You Really Get Hired,* 1986. Used by permission of the publisher, ARCO/A division of Simon & Schuster, New York.

Chapter Fourteen

Communicating Interpersonally

PREVIEW

Effective oral interactions—activities like talking out a problem, kicking around an idea, settling differences, and building trust—often make the difference between a productive and an unproductive business organization. This chapter presents a useful model for interpersonal communication. Then it covers two essential aspects of processing incoming information. Active listening is a group of skills rarely taught in any deliberate way yet crucial to business success. Perceiving and evaluating nonverbal communication are closely related to active listening. People's nonverbal communication is more often misunderstood than is their verbal communication. We will look at why that is so, explain what to do about it, and describe how to control the nonverbal signals we ourselves send. ●

**Jason Witter
Production Supervisor**

$\mathscr{F}$rom the desk of...

My co-supervisor, Paul, and I began working together about four months ago. Together we are overseeing the critical first six months of production of a component several large equipment companies are relying on. Each of us runs one line. He's a competent guy—I think.

So why am I worried? When we exchange information about routine problems and solutions, he searches my face as if he's not sure what he's saying is right, or not sure it's okay with me—I don't know, exactly. What he says is okay—the words are, anyway. He hesitates a lot when he talks, and acts nervous. He's really knowledgeable. He reads everything, and he's on top of an amazing amount of production detail. But I've realized several times, after we've solved a problem, that he remembers all the detail in the conversation but not the main idea. He evidently goes and works it out correctly himself—so far. . . .

Frankly, I'm on edge. Our job is to spot and solve production problems. If we can't communicate better we could miss something, and it could be horrendously expensive. But I'm not even sure why I'm uneasy. So how do I bring it up with *him?*

PERCEPTION AND ATTITUDE

Considering the receiver is as important in interpersonal communication as it is in writing.

Chapter 1 discussed the differences in the way different people perceive the same experiences and the different attitudes, backgrounds, experiences, emotions, values, and needs creating their differences in perception.

Other earlier chapters touched on the need to examine the nature of the audience or the reader before writing a business message. The same need characterizes ordinary daily dialog, in which we easily revert to the me-centered focus that comes to us so naturally. We forget that those differences we examined are still present and active. In the spontaneous stream of speech, often we speak before we think enough about what might be misunderstood. As listeners, too, we settle comfortably into our own frame of reference and thereby isolate ourselves from another's intended meaning. As both senders and receivers, we lose out—and so does our organization.

INFLUENCING AND INFORMING

We cannot purposefully influence others unless we know who they are, how they think and feel and how strongly, why they feel that way, and how they view us and the surrounding situation. We cannot inform others unless we know who they are, what they already know, what they need, and why they need it. When we receive, process, and evaluate incoming information accurately, we begin to know how to influence and inform.

TEAMWORK

The most effective teams value cooperation more than competition.

In response to international competition, U.S. organizations are increasing emphasis on teamwork. Teamwork relies on the willingness of group members to understand the needs of co-workers and of the organization and to value cooperation more highly than personal competition.

This team orientation comes harder to Americans, on the average, than to many other peoples. From the time of the first European migrations, Americans have been—not selfish, necessarily—but self-absorbed. Until recently, our history, biography, and fiction have featured individuals, not groups, who conquered obstacles and became heroes. Now, as the global business perspective

EXHIBIT 14–1   Johari Grid

Johari Grid

	Person A is aware	Person A is unaware
Person B is aware	Public or Open **A**	Blind **B**
Person B is unaware	Hidden **C**	Unknown or Unconscious **D**

Source: Joseph Luft, *Of Human Interaction* (Palo Alto, Calif.: National Press Books, 1969).

expands, Americans are learning the value of interdependence in addition to independence and initiative.

The synergy principle says that a functional group produces more than the sum of individual members' efforts alone. The payoff "increases the size of the pie to divide," and everyone's reward rises. In this light, contributing one's best to a group makes excellent sense. Still, to work effectively as team members, individuals must learn and incorporate the perspectives of others and must master the skills needed to exchange those perspectives.

A synergistic group produces more than the sum of individual members' efforts.

COMMON GROUND AND TRUST

Mastering these skills is not easy. People have to start with self-knowledge, and self-knowledge, as Kurt Vonnegut has said, "is always bad news." We like looking at the pleasant things about ourselves and tend to avoid the unpleasant things. From this semi-stable basis, we take in and process information about others—at least, as much information as they are willing to give us. Each side builds trust cautiously. We rarely have as much information as would be ideal; yet we must act anyway.

Before we take up listening and nonverbal communication, let us lay some groundwork. Two theorists, Joseph Luft and Harrington Ingham, diagrammed the information about a sender that is or could be available to another person in a communication encounter. This diagram, called the **Johari Grid,** is shown in Exhibit 14–1.

Johari Grid

Quadrant A of the Johari Grid, called the Open or Public area, contains the information both sender and receiver know. Quadrant B, the Blind area, contains the information the sender is unaware of but the receiver is aware of. Quadrant C, the Hidden area, contains the information the sender is aware of but is concealing from the receiver. Quadrant D, the Unknown or Unconscious area, contains the information that neither sender nor receiver knows about but that may still influence the interaction. Let's look at a case using the Johari Grid.

The Johari Grid diagrams the complexity involved in understanding another person's messages.

Communicating Interpersonally

The sender is Jerry, and the receiver is Mike. The two have worked for the same company for three years and sometimes play slow-pitch ball together on weekends. Outside the job, Mike has what he considers a very solid project in which he would like to involve Jerry. They have talked about it from time to time. Jerry has been mildly interested but noncommittal. Today Mike says that he mainly needs Jerry's time and expertise to add to his own, but the $1,000 he has already laid out in materials didn't quite stretch. He is nearly ready to sell the project and has located a buyer, but he also needs $250 from Jerry.

- In Quadrant A, the Open area, we place all of Jerry's verbal and nonverbal signals he knowingly sends today that are received as he intended them. We also place there the history accumulated over the last three years of which both men are aware.
- In Quadrant B, the Blind area, we place what Mike can see that Jerry is unaware of. For instance, Mike thinks Jerry's hands fidget more than usual. Jerry seems less attentive than usual. His eyes look red. Mike thinks, "Tears? Smoke? Too much liquor?" and doesn't mention it. Mike remembers a stupid argument the two had a year ago about a softball game loss and wonders whether Jerry's wish to change the subject means he is still sore about it.
- In Quadrant C, the Hidden area, we place what Jerry knows but conceals from Mike. For example, Jerry hates to part with money, dislikes this trait in himself, and has therefore given generously to office collections for good causes. Jerry is working on a project of his own, not similar to Mike's but one Jerry has financed on his own. Although he knows Mike's work is good, he disapproves of the inadequate money planning. He also worked late last night, and his head aches. And so on.
- In Quadrant D, the Unknown area, we place such things as Jerry's repressed and forgotten guilt over a very foolish $300 bet he once placed and lost, as well as Jerry's unrecognized partiality to people who remind him, as Mike does, of his dad's youngest brother, the uncle who used to take him often to the video arcade and supply him with quarters. And so on.

We would need to make a second grid to diagram the encounter with Mike as sender and Jerry as receiver. You can see from this one sketchy analysis the built-in problems in an interaction in which each communicator considers that he is "acting normal."

In a successful interaction, the Open area grows. Ideally, with each interaction senders become more aware of what they are sending. The Blind area diminishes, and receivers help senders by being tactful and candid. Ideally, senders decide to reveal more of (or diminish the importance of) the Hidden area's content, and receivers help them by being worthy of trust. Sometimes continued interaction even brings to the surface some of the repressed or unrecognized content of the Unknown area. As a relationship develops and trust grows, Quadrants B, C, and D become less influential.

Agendas in Interpersonal Communication

The reason or goal for a communication is the communicator's **agenda.** In an ordinary conversation, a sender's agenda might be "getting to know you." In addition, however, a second agenda might be "learning how you might be of use to me and making you willing to be." This **hidden agenda** also "drives" some of the interaction. Many hidden agendas are manipulative or even sinister.

Agendas can be overt or hidden.

If the sender creates and maintains a facade and the receiver perceives the sender pretending to be what she is not, the receiver is likely to do the same. The open area will not grow much. Both communicators might develop hidden agendas.

If problems arise between two communicators in the same culture, consider how much more troublesome these areas of blindness, dissimilar expectations, and inaccurate interpretations become in intercultural or international settings. In cultures valuing soft speech and self-control, a communicator who uses a forceful voice to convey authority makes the opposite impression. When communicators from different cultures converse to "break the ice" before beginning business, different personal topics are acceptable or unacceptable. Americans might mention or inquire about a spouse and children, but to many businesspersons in the Middle East such a topic invades privacy. Such interpersonal and intercultural errors might diminish rather than expand trust.

Successful interpersonal behavior in organizations depends on communicators' willingness to work toward openness, cooperation, trust, teamwork, and group or organizational goals. An essential skill set for achieving this is active listening.

ACTIVE LISTENING

Most people believe they are good listeners. Few are. Studies show that after an interval of just a few hours, most people retain only about 25 percent of what they heard. Hearers tend to pass the responsibility for their inattention on to the speaker: "If you want me to listen, you have to keep me interested." Active listening and simply hearing are very different. Many people just hear.

Most listeners retain only about 25 percent of what they hear.

Causes of Poor Listening

Research on listening has pointed out causes of poor listening in American culture. First, unlike many Asian nations' schools, our schools reward young children for asserting themselves ("I know, Teacher! I know! I know! Call on me!") rather than for working silently to absorb what they are taught. As children become adults, they perceive that others pay attention to the talkers rather than to the listeners. The listeners seem to be unimportant, passive, and compliant.

Then too, every day and from all sides Americans are bombarded by demands for their attention: radio and television programs, advertisements, conversation, traffic, ringing phones, and much more. In these noisy surroundings, many people form habits of inattention just to let themselves concentrate. These habits create unrecognized barriers when others talk to these people.

PEANUTS reprinted by permission of UFS, Inc.

Lucy Van Pelt is a serious bad-listening case. She doesn't even *pretend* to listen.

A communication barrier called **allness** inhibits good listening. "I already know all about that," we often think when we simply don't want to be bothered with new information. We also tend to write off people who don't communicate very effectively. "I'm never going to hear anything I need from him," we think, and the mental wall goes up as this person tries to tell us something. The speaker believes we need the information. Some of the time he will be absolutely right—and we will lose.

Research shows that the mind can process information about three times as fast as most people speak. Our minds have spare time. The extra time is best used to integrate the new information with what we already know. Unfortunately, many people leave this spare time idle or work out what they will say next (which makes them begin debating the speaker and perhaps even stop processing the new information). Or they daydream, looking at the speaker but only pretending to pay attention.

Daydreaming, if controlled, is healthy. People's attention spans (their capacity for unbroken concentration) vary from a few seconds to a few minutes. At these intervals, the mind takes short side trips to other topics, lingers there briefly, and then (if we are trying) comes back, refreshed, to the here and now. The trick is to make oneself come back. Those side trips may be pleasure jaunts, as the person imagines driving the dream car fast on a long stretch of open road. They may be work trips, where a continuing worry reasserts itself and the person hunts for the solution. Poor listeners tune out without even being aware of it.

Use spare thinking time to integrate new information.

Effective Listening Behaviors

Effective listening is a set of behaviors. Making the behaviors into habits and retaining the habits take constant effort. All our laziest impulses get in the way, and we backslide constantly. Our best advice is to review the following list every six months. Good listeners know that these habits need reinforcement.

- *Do not interrupt.* All that extra brain time gives you ample material, and the temptation to assert yourself is strong.

- *Defer judgment* of what you are hearing. A poor listener takes in the first few words, thinks "Oh, that again," or "This is boring" (too difficult, irrelevant, disorganized, stupid, a typical tech mindset, beancounter mentality, touchy-feely, the union line, and so on) and tunes out. The good listener hears the speaker out before evaluating what she hears.

Undisciplined emotional reactions create barriers to listening.

- *Do not react emotionally* to a point you may disagree with. Good listeners look for common ground and try to increase it. Poor listeners look for differences, get involved emotionally, and close their minds.

- *Watch nonverbals* to be certain you are receiving the whole message or, indeed, the real message. Use your sight as well as your hearing. Try to be empathetic and intuitive. Observe nonverbals, not to criticize them but to comprehend more fully. As we will discuss in more detail shortly, sometimes nonverbals carry far more information than verbal messages do—or even contradict them.

- *Listen to learn.* Be a curious person with an open mind. Do not dismiss topics or ideas as dull. Usually it's not the topic that is dull; it's the dull mind that shuts it out.

- *Do not be distracted by the speaker's differences from you.* Our biases are triggered by differences in age, race, sex, or type of word choice;

by nonverbals such as stance, grooming, and clothing; and even by differences in personal attractiveness.

- *Minimize distractions.* In noisy surroundings, move the encounter to a quieter place, if possible. If not, concentrate harder to filter out the intrusive signals.

- *Sift the main ideas from the details,* and try to remember the important points. The mind distracted by the interesting small stuff misses what is critical. The result is cluttered, hard to organize, and even harder to remember.

- *Control your outward behavior as a listener.* The speaker is watching you. Your high eye contact, your murmured "Mm-hmm," "I see," "Go on," your open posture, and your encouraging facial expressions help the speaker continue confidently and enhance the speaker's trust in you. If you avert your face, turn your shoulder to the person, sigh, or rattle papers (you can fill out the list), the speaker must deal with disappointment and struggle to go on. He might give up. Worse, to try to please you, he might alter what he was going to say. You don't just lose a truth. You gain a distortion.

- *In highly charged situations, paraphrase.* Occasionally both speaker and listener feel stressed. Both are tempted to forget courtesy, turn taking, and the other conventions of productive conversation. Active listening nearly goes out the window.

  Then the listener remembers the technique of paraphrasing. He says, "We're probably not understanding each other fully. After you tell me your point, I'll try to put it in my own words. You tell me if I'm right or not. If I'm right, then I'll respond. If you aren't satisfied that I understand, tell me again until I can summarize to your satisfaction what you have said."

  Paraphrasing forces both communicators to try harder. They have to agree on words and on meanings of words. Their consensus on what was said lays the groundwork for agreement, or at least understanding, on the point at issue. Cooperation becomes possible.

The Payoffs of Good Listening

Knowledge is power. Information gives the edge to those who possess it. The most current information usually has not been written down yet. To obtain it, stay tuned in. Listen.

Good listening raises productivity.

Good listening is closely linked to productivity. To perform a task correctly, an active listener needs to hear a set of instructions only once. Poor listeners waste the organization's resources, giving rise to the adage, "There's never time to do it right, but there's always time to do it over."

People deeply need to be heard. When you listen to another person, you help that individual develop, motivate him, and usually earn or increase his loyalty to you. Denied listening is punitive. It makes people feel angry and diminished, and it makes them avoid you.

No doubt you know a few people whose talk offers little of value to you. Yet one day one of them will know something that will make a great difference to you. If you have rebuffed that person's attempts to talk to you previously, you will not hear from her on the day you need to.

As you listen actively to subordinates and co-workers, you model correct listening behavior to them. An organization whose workers are good listeners is more productive.

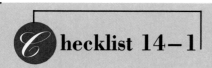

Checklist 14–1

Good Listening Behavior

As a listener, do I

- Use spare mental processing time to integrate the new information?
- Resist distractions?
- Maintain high eye contact?
- Control daydreaming?
- Defer judging or second-guessing until I have heard the whole story?
- Watch the speaker's nonverbals to understand better?
- Learn from listening (WIIFM)?
- Listen for the main ideas?
- Empathize with the speaker to see the matter as he or she does?
- Offer supportive nonverbals to encourage the speaker?
- Paraphrase or question in cases of ambiguous information or stress?

As a listener, do I *avoid*

- Prejudging the speaker?
- Prejudging the subject?
- Interrupting or finishing the speaker's sentences?
- Internally debating the speaker?
- Faking attention?
- Reacting emotionally?
- Getting distracted by the speaker's differences from me?
- Giving discouraging nonverbals such as fidgeting, turning away, or doing other work?

When Do You Stop Listening?

Does all this mean that you should listen to everyone just as long as each of them wants to talk to you? That would be foolish. Time is money, and not all talkers understand brevity or staying to the point.

Listen until you are sure you have understood. Then, if you are busy, close the conversation in a tactful way. Refer to the work you must do, and use nonverbals to reinforce what you say. Be pleasant. If appropriate, suggest that the two of you talk again later.

Poor listeners sometimes find out too late what they missed. Often they never find out at all. Good listeners include many of the world's most powerful and influential managers. Some explicitly cite the importance of listening, as does Lee Iacocca, well-known chairman and CEO of Chrysler Corporation during the 1980s:

> I only wish I could find an institute that teaches people how to *listen.* After all, a good manager needs to listen at least as much as he needs to talk. Too many people fail to realize that real communication goes in both directions.
>
> In corporate life, you have to encourage all your people to make a contribution to the common good and to come up with better ways of doing things. You don't have to accept every single suggestion, but if you don't get back to the guy and say, "Hey, that idea was terrific," and pat him on the back, he'll never give you another one. That kind of communication lets people know they really count.
>
> You have to be able to listen well if you're going to motivate the people who work for you. Right there, that's the difference between a mediocre company and a great company. The most fulfilling thing for

Superstock, Inc.

Nonverbals are eloquent but sometimes ambiguous. What is in these nonverbals, viewed left to right? Passivity, dominance, engrossment, and suspicion? Or avoidance, earnestness, boredom, and admiration? To be certain, we would need to observe longer.

me as a manager is to watch someone the system has labeled as just average or mediocre really come into his own, all because someone has listened to his problems and helped him solve them.[1]

To conclude this section, consider these maxims:

- Nature gave us two ears but only one mouth. That should tell us something.
- Our ears won't shut, but our mouth will.
- Nobody ever learned anything with his mouth open.

Checklist 14–1 will help you assess your listening behaviors.

NONVERBAL COMMUNICATION

Actual words convey only 10 to 30 percent of a spoken message's meaning. The rest is nonverbal.

Experts say that between 70 and 90 percent of a sender's meaning is transmitted nonverbally. As is true of active listening, we rarely stop to examine this communication component. But we have excellent reason to examine it. For instance, research shows that many job interviewers decide only a minute or two into an interview whether a candidate will be a good hire and then spend the remaining 20 or 30 minutes selectively perceiving evidence that confirms their quick judgment.

Ambiguity and Multiple Meanings

When we send worded messages, we take care to choose unambiguous words and clarify through context when a word has multiple meanings. Nonverbal signals carry higher risks of ambiguity, for several reasons.

[1]Lee Iacocca with W. Novak, *Iacocca: An Autobiography* (New York: Bantam Books, 1984), p. 58.

Nonverbals occur in clusters—in infinite combinations. These clusters include what the eye muscles do, what the hands do, the use of surrounding space, and so on. In practice, a nonverbal signal rarely occurs alone. For instance, a person who widens his or her eyes could be signaling surprise but could also be communicating horror or disgust. Interpreting correctly depends on what else the person does. If the eyebrows lift and the mouth smiles or remains relaxed, we read pleasant surprise. If the eyebrows do not move and the head is pulled sharply backward, the negative interpretation is probably correct.

Different cultures' meanings for nonverbal signals differ. After a class, an American student waved "bye" (extending her hand, palm down, and wiggling the fingers) to an acquaintance from Southeast Asia. The Asian student, who had nearly reached the door, returned at once and asked, "Yes? What else did you need to say to me?" In her country, that gesture is a polite "Come here," and Americans' gesture for "come here" (palm *up*, fingers wiggling) is used only to summon dogs or inferiors.

People assume that some nonverbals are universal. Some, such as a smile, may be nearly so, but a smile under the wrong circumstances can be insulting. Some Asian peoples cover anger or embarrassment with a fixed smile.

Desmond Morris's book *Gestures* examines 20 nonverbal hand signals.[2] Researchers interviewed residents in more than 1,000 localities all over Europe and the Middle East. Several of the signals, such as pursing together the fingers and thumb or tugging the lower eyelid downward, mean nothing to most Americans. In the United States, these signals are used only in population enclaves containing residents from countries where they do have meaning. They carry definite but varying meanings abroad. The hand-purse gesture means "What is it? What do you mean?" in much of Italy, "I'm afraid" in Belgium, and "Many, lots" in Spain. The eyelid tug can mean "Be watchful" or "I'm suspicious of you," depending on where you are.

The American "A-OK" gesture, in which one makes a ring of the index finger and thumb and extends the other three fingers, is understood in Brazil as an indecent sexual comment. In Japan the same finger-and-thumb ring means "money." In France it means "zero."

When a nonverbal message contradicts a verbal one, receivers tend to believe the nonverbal message. Businesspeople usually speak deliberately. Although they control what they say, they may not always control or even realize what they are *doing* as they speak. For this reason, observers infer that a speaker's real intent shows in the less deliberate nonverbal behavior accompanying the verbal message. When verbal and nonverbal behaviors reinforce each other, all is well. When they conflict, however, receivers perceive the nonverbal behavior as more revealing.

Suppose a subordinate has made a serious error. She tries to explain at some length the reason for the mistake. Meanwhile her supervisor listens, with face rigid and averted. The explanation finished, a long pause ensues. Then the boss says unsmilingly, in an even, controlled tone, "Well, Jane, don't worry about it. That'll be all." Jane couldn't even get eye contact from the boss. She leaves the office feeling doomed.

When a nonverbal conflicts with the speaker's words, the receiver will believe the nonverbal message.

[2]Desmond Morris, Peter Collett, Peter Marsh, and Marie O'Shaughnessy, *Gestures* (New York: Stein and Day, 1979).

The same nonverbal signal can send different messages. Interpretation can depend on the perceiver. A woman tells of looking at packaged light bulbs in a store. Deep in thought but perfectly content, she was pondering wattage, brand, tint, and price. Someone passing by in the aisle glanced at her frown of concentration and said, "Cheer up! Life can't be that bad."

Interpretation can depend on the situation. The identical behavior—a chuckle, for instance—can be exactly right at a business lunch but highly out of place in a courtroom.

The same nonverbal message can be sent by the same person in multiple ways. In some circumstances, a person might communicate anger by raised voice and contracted facial muscles. In another setting, the same person might communicate anger by an impassive face, a long silence, and short, noncommittal words.

We cannot NOT communicate nonverbally. Even if a person opts to sit rigidly in a chair, a passerby might notice him and wonder, "Why is that guy sitting there like a rock? Wonder if I should ask if he's sick. Maybe he's angry. Maybe he's a nut." If the same person relaxes his posture, hoping to avoid making that rigid impression, a viewer might think, "That fellow sure has it easy. I wish I had time just to sit around like that." Others interpret our behavior constantly, even when we may have no intention of communicating.

We lack the words and a supporting environment for discussing nonverbal communication in the workplace. Hence we can be uncertain about it but have little opportunity to check our impressions with another observer. A given cluster of nonverbals might puzzle us, but we might feel foolish asking, "What does Bill mean when he holds his eyebrows just like that?" The other observer might ask, "Huh? Like what?" "Didn't you see?" "I didn't notice anything." If you ask Bill, Bill might say, "I wasn't," "I didn't mean anything," or "Do you have an eyebrows problem?" and laugh at you. Yet you know what you saw, and you still don't quite understand.

One option is to try to put into words what you think is intended: "You seem to feel a little skeptical. Is that right?" or "I hope I hear you saying that you've found the funny side of this dilemma."

Lacking words for talking about specific nonverbal messages makes those messages' ambiguity even more a problem.

Evaluate others' nonverbals cautiously. Refrain from snap judgments. Before you decide that a given nonverbal "means" this or that, watch the individual for a while to see what nonverbals are simply part of his or her ordinary patterns, that is, the individual's **behavioral baseline.** One person, for instance, keeps her hand near her mouth much of the time when conversing. This nonverbal sometimes means an individual is lying. After a few minutes, though, the person she is talking to realizes that her front teeth are a little crooked and she is self-conscious about it.

Some writers on nonverbal communication advise observers to watch a speaker's nonverbals closely for signs of untruthfulness. They use the term **nonverbal leakage** to refer to a speaker's unintentional nonverbal disclosure of negative or contradictory information. However, the hand-to-face nonverbal just mentioned *also* sometimes accompanies doubt, hesitation, or thoughtfulness on the part of the speaker.

Our best advice is to watch nonverbals but remain aware of the multiple meanings many of them have. Also, remember that people sometimes conceal information for inoffensive reasons. The person touching her cheek, for in-

Interpreting: Establish Behavioral Baseline First

Withhold judgment of a speaker's nonverbals till you know what is ordinary behavior for him or her.

stance, may actually be uncomfortable about the subject matter or uncertain about her authority to speak about it, while what she *says* about it will be perfectly true. People do lie sometimes, but convicting them on the basis of nonverbals alone would be foolish.

Recognize cultural differences in behavioral baselines too, domestically as well as abroad. We will refer to some of them as we discuss the nonverbals typical of the mainstream U.S. culture. Each culture evolves its own "rules" of behavior. No single set of rules is better or worse than any other, although the usefulness of a set or of a given behavior may be less functional in some situations than in others.

For instance, many women in Asian countries are socialized to speak very softly. In the United States, they may be at a competitive disadvantage not only with men but also with women who speak strongly and assertively. Conversely, if an American frowns, paces, or pounds a fist on a table in a nation where people cover annoyance with light laughter, a smile, or an impassive face, the American may be seen as lacking self-control.

Be Aware of and Control What You Send

Control the nonverbal signals you send. Replace bad habits with habits that support your communication goals. As you read the material to come, reflect on your own practice in each of the categories. Each of us develops an image. John T. Molloy has this to say about image, based on interviewing 1,000 executives:

> Almost all the men and women we interviewed agreed that success has more to do with . . . energy than image. However, 98.5 percent of those interviewed also believe that successful image— including dressing correctly, moving correctly, and speaking correctly—is critical to getting ahead. They believe that a person who dresses conservatively, speaks standard English, and carries himself in an erect manner has a better chance of impressing people, and succeeding, than someone who does not.[3]

With respect to image, Molloy also says that people succeed best in business when they project upper-middle-class dress, carriage, and speech patterns. Not leisure class or jet set, not blue-collar, not ethnic, "normal" in business is the upper-middle-class image.

Power, Status, and Nonverbals

People convey dominance or submissiveness nonverbally.

In the discussion of active listening, you read about the set of nonverbal behaviors that encourages another person to communicate. As we look around us, however, we can readily see that these nonverbal behaviors are not always forthcoming.

People with power and status often display dominating nonverbals. These include frowning or staring, taking up more physical space, standing over a less powerful person, and so on. Often the spoken words accompanying these behaviors are mild and encouraging, but the less powerful person "gets the message" all the same. Typically he or she displays submissive nonverbals in response, such as nodding a lot, lowering the head, averting the eyes, and so on.

Research suggests that women more often display submissive nonverbals and men more often display dominating ones. If you observe this to be true of yourself or of others, some behavior modification may be in order.

[3]John T. Molloy, *Molloy's Live for Success* (New York: Bantam/Perigord Press, 1981), p. 2.

Most of what we say about nonverbal communication addresses nonverbal behavior typical of mainstream American culture. As we go along, we will point out some (but by no means all) differences between this culture and that of other nations and of important alternative cultures within our own borders.

Mainstream U.S. Nonverbal Communication

The United States has always been home to many cultures. Still, a fairly well-understood set of nonverbal behaviors has come to represent desired and expected behavior in business. Although some businesspeople are learning to understand alternate behaviors, most newcomers understand that acceptance comes most quickly when they learn and accommodate mainstream culture.

Foreign-born workers in America have managers, co-workers, and subordinates. These American-born employees need to understand the boost to productivity that will occur when they try to learn more about what may seem unusual or inappropriate nonverbals on the part of newcomers. To the newcomers, their own nonverbals are the way things should be. The newcomers are usually dealing with considerable culture shock and trying to decipher the sometimes incomprehensible messages they are receiving.

In former times, the newcomers were expected to blend in. More recently, global business influences have made it worth Americans' while to learn about other cultures. Some have eagerly sought the new knowledge. Some have avoided it. Many business experts believe that avoiding it will not remain a successful strategy for long.

Although nonverbal signals usually occur in clusters, examining each category helps focus awareness on components of these messages. The categories are facial expression, posture, gesture and movement, time, space, touch, dress, surroundings and artifacts, and voice.

Categories of Nonverbals

Are any facial expressions universal? Probably not. Our many dozens of separate facial muscles permit almost infinite variations in expressions. So even a smile—probably our best candidate for universality—is not necessarily an expression connoting friendship and goodwill. Consider the forced smile, the frozen smile, the bland, impassive smile, the seductive smile, and the contemptuous smile. We can be sure that facial expression will differ in meaning from one culture to another. Indeed, they differ from one *person* to another and from one *situation* to another.

Meaning and Facial Expression

When facial expressions are well matched with verbal content, meaning is enhanced. When they are inconsistent, the receiver is puzzled and has to guess which message the sender intends. Most of the time, the receiver believes the nonverbal signal.

The muscles surrounding the eyes convey the greatest variety of expressions. People look at eyes when they are trying hard to understand what another person means. Mainstream American culture has well-understood (but seldom worded) rules about how long one person can look straight at another's eyes and convey only a neutral meaning. If gaze exceeds this time limit, the look takes on other meanings. The most common meanings for a lengthened gaze are hostility/threat and sexual interest.

Rules in other cultures differ greatly. Looking time in the Middle East is considerably longer than in America. Among American Navajos, looking straight at another person for more than a second or two is considered rude and intrusive. In Japan, people seldom look at eyes. A respectful gaze is directed at about the level of the other person's neck.

Mainstream American culture responds favorably to open, expressive faces. Certainly a speechmaker with a communicative face holds an audience's attention more easily than one with a wooden face. There are uses for the "poker face," however. Sometimes powerful people put on an inexpressive mask to intimidate others. When a face is unreadable, behavior is much harder to predict and the level of risk in the exchange might rise. Negotiators, too, are careful not to let their faces communicate information that puts them at a disadvantage.

Meaning and Posture

Businesspeople's standing posture should be erect and controlled, for both men and women. Feet should neither be tightly together nor too far apart. The person should appear evenly balanced and stable. Changing weight from foot to foot implies nervousness to most people. A slumped posture conveys fatigue, lack of energy, negative attitude, or other undesirable attributes.

When people communicate while seated, their posture should be erect. Expectations for women differ somewhat from those for men. Men can communicate attentiveness even when leaning back (but not slouching) in the chair. Women must sit erect and even lean forward a little to communicate attentiveness.

Meaning, Gesture, and Movement

Gestures can be meaningful in themselves or modify worded messages.

Gestures can carry meanings of their own and can modify or reinforce the meanings of worded messages. You can probably think of a gesture that substitutes clearly for

- I want to hurt you badly.
- Take it easy. Simmer down. Don't get all worked up.
- I'm so glad to be here! I love you all.
- We won! We won!
- Maybe yes, maybe no; I feel both ways about it.
- Get over here, and hurry up!

No accompanying words would be needed.

Gestures are also one means by which we regulate turn taking in conversation. We hold up a hand to mean "Wait, I'm not done yet" or extend a hand and nod the head to mean "Okay, your turn."

Sometimes we gesture to emphasize and add conviction to what we say. "Mark my words," we might say, jabbing a forefinger into the air with each word. "It's tough, but there's nothing I can do for you" might be accompanied by shrugged shoulders and extended hands, palms upward and out to the sides.

Sometimes we gesture to complement or further explain a worded message. "The shortest route turns north here and goes through Kentucky," we say as we move a finger along a line on a map. "The desktop should be this high," we explain, holding a hand palm down 30 inches from the floor.

Body position, degree of tension, degree of control of movement, speed and force of position change—all these communicate meaning to an observer. People control space with their bodies. Those who gesture in an expansive but controlled way seem larger and more powerful. People who "stand and sit small" and who gesture timidly give up perceived power by doing so.

Meaning and Time

The United States, Canada, and much of Europe adhere rather tightly to schedules. Many other places, however, have other ideas about time.

In the mainstream U.S. culture, lateness is usually an error—at times a grave error. For instance, an applicant who is 10 minutes late to a job interview has made a bad impression from which she probably cannot recover.

We speak of budgeting our time. We study time management. We carry our daily calendars with us and cram our days with tasks and appointments. We "make time" for people. We say people "waste our time" when we disagree with them about how time should be spent. *Spent* is the right word in the U.S. business culture. Time is a resource. We routinely place a dollar value on it, buy it, and sell it. If communications are late, their value drops drastically.

Status influences time and the value of time. The higher a person's status, the higher perceived value (sometimes monetary, sometimes intangible but still very real) placed on his or her time. A higher-status person typically controls time in an interview and gets to talk longer.

In Germany the trains run on time—period. In Ireland, they run on time sometimes. In Ireland, if a friend asks you to meet him "about 7 this evening," he might appear at 9:30 P.M. Do not be annoyed at his lateness. To him, this is not lateness.

In Mexico some lateness is expected, especially of a higher-status person. In the Middle East, time is viewed much more flexibly than in the United States. Things can be planned, but if they do not happen as scheduled, people say, *insh'allah* ("as God wills").

At a business appointment in the United States or Germany, people do one thing at a time. At a business appointment in Saudi Arabia, many activities might proceed simultaneously. Americans must not take it amiss when a Saudi conducts business with them in a roomful of people. Interruptions will be frequent. As Amelia Lobsenz writes, "In answer to the American who asks 'couldn't we speak privately?' the Arab will simply lean closer."[4]

Businesspeople in other cultures are aware of Americans' preoccupation with time and sometimes use it to their advantage. For instance, an American negotiating with a Japanese must be prepared to spend as much as a week or more just getting acquainted. After the actual negotiation opens, Japanese concessions are likely to be small and slow in coming. The American may feel he is getting nowhere. If he has told the Japanese the date of his return flight, he probably *is* getting nowhere. Often nothing much will happen until this known departure date nears and he is getting desperate. At this point, the American may well make large concessions just to get *some* business. He will do much better in this negotiation if he has an open-ended return ticket and lets the negotiation take all the time it requires.

Meaning and Space

Each culture generates "rules" about interpersonal space. If someone comes to America from a culture where people stand close together, she may mistakenly think, "They don't like me" when Americans take a step back from her.

Americans are used to having considerable personal space. We speak of four **zones** in interpersonal distance. Think of each as a circle with the individual at the center:

- Intimate—ranging from physical contact out to about 18 inches from a person.
- Personal—ranging from 18 inches to about 4 feet.

[4]Amelia Lobsenz, "When a Nod Means No," *Public Relations Journal,* October 1987, p. 36.

- Social—ranging from about 4 out to 10 or 12 feet from the individual.
- Public or impersonal—the distance beyond the social, out to infinity.

In business, the intimate zone would rarely be used. Such near approaches are reserved for family members, lovers, and the like. This rule is well understood and quite firm. If, for instance, a man in a workplace were repeatedly to invade this zone belonging to a specific woman, the woman would probably regard the behavior as a sexual message. It could even lead to a sexual harassment charge.

The personal zone is used for many interpersonal business exchanges. When two people meet and shake hands, they rarely approach closer than about 18 inches. When they continue their talk, they generally stand within four feet of each other. This distance implies, "I am paying attention mainly to you." If either one moves farther away, the other infers that she might be getting ready to end the exchange.

When several people meet in a hallway and stop to discuss something important, they use the personal zone. When they stand at this distance from one another, they are said to be "huddling." Seeing a small clump of people standing at this distance, intent in conversation, often discourages others from joining.

The social zone is suitable for less concentrated exchanges. Casual or brief exchanges occur in this zone.

To test the idea of public or interpersonal space, consider this: You are standing in a fairly large area. If someone walks by at about seven feet from you and looks at you, you think she is fairly likely to speak to you. If that same person walks by at about 14 feet from you and looks at you, you do not necessarily think she wants your attention.

Invading people's space bothers them and sometimes makes them feel threatened. Most people observe the conventions even though many would be unable to put those rules into words. For instance, suppose a large group in your firm is gathering in an auditorium. You go in, see a co-worker you like, and go to join him. If there are numerous open chairs, convention causes you to ask, "Mind if I sit here?" even when you know (1) he has no "rights" to any chair but the one he is sitting in and (2) it will be perfectly okay with him if you sit next to him. If there are numerous open chairs and you do *not* know the person sitting there, you will *not* select the chair right next to him. Convention demands that you leave space. The space will fill as more people come, but you will not sit down right next to someone unless most other spaces are taken.

The zone space in front of a person is more important than that at the side or in back. In the workplace, looking at someone face to face at a distance of 12 inches is quite threatening. It invokes the image of the drill sergeant shouting down the throat of the trembling recruit.

Certain situations permit people to stand closer for specified periods of time. Everyone knows about "elevator behavior," and on a crowded bus people sometimes squeeze so tightly together that they seem to challenge the physics law that two bodies cannot occupy the same space.

More powerful people are accorded more space around them than less powerful people are.

Finally, a person's physical size influences the amount of power he or she projects. Tall, strongly built people seem more imposing to others. A number of studies have shown that they are listened to and deferred to more than

Business uses the personal and social interpersonal zones heavily.

smaller people are. Electoral votes tend to favor taller candidates. Although smaller people can and do obtain power, they must contend with people's unconscious bias in favor of taller persons.

Among businesspeople, the handshake is the usual touch exchange. In mainstream U.S. culture, a firm but not crushing handshake of one or two seconds' duration is customary. This is true for both women and men, although formerly customs differed. Before women entered business and management in high numbers, they were treated as delicate creatures. A man shook hands with a woman *only* if she extended her hand first, and then he shook her hand lightly and softly. This is no longer the case. Businesswomen dislike the soft little handshake. It seems to relegate them to an outdated position of weakness.

In business, any touch beyond the handshake can be a minefield. The reasons include

- The inherent ambiguity of nonverbals.
- The perception that initiating touch is often an assertion of power.
- The multiple simultaneous agendas that a single communicator can have.
- The growth of sexual harassment suits.
- The great differences among people in what they perceive to be the "right" amount of touching.

Even touches that do not suggest sexual interest (a touch on the forearm, a pat on the shoulder, a light slap on the back) can create problems.

In the United States, different cultural groups have developed different touching behavior in both amount and kind of touching. Often the groups who gesture more also touch more. Outside business, this need not concern us. In business, however, someone socialized to expect little or no touching behavior might feel irritated and resentful if touched (touched on the forearm, hugged, patted on the shoulder), especially by someone he or she regards as inferior in status. One unwritten rule in business is that a superior can initiate touch but a subordinate cannot.

This convention sometimes astonishes people from groups in which touching is a normal part of conversation. Many Italian Americans touch a lot. Many Chinese Americans do not. Many German Americans touch very little. Many African Americans touch a lot. These differences have no relationship to the capacity of any group for love or for respect for others; these human emotions are constant across ethnic groups.

The fact that touch can so easily miscommunicate should make us cautious. Use a firm handshake freely, but refrain from other touches unless you are certain they will not offend. The most troublesome touch *mis*communications are "I am asserting my more powerful position" and "I am sexually interested in you."

Aside from the handshake, touching in business can be risky.

Sexual harassment lawsuits against businesses have resulted in numerous multimillion-dollar awards to individuals, and the cost continues to rise. Sexual harassment—unwelcome sexual attentions in the workplace—is defined fully in Exhibit 14–2 on page 478.

Many sexual harassment offenses are mostly or entirely nonverbal. Unwelcome sexual advances in the workplace are illegal and can be very costly to an organization. The federal guidelines show that businesses can be held respon-

1980

§1604–11 Sexual harassment.

(a) Harassment on the basis of sex is a violation of Sec. 703 of Title VII. Unwelcome sexual advances, requests for sexual favors, and other verbal or physical conduct of a sexual nature constitute sexual harassment when (1) submission to such conduct is made either explicitly or implicitly a term or condition of an individual's employment, (2) submission to or rejection of such conduct by an individual is used as the basis for employment decisions affecting such individual, or (3) such conduct has the purpose or effect of unreasonably interfering with an individual's work performance or creating an intimidating, hostile, or offensive working environment.

(b) In determining whether alleged conduct constitutes sexual harassment, the Commission will look at the record as a whole and at the totality of the circumstances, such as the nature of the sexual advances and the context in which the alleged incidents occurred. The determination of the legality of a particular action will be made from the facts, on a case by case basis.

(c) Applying general Title VII principles, an employer, employment agency, joint apprenticeship committee or labor organization (hereinafter collectively referred to as "employer") is responsible for its acts and those of its agents and supervisory employees with respect to sexual harassment regardless of whether the specific acts complained of were authorized or even forbidden by the employer and regardless of whether the employer knew or should have known of their occurrence. The Commission will examine the circumstances of the particular employment relationship and the job junctions performed by the individual in determining whether an individual acts in either a supervisory or agency capacity.

(d) With respect to conduct between fellow employees, an employer is responsible for acts of sexual harassment in the workplace where the employer (or its agents or supervisory employees) knows or should have known of the conduct, unless it can show that it took immediate and appropriate corrective action.

(e) An employer may also be responsible for the acts of non-employees, with respect to sexual harassment of employees in the workplace, where the employer (or its agents or supervisory employees) knows or should have known of the conduct and fails to take immediate and appropriate corrective action. In reviewing these cases the Commission will consider the extent of the employer's control and any other legal responsibility which the employer may have with respect to the conduct of such non-employees.

(f) Prevention is the best tool for the elimination of sexual harassment. An employer should take all steps necessary to prevent sexual harassment from occurring, such as affirmatively raising the subject, expressing strong disapproval, developing appropriate sanctions, informing employees of their right to raise and how to raise the issue of harassment under Title VII, and developing methods to sensitize all concerned.

(g) Other related practices: Where employment opportunities or benefits are granted because of an individual's submission to the employer's sexual advances or requests for sexual favors, the employer may be held liable for unlawful sex discrimination against other persons who were qualified for but denied that employment opportunity or benefit.

(Title VII, Pub. L. 88–352, 78 Stat. 253 (42 U.S.C. 2000e et seq.))

sible for their members' actions in the workplace. Even when the matter does not go to court, the ill will ensuing from a sexual harassment situation costs the business heavily in loss of trained personnel and sharply lowered productivity among those who stay. One source compared a sexual harassment inquiry to "the nastiest divorce case."[5]

[5]Katherine Morrall, "Education, Training Prevent Sexual Harassment Problems: Precautionary Measures Help Avoid Lawsuits, *Savings Institutions* 108 (February 1987), p. 121.

"I believe young Lewis may be on to something."

Drawing by Shanahan; © 1992 The New Yorker Magazine, Inc.

Corporate norms on business dress seem to be dysfunctional here.

What people wear communicates a great deal about them and influences the way others, both outside and inside the firm, view the firm itself. Much has been written about clothing as a nonverbal in business. The navy blue or gray suit (with a tie, for men) is a virtual uniform for managers. Men or women can choose this garb and rarely look inappropriate. Having said this, we need to discuss how far and under what circumstances a businessperson can deviate from this "uniform."

The main variable is the corporate culture where you work. Apple Computer has a more informal style than IBM does. Account executives in an advertising agency generally wear more high-fashion styles of business clothing than the blue-pinstripe-clad people at a bank. Note that the ad agency's artists and writers might be able to dress quite informally but will probably dress up when the team makes a presentation to a client.

Businesspeople on the East Coast dress more conservatively than those on the West Coast. For a man, for instance, a brown, camel, or beige suit might be acceptable in California but inadvisable in New York.

People dress conservatively when getting others to develop trust in them is essential. For instance, older brokerage clients are more likely to invest their money with a young broker who wears a good-quality, blue or gray, conservatively cut suit than with the same broker in a high-fashion, baggy-styled, Italian-silk suit.

People just beginning a business career need a couple of good-quality, conservative suits in navy or gray. Conservative dress is expected at interviews, even in firms where most people work in shirtsleeves after hire. If the "latest-fashion" look is avoided, the suits can serve for several years.

Communicating Interpersonally

What people buy after working for a while depends on factors like those just discussed. Two other considerations sometimes tempt business shoppers to move away from the conservative image. First, many workers look to the workplace (where they invest most of their time and energy) when they look for love relationships. Second, the fashion industry needs to make each season's clothing obsolete to build a market for next season's. Both these facts are perfectly legitimate. But common sense needs to govern choices. The individual worker must still consider his (and more often her) professional image.

Because women's positions in managerial ranks are recent and still not very secure, image matters even more for women than for men. Where there are few women in a formerly all-male occupation or workplace, the behavior of these few is much more rigidly scrutinized than is the behavior of the male employees. If something displeases, adverse inferences are drawn about this woman and the suitability of women in general for management. (The first minority members to break into a workplace are similarly scrutinized, perhaps to an even greater degree.)

Managerial dress for women is a good-quality skirted suit and conservative blouse or a good-quality conservative dress and blazer. The *jacket* has been cited again and again as the means of conveying that the woman holds a position of authority. Shoes are mid-heel, closed-toe pumps. Jewelry, if worn, is understated and of good quality. Skirt length is debatable; in fall 1992 many fashion houses were promoting above-the-knee skirted suits.

The point about short skirts, superhigh heels, tight or clingy clothing, or other fun clothes is this: Other people will infer from nonverbals a woman's primary goal in coming to work. If she can be certain that above-the-knee skirts will not communicate any impression other than a businesslike one, then above-the-knee skirts are fine. A woman who chooses to wear very short or sexy clothes, though, might as well forget about rising in the managerial ranks. It's tough enough to be taken seriously even when she does everything right.

Some organizations do not care what people wear as long as their work is done where the public does not see them. Some care a great deal and either set forth a written dress code or communicate their displeasure orally to those who deviate. Learn and meet the expectations of your organization.

Business dress must meet the expectations of one's organization and business contacts.

Meaning, Surroundings and Artifacts

In the work place, workers at every status level have space that "belongs" to them alone. The president of the firm has the corner office with window walls, a beautiful view, thick carpet, and mahogany furniture. The worker on the assembly line has a work space he or she always occupies, space for storing tools, and perhaps a locker for securing possessions. The data-entry worker has a doorless, partitioned cubicle.

To the extent possible, workers arrange artifacts (decorations, pictures, and other personal possessions) in their space. High-level managers surround themselves with decor and objects that project a desired image: maybe a Steuben crystal piece, a tasteful painting with its colors repeated in the room's fabrics, award plaques, an expensive desk set, and the portrait of the family.

The data-entry clerk's space would probably fit 15 or 20 times in the president's office. Still, Jack, the data-entry worker, "owns" his space. Although guidelines usually exist on what may and may not be displayed, he too might have the family picture on his desk, along with a plant and some small decorations. When another worker wants to talk to Jack, she pauses at the opening of the cubicle and waits for a signal.

Where people do not have their own space or where the space is repeatedly invaded by others, stress rises. The "open office" met resistance in the United States until managers realized that they had to let workers individualize their surroundings a little.

Each person's voice is unique. When a computer digitally stores the sounds of two people with similar voices saying "Good morning," the stored signals differ enough that they can be used as keys to secured areas. Jane says "Good morning" and the gate unlocks. Jane's sister Joan says "Good morning" and the gate stays shut.

Meaning and Voice

Voices differ in quality and resonance. They also differ in the degree to which individuals are able to vary and control range, pitch, speed, volume, and extent. Some voice characteristics are inborn; some are habits formed as we acquire language by imitating the people around us.

People dissatisfied with their speaking voices can improve them by setting goals and practicing. Inborn characteristics, such as a high-pitched voice, are harder to change, but improvement is possible. Speech trainers help people change nasal voices, regional accents, monotone voices, poor articulation, and any other vocal characteristic they perceive as a drawback.

Most speakers can improve voice characteristics with practice.

Most of the characteristics treated in this section are important in interpersonal speech but even more so in giving oral presentations. Most of us need more variety in our speech. Indeed, people can vary their patterns too much, but most of us are far from doing that.

Range. A person's range is the array of tones between the highest and the lowest note the person can speak or sing. We are born with vocal cords that will develop to a certain length and thickness, both of which determine range. Yet some singers and speakers have carefully pushed the limits of the voices they inherited and extended their range.

When we speak, we rarely use the extremes of the notes we can sing. (We would sound foolish if we did.) By the same token, most of us can extend the range of our everyday speaking voices if we try. This gives us better expressiveness.

Speakers with relatively high voices can and should work to extend the lower register of their voices. Quite unfairly, a high voice projects low authority and can sound shrill and ineffectual at higher volumes.

Pitch. Many people who can sing a two- or three-octave scale speak, unfortunately, with little variation in pitch. Most people should vary pitch more than they do. Variation is expressive, and listeners like it.

Monotone speaking makes a low-energy impression. In a business presentation, it is deadening. Interpersonally it conveys listlessness and lack of interest, even when the speaker is in reality an active, involved individual.

We use changes in pitch to convey meaning. When we pronounce phrases and sentences on a rising inflection—that is, when our pitch rises toward the end of the utterance—we might intend a question: "What did you say?" Or we might be tentative about a statement: "So I'll leave early today and stay late tomorrow?"

Downward-ending inflections can convey confidence: "So from this evidence we conclude that $50,000 will buy the equipment we need." Some speakers (more women than men) have formed a bad habit of making informative statements and assertions with a rising inflection. They seem constantly to be asking, "Is it okay?" "Can I say this?" "Do you like me?" This disempowers them. They need to change the habit.

Speed.   Some people talk fast, some slow. New Yorkers tend to speak more rapidly than Nebraskans, who in turn speak more rapidly than Mississippians. Someone used to slower speech might not readily process "WellIgoddageddadahih." (The Manhattanite is about to leave.) Note that very slow speech is sometimes "read" as slow-wittedness. (This has been successfully used by slow talkers to lay traps for the unwary: "I'm just country folks. You just explain it to me, now, won't you?" and the city folks give away their negotiating strategy to the smiling, leisurely genius from Tupelo or Vicksburg.)

People tend to accommodate to the speed of those they spend time around. However, some slow talkers simply have a problem with fluency. They grope for the perfect word, while others grow impatient. Listeners will tolerate some pauses, even some fairly long ones. But the speaker who cannot seem to get his or her thoughts out at a reasonable pace might need some work to improve fluency. Some fast talkers allow nervousness to speed up their speech. Such persons need to know that too-fast speech can be hard for listeners to understand or could be perceived as an effort to intimidate. If a nervous rush of words is accurately read as stress, the speaker's power position can suffer.

Volume.   We might increase volume to make ourselves better heard; we might lower volume to convey confidentiality. On the speaker's platform, we need higher volume without higher pitch. Good presenters project their voices, that is, speak from the diaphragm. People who learn to do this well can often speak to a large group of people all day without fatigue, while those who allow this important "belly" muscle to grow lax get worn out and hoarse after only an hour or so.

We also need to control and vary volume. It isn't only that our voices often need to carry across distance. Volume, especially in conjunction with the other vocal characteristics, can change meaning greatly. Imagine a person saying, factually, "You will never do that again." Then imagine a person saying the same words, but this time making the words an order, indelibly printed on the hearer's memory, with the threat that any violation will result in heavy punishment. The speaker might slow the words down or leave a little space between the words, but the main difference is in volume.

Extent.   Extent means the degree to which we draw out syllables, words, and even sentences. We might stretch out a "We-e-e-e-ll" to convey skepticism or hesitancy. We might clip syllables short to convey that we are in a hurry or to energize other people. Sometimes speakers extend syllables to sound soothing, sometimes to seem thoughtful, and sometimes to slow another person down.

Voice and shades of meaning.   Speakers of English infer shades of meaning from stressed syllables and changes in pitch. Consider how the changes in stress alter the meaning of this sentence:

She is the senior engineer.	You are mistaken to think that someone else is.
She *is* the senior engineer.	No, you can't "talk to her supervisor."
She is *the* senior engineer.	She is the only, or most important, or most respected senior engineer.

| She is the *senior* engineer. | The other veteran engineers will have to defer to her. |
| She is the senior *engineer*. | She is not the senior finance officer or marketer. She decides on engineering matters only. |

These changes are in no way universal. English speakers in different nations interpret some stress and pitch patterns differently. When we move into different languages, all bets are off. For instance, while we use pitch changes to convey shades of meaning, denotation generally remains constant. In contrast, speakers of Chinese infer entirely different *denotations* of words from "tones," that is, from changes in pitch.

Human beings process an amazing amount of information when they communicate interpersonally: words, visual cues, voice cues, situational cues, and much more. Much processing is intuitive and proceeds at a speed beyond our noticing it. Yet all of us can become better at both receiving and sending these complicated interpersonal messages. Awareness precedes all deliberate change.

Communications trainer Sondra Thiederman discusses numerous possible barriers to successful communication with non-U.S.-born newcomer employees."[6] The concept of saving face becomes especially important. Americans dislike losing face, of course, but to most it is a momentary inconvenience, a transient embarrassment soon forgotten. To people from Mexico, Korea, Central America, the Philippines, China, and many other places, however, loss of face might be a profound, burning humiliation, dreaded beyond many other misfortunes. Also, while America values individual initiative highly, many other cultures do not.

Having a work error pointed out in front of others might seem radically different to Americans than to newcomers from these countries. A Filipina might be thinking, "How could she make me seem such a fool? I do not know if I can bear to come back to work here tomorrow." The American is thinking, "Why is she smiling with tears in her eyes? Does she even know how to do the work *now?* I'll never understand these people. They can't take a simple criticism."

Equally important might be some newcomers' very strong respect for authority. A non-native-born employee might think that if he seems not to understand a set of instructions, he might be implying that the supervisor has not explained the material well.

Thus, Thiederman says, when an employee nods and smiles repeatedly, says, "Yes, yes, I understand," never has any questions, and exhibits a distracted facial expression, he or she may not actually understand well.

A supervisor needs to involve the whole work group in making communications succeed, Thiederman says. She offers these suggestions:

- Be patient, but do not patronize.
- Share responsibility for the communication.
- Speak slowly and distinctly, but do not patronize.
- Minimize the use of English slang.

Avoiding Communication Pitfalls with Non-Native-Born Employees

New worker populations in the United States bring new communication challenges.

[6]Sondra Thiederman, "Breaking Through to Foreign-Born Employees," *Management World* 17 (May–June 1988), pp. 22–23.

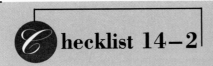

Checklist 14-2

Sending and Interpreting Nonverbal Communication

As a sender, do I understand that

- My nonverbals affect my verbal messages?
- Many different nonverbal "senders"—face, hands, stance, voice, and many others—operate both singly and in clusters?
- I have to be conscious of what I am doing as I speak or listen?
- Nonverbals are harder to watch and control than words are?
- The situation can affect the meaning of my nonverbals?
- Different organizations have different expectations about nonverbals?
- Nonverbals affect the perception of an individual's relative power and status?

- I might have to modify some of my nonverbals for others who might otherwise misunderstand?

As a receiver, do I understand that

- I must watch others' nonverbals for a time before making judgments based on them?
- Cultural differences affect both sending and interpreting of nonverbals?
- Nonverbals can be ambiguous?
- Many unacknowledged biases affect the way we perceive others' nonverbals?

- Follow up any questionable conversations with written memos.
- Watch for nonverbal signs that show lack of understanding.
- Support verbal messages with nonverbal means of communication.
- Repeat what has been said if any confusion exists.
- Check frequently for understanding.
- Teach any jargon or specialized language necessary for the work.

Give the employee positive reinforcement when he or she (1) admits any lack of understanding, (2) speaks slowly and distinctly, (3) tries again if understanding fails, or (4) understands that management also loses face if tasks are not completed correctly by employees. When barriers like these are overcome, productivity can only rise.

Diversity and Nonverbal Communication

Many writers point out that the United States is and will be multiracial and multiethnic. According to projections, by the year 2000 America will have 67 million nonwhite residents, with their percentage growing to 25 percent. In some states, numbers of nonwhite residents approach 50 percent of the total population.

To be sure, people who work in business expect to learn the work behaviors of mainstream American culture. But because of the shifts in numbers, mainstream American culture must be ready to adapt as well and be more accepting of others' cultural differences. Without such adaptation, subtle obstacles will arise and interfere with some workers' ability to contribute fully to organizations. We all need all of us.

To assess your awareness of nonverbal communication, study Checklist 14-2.

Synergy in organizations depends on workers' ability to depend on one another and work toward group goals. Good teamwork makes businesses more competitive internationally. The Johari Grid diagrams two communicators' differences in perception during an interaction. Each communicator has one or more agendas, sometimes overt, sometimes hidden.

Although active listening yields many benefits, most people do not listen very well. Reasons include noisy surroundings, cultural emphasis on assertiveness, allness, excess mental processing time, and uncontrolled daydreaming. Adhering to 10 principles for good listening offers individuals and organizations many benefits. These include information power, increased productivity, and the ability to motivate others.

Nonverbal communication affects the success of interpersonal business communication but, like listening, receives less analysis and emphasis than it deserves. Senders convey between 70 and 90 percent of their meaning via nonverbal signals. Nonverbal messages have different meanings in different combinations, in different situations, and especially in different cultures. As senders and as interpreters, people choose and assign meaning differently to nonverbal signals. Senders must recognize and control their nonverbals. Because interpretation is inexact, receivers must establish a behavioral baseline for a new sender before drawing inferences.

Nonverbal business communication includes facial expression, posture, gesture, use of time, use of space, touch, business dress, surroundings and artifacts, and voice.

With the increasing diversity of the American work force, managers must become more sensitive to nonverbals as sent and received by non-native-born employees.

APPLICATION EXERCISES

1. Developing the trust necessary for teamwork involves risk. People have to share work information and disclose information about themselves. Discuss the advantages of doing so. Next, honestly and pragmatically, discuss the *dis*advantages.

2. Describe the Johari Grid, naming the quadrants and telling what kind of information would be classified in each.

3. Recall a recent communication encounter in which the person to whom you were talking *unknowingly* revealed information he or she would rather have concealed. What did you learn, and by exactly what kinds of signals?

3. Describe the several contributory causes of poor listening.

4. In interpersonal communication, what is paraphrasing?

5. What advantages does a businessperson gain by listening to superiors? To co-workers? To subordinates?

6. Analyze the listening behaviors of selected persons. Then answer the following questions.
   a. Who is the best listener you know? List his or her behaviors as a listener.
   b. Who is the most important listener in your life? List his or her behaviors as a listener.
   c. Who is the worst listener you know? List his or her behaviors as a listener.
   d. Using the checklist on page 468 as a guide, list your own typical listening behaviors. Which weaknesses would be hardest for you to correct? Set some reasonable, achievable goals, and assess your progress daily for a month. *Resolve to repeat this exercise every six months throughout your business career.*

7. What makes listening difficult for you? What makes it easy?
   a. To whom do you have greatest difficulty listening? List this person's communication behaviors that give rise to your difficulty. In response to this person, which good listening behaviors are hardest for you to perform?
   b. To whom do you listen most easily and gladly? List this person's communication behaviors that ease your listening task.

8. Words have the power to create listening problems. Think of different communication encounters in which people were angered or offended by a speaker's poorly selected words. (Example: Teachers laugh and fume simultaneously when students return after an absence and ask, "Did I miss anything important?" The teachers know what the students mean, but better wording would avoid the implication that nothing important had gone on during the absence.) What words are "hot buttons" for *(a)* you? *(b)* your spouse or significant other? *(c)* your father or mother? *(d)* your boss?

9. Do the following exercise with a classmate. Each partner writes down an emotion (fear, disgust, joy, anger, uncertainty, pity, and so on) on an index card or piece of paper. Neither shows the other what was written. Then one partner uses *nonverbals* such as facial expression, stance, and gesture to communicate the selected emotion to the other. The second partner writes down what he or she believes the first is communicating.

   Next, change roles. The second partner uses nonverbals to communicate his or her selected emotion, and the first partner writes down the emotion he or she thinks is being portrayed.

   Then discuss *(a)* the accuracy of the perception and *(b)* the ease or difficulty of communicating that particular emotion nonverbally. Exchange your findings with other pairs of class members who have selected other emotions to try to communicate nonverbally. Compare what you observed about the accuracy of perceived nonverbals.

10. From TV newscasts, try to think of a public figure who is currently having a credibility problem. Watch nonverbals as he or she is shown speaking in newscast clips. What do you see? Are the person's nonverbals in any way a problem?

11. Think of an occasion when your nonverbal communication was misinterpreted. (A business example would be best, but also consider school and outside-school experiences.) What exactly went wrong? What did you intend that differed from what others said you meant?

12. Either on television or in person, examine the ways others behave toward a person of high status. For instance, observe the mayor of your city with the city council, the president of your school with deans or department chairs, or an influential business leader with a community group or in his or her workplace. Look at interpersonal space, use of eye contact, gesture, posture and body orientation, and other categories of nonverbals. Do you see any nonverbal signals indicating who is the person of highest status in a given group?

13. In your workplace, what is standard dress for managerial employees when meeting persons from outside the organization?

14. Discuss your observations about interpersonal distance in the following situations:

    a. In an elevator.
    b. In a lecture hall.
    c. In a waiting line for ticket purchases.
    d. On a bus.
    e. In a manager's office.

15. In five versions of the following sentence, five different words are emphasized. By paraphrasing, show how the different emphasis changes the meaning.

    a. *He* won't pay that price.
    b. He *won't* pay that price.
    c. He won't *pay* that price.
    d. He won't pay *that* price.
    e. He won't pay that *price.*

CASES

Examine each of the following cases in terms of (as appropriate) differing perceptions, the Johari Grid, teamwork, trust and the earning of trust, listening skills, and nonverbal communication. Try to estimate *costs,* in both "soft" terms and, if possible, in actual dollars.

1. **Who's Running This Ship?**   The corporate culture of a software engineering firm called for a relaxed, casual dress code. Even sloppy clothing was okay. The engineers liked this arrangement. Ken, a bright, newly hired engineer, came to the organization from the U.S. Navy. He had formed the habit of sharp creases and lots of starch. In itself this was not a problem, but visitors to the firm assumed he was the manager instead of a junior software engineer. The senior members of the group felt threatened by him. They were unwilling to work with him on a one-to-one basis. If you were a consultant to the group, what actions would you recommend, and to whom? Be prepared to discuss and defend your answer.

2. **Don't We Share a Goal in This Booth?**   Chuck, one of several district sales managers for a computer peripherals company, worked as a loner and kept to himself. Before a major trade show, while others were setting up the booth and moving product around, he was making phone calls to his own customers. During the show, when district sales managers were expected to be working the booth and greeting all customers from everyone's territory, Chuck was often absent from the booth, meeting privately with his own customers. When he worked the booth he talked only to people he recognized, ignoring others and leaving them disgruntled.

3. **Oh, Sorry—My Brains Are All on Break!**
Alvin, a customer service worker in a financial institution, was often asked for information on a computerized funds transfer system and how to correct problems with it. He was bright but unwilling to learn the system thoroughly enough to be able to answer the questions all on his own. Instead, when a superior or outsider called with a problem, he would "get back to them with an answer." He would then ask others for help and call the caller back with the correct answer. His co-workers resented what he was doing but did not feel it was their place to blow the whistle on him. One day, his fakery backfired when one institution that had spoken to him before called with a serious problem and no one was around for him to ask. He took a chance, guessed at an answer, and relayed it confidently. The customer, a bank, proceeded to lose $1 million in a transfer that was processed incorrectly.

   Now think back to the time *before* Alvin was exposed. What would you have done if you were in the position of his co-workers? If you were Al's supervisor, what would you do *now* to keep mistakes like this from occurring in the future?

4. **How *Not* to Motivate.**   Garth, the director of registration at STH, a health-care organization, picked up a patient's record completed by Diane, an intake worker. He called a supervisor at another hospital to find out how to handle a record of this type, which involved a particular procedure and a patient who had applied for Medicaid. Hearing what the correct procedure was, Garth approached Diane and, in front of co-workers, instructed her how to do it. His approach was oversimplified and patronizing. His manner implied Diane had completed the record incorrectly, which was not the case. Diane was humiliated. She wished Garth had simply asked her in the first place rather than phoning a supervisor. She did not feel free to object, since he was the boss. She could not make any sense out of the incident or figure out why he seemed to have picked up a record at random and singled her out for unjustified criticism.

5. **And How Did You Want to Pay for This?**   Bob, a sales rep, was on the phone one day when Mary, a new sales manager, heard him tell a customer that the firm could not meet the customer's needs. With gestures, Mary pantomimed to Bob

that she was going to her office and would pick up the phone line he was on. She listened to the customer briefly and then assured him that yes, they could certainly sell him the items he wanted. Bob was made to look foolish, but not as foolish as Mary looked later when Bob told her that this customer was a bad-pay and had already defaulted on a couple of good-sized bills.

6. **What Could I Possibly Learn There?**   Barbara had recently been denied a promotion. She felt she had deserved it because she could do all her assignments more quickly than her coworkers. She disliked the thought of participating in the company's semiannual retreat, scheduled to start in one week. This service-oriented organization stressed cooperation and interpersonal communication skills. The retreat's activities included brainstorming sessions, problem-solving sessions, and appreciation gatherings for "champion" workers who, Barbara believed, did much less than she and spent far too much time just talking to one another.

7. **Is a Necktie More Important than a Sale?** John Rosenzweig, president of a company based in Hawaii, flew to Detroit in July to meet with James Marks, president of a Michigan company. It was hot and humid, and Rosenzweig wore a short-sleeved, open-necked shirt and slacks, the usual business garb in Hawaii. Marks wore a suit and tie, although perspiration soaked his collar. Marks narrowed his eyes when he first saw Rosenzweig as they met at the airport. At lunch, Rosenzweig asked whether Marks wouldn't like to shed his jacket. "No, thanks," Marks said curtly. They didn't get far into their business discussion. Rosenzweig didn't feel that he was getting the price concessions he should; Marks wondered whether Rosenzweig really had the authority to negotiate. He didn't feel sure he was really talking to the president of a company.

8. **Thanks, I've Had about All the Help I Can Stand.**   Kelly was hired by a construction firm as a tax manager. The firm was a collection of departments, each ruled by a fairly autocratic manager. They cooperated but did not challenge one another's authority. Kelly, feeling she had to prove a woman could hold her own in this environment, overcompensated. Her manner was abrasive both to the people she supervised and to those she reported to. In quite a tactless manner, she freely pointed out what she felt were errors in judgment and procedures. She loved to get what she called a "major bust"—finding an error in a tax return or a violation of the building code and pointing it out with great zeal to the vice president. Many people in the organization wanted her out and expended effort to make it happen. She lasted six months and then resigned.

9. **One Size Fits All.**   In a large urban bank, 17 of the 18 women in a department followed an unspoken dress policy. They wore tailored dresses with jackets or skirt suits. The company handbook merely stated that employees should dress in "proper business attire." Debra, a very bright woman who felt she was too heavy, wore polyester pants and overblouses because she felt better and believed she looked better in these garments. The manager of the department could not perceive her intelligence and overlooked her work record. He saw only that she did not conform to the dress code—which had never been explicitly stated. He constantly berated her and made her feel inadequate. Because she did not want reasons to communicate with him, she stopped trying to excel on the job. She didn't want to draw his attention for any reason, good or bad.

10. **But I Thought You Said . . .**   While out conducting fieldwork, Beth found that she did not understand which information was necessary to include on a workpaper. Beth asked the manager in charge what she thought was a very specific question. The manager responded in a way that let Beth know the question had not been understood. She asked again, and the manager acted annoyed because he felt he had answered the question. After the second explanation, Beth was still confused, but rather than make the manager angry she did the workpaper the way she thought was probably right. As a result, the workpapers lacked vital information and the two found themselves answering to one of the partners in the firm. The manager said he had explained the matter twice. Beth stated she had never understood. Who was at fault?

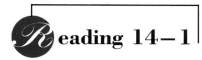

USING THE MAGIC BULLET

Reading 14–1

Roger Ailes

If you want to influence others, one trait is so much more powerful than all others: I call it the "magic bullet." With it, your audience will forgive just about anything else you do wrong. Without it, you can hit every bull's-eye in the room and no one will be impressed.

The magic bullet is being likable as a speaker. In politics, the "like" vote can swing elections. The same phenomenon shapes our business environment and forms the basis of most negotiations.

Those who can be tough-minded but likable will be the future's management elite. That's because the leaders of the next 10 years will no longer be able to maintain the low profiles they are accustomed to. The arena will be wide open to public scrutiny and will require winning the good-will—the "like" votes—of constituencies such as employees, investors, government regulators, consumer activists, and the news media. As Irving Shapiro, former DuPont CEO, said in an interview: "Today, [the CEO] is a quasi-public official, who needs as much skill in dealing with people as any Senator."

The most common failings of today's business leaders are qualities that used to be considered "natural" in a boss. At least one-third of my clients are too arrogant or aggressive. Many of them are technically brilliant executives, but they fail to win support from subordinates and co-workers.

Sometimes they alienate clients. Their logic and analysis may be correct, but their manner is so abrasive that they lose "like" votes—which can torpedo their progress (and even their jobs).

One CEO of a major retailing firm told me that he was on the verge of firing a $400,000-a-year executive who was a consistently good bottom-line performer: "I hate his guts. Not only that, everybody on the board hates his guts. He has a big mouth and he irritates his peers as well."

I met with the executive. I told him that I had heard that he was rude, condescending, thin-skinned—and enormously talented. He shifted in his chair and looked at me disdainfully. But he was disarmed by my candor.

We had six two-hour meetings. When we played back tapes, he was shocked at how intensely unlikable he appeared. He used put-down phrases: "You don't understand," "Well, obviously," and "Let me explain something to you."

He communicated impatience and disrespect: interrupting frequently, scowling, rolling his eyes, and sighing. Over time, he learned to listen better, elicit others' ideas, exercise diplomacy and laugh—especially at himself.

No one can tell you how to be more likable. For the executive I advised, showing made the difference. But the suggestions that helped him may help you as well:

1. Be considerate. Make listeners comfortable.
2. Get off to a good start. A strong, warm, responsive beginning puts you in control.
3. Choose your words. Try to talk so your listeners can understand you.
4. Persuade. Requests work better than orders.
5. Relate. Be enthusiastic and react naturally. Don't hide behind a deadpan expression.
6. Be patient. People think at different speeds.
7. Read between the lines. Some people have personal problems. If someone doesn't seem to be absorbing what you're saying, don't immediately assume that he isn't buying your story.
8. Admit your weaknesses, when appropriate. You will gain respect and understanding.
9. Pay compliments. They express your awareness and make people want to please you.
10. Express thanks. You'll gain support.
11. Finally, consider Lord Chesterfield's advice: "Be wiser than other people, if you can, but do not tell them so."

Source: Roger Ailes, "Using the Magic Bullet," *Newsweek,* Special Section: Management Digest, September 2, 1991.

MIMIC YOUR WAY TO THE TOP

Reading 14–2

Larry Reibstein and Nadine Joseph

Here's the scene: the top executives of Microsoft Corp. are in a meeting and cofounder and CEO Bill Gates is talking. As he grows intense he starts rocking and bobbing back and forth in his chair, the rocking and bobbing speeding up as he continues. Seated around him, several of his lieutenants soon are rocking and bobbing, rocking and bobbing. Gates periodically pushes his glasses up on his nose; his associates push their glasses up.

What's wrong with this picture? Nothing, actually. Psychologists call the phenomenon "modeling," or "mirroring" or "patterning." The guy in the next office calls it sucking up to the boss. Whether done consciously or not, subordinates show a relentless tendency to copy their

Source: Larry Reibstein and Nadine Joseph, "Mimic Your Way to the Top," *Newsweek,* August 8, 1988, p. 50.

boss's mannerisms, gestures, way of speaking, dress and sometimes even choice of cars and homes. It's an acceptable mode of behavior—up to a point. Some people become so absorbed in their boss's identity that when the boss moves on, the subordinate may feel abandoned.

Experts say the motive to mimic derives from the same forces that lead children to imitate a parent. "We pay homage and show allegiance to the most powerful through mimicry," says Robert Decker, director of the Palo Alto Center for Stress Related Disorders. In groups, he notes, the real power is the person being mimicked, not the person with the biggest title.

When they do it intentionally, subordinates are trying to win the boss's approval. At one IBM office, corporate culture used to demand that the desks be steel and the chairs gray. But one top manager brought in a curvy, bright orange ashtray, and within days colorful objects materialized in offices. "When an executive believes he can evoke interest from the boss he'll fly the same airline, order the same cucumber salad at lunch, wear the same kind of cuff links," says Jean Hollands, a Silicon Valley consultant.

The danger is when such behavior slips into toadyism or steps on a boss's ego. Letitia Baldrige, an adviser on executive manners, recalls the young assistant who wore a plaid suit to please his boss, who always wore plaid. The boss promptly ordered him home to change clothes. The subordinate had diluted the boss's uniqueness. But most bosses bask in imitation. Hollands cites a California company whose top managers developed an interest in politics when their boss, a former Washington pol, took over.

'Like a jerk': Lots of traits are picked up unintentionally, sometimes as a way to cope with stress. An Oakland lawyer who nodded like her boss says, "I felt like a jerk because I couldn't stand him." Yet unintentional traits are easily dropped. Maureen McNamara, media director at Emerson Lane Fortuna, a Boston advertising agency, says that she inherited a subordinate who gulped loudly to express surprise, a trait she picked up from the previous boss. Within a week, the aide dropped the gulp and picked up McNamara's way of saying "Really?!" It was a shrewd move. As McNamara puts it, "I tend to mimic up."

Mimicking's benefits—like career advancement—aren't necessarily available to all. Minorities and foreigners often find it puzzling to decipher the nonverbal traits of a boss of a different culture or sex, according to Jane Falk, a linguist. That reluctance to mirror the boss, Falk adds, may play at least a small role when minorities and foreigners are overlooked for top jobs. Says Falk, "They're not marching to the same drummer."

Chapter Fifteen

Communicating in Organizations

PREVIEW

An organization contains many smaller organizations. Businesspersons must become effective in groups of all sizes and configurations. This chapter examines some means of working well in groups and increasing the effectiveness of the organization itself. We will examine corporate culture, power in organizations, organizational networks, and meetings. ●

**Anna Cuevas
Account Executive**

Molly erred as many do when she inferred only part of a set of unwritten rules. Newcomers must acculturate. Doing so takes time, and mistakes are part of the reason newcomers do not immediately create full value in return for their pay.

CORPORATE CULTURE

Newcomers to organizations must learn from others the basic assumptions and rules governing appropriate behavior and other responses.

Terrence E. Deal and Allan A. Kennedy's book *Corporate Cultures* describes how business organizations generate an internal atmosphere in which managers and employees work.[1] In some organizations, the culture is strong and well understood by all. In others the culture is weak, poorly understood, or even different from one department to another.

This internal environment conveys the organization's values and permeates what the organization is and does. The culture can be relatively formal or informal, open or close-mouthed, punitive or indulgent, innovative or conservative. Adjectives usually applied to people can be applied to organizations: *brash, gutsy, energetic, staid,* and so on.

Some organizations, like IBM, let their employees know exactly which activities are okay and which are not. "Big Blue" even recommends a conservative style of dress. IBM also believes in helping employees set reachable goals to make success probable and to generate high motivation in employees. Even if forced to downsize (as seemed likely as this book went into production), IBM is unlikely to stop shaping and reinforcing its employees' success.

Other organizations create other kinds of internal climates. Apple Computer, Inc., cares little about a particular style of business dress but cares a great deal about innovation. Some organizations hold formal orientation sessions in corporate culture. In others, employees have to infer for themselves what the "rules" are for success in those organizations.

Some organizations create their cultures deliberately. Others simply let their cultures evolve, sometimes remaining unaware of the importance, or even the existence, of a culture. Some organizations encourage "intelligent failure," preferring that individuals try out good ideas even if they fail and

[1]Terrence E. Deal and Allan A. Kennedy, *Corporate Cultures* (Reading, Mass.: Addison-Wesley, 1982).

examining errors eagerly for what can be learned. Some firms punish failures whether the idea was good or bad.

Learning the Ropes

Most firms train new hires, even when newcomers' education and experience suit the job. Training is expensive but essential. You may know that in many jobs a new employee works his or her best for six months or more before the firm begins to realize any profit on that employee. Some organizations train new people in organizational culture as well as in job content. Most of the time, however, culture is subtle and situational. It does not lend itself well to formal instruction.

What can new employees do to learn about culture? They can watch the behavior of others to see what succeeds and what does not. For instance, some organizations encourage individuals to make their own successes known. In other organizations, individuals must share credit for successful projects even when most of the work was their own. If employees "toot their own horn" in the latter kind of firm, they might be limiting their career opportunities in that organization.

Employees can familiarize themselves with whatever policy the firm has put in writing. Many organizations have policy manuals, some extensive and some minimal. Some firms refer to policy frequently; others write it down and then mostly forget about it. Employees rarely need to read through a foot-thick manual, but they should look at the table of contents and read carefully any written policy affecting the whole firm and any written policy dealing with their own areas.

Employees can listen actively. Active listening, as you read in Chapter Fourteen, builds trust. The good listener is much more likely to receive useful information and advice than the constant talker, the know-it-all, or the loner. Although excess socializing on the job is rightly discouraged, brief, friendly, and time-effective social exchanges build an environment conducive to learning how to meet expectations and how to avoid career-limiting errors.

Finally, employees can seek a mentor or mentors. A **mentor** is an experienced, senior person in the organization who is well thought of and willing to share experiences and offer advice. Two warnings are important in choosing a mentor. First, be sure the mentor really does understand the culture. Seniority and friendliness do not in themselves make a good mentor. Second, be aware that in a changeable business environment, individuals can ascend or descend the organizational ladder unexpectedly. If a mentor loses power, the protégé may go down as well.

Written and Unwritten Rules

Some organizational rules are explicit.

Most organizations have a mission statement setting forth their strongest, most basic beliefs about the purpose underlying all their efforts. Many firms also make formal organizational plans for one year, five years, and even ten years. Many create formal, written goals and objectives for the firm and its divisions and departments. Those subunits often carry the formal planning process much further, sometimes proceeding to formal, written goal setting for individual employees.

The plans, goals, and objectives cover *what* the firms and their employees are to do. Often other kinds of policies and rules cover *how* they are to do it. Some organizations are explicit about policies. For instance, an organization might clearly tell its employees, "We are a collaborative organization. Our employees share what they know." Another organization might say little but instead create the kind of atmosphere that encourages this sharing. The firm might find ways to reward employees who share freely and discourage employees who hoard information.

Another organization might say little about information sharing and even frown on employees who ask for or offer information on the job. Such employees might hear, "Isn't that outside your area of responsibility?" or even "Mind your own business," "I'm really busy," or "Go bother somebody else." Only time and experience tell employees whether the discouraging words represent individual co-workers having a bad day or whether they reflect the reigning corporate culture and its unwritten rules.

People readily learn meta-rules, that is, "rules about rules." For instance, Jones, the manager, hurries over to two budget analysts and demands, "Haven't you got those figures yet? I gave you a five o'clock deadline! This is the last time I'm going to tell you!" As the door closes behind Jones, one analyst says to the other, "Don't sweat it—Jones isn't even yelling yet. And Jones's counterpart in Denver says the real deadline isn't till this Friday anyway." The usual "rule" says to believe what your supervisor says. The rule about what *this* manager says, however, is that unless he seems very stressed, he is probably overstating the urgency of the deadline. Employees learn whom to believe, which pronouncements are real and which are window dressing, who the influential people are, and so on.

Hard kinds of cultures for employees to learn are those of the organizations that say one thing and do another or those that say little or nothing and behave inconsistently. In these kinds of atmospheres, employees proceed uncertainly, make judgment errors, and sometimes displease management despite their best efforts.

Where "the ropes" are hard to learn, workers learn to minimize risk to themselves. They use the CYA (cover your "anatomy") strategy, qualify their statements, and learn where the exits and hiding places are. Cultures of this kind are often dysfunctional. The energy employees spend protecting themselves could be better spent furthering corporate goals.

Rosabeth Moss Kanter, Edgar H. Schein, and other theorists believe corporate cultures can be guided and changed.[2] Cultural change occurs slowly, however, even where management desires it. Employees believe what they see more than what they hear, and changing established behaviors and beliefs of large numbers of people is difficult.

POWER, POLITICS, AND INFLUENCE

Although organizational reporting relationships can be charted neatly, much communication and much influence travel along informal lines. Who talks to whom and who influences whom can depend in part on how much power individuals are perceived to have.

Kinds of Power

Most theorists discuss five kinds of power: position power (sometimes called legitimate power), reward power, punitive power, expert power, and referent power.

Position power is the right of superiors in organizations to expect subordinates to carry out instructions and orders. The higher an individual's position in the hierarchy, the more position power the individual holds and the greater his or her authority.

> Some rules are unwritten and learnable only by watching, drawing inferences, and cautious trial and error.

[2]Rosabeth Moss Kanter, "Change Masters and the Intricate Architecture of Corporate Culture Change," *Management Review* 72, October 1983, pp. 18–28; Edgar H. Schein, *Organizational Culture and Leadership* (San Francisco: Jossey-Bass, 1985).

People use **reward power** when, by conferring something that another person values, they can motivate the person to do something. Rewards can include money, gifts, or praise, for example.

Conversely, people use **punitive power** when they motivate either by withholding something of value or by giving something disliked (for instance, humiliation or ridicule).

Expert power comes from superior knowledge or experience about the matter in question. As workers become more and more specialized and highly trained, expert power becomes both narrower in its application and more critically needed.

Referent power derives from an individual's personality, likability, forcefulness, and credibility. The leadership characteristic called **charisma** exemplifies a strong form of referent power. People do what a person says because they like, admire, and respect him or her.

A knowledgeable executive might possess large amounts of all five kinds of power and a low-level worker only modest amounts of one or two kinds.

Organizational Politics

In virtually all firms, employees must learn and continue to watch organizational politics. Although the word **politics** has negative connotations for many, coalitions and tactics are necessary where different people see things in different ways. Politics can be ethically positive, negative, or neutral, but it will exist. The organization's work has to go on; thus, people will work out their disagreements.

Whether organizational power is centralized or dispersed, employees can work well and gain satisfaction from their work. In general, both organization and employee prosper when the employee's personal work goals are well matched with the organization's goals.

Different employees have different attitudes toward personal power. Some are ambitious to direct the work of others. Some feel empowered when they are allowed to direct their own activities without undue interference from others.

Employees might experience conflicts in loyalty. For instance, an employee who considers himself loyal to the firm might find himself working under a powerful individual manager who is empire building by undermining a rival department's power. The manager believes she is acting in the firm's best interests. The uneasy employee has to decide what, if anything, he can do, what ethical options he has, whether he can learn enough to make a sensible decision, and whether it is any of his business in the first place.

Developing Personal Power

Power and the ability to persuade are intricately linked. Often the more "clout" people are perceived to have, the less persuading they have to do. Similarly, people's ability to persuade is part of what creates others' perceptions that individuals hold power.

Power adds weight to persuasion, and often the ability to persuade increases power.

Means of building power in organizations include (obviously) job knowledge, education, competency, and productivity. But they also include the ability to *make and sustain connections.* Some means of doing so are

1. **Environmental scanning**—paying attention to what is happening in your industry, your profession, the economy, and so on.
2. **Boundary spanning**—participating in organizational activities that let you move outside your own work group, work cooperatively with other work groups, and learn how other functional areas operate.

3. **Networking**—developing contacts in other businesses, among professionals, with government representatives, and with others with whom you can exchange useful information and opportunities.

People in organizations ally with others. They call on one another for support and information. You can "create debt" by helping other people and expect help or support in return. These many contacts put you in the right places for hearing what is important. When you are one of the earliest people with accurate information about what is really happening, your power grows.

The more "tuned in" you are, the less risk you run of making a CLM (career-limiting move) or CLR (career-limiting remark). People make serious political mistakes when they fail to pay attention to power factors, as, for instance, when they assume they have more power than they do or when they try to use one type of power when a different kind is called for. Paying attention takes time, of course, and your work must not suffer. Somebody who knows everything but does nothing will not be esteemed.

You also have to look the part. The material in Chapter Fourteen on non-verbal communication will help. "Power dressing," for instance, often gains a person preferential treatment.

Ignoring power factors is risky.

Influencing Peers

Peers exert considerable influence on one another. Look on any playground to see young children already wielding rewards and punishments. An influential five-year-old decides who can and cannot be included in the play group that day. Reacting to referent power, the child's "posse" excludes the less influential child. With the exclusion, the follower children place a higher value on being included, because they have seen how hard to get inclusion can be. As people grow and mature, they further develop their ability to influence others. Influence strategies and tactics become subtler but no less effective.

When you seek to get people to work with you, think hard about what is in it for them (the WIIFM factor) to do so and where disagreement is possible. Through active listening, find out what they want and need. If you plan your persuasion strategy, they will be motivated to help you because they will perceive that they are moving toward their own goals as well.

If you are developing the personal power discussed earlier, your peers are likely to seek out your help and support. You will, of course, be glad to assist, unless doing so will lose something for you. If you have to disagree with or oppose someone, "fight fair."

You lack position power over peers, but the other four kinds of power offer many possibilities. Referent power? You "look promotable," although you do not discuss your ambitions. You seek common ground with those on your own level, behave as though you respect them, give compliments as deserved, and stroke egos. You treat the boss respectfully but are not servile. You're a "good guy." Expert power? You know a great deal that others need to know. Reward and punishment power? You can give information and support (and many other benefits), and you can withhold them as well.

With peers, an individual might be able to exercise all forms of power except position power.

You can empower peers and subordinates. By assisting them, sharing information, and promoting their efforts and goals, you can help them develop their capabilities and self-confidence. Empowered people have more to give, and they will be well disposed toward those who have helped them.

Influencing the Boss

In the boss-subordinate power relationship, most of the influence is downward. The boss says, "Jump"; the subordinate says, "How high?" To be sure, subordinates work more willingly when bosses minimize the use of "hard" influence tactics. Still, unless superiors have behaved previously in ways that have eroded their influence, superiors' position power causes subordinates to obey orders simply because the boss is the boss.

Subordinates can direct influence upward, but their tactics are limited to "soft" and indirect means. You have no position power, and it's not a good idea to try to punish the boss, but consider these possibilities. First, you can make the boss look good. When your good work reflects well on him, you have gained some reward power. Second, you can help him: Pay attention, read, think, listen, learn, be a voice of reason, and be a resource for him. This gives you some expert power. Third, you can cultivate some of the same things he likes and avoid the things he dislikes. Learn what he knows. Find out how he thinks and, within reason, try to think the same way. If perceived similarity creates liking, as it usually does, you will gain some referent power.

Preparing for a business career, though, you need to analyze yourself and your career goals to discover how much you can comfortably adapt to a boss. Realize also that working positively toward the boss's goals is not the same as being a "yes" person intent only on getting ahead.

ORGANIZATIONAL COMMUNICATION NETWORKS

A classic definition states that a formal organization is "a system of coordinated activities of a group of people working cooperatively toward a common goal under authority and leadership."[3] Lines of communication link individuals and groups; without communication networks, coordination and cooperation would be impossible. Most organizations operate with a formal organizational network and one or more informal ones.

Formal Network: The Chain of Command

The typical business organization is a pyramid-shaped hierarchy, exemplified in Exhibit 15–1 (page 500), with

- A president or chief executive officer (CEO) at the top.
- Several vice presidents reporting to the president or CEO.
- Several managers reporting to each vice president.
- Supervisors reporting to each manager.
- A number of workers reporting to each supervisor.

Numerous variations in and exceptions to this pyramid pattern exist, but most organizations have this basic overall shape.

The sequence of reporting relationships, from low to high, is called the **chain of command.** The number of people reporting directly to an individual is called that person's **span of control.**

Currently, in response to competition, the pyramid in many organizations is becoming flatter. These "leaner and meaner" organizations are paring some middle-management positions in the hope of becoming more responsive to customers in less time. In such organizations, fewer levels separate the CEO from the lowest level of workers.

Project management organizations, although still hierarchical with the few supervising the many, reconfigure reporting relationships to serve the needs of particular projects. A senior engineer, for example, might report both to the chief of her department and to the head of a project team. That engineer might use the services of support workers in several departments.

[3]William G. Scott, *Organization Theory* (Homewood, Ill.: Richard D. Irwin, 1967).

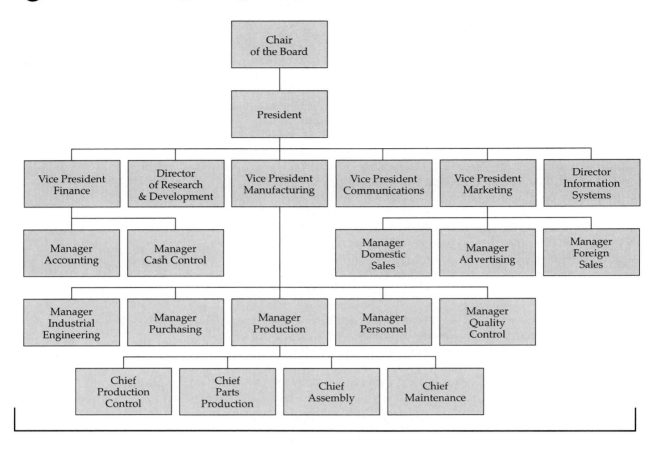

Heavy information traffic follows the chain of command. Orders, instructions, specifications, budgets, and many other messages flow downward. Reports of many kinds—product, cost, design, personnel, and so on—flow upward. Efforts to bypass levels in the chain, especially when communicating upward, are discouraged. "Go through channels," a person will be told.

The formal organization also supports considerable lateral communication for the purpose of coordinating activities among departments. People in organizations do, of course, "meet informally" for the organization's purposes outside their usual departments or areas. However, these meetings are not daily occurrences for most workers.

Informal Networks

The informal communication networks in an organization also carry heavy traffic. **Informal networks** are composed of people who know and talk to people. A person's level in the organization may or may not be important; what is important is whether the person hears what is going around. Some people—often those with high referent power—hear everything. Others hear little or nothing. Some people gain the reputation of being reliable sources. Others talk a lot but are taken seriously by no one.

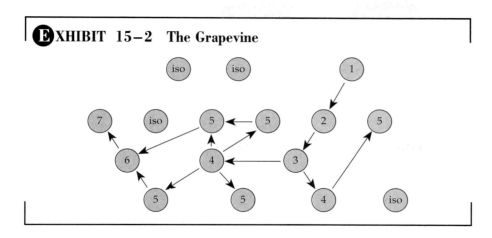

EXHIBIT 15–2 The Grapevine

The best description of an informal network is Keith Davis's classic piece on the organizational **grapevine**.[4] Exhibit 15–2 diagrams the travel of an organizational grapevine message. The numbers on the "heads" show the number of people in the chain between the source (person 1) and the numbered receiver. For instance, before the 5s heard the message, it passed through four others.

Information might originate anywhere. People who hear it either keep quiet or tell it to one or more others, who in turn either keep quiet or pass it on. Once information is in the grapevine, many, many people hear it, with astonishing speed. But not everyone hears it. A few people, called **isolates** ("heads" marked *iso* in Exhibit 15–2), have no grapevine connection. Somehow they remain oblivious while information races through the ductwork.

Grapevine content is usually high-interest material. A possible layoff, a rumor, a scandal, a grievance, a pregnancy—all these are food for the grapevine. Researchers on this informal network report that the content is fairly accurate most of the time, although often the most fascinating part of a complicated story is what turns out to be inaccurate. For instance, one week a firm's grapevine carried the electrifying news that the president's daughter was to marry a particularly unprepossessing company assembly-line worker. The story had the wedding date right, the bride right, and many other details right. The groom, however, did not work for the company but did bear a common name that happened also to be the name of that particular assembly-line worker.

Whereas chain-of-command messages flow upward, downward, and laterally, grapevine messages go in any direction. They travel diagonally; they leap over levels in the hierarchy; they go from anybody with a mouth to anybody with ears.

Managers and employees alike must access the grapevine. Without it, they miss information that could be critical to them. Managers, especially, need to stay in touch with the grapevine. Management often goes to great effort to prepare and disseminate employee communications that, once they have arrived through slow, official channels, are disbelieved because the grapevine got there first—and more convincingly.

The grapevine is flawed but inevitable and often highly useful.

[4]Keith Davis, "Management Communication and the Grapevine," *Harvard Business Review* 31 (September–October 1953), pp. 43–49.

Out of the loop. **Way out of the loop.** **Doesn't know there is a loop.**

Organization members must access the informal network as well as formal information channels, or they risk being isolated.

Sometimes information must be deliberately fed into the grapevine. One instance would be a need to squelch an untrue and potentially harmful rumor. In such a case, management needs to find out exactly what the grapevine says and feed it accurate information in a sufficiently interesting and convincing way that the grapevine will transmit it.

Harmful rumors, in fact, typically start because employees are not getting information they view as crucial. When they perceive that management is "holding out on them," their fear and anxiety levels rise. So does their eagerness to make much of little. Under these circumstances, a hint, doubt, or worry becomes a certainty, and the grapevine hums. Suppose a 10 percent layoff is a distant possibility. Suppose the work force, hearing nothing and fearing much, believes a 20 percent layoff is imminent. This rumor might be enough to cause a number of people to quit and look for better prospects early, before competition becomes too heavy.

Barriers to Effective Organizational Communication

Any existing interpersonal communication problems are compounded when people work in organizations. Where communication is faulty, many people, not just one or two, may get wrong information or none at all. Additional problems that grow out of the nature of organizations include too many transfer stations, overload, bottlenecks, withholding of information, and cliques and in-groups.

In business, ideas must move through and past many people in the course of becoming useful. These receiver-transmitters are called **transfer stations.** Recall the communication model from Chapter One as you consider the way information moves. Each person receives through the filter, decodes, interprets, selects, reencodes, and sends through the filter. Human differences, noise, bias, fears, agendas, and many other factors may influence the accuracy of the reconveyed information.

If information passes through five people from initiator to ultimate receiver, five people have the chance to modify it. Whether intentionally or unintentionally, benignly or maliciously, people might change messages they carry. People hear and understand imperfectly, and if they miss something they do not like to send an incomplete message. Often, when something is missing, they think, "Oh, it must be X," and they fill in X. Extra care must be taken to move messages accurately when there are many transfer stations.

Each person receiving and forwarding a message might distort it, either deliberately or accidentally.

In the course of a business day, you will process scores of messages. Some are trivial and some essential, but you get them all. Sometimes messages arrive simultaneously. Sometimes you get messages meant for someone else, messages that require time to study, messages you have to supplement by looking something up, messages you have to divide and pass to others, and so on. You will get many messages just because they are routine. You will get many messages just because you end up on someone's "pc" list. You will get 10-page messages that should be one paragraph. You will get messages by phone, by an anxious person standing in front of you, by a shout down the hall, by E-mail, by memo, by fax, by car phone. How can anybody process all that information?

Overload

Information overload is the condition of having too much information to handle. At some point the employee's stress level spikes, the brain balks, and fatigue sets in. In some ways an organization is an information machine, continuously pumping data through, sometimes without any real justification. "We sent this report because we've always sent this report. Of course you're supposed to read this report. Do with it? I don't know. Anyway, here. Take it."

Many employees have excellent ideas that someone higher in the organization should see. The employees write up their ideas, give them to their immediate superiors to pass upward to the next level, and wait for feedback. Some managers, for various reasons—inattention, malice, overwork, feeling threatened, who knows why?—create a bottleneck. They never transmit the ideas of subordinates. Often these same managers keep their subordinates undersupplied with information from higher management.

Bottlenecks

We would like to offer a formula for a solution, but sadly, channels are firm, upper management supports middle management before employees, and the problem is all too familiar. Employees with much talent typically work for such a manager long enough to learn what he or she knows and then get a better job in a different firm. The loss to the original firm is considerable.

A bottleneck can also occur when one transfer station cannot process information as fast as senders, receivers, and other transfer stations can. Messages pile up. Many arrive late, and some never get through at all.

Communicating in Organizations

Withholding Information

Hoarding information others need to do their jobs well is dysfunctional to an organization.

Information is an organization's life blood. It is also a source of power for people who have it. Whereas most employees understand the need to make sure others have the information they need to do their jobs effectively, some people are information misers. They take it in but then hold onto it. The more information becomes a centrally stored resource in a firm's computer information system, however, the less any individual can hoard it.

Another occasion when information might be withheld occurs when a subordinate does not want to displease a superior. At times the employee edits or filters disappointing information, sometimes without realizing it, before transmitting the message upward.

Cliques and In-Groups

Every organization has its informal opinion leaders. Many of these people hold no leadership position on the organizational chart but nevertheless heavily influence the attitudes and opinions of an informal group. Some opinion leaders are the steadfast friends of the company. If they are hostile to the organization or to individuals, though, trouble arises.

Negative opinion leaders gain ego gratification from keeping others out. The group is "by invitation only"—a **clique.** Sometimes they make life hard for employees whom they ostracize. Sometimes they start petty mutinies. Sometimes they merely waste time.

Managers must try to change the behavior of negative opinion leaders.

Managers can counsel such employees, discipline them, or ignore them. Sometimes they can co-opt them—take them in as Genghis Khan made his conquered tribes his faithful followers. Managers can scoop up their complainers, put them to work on a special task so demanding that they lack the time to play games, and praise their output. Managers should try to modify the behavior of these workers, though. Intransigent, disaffected opinion leaders are a source of potential harm.

Technological Communication Networks

Local area networks *(LANs)* are cables connecting the computers and computer-assisted devices within an organization. Network software permits users to access other users, stored information, communication devices, and external communication networks—all subject, of course, to availability and clearances.

External communication networks and services are becoming more numerous. We now have multiple phone companies, and the telephone network's infrastructure is being upgraded from copper wire to fiber optics.

For years, subscribers to information services such as CompuServe and Prodigy have sent electronic mail to other subscribers, accessed weather services and airline schedules, entertained and educated themselves with computer bulletin boards and special-interest groups, downloaded public-domain software and shareware, and used many other options. Dow Jones News Service offers instant news. Many other services are available, most, like DJNS, at a cost.

Businesses have numerous options for digital communication outside the organization. One innovation in particular holds promise: ISDN (Integrated Systems Digital Network). This system of switching equipment for the phone network eases the problem of obtaining connectivity among different makes of computers and computer-assisted devices.

Electronic Mail and Organizations

Chapter Two introduced electronic mail. In this section we will note some further points about this important technology.

Chapter Fifteen

Electronic mail is fast, convenient, and unintrusive. It has reduced **information float**—the time between when a message is sent and when it is received—to near zero. E-mail boosts efficiency and productivity when used responsibly. However, some users abuse E-mail, clogging it with trivia, personal messages, jokes, ads, or solicitations. Some fail to read their mail, which negates the information-float gain. Some write long, incomprehensible messages with the important elements buried on the fourth screenful. In response to these problems, some organizations have developed policy on E-mail use.

Employees and organizations have sometimes disagreed about how they can use E-mail. Some employees have complained when managers have tried to regulate use, calling such efforts invasion of privacy. A few cases went to court. In one case, a woman accused her manager of opening her E-mail mailbox and reading her personal mail. Thus far, the courts seem to favor organizations. Companies bought their E-mail systems and can use them as they see fit. At least for now, employees do not have a proprietary right to what they put into their organizations' E-mail systems.

Electronic mail reduces information float.

Thanks to LANs and WANs (wide area networks), computers, phones, modems, fax machines, and other technological tools, many workers need not make a daily trip to the office. Some occupations permit businesspeople to work in the office perhaps two days a week and work the other days either out of a home office or on the road. They send and receive information to and from the office in the course of the workday. Salespeople, auditors, programmers, brokers, writers, data-entry workers, and many others report increased productivity and lower stress due to avoiding the commute.

Not everyone is cut out to be a telecommuter, however. An ideal telecommuter is a motivated self-starter able to concentrate on work even if home needs beckon. Telecommuters need equipment at home and a specific area in the home set aside purely for work. They also need to be able to keep neighbors, dogs, and other friendly creatures from making demands on their work time.

Organizations can gain much from judicious use of telecommuting. Sometimes they can use the same office space for more than one person or purpose. They gain good-citizen points for taking a commuter off the streets and highways a couple of days a week. They reap the product of the worker's increased ability to concentrate on a task and sometimes all or most of the time the worker formerly spent traveling. These and other advantages are leading more organizations to consider telecommuting.

One drawback is possible isolation of workers. A telecommuter must work to prevent isolation. He or she must be enough of a people person to check in by phone frequently and to maintain a presence in the office on the days spent there. A second drawback is that some managers need to actually see their employees working. They worry that their telecommuters might be "toiling" over a beer and a good book in a hammock. Several solutions are possible here. Telecommuters should be carefully selected. Managers should put controls in place to ensure telecommuters' productivity. Co-workers should be able to rely on the telecommuters to be where they say they will be and to provide product and information on schedule.

Telecommuting can work well. Knowledge workers, in particular, will appreciate the chance to work when and where they work best. It is essential, however, that the workers, their managers, and their co-workers make sure they are integrated within the company's network.

Telecommuting and Organizations

Organizations can gain much from motivated telecommuters but must ensure that they are integrated in the organization's communication networks.

SMALL-GROUP MEETINGS

The Cost of Meetings

Many meetings waste time because leaders and participants do not think about their high cost.

Because organizations unite the efforts of many people and work toward common goals, meetings are essential.

Meetings are such a routine part of the business day that participants sometimes lose sight of their cost. Each manager or employee earns a specified amount for a workday hour, whether on a wage or a salary basis. Each person at a meeting earns that amount for the typical one-hour meeting. When you add the hour's wage or salary of each participant, the cost mounts rapidly.

Instead of each person working on his or her individual task, at a meeting all participants center on one task. While they do this, their other work, for which the organization also pays them, is not getting done. When the other work takes more time to complete, they are paid for that time, too.

Consider also that many meetings start late, last too long, and run inefficiently. Agenda items that managers could take care of with a memo crowd out necessary discussion items, which are put off until another meeting can be held. Finally, some meetings are held only because they have always been held.

Because of these costs and inefficiencies, meetings deserve extra attention. Careful planning, thorough preparation, and an eye on the wristwatch will help ensure that the meeting is worth its high cost.

BIZARRO   By DAN PIRARO

IT DOESN'T WANT TO GO TO THE MEETING...

BIZARRO By Dan Piraro is reprinted by permission of Chronicle Features, San Francisco, CA.

If meetings do not make good use of time, most participants would rather not go.

Jim Pickerell/Stock Boston

Meetings are essential for reaching the goals of most organizations.

Participating in Meetings

Sometimes you will chair or facilitate a meeting. Most often you will be one of the participants.

Meetings offer you many opportunities to advance both the organization's goals and your own. Thorough preparation will let you contribute intelligently. You can present your ideas in front of several people at once. You can "look promotable."

Read the agenda and supporting materials in advance. Think the items over. Analyze your own views, and obtain any information you will need when you present them at the meeting. Consider who else will attend and what they will want and need to hear in support of your views.

Don't jump in with ideas before you understand the issue. In fact, writers on the politics of meetings say that a smart participant waits to "see which way the wind is blowing" before speaking. It is foolish to commit yourself prematurely to a stand others will not support.

Don't try to take over the meeting, but do be available to help the meeting chair, if necessary. Avoid being an unproductive participant like those we will discuss on pages 510–511. When action items emerge from the discussion, volunteer for those that will permit you to use your time and strengths efficiently and effectively. Watch and analyze the strengths and weaknesses of the chairperson and other participants with a view toward strengthening your own performance in both roles.

Facilitating Meetings

Some meeting chairpersons make the mistake of thinking it is their show. For the chair to talk all or most of the time is usually an error. Given the cost of meetings, if the presence of the other participants is not integral to the task, the chair should question whether to hold a meeting at all. Meeting chairs should think of themselves as **facilitators:** people who elicit contributions from all participants, clarify unclear comments of others for the group, integrate contributions to create consensus, and handle turn taking.

Because being the chair adds weight to what the person says, the meeting leader should downplay his or her opinion, at least until other opinions have been aired. If the chair leads with an opinion, that opinion is fairly likely to become the group's opinion, even when a different one might have more merit. The following sections will include some techniques for spreading out the input.

Planning and Organizing Meetings

The success of a meeting often depends on planning that began weeks ahead of time.

Deciding on an Objective

A meeting without a clear objective will rarely yield a good product.

A meeting should serve one main purpose, with other issues subordinated or omitted. Will the meeting be a decision-making meeting? If so, state the objective:

> We will discuss the two feasibility studies, the one from our internal planners and the one from our outside consultant, and decide whether to lease 5,000 square feet more space in December.

Will it be a brainstorming meeting? State the objective:

> Revenue is down owing to a dip in the economy. We will explore the possible ways we can reduce expenses without cutting personnel.

Is it to be an information-sharing meeting? State the objective:

> Marketing, finance, accounting, facilities, and production will discuss their perspectives on the effects of offering the cleaning-product line in institutional sizes.

If the objective comprises several different issues, be sure they are ranked in order of greatest to least importance. If a department meets monthly, for instance, the objective might be to treat all matters of importance to the department that cannot be dealt with in any less time-consuming way.

Take care not to try to cover too much in one meeting, particularly one that participants will view as a typical one-hour meeting. A serious and complex issue might require several meetings. Or it might be best explored using a number of different communication media and channels.

Setting the Agenda

A clear agenda sets the stage for an efficient and effective meeting.

With the meeting's objective in mind, list in logical order the separate topics the meeting must cover. Make sure the objective is clear so that participants shape their expectations to meet it.

Schedule only the amount of time needed. If you will need less than an hour, schedule less. Nothing is magical about the one-hour time slot. People can do valuable work in the 15 or 30 minutes they are *not* sitting needlessly in a meeting. Beyond 90 minutes, most writers on meetings have suggested, productivity drops away rapidly. Schedule routine meetings for the customary amount of time, but increased efficiency might permit you to begin allocating less time even for these meetings.

Schedule the day, date, and time. Your ability to find a time when all needed persons can meet will depend on how much position power they have compared to you, how busy they and you are, and how firmly scheduled their other duties are. The harder they are to get, the earlier you must start trying to get them.

As you prepare the agenda, plan ways to engage others' participation at once, so that attenders hear voices other than yours from the very outset. If background must precede the statement of the objective, for example, assign a participant the task of presenting it.

Limit sharply any extraneous items. Announcements, for instance, should take little of a meeting's time. Do not let any announcements become discussion items. Such sidelights have run away with many a meeting.

Several days before the meeting, send all participants a copy of the agenda and any necessary support material. (Prepare extra copies to take to the meeting.) Send only what is necessary. Receiving an inch-thick stack of paper to read will daunt even well-meaning participants, and your stack will go unread. Do not send the agenda too early. Businesspeople's days are crowded with details on countless subjects and tasks. Too great a time lag—more than 10 days, for instance—can prevent their associating your agenda with the upcoming meeting. They may misplace the material and show up without it.

Selecting the Participants

Invite persons whose input is essential, who must take part in the decision, or who must be informed. Outside of these people, invite only those whom it would be impolitic to omit—for instance, an interested person whose support is needed in implementing decisions. With each added person in a meeting, group processes can grow more complex, and hearing from everyone takes more time.

Group processes grow more complex as the size of the meeting increases.

Others, if interested, can receive a copy of the agenda and a report of the meeting's minutes. Typically, people are glad to keep the hour free to do their own work.

Assign someone in advance to take minutes. Consider what each invitee can contribute. Sometimes you will want to ask one or more people formally to cover or present specific items. If you want specific questions asked but do not want to be always the one asking them, tap individuals in advance to do so.

Choosing the Physical Surroundings

Try to find the right space for the number of people and the meeting type. Five people huddled in one corner of a huge room will find the great space a barrier. The same five people crowded into one person's office will knock their knees and elbows together and set briefcases down on one another's feet. Furniture should be comfortable ("The mind can absorb no more than the seat can endure") but not sleep inducing.

In a meeting that is mainly informational, seat people in rows facing the speaker. If you seat them in a circle, they will feel like discussing the information instead of absorbing it. If they are supposed to discuss but cannot look at one another's faces, they will not discuss as effectively.

If audiovisual material or equipment is needed, order it. Make sure everything works in advance of the meeting.

Conducting Meetings

After your careful preparation, run the meeting you planned. Start on time, follow your agenda, elicit contributions from all attenders, control nonproductive or dysfunctional meeting behavior, and end on time.

Start on Time

If the schedule says to start at 9 A.M., at 9:01 the meeting should be under way. Stress the importance of sticking to the agenda and announce (good-naturedly) your intention to drag digressers back to it. Do not wait for latecomers, and do not stop to update them. If you start 10 minutes late, you will pay all participants one-sixth of an hour's pay for nothing. If this pattern establishes itself, the time wasting will continue, meeting after meeting. Starting on time rewards those who are prompt.

Follow the Agenda Efficiently

Meeting leaders must keep to the agenda.

Keep the discussion to the agenda. Give each item the time you allotted. At appropriate intervals, ask for consensus and then move on to the next item. If you inadvertently underscheduled time for an item, permit the group to develop it as needed, but be sure the need is justified. If you have sat in many meetings, you will often have seen the first couple of agenda items discussed far beyond any need, leaving time for only sketchy coverage of the last few.

Obtain Productive Input from All Participants

The chair must make sure all attenders contribute to the meeting.

Ideally, all members will contribute ideas in a courteous, orderly, intelligible manner. You may have to help. Some are weaker communicators than others, but give them time, and make sure others do not interrupt them. If someone has trouble expressing himself, try to paraphrase, but ask him to correct anything you have not stated to his satisfaction.

Make sure individuals feel genuinely welcome to disagree. Meetings at which intelligent objections are suppressed result in bad decisions. (See the section on groupthink on page 511.) Keep conflict constructive and nonhostile. If tension arises, clear the air with some low-key humor.

Productive contributors initiate ideas, expand them, critique them, support them, ask for clarification of them, and build on them. Because human beings are political, playful, and competitive, some "one-upmanship," or jockeying for influence, may occur. This is natural, typical, and harmless unless it gets out of hand.

Modify Nonproductive Behavior

Most participants will contribute positively, but the facilitator must deal with occasional exceptions. When a group member's behavior interferes with business, you must stop the behavior without losing the goodwill either of the problem person or the group. Coming on as a "heavy" will often alienate both. Above all, do not seem upset, defensive, or angry. Following are some familiar problem behaviors and at least one courteous means of dealing with each.

The dominating motormouth.   Is one person talking too much? Unable to get to the point? Feel free to interrupt her courteously. Break in and say, "Eileen, could you just summarize your main point?" Or, "Interesting, Eileen; I'd like to hear from Bruce how your idea strikes him. Bruce?" In a serious case, say, "Mm-hmm. Un-huh. Time is pressing us. We have three more agenda items, and we just have to move on. Let's talk about this after the meeting." Then smile.

The humorist.   A little humor can break tension, support group processes, smooth embarrassment, and even make a point memorably. Too much humor, though, especially when several people are investing costly time in an important task, is at best wasteful and at worst disruptive. If a would-be comedian is taking up valuable meeting time, stop the behavior even if everyone is having fun. The clock is running. Referring to the remaining agenda items, the meeting's unmet objective, and the possible need to schedule another meeting is usually a sobering thought.

For a tough case, some writers suggest dead seriousness. The comic cannot continue if the chair does not "get" the joke. Courteously ask him to repeat it. Then ask him to explain it. Then ask him how it relates to the task under discussion. Usually he will give up, and you can continue business.

The side-of-the-mouth saboteur.   Members of cliques and coalitions sometimes arrive at meetings and sit together. Sometimes, while chair and participants are trying to brainstorm or problem solve, two dissidents will be having their own minimeeting there at the table. Their running undercurrent of negative or sarcastic comments is distracting at best; at worst, others are drawn into their exchange, and the meeting falls apart.

Sometimes you will be able to pause, look at them inquiringly, and ask them to state their views for everyone. Do this (1) if you believe they are not generally supported and (2) if they have the habit of grumbling after the meeting to others who were there. The group will tend to unite with you and isolate them. Peer pressure can bring them back into line.

If you suspect in advance that you might have one or more muttering malcontents at your meeting, assign one a task that will occupy her too much to permit the whispered commentary. Or find her ideas so indispensable that she *has* to sit next to you. Are two pests already in place? Pull up a chair and sit between them, or send somebody else to do so. If they are on the same side of the table with someone between them, they cannot make eye contact with each other.

You might assign one the task of summarizing the comments of others to the others' satisfaction. If the summarizer tries to distort the comments, other participants, as well as the original commenter, are likely to object. This tactic gets the adverse message out into the open under conditions that do not favor it.

The shy violet.   Some people are slow to contribute. They ponder, and by the time they feel ready to speak, the discussion has moved past them. Or they are bright but unassertive. Or they are having a bad day. They were invited for a purpose, though, and are being paid for being there. The chair needs to elicit good value from them.

Address a specific question to them by name. Make sure it is a question on which they are likely to have some useful thoughts. Hitting them unexpectedly with a question they have not thought about will only reinforce their retiring ways. Give them a little extra time to answer. Drawing them out in ways the group approves will reinforce their willingness to contribute the next time.

The yes-person.   A meeting chair likes to feel supported. Sometimes, though, one group member will eagerly second everything said by the chair or by someone else perceived as influential. This tactic adds nothing, becomes ludicrous, and gets old fast. If her only comment is "I agree" or "Right! Right!" direct to her a question that forces her to develop the idea. Frame a question that cannot be answered with *yes* or *no:* "Tell about . . . ," "What do you see as a result of . . . ," "Compare what Bob said with . . . ," "How would you explain . . . ," "Why do you favor Bob's solution over Mary's suggestion that . . . " and the like.

If you know in advance about a person's *yes* habit, talk with her before the meeting. Assign her the job of finding the weaknesses in an idea you or the other influential person will cover. In the meeting, approve her efforts.

Groupthink is a dysfunctional meeting behavior in which the group is so cohesive that it fails to perceive its own weaknesses, the strengths of the opposition, and the pitfalls in its decisions. Groupthink plagues long-time work groups more than groups whose membership is more fluid. Group members become cheerleaders for the group and for one another.

Group members chide those who bring up negatives, indulge in excessively optimistic predictions and value statements, and suppress their own disagreement, often unaware that they are doing so. These habits lead to premature

Avoid Groupthink

Long-term, cohesive work groups are sometimes prone to groupthink, a dysfunctional meeting behavior.

Communicating in Organizations | 511

decisions based on faulty and incomplete information. Sometimes such decisions are disastrously costly.

As William J. Altier writes, "A problem that hasn't been anticipated can't be prevented."[5] Fostering constructive disagreement is essential, even if the chair has to prime a participant to act as devil's advocate.

Wrap Up and End on Time

If you have scheduled an hour for the meeting, by 10 minutes before the hour's end a summary should be in progress and action items specified and assigned. Explicitly say how the meeting's objective has been met. Finally, participants, having worked hard for an hour, will appreciate thanks from the chair.

Following Up

Meetings generate action. The chair and participants need to follow up.

Make sure the minutes are prepared, checked, photocopied, and distributed promptly. Check with all those who received assignments at the end of the meeting so that the action items see action and decisions are implemented.

Meetings Using Group Decision Support Systems

Although decision-making meetings need every member's best input, several elements of human nature tend to decrease members' candor and distort their judgment. As they sit around the meeting table, participants contemplate more than just the quality of the decision. They think about politics, personal risks and benefits, and other members' status. Considerations like these make them voice some ideas and withhold others. Good ideas from unregarded members are undervalued; those from highly regarded members are overvalued.

Obtaining thorough Input

A GDSS streamlines the stages of problem solving without loss of thoroughness.

In the late 1980s, researchers developed software for meetings to lower risk and equalize status. Using **group decision support systems** *(GDSSs),* participants can offer their comments, questions, and criticisms anonymously. A facilitator both operates the meeting software and moves the meeting through its phases. Unlike a meeting chair, the facilitator usually does not give input to the decision.

Most GDSS facilities contain a circle or semicircle of a dozen or so networked computers. Because all users face the center of the circle, no one can see any other user's screen. The software links them.

Participants key in ideas in response to the facilitator's prompts, which change as they progress through the phases of the decision process. The facilitator might first ask them to define the problem. If the problem is well defined, the first question to be answered in the meeting might be "What are the criteria for this decision?" The group can perform a brainstorming session, then derive the few best ideas from the brainstorming, then select a single strategy by applying the criteria, then decide how to implement the strategy. The facilitator sets the group a task, watches to see when the inputting slows down, asks them for consensus, takes their vote, and moves the group to the next part of the task.

GDSSs remove the political risk of contributing possibly unwelcome ideas.

Any participant can respond to any other participant's comment. Because no one knows who said what, comments center on the ideas rather than on personalities or status. Groupthink is unlikely because no one fears to point out the weaknesses in an idea. No one can show off. No one can intimidate anybody else. If the boss keys in a poor idea, the group is likely to discuss its shortcomings. As they do so, the boss does not lose face. Although they may suspect, no one knows for sure who keyed in the idea.

[5]William J. Altier, "The Power of Negative Thinking," *Business Horizons,* January–February 1991, p. 5.

Besides more thorough and representative input, the decision support system's other great advantage is time saving. In conventional meetings, members sometimes talk around and around a subject before finally meeting it head on. If the issue is sensitive, they defer, hedge, banter, complain, and dance all around it, sometimes spending hours, days, or even months before getting down to business.

Using a decision support system, members are aware of the clock. The meter is running. They are disinclined to respond to people with personal agendas or issues that do not address the problem. If no one supports an idea, the group moves around it and goes on. If several defend an idea, the group needs to consider it.

Studies of groups using decision support systems report that making decisions takes a fraction of the time that it does in around-the-table meetings. When multistep projects use decision support systems, the time line can be shortened still more.

Saving Time

After its riots of May 1992, Los Angeles appointed a committee to examine how best to rebuild South Central Los Angeles, the part of the city hit hardest by the disturbances. On the committee sat representatives of all stakeholders in the decision: Korean Americans, African Americans, Mexican Americans, Anglos, and many other ethnic groups not in those categories. They represented business interests, government interests, neighborhood groups, religious organizations, and many other coalitions. Their problem was how to make best use of the funds available for rebuilding. You can see immediately that such diverse groups would have strong ideas and even stronger feelings about the decisions to be made.

Consider the effect a decision support system might have in such a case. Although it would not create perfect group processes, it would give all participants an equal chance to express themselves and would diminish the filtering distortion caused by bias. How good an idea sounded would not depend on who expressed it; it would be judged on its own merits. Participants would not always have to show "solidarity" with their own group if a good idea came from outside it.

An Example of a GDSS's Usefulness

Business **teleconferencing** (*tele* means "far off, distant") began as an effort to decrease travel expenses when a number of people in locations remote from one another needed to meet. The earliest form was the **audioconference,** very much like the now familiar conference call.

Computer conferences let computer users join any other users who share the same network, whether a company's own network or one provided by an external vendor. Computer conferences differ from GDSSs, which are "real-time"; that is, all users are on the system at once, interacting with the facilitator and the other participants. GDSS users key input simultaneously and see others' messages as they are being keyed in. Computer conferences are not real-time. Messages are keyed in and sent to a central computer, which stores them until other users call them up. Some computer conferences end in a few hours; others can go on indefinitely.

Videoconferencing gives communicators much more information about one another than audioconferencing or computer conferencing does. Seeing others' facial expressions, posture, and gestures along with hearing their voices conveys meaning faster and more accurately.

Teleconferencing

All forms of teleconferencing let people hold a meeting despite geographic distance among members.

Communication in ad hoc
videoconferences is mostly one-
way video with limited two-way
audio communication.

Three kinds of videoconferencing are ad hoc, freeze-frame (or slow-scan), and full-motion, fully interactive. Businesses use **ad hoc** videoconferencing to send one visual conference one way to a large number of receivers. The receivers cannot send a return video signal, but some have the opportunity to send audio messages. Ad hoc teleconferences work well for events such as new-product introductions. Automakers, for instance, have put on ad hoc videoconferences to introduce a year's new models. They schedule sales meetings in one large city in each state, gather dealers and representatives in conference centers in those cities, and beam a polished, high-quality informational and promotional broadcast to those locations. The broadcast is both festive and motivating. Educational institutions use ad hoc videoconferences to send major events of academic meetings to other interested schools. Ad hoc videoconferences are not meetings in the full sense; communication is mostly one way.

Freeze-frame and **full-motion** videoconferences are meetings in which senders and receivers interact in both directions. These two media differ in quality of realism and in price. Freeze-frame is relatively inexpensive but not very natural-seeming. The receiver sees a picture of a person, but it is a still picture that changes, or "refreshes," every few seconds. The full-motion video is expensive, but it provides far greater realism. It offers the picture quality of network television, although the "performances" are less polished. While people should—and do—prepare carefully for the meeting to conserve time and get the job done well, the video captures the everyday communication of business professionals.

In both types of videoconference, participants sit at a half-table facing a screen on which they see the participants in a remote location, sitting at a similar half-table. Both full-motion and freeze-frame conferencing allow the use of ancillary technologies. For instance, a person at either end of the conference could say to the camera, "Here's a copy of the contract" and send a fax immediately. Participants in both kinds of conference have reported some difficulty in liking people whom they met for the first time via videoconference. The "vibes" that occur when people first meet, shake hands, look at each other's eyes, and smile do not seem to transmit across distance. If the people have met before in person, liking is not a problem.

Without getting far into technicalities, we need to mention that the line separating a freeze-frame from a full-motion videoconference is blurring. Two changes—new and better transmission channels and better codecs (compression-*de*compression devices)—are making them more similar.

In the past, videoconferences had to be transmitted through whatever channel was available, often only a telephone wire. The phone wires could not carry a very dense signal, which restricted the speed at which a freeze-frame image could refresh. Where channels with greater capacity are available, such as a fiber optic network or microwave via satellite, much more data can be sent per second. The eye perceives the illusion of motion when an image refreshes at the rate of about 30 frames per second.

The other change is the continually improving codec. This device processes the signal to send it in its most stripped-down useful form. A full-motion picture can lose a little of its sharpness and still be very useful and natural seeming. Thus, the price of full motion is coming down, and freeze-frame is becoming less and less "frozen."

In the early 1980s, only a handful of the largest organizations had full-motion videoconferencing, including Arco, Boeing, and Allstate. Improvements and price drops are bringing this technology within reach of many more.

Although videoconferencing is a tool and not a show, most participants feel the need to prepare their remarks. Many even practice them ahead of time, wishing to avoid seeming thoughtless or disorganized. Some videoconference content, of course, is spontaneous; yet the condensed time frame intensifies the impressions made. Then, too, the meter really *is* running; in addition to equipment and facilities costs, operating costs are considerable. Thus, people tend to keep to the agenda and proceed efficiently.

Organizations with teleconferencing report productivity gains, travel savings, and increased flexibility. With the technology improving continually, the business future of many workers is likely to hold some form of teleconferencing.

Two-way videoconference participants should try to seem knowledgeable, articulate, and organized.

REVIEW

Whether an organization's culture is strong or weak, employees must learn both written and unwritten rules to fit in and succeed. As they learn acceptable behaviors in their organization, they develop their own power and influence. The chapter discussed five kinds of power: position (legitimate), reward, punitive, expert, and referent. Different kinds of power offer different means of influencing peers, co-workers, and, to some extent, superiors.

The formal organizational communication network follows the structure of the organization. Informal networks, notably the grapevine, are amorphous, fast, and only partly accurate. Yet organization members must access them to stay aware of events and sometimes to correct what they contain. Barriers to an organization's communication include too many transfer stations, information overload, bottlenecks, hoarding or withholding information, and cliques and in-groups. Technological advances in organizational communication include local and wide area networks and information services, electronic mail, and telecommuting.

The pervasiveness of meetings should not distract from their high cost. This chapter discussed effective means of participating in and leading or facilitating meetings. The technological innovations of group decision support systems and of teleconferences typically improve the effectiveness of meetings and save on travel and time.

APPLICATION EXERCISES

1. If you now work or have worked, consider the culture of the organization you know best. (If not, think of a club or other group in which you participate regularly.) Mentally analyze the culture. Is the atmosphere tense? Relaxed? Casual? Businesslike? How do people exchange information? Casually? Generously? Formally? Cautiously? Who are the influential people? How do you know? Consider other rules, both explicit and implicit. Write a paragraph describing the culture of this organization.

2. In the organization you described in Exercise 1, what types of power do you hold? Who holds the most position power? Expert power? For these individuals, does high referent power accompany high position and expert power? Why or why not?

3. Over whom do you hold at least some reward power? Punitive power? Who holds these types of power over you? Think in both tangible and intangible terms.

4. Think of a case where you saw an individual break an "unwritten rule" of an organization. What should that individual have known, and how should he or she have known it?

5. What means of developing personal power are open to employees? Tell how they can be used with subordinates, with peers, and with superiors.

6. Explain the differences between formal and informal communication networks in organizations.

7. What is the grapevine? What are its advantages and disadvantages?

8. What grapevines do you access at present, and for what purposes? How reliable are they?

9. What is information overload? Under what conditions do you become overloaded? In what different ways do you respond to overload?

10. In the organization you considered in Exercise 1,
    a. Do cliques, in-groups, or informal opinion leaders exist?
    b. How does a newcomer become aware of them?
    c. How does a newcomer know what to do about them?

11. What is "information float"? How is it affected by E-mail?

12. In the organization you considered in Exercise 1,
    a. Describe a typical meeting: agenda (Is there one? Do you receive it beforehand? Is it appropriate?), effective or ineffective use of time, type of leadership, members' willingness to contribute, incidence of "political" behavior (good or bad), incidence of disruptive behavior.
    b. Do the meetings typically accomplish a known objective in a timely way? Discuss.

13. What is a group decision support system? What are its advantages over a standard around-the-table meeting? Do you see any disadvantages? Explain.

14. The chapter gave the "Rebuild Los Angeles" group as an example of a problem-solving group with much to gain by using a group decision support system. Think of an example from your own business or community in which a GDSS would produce better results in less time than a standard meeting. Discuss.

15. Differentiate among these types of teleconferencing: computer, audio, ad hoc, freeze-frame, and full-motion.

CASES

As you analyze these cases, recall and apply the chapter's discussion of organizational culture, rules, kinds of power and politics, formal and informal communication networks, and appropriate meeting behaviors for leaders and participants.

1. **Junior CIA Man.** Brian, an inventory control worker, disliked Kirk, his immediate supervisor. Brian decided to keep a file on Kirk. Every time he observed Kirk taking a break, kidding around, or being what Brian considered unproductive, he noted these impressions in the file. His fellow employees noticed what he was doing and wondered what he intended to do with the file. Before he could do anything with it, the file fell into the hands of higher management. Ms.

Greeley, purchasing manager, told Brian coldly, "We like the morale Kirk has going in inventory control. I seriously wonder how productive *you* can be, if this is the way you spend your time."

2. **Don't Look for Me to Say Anything Next Time.** A computer program was put in place at Fidelity Liberty to generate letters notifying customers who bought travel insurance of an across-the-board refund ranging between $1 and $9. The program had a glitch. Instead of $1 to $9, the letters said $10,000 to $90,000. The letters were signed using an automatic signature machine and were never reviewed. No one caught the mistake until the mailroom people had the good sense to question why a $90,000 refund would be

due on a $200 policy. They put the letters on hold until they ascertained whether to mail them or destroy them. The letters were destroyed, of course. Once the error was discovered, the managers and supervisors all blamed one another. For two weeks, little got done and the mailroom personnel struggled with a backlog. Other employees had to pitch in and help get the new letters out. The person who had brought the error to the appropriate manager's attention was called derogatory names, deemed a troublemaker, and accused of trying to climb the corporate ladder at the expense of the other supervisors.

3. **Who Butters the Bread Around Here?** Claude, a technical writer at an engineering firm, put in long days working on a proposal with several senior engineers and architects. Claude's supervisor, Penny, reviewed their draft, made corrections, wrote the final draft, sent it out on time, but did not inform the engineering side or send them a copy. Two days after the deadline, Penny wrote the vice president a long memo criticizing the engineers and architects and taking full credit for meeting the deadline "despite the many writing problems created by the technical side." She did not send engineering a copy of her memo. Senior management laughed at the memo and faxed it to others with "Warning! The spellchecker's [sic] are in revolt" written across the top. Penny—and Claude—sank to the bottom of the credibility list. "What nerve!" one architect scoffed. "This is a technical firm. We create the value. Those writers are nothing but overhead."

4. **But My Teammates Are Such Pros!**
Consultants at Inno-Getics, a management services firm, have considerable autonomy. Professionalism is a "given," although the corporate culture is relaxed. Jake, a highly capable consultant hired four months earlier, was project team leader on a new project. He put heavy effort into the work and relied strongly on his teammates. He considered the others to be just as important as he. The first Tuesday in May was the kick-off meeting to launch the project. It rained heavily that day and Jake, who had a two-hour commute to the meeting site, decided his teammates could handle the meeting without him and did not go. The general ledger and accounts payable team members were there; so were two other Inno-Getics people and three representatives of the client. At 11 A.M., Jake's manager reached him by phone. "Since you didn't show up, we canceled the meeting," the manager said. "You stood up your client. Just why did you think that would be acceptable?"

5. **The 10-Minute Expert.** One purpose served by the two-hour weekly staff meetings at Liffey Inc. was to pass on and discuss information received from higher management and to establish requirements based on the new material. Supervisors got this information at a weekly supervisors' meeting the evening prior to the staff meeting. Martin, a 10-year supervisor of one operations department, knew that Jeremy, one of his subordinates, was applying for a supervisor's job. Martin took Jeremy along to the supervisors' meeting to give him more exposure to the new duties he hoped to take on. The next day, at the staff meeting, Jeremy disagreed with what Martin said about a procedure they had both heard discussed the night before. Martin told him, "The information you heard last night is general. Supervisors have some leeway in adjusting it to the environment and the group's work style." Jeremy pushed it: "All the same, that's not what they said at the supervisors' meeting last night." Martin silenced Jeremy with a few sharp words and continued with his interpretation of the procedure.

6. **You Consult with Me. I Don't Consult with You.** Karen broke "the glass ceiling" and moved into a vice president−personnel position in her manufacturing firm. Eager to show top management they had made a good decision, she developed and launched a new, corporationwide performance appraisal program. Managers and supervisors had deep reservations about several appraisal criteria in her plan. They asked her why she hadn't asked for their input. Several offered some simple modifications to her plan that they said would make it much more workable. She told them, "Look, I don't have time to do PR for this program. My job is personnel; I know the field inside and out, and my nameplate says vice president. Implement this program." Resistance hardened. The program failed embarrassingly and expensively.

7. **A Logical Deduction, Not an Information Theft.** Frank, a high-ranking manager in a government agency, heard a rumor that Tom, one of his subordinates, had accessed a personal records database he was not authorized to use. In a staff meeting, Frank turned the discussion to budget line items and casually inquired, "What do you suppose Mary Kay is making?" "I'd say at least $45,000," Tom said. "That proves it," Frank snapped. "How did you crack the password code on that database?" Tom turned pale, and the rest of the staffers stared at Frank. Finally, Tom said, "Mary Kay's job is the same as the one being advertised this week in the *Star*. Salary range is

$42,000 to $45,000 to start. Mary Kay has been here four years. I hope you don't really think I've broken into the records database." Frank glared at Tom and said, "Well, just watch yourself."

8. **Monkey See, Monkey Call in Before Monkey Do.** Edu-Ware sells educational products by appointment to buyers for school districts. Helen, a new and promising sales rep, arrived at 9:25 A.M. for a 9:00 A.M. appointment with one of these clients. She did not seem worried. "I've seen other people come skating in 10 or 15 minutes late," she said, "so why single me out?" "Because your appointment steamed out of here at 9:15 complaining about bad service in front of a lobby full of customers," the supervisor replied. "Anybody you ever saw arrive 15 minutes late had called to let us know. Then we can reassure the client, and sometimes somebody else can cover. Didn't you look at this client's file? Last year her orders totaled $20,000."

9. **And I Don't Like Standing When the Judge Comes in, Either.** Blake, a young police officer, arrested and brought in a suspect who was the son of another officer, Parker. Blake treated the son the same as any other individual, since he was 18 years old. Blake did not communicate to Parker what had occurred. Parker felt betrayed. The culture dictated that officers look out for their own. Mabrito, a friend of both Blake and Parker, told Blake, "Nobody is saying you shouldn't have arrested the kid, but you could have at least let Parker know. You look like a jerk." Blake said, "I followed the law. This stupid culture needs changing." "You *are* a jerk," Mabrito said.

10. **Nine × ($280 + Overhead + Travel + Cost of Undone Work) = Waste.** Regional managers, the corporate planning officer, and corporate staff support people in a large automotive parts supplier met for a day-long strategic planning retreat. Harry, the corporate planner, handed out an agenda. "Okay," he said, "Let's start with a budget overview. Vera," he said to one of his staffers, "what did you bring us on budget?" Vera handed around a paper. "Where are the projections, Vera?" asked Harry. Vera said, "Was I supposed to get you projections?" "Well, I'd have thought strategic planning rather implied as much," Harry replied. Eddie, a regional manager, glanced down the agenda and said, "Harry, these weren't the topics I thought would be on the agenda. The records I've brought don't apply, and I'm not really prepared to generate ideas on what you have here." "This is different from what I expected also," Carrie, another regional manager, said. "Don't you people know what strategic planning is?" Harry demanded.

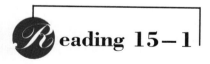

$\mathcal{R}$eading 15–1

"COMPUTERIZING" DULL MEETINGS IS TOUTED AS AN ANTIDOTE TO THE MOUTH THAT BORED

William M. Bulkeley

Just about the most expensive and inefficient thing companies do is hold meetings. Talkers filibuster. Dreamers daydream. Everyone walks out complaining that nothing was accomplished.

But evidence is accumulating that computers can make this most human of activities much more productive. Some professional meeting facilitators are using numeric keypads connected to a personal computer to let everyone at a meeting secretly vote on issues. A few companies and universities are building meeting rooms costing $50,000 to $200,000 equipped with a dozen or more connected personal computers; those at the meeting hammer away on keyboards instead of jabbering at each other.

"We're having the quietest, least stressful, most productive meetings you've ever seen," says Carl DiPietro, vice president, human resources at Marriott Corp.'s architecture and construction division. Marriott, which uses a program called VisionQuest from Collaborative Technologies Corp., Austin, Texas, finished a computerized meeting room last fall. In two months, 1,000 people used the room to generate and organize 10,000 ideas, he says. Mr. DiPietro and his associates estimate traditional meetings would have taken nine to 12 times longer to accomplish as much.

Advocates of computerized meetings say the computer helps leaders stick to an agenda, partly because people digress less with a keyboard than they do orally. Meetings typically include some oral discussion, but most of the progress occurs on computer screens. Voting on the importance of each issue means those at the meeting often

Source: William M. Bulkeley, "'Computerizing' Dull Meetings Is Touted as an Antidote to the Mouth That Bored," *The Wall Street Journal*, January 28, 1992, p. B7.

discover that everyone agrees and that there isn't any need for passionate speeches extolling a particular viewpoint.

Several studies seem to prove computerized meetings work much better. Boeing Co. analyzed 64 groups using a meeting room equipped with personal computers and TeamFocus software sold by International Business Machines Corp. It found that total time involved in meetings was cut by 71%. The calendar time required for team projects involving meetings was cut a whopping 91%.

IBM has built 45 computerized meeting rooms for its own use. In a 1990 study of 30 meetings in such rooms, it reported average time reductions of 56% compared with expectations of those at the meetings.

The most elaborate computerized meeting systems save time in a variety of ways. Typically, a meeting starts out with everyone typing out ideas on a subject for half an hour. Ideas appear on a big screen in front of the room as fast as people write them. Everyone is writing simultaneously, often conforming to tight limits on length. Everyone is anonymous so there isn't any showing off or intimidation.

"It definitely improves the productivity of brainstorming," says Lynn Reed, vice president, technology, at New York bank J.P. Morgan & Co., which built a computerized meeting room late last year. "We'll have 10 or 12 managers generating 60 to 100 ideas in half an hour."

Then participants categorize and rank ideas. "The difficult thing isn't getting the ideas thumbtacked on the wall—it's how do you reduce this to something manageable," says Dana Cound, vice president, quality management, at GenCorp, an Akron, Ohio, rubber and plastic maker. GenCorp executives used a voting system called OptionFinder made by Option Technologies Inc., Mendota Heights, Minn., in a recent strategy meeting. "It was incredible, the ability of this technique to bring order out of chaos," Mr. Cound says.

"Naming a new product, we got 75 names. We were able to narrow it to 10 names in 45 minutes," says Bruce Ezell, business development manager at Dell Computer Corp., Austin, Texas, which uses VisionQuest. "On problems where people like to discuss and discuss and discuss, this gives a way to quickly list and prioritize."

When users rank issues by importance, they quickly see whether they are talking the same language. Proponents of teamwork—one of the management buzzwords of the '90s—say that American teams tend to slide over disagreements by talking in vague generalities. Then they say they have consensus while each goes his own way after leaving the meeting. "With the John Wayne management style,

there's no real need for this sort of thing," says Mr. Cound of GenCorp. "It's easy for the boss to get 12 people in a room for half an hour and then say, 'We're all in agreement here.'" Team organization "is a messier process," he notes.

At Greyhound Financial Corp., a Phoenix, Ariz., unit of Dial Corp., each department head orally presents annual plans to a computerized meeting of the other department heads. Listeners then type in comments, criticisms or areas where they can provide support. Greyhound has used meeting software made by Ventana Corp., Tucson, Ariz., for three years. The computerized method is "much faster and more inviting than sending out long memos for comment," says Samuel Eichenfeld, Greyhound president.

Users claim computerization enhances many types of meetings. Instead of doing an employee survey, Marriott conducted a one-hour computerized focus group with a few employees to help a new manager prepare his initial speech to his employees. Maryam Alavi, a professor at the University of Maryland, says corporations pay $2,000 to $3,000 a day to use its computerized meeting room. She says groups have designed employee-recognition programs, developed training requirements for a quality-management program, come up with ideas for an annual conference, developed annual objectives for different departments and even specified attributes for a high level job opening.

Nevertheless, with only an estimated 200 computerized rooms installed around the country, sales have "been slower than expected. I would have liked to have sold twice as many," says Sterling Phillips, who heads IBM's program selling TeamFocus. "While people think meetings are unproductive, there's an intuitive reaction that they can't imagine people sitting around pounding on PCs." Even at IBM many employees are unfamiliar with the technology.

"You're really changing the culture," says Jay Nunamaker, a University of Arizona professor who founded Ventana. "Managers have been promoted based on their ability to go into a meeting and drive home their agenda. Now we're moving into the age of teams."

For all those companies that want to make their meetings more productive without changing their culture, Bernard de Koven has just the product. Mr. de Koven is president of the Institute for Better Meetings, a Palo Alto, Calif., consulting firm. His $40 Meeting Meter software displays on a computer screen the running cost of a meeting based on room charges and participants' salaries. "It's tongue-in-cheek," he says. "But it's useful—like knowing how to count calories."

Chapter Sixteen

Communication in Managing and Supervising

PREVIEW

Many new graduates begin almost immediately to oversee the activities of others. This chapter will help you fulfill these responsibilities with maximum benefit to the task and to the people involved. New graduates also represent their employers to many groups. In this chapter you will read about managerial interviewing, appraising performance, disciplining and motivating, managing conflict, and communicating with a business's many "publics." ●

Rita Carmody
Technical Services Manager

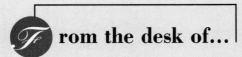

rom the desk of...

Unresolved Conflict—at the Worst Possible Time

I work at a flavors and fragrances firm. Last winter, a new and complex problem related to product quality arose. Sales told a major customer that we could supply a new mix before asking Technical if we could actually do it.

Sales and Technical have traditionally had tensions. The vice president who supervises both functions always just says, "Work it out." Usually we do. This time we tried, but not hard enough, as became clear.

I was pretty sure we could solve the technical problem by changing our monitoring process, but I needed more time. Communications flew back and forth, gradually becoming accusatory. Finally, *in a meeting with the customer*, the sales manager, Kirby, astonished me by first trying to blame the problem on our suppliers but then reversing himself and saying Technical did not know yet how to solve his problem. I had to think and act quickly to minimize the damage done by Kirby's double message, and was fairly successful—by which I mean we lost only $125,000 instead of much more.

Kirby and I are both to blame for this, but I think the vice president let us down. He left us on our own, and we didn't get it right.

The communication failure described above could have been headed off by skillful interviewing and conflict resolution. Instead, despite good intentions, this firm made a bad impression on important internal and external groups, including a high-value customer. We will begin this chapter by discussing managerial interviewing.

INTERVIEWING: FROM THE ORGANIZATION SIDE OF THE DESK

When most business students think of interviewing, they envision themselves eagerly communicating their credentials to a prospective employer. Once they are hired, however, their perspective changes. They will be "on the other side of the desk," giving and receiving information as members of an organization rather than as outsiders vying for the invitation to join it.

The Objective: Obtaining and Sharing Information

People interview to give and receive business information.

An **interview** is a meeting in which two or more individuals give and receive information. In a business interview, the participants typically serve both the organization's goals and their own goals.

For the most effective interview, the participants should plan beforehand what the interview is to accomplish. For instance, a supervisor about to correct an employee's problem behavior needs to make at least a mental agenda. The agenda tasks include objectively describing the problem, drawing from the employee his or her ideas and explanations, and outlining means and expectations for correcting the problem. A manager with a conflict to manage or resolve mentally lists what is already known and what must be learned from the persons in conflict.

Types of Interviews

Many new graduates are likely to engage in some supervision, often including hiring, problem solving, and performance appraisal. This section examines the recruitment interview and the problem-solving interview. Performance appraisal is discussed in a later section.

Interviewers and interviewees share a common goal in employment interviews: Both want an excellent fit between person and job. Although each communicator in such an interview seeks to emphasize some things and de-emphasize or conceal others, both sides gain when the genuinely important facts about applicant and organization are brought to light.

Both sides must tell the truth and nothing but the truth. Recall that telling the *whole* truth is not possible and would be unwise even if it were possible. The unwritten rules about employment interviews say that each side will present itself in the best light that the truth will support.

Each side knows the other is likely to conceal some information. Ethics demands, however, that each side avoid deliberately misleading the other on any essential point. Doing so is foolish in any case, and sometimes punishable. For instance, an applicant who says she has a degree she does not have can be fired if the falsehood comes to light after hire. Similarly, an interviewer who implies a promise of benefits that cannot be delivered is behaving unethically. Legal actions sometimes result when an organization abuses an applicant's trust.

An application interview contains elements of a negotiation. The interviewer holds more negotiating power than does a new graduate but should not make an issue of it. Also, many applicants will be experienced. The more

BIZARRO   By DAN PIRARO

...I ASK ALL PROSPECTIVE EMPLOYEES THE SAME TWO QUESTIONS, MR. TRENT: ARE YOU FILLED WITH THE SPIRIT OF VOLUNTEER-ISM, AND DO YOU LIKE MAGIC?

BIZARRO By Dan Piraro is reprinted by permission of Chronicle Features, San Francisco, CA.

This managerial interviewer is *not* a good role model for you.

desirable credentials the applicant acquires, the more power she holds in the exchange.

Both participants are buying *and* selling. The interviewer is promoting his organization as well as drawing out information about the applicant's qualifications. If the applicant draws unfavorable inferences about the interviewer, the job, or the organizational environment, not even "senior-year job hunger" can maintain the candidate's interest in a job or company she suspects she will dislike.

If the applicant's education and training are inappropriate but she is hired anyway, no one wins. Either too much or too little preparation for a specific vacancy can lead to wasted time and money. If the dissatisfied new hire quits, she takes on the stress and expense of another job search, and the organization must spend again to rehire and retrain. If she stays but underproduces or, worse, makes expensive errors, she acquires a weak work record, and the organization incurs costs. Sometimes an overqualified person can be moved to a more appropriate job, but often another person with longer tenure in the organization deserves—and receives—the job instead.

If you are asked to interview job applicants, request some training. At minimum, read about interviewing, familiarize yourself with your organization's needs, and brush up on the laws and regulations covering employment. For each interview you conduct, familiarize yourself fully with the position description and the preparation needed.

Cultivate a completely open mind about types of applicants, and concentrate on credentials. Women, racial and ethnic minorities, older workers, workers with disabilities, and several other categories of workers are accorded equal access to employment under the law. Exhibit 16–1 shows the pertinent laws and dates, the categories protected, and the types of employers regulated. One additional law, the Americans with Disabilities Act passed in 1990, prohibits all employers, even private businesses, from discriminating against disabled persons in employment decisions. Employers must provide "reasonable accommodation" to employees and applicants with disabilities, though those accommodations need not be provided if they constitute "undue hardship" to the businesses.

Prejudice is still active. Make sure it does not cloud your judgment. Similarly, avoid practicing reverse discrimination—discrimination against white male applicants. Look for the best applicant for the job.

The interview itself typically proceeds as follows: After the applicant and the interviewer meet and shake hands, the interviewer makes brief "small talk" to help the applicant relax. Topics can address interests and experiences but not those (religious activities or national origin, for instance) that would bring up possibly discriminatory information. Note that any such information *volunteered* by the applicant can be discussed—but do not probe for more. Devote most of the interview to exploring (1) whether the applicant has the appropriate level of preparation for the job or can be cost-effectively trained for it and (2) whether the applicant will mesh well with the work group and the organization.

During the interview, watch nonverbals but remember how inexact a science the interpretation of nonverbals is. Do not judge anything too soon. Be willing to revise an opinion. Realize that the condensed format of the interview tends to push an interviewer toward premature closure.

Because you will often interview multiple applicants, make sure you ask all of them the same questions in the same way. It is a good idea to *list the*

In recruitment interviews, the applicant and the organization are both buyers and sellers.

A bad hiring decision by an unskilled interviewer can be costly.

Nonverbals should be observed but not overemphasized.

Major Equal Employment Opportunity Laws	Objectives	Jurisdiction
Equal Pay Act (1963)	Equal pay for equal work regardless of sex	Employers engaged in interstate commerce and most employees of federal, state, and local governments
Title VII of the Civil Rights Act (1964) (as amended in 1972)	EEO for different races, colors, religions, sexes, and national origins	Employers with 15 or more employees; unions with 15 or more members; employment agencies; union hiring halls; institutions of higher education; federal, state, and local governments
Age Discrimination in Employment Act (1967) (as amended from age 65 to 70 in 1978)	EEO for ages 40 to 70	Employers with 20 or more employees; unions with 25 or more members; employment agencies; federal, state, and local governments
Vocational Rehabilitation Act (1973)	EEO and reasonable affirmative action for people with disabilities	Federal government agencies and government contractors with contracts of $2,500 or more
Pregnancy Discrimination Act (1978)	EEO during pregnancy	Same as for Civil Rights Act

Source: Keith Davis and John W. Newstrom, *Human Behavior at Work: Organizational Behavior* (New York: McGraw-Hill, 1985), p. 402.

questions in writing and to make notes of the applicant's responses. Fill out your notes as soon as possible after the interview ends. Memory can fail you. Active listening is hard work, and you usually see a series of applicants in one day.

Employers are not supposed to ask, either on job applications or in interviews, any questions with answers that might permit them to discriminate against underrepresented groups. *If* a person who was refused a job can prove in court that such discrimination took place and resulted in the loss of a job to which he or she was entitled, money damages can be awarded and the job gained after all.

An exception is the **bona fide occupational qualification** *(BFOQ)*. A BFOQ is a characteristic that is integral to the job itself. Ethnic origin, sex, and age are usually *not* specific to a job. However, in a job requiring heavy lifting, for example, an employer could set as a BFOQ the ability to lift 80 pounds to shoulder height. This requirement might keep some women (but not all) out of the job. It might exclude persons with certain disabilities, but not others. It might also exclude some men.

A BFOQ is a characteristic that is integral to the job.

Questions like those in Exhibit 16–2 are probably nondiscriminatory. Notice that the questions are open-ended—designed to get the applicant talking—rather than questions that can be answered with only a word or two.

The questions in Exhibit 16–3 might be grounds for unfair discrimination.

EXHIBIT 16–2   Questions that Are Probably Nondiscriminatory

1. What kind of position interests you most?
2. What two or three things that you've done have been most satisfying? Why?
3. Why did you choose to apply to this organization?
4. What are your career objectives? What do you see yourself doing in five years? Ten?
5. How would you describe yourself?
6. What made you choose the career you're preparing for?
7. What made you choose the college or university you're graduating from?
8. What do you know about our organization?
9. What studies did you like most in college? Least?
10. Why should I hire you?
11. What job have you liked best? Least?
12. Describe the ideal boss.
13. How do you feel about relocating?
14. What are your greatest strengths? Weaknesses?
15. In your opinion, do your grades indicate well what you've achieved academically?
16. How do you think you can contribute to our company?
17. If you could go back five years, what would you do differently?
18. How do you feel about overtime work? Traveling on the job?
19. Describe your least favorite boss or teacher.
20. What kinds of references would you receive from former employers?
21. What do you think is the most important contribution you've made in your present job?
22. What do you feel this company can do for you?

EXHIBIT 16–3   Questions that Might Be Discriminatory

1. What is your maiden name?
2. How old are your children? How old is your youngest child?
3. What is your birth date?
4. Have you ever declared bankruptcy?
5. Are you married? (Single? Divorced? Separated? Widowed?)
6. (More subtle form of the same question): Is there anyone in your life who strongly influences your decisions?
7. Who will care for your children while you are working?
8. How long have you lived at your present address?
9. What is your father's name?
10. Have you ever had your wages garnished?
11. Where do you bank? Do you have any loans outstanding?
12. Do you own or rent your home?
13. Were you ever arrested?
14. What religious group do you belong to? What is the name of your priest? (Rabbi? Minister?)
15. Where does your husband (wife, father, mother) work?
16. How did you learn to speak Spanish (German, Russian, etc.)?
17. List for me all the societies, clubs, and lodges you belong to.

Think hard about what you can ask. Think equally hard about what you really want to find out. Frame your questions so that you learn what the organization really needs to know but do not discriminate.

For example, you—and your organization—would like to know whether a parent of small children will miss work often to take care of family needs. But you cannot safely ask about family responsibilities. If you do, you could lay the organization open to ill will or even to a lawsuit. *Even if you could ask questions such as this, obtaining the information would not necessarily predict anything useful.* Workers differ greatly in their ability and willingness to handle multiple responsibilities. Rather than probing into applicants' personal lives, which is dangerous, interviewers do better to sketch scenarios in which they set the applicant a hypothetical *work* problem and ask "what-if" questions about it. For instance:

> Suppose you are on your way to an 8:30 A.M. meeting and you are involved in a three-car fender bender at a downtown intersection. No one is injured, and your car is drivable, but the property damage is high enough that those involved are required to stay and give statements. You cannot get to the meeting before about 8:55. In your briefcase you have several exhibits that will be needed in the meeting. What would you do?

Look for maturity and flexibility in the responses. If the applicant says, "I guess I'd just kiss my raise goodbye and hope for another chance," or "Oh, no! Not my Beamer!" it matters little whether the person is a single father of tonsillitis-prone toddlers, a genius, or both. He is not a problem solver. If he says, however, "Most coffee shops downtown have installed faxes to appeal to the business crowd. I'd call . . . ," you are listening to a person with considerable presence of mind and good attitudes toward work and responsibility.

Use the interview time efficiently. Do not talk too much yourself, but be ready to address the interviewee's questions and to present the company favorably to the job seeker.

At the end of the interview, tell the candidate the decision time line if you can. Express appreciation for the interest shown. Leave him or her with a positive impression of you and your organization. Only one (or at most a few) can be hired, but each applicant is likely to convey impressions of your organization to others. Afterward, do what you say you will do. If you promised a phone call when the decision is made, make sure the applicant gets a call.

Researchers have repeatedly shown that the employment interview itself is less valid in predicting employee behavior than various preemployment tests are. However, organizations continue to prefer the interview despite its flawed validity. Try to question impartially, interpret intelligently, and represent your organization with integrity and tact.

Although recruitment interviews are not good predictors of employees' job success, organizations are unlikely to give them up.

Interviewing to Solve Problems

Problem-solving interviews do not fall into easy categories. Managerial work means dealing with many unpredictable elements. Shortages, mistakes, communication gaps, schedule crises, disappointing defect rates, and dozens of other things might move a manager to hold a one-on-one meeting to analyze and solve a problem.

The usual problem-solving interview moves through these steps:

1. Recognizing and defining the problem.
2. Determining source or cause.

R. Llewellyn/Superstock, Inc.

Interviewing to solve problems calls for active listening, logical thinking, and an attitude that is both empathetic and impartial.

3. Considering alternative means of solution.
4. Determining objectives to be achieved.
5. Choosing a means of solution.
6. Devising means of implementing the solution.
7. Monitoring and following up.

Let's follow this process through an example.

Through grapevine contacts, you hear that Rich, one of your supervisors, favors a newcomer named Lloyd and expects too much from his other people. You know their productivity is down; end-of-month reports have been late twice out of the last five months. Rich is stressed because he needs his department's effort to prepare for an external audit scheduled for next month. You ask Rich to your office to get his perspective. Your objective is to gain information that will show how to solve the problem.

Rich agrees his people are unproductive and discontented. He blames Glynis, whom he views as a troublemaker. You ask more low-key questions: When did the problem start? What other disagreements have there been? You want to get to the root of the problem but are also aware of an organization's responsibility to support its managers unless they are behaving incompetently.

The two of you talk to Lloyd and, one by one, to the seven other women and men in the department. Finally one employee, Marie, reluctantly tells you both how the employees see the case: They think Rich promoted Lloyd to "show" Glynis. You ask why they think that. After reassurances from both you and Rich, Marie says Glynis is a close personal friend of a woman Richard dated briefly and broke up with six months ago. The two women went to school together.

Rich is astonished. He says his former friend never mentioned Glynis; he had no idea they knew each other. Marie says, "It adds up, though. You hired Lloyd instead of promoting Glynis; you took her off the information systems audit; . . . " and she mentions other circumstances that looked prejudicial to the employees. After Marie leaves, you consider. Rich's life outside the job is irrelevant. He hasn't done anything unprofessional. He was leaning on his people, but for a valid reason. He may have been imperceptive, but his managerial behavior was basically sound.

What to do now? Should Rich open up the matter with his department and hash it out? Use a mediator? Transfer Lloyd? Counsel Glynis? Discipline Glynis? Since you and he agree on the objective—a smooth-running and productive department—you discuss these possible solutions and a number of others.

Finally, Rich says that he and Glynis should meet, with the human resources manager sitting in. You agree and strongly recommend that he listen actively to what both say. You opt out of the meeting because you do not want to send any message to Rich's subordinates that you are disciplining him. Setting the agenda for the meeting and deciding what to do as a result of it are Rich's decisions. You express confidence in his managerial ability and motivation to set the department in order. You set a date when you will check back.

Is this a typical problem-solution interview? Maybe no such interview is "typical." Problems are individual. Often the difficulties exist because people have jumped over steps in the problem-solving process straight into faulty and premature judgments. Managers need to approach problem-solving interviews according to the steps outlined earlier.

Problem solving is a stepwise process. Skipping steps can lead to flawed solutions and new problems.

PERFORMANCE APPRAISALS

Even as a new graduate, you might incur immediate supervisory responsibilities. If you do, you will be appraising performance. For several reasons, many businesspeople count performance appraisal among their most disliked tasks:

- Important elements of a subordinate's work life depend on a favorable appraisal.
- Superiors and subordinates have different perspectives on a given performance. Superiors see a broader picture but may know much less about a single individual's contribution.
- People do not like to criticize or to disappoint.
- Unfairness is always a hazard, since no one can supervise anyone else constantly.
- Many organizations offer little training or support for the appraisal process.
- Subordinates who believe they were unfairly appraised sometimes bring legal action.

You yourself may already have received one or more performance appraisals. Your superior may have done an effective job, but many do not. Many people report that they leave appraisals dissatisfied because, for instance,

She didn't seem to know about anything I'd done.

His ratings were inconsistent. They didn't make any kind of sense.

After 10 months on this job, I finally had my first appraisal, only to find out that the objectives I've been working toward weren't what the company wanted. I was shocked, and of course I got a terrible evaluation.

Others complain that they have never received an appraisal:

> I've worked in this job 15 months, and I've never had a performance appraisal. I have to guess I'm doing okay, but I don't really know.

Recall, from the communication model in Chapter One, the importance of feedback. When employees work, they are trying to respond to what they believe are managers' wishes, which are not always explicit. They need information on the effectiveness of what they do. They need managers' feedback.

Although probably only the top performers genuinely look forward to the appraisal interview, most employees value their jobs and want to know how to do them better. Performance appraisals can raise or undermine motivation and, thus, productivity. The appraisal process is well worth the time and effort needed to do it well.

Preparing to Appraise

Even if you are not a people person, try to make daily contact with your subordinates. Kenneth Blanchard and Spencer Johnson advise managers to take one minute each day to interact with each person they supervise.[1] Catch them doing something right, these authors say, and spend the minute on praise and reinforcement. If you catch them in an error, be supportive and spend the minute on instruction and coaching. Some experts call this process **managing by walking around** *(MBWA).*

Keeping this continual contact with employees offers many advantages. First, it helps avoid one pitfall of evaluating: the **halo** or **horns effect.** If managers have few contacts with employees, they may exaggerate, in either direction, the inferences they draw about those employees' competence. If an employee makes a good impression once, the manager may always view more favorably what that employee does (the halo effect). If the one or two contacts a manager has with an employee are unfavorable, the manager may always expect that employee to perform poorly (the horns effect). Managers are human. They see what they expect to see.

Second, daily interaction makes the appraisal task less heavy. Managers must evaluate even if they have little or no information about subordinates. The longer they postpone appraisal, the harder it is to construct an intelligent basis on which to evaluate. Furthermore, when previous interaction has been frequent, the manager and the employees will not be approaching the appraisal as strangers. They will know each other. Moreover, employees will have a good idea how they have been doing. The manager will not be in the position of having to administer an unpleasant surprise.

Managing by walking around can take the unpleasant surprises out of appraisals.

Critics of the one-minute method complain that it can become mechanical and seem unnatural. Used intelligently, it need not be so, and even supposing it did, the benefits far outweigh a minor drawback.

In your walking around and in appraisals, help your subordinates set specific, verifiable objectives, and let them know how these objectives will be measured. Recall from earlier chapters the potential for misunderstanding when ideas are presented at too abstract a level. Say what you mean by "decrease the error rate": "Six or fewer requests for recount during the next 90 days."

---

[1]Kenneth Blanchard and Spencer Johnson, *The One-Minute Manager* (New York: Berkley Books, 1983).

Familiarize yourself with your organization's appraisal practices. Study carefully the appraisal forms in use, which you will mark and which will become part of the employee's personnel file.[2]

Let employees know that appraisals will be scheduled. Treat appraisals as part of employees' continuing development rather than as all-or-nothing, win-or-lose ordeals. Appraisals do influence some of the rewards a company can give employees, but they should not assume unrealistic importance.

Companies and their managers must be careful about what their appraisal policies might imply. Some organizations' policies, for instance, set out a 90-day probationary period. An employee who continues in the job beyond that time considers that he has passed the probationary period successfully. If managers delay appraising or forget to appraise, they may discover too late that they have an unsuitable employee. Managers must also avoid promising what is beyond their authority (or common sense) to promise. The supervisor who tells an employee distraught over a serious mistake, "Don't worry, your job won't be in any danger" may find these comforting words treated as a contract later.

Schedule the interview several days in advance. Do not do as one appraisal-averse supervisor did. The first notice the employee got of the impending appraisal was, "Mary Ellen. In my office. Now."

At the time of scheduling, give the subordinate due for appraisal a copy of the appraisal form, together with your request to fill it out as objectively as possible. If the form does not lend itself to this use, write out before the meeting an agenda containing the points to cover.

When you begin the appraisal interview, you will wish to spend a minute or two in small talk to break the ice. Then move to appraisal specifics. If both you and the employee have made a conscientious effort to evaluate the person's performance on the appraisal form, you can use the form to structure the interview. Otherwise, use your prepared agenda and stick to it. Empathy and objectivity will enhance your ability to evaluate subordinates at any level of performance.

Interviews with superior performers are usually a pleasure. Outstanding employees tend to motivate themselves. One boss says, "Just tell them what the task is and get out of their way." Give praise where it is due. Be careful, however, not to imply that they have no need to reach for improvement. Also, be wary of the halo effect. Even outstanding employees sometimes have weak suits. Be aware of these weaknesses and of a possible need to help them set some goals.

Begin and end the evaluation on a strong positive note. Concentrate on accomplishments and encourage more. In helping them set objectives, do not let their enthusiasm (or yours) lead you to overestimate what they can achieve. Goals should stretch people's capabilities but should be reachable; missing a goal demotivates. Sandwich your discussion of "growth areas" between positive comments on strengths.

---

[2]Discussion of the types of appraisal forms is beyond the scope of this chapter. Not all forms are equally well designed and your company's form might not be ideal—but you will still need to use it. Enter your information as impartially as possible, and make fairness a priority.

┌───┐

Ⓔ XHIBIT 16–4   **Communication Behaviors to Increase the Chance of Productive Conflict Resolution**

1. Use neutral rather than emotional terms. "I still tend to prefer my approach" is better than "Your idea is really lousy."
2. Avoid absolute statements that leave no room for modification. "I think this is the way . . ." is better than "this is the *only* way."
3. Ask open-ended questions so that others will be inclined to offer their viewpoints.
4. Avoid leading questions that induce people to agree verbally even when they disagree. This rule is especially important where status differences are present.
5. Repeat key phrases to make sure that all parties are communicating on the same wavelength.
6. Use terms that all parties clearly understand, and be sure that the conflict is not over the meaning of terms rather than substantive issues.
7. Allow the other person to complete statements. Interruptions only add to the felt conflict and may lead to hostility.
8. Use effective listening skills to ensure that the other person's ideas are fully understood.
9. Maintain a pleasant expression. A facial expression that implies a challenge can increase perceived conflict.
10. Use a face-to-face format, if at all possible. Telephoned or written messages are less effective than face-to-face meetings for resolving conflicts.
11. Be aware of the importance of physical arrangements. For instance, sitting in front of a big desk may cause a person to feel defensive.

└───┘

Source: Larry R. Smeltzer, John L. Waltman, and Donald J. Leonard, *Managerial Communication: A Strategic Approach* (Needham Heights, Mass.: Ginn Press, 1991), pp. 382–83.

other strategies. Also, the positive, cooperative attitudes required for optimization often carry over to other business behaviors in productive ways.

Exhibit 16–4 offers 11 communication principles that increase people's ability to generate a win-win resolution. These principles make good ground rules whether managers are parties to the conflict or whether they are instructing two antagonistic subordinates to use them.

Conflict, though one of the more challenging aspects of managers' communicating, is inevitable but can be managed. Well handled, it can lead to increased creativity and cooperation.

COMMUNICATING WITH PUBLICS AND STAKEHOLDERS

A company's stakeholders have something to gain or lose by what the company does.

Many groups have a "stake" in a company's success. The task of business is to create value, and this value passes to many people in many forms. Businesses enable employees to earn livelihoods, buyers to obtain products or services they need, and communities to grow in size and importance. For these benefits to occur, business needs the support of its many constituencies, or "publics."

The goodwill of many different groups affects a business's fortunes. Any group believing a business guilty of a wrongdoing has the potential to interfere with people's willingness to do business with that firm. Thus, the employees and managers in a business, while pursuing profit, must neither act harmfully nor *appear* to do so. Business conduct must be both ethical and profitable.

Many business plans and transactions are complex. Many cannot be explained fully in as brief a time as people are willing to listen. Many such plans are kept secret from competitors. A few businesspeople *are* unethical, and as

Familiarize yourself with your organization's appraisal practices. Study carefully the appraisal forms in use, which you will mark and which will become part of the employee's personnel file.[2]

Let employees know that appraisals will be scheduled. Treat appraisals as part of employees' continuing development rather than as all-or-nothing, win-or-lose ordeals. Appraisals do influence some of the rewards a company can give employees, but they should not assume unrealistic importance.

Companies and their managers must be careful about what their appraisal policies might imply. Some organizations' policies, for instance, set out a 90-day probationary period. An employee who continues in the job beyond that time considers that he has passed the probationary period successfully. If managers delay appraising or forget to appraise, they may discover too late that they have an unsuitable employee. Managers must also avoid promising what is beyond their authority (or common sense) to promise. The supervisor who tells an employee distraught over a serious mistake, "Don't worry, your job won't be in any danger" may find these comforting words treated as a contract later.

Schedule the interview several days in advance. Do not do as one appraisal-averse supervisor did. The first notice the employee got of the impending appraisal was, "Mary Ellen. In my office. Now."

At the time of scheduling, give the subordinate due for appraisal a copy of the appraisal form, together with your request to fill it out as objectively as possible. If the form does not lend itself to this use, write out before the meeting an agenda containing the points to cover.

When you begin the appraisal interview, you will wish to spend a minute or two in small talk to break the ice. Then move to appraisal specifics. If both you and the employee have made a conscientious effort to evaluate the person's performance on the appraisal form, you can use the form to structure the interview. Otherwise, use your prepared agenda and stick to it. Empathy and objectivity will enhance your ability to evaluate subordinates at any level of performance.

Interviews with superior performers are usually a pleasure. Outstanding employees tend to motivate themselves. One boss says, "Just tell them what the task is and get out of their way." Give praise where it is due. Be careful, however, not to imply that they have no need to reach for improvement. Also, be wary of the halo effect. Even outstanding employees sometimes have weak suits. Be aware of these weaknesses and of a possible need to help them set some goals.

Begin and end the evaluation on a strong positive note. Concentrate on accomplishments and encourage more. In helping them set objectives, do not let their enthusiasm (or yours) lead you to overestimate what they can achieve. Goals should stretch people's capabilities but should be reachable; missing a goal demotivates. Sandwich your discussion of "growth areas" between positive comments on strengths.

Using Forms and Processes

Conducting the Performance Appraisal Interview

Empathy and objectivity improve appraisal interviews.

Superior Performers

---

[2]Discussion of the types of appraisal forms is beyond the scope of this chapter. Not all forms are equally well designed and your company's form might not be ideal—but you will still need to use it. Enter your information as impartially as possible, and make fairness a priority.

Average Performers

Sometimes appraisers control none of an employee's tangible rewards. They must search for intrinsic motivators.

Take particular care in appraising average performers. The definition of *average* requires that most employees will fall into this category. People do not, however, like thinking of themselves as average, especially when they are reliable and experienced. You cannot promote them; they may not be due for a raise for some time; but you would hate to lose them.

Sometimes average performers do not easily see the difference between what they do and what a superior performer does. To the extent that time and support material permit, try to explain the difference without citing specific individuals or diminishing anyone. If your firm has a well-designed appraisal form, the form might help define performance categories. For instance, a brief explanatory note to *outstanding* might say "Consistently exceeds standards for speed and accuracy. Takes initiative in solving problems."

Underscore the value of the average performer's work and his or her value as a person. Such reinforcement is motivating to employees, especially when they already make as much money as their performance justifies and you cannot give a tangible reward. Even in cases where promotions and perks are your decision, you cannot give these rewards to average employees. A later section on motivation will discuss intrinsic motivators. For average employees, consider the motivational potential of giving favorable recognition, adding interest to the job, or offering opportunities for additional learning.

Below-Average Performers

With poor performers, your task may not be pleasant, but it is straightforward. Whereas you want to maintain average performers' work at its present level or a little higher, below-average performers' work behavior *must* change.

Be empathetic but objective. Avoid generalizations, and stick to specifics. If you make an assertion, be prepared to back it up with evidence. Set realistic objectives, make sure they are understood, and be frank about your expectations. If this is a person whom you might eventually need to discharge, document the appraisal with extra care.

Documenting the Appraisal

A critical incident is a brief summary of a work task or interaction typical of the employee's work.

An employee may rebut all or part of an appraisal.

Fill out your company's appraisal form carefully. Use objective, impartial language to support and explain any ratings you make. Make use of **critical incidents**—brief summaries of work tasks or interactions that exemplify the employee's typical work. These summaries may be positive, negative, or mixed, but they must be factual and free of value judgments.

Listen to the employee in the appraisal. If you have prepared thoroughly, you are unlikely to wish to change any rating or comment; yet you do retain that option. The employee needs to read what you have written and sign the appraisal. If the employee disagrees sharply with you, he or she may write a rebuttal, which also goes into the file.

Between appraisals, when in doubt whether to document, *do* document. With luck and good management, you may never need to produce these files. If you do need to defend your own or your organization's decisions, however, the records will be crucial.

DISCIPLINARY COMMUNICATION

In any employee category, you might have to change employees' behavior. Employees might, for instance, behave dishonestly, miss work too often, quarrel with others, fail to learn, or perform job tasks poorly. Although managers' responses will depend on the situation, the individual, and the organizational culture, when employees are doing their jobs poorly managers must act. To protect both the employee and the organization, written documentation is essential, as the section on progressive discipline will make clear.

Infractions range from high-dollar embezzlement to sneaking personal copies on the company copier. In some firms managers would ignore the latter practice, but no manager in any firm can afford to protect someone who steals.

Coaching, Correcting, and Supporting

Many employees make mistakes out of ignorance, others out of low motivation. Managers can intervene in these and similar cases in a positive rather than a negative way: They can correct and coach.

Managers can learn what rewards employees value and offer those rewards in return for improvement. They can clarify instructions, provide training, or simply encourage people who are dealing with frustrations. They can assign a mentor or let an employee "shadow" a more experienced worker and learn by observing. If the employee is a poor fit where she is, they can move her to a different position. They can explain, coax, or even kid an employee into trying harder or trying again. They can affirm their belief in the employee's ability.

Managers must listen actively to hear what employees really need. "I just can't do this" can carry very different meanings. Some very capable employees need more ego stroking than others. Some just need more time and less stress. Some need to overcome learning anxiety.

> In coaching, active listening is essential.

Managers are unlikely to learn what employees need if they avoid interacting with them. Also, as we will see later, the mere fact of a manager's attention, whether positive or negative, motivates most employees.

Using Progressive Discipline

When employees break a law or an essential company policy, when job incompetence is extreme, or when correcting and coaching do not correct bad behavior, managers must discipline. The ideal result of coaching and correction is changed behavior, but it does not always occur. In these cases, managers must begin the **progressive discipline** process.

A manager using progressive discipline begins in a timely way, follows up at regular intervals, remains humane and empathetic, increases stringency, and stops as soon as the undesirable behavior is corrected—if it is corrected. Early phases might be relatively positive. Fairness is essential. *All* employees must meet the firm's reasonable expectations; managers cannot play favorites or afford exceptional treatment.

> To discipline effectively, supervisors must never play favorites. All rules must apply equally to all their subordinates.

Suppose an employee—call him James—is experiencing marital difficulties that impair his job effectiveness. An empathetic manager will usually support such a person for a time, hoping the crisis will pass and the employee will resume performing adequately. Suppose James cannot make a decision that would let him move on with his life, and his work continues to suffer. He fails

Constructive evaluation from managers is supposed to feel better than this.

to return clients' calls, his work contains errors that require another employee to check everything he does, he has outbursts of temper about twice a week, and he sometimes just sits at his desk looking into space.

You have spoken with James often, listened actively, and encouraged him. You have made informal notes but have made no entries in his personnel file. You now begin to think that if he were going to correct his behavior, he would have begun to do so by now. You estimate what he is costing the company. The cost is growing hard to justify.

In the first stages of progressive discipline, you listen and coach. When problems become serious, you mention disciplinary action to the employee and state your expectations. If problems persist, you speak to the employee again and this time document what you said. Then you place the record in the employee's file. How much time you give the employee to correct the behavior depends on situational factors, but once you begin to consider termination, documenting your own and the employee's actions becomes essential.

Suppose that after counseling James, you tell him you cannot let his problem continue to harm the company. He *must* change. He promises to do so, but does not. You speak to him again and this time, in his presence, make a written record. Again he promises to change. Two weeks later, when other employees tell you he has begun to come to work in the afternoon having clearly been drinking, you call him in and order him to make an appointment at the firm's Employee Assistance Program (EAP) office.[3] You make a written record of your order to James.

The EAP worker evaluates James and recommends counseling and stress medication. The evaluation says James is not an alcoholic. You order James to begin the counseling and never again appear at the office under the influence of alcohol, under penalty of suspension. You make written records of all these proceedings.

James protests and makes promises, but he does not comply. At this point you know you will probably fire him, but you suspend him for three days. You make a written record. James is shocked at the suspension. He spends the three days soul searching. He returns to work and says he and his wife are getting things worked out. You make a written record. One week later, he comes back from lunch clearly intoxicated. You fire him.

A sad case? Yes. Cruel? No. People are responsible for their own actions, and businesses cannot indefinitely absorb the costs of their failure to take responsibility. At any point in the progressive discipline, James had the chance to correct the problem behavior. Whether he and his wife divorced or mended relations is not the company's or the manager's business. The quality of his work *is* their concern.

The preceding case stressed creating written records, the so-called "paper trail." Managers are wise to record all pertinent information. Events, witnesses, and patterns of behavior should all be written down. The human resources department serves as a valuable resource. In view of the skyrocketing number of wrongful-discharge cases, companies must protect themselves. They must be prepared to show that a discharged employee received all the job protection afforded by law or by any existing union contract.

Laws vary by state and locality, and union contracts differ. Although most regulations afford businesses the right to terminate for cause, nothing prevents

The paper trail is the series of written records a manager keeps to document any procedure, such as a firing, that may be called into legal question.

---

[3]Employee Assistance Programs put troubled employees in contact with appropriate counselors or care providers. Sometimes counseling is in house, sometimes by referral.

a disgruntled employee from initiating a proceeding. True, at some point the union may decline to support the employee or a judge will decline to hear the case. But as long as the employee presses the case, the company has to deal with it and pay whatever it costs, as far as it gets.

If the case goes to court, the company might win, but it will rarely recover costs from an individual employee. The legal system often assumes businesses have "deep pockets"—that is, high-value assets—and companies can be hit with heavy costs if they lose. Many cases settle out of court. When legal actions drag on and on before going to trial, legal fees mount, the action requires attention by the company, and sometimes other animosities develop. Thus, even if a firm believes it is in the clear, it may offer a cash settlement just to move on and return to normal.

Because ineffective performance appraisal practices can cost a business in many different ways, managers and supervisors must ensure that their practices are sound and well documented.

COMMUNICATING TO MOTIVATE

Most people would say that they work in return for money and benefits needed to sustain life, well-being, and security for themselves and their dependents. People also go to work to fulfill their need to be part of a group.

Motivation of employees is so essential to the success of a business that businesspersons are keenly interested in the subject. Despite considerable research on motivation, many questions remain. Although low-skill workers seem to be motivated by possibilities such as the threat of job loss, low-skill workers are individuals, just as are all other groups of workers. Many of them are keenly interested in the job as much for its own sake as for the money. Salespeople respond well to bonuses and contests, yet not all salespeople excel in a bonus-and-contest environment. Knowledge workers, such as engineers, economists, or architects, are probably the most heterogeneous of all. Motivation is not simple. We cannot say one size fits all.

In earlier times, to get employees to work hard, managers relied on employees' need for money and their fear of losing it. Yet employees can work just hard enough to meet the minimum requirements of a job—and get their money—or they can strive to excel. What makes them strive to do their most productive work?

Abraham Maslow, an early theorist, said that workers put forth effort to fulfill different levels of needs, which he arranged in a **five-level need hierarchy.**[4] Maslow proposed that once workers are assured of the essentials for sustaining life, they work to obtain security and safety. Once assured of that, they become motivated by the need to belong. After that, they work for the esteem of others. Finally, they work to self-actualize, that is, to develop their best self—to "grow" in intellect and spirit. Maslow's ideas are still influential, although many now believe people work to satisfy more than one level of these needs at a time.

Further probing the reasons why people work, Frederick Herzberg divided motivational factors into two groups.[5] He classified as **motivators** such elements as recognition, achievement, advancement, increased responsibility, the potential for personal growth, and the level of interest in the work itself. He believed that employees would increase effort in return for increases in these areas.

Herzberg's motivators are intrinsic factors.

[4]Abraham H. Maslow, *Motivation and Personality* (New York: Harper & Row, 1954).

[5]Frederick Herzberg, *Work and the Nature of Man* (Cleveland: World Publishing, 1966).

Maintenance factors dissatisfy and demotivate if the employee finds their level insufficient.

Herzberg called his second category **maintenance factors.** Here he listed pay; job security; supervision; personal relations with supervisors, peers, and subordinates; working conditions; status; and company policy. He sometimes referred to these factors as **dissatisfiers** but did not consider them motivators. As long as these factors are at an adequate level, he said, the worker is not dissatisfied. However, once they are adequate, increasing them—for instance, offering better working conditions or pay—will not call forth increased effort from the worker. Unacceptable levels of any of these factors might create anger, apathy, or other negative emotional states. Attempting to manipulate these factors as motivators, a firm could lose but not gain.

You may feel you would strive to excel in return for a promised raise or end-of-year bonus. Many agree. Notice, though, that the motivators are intrinsic to the worker, whereas the maintenance factors depend on extrinsic factors. As managers, we should see opportunity in these facts. Many of the extrinsic factors cost money and are often outside managers' discretionary choice. Creative thinking and active listening, however, might let managers tap into highly motivating attitudes *intrinsic to the employee* at no cost except managers' time and effort.

Expectancy theory looks at five factors affecting whether employees believe extra effort is worthwhile.

Victor Vroom's **expectancy theory** holds that employees put forth effort to reach a performance level resulting in rewards they value.[6] Employees have choices. Whether they choose to work hard depends on what they expect to gain, how much they value the reward, and the probability of gaining it. On this basis, we can infer that employees' motivation will improve if they

- Value the reward offered.
- Believe a given amount of effort will gain them the reward.
- Believe they can put forth the effort required to get the reward.
- Receive sufficient instructions.
- Receive needed materials and resources.

Not all motivation is positive. People modify their work effort to avoid disliked consequences as well as to obtain rewards. The strength of their positive or negative preference for an outcome is called **valence.** For instance, a person with high potential and strong support from the boss might underperform because he dislikes feeling that others envy him. The negative valence of envy is stronger than the positive valence of the boss's encouragement.

For you as a manager, motivating effectively means more active listening, greater creativity in developing appropriate intrinsic and extrinsic motivations, more monitoring of performance, and more feedback and following up. Can you devise more variety in a job? More autonomy? More of a feeling that what an employee does matters to the firm and reflects favorably on the employee? View employees as individuals. Learn what they value in their work, and help them attain it.

COMMUNICATION AND CONFLICT

No one makes it through a career without conflict. Conflict occurs when two or more parties have incompatible goals, attitudes, or emotions that lead them to oppose or fight each other. Persons and groups in organizations depend on one another and on the organization for support and resources. Because support and resources are not infinite, disagreements over who gives what and who gets what are inevitable.

[6]Victor H. Vroom, *Work and Motivation* (New York: John Wiley & Sons, 1964).

In your work life you will participate in conflict, observe conflict, and manage conflict. Conflict can be constructive and creative or damaging and destructive. In this section we will look at the stages of conflict, the benefits of managing it effectively, and the means of resolving it.

Managed conflict can be constructive.

Organizational conflict may be latent (coming but not yet apparent), perceived or felt, or manifest (out in the open). Since no fight continues forever, an aftermath stage follows the close of conflict.

Stages of Conflict

Conflict in a business organization begins before anyone realizes it. When limited amounts of resources must serve the needs of all, inevitably some receive more than others. When one person or department has to depend on another person or department for work, support, information, or any other necessity of a job, potential exists for lateness, failure, or other disappointing outcomes. The very structure of organizations creates conditions making conflict likely. Any kind of imbalance or inequity in an organization can create latent conflict.

Latent Conflict

Human nature itself creates conflict. We are touchy, vain, insecure creatures who view experience through our individual filters. We have needs others may not even know about, let alone be able to fill for us.

At some point, the inequity or imbalance starts to bother someone. At times, people *perceive* clearly that one or more others have something they want. At other times, people *feel* that others are better off than they are. If you asked them, they would speak of feeling irritated, slighted, pushed, or threatened, but they might be unable to identify the source or cause. Whether the conflict is perceived intellectually or felt, people are aware of it but not yet ready to talk about it or fight about it.

Perceived or Felt Conflict

Being equal or "even" is important to people. Some conflicts begin because one person takes offense at something another meant harmlessly, or even as an offhand compliment. Suppose Jack finishes a report in record time and Philip says, "Way to go, Jack! Always dragging out a job." Maybe the boss is present and smiles, understanding that a compliment is intended. But Jack remembers a couple of deadlines he missed a year ago, imagines that the boss does too, and blames Philip for bringing it up.

Sometimes people in Jack's position carry a long-standing grudge about something others have forgotten, understood differently, and never viewed as important. Such people feel "one down," damaged, and needful of something to make them feel as good as the other person again. Suppose Jack does something to get even with Philip. To Philip, Jack seems to have harmed him for no reason at all and feels, in his turn, "one down" and not disposed to stay that way. Once conflict is manifest—out in the open—it must be dealt with or it will escalate.

People do not like feeling out of balance, unequal, or "one down."

At the stage when conflict becomes manifest, people are ready to accuse, fight, bully, complain, threaten, or, if you are lucky, discuss it calmly. As a manager, you will often have to handle conflict among those reporting to you. As such, you will have to be able to empathize with the parties. As both an employee and a manager, you will often *be* one of the parties. We will discuss this stage in more depth shortly.

Manifest Conflict

The conflict gets resolved in one of several ways. If the manager and the participants have addressed the conflict fairly and all parties are satisfied, the conflict will fade into memory. If the resolution strategy left one or more parties dissatisfied, the conflict is likely to erupt again. Managers do well to monitor the parties to a resolved conflict to make sure the solution was genuine.

Resolution is not always fair. Sometimes one party wins big and the other loses big. Depending on the conflict's magnitude, the personalities of the antagonists, the length of their relationship, the organizational climate, and many other factors, the result could be trivial or damaging. The loser might say, "No hard feelings" and mean it. Or she might begin a campaign of hostility or sabotage that could end by costing the whole organization heavily.

When conflict does not end fairly, it can erupt again.

Managing Conflict

Some organizations promote a certain level of conflict, particularly where a turbulent environment requires creativity and quick adaptation to change. Managers in such firms may feel that active conflict reveals the merits or drawbacks of an idea faster than calmer, slower analysis would. Conflict may also spur people to outdo themselves, surpass other employees, and think outside old patterns.

While conflict can offer positive outcomes, managers must control its darker aspects. Friendly rivalry helps. Interpersonal or interdepartmental warfare grinds business to a halt. Conflict should not get personal and should not promote aims unbeneficial to the organization. Managers need to stay on top of conflict, prohibiting the damaging kinds and moving to resolve conflicts that further no useful ends.

Communicating to Resolve Conflict

Of the five managerial responses to conflict, many approach conflict using their habitual response rather than the best response.

Theorists on conflict describe five common means by which managers address conflict in their departments: **withdrawal, smoothing, forcing, compromise,** and **optimizing.** Most managers are predisposed by personality, experience, and habit toward one of these means. Different kinds of conflict, however, call for different managerial responses, and all managers should develop the full repertoire of responses. Although not all conflict is amenable to it, optimizing is the best of the five responses for long-term resolution.

Consider an example. Two staffers are weary of gathering data for and preparing a dull but critical periodic report. Their job titles are the same, their seniority and competence are about equal, they view this task with equal distaste, and they continually try to dump the job on each other. Now they are arguing about it. Here are five scenarios:

The boss withdraws from the conflict: "I don't want to hear about it. You've got the work to do; do it. I've got too much to do to listen to this. I'm going into my office."

The boss smoothes the conflict over: "Now, Beth, you and Milly have been working together for five years. Think of all the projects you've helped each other on, working side by side. Put this disagreement back into its proper perspective. We're a family here. You don't really mean these things you're saying."

The boss forces a solution: "Enough of this! Take 45 minutes, go into the conference room, and work it out in that time. If you can't do that, well, I'm sure I can find another crummy task so you'll *both* have one to do."

Bruce Ayres/Tony Stone Images

Managing and resolving conflicts holds down costs and promotes productive use of organizational resources.

The boss offers a compromise: "Look. Beth, you do the tedious job one week and Milly does it the next. That way neither of you gets stuck with it all the time."

The boss optimizes, that is, tries to offer some advantage for each: "Milly, what about this task seems most tedious? Beth, how about you? Can we divide it into multiple pieces so that you can each choose what you don't dislike quite as much? How might we be able to make parts of it more interesting? Will it be easier if you can do it over a period of time with more interesting tasks in between?"

Which strategy works will depend on Beth, Milly, and the boss. If both employees are candid and willing to trust, optimizing can work. If either or both have a hidden agenda, however, the boss has to use a different response. Suppose Beth thinks Milly will not play fair. If she thinks Milly will stick her with whatever she says she dislikes, Beth will claim to dislike a task she actually likes. If the antagonists seem to be playing games, the boss might decide either to compromise or to force the issue. If the boss knows from experience that the two will find something else to disagree about but the job will get done anyway, she might opt for a withdrawal or smoothing strategy.

Most people habitually "default" to one strategy, or at most two, when faced with conflict. Some people immediately try to force an issue. Others habitually withdraw, smooth, or compromise. Many would never dream of trying to optimize until someone pointed out the possibility. Preferred strategies are closely linked to personality types. Many of us must consciously work to employ strategies other than the one or two that are most natural to us.

Dealing with conflict involves more than just dispute over an issue. It involves winning and losing, gains in status and loss of face. Is forcing ever right? Is smoothing always wrong? Let's look at some factors that influence a manager's choice of strategy.

Withdrawal

Managers—and participants—can withdraw from a conflict. They can withdraw explicitly ("I'm leaving"), or they can simply not *be* there. Sometimes a participant's withdrawal loses the game. Sometimes withdrawal prevents the other from winning the game. Depending on circumstances, a manager can gain or lose stature using withdrawal. (Sometimes withdrawal saves one's sanity.)

A conflict is not always a manager's problem. Some antagonistic co-workers, for instance, simmer for years but do not erupt except with name calling during the weekend softball games. On the job, the two get their jobs done. The manager is in error only if she withdraws when the conflict is present and unlikely to disappear or resolve itself.

Fortunately, many workers are solution minded and do not need a manager's intervention. If the antagonists seem likely to work out their difference, the manager is right to withdraw. Later the manager can congratulate them on having resolved the conflict.

Smoothing

Managers might choose smoothing if disagreements are not very serious and seem likely to blow over soon. If two subordinates have a "personality conflict"—that is, if deep-seated personality traits cause them to view experience in incompatible ways—nothing is gained by investing time trying to help them understand each other. A better strategy is to minimize the importance of the conflict, appeal to their concern for the department's welfare, and keep them apart.

Still, parties to a conflict whose boss just says, "Be nice. Love one another. Be happy," might not be as frank or trusting in the future. They probably perceive their disagreement as more important than the boss does. His smoothing is, in effect, denied listening. At some point in the future their input might be critical, but the boss might not hear from them.

A smoothed-over conflict is not resolved. Hostilities could break out again.

Forcing

Forcing may create a win-lose or a lose-lose outcome.

Forcing is the old-line manager's default response. A manager who uses forcing either demands that the parties reach agreement under threat of punishment or imposes his own solution, which may not be agreeable to either party. The latter is a lose-lose outcome. If he forces them to resolve the struggle themselves, the tougher side defeats the weaker side in a win-lose outcome.

When the parties are uncooperative, managers sometimes use forcing. Forcing is a fast solution, but rarely permanent. The present conflict may erupt again, or residual anger may carry over and create new conflicts in other activities.

Compromising

Compromise is rational. What could be simpler? What are the parties fighting over? Just divide it 50-50; each person gets half of what he or she wants, and everything is solved—right? Solved, yes, but not necessarily solved in the best way.

Consider the story of two sisters who are quarreling over an orange. Neither will give it up. The parent listens to their bickering and finally says, "We're going to divide the orange exactly down the middle, and you can each have half." Each sister grumpily accepts her half and goes away. Later the parent says, "Did you eat your half of the orange?" "No," one sister says. "I just wanted the juice. I drank it, but there wasn't much." "No," the other sister says. "I needed to grate the rind for a cake I was making." Many compromises end this way.

Compromise is useful when the size of the "pie"—the amount or array being contested—cannot be changed. When opponents' rights are equal and nothing of value can be added, we try to divide the pie fairly.

When the parties are generally cooperative and a relationship continues, compromise can work well enough to go on with. In a 50-50 split, both win and both lose. Many compromises, of course, are 60-40 or even more unequal. "You win some, you lose some, and some get rained out," the saying goes. If a person loses an advantage one day, another day will come when he will win one. Sometimes, though, people can do better. They can optimize.

In compromise, those in conflict partly win and partly lose.

Optimizing is sometimes called the **win-win strategy.** The story of the sisters and the orange shows a case where each party could have had all of what she wanted, had anyone probed to find out exactly what each valued. Although few conflicts permit such neat and fulfilling resolution, optimizing can usually uncover more possible benefits to divide. Optimizing works best if the parties are basically cooperative, communication is candid, and people are able to "think outside the box" of established habits and patterns.

Optimizing

In optimizing, both parties to the conflict win.

Optimizing requires "thinking outside the box."

For instance, suppose your firm implements flextime, the scheduling arrangement permitting some workers to work an early schedule or a late schedule. Your firm's needs require a balance between those who work from 7 to 4 and those who work from 10 to 7, with an hour for lunch for each group. Seniority gives most workers their preference, but you have two newcomers who both really want to work the early schedule. There is only one slot open. One of them must work the later shift.

Why do the two employees want the earlier shift? Jorge, a single parent, has to pick up his daughter from preschool before 5 P.M. Bill, the other newcomer, needs the time to do banking and other errands before many businesses close. Jorge's reason appears more important than Bill's. But why not explore options? See if there is a way to make both of them willing to take the later shift.

First, you ask, if it weren't for these reasons, would each take the later time? Each says yes. Now you probe for ways to solve their individual problems. Begin with Jorge: "What are you going to do about your daughter next year, when she enters public school? She'll be getting out even earlier." "Oh, she's starting kindergarten in six months. That's arranged. My nephew will get her and take her home with him." "So this situation is temporary? When you don't have your daughter to pick up, could you work the late shift?" He says yes. Now you can give him the preferred shift on a temporary basis—until he makes the arrangements to which he has agreed.

Then you say to Bill, "Jorge has agreed to work the late shift in the future. Would you be willing to work it now, if I can arrange for the early shift for you later?" Bill points out that this solution doesn't help him now. So you offer another temporary solution, where *you* bend a little: "Bill, why don't you come in an hour early, at 9, three days a week, and I'll arrange for you to have a two-hour lunch break on those days—say, from 2 to 4—to take care of your business until an earlier shift opens up." Bill likes that.

The larger context contained alternatives. You have established that in the future, both will be willing to work either shift. You and both employees win. The cost to you is a few minutes' thinking time and a small schedule concession to one employee.

Optimizing often takes more time and energy than in this case. The most frequently cited disadvantage of optimizing is time. Most of the other strategies are quick, by comparison. Yet the results of optimizing often outlast those of

---

EXHIBIT 16–4 **Communication Behaviors to Increase the Chance of Productive Conflict Resolution**

1. Use neutral rather than emotional terms. "I still tend to prefer my approach" is better than "Your idea is really lousy."
2. Avoid absolute statements that leave no room for modification. "I think this is the way . . ." is better than "this is the *only* way."
3. Ask open-ended questions so that others will be inclined to offer their viewpoints.
4. Avoid leading questions that induce people to agree verbally even when they disagree. This rule is especially important where status differences are present.
5. Repeat key phrases to make sure that all parties are communicating on the same wavelength.
6. Use terms that all parties clearly understand, and be sure that the conflict is not over the meaning of terms rather than substantive issues.
7. Allow the other person to complete statements. Interruptions only add to the felt conflict and may lead to hostility.
8. Use effective listening skills to ensure that the other person's ideas are fully understood.
9. Maintain a pleasant expression. A facial expression that implies a challenge can increase perceived conflict.
10. Use a face-to-face format, if at all possible. Telephoned or written messages are less effective than face-to-face meetings for resolving conflicts.
11. Be aware of the importance of physical arrangements. For instance, sitting in front of a big desk may cause a person to feel defensive.

Source: Larry R. Smeltzer, John L. Waltman, and Donald J. Leonard, *Managerial Communication: A Strategic Approach* (Needham Heights, Mass.: Ginn Press, 1991), pp. 382–83.

other strategies. Also, the positive, cooperative attitudes required for optimization often carry over to other business behaviors in productive ways.

Exhibit 16–4 offers 11 communication principles that increase people's ability to generate a win-win resolution. These principles make good ground rules whether managers are parties to the conflict or whether they are instructing two antagonistic subordinates to use them.

Conflict, though one of the more challenging aspects of managers' communicating, is inevitable but can be managed. Well handled, it can lead to increased creativity and cooperation.

COMMUNICATING WITH PUBLICS AND STAKEHOLDERS

A company's stakeholders have something to gain or lose by what the company does.

Many groups have a "stake" in a company's success. The task of business is to create value, and this value passes to many people in many forms. Businesses enable employees to earn livelihoods, buyers to obtain products or services they need, and communities to grow in size and importance. For these benefits to occur, business needs the support of its many constituencies, or "publics."

The goodwill of many different groups affects a business's fortunes. Any group believing a business guilty of a wrongdoing has the potential to interfere with people's willingness to do business with that firm. Thus, the employees and managers in a business, while pursuing profit, must neither act harmfully nor *appear* to do so. Business conduct must be both ethical and profitable.

Many business plans and transactions are complex. Many cannot be explained fully in as brief a time as people are willing to listen. Many such plans are kept secret from competitors. A few businesspeople *are* unethical, and as a result the public is somewhat suspicious of most businesses. Add to this the fact that bad news has more media value than good news.

From this discussion, you can see that businesspeople have to be careful not just about what they do and say but also about how it looks and sounds to the many groups observing their behavior, each group with motives of its own. "You can't please all the people all the time," the old saying goes. The fewer people a business *dis*pleases, however, the fewer ill effects on the business.

Many different persons and groups observe and judge a business's actions.

Businesspeople—and the business itself—need to keep in mind the perceptions of groups, or **publics,** both inside and outside the organization. These groups will expect to give and receive messages. Specialized corporate communicators address many of a firm's publics. Their functions take various names—corporate communication, public relations, public information, public affairs, employee relations, investor relations—depending on what kinds of messages are needed for what kinds of audiences. Managers and employees should regard these specialists as resources and call on them for counsel.

Internal publics include management—which contains various subgroups—and employees.

Internal Publics

At first, you might think a company's leadership holds all the cards and therefore need not be considered a public. Management is not a monolith, however, and it does not, either collectively or separately, hold all of an organization's power. The president, for example, can lose the support of the employees, of the other executives, or of the board of directors. Suppose the employees go out on strike. In such a case the president's real alternatives are sharply curbed.

Management, Executives, and Directors

Consider that the board usually consists of some senior firm members and some members from outside the organization. They often think alike but sometimes cannot reach consensus on an issue. They make recommendations to the president rather than give him or her orders, but they can vote the president out of position if seriously displeased.

A company's executives reach consensus on important strategic issues but might differ on many important attitudes and beliefs. They might hold different ethical beliefs, prefer different human resource practices, view the economy differently, and so on. One or more might hope eventually to hold the presidency. The same things may be true of upper-level managers and even of middle managers. Individual managers, employees, or departments should consider these differences as they view the firm's leadership and shape communications intended for high-level receivers.

In what sense are the employees a public? In unenlightened eyes, they are not. Some managers pay little attention to the people who work for them. Their attitude is "They can do what I tell them to do or hit the road." If employees quit, however, replacing them and training the new hires will be costly. If they stay, they might take heavy sick leave, or file for worker's compensation for stress, or come to work and underproduce, or air their grievances all day to co-workers. Employees have considerable "won't power." Goading them to exercise it is foolish.

Employees

Study after study shows that employees show appreciation for managerial consideration in ways that improve the balance sheet. At every supervisory and managerial level, considering the effects of one's behavior on employees makes good sense.

Employees want information about their jobs and their performance, appreciation when they do well, instruction when they do not, some measure of self-determination, information about the company, a sense of belonging, an acceptable level of job security, and a number of other reasonable job expectations. They want pay comparable to what others like them are earning, but money and benefits alone will not make employees loyal if intrinsic needs go unmet.

Some firms communicate effectively with employees. They hold informational and motivational meetings, publish a readable and interesting house periodical, and support managers' efforts on employees' behalf. If you manage or supervise in a less enlightened or even in a repressive organization, you as an individual can often do better within your span of control than the firm does. But you will not be free to make all the changes you might wish.

External Publics

Among an organization's external publics are customers, the community, the stockholders, activist groups, the government, the industry, competitors, and the mass media. In some cases, individual employees make the contacts and create the impression. In some cases, only selected spokespersons communicate for the firm.

Customers

Because much of this textbook has stressed the importance of a business's communications with its customers, little need be said here. All customer communications should put the customer first. They should also show the organization to be well organized, ethical, and reliable. Customers want an organization to "have its act together."

Community

A business needs to be a good citizen of its community.

Organizations need to be good citizens of the place or places where they produce their goods and services. Businesses, and individuals within them, should support the locality in hiring and buying, take care not to pollute or spoil the area, and interest themselves in local issues for the betterment of the community. Sometimes they can give money and time to charities. Managers and employees can become active in community organizations such as Junior League, Rotary, and Big Brothers. Often individuals volunteer as speakers and in so doing build goodwill for the business.

Stockholders

Any publicly held company is responsible to those who buy its stock. Stockholders own the company. Their shares represent equity. Holders of large blocks of stock can wield power if they choose; and if small stockholders become angry or alarmed and pool their voting power, management is in trouble.

Companies communicate carefully with their stockholders. You are already aware of the time, money, and effort spent preparing the annual report. Some firms have investor relations departments that specialize in maintaining favorable contact with stockholders and marketing the stock to new prospects. Executives make their public statements with an eye to their probable effect on stockholders.

Nervous stockholders might dump their stock. Enough angry stockholders can expel a whole management team, although a "stockholders' revolt" is infrequent. Stockholders want the company to make money. Often what they want is directly opposed to what activists want.

Activist groups require the most careful handling. Such groups consist of well-intentioned people who devote time and energy to a cause they believe in passionately. Various activist groups protest against the use of animals in testing laboratories, the use of agricultural chemicals, the creation of landfills, the building of nuclear power plants, the use of fishing nets that snare marine mammals, and thousands of other causes. You probably feel considerable sympathy for some of these causes. On the other hand, every day we all use products that arouse the ire of one or more activist groups. Agreement or disagreement is not the issue here.

What is important for businesspeople to remember is that the groups are generally not interested in compromise or discussion. They are trying to stir a jaded public to action. They need the energy and drive that come from simple conviction. They have a First Amendment right to speak, and they will speak—especially to reporters.

For best results, a business listens carefully to activists, accommodates where it can, and thereafter makes its best decision on the point at issue. Animal testing, nuclear generating plants, and other causes are not simple matters of right and wrong. To explore the complexities of just one issue would take hundreds of pages. Because so many activist groups exist, pressing so many positions, only a rare business is able to avoid attack altogether. In pleasing one group, a business can mortally offend another.

What to do? First, a business should conduct itself well and reasonably and try not to draw activists' attention. If attacked, the business presents its side—not usually to activists but instead to the public via the mass media.

The business must make its case as simply as possible in a low-key and truthful statement. Often only a long statement would convey complete accuracy, but a long statement will not reach the public. The mass media will not use it; the public will lack the patience to hear or read it. Conveying a situation accurately in a few short sentences is so difficult that only top management and public relations people prepare and issue these communications.

National, state, and local governments regulate many aspects of business. Laws govern financial reporting, personnel practices, selling and advertising, contracts, and many other business activities. Businesspeople must understand the legal environment in which they act.

> Government agencies monitor many business practices regulated by public policy.

Government agencies monitor business practices by requiring specified reports. As long as the information appears on time and shows sound practice, government tends to leave businesses alone. Recently, however, the federal government had to step in when a large number of firms in the savings and loan industry had, without due warning, placed their investors' funds at high risk. In many cases, investors lost everything they had. The Resolution Trust Corporation (RTC), a government agency, took over many firms at great public cost and presided over the bankruptcy, merger, or whatever other disposition seemed best.

Whether one firm or an entire industry runs afoul of the law, costs are high and credibility is destroyed. Fines and penalties, although often heavy, are less harmful than the ill will generated.

Each industry maintains standards, some carefully spelled out and others loosely agreed on and understood. The American Institute of Certified Public Accountants (AICPA), for example, is responsible for Generally Accepted Accounting Principles (GAAP), the formal standards by which accountants perform audits. Businesses and their members need to work and communicate to meet the expectations of their industry.

Competitors are not always enemies. In fact, competitors prefer to respect one another, and sometimes they cooperate. For instance, a store that does not carry an item you want to buy will often suggest that you check at a rival store. The rival will do the same in return. If you take all your business somewhere else, both lose.

Businesspeople should not malign the competition. Even when feeling pressed, they can say, "Our competition works hard. They keep us on our toes." Bad-mouthing the competition reduces the stature of the speaker and often prompts the hearer to check out the competition personally.

Many businesses, even large ones, never appear in the mass media. For instance, until recently the public never thought about the nation's foremost waste management firms and never heard or read about them. The firms wanted it that way. They had to dispose of a nation's garbage, and nobody wants any of it anywhere nearby. Who wants public attention with that kind of a job to do?

These firms are in the news now because of increased interest in ecology. Their specialized communicators prepare informative pieces to educate the public about levels of hazard, types of disposal, modern means of waste treatment, resource recovery, and many other related topics. The pieces are factual, balanced, and highly credible.

Most firms' public relations staffs prepare communications for the various mass media. Their work is generally worth the money it costs. Informative news pieces and interesting feature articles from or about an organization create a favorable climate for it. They offer the media news about

Many favorable corporate events interest the public. Organizations' skilled communicators convey this information to the mass media.

- New product or service offerings.
- Promotions and appointments.
- Employee accomplishments.
- Company-sponsored community events and programs.
- Company expansion or new construction.
- Newsworthy speeches by executives.
- Corporate giving.

These are just some of the many possible topics. Thanks to the goodwill created by news of these company activities, public opinion is not merely neutral if an unforeseen crisis should occur.

Crisis communication is another function of public relations. Examples of crises include, among others,

- A violent crime on the premises (hostage, homicide, etc.).
- A hurricane, tornado, flood, earthquake, or other natural disaster.
- Evidence of wrongdoing by a member of the organization, such as embezzlement or sexual harassment.

Crisis communication plans ensure that the public is informed coherently, credibly, and consistently if an organization is hit by a human or natural disaster.

- A fire or explosion.
- A product liability suit.
- A strike.
- An organized demonstration.

Many organizations prepare crisis communication plans, with procedures to be followed in the event that specific emergencies arise. *Virtually all such plans direct that employees refer all requests from the mass media to designated spokespersons.* Organization members will be well informed about some things and ignorant of others. If each person feels free to talk to the media, stories will be incomplete and therefore possibly contradictory. Both the media and the public will infer that someone is lying, especially when the emergency is making everyone nervous.

Most line and staff managers and employees should decline to speak for the firm unless so authorized by the public relations department. Sometimes employees will be *asked* to do so. A public utility in Arizona encourages its employees to answer neighbors' and friends' questions, trains them, and keeps them supplied with updated facts. The utility regards its people as ambassadors to important opinion groups. Queries on sensitive subjects, of course, are referred to corporate spokespersons. Some organizations, including this utility, encourage their members to give talks to community groups in their areas of expertise.

The Communication Audit

The most thorough communication audit procedure was developed by the International Communication Association (ICA). A **communication audit** is a systematic review of all the company's communication practices to see whether their communication is actually doing what the firm intends it to do and believes it is doing. Some organizations conduct an audit periodically, as a preventive measure. Some firms conduct one when they discover or suspect a problem.

A communication audit traces and analyzes the information flow within an organization.

A company's communication should further the company's objectives. The audit can help solve existing problems, discover unrecognized ones, and head off potential ones. A motivated organization can derive great benefit from an audit. At minimum, a company performing one must examine its communication practices closely—which many companies do not often even think about, let alone do.

Usually, trained employee relations managers or consultants perform the audit. Using questionnaires, interviews, communication diaries, experience reports, and other instruments and techniques, they gather many different kinds of data. Wherever possible, they treat the data statistically. They compare results internally and also externally with the bank of data accumulated by the ICA.

Because those conducting the audit seek to discern patterns rather than incriminate individuals, employees can communicate freely with them. All members of the organization can benefit when problems are uncovered and solved. Examined areas inside the company include, among dozens of others,

- Whether employees get enough information to do their jobs well.
- Whether information is timely.
- Whether people are told how well they are performing.
- Whether employees learn about company errors.
- How people hear different kinds of information.
- What employees would suggest to improve communication.
- What informal communication lines exist.

The cumulated and treated data permit auditors to map the firm's communications, both formal and informal, and to show what works and what does not.

They can recommend changes in policy and procedure, show areas of strength, and suggest training if needed.

Individuals in a company, whether managers or employees, can monitor their own communication practices and those of others with whom they work. If they give and seek feedback, clarify instructions and statements of goals and objectives, and give and seek accurate and timely company information, they further beneficial communication and prevent problems. As they rise in the organization, they can make open and supportive communication basic to their leadership styles.

Interviewers of job applicants must strive to recruit the best applicant for the job while observing fair and legal hiring practices. When interviewing to solve a problem, managers and supervisors define the problem, search for the cause, consider various solutions, determine objectives, choose a means of solution, implement the solution, and follow up.

Ideally, performance appraisal combines interviewing and "walking around." Frequent interaction with employees lets supervisors convey expectations, standards, praise, critiques, and other matters that take the mystery out of appraisals. In appraisal interviews, supervisors and employees compare ideas about employees' job competence and productivity. The completed appraisal form becomes a permanent record, as does any written comment the employee wishes to make.

For problem employees, supervisors should first try teaching and correcting them. If this approach fails, supervisors must discipline. Progressive discipline often turns a poor performer around. If it fails, the individual may have to be discharged. Documentation of all steps in progressive discipline is essential.

As theorists have pointed out, employees work to fulfill needs, both extrinsic and intrinsic. Managers should learn what individuals value in their work and what interferes with their motivation. Then they should set the stage for employees' best work by providing the necessary rewards, instructions, and resources.

Organizational conflict proceeds in four stages: latent, perceived or felt, manifest, and aftermath. When well managed, conflict can be productive, generating creativity and encouraging healthy competition. When poorly managed, it is often destructive and wasteful of time and resources. Five typical responses to conflict include withdrawal, smoothing, forcing, compromising, and optimizing (win-win). Each response might suit a given problem, but people can optimize more often than they do. To optimize, participants must explore or develop additional benefits to divide.

Organizations have many internal and external constituencies or publics—groups with a stake in the organization's success. Internal publics are managers, executives, directors, and employees. External publics include customers, the community, stockholders, activist groups, government, the industry, competitors, and the mass media. Because organizations wish to displease as few of these constituencies as possible, communications must emanate from appropriate and credible sources and must be thoughtful and carefully tailored to the specific audience.

APPLICATION EXERCISES

1. When we say interviewers serve both their own and the organization's goals, what goals of their own might they be serving?

2. In recruitment interviews, to what extent may organizations and applicants conceal their weaknesses? Discuss.

3. What are the consequences of hiring a person who is not a good fit for the organization and the job?

4. What is a BFOQ? What kind of job might legitimately require a male? A Latino applicant? A female? An Anglo? A person under 30? A person without a hearing disability?

5. Why is it important to ask all applicants for a job the same questions in the same way?

6. Lately several of your workers have had family problems. You are interviewing and want to be sure you are hiring someone with a stable home life. Think of a nondiscriminatory "what-if" situational question whose answer would give you some indication of this stability.

7. What problem in your business, school, or professional life caused you to perform all or most of the steps given in connection with the problem-solving interview? How did you proceed?

8. What are the advantages of conducting regular, careful performance appraisals?

9. Explain the "halo" and "horns" effects, and give an example of each.

10. Discuss the connection between "managing by walking around" and giving performance appraisals.

11. Why are evaluations of average performers more difficult to do than those of outstanding performers?

12. Discuss the purposes of documenting performance evaluations. Give particular attention to cases involving progressive discipline.

13. Think of several of your working friends and relatives. Are they motivated by the same or by different things? Are they demotivated by the same or by different things? Are your motivations similar or dissimilar to theirs? Discuss.

14. Define and give an example of (*a*) latent conflict, (*b*) perceived or felt conflict, (*c*) manifest conflict, (*d*) aftermath of conflict.

15. Again think of several of your friends and relatives. Do you know a person whose "default" means of conflict resolution is to withdraw? To smooth over the conflict? To force it? To compromise? Do you know anyone who usually tries to optimize? Describe an incident that exemplifies each kind of behavior.

16. Divide into groups of five. Suppose you and your teammates are equal owners and managers of a 100-person business. Agree among yourselves what kind of business you are operating. Then think about the many other stakeholders: hourly employees, salaried employees, customers, community, activist groups, government, industry, competitors, the mass media. Consider, describe, and solve a problem you might have to address with each of these stakeholders.

CASES

The following cases require you to apply what you have learned about interviewing, appraising, coaching and disciplining, motivating, handling conflict, and communicating with organizational publics, both internal and external. Most of the cases involve more than one of these topics—just as everyday business supervision does.

1. **Not Everything Useful Is Permissible.** Kristin VanMeter is in charge of recruitment for an engineering firm that does a great deal of its work in the field. In interviews, she makes this fact clear and asks if that's okay with the applicants. Typically they say yes. She has recently started asking one further question of female applicants: "How does your husband or boyfriend feel about your being away at night this much?" She defends her practice this way: "Women expect their men to have to be away. They don't fuss about it. But

the guys! I can't tell you how much static we get from the women engineers we hire, and they're in turn getting pressure from their husbands or live-ins. Some of the women have wiggled out of their field work responsibilities. Some have quit. We want to hire women, but we can't afford to spend $30,000 training these people and then have them do that—not when we're up front with them."

2. **For a Complex Problem, Where Do You Begin?** Production and sales at your firm do not seem well coordinated. You, a staff assistant to the vice president of operations, are charged with finding out why. Jack Bowie, a high-level line manager, says they need more lead time for large orders. "Between large runs, we fill in by making product to the specs of smaller customers, and we make commitments to them," he tells you. "We

try hard to fill the high-volume orders—they're 80 percent of our revenue. But we can't reset at a moment's notice." Jennifer Purnell, sales manager, says she wishes she could give them more lead time. "We make a lot of calls and a lot of bids," she says, "but we can't predict which will turn into sales. This industry is hotly competitive. When the buyers say yes, we have to get the product to them at least as quickly as our competitors can. We've lost two repeat customers this quarter." "How often do sales and production meet?" you ask Bowie. "We're supposed to meet twice weekly," he says, "but Jennifer is gone a lot." Purnell tells you the biweekly meetings don't accomplish anything one weekly meeting couldn't. You wonder: Is the problem lack of information flow? At what point? What factors or patterns might predict orders? Would research give us anything solid enough to help Bowie do better production planning? How do you define what the real problem is?

3. **Anxiety Fills an Appraisal Vacuum.** Carl, an accountant at a heavy manufacturing firm, had not been appraised since his 90-day post-hire appraisal two years ago. He was shy and anxious by nature and did not deal well with normal ups and downs on the job. Michael, the department supervisor, often kidded around with some of the other staffers, although he thought Carl was humorless and did not banter with him. Seeing Michael and several other accountants so comfortable together, Carl began to believe Michael was displeased with his performance. He began to avoid Michael and tried to look too busy to interrupt when Michael would walk through the department. Near the close of business one day, Carl approached Michael and said, "My work has not been up to your standard, has it? I'm trying my best—really!" Michael said, "Carl, you funny duck, relax! Things are fine." Carl did not think so. He became more and more certain he would be replaced soon. A few months later, he left the firm on his own.

4. **A Message Is Sent: "Problem Behavior Pays."** Liz was hired as a supervisor at the central office of a government forestry agency. Most other workers there believed she was hired because she was a female rather than for her education or work experience. Her work, for which she had to be specially trained, was mainly timekeeping. She made numerous errors, which had to be traced and corrected. After about six months, her supervisor found out that Liz had a cocaine problem. She was sent to a drug treatment program and shortly thereafter was transferred to a higher-paying position with less responsibility and stress. Her co-workers believed that she should have been fired but that the agency would look bad if they fired a woman when they employed so few.

5. **Let's Shut Our Eyes—Then the Problem Will Go Away.** Colette had started as a clerical worker and worked her way up in a manufacturing firm. She now co-managed 18 employees. She had no management training, and her communication skills were mediocre. Because she worked so hard and treated people well, her subordinates respected and supported her, and the department ran smoothly. New hires were usually "socialized" by co-workers, since Colette was ineffective at conveying company policies to newcomers. Del, a new employee with significant experience in the industry, quickly identified her lack of effective communication. He began to come to work late, take long breaks, and in other ways take significant advantage of his manager. His co-workers tried to coach him, but he said, "The boss lady doesn't seem to have any problem with what I do," and continued to flout the department's standard practices. When Del's co-workers told Colette of their annoyance, she said, "Everybody has come around eventually. Del will fit in after a while." One morning Del's tardiness resulted in a meeting fiasco that made Colette and her whole department look incompetent to higher management.

6. **You Call That Music?** You manage a department of a company that does chemical and biological testing. The workers are a cohesive group. They often work 10-hour days and are sometimes willing to work an all-night shift if demand becomes heavy. To counteract the routine nature of the work, they really enjoy listening to KUKN, a classic-rock station. The exception is David, who does not like KUKN and changes the station when the others aren't paying attention. Tension mounts until someone changes the station back to KUKN. Nobody wants to make a big issue out of this, but everyone's feelings are strong. David is an excellent employee. The periodic accuracy audits that your lab commissions from an independent audit agency show his error rate to be virtually zero.

7. **Achtung, Stupid! More Work, Less Humanism!** Nancy Booth obtained her first supervisory position at Prospero Development, a real estate development firm with a humanistic culture. She knew the development business thoroughly and was determined to excel in her new job. This pleased the vice president. He had been glad of the way Nancy's predecessor had handled the department's routine problems without needing much of his attention. He counted on Nancy's

doing the same thing. "We're all going to get more out of our hours," Nancy announced to the employees. "No more chitchat." She made numerous changes in operations right away to improve efficiency but did not communicate them well. People made mistakes, which she would use as don't-do-this examples for the others. She insisted on punctuality from them but not from herself. She watched them all closely and constantly. Her employees began to resent her style, which they considered micromanagement. They began calling her "Nazi" instead of "Nancy" behind her back. One day, Nancy let it slip that she wouldn't mind getting rid of some of the staff she had inherited. In this she succeeded. Most of the department resigned within the first year, and a budget cutback permitted replacing only half of them. Nancy—and the vice president—were left with 50 percent of a staff, very few of whom knew much about how Prospero Development operated.

8. **I'm Right and the Auditors Are Wrong. I Win!** Ed was a program manager in an institution that receives government entitlement monies. Ed kept records his own way, and when an auditor representing the government came to audit Ed's program, numerous problems and findings had to be brought to the attention of the administration. A meeting was held with the auditors, the administrators, and Ed. Every finding they discussed enraged Ed. He argued with the auditors, raised his voice, blamed others for his errors, and insisted that the auditors owed him an apology. The meeting was an embarrassment. The administrators accepted the findings of the audit and assured the auditors that Ed would make appropriate corrections, but the penalty was still severe. A large sum of government money had to be paid back, and the program was discontinued.

9. **It's *Your* Newsletter (If You're the Boss's Pal).** Kay, in human resources, coordinates a monthly corporate newsletter for a food service distributor. She is keenly aware of the need to involve rank-and-file employees and believes the six-page newsletter, *Everything Fresh,* is one of the best media for doing so. One day a warehouse supervisor, Rob Tokharian, approached her rather uncertainly to mention an idea for a human-interest story about one of his employees. "I've read the two features on individual employees in this month's edition, and I'm sure this guy's story is newsworthy." "Great," Kay said. "E-mail me the names of people to talk to, and we'll take it from there." "Really?" Rob said, "that's all?" "Sure," Kay replied. "Hasn't your manager told you that we're always looking for articles about our employees?" "No," Rob said, "I thought just the managers picked out who you'd write about." Kay thought about Rob's manager, a bright, ambitious, young fellow, and remembered that the two features she had received from his department showcased chums of his. She wondered how many other managers were gatekeeping, how many employees felt shut out, and what she should do about it.

10. **Lifesavers Have Their Own Communication Policy.** Communication with the press and the public is a touchy subject in the health-care field. Santa Inez Hospital's communication policy directs all media calls to public relations and marketing to ensure proper patient confidentiality. All personnel follow it except the top people in the emergency and intensive-care units. These individuals, with so many life-and-death crises to attend to daily, hold the policy in some contempt and freely give information to the press when they see fit. One evening, head ER nurse Mitzi Fields, exhausted after assisting in the treatment of five auto accident victims, was relaxing in the break room with Mary Blalock, a newspaper reporter who had spent many hours at Santa Inez recently working on an in-depth feature article on the costs of medical care. Mary asked, "Did I hear the head trauma case called Laurie Mortensen? Is that Laurie Mortensen the mayor's daughter?" Mitzi asked, "Off the record?" and continued, "Yeah, you're right. And I get so tired of patching up these irresponsible kids. If it isn't pot, it's coke or booze." The next morning's newspaper led off with "Mayor's daughter badly injured. Substance abuse mentioned."

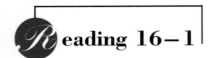

GETTING PAST PERSONALITY CONFLICTS

Andrew S. Grove

All of us work in the company of others. We all have idiosyncrasies, we approach problems and situations uniquely, and we don't always like the differences in style and attitude that we encounter. Of course, not all problems are worth worrying about. But how do you know when a person's style is legitimately your business, and how do you decide when it isn't? It is as important to know which battles *not* to engage in as it is to choose the ones you want to fight.

- One of my junior colleagues tends to giggle nervously when she has to deal with senior people. Her lack of poise is hampering her own career, and people are starting to make fun of her. I don't want to scare her by being critical, but I'd like to help her before she completely undermines herself. What should I do?

Asking people to change their habits is about as effective as telling the rain to stop—even if they desperately want to change, they'll still lapse into ingrained behavior periodically. On the other hand, it's clear that you want to help your employee. So arrange a conversation in which you describe her habit and the effect it has on her work and on her co-workers' perception of her. Then ask, "What can I do to help you break this habit?" Work at coming up with an unembarrassing signal for when she starts giggling that will be obvious only to you and her. You might even set up a system whereby you rate her on how well she avoided this habit after each presentation. You should realize that a single mention will probably have no impact, so don't set your initial expectations too high. This has to be a patient and ongoing process on both your parts.

- A recent transfer into my division doesn't understand my work style. I prefer to be informal; she's a memo-maniac. I call meetings when I feel there's something to discuss; she wants a weekly schedule. I feel as if I'm being nitpicked to death. What should I do?

There's nothing right or wrong with either of your styles—both approaches can work. But take care that the differences in style don't overwhelm getting the work done. I think you need to meet your colleague halfway. Propose a compromise by saying something like "Look, we obviously approach things differently. Let's not let that cut down on the efficiency of the office. I'll try to do things your way, and I'd appreciate it if you'd try to approach things my way some of the time." In other words, you'll have to write a few more memos; in return, you'll expect her to accept your informality.

- I've let my personal dislike of a colleague get to the point where I can't stand to be in the same room with him. I don't approve of the way he handles his work or how he deals with co-workers and subordinates. Even his voice bugs me. But we've just been assigned to work on a project together. What can I do to work successfully with him?

Simply concentrate on the work and discipline yourself to set aside other considerations; this is the hand that you've been dealt, and you have to learn to play with it. The more you think about your dislike of this person, the more you're going to be aware of it and the more you're going to be bothered by him. Try not to get worked up; just tell yourself: Hey, that's not my problem—my problem is to fill this order (or make this machine work, or whatever). If you focus on getting on with the work, the undesirable factors will fade by comparison in your mind.

- My immediate subordinate won't be subordinate. He grabs the limelight on joint sales calls, continually interrupts my presentations and doesn't keep me informed about his own sales calls. I've spoken to him about this, but the behavior continues. The problem, is, he's producing a lot of revenue, so I can't just fire him. What do you suggest?

This is a style issue that has been transformed into a substance issue. It's annoying and counterproductive when your subordinate steals the show, but that's something you can live with. When he goes out on his own, however, and doesn't keep you informed about his activities, then future development is threatened and you have no choice but to stop this behavior.

Use your formal authority to good advantage. Address the issue without apologies, illustrating your points with examples, and tell him to stop. Point out that you can't do your job unless he is diligent about informing you of the relevant aspects of his work. Be alert to any repetition of his misconduct; when it happens again (and it will), jump on the issue immediately. If the behavior continues, make it clear that it's something you are not prepared to live with, current productivity notwithstanding.

It's important not to dilute this issue by including complaints about your employee's grabbing the limelight in the same conversation. The latter is an annoyance; the former is a problem. Keep at the substantive issue until it's gone; you'll have plenty of time to work on style later.

- I've inherited an apologist who begs my pardon every time she enters my office. I've actually caught myself snapping at her because she acts so meek. How can I respond to her without seeming harsh?

Andrew S. Grove, "Getting Past Personality Conflicts: What to Do When Your Staff and Colleagues Drive You Nuts," *Working Woman*, February 1993, pp. 34–35.

Forget it. You have met the enemy and she is you. You can't expect all the people you come across in the course of your work to follow a code of conduct that you have defined someplace in the deep recesses of your mind. Although they are frustrating to you, your employee's actions are completely harmless. Lighten up and shrug it off; it's merely a matter of somebody acting in a way you prefer she didn't.

- I've heard that one of my assistants takes advantage of the secretaries by making them do tasks that are his responsibility. He's a cocky young man, and I've had problems with him before—he can't seem to deal with a boss who's a woman. How do I get him to knuckle down and improve his attitude without coming across like his high school English teacher?

Try to avoid chasing after vague notions like attitude and respect and instead go after concrete issues. That's where your best case can be made. He didn't do his filing—that's a problem. He didn't prepare a report when asked—that's a problem. He isn't respectful? I don't know what that means, and neither will he. Is the cocky young man in question doing his work or not? If he is, you surely have other things to worry about. If he isn't, then you clearly have something concrete to discuss.

- One of my top staffers gets up on the wrong side of bed every morning. Her sour attitude and nonstop criticisms are becoming a real drag on office morale, but I'm afraid that if I say something to her, the griping will increase. What's the solution?

Don't be afraid. This isn't an instance of an overlookable bad day. You get paid to keep your group's productivity at a certain level, and it's clear that this person's actions interfere with that productivity. Therefore, it's your job to stop that behavior. Address the issue privately, using lots of examples, and be prepared to persist in your reminders—one mention won't do the trick. But for your own peace of mind, remember that this is a serious issue concerning work flow and that ignoring it would be shunning your responsibility to your company and to your staff.

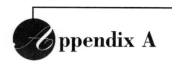

ppendix A | FORMATS FOR BUSINESS MESSAGES

BUSINESS LETTERS: PARTS AND FORMATS

Readers of business letters have certain expectations. Letters must present a clean, attractive, professional appearance. They should be centered on the page, with adequate margins. They should present an open, readable appearance, with no lengthy, gray paragraphs. The appearance of a letter creates an impression of its writer's care and pride in workmanship. It also reflects on the organization from which it is sent.

Reader expectations also determine a letter's parts and their placement. A letter's parts are the heading, the inside address, the salutation, the body, the complimentary close, and the signature. After the signature, several abbreviations sometimes appear. Exhibit A–1 labels these parts.

Readers also expect to see an acceptable business-letter format. Business letters may appear in a traditional format such as full block style, in the simplified format developed by the Administrative Management Society, or in a newer format allowing for several variations, often called the creative format.

The Parts of a Business Letter

The **heading** contains the writer's address and the date (see Exhibit A–1). Most business letters appear on an organization's letterhead stationery, which usually includes the address in preprinted form. In these letters, the heading contains just the date and starts two or more spaces below the letterhead, either at the left margin—full block style—or at the center of the line—modified block style (see Exhibits A–2 and A–3).

The **inside address** contains the reader's name, title, and full address. Its vertical placement varies with the length of the letter. If the letter is long, only a couple of lines separate it from the date. For a short letter, the writer inserts as many lines between date and inside address as will center the letter attractively on the page. The inside address always appears at the left margin.

The **salutation** greets the reader or readers and is traditionally followed by a colon. Traditional salutations include the reader's name, if known, or a courteous substitute:

Dear Ms. Casey: Dear Sir:
Gentlemen: Dear Sir or Madam:
Dear Mrs. Maxwell: Dear Mr. and Mrs. Peterson:
Dear Col. Carter: Ladies and Gentlemen:
Mr. Higgins: Dear Dr. Bishop:

Punctuation is sometimes omitted in a style called **open punctuation.** Less frequently, the colon is replaced with a comma. The comma, though, is usually associated with the format for personal letters rather than that for business letters.

The main part of a letter is called the **body.** The body of most business letters is single-spaced, with a blank space between paragraphs. Today's practice favors block-style paragraphs, but paragraphs may be indented if the writer or the firm prefers that style.

Paragraphs in business letters should be short. Long paragraphs in letters discourage readers from reading the letter completely and carefully.

Two vertical spaces below the body and four vertical spaces above the signature, the **complimentary close** appears. Typical complimentary closes include *Sincerely, Yours truly,* and *Sincerely yours.* Less frequently used are *Respectfully yours,* and *Very sincerely yours. Thank you* and *Best wishes* are gaining acceptance as complimentary

Source: Adapted from Jeanette W. Gilsdorf, *Business Correspondence for Today* (New York: John Wiley & Sons, 1989), pp. 361–370.

Heading

4622 North Basswood Drive
St. Louis, MO 63116
January 2, 19—

Inside address

Jordan L. Tomlinson
Personnel Director
Anheuser-Busch, Inc.
One Busch Place
St. Louis, MO 63118

Salutation

Dear Mr. Tomlinson:

Your advertisement in Sunday's St. Louis Post-Dispatch for an area distributor matched my qualifications closely. Two years as college rep for Anheuser-Busch, an associate's degree emphasizing transportation and marketing, and entrepreneurial experience make me an ideal candidate for this position.

Much of my energy propelled Anheuser-Busch's marketing efforts on the campus of Santa Ynez Community College, where I combined A-B's excellent materials and promotions with what my marketing classes were teaching me.

Body

Because a beer distributor must be a planner, a self-starter, and a motivator of others, my experience operating my own business is pertinent. I ran a lawn and pool service April through October 1990 and 1991, with seven people working for me during the high-volume months. Profits enabled me to upgrade my truck and equipment while maintaining high customer satisfaction and repeat business.

The attached resume will show my other work experience and my education more fully.

Working and attending college in California, I observed some interesting things about area preferences in beers. In particular, I have some ideas I'd like to discuss with you about how Anheuser-Busch can market to those who seem to prefer some of the imported beers over domestics.

Since I'll be in St. Louis until January 21, I'll call later this week to arrange a convenient time to meet and talk. I'll surely appreciate a chance to show you why Anheuser-Busch needs to hire me as an area distributor.

Complimentary close

Sincerely,

Typed signature

Robert J. Galbraith

Enclosure line

Enclosure

Pact-Wel Foods

QLF INTERNATIONAL

A QLF GROUP COMPANY
Kaywood Plaza
Mankton Gardens, RI 00711

*All elements
lined up at
left margin.
Alternative
form could
indent first
line of each
paragraph*

November 17, 19—

Mr. James E. Marantz
8549 E. San Gabriel Drive
Shawnee Mission, KS 66287

Dear Mr. Marantz:

Please use the enclosed full-price coupon to replace your
container of delicious Cheddar-Creme spread, in accordance
with our guarantee.

From your description, we think that the container may have
had a defect in the actuator button. We're enclosing a
postage-paid label for your convenience in returning the can to
our Quality Control department. With the product for
examination, we can determine why it may not be operating
properly. This helps us a great deal—we want to make sure
nothing about the product interferes with people's enjoyment
of it.

Thanks for getting in touch with us. We're glad to have the
opportunity to help you enjoy our popular Cheddar-Creme, and
to make sure that the next purchaser can do so as well.

Sincerely,

Jessamyn Rooney

Jessamyn Rooney
Consumer Service Representative

Jr: ac

Enclosure

c: Quality Control

Pact-Wel Foods

QLF INTERNATIONAL

A QLF GROUP COMPANY
Kaywood Plaza
Mankton Gardens, RI 00711

*Date
centered*

November 17, 19—

Mr. James E. Marantz
8549 E. San Gabriel Drive
Shawnee Mission, KS 66287

Dear Mr. Marantz:

*Alternate
form could
indent
paragraphs*

Please use the enclosed full-price coupon to replace your
container of delicious Cheddar-Creme spread, in accordance
with our guarantee.

From your description, we think that the container may have
had a defect in the actuator button. We're enclosing a
postage-paid label for your convenience in returning the can to
our Quality Control department. With the product for
examination, we can determine why it may not be operating
properly. This helps us a great deal—we want to make sure
nothing about the product interferes with people's enjoyment
of it.

Thanks for getting in touch with us. We're glad to have the
opportunity to help you enjoy our popular Cheddar-Creme, and
to make sure that the next purchaser can do so as well.

*Closing
centered*

Sincerely,

Jessamyn Rooney

Jessamyn Rooney
Consumer Service Representative

Jr: ac

Enclosure

c: Quality Control

A: Full block style, mixed punctuation

B: Modified block style, open punctuation

C: No letterhead, block form, indented
paragraphs, mixed punctuation

D: Memo form

closes. Traditional punctuation after this letter element is a comma. In open punctuation, no punctuation appears.

The signature block, typed four spaces below the complimentary close, shows the writer's name and often his or her position in the firm. In the four-line space between complimentary close and typed name, the writer *signs* his or her name in ink.

The complimentary close and the signature block start at the left margin if the letter's date does so (full block style), but start at the center of the line if the letter's date starts there (modified block style).

Several symbols may appear after the signature. Two more vertical lines separate the signature from whatever follows. The symbols may include the initials of the person who originated the letter, the initials of the person who typed it, the word *Enclosure,* and the symbol *c* (copy) or *pc* (photocopy) and one or more names of recipients of these copies.

A business letter written on plain stationery—stationery that has no preprinted letterhead—might look like Exhibit A–1. This letter uses the modified block style with no paragraph indention. Note vertical spacing of the element in Exhibits A–1, A–2, and A–3. Exhibit A–4 gives a quick comparison among layout types.

Format Variations

Today's traditional format is either full block style or modified block style. (An older format, the indented style, is rarely used.) The letter in Exhibit A–2 is in **full block style.** Notice that all elements begin at the left margin. Full block style is quick and easy for typists. The appearance is crisp.

In the **modified block style,** shown in Exhibit A–3, the date, the complimentary close, and the signature start at the center of the line. This letter does not indent paragraphs. A different variation of modified block style does indent paragraphs.

Not every letter must have the dictator's initials *(JR)*. Often just the typist's initials *(ac)* appear. Sometimes the two sets of initials are separated by a slash instead of a colon. Sometimes no typist's initials appear. Not all letters have enclosures. Similarly, copies or photocopies (indicated by *c* or *pc*) are not always necessary.[1]

The **simplified style** omits the salutation and the complimentary close (see Exhibit A–5). You may have asked yourself just why every recipient of every letter is "dear" and why nearly every writer must claim to have written "sincerely" or must affirm that he or she is "yours." The effect of telling someone who is both "dear" and "very truly yours" how annoyed you are with a bad product would be comic, if anyone ever thought hard about it.

The Administrative Management Society thought hard about it and decided yesteryear's forms could be dispensed with. Their recommended simplified format has been gaining popularity. It not only does away with archaic language but also solves another problem: avoiding sexist language.

Forty years ago, so few women held high positions in business that unknown letter recipients could safely be addressed as *Dear Sir, Dear Sirs,* or *Gentlemen.* Assuming unknown business recipients to be male is no longer safe. But what do we do if our best effort has not discovered the name of a person we need to write to? Or what if we have the name but do not know whether T. R. Cadwallader or Terry R. Cadwallader is male or female?

We do have some options. We can write, *Dear Sir or Madam, To whom it may concern, Dear Committee, Gentlemen and Ladies, Dear Chairperson,* and the like. We can write *Dear Mr. or Ms. Cadwallader,* or *Dear T. R. Cadwallader.* But most of the solutions that avoid the sexism pitfall are graceless and a bit strange to the eye and ear. Because of their unfamiliarity, they call attention to themselves and thus to the fact that the writer doesn't know the recipient.

The simplified style usually uses the salutation position for a useful business message. Sometimes it's a subject line:

SUBJECT: Your order for silk brocade.

Sometimes it's an attention line:

ATTN: Freight Expediter

[1]Although photocopies are often referred to as "xeroxes," Xerox is not a generic word for photocopy. It is a trademark, and its use is protected by law. Therefore, avoid using "xc" as an abbreviation at the end of a letter.

Pact-Wel Foods

QLF INTERNATIONAL

A QLF GROUP COMPANY
Kaywood Plaza
Mankton Gardens, RI 00711

November 17, 19—

Mr. James E. Marantz
8549 E. San Gabriel Drive
Shawnee Mission, KS 66287

Please use the enclosed full-price coupon to replace your
container of delicious Cheddar-Creme spread, in accordance
with our guarantee.

From your description, we think that the container may have
had a defect in the actuator button. We're enclosing a
postage-paid label for your convenience in returning the can to
our Quality Control department. With the product for
examination, we can determine why it may not be operating
properly. This helps us a great deal—we want to make sure
nothing about the product interferes with people's enjoyment
of it.

Thanks for getting in touch with us. We're glad to have the
opportunity to help you enjoy our popular Cheddar-Creme, and
to make sure that the next purchaser can do so as well.

Jessamyn Rooney

Jessamyn Rooney
Consumer Service Representative

Jr: ac

Enclosure

c: Quality Control

A sales letter could say, where the salutation usually appears,

DISKETTES FOR LESS—GUARANTEED!

and then begin the body of the letter.

At the end of the letter's body, the writer simply leaves four vertical spaces for the signature and types the signature block as usual. The omission of the complimentary close is not as noticeable as the omission of the salutation.

The **creative style** develops the simplified style one step further. As the term suggests, this format permits the writer some freedom.

Not all letters are suited to format creativity. The creative style suggests lightness, even playfulness at times. The writer's judgment about the communication task comes into play.

Instead of the standard salutation, the writer of a favorable adjustment letter might say,

Here is your $30, Mr. Parker . . .

and continue with the body of the letter.
A job offer might begin,

Schilling Associates likes your ideas, Ms. Larson . . .
. . . and we'd like you to start putting them to work for us on March 3, the date you said you'd be available. Starting salary for someone with your excellent experience and qualifications is $41,500 . . .

A writer might choose the creative format for any letter whose content is basically positive. The creative format is *not* suitable for bad-news letters, collection letters, letter reports, transmittal letters for formal reports, or any letter whose content is not light. Using the creative format for an auditor's letter report, for instance, would detract from the seriousness of the content. The letter's credibility would suffer. Exhibit A−6 shows a letter that appropriately uses the creative format.

As you can see, business communicators have many letter format options. Unless your organization has a set policy on letter format, consider which format best suits each letter you write.

BUSINESS MEMO FORMATS

Many organizations have preprinted forms, in half-sheet or whole-page length, for memorandums. If yours does, use its forms. Readers become accustomed to looking for the same information in the same place. You will save memo readers' time by putting information where they expect to find it.

Some organizations do not have preprinted memo forms but do follow a set memo style. If yours does, follow that style.

Memos are written either on plain stationery or on letterhead designed for internal use.

Most memos contain four elements near the top of the page:

TO: [name of receiver, and title, if needed]
FROM: [name of sender, and title, if needed]
DATE: [date sent]
SUBJECT: [phrase concisely describing most important idea]

Placement and order can vary, but all four of these elements are important. Exhibits A−7 and A−8 show two common memorandum formats. Others can be found in many chapters in this textbook and in Exhibit A−4.

Both letters and memos are generally folded for insertion into envelopes. The most common folds are shown in Exhibit A−9. The first is for a "business-size" (number 10) envelope, which measures $9\frac{1}{2}'' \times 4\frac{1}{8}''$. The other is for a smaller envelope (number $6\frac{3}{4}$). This envelope measures $6\frac{1}{2}'' \times 3\frac{5}{8}''$.

GENTLEMEN'S BIMONTHLY MAGAZINE

700 Talbot Avenue – Suite 601
Hartford, CT 06100

June 20, 19—

> Help the American Cancer Society,
> the American Heart Association,
> the United Way, or the March of Dimes–

For your 5 minutes, your favorite charity gains. . . .

We'd like to ask a favor of you. And to show our appreciation, we'll make a contribution to the charity of your choice.

Surveying GENTLEMEN'S BIMONTHLY MAGAZINE subscribers will help us make the magazine exactly what you want it to be. If you'll take a minute or two to fill out and return the enclosed questionnaire, you'll help us make your magazine more valuable to you.

. . . and you'll also lend a hand to the American Cancer Society, the American Heart Association, the United Way or the March of Dimes—the choice is up to you.

To let us know which organization you wish to receive the contribution made possible by your reply, please check the appropriate box at the end of your questionnaire.

Naturally, the answers you give will be held in confidence. So won't you complete your Subscriber Survey and return it today? We've enclosed a postpaid envelope for your reply.

Help improve YOUR magazine, and assist your favorite charity. . . .

John R. Shelley

JRS/lf

Enclosures

MEMORANDUM

March 5. 19--

Date can also be at left margin

To: District 7 Sales Force
From: Bert Wong, District Director
Subject: Four District 7 Champions Gain Honors for February

Emphasize subject by underlining, bold, or all caps

Your effort made district 7 the sales leader for February.

No other district had more than two sales reps on the OVER FIFTY-K list. Ours had four: Ollie Bellmar, Beverly Harris, Amy Potter, and Ken Swain. Two others, Harry Abraham and Patricia Wildde, were very close to reaching the $50,000 sales figure.

You made February a month to be proud of. Nice work!

pc: M.C. Pitmann
    Southeast Region Sales Manager

An alternative way to fold an 8½″ × 11″ page into a number 10 envelope is the *Z* fold, which allows the top of the page to show when the recipient takes it out of the envelope (see Exhibit A–10).

ENVELOPES AND OCR HANDLING

As with stationery, the quality of the envelope paper should contribute to your firm's image. The sender's return address, usually printed like the letterhead (or typed), should appear in the upper left-hand corner of the envelope. Traditionally, the main address—blocked the same way as the inside address, and with the zip code—should go in the lower half of the envelope, with the address beginning approximately five spaces to the left of the horizontal center point of the envelope.

If you want the letter to get to the attention of someone, type the word *attention* and the person's name in the lower left-hand corner of the envelope *(Attention: Anthony Boggs* or *Attn: Anthony Boggs)*, or put it under the company name:

Shearson Lehman Hutton, Inc.
Attention: Anthony Boggs

To speed up and economize on mail handling, the U.S. Postal Service has moved steadily toward machine sorting of mail—LSM (letter-sorting machine) and OCR (optical character recognition) handling. How you address your letter will determine its handling—and the difference could determine whether it goes out in today's mail!

For the faster OCR handling, you must follow specific requirements for the main address, as explained and illustrated in Exhibit A–11 on a number 10 envelope:

1. Single-space, capitalize everything, omit all punctuation, and use block style. No proportional spacing of characters, no italic or script, and no spelling out of numbers. All address information must be in the last three lines, with the street address or box number immediately above the city–state–zip code (which should be the last line). If the zip code will not fit, it may go in the next line immediately below the city and state.

O–RING *INTERNATIONAL*

I N T E R O F F I C E   M E M O R A N D U M

Emphasis on subject line

     To: All Production Personnel
   From: Plant Maintenance Supervisor
Subject: <u>Scheduled Maintenance</u>
   Date: November 16, 19—

This notice reminds all production personnel that scheduled cleaning, lubrication, and safety inspection will be performed on line machinery the Friday after Thanksgiving.

So that the maintenance can be completed rapidly, please shelve all tools and clear your work area completely at the end of the Wednesday before the holiday.

If the maintenance crew has to clear work areas, the work may run into Monday, causing production downtime.

But with your cooperation, the maintenance can be completed within one day's time—Friday—which is a paid holiday for production personnel.

Enjoy your four-day weekend and come in Monday to an up-and-running line of safe, clean machinery.

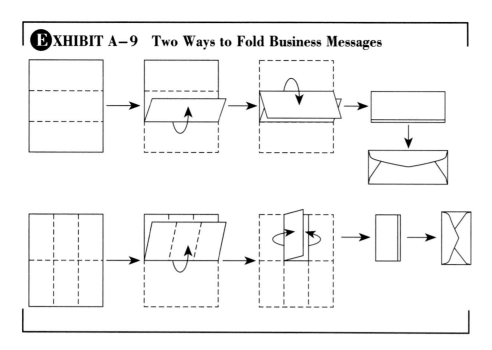

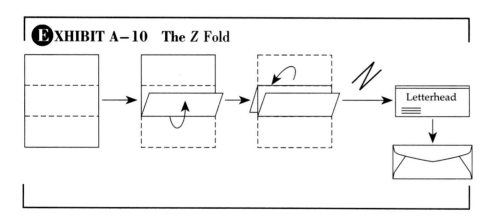

Put a minimum of two to four spaces between the state and the zip code. The two-letter state abbreviation is preferable for OCR. Put apartment numbers, suite numbers, and so forth on the same line as the street address, if possible. For mail addressed to a foreign country, follow the same rules. Include the postal delivery zone number (if any). The name of the country must be the last item in the address.

2. Put nothing to the left or right of or below the address. The address must begin at least an inch from the left edge and be more than half an inch from the bottom. Any codes should be part of the address and go immediately above the addressee's name.

3. Use both the zip code plus four figures and the two-letter state abbreviation.

4. Keep typewriter or printer type clean and ribbons fresh to provide clear, crisp impressions.

EXHIBIT A–11 Number 10 Envelope Addressed for OCR Handling

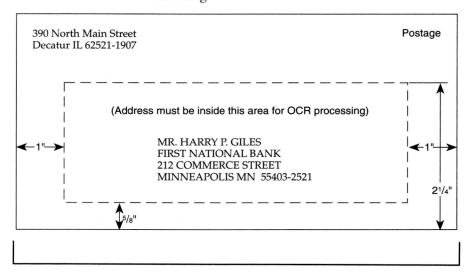

Enjoying the economies of window envelopes (gained largely by typing the addresses only once) requires folding the letter so that only the inside address shows through the window. For OCR handling, window envelopes must follow additional rules. Consult your postmaster.

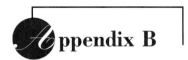

Appendix B | WRITING HANDBOOK

This alphabetical list of short, easy-to-remember **symbols** will save instructors time in marking papers and will help students by giving brief explanations of many writing and business communication problems. Note that all forms of punctuation (period, comma, colon, etc.) are discussed under the symbol **Punc.**

Abbreviation Before using an abbreviation, make sure it is appropriate, understood, and standard (including capitalization, spacing, and punctuation).

Accuracy Get facts, names, addresses, and statements right.

Adapt Adapt to your reader's interests, reading ability, and experience. Personalized messages written for and adapted to specific readers are more effective than mass broadcasts. What seems to be for everybody has less interest to anybody. Even form letters should give the feeling that the message is directed to each reader. Expressions such as "Those of you who . . . " and "If you are one who . . . " give just the opposite impression.

Adj/Adv Be sure to use the right form of a word for its function in the sentence. For the comparative and superlative forms, see **Compr** 3.

Agreement Agreement of subjects with their verbs and of pronouns with their antecedents is essential to clear, inconspicuous communication. Don't be confused by other words that come between two words that are supposed to agree.

1. Notice that the first sentence about agreement is an illustration of the first point: *Agreement* (singular) is the subject of the verb *is,* but between them is a prepositional phrase with four plurals. Consider the following other illustrations:

   Selection of topics *depends* on the reader's knowledge and interests.

   Lee also tells how important the arrangement of the records offices *is.*

   Part, series, type, and other words usually followed by plural phrases are frequently pitfalls to the unwary writer:

   The greatest part of their investments *is* in real estate.

   A series of bank loans *has* enabled the firm to stay in business.

2. *Anyone, each, every, everyone, everybody, either,* and *neither* all point to singular verbs (and pronouns), except that in an *either-or* situation, with one noun singular and one plural, verbs and pronouns agree with the closer noun:

   Each of the women in the group *is* willing to give some of *her* time to helping the group when asked.

   Either board members or the president *has* power to act on the point.

   Neither the mayor nor the council members *are* allowed to use city-owned automobiles in transacting *their* own business.

Source: Adapted from Gretchen N. Vik, C. W. Wilkinson, and Dorothy C. Wilkinson, *Writing and Speaking in Business* (Homewood, Ill.: Richard D. Irwin, Inc., 1990), pp. 600–630.

3. Two separate singular subjects combined by *and* require a plural verb or pronoun; but when combined by *besides, either-or, together with,* or *as well as,* they take a singular:

Mrs. Davis and her secretary *do* the work in the central office.

Considerable knowledge, as well as care, *is* necessary in good writing.

But note:

The honorary president and leader of this group *is* Mr. Anderson (one person, two titles).

4. Be sure pronouns agree in number and gender with their antecedents (words they stand for):

Find out whether Coronal Supermarkets is dissatisfied without emphasizing its (not *their*) possible dissatisfaction.

The benefits students get from studying the practical psychology, writing skills, and ways of business in good courses like letter writing and report writing will help *them* throughout life.

5. Relative clauses beginning with *who, that,* or *which* require that verbs agree with the antecedents of those words:

The manager is one of those *persons who* expect unquestioning loyalty.

The *actions* in the life of any animal *that* interest a biologist are those concerned with food, shelter, protection from enemies, and procreation.

6. Plural-sounding collective subjects take singular verbs and pronouns when the action is that of the group but plural verbs when the action is that of two or more individuals in the group:

The board *is* having a long meeting. (Board acting in unison.)

The board *have* been arguing and disagreeing on that point for months. (Board acting divisively.)

7. Beware of letting the complement tempt you to make the verb agree with it instead of with the subject:

Our main difficulty *was* errors in billing.

The biggest cost item *is* employees' salaries and wages. (In most such situations, however, rewriting would be better.)

8. Certain words deserve careful attention because their form is an uncertain or misleading indication of their number:
   a. The meaning of the whole context determines the number of *any, all, more, most, some,* and *none.*
   b. *Acoustics, economics, genetics, linguistics, mathematics, news, physics,* and *semantics* are all singular despite their look and sound; *deer* and *fish* are both singular and plural; and *mice,* like *men,* is plural.

9. Beware of words whose forms are in transition, like *data.* The original forms, from Latin, were singular *datum* and plural *data.* In modern usage, *datum* is disappearing and *data* is coming into use as both the singular and plural form:

All the data are in.

All the data is in (commonly seen in modern usage).

Ambiguous   This means there is more than one possible meaning and confusion might result. Usually you can clear up the temporary confusion by (1) correcting a faulty pronoun reference (see **Ref**) or (2) rewording to straighten out a modifier so that it modifies only what you intend (see **Mod**).

He took over the management of the business from his father when he was 55. (When his father reached 55, Carl took over management of the business.)

We agreed when we signed the papers that you would pay $100. (When we signed the papers, we agreed that you would pay $100 *or* We agreed that you would pay $100 when we signed the papers.)

And   *And* is a strong coordinating conjunction—one of the most useful and most troublesome words.

The symbol ∅ alerts you to a **bad** example.

1. It should connect (in the sense of addition) only things of similar quality and grammatical form. Used otherwise, it produces faulty coordination between an independent and a dependent clause, misparallelism, or sentence disunity. See **Subord, Para,** and **Unity.**

   ∅   The plans call for a new four-story building, and which will cost $4.5 million. (Omit *and;* it can't connect an independent clause to a dependent one.) See **Coh.**

   ∅   In this course you learn the ways of the business world, the principles of practical psychology, and to write better. (The infinitive *to write* is not parallel with the nouns *ways* and *principles.* Make them all the same form before connecting them by *and.*) See **Para.**

   ∅   We feel sure that the saw will serve you well, and we appreciate your order. (The two ideas are not closely enough related to appear in the same sentence—probably not even in the same paragraph.) See **Unity.**

2. *And* is properly the most often used connective, but don't overuse it to connect a series of independent clauses into a long, stringy sentence. If the clauses deserve equal emphasis, you can make separate sentences. If not, subordinate the weaker ones. See **Subord.**

   ∅   The consultant first talked with the executives about their letter-writing problems *and* then took a sample of 1,000 carbon copies *and* classified them into two groups *and* 45 percent of them were for situations that could just as well have been handled by forms. (After talking with the executives about their letter-writing problems, the consultant classified a sample of 1,000 carbon copies from the files. Forty-five percent of them were for situations that could just as well. . . .)

3. *And* may properly begin a sentence, but only if you want to emphasize it.

4. *And* is not proper before *etc.;* the *et* in *et cetera* means *and.*

5. Except in formal writing, *and/or* is acceptable to mean either or both of two mentioned possibilities.

Appear   The appearance of a written message (as of a person) should be pleasant but unobtrusive and should suggest that the writer is competent, accurate, neat, and alert. Because of the many choices of typefaces, special characters, boxes, and lines available through word processing and desktop publishing software, creating a document that confuses rather than communicates is all too possible. Here are some tips from design experts:

- Don't overdo the *design* of a document. Readers are distracted by too many typefaces, lines, boxes, colors, and types of exhibits. Remember the ransom note newsletter in Chapter Two.
- Help the reader move through your document with headings, transitions, itemized lists, and graphics. Use layout to convey meaning and emphasis.
- Turn off right justification for better readability of a document.
- In a single-column document (such as a letter, memo, or report), use short paragraphs, frequent headings, and adequate margins to make the document easier to read.
- For documents other than letters, memos, and reports, choose a grid that contains columns of different widths. Off-centered column formats give white space in a *scholar's margin,* which can appear always on the left, always on the

Appendix B   569

right, or always on the outside of the page.[1] Use a consistent grid for similar pages.

- Consistently unequal margins (wide right, wide outer, wide left, wide top) make pages more interesting than one-inch-all-around margins.[2]
- Make column dividers narrower than margins.[3]
- Encourage reading by using wider top margins and ragged bottom margins (where all columns don't end at the same line).[4]
- For reading ease, limit the number of typefaces used in a document to two: a serif for text and a sans serif for headings. Since a typeface is a family of type that includes different sizes and styles such as bold and italics, this still gives you variety within a long document.

Apostrophes   An apostrophe (a punctuation *and* spelling problem) should appear in

1. Possessives (except *its* and the personal pronouns): before *s* in singulars *(man's)*; after the *s* in plurals if the *s* or *z* sound is there to make the word plural *(ladies'* but *women's)*.
2. Contractions: to mark the omission of a letter *(isn't, doesn't, it's*—meaning "it is," quite different from the possessive *its)*.
3. In decades *(in the '60s)* to show omission of *19* but not in temperatures *(in the 60s)*.
4. Plurals of symbols: figures (illegible *8's*), letters of the alphabet (one *o* and two *m's*), and words written about as words (too many *and's* and *but's*), though some authorities now restrict this use to avoiding confusion.

Awkward   An awkward expression calls attention to itself, and it may confuse the reader. Reconstruct your sentence or change word order for a more natural flow.

A so-called split infinitive (putting a modifier between *to* and a verb) is not incorrect as much as it is awkward. It calls attention to itself and often emphasizes the infinitive much more than the writer intends.

Capitalization   Capitalization is pretty well standardized (except that newspapers set their own practices and hence are not guides for other writing).

1. Capitalize the names of specific things, including the titles of people, but not general words. For instance, you capitalize the name of any specific college, university, or department, but you write:

   A university education may well cost $22,000, regardless of the department in which one studies.

   L. W. Wilson, president of the University of. . . . When President Wilson came. . . .

   You capitalize any specific course, room, lake, river, building, and so on, but not the general words. So you might write:

   I am taking Economics 215.

   I am majoring in engineering.

   Now I must go to a history class in the Liberal Arts Building, after stopping to see a professor in Room 115.

---

[1]Jeanne L. McLaren and Judy Stopke, *Do's and Don'ts of Desktop Publishing Design,* 2nd ed. (Ann Arbor, Mich.: Promotional Perspectives, 1992), pp. 5–6.

[2]McLaren & Stopke, p. 7.

[3]McLaren & Stopke, p. 10.

[4]McLaren & Stopke, p. 11.

Next summer I may fish mostly in Portage Lake and some in the Ausable River, although I prefer river to lake fishing.

Of course, you capitalize languages—*English, French, German*—because they derive from the names of countries.

2. In titles of books and articles, capitalize the first word and (although library materials don't) all others except articles *(a, an, the)*, prepositions *(of, to, in, on, for)*, and conjunctions *(and, but, or, nor, although)*.

3. Capitalize the seasons (spring, summer) only when you personify them (rare except in poetry).

4. Capitalize sections of the country (the South, the East Coast) but not directions (east, west).

5. Capitalize people's titles *(Mr., Mrs., Ms., Miss, Dr., Colonel, Professor, Judge, Governor, President)* and terms of family relations *(Uncle Jim)* when used before names, but only to show a high degree of respect when used in place of or after names.

6. Capitalize the first word after a colon only if it starts a complete sentence. (In an itemized listing, you may capitalize the first words of items even though they are incomplete sentences.)

Case   One form serves for all cases of nouns except the possessive, and the only problem there is remembering correct use of the apostrophe. For personal pronouns,

1. Use the nominative case *(I, we, he, she, they, who)* for the subject of a verb (other than an infinitive) and for the complement of a linking verb (any form of *to be* except the infinitive with a subject).

2. Use the objective case *(me, us, him, her, them, whom)* as the object of a verb or a preposition and as the subject or object of an infinitive (except *to be* without a subject). In informal speaking and writing, however, *who* is acceptable as the object of a preposition (especially if it is in the usual subject position) unless it immediately follows the preposition:

   Who was the letter addressed to?

3. Use the possessive case to show possession and to serve as the subject of a gerund (a verb form ending in *ing* and used as a noun):

   His accusing me of dishonesty. . . .

   My thinking that a. . . .

4. Watch case particularly after *than* and *as* and in compounds with a name and a personal pronoun:

   He is better informed on the subject than I (*am informed* implied).

   I am a more cautious man than he (*is* understood).

   Virginia and she went . . . (subject).

   I am to pick up Virginia and her . . . (object of verb).

   He told the story to Virginia and her (object of preposition).

   Remember that *myself* is not used in place of *me*.

Choppy   Jerky, short sentences are slow and awkward. Usually the trouble is (1) incoherence (the sentences don't follow each other naturally—see **Coh**); (2) poor control of emphasis (all the ideas in independent clauses, although of different importance—see **Subord**); or (3) lack of variety (all the sentences of the same pattern, usually all beginning with the subject or nearly the same length—

see **Var**). Try combining several of the sentences, subordinating the less important ideas and stressing the important ones in the independent clauses.

Clarity Immediate clarity is a fundamental of good writing. Make sure your reader can get your meaning quickly and easily.

Coherence *Coherence* means clearly showing your reader *the relationships among ideas.* It is usually achieved from a logical sequence (proper organization), with major emphasis on the important ideas, less on the related but less important ideas, and any necessary conjunctions to indicate what relationships exist. Incoherence comes from mixing unrelated ideas together in the same sentence or paragraph, but particularly from (1) using a causative word when the named cause is not the whole cause of the named effect and (2) linking unrelated ideas or ideas of different importance by *and.*

1. Plan ahead—get your ideas in logical sequence *before* you write. You can group seemingly unrelated ideas with a topic sentence such as "Three factors deserve special consideration."

2. Give your ideas proper emphasis (see **Emph** and **Subord**). Important ideas should be in independent clauses or separate sentences. Two closely related and equally important ideas can be together in a compound sentence. Put a less important idea in a dependent clause attached to an independent clause, making a complex sentence.

3. Carefully choose transitional words or phrases if you need them to smooth the natural sequence of ideas (see **Trans**). Consider the following as examples:

    And . . . moreover, besides, in addition, also, furthermore.

    But . . . however, nevertheless, yet, still, although, while.

    Either-or . . . neither-nor, else, whether.

    Therefore . . . consequently, hence, as a result, accordingly, so, thus. (Check for *true* cause-effect relation.)

    Because . . . since, as, for, the reason is.

    Then . . . after that, afterward, later, subsequently.

    Meanwhile . . . during, simultaneously, concurrently, while.

    Before . . . preceding, previously, prior to.

    If . . . provided, assuming, in case, unless.

4. In papers longer than a page or two—and even more so in oral presentations —you probably will need even more than the three preceding means of showing the relationships of ideas and thus keeping the reader on the track. (See Topic and Summary Sentences and Headings and Subheads in the Index.)

Compr Comparisons require special attention to these points:

1. Things compared must be comparable. Usually the trouble is omission of necessary phrases like *that of, that on, other,* or *else.*

    The markup on Schick razors is higher than *that on* Gillettes. (If you omit *that on* you'll be comparing the markup on Schicks—a percentage—with the height of a Gillette—measured in inches.)

    Frank Mosteller sells more Fuller brushes than any *other* salesperson. (Without *other,* the statement is illogical if Frank is a salesperson; he can't sell more than he himself sells.)

2. Incomplete comparisons mean nothing; complete them.

    You get more miles per dollar with XXX. (More than with what?)

    This material has a higher percentage of wool. (Higher than what?)

3. Be sure to use the correct form of comparison words. Comparisons involving two things usually call for adding *-er* (the comparative) to the simple form *(cold, slow* become *colder, slower).* Those involving more than two usually require the *-est* (or superlative) form *(coldest, slowest, fastest).*

   For words of three syllables or more —and for many with two and some with only one—the preferred form is *more* plus the simple form (for the comparative) or *most* plus the simple form (for the superlative): *more frequently, most hopeful.* Some words can go either way: *oftener* or *more often; oftenest* or *most often.*

4. Watch these idioms: Complete the *as much as* phrase and use *to* after *compare* when pointing out similarities only, *with* when pointing out any differences:

   Price increases may be worth *as much as,* if not more than, the dividends on a common stock purchase.

   Comparison of X *to* Y shows that they involve the same principles.

   Comparison of sales letters *with* application letters shows that they have minor differences.

5. Some words (*unique, empty, final,* for example) are logical absolutes and hence cannot take comparative or superlative forms.

Conciseness   Conciseness, which is not necessarily brevity, depends on leaving out the irrelevant, leaving unsaid what you can adequately imply, and cutting out deadwood.

Connotations   Connotations, the overtones or related meanings of words, are often as important as the denotations, or dictionary meanings. Be sure the words you use are appropriate in connotation as well as in denotation. Consider the connotations in the following: *cheap, inexpensive, economical; secondhand, used, previously owned; complaint department, customer service department; bargain basement, thrift store, budget floor.*

Copy   Copying from the assignment, the case's wording, or from other people produces writing that doesn't sound like you. Put your ideas in your own words.

CS   *Comma splice*   This a serious error. Except when they are in series or are short and parallel, two or more independent clauses require separation by a period, a comma and a coordinating conjunction, or a semicolon (which may or may not require a following transition like *that is* or one of the conjunctive adverbs).

Diction   This means use a more suitable word. The big test, of course, is whether the word, including its connotations, conveys your thought accurately. Consider whether your words are easy for your reader to understand; whether they give a sharp, vivid picture by being natural and fresh instead of pompous, jargonistic, or trite; whether they give a specific, concrete meaning instead of a fuzzy or dull concept because they are general or abstract; and whether they are appropriately informal, formal, standard, technical, or nontechnical according to the topic and the reader.

   Watch especially the following often confused pairs: *accept, except; adapt, adopt; affect, effect; all ready, already; all together, altogether; allude, elude; almost, most; among, between; amount, number; appraise, apprise; beside, besides; capital, capitol; complement, compliment; compose, comprise; copy, replica; disinterested, uninterested; farther, further; fewer, less; flaunt, flout; formally, formerly; imply, infer; in regard to, with regards to; it's, its; loose, lose; marital, martial; may be, maybe; moral, morale; oral, verbal; parameter, perimeter; personal, personnel; pinch hitter, substitute; pore over, pour over; principal, principle; reign, rein;*

respectfully, respectively; stationary, stationery; some time, sometime; your, you're; and *to, too, two.*

Date   Date all messages in the standard form *(November 2, 1994)* unless you have good reason to do otherwise. Your most likely good reasons could be: (1) You are in the armed services, where the form *2 November 1994* is standard; or (2) you are writing a formal notice, where you use words with no figures; or (3) you are writing an informal note and may well use the form *11/2/94;* or (4) you are writing to someone in a country where practice differs *(2 November 1994)*. Modern business writing usually does not abbreviate months and does not use the ordinal forms.

Deadwood   Deadwood phrases add nothing to the meaning but merely take up writing and reading time.

Develop   You need to develop your point more thoroughly with more explanation, definition, specific details, classifications, comparisons, or examples to make it clearer, more interesting, more convincing, or more emphatic. See **Spec.**

Directness   By being direct, you save words, speed up reading, and make your ideas clearer. Don't waste words by beginning too far back in the background of the subject or stating what the reader already knows. Write direct, active-voice sentences beginning with the important word as the subject. The expletives *"It is . . ."* and *"There are . . . "* are indirect and unemphatic (see **Expl**).

Dng *Dangling modifier*   See **Mod** 1.

Documentation   When you use the ideas of others, telling your sources is necessary to avoid plagiarism and show your reader that what you say has the backing of cited authorities.

Emphasis   Dividing emphasis among your ideas according to their relative importance is basic to good communication.

1. When you state important ideas, give them deserved emphasis through length of discussion; placement at beginnings and endings of documents, paragraphs, and sentences; use of headings and itemized lists; and use of underlining, bold type, larger type, or a different font where appropriate. Writing something in all capital letters makes it emphatic but more difficult to read than capitals and lowercase letters, so save this method for headings or other limited uses.

2. When you have negative, unimportant, already known, or other ideas that do not warrant emphasis, avoid overemphasizing them:

$\emptyset$ Spring is just around the corner. You'll be needing. . . . (With spring just around the corner, you'll. . . .)

$\emptyset$ On October 3 you asked me to write a report on. . . . I have finished it and am. . . . (Here is the report requested in your letter of October 3. . . .)

$\emptyset$ I have your letter of April 20 in which you ask for quotations on X. I am glad to give you our prices. Our present prices on X are. . . . (Just omit the first two sentences. They're implied in the third.)

3. Transitional words like *and* and *but* usually do not deserve the emphasis they would get at the beginning of a sentence.

Etc.   This abbreviation of the Latin *et cetera,* meaning "and so forth," is appropriate only when the reader can easily fill out the incomplete list (as in "Please take even-numbered seats 2, 4, 6, etc."). Otherwise it can mean only "Reader, you guess what else I mean to include." Because *etc.* is an abbreviation, it takes a period. In no case should you write "and etc." *(et* means *and)* or "etc. . . ." (the middle three dots mean the same as *etc.* here).

Exaggeration   Exaggeration creates distrust, especially in intercultural communication.

Expletive   Expletives *(it is, there are)* slow the reader up in getting to significant information and, overused, make your writing unnecessarily wordy, weak, and passive. However, sometimes expletives help soften a command, avoid presumptuousness in a recommendation, or ease reader acceptance of bad news:

⊘   It was thought that you would prefer. . . . (I thought you would. . . .)

⊘   There are four important factors involved. These are: . . . . (The four important factors are. . . .)

⊘   It will be necessary to have your. . . . ("You must send . . . " might be too commanding.)

Figure   Use figures if the quantity is above nine, but observe these exceptions and guidelines.

1. If a quantity comes as the first word of a sentence, write it in words or recast the sentence.

2. When a sentence involves two different series of quantities, use figures for one and words for the other to avoid confusion; if more than two, use a table.

   On the qualifying exam, ten percent of the applicants scored 90–100; thirty percent, 80–89; . . . .

   Please make six 2″ × 3″ and three 5″ × 7″ black-and-white prints.

3. The old longhand practice of stating quantities twice—in figures followed parenthetically by words—is unnecessary and undesirable in type or print, although it still sometimes appears in legal documents, and always in checks, for double certainty and security.

4. Except in dates, street numbers, and serial numbers, use a comma between groups of three digits, counting from the right.

5. Except in tables involving some cents, periods and zeros after money quantities are wasted typing and reading.

6. Cardinal numbers (*1, 2, 3, 4,* etc.) are preferable to ordinals *(1st, 2d, 3d, 4th)* in dates except when the day is separate from the month.

7. Since ordinals are either adjectives or adverbs, an *-ly* ending is never necessary or desirable (not *secondly* or *thirdly*).

Flattery   Flattery, especially if obvious, is more likely to hurt than to help.

Fragment   Fragments (phrases or subordinate clauses posing as sentences) are serious errors (because they show ignorance of sentence structure) except when perfectly clear and intentional. Attach them to the independent clauses to which they belong, or change their wording to make them the complete, independent sentences they pretend to be.

⊘   The latter being the better way. (This is a phrase fragment that should be attached by a comma to the preceding sentence. Or you could simply change *being* to *is*).

⊘   One job in revising any paper is checking for and correcting any fragments. Which is easy to do. (The second "sentence" is a dependent clause and hence a fragment unless attached—by a comma—to the preceding.)

Gobbledygook   Avoid big-wordy, roundabout, long-winded, or stuffed-shirt language.

Graphic   Graphic devices of various kinds can often supplement words to make the information clearer, easier, or more interesting. Use them where they will help, but only if they will.

Gw *Goodwill*   The symbol indicates that goodwill, a basic requirement of a business letter, is lacking or poorly handled.

Headings   Heads and subheads can improve coherence and transitions.

Idiom   Idiom violated. Follow the natural, customary (idiomatic) way of expressing your idea. An error in idiom can be use of the wrong preposition, omission of verb endings, or misuse of articles. Consider *possibility of, possible to, necessity of, need for,* and *ability to.*

Itemize   Itemize complex series and lists (like this) and make them parallel to (1) emphasize the points, (2) avoid complex punctuation, (3) force yourself to state your points more precisely and concisely, and (4) grab your reader's attention. This point is particularly important in oral communication.

Jargon   Jargon is the specialized technical language of an occupational group. It is inappropriately used if the reader is not a member of that occupational group.

KM   *Keyboarding Mechanics*   If you are an untrained typist or keyboarder, these tips may help:

1. Use standard within-line spacings.
   a. Use five spaces *(Tab)* for paragraph indentation. Or use the *first-line indent* command on a word processor, which will indent the first line of each paragraph if you signal a paragraph by hitting *Return.* (Other lines in the paragraph will be wordwrapped without hitting *Return.*)
   b. Use one space after a colon or end-of-sentence punctuation (including an enclosing end parenthesis) if using any proportional-spaced type.
   c. Use two spaces after a colon or end-of-sentence punctuation (including an enclosing end parenthesis) if using Courier or other monospaced type.
   d. Use one space after all other punctuation except as explained below.
   e. Don't put any space after an opening parenthesis or before or after a hyphen or dash.
2. Abbreviations pose a spacing problem. Some, like *HEW, IRS, SEC, UN, AFL-CIO,* are solid. Others have internal periods but no spaces, such as *B.A., J.D., M.B.A., Ph.D., U.K., R.N.* Initials used in a person's name have a period *and* a space, as in *T. S. Eliot.* Since a set rule does not exist for which abbreviations are solid and which have periods but no spaces, learn the ones you use most often and look the others up in a dictionary or style manual.
3. Do not put a space on either side of a hyphen when joining words, as in compound adjectives such as *follow-up activities.* A suspension hyphen joining the first of a series of compound adjectives made with one element in common has a space after it, as in *two- and four-year colleges.*
4. An en dash (a printing mark that is the width of the letter *n*) is used between words indicating duration, such as *Monday–Friday.* A thin space or no space can be inserted on each side of the en dash. According to Robin Williams, author of *A PC Is Not a Typewriter,*[5] "Also use the en dash when you have a compound adjective and one of the elements is made of two words or a hyphenated word, such as: San Francisco–Chicago flight, pre–Vietnam War period, and twenty-three–purple-toed Venutians." This is a fine distinction that will not come up much in business.
5. An em dash (which is the width of the letter *m*) is used in place of the old typing dash made up of two hyphens. Desktop publishing experts vary on spacing. Robin Williams says that the old typing rule holds: Use no space on either side of an em dash.[6] Others use a small space on each side. When

---

[5]Robin Williams, *"A PC Is Not a Typewriter"* (Berkeley Cal.: Peachpit Press, 1992), pp. 19–20.

[6]Williams, p. 20.

using two hyphens for a dash, if you do not put a space on each side, the computer may separate the hyphens when wordwrapping. You can easily correct this by proofreading for line divisions and hyphen use.

6. For quotations of more than four lines, space above and below, indent from each side, single-space, and use no quotation marks.

7. Check your word processing software manual for features such as *right-aligned tab,* used to align numbers in a list by tens; *centered tab,* to automatically center lines on a page; and *decimal tab,* to align decimal points or periods.

8. Create quotation marks, apostrophes, and special characters such as superscripts, subscripts, and bullets on your word processor by using special key combinations or codes. For example, a WordPerfect solid square for your résumé is *Control V 4,2.* See your manual or *A PC Is Not a Typewriter* for details. The usual typed quotation and apostrophe marks are the characters for inches and feet. Thus, one sign of professional word processing is using real quotation marks and apostrophes.

9. Set your word processor to avoid widows and orphans. A *widow* is fewer than seven characters on the last line of a page; an *orphan* is the top line of a page that is the end of the previous page's last paragraph. Both look like a small "lost" bunch of type.

10. Generally, choose a type size of 9 to 14 points for text and 15 or larger for headings. Overhead transparencies usually require still larger type sizes for good readability.

lc *Lowercase* Indicates that the student should use lowercase instead of a capital letter. See **Cap.**

Logic Avoid statements that will not stand the test of logic or for which the logic is not readily clear. Perhaps you need to supply a missing step in the logic. Maybe you need to state your idea more precisely. Or maybe you need to complete a comparison to make it logical.

Modifier Make sure that each modifier relates clearly to the thing it is supposed to modify. As a general rule, the two should be as close together as natural sentence construction will allow.

1. Participles (usually phrases including a verb form ending in *-ing* or *-ed* and usually at the beginning of a sentence) require careful attention lest you relate them to the wrong word (or nothing at all) and produce "dangling modifiers" **(Dng).**

∅ Smelling of liquor, I arrested the driver.

∅ After soaking in sulfuric acid overnight, I set the specimen up to dry.

Infinitives can dangle the same way:

∅ To enjoy the longest, most dependable service, the motor must be tuned up about every 500 hours of operation. (The motor cannot enjoy dependable service.)

∅ In order to assist you in collecting for damages, it will be necessary to fill out a company blank. (The two infinitives dangle because they do not relate to any proper doers of the actions indicated.)

But absolute phrases (a noun plus a participle) and participles, gerunds, and infinitives that name an accepted truth rather than the action of any particular person or thing do not need to relate to any subject:

The sun having set, the fish began to bite.

All things considered, Steve is the better man.

2. Misplaced modifiers, like danglers, can also make you look silly.

⊘   The girl riding the horse in the blue sweater is my sister.

⊘   There is a meeting at 3 this afternoon about morality in the president's office.

Watch especially where you put such limiting qualifiers as *only, almost,* and *nearly.* Consider the varied meanings from placing *only* at different spots in "I can approve payment of a $30 adjustment" or in "He mourned for his brother."

Natural   Natural writing avoids triteness, awkwardness, and pomposity. Clichés, hackneyed expressions, and inappropriately used jargon suggest that you are not thinking about your subject and your reader; awkwardness suggests carelessness; and big words and pomposity suggest that you are trying to make an impression. Think through what you want to say and put it simply, smoothly, and naturally. Although you cannot write exactly as you talk, try to write with the same freedom, ease, simplicity, and smoothness.

Negative   In letter and memo writing, *negative* means anything unpleasant to your reader. Avoid the negative when you can and subordinate it when you can't avoid it. Insofar as possible, stress the positive by telling what you have done, can do, will do, or want done instead of their negative opposites.

Objectivity   Use of emotional words suggests a prejudiced rather than an objective view and therefore causes the reader to lose faith in the writer—especially a report writer.

Obvious   Obvious statements—when unnecessary as bases for other statements—waste words and may insult the reader's intelligence. When you need to establish an obvious fact as the basis for something else, put it in a dependent clause or imply it. (See **Emp** and **Subord.**)

   New York is America's biggest city. Therefore, . . . (Since New York is America's biggest city, ...)

Paragraph (¶)   Paragraphs in letters and reports are the same as in other writing—unified and coherent developments of topics—except that they tend to be more compressed and shorter for easier readability. Six to eight typed lines are a good business paragraph length.

1. Keep paragraphs reasonably short. Long ones are discouragingly hard to read. Especially the first and last paragraphs of letters and memos should be short (rarely more than three or four lines). Elsewhere, if a paragraph runs to more than about eight lines, you should consider breaking it up for easier readability. Remember that a paragraph can be merely one sentence if you want to emphasize an idea.

2. Still, develop your paragraphs adequately to clarify and support your points—by explanation, detail, facts and figures, or illustrations and examples.

3. Make each paragraph unified and coherent by taking out elements irrelevant to the topic, organizing carefully, and showing the interrelationship among the ideas. Consider beginning with a topic sentence and/or ending with a summary.

4. Show the relation of the paragraph to the preceding one (by following logical sequence, carrying over key ideas, and/or using transitional words) and to the purpose of the whole paper or section (by pointing out the significance and/or using transitional words or sentences).

Paragraph unity also includes. . . . (*Also* means that some of the explanation has preceded.)

Carrying over key words and using transitional words are both means of providing unity between paragraphs as well as within them. (As *well as* means we have discussed unity *in* paragraphs and now will discuss it *between* them.)

5. **Para** with **No** before it means "No new paragraph needed here because you are still on the same topic and within reasonable paragraph length."

Parallelism   Parallelism means using the same kind of grammatical structure for ideas that you use coordinately, as in pairs, series (including lists), comparisons, and outlines. These structures state or imply relationships usually indicated by *and, but,* or *or* and hence should relate only full sentences to full sentences, nouns to nouns, verbs to verbs, active voice to active voice, plural to plural—indeed *any* grammatical form only to the same grammatical form in the related part. Watch for parallelism with *not only . . . but also, as well as, larger, less expensive,* and the like.

Ø   One of the duties of the flight attendant is to offer customers magazines, pillows, and hang their coats (two plural nouns and a verb improperly connected by the coordinating conjunction *and*).

Ø   The No-Skid knee guard is long wearing, washable, and stays in position (two adjectives improperly connected by *and* to a verb).

Ø   John Coleman is 39, married, and a native (two adjectives and a noun).

Ø   If we fair each side of the arc, we produce a more practical airfoil section and an increase in performance is attained. (Active voice related to passive. Rewrite the last part as "increase performance.")

Ø   The next step is baking or catalyzation. (Use "baking or catalyzing.")

Ø   Swimming is better exercise than to walk (a gerund compared with an infinitive).

Parallelism in pairs, series, and comparisons is largely a question of logic; you can add together and compare only like things. See **Logic.**

Passive   Passive voice, in which the subject of the sentence is the receiver of the verb's action, is often wordy, awkward, and weak. Use it when subordinating *who* took the action, as when you wish to avoid blaming someone directly. Also use passive voice to convey negative information, to avoid blaming, and to soften commands.

Active voice, in which the subject of the sentence is the doer of the verb's action, is livelier, more vivid, and easier for the reader to picture mentally. Writing that uses much passive voice, such as government writing, is dull and heavy because nobody exactly ever *does* anything; things just are *done.*

People prefer to read about people doing things: "The Snow Valley branch reports increased walk-in business for July." If it is not possible to write about people doing things, let the reader see *things doing other things:* "The low default rate frees up more funds to lend at lower risk."

Pompous   Try to express the thought simply, not to impress the reader.

Preposition   Prepositions indicate relationships within a sentence.

1. Be sure to use the right prepositions for your construction. Some words require certain prepositions; others vary prepositions for different meanings. Ability *to;* agree *to, with,* or *in;* compare *to* (for similarities only) or *with* (for likenesses and differences); different *from* (not different *than*).

2. When you use two words that require different prepositions, use both: Because of your interest *in* and aptitude *for . . . .*

Pt. of V   *Point of View*   Insofar as possible, keep the same point of view in a sentence, a paragraph, or a whole letter. Make only logically necessary shifts, and alert your reader by providing the necessary transitional words. Watch carefully for shifts in time, location, and those whose eyes you seem to be looking through.

* * * * *

Punctuation   Punctuation that follows the conventions of written English is a *helpful device for both reader and writer in communicating clearly, quickly, and easily.* Here are the conventions most commonly violated.

- **Brackets**   Brackets [ ] are useful for two purposes:

  1. To make a comment inside a quotation.
  2. To enclose a parenthetical expression that has parentheses or a pair of dashes inside it.

- **Colon**   The colon is either an anticipating or a separating mark. As an anticipator, it appears after introductory lead-ins to explanations or quotations, especially if the lead-in includes such formalizing terms as the word *following* or if the explanation is lengthy or itemized.

  > The X Company's ink was even redder: its third-quarter loss of. . . .

  > Three main benefits deserve your attention: . . . . (Enumeration follows. Notice that you do not need a word-wasting expression like "these benefits are" before or after the colon!)

  > On the use of the colon, Perrin says: . . . . (Long quotation follows.)

  Because the colon is also a separating mark, however—used to separate hours from minutes and volume numbers from pages, for example—it should not serve as an anticipating mark when the lead-in phrasing fits well as an integral part of a short, informal statement.

  > The three main advantages are (colon would be obtrusive here) speed, economy, and convenience.

  > Perrin reports that (no colon; not even a comma) "*Will* has practically replaced *shall* in . . . "

  Almost invariably words like *namely, that is, for example,* and *as follows* are wasted when used with a colon. The introductory phrasing and the colon adequately anticipate without these words.

  > We have several reasons for changing: namely the . . . (Omit *namely.*)

  > We had several reasons for changing. These reasons are: . . . (This is worse. Omit *These reasons are;* put the colon after *changing.*)

  Although practice varies, usually you should capitalize the first word after a colon only if it begins a complete sentence. But if itemizations follow, you may capitalize even though each item depends on the introductory statement for completeness.

  The same idea applies to the end punctuation of items following a colon. If the items make complete sentences, put a period after each. But if all are to be considered one sentence, use a comma or a semicolon at the end of each (except the last, of course) as in other series. Or you may use no end punctuation if the items listed are fairly brief.

- **Comma 1**   Use a comma between two independent clauses connected by *and, but, or,* or *nor* if no other commas are in the sentence. But be sure you are connecting two clauses rather than a compound subject, verb, or object.

  > You may buy the regular Whiz mixer at $78.75, but I think you would find the Super Whiz much more satisfactory (two clauses).

  > We make two grades of Whiz mixers and sell both at prices lower than those of our competitors' products (compound verb; one subject).

Be sure too that you don't use obtrusive commas before the first or after the last item in a series or between a subject and its verb, a verb and its object, or a noun and its adjective. Also, you do not usually need a comma after *and, but, or, nor.*

- **Comma 2**   Use a comma after first-of-sentence dependent clauses longer than five or six words, long phrases, or other phrases containing any form of a verb. But when these forms or appositives or transitional words appear elsewhere in a sentence, use commas only with nonrestrictive (nonessential) ones. Nonrestrictive statements add descriptive detail about an already identified word and are not necessary to the logic or grammatical completeness of the sentence. Restrictive statements define, limit, or identify and are necessary to convey the intended meaning or complete the sentence. If, on reading aloud, you naturally pause and inflect your voice, the statement is nonrestrictive and requires the comma(s).

> Because the dependent clause comes at the beginning, we have to use a comma in this sentence.

> We do not need a comma in a complex sentence if the dependent part comes at the end or in the middle and restricts the meaning the way this one does.

> Having illustrated the two points about dependent clauses at the beginning and restrictive clauses elsewhere in the sentence, we now use this sentence to illustrate the use of a comma after a long phrase at the first of a sentence. (Because it includes a verb form, it would require a comma even if it were short, like "Having illustrated the point, we now leave the topic.")

> The three points already illustrated, which are certainly important, are no more important than the point about using commas to set off nonrestrictive clauses anywhere, which this sentence illustrates. (In fact, it illustrates twice: you could omit both the *which* clauses; they are nonrestrictive because they merely give added information unnecessary to either the meaning or the grammar of the basic sentence.)

Sometimes you need a comma to prevent misreading—especially after a gerund, participle, or infinitive:

> In the office, files were scattered all over the floor.

> By shooting, the man attracted the attention of the rescue party.

> Thinking that, he was unwilling to listen to reason.

> Seeing the foreman's unwillingness to help, the men gave up.

- **Comma 3**   Use *pairs* of commas, parentheses, or dashes as needed to mark off parenthetical expressions within sentences. The "as needed" in the preceding sentence is a reminder that some parentheticals need no surrounding punctuation. Like dependent clauses, some appositives are restrictive or so closely related that they require no punctuation, while others are nonrestrictive or so loosely related that they do.

> Our starting point that good punctuation is a matter of following the conventions has not had enough attention.

> Our second point—the importance of writing letters so smoothly and naturally that they require little internal punctuation—would preclude most punctuation problems.

1. Commas are normal for short, unemphatic, and otherwise unpunctuated direct addresses like "Yes, Mr. Thomas, you may . . . ," tucked-in transitions like *however* and *on the other hand,* and brief appositives.
2. As the length increases in a side comment or an appositive (a restatement like this one, following immediately to explain a term), the call for stronger marks like parentheses becomes more likely. Commas within a parenthetical (as in the preceding sentence) or a desire to deemphasize it also make parentheses necessary around it.

3. If you want to emphasize a parenthetical expression—or if it contains complicated punctuation or is long—a pair of dashes such as we are using here will be your best punctuation to fence it in.

- **Comma 4**   Use commas to separate coordinate adjectives. As two tests for coordinacy, see if you can put *and* between the adjectives or invert their order without producing awkwardness. If so, they are coordinate and require a comma.

    Proper punctuation can help greatly in writing a clear, easy-to-read style.

    Fairly heavy white paper is best for letterheads.

- **Comma 5**   A comma is the usual punctuation *between* (but not before or after) items in a series (preferably including one before the *and* with the last item, because it is sometimes necessary for clearness and is always correct). But if any item except the last has a comma *within* it, use semicolons at all points *between* items. (Suggestion: If only one of a series requires an internal comma, consider putting it last and using commas between the items.)

    Make your writing clear, quick, and easy to read.

    Use commas between independent clauses connected by *and, but, or,* or *nor;* semicolons between independent clauses with other connectives or no connecting words; commas for dependent clauses and verbal or long phrases at the beginnings of sentences, for nonrestrictive ones elsewhere, and for simple series; and semicolons for complex series like the one in this sentence.

- **Dash**   Dashes are also acceptable (in pairs) around parenthetical expressions that interrupt the main part of the sentence.

    If the parenthetical part contains internal parentheses, dashes must surround it; if it contains commas, then dashes *or* parentheses must surround it. (Of course, only a pair of parentheses can surround a sentence giving explanations, relatively unimportant additional detail, or side information, as this sentence does. In that case, the period goes inside the closing parentheses, although it goes outside otherwise.)

    Except as explained in the preceding paragraph, the choice depends on the desired emphasis and on the other punctuation.

    1. Two dashes (called "bridge dashes") emphasize most:

        Your main weaknesses in writing—misspelling, faulty punctuation, and incoherence—deserve attention before you write letters.

    2. A single dash—made by two hyphens without spacing before, between, or after—may mark an abrupt change in the trend of a sentence or precede an added statement summarizing, contrasting, or explaining the first part. In this second function, it is the "pickup dash."

        Errors in spelling, punctuation, or coherence—all of these mar an otherwise good letter.

        A letter writer must avoid the common errors in writing—misspelling, bad punctuation, and incoherence. (Of course, a colon could replace the dash here; but ordinarily it should not unless the preceding statement is a formal introduction, usually indicated by the word *following,* or unless it is an introduction to an itemized list.)

    3. The em dash used in word processing may use spaces before and after to make computerized spacing easier.

- **Ellipses**   Ellipses (three *spaced* periods) mean that you have left out something. You *must* use this mark when giving an incomplete quotation. Note that if an omission comes at the end of a sentence, you need to add the appropriate end-of-sentence punctuation—a fourth dot for the period, a question mark, or an exclamation point. Ellipses are also coming into wide use, especially in business, as an additional way to mark parenthetical expressions, but this practice has not yet achieved total acceptance.

"We the people of the United States . . . do ordain and establish this Constitution . . ."

- **Ends of Sentences**

    1. Use a period at the end of a sentence unless it is a question, is questionable, or is an exclamation. Less than full-sentence expressions used as outline items may end with periods or remain open-ended.

    2. Use a question mark at the end of a question and (in parentheses) after a spelling or statement about which you can't be sure.

        Though I've heard of Mrs. Muennink's (?) varied interests and accomplishments, I've never met the lady. (The question mark means only that I'm not sure of the spelling.)

        When Colby first moved to Miami in January 1981 (?), I thought . . .

    3. Use exclamation marks *(sparingly)* after sentences or (in parentheses) after lesser expressions that you want to give dramatic emphasis.

        He said he wanted (!) to be the first to. . . .

        The general's succinct reply was "Nuts!"

- **Hyphen**   Hyphenate two or more words (unless the first ends in *-ly*) used to make a compound adjective modifying a following noun.

    Fast-selling product, wrinkle-resistant material, long-wearing soles, never-to-be-forgotten experience, high-level executive.

Note that you do not hyphenate when the adjectives follow the noun.

    The material is highly wrinkle resistant and long wearing.

Certainly it does not apply when the adjectives modify the noun separately.

    These slacks are made of a hard, durable material.

The compound-adjective principle does apply, however, to double compounds made with one element in common, where the "suspension hyphen" follows the first: three- and five-pound cans.

The hyphen also marks the break in a word at the end of a line.

Other less frequent uses of the hyphen include (1) spelling of fractions as modifiers (*three-fourths* majority) and (2) prefixing words or syllables to names (*post-Bush* Washington).

- **Question Mark**   Besides its well-known use at the end of a question, the question mark (in parentheses) immediately following a statement or spelling indicates that the writer is uncertain and unable to determine. Obviously, it should not be an excuse for laziness; but if you have only heard a difficult name, for example, and have to write to that person, you will be better off using the mark than misspelling the name.

    A question mark should not appear after indirect questions and is unnecessary after commands softened by question form, but some writers feel that it further softens commands.

    We need to know what your decision is. (This is an indirect question.)

    Will you please ask the secretary in your office to change my mailing address. (This is a softened command, with or without the question mark.)

- **Quotation Marks**   Quotation marks are used primarily for short, exact quotations (not paraphrasings) of other people's words and for titles of *parts* of publications, such as magazine and newspaper stories or book chapters. (Italicize the titles of whole journals and books—underlined in typed copy.) If a quotation is more than four lines long, you should indent it from each side, single-space it, and omit quotation marks.

When closing quotation marks and other marks seem to come at the same place, the standard *American* practice is as follows: Place commas or periods *inside* the closing quotes; place semicolons or colons *outside;* and place question or exclamation marks inside or outside depending on whether they belong to the quotation or to the sentence that encompasses it. See **KM** for a comment on word processing these characters.

- **Semicolon** The semicolon is a pivotal mark; avoid using it between expressions unless they are of equal grammatical structure (usually two independent clauses or two items in a complex series). Use a semicolon between two independent clauses unless connected by *and, but, or,* or *nor;* and even then use a semicolon if the sentence already has a comma in it (as in this one). Typical weaker connectives requiring the semicolon between two independent clauses are *therefore, so, moreover, hence, still, accordingly, nevertheless, furthermore, consequently,* and *however.* When these words are simple connectors not between two independent clauses, however (as right here), set them off by a pair of commas unless they fit so smoothly into the sentence that they require no marks.

  > New developments in office machines have made maintenance workers relearn their jobs; the new manuals are twice as thick as those of only a few years ago (no connective).

  > The preceding sentence could be two, of course; but because the ideas are closely related, it is better as one. (Commas elsewhere in this sentence require a semicolon before even a strong conjunction.)

  > Good business writing requires proper punctuation; therefore, you must know how to use the semicolon (weak connective).

  > The proper style for letters is simpler and less involved than for most other writing, however, and therefore does not require very complex punctuation procedures. (*However,* is a simple transition, *not* used between two clauses here and *not* closely knit into the phrasing the way *therefore* is; so it needs commas, while *therefore* goes unmarked. Note, too, that the weak connective *so* requires the semicolon because it connects two clauses.)

- **Semicolon and Comma Confusion.** Look at the following example, which shows four equally acceptable ways of punctuating two independent clauses:

  1. I don't enjoy writing. I enjoy having written.
  2. I don't enjoy writing; I enjoy having written.
  3. I don't enjoy writing; nevertheless, I enjoy having written.
  4. I don't enjoy writing, but I enjoy having written.

  A semicolon is more of a pause than a comma and less than a period. To use it correctly, think of a semicolon as being formed from a comma and a period rather than being related to a colon.

  The differences in the sentences in the example are stylistic; choose the one that best fits your audience. The first sentence, with its two independent clauses, is emphatic because of its structure. The second joins the two ideas so the reader is forced to deal with them as related ideas but is left to figure out how they are related. The third joins the two ideas *and* gives a transition word that shows the relationship between them. The fourth joins the two ideas with a simpler transition.

- **Underline** Underlining in typed or handwritten copy specifies italic type when printed. Its main uses are to mark titles of books and journals, to emphasize, and to indicate unanglicized words. In copy not to be printed, underlining should go with any heading not written in solid capitals. Otherwise the heading, which is really a title for the copy over which it stands, does not stand out sufficiently. (A printer would make it stand out by using big or boldface type.)

Typed underlining is preferably continuous rather than broken by individual words, because it is easier both to type and to read that way.

* * * * *

RB *Reader Benefits* Bring your reader into the picture early—and don't forget later. The reader is the most important person involved with your message.

Psychological description (interpreting facts and physical features of a product in terms of *reader benefits*) is the real heart of selling. Unless your reader readily makes the interpretation, pure physical description is ineffective in selling. So when you name a physical feature of a product you are selling, show the reader what it means in terms of benefits.

> The Bostonian Sporty shoe has Neolite soles and triple-stitched welt construction. (Better: The Neolite soles and triple-stitched welt construction cause the Bostonian Sporty to last long and keep your feet dry.)

Reference The references of your pronouns must be immediately certain and clear to your reader—not ambiguous, too far away, or merely implied. Except for the few indefinite pronouns *(one, everybody, anybody,* and *it),* a pronoun confuses or distracts a reader unless it refers clearly to a preceding noun and agrees with it in number and gender. *Each, every, any,* and their combinations *anybody* and *everybody* are singulars requiring singular verbs and pronouns. (See **Agree** for further explanation of agreement.)

1. Often the trouble with a pronoun reference is that the antecedent is too far away. Ordinarily a pronoun tends to "grab onto" the closest preceding noun as its antecedent. So construct (or reconstruct) your sentences with that tendency in mind.

2. Guard particularly against *this, that, which, it,* and *they* making vague reference to ideas of whole preceding clauses instead of clear, one-word antecedents. Current usage allows a *clear* reference to a clause.

⊘ > Dayton adopted the plan in 1914 and has kept it ever since, which is a good example of the success of the council-manager form of government. (What does *which* refer to?)

⊘ > After reading a book about television engineering, the young man wanted to be one of them. (One of what? The antecedent is only implied.)

3. Don't use the same pronoun with different meanings in the same sentence:

⊘ > The directions say that it is up to the owner to change the filter whenever it needs it.

Repetition Repetition of words or ideas is wordy and monotonous unless it serves a justified purpose. Although restatement of important ideas deserving emphasis is often desirable, even then the restatement usually should be in somewhat different words to avoid monotony.

Resale Resale material—reassuring a customer that a choice of goods and/or firm was a good one—not only shows your service attitude but also helps keep incomplete orders and delayed shipments on the books, rebuilds reader confidence in adjustment situations, and serves as a basic idea in collections. Look it up in the index to this book and read about it in connection with the particular type of message involved.

Serv Att *Service Attitude* Service attitude—showing a genuine desire to give the kinds and quality of goods and services wanted, favorable prices, and various conveniences, plus unselfish reassurance of appreciation for business—can go a long way toward overcoming a reader's feeling that you are indifferent.

SC *Success Consciousness* In your writing, show success consciousness. Be self confident and positive. Avoid *if, hope, trust* (as in *"we trust* this is the information you needed").

Shift   Shifting of tense (time), voice (active-passive), mood (indicative, imperative, subjunctive), or person (first, second, third) should occur only when the logic of the situation dictates it. Otherwise it leads to incoherence and loses or confuses readers.

Simplify   Needlessly big words or complex sentences are hard to read.

Sincerity   Sincerity is essential if you are to be believed. Don't pretend or overstate your case.

Slow   Slow movement is desirable only in a disappointing message, where you must reason calmly with the reader to justify the unpleasant point you are preparing to present. Otherwise it is objectionable.

1. Don't use too many words before getting to an important point. Starting too far back in the background, giving too many details, or saying things that you should imply are the most frequent faults.
2. Don't use too many short, choppy sentences and thus slow up a message that should move quickly.

SOS   *Sentence Out of Service*   Errors in sentence organization and structure are sometimes serious enough to justify the distress signal.

1. Don't present a phrase or dependent clause as a sentence. Usually correction requires only attaching the dependent element to the preceding or following sentence (on which it depends). See **Frag.**

Ø   In answer to your request concerning what the company is like, what has been accomplished, and the future prospects. Here is the information I have been able to acquire. (Replace the period with a comma.)

2. Don't use a comma—or omit punctuation—between two independent clauses unless a strong conjunction *(and, but, or,* or *nor)* is there. The error is not basically one of punctuation but the more serious failure to recognize what a sentence is. You need a period if the two statements are not so closely related that they ought to be in the same sentence, or a semicolon if they are.

Ø   The credit business is big business some people estimate that it is as much as 86 percent of American business (period needed before *some*).

Ø   Running two sentences together without punctuation is about the worst error a writer can make, however it is little worse than using a comma where a semicolon is required, as in this sentence.

3. Don't put words together in unnatural, confusing relationships that the reader has to ponder to get the intended meaning.

Ø   Just because you want to sell I don't want right now to buy. (The fact that you want to sell doesn't mean that I want to buy.)

4. Don't put ideas together with connectives that falsely represent their relationship.

Spelling   Spelling errors rarely confuse or mislead, but they nearly always have the unfavorable effect of making the writer look careless. Here are the most important tips on spelling and a list of words frequently misspelled in business writing. If you have spelling problems, study both—carefully. Don't rely entirely on your computerized spell checker. While this software will catch the majority of your typos, repeated words, and spelling errors, you still need to check manually for substitutions such as *of* for *or* and *you* for *your* where the wrong word is still correctly spelled. You also need to check for homonyms such as *affect/effect* and *their/there/they're,* because each version is a word in its own right.

1. *Ie* or *ei:* When pronounced like *ee,* write *ie* except after *c,* as in *brief, believe, piece, wield; receive, deceive, perceive.* The exceptions are *either, neither, leisure, seize,* and *weird.* When pronounced otherwise, write *ei* (as in *freight, height, forfeit*) except in *die, lie, pie, tie, vie,* and *science.*

2. Double a final single consonant preceded by a single vowel *(a, e, i, o, u)* in an accented syllable when you add a suffix *(-ing, -ed, er)* beginning with a vowel *(plan, planning; shop, shopping).* Note that if the word already ends in two consonants, or one preceded by two vowels, you do not double the last consonant *(holding, helping; daubing, seeded).* Note too that you usually do not double the consonant unless in an accented syllable *(refer, referred, references).* Two new exceptions, *benefitted* and *travelled,* can now go either way.

3. Drop a final unpronounced *e* preceded by a consonant when you add a suffix beginning with a vowel *(hope, hoping; owe, owing);* but retain the *e* after *c* or *g* unless the suffix begins with one of the front vowels, *i* or *e (noticeable, changeable, changing, reduced).*

4. Change final *y* to *i* and add *es* for the plural if a consonant precedes the *y* *(ally, allies; tally, tallies);* otherwise, just add *s (valley, valleys).*

5. Add *'s* for the possessives of all singulars and of plurals that do not end in *s* *(man's, men's, lady's).* Add only an apostrophe for *s*-ending plurals *(ladies', Davises', students').*

6. Hyphenate double-word quantities between 20 and 100 *(twenty-one, thirty-two, forty-four, ninety-eight)* and fractions used as modifiers *(nine-tenths* depleted) but not fractions used as nouns (increased by *one fourth).*

7. Most words ending with the sound of *seed* are like *concede, precede,* and *recede;* but three require *ee (exceed, proceed,* and *succeed),* and one takes an *s* instead of a *c (supersede).*

8. Get somebody to pronounce for you while you try to spell the following frequently misspelled words. Then study those you miss (along with others that give you trouble from whatever source).

a lot	explanation	personal
accessible	gauge	personnel
accidentally	government	precede
accommodate	grammar	prejudiced
achievement	height	principal
acquaintance	hindrance	principle
acquire	incidentally	privilege
affect (to influence)	interest	procedure
among	it's (its)	quantity
argument	laboratory	questionnaire
attorneys	lose (loose)	receive
basically	maintenance	referring
believe	moral (morale)	renowned
calendar	mortgage	separate
conscientious	noticeable	stationary
consensus	occasionally	stationery
convenience	occurrence	surprise
definitely	offered	temperament
disastrous	omitted	than (then)
effect (result)	paid	their (there)
efficiency	parallel	too (to, two)
embarrass	passed (past)	undoubtedly
environment	perform	whether (weather)
equipped	permissible	writing (written)
existence		

Specific   Specific wording, like a sharp photograph, helps the reader get a clear idea. General words give only a hazy view.

1. If you are inclined to use the general word for a class of things, consider the advantages of giving the specific kind in that class (machine—mower; office equipment—files, desks, chairs, and typewriters; employees—salesclerks, janitors, secretaries, and others).

2. Another kind of specificness is giving supporting details, illustrations, examples, and full explanations for general statements made. If you use generalities to gain conciseness in topic and summarizing statements, be sure to provide necessary supporting explanations or further details. Otherwise, your unsupported statements may not be accepted, even if understood.

3. Still another important kind of specificness is giving the evidences of abstract qualities you may use. If you are inclined to say that something is a bargain, an outstanding offer, of the highest quality, revolutionary, best, ideal, or economical, give concrete evidence for these qualities instead of the abstract words.

In an application letter, if you want to convey that you are intelligent, industrious, honest, dependable, and sociable, give the evidence and let the reader draw the conclusions. You will sound boastful if you apply these words to yourself, and your reader will not believe them anyway unless you give the supporting concrete facts.

Strategy   Choose your best strategy for your message and audience—direct strategy for positive or neutral news and indirect strategy for negative or persuasive messages.

Subordinate   Don't overstress negative ideas, facts the reader knows, or insignificant points. If you must say them, put them in the middle of the paragraph or letter, devote little space to them, and/or put them in dependent clauses or phrases. Dependent clauses are particularly useful in subordinating. Here are some of the main beginning words that make clauses dependent: *after, although, as, because, before, if, since, though, till, unless, until, when, where, while.*

SX   *Sexist*   Phrase your message for equal treatment of females and males. Using plurals where possible is one easy way.

> Each auditor should turn in his or her time card.

> Auditors should turn in their time cards.

Syllable   Divide words at the ends of lines only at syllable breaks, and then only if each part has at least two letters and is pronounceable. If in doubt about where to divide a word, check your dictionary. Don't rely on your word processing software to divide syllables properly; check divisions as part of your proofreading.

Tabulate   Tabulate or itemize when you have lots of figures to present or a series of distinct points to make. Itemization will make you think more sharply and state your ideas more precisely and concisely. Thus, you will produce clearer, quicker reading and more emphasis. Furthermore, itemization grabs readers' or listeners' attention.

Tense   Watch tense (time indicated by your verbs) for appropriateness in the individual verb and logic in the sequence of verbs.

1. Normally you use the present, past, or future tense according to the time of the action you are reporting.

2. The tense of the key verb in an independent clause governs a sentence. Thus, the tenses of other verbs or verbals should indicate time *relative to* the time of the main verb.

I will do it as soon as I am able (a future and relative present).

I had hoped that I would be able to go (a past perfect and relative future).

3. A special use of the present tenses deserves careful attention, however, for some situations: You use the present (called the *universal present*) for statements that were true in the past, are true now, and will be true later. We say "The sun *sets* in the west" (universal present) even though it may have set hours earlier. Any statement you might make about what a book *says* fits the conditions. If you now read a book written even in 1620, it still *says* . . . . Similarly, in reporting on your research findings (which presumably are still true), you use the universal present tense. To do otherwise would imply doubt about the present validity of your results.

The law of supply and demand *means* . . . .

The 1986 edition *says*. . . .

In all the groups surveyed, more than 80 percent of the people prefer (not preferred). . . .

4. Do not shift tenses unless the logic of the situation requires that you do so.

5. Be sure to spell the appropriate verb form correctly. Remember that English has two classes of verbs. The Old English weak verbs became our regular verbs, whose principal parts go like *plow, plowed, plowed.* Old English strong verbs became our irregular ones, which change internally *(think, thought, thought; throw, threw, thrown; lead, led, led;* and *meet, met, met).*

Tone   Watch out for a tone of distrust, indifference, undue humility, flattery, condescension, preachiness, bragging, anger, accusation, sarcasm, curtness, effusiveness, or exaggeration.

Transition   Transitions between sentences in a paragraph, between paragraphs, and between sections in longer presentations must show their relationships. Your best method is to use a thread of logic (based on careful organization) that will hold your thoughts together like beads on a string. When the logical thread does not make the relationship clear, however, you need to do so by repeating a key word or idea from the preceding paragraph or by using a connecting word, phrase, sentence, or heading that shows the relationship. See **Coh** and **Unity.**

Trite   Trite expressions are overused and hence worn-out figures of speech that dull writing. The remedy is to state your idea simply in natural, normal English or to use an original figure of speech.

Unity   Unity (of sentences, paragraphs, or whole pieces of writing) requires that you show how each statement fits in or belongs (is not irrelevant). Applied to a sentence or paragraph, **unity** means the statement seems irrelevant or the various ideas are not closely enough related to be in one sentence or paragraph. Applied to a whole letter or report, it means the content seems so varied as to lack a central theme and you should put it in two or more separate papers. Often, however, the writer sees relationships that justify putting things together as they are, and the fault is in not showing the reader the relationships—an error of coherence (see **Coh**).

 Please put your answers in ink and have your signature witnessed by two people. One of our envelopes is enclosed for your convenience. (The envelope is not a convenience in doing what is requested in the first sentence. The two unrelated ideas should not be in the same paragraph. Or adding "in returning your answers" would help.)

Usage   Usage refers to the appropriateness of the language to the situation. A passage or expression marked with this symbol may be too formal and stiff, literary, flashy, or highbrow or too slangy, familiar, crude, or lowbrow. The normal, natural

English of educated people conducting their everyday affairs is neither formal nor illiterate but informal and natural. That is what you should use for most letters, memos, and reports.

Guard against the following illiterate forms (mostly the result of bad pronunciation): "He is prejudice" *(prejudiced),* "He is bias" *(biased),* "usta" or "use to" *(used to),* "had of" *(had),* "would of" *(would have),* "most all" *(almost all),* "a savings of" *(a saving of),* "She lead the meeting" *(led).*

Variety   Variety (of diction and of sentence pattern, type, and length) is necessary to avoid monotony. Achieving variety should be a part of the revision process, however, and should not distract you from saying what you want to say in writing a first draft.

In your revision, see that you haven't begun too many successive sentences the same way (especially not with *I* or *we).* If you have repeated yourself, cut out the repetition unless you need it for emphasis.

The usual English sentence pattern is subject-verb-complement; in revision, vary the pattern to avoid a dull sameness.

Good style also requires variety in sentence type. Some of your sentences should be simple (one independent clause); some should be compound (two independent clauses stating two closely related ideas of nearly equal importance); and some should be complex (at least one independent clause and one or more dependent clauses, all expressing ideas that are related but of unequal importance). Especially avoid too many successive simple sentences for ideas not deserving equal emphasis or too many compound sentences connected by *and.* (See **Subord.**)

Although most of your sentences should be relatively short (averaging 16–17 words for easy readability), you will produce a monotonous choppiness if all your sentences are in that range. See **Simp** and **Chop,** and revise accordingly.

Wordy   Use only words that add to your meaning. Edit for extra words, vague words, passive voice, and expletives.

YA   *"You" Attitude*   The "you" attitude is one of the three most important points about letter writing. People do things for their own benefit, not yours. If you want to persuade them to act, you have to show them the advantages of the action to themselves.

To show readers what is in the situation for them (WIIFM), you have to visualize their ways of life and show how your proposal fits in.

PROOFREADER'S SYMBOLS

These marks may be useful to you in revising your rough copy.

all samples

Symbol	Meaning	Example
∧	Insert text	Weigh to the nearest .01 ounce.
∨	Insert apostrophe	The report doesnt explain the discrepancy.
∧	Insert comma	Eleven crates broken at the site spilled
⊙	Insert period	Mr Gabe Justis called at 10 a.m.
∨ ∨	Insert quotation marks	He said, Not under any circumstances!
⌠	Insert space	Mail goes at 4 p.m Have it here on time.
ℰ	Delete	Campden and Cowdery are very displeased.
⌣	Close up space	Her has te led to error.
l.c. ///	Use lower case	*l.c.* Four CASES in an UNACCEPTABLE overrun.
caps	Use capitals	*caps* Four CASES is an <u>unacceptable</u> overrun.
STET	Let copy stand as originally typed; do not correct	Campden and Cowdery are very displeased. *STET*
(*sp*)	Spell out fully.	(*sp*) Flannery and Baird Co's both ordered 6 weeks ago.
¶	Start new paragraph	. . . summarizes the week. Next we . . . ¶
no ¶	Don't paragraph	
s.s.	Single space copy	
d.s.	Double space copy	
∼	Transpose copy	The director left out that
italic	Underline (printers would use italics)	Today's <u>World</u> reported more inflation.
⊢OR ⊏	Move copy left	⊢Choose one of these. Choose one of these.⊏
⊣OR ⊐	Move copy right	Choose one of these. ⊐Choose one of these.

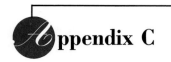

THREE COMMON BIBLIOGRAPHIC STYLES: APA, MLA, AND UNIVERSITY OF CHICAGO

This appendix illustrates the three most common bibliographic styles:

- **APA.** American Psychological Association, *Publication Manual of the American Psychological Association,* 3rd ed. (Washington, D.C.: American Psychological Association, 1983).
- **MLA.** Walter S. Achtert and Joseph Gibaldi, *The MLA Style Manual* (New York: Modern Language Association, 1985).
- **University of Chicago.** Kate L. Turabian and B. B. Honigsblum, *A Manual for Writers of Term Papers, Theses, and Dissertations,* 5th ed. (Chicago: University of Chicago Press, 1987).

Note that the publisher of this textbook, Richard D. Irwin, Inc., requires the use of its own style, which conforms to *none* of these styles. For your papers, use the style your instructor recommends—APA, MLA, or University of Chicago. Follow the appropriate examples in this appendix. The examples that follow illustrate *reference list* (bibliography) and *citation note* format for these nine common kinds of reference sources:

Book, one author.

Journal article, two authors.

Work contained within another work.

Newspaper article, one author.

Newspaper article, no author.

Magazine article, multiple authors.

Unpublished paper presented at a meeting.

Interview.

Government document.

Like other publications, government documents come in many different forms and media. For instance, you may find a document with an individual author, a government agency as author, or no author. You may find that your document is a pamphlet, a book, a journal article, or a videotape. We give only one example of a government document. For further style manual assistance in documenting government publications, refer to Diane L. Garner and Diane H. Smith, *The Complete Guide to Citing Government Documents: A Manual for Writers and Librarians* (Bethesda, Md.: Congressional Information Service, Inc., 1984).

APA: PUBLICATION MANUAL OF THE AMERICAN PSYCHOLOGICAL ASSOCIATION

- Authors' names are in reverse order (last name first). Initials rather than first and middle names are used.
- The date follows the name of the author(s).
- For titles of articles (not underlined) and books (underlined), "sentence-style capitalization" is used. Only the first word of the title and the first word after an internal colon are capitalized.
- Journal titles are in italics or underlined. Journal titles are given "headline-style," meaning that all important words are capitalized. After a journal title, give the volume number, in arabic numbers and in italics or underlined. If there is an issue number, give it in parentheses after the volume number. Do not put it in italics or underline it.

- Book titles are in italics or underlined but capitalized "sentence-style." For states, APA uses two-letter postal code abbreviations.

Book, One Author

Reference List Entry
Henze, G. (1992). *Winning career moves: A complete job search program for managers and professionals.* Homewood, IL: Business One Irwin.

In-Text Note
Among techniques for overcoming job-search anxiety is generating, on paper, a long list of "worst-case" possibilities. Once on paper before the job seeker's eyes, many of them are far-fetched, improbable, and ridiculous. The anxiety tends to diminish, and the job seeker's worries assume more sensible proportions (Henze, 1992, p. 42).

Journal Article, Two Authors

Reference List Entry
Lewis, P. V., & Speck, H. E., III. (1990). Ethical orientations for understanding business ethics. *Journal of Business Communication, 27*(3), 213–232.

In-Text Note
A recent discussion of business ethics helpfully lists the many subsets of ethical theory (Lewis & Speck, 1990, p. 215).
   or
Lewis and Speck (1990) offer an exhibit dividing the subsets of ethical theory into teleological theories and deontological theories (p. 215).

Work Contained within Another Work

Reference List Entry
Dumaine, B. (1990, January 15). Creating a new company culture. *Fortune,* pp. 127–131. In P. J. Frost, V. Mitchell, & W. R. Nord (Eds.) (1992). *Organizational reality: Reports from the firing line* (4th ed.) (pp. 443–448). New York: HarperCollins Publishers Inc.

In-Text Note
Change in corporate culture can take five to ten years, but without change, the organization might die (Dumaine, 1990, p. 444).

Newspaper Article, One Author

Reference List Entry
Applegate, J. (1990, June 15). Service without a smile can be deadly. *Los Angeles Times,* pp. D3, D7.

In-Text Note
Small businesses, many having to depend on word of mouth in place of expensive advertising, can least afford to send customers away unhappy, a recent *Los Angeles Times* article said. "Customer service experts say the average unhappy customer complains to about half a dozen friends, neighbors and colleagues about poor service. Imagine the impact that 10 unhappy customers could have on your earnings" (Applegate, 1990, p. D3).

Newspaper Article, No Author

Reference List Entry

Overseas work appeals to more U.S. managers as a wise career move. (1983). *The Wall Street Journal,* July 19, p. 1.

In-Text Note

Despite encountering difficulties on both leaving and re-entering the American culture, ambitious executives seek overseas assignments eagerly, according to a survey (Overseas work, 1983, p. 1).

Magazine Article, Multiple Authors

Reference List Entry

Begley, S., Wright, L., Church, V., & Hager, M. (1992, April 20). Mapping the brain. *Newsweek,* pp. 66–70.

In-Text Note

Neuroscientists, using an array of new imaging technologies, are able to map different areas of the human brain that become active upon the person's engaging in different activities (Begley, Wright, Church, & Hager, 1992, p. 66). The brain is compared to "a society of specialists" (p. 70).

Unpublished Paper Presented at a Meeting

Reference List Entry

Hellweg, S. A., & Phillips, S. L. (1983, March). *Communication policies and practices in American corporations.* Paper presented at the Western Regional Meeting of the American Business Communication Association, Marina del Rey, CA.

In-Text Note

Though Hellweg and Phillips (1983) reported that 53 percent of their 98 Fortune 500 respondents had a corporate communication policy, respondents did not specify form and coverage.

Interview

Reference List Entry

Garcia, H., partner, Ibanez and Garcia, CPA, Inc. (1993, March 22). Interview by Margaret Fox. Burbank, CA.

In-Text Note

Still another interviewee commented on the substantial amounts of writing required of CPAs (Garcia, 1993).

Government Document

Reference List Entry

Department of the Navy. (1983). *Correspondence manual* (SECNAVINST 5216.5C). Washington, DC: U.S. Government Printing Office.

In-Text Note

In the following mock exchange, the U.S. Navy's *Correspondence Manual* reduces to absurdity the timeworn military preference for passive voice:

> *Doctor:* When did you first notice your use of verbs in the passive voice?
> *Patient:* The utilization was first noticed by me shortly after the Navy was entered. The Marine Corps has been joined by my brother. The same condition has been remarked on by him.
> *Doctor:* Did you know that most of the verbs we speak with are active? So are most of the verbs in newspapers and magazines, the kinds of writing we like to read.
> *Patient:* Well, it is believed by me that most verbs are made passive by naval writers. In the letters and directives that have been prepared by this speaker, passive verbs have been utilized extensively. Are problems caused? (Department of the Navy, 1983, p. 1–19).

(The preceding document's pages are numbered 1–1, 1–2, 1–3, and so on. Page 1–19 is one page, not 19 pages.)

MLA: THE MLA STYLE MANUAL

MLA style differs from APA in several ways:

- The in-text note has no comma between author's name and page number. The abbreviations *p.* and *pp.* (for *page* and *pages*) are not used. A typical note would be (Barton 166).

- In the in-text note, the year of publication is usually not given. Including the year in the in-text note is permissible in the social and physical sciences. (Business is considered a social science.) The form is (Barton 1987, 166).

- In the bibliographic note, book and journal titles use headline-style capitalization. Both are in italics or underlined.

Book, One Author

Reference List Entry

Henze, Geraldine. *Winning Career Moves: A Complete Job Search Program for Managers and Professionals.* Homewood: Business One Irwin, 1992.

In-Text Note

Among techniques for overcoming job-search anxiety is generating, on paper, a long list of "worst-case" possibilities. Once on paper before the job seeker's eyes, many of them are far-fetched, improbable, and ridiculous. The anxiety tends to diminish, and the job seeker's worries assume more sensible proportions (Henze 1992, 42).

Journal Article, Two Authors

Reference List Entry

Lewis, Phillip V., and Henry E. Speck, III. "Ethical Orientations for Understanding Business Ethics." *Journal of Business Communication* 27 (1990): 213–232.

In-Text Note

A recent discussion of business ethics helpfully lists the many subsets of ethical theory (Lewis and Speck 1990, 215).
   or
Lewis and Speck (1990) offer an exhibit dividing the subsets of ethical theory into teleological theories and deontological theories (215).

Work Contained within Another Work

Reference List Entry

Dumaine, Brian. "Creating a New Company Culture." *Fortune* (15 Jan. 1990): 127–131. Rpt. in *Organizational reality: Reports from the firing line.* Ed. Peter J. Frost, Vance Mitchell, and Walter R. Nord. 4th ed. New York: HarperCollins Publishers Inc., 1992. 443–448.

In-Text Note

Change in corporate culture can take five to ten years, but without change, the organization might die (Dumaine 1992, 444).

Newspaper Article, One Author

Reference List Entry

Applegate, Jane. "Service Without a Smile Can Be Deadly." *Los Angeles Times* 15 June 1990: D3, D7.

In-Text Note

Small businesses, many having to depend on word of mouth in place of expensive advertising, can least afford to send customers away unhappy, a recent *Los Angeles Times* article said. "Customer service experts say the average unhappy customer complains to about half a dozen friends, neighbors and colleagues about poor service. Imagine the impact that 10 unhappy customers could have on your earnings" (Applegate 1990, D3).

Newspaper Article, No Author

Reference List Entry

"Overseas Work Appeals to More U.S. Managers as a Wise Career Move." *The Wall Street Journal* 19 July 1983: 1.

In-Text Note

Despite encountering difficulties on both leaving and re-entering the American culture, ambitious executives seek overseas assignments eagerly, according to a survey ("Overseas Work" 1983, 1).

Magazine Article, Multiple Authors

Reference List Entry

Begley, Sharon, Lynda Wright, Vernon Church, and Mary Hager. "Mapping the brain." *Newsweek* 20 Apr. 1992: 66–70.

In-Text Note

Neuroscientists, using an array of new imaging technologies, are able to map different areas of the human brain that become active upon the person's engaging in different activities (Begley, Wright, Church, and Hager 1992, 66). The brain is compared to "a society of specialists" (70).

Unpublished Paper Presented at a Meeting

Reference List Entry

Hellweg, Susan A., and Steven L. Phillips. "Communication Policies and Practices in American Corporations." Western Regional Meeting of the American Business Communication Association, Marina del Rey, March 1983.

In-Text Note

Though Hellweg and Phillips (1983) reported that 53 percent of their 98 Fortune 500 respondents had a corporate communication policy, respondents did not specify form and coverage.

Interview

Reference List Entry

Garcia, Howard. Personal interview. 22 March 1993.

In-Text Note

Still another interviewee commented on the substantial amounts of writing required of CPAs (Garcia 1993).

Government Document

Reference List Entry

United States Department of the Navy. *Correspondence Manual* SECNAVINST
      5216.5C. Washington, DC: U.S. Government Printing Office 1983.

In-Text Note

In the following mock exchange, the U.S. Navy's *Correspondence Manual* reduces to absurdity the timeworn military preference for passive voice:

> *Doctor:* When did you first notice your use of verbs in the passive voice?
> *Patient:* The utilization was first noticed by me shortly after the Navy was entered. The Marine Corps has been joined by my brother. The same condition has been remarked on by him.
> *Doctor:* Did you know that most of the verbs we speak with are active? So are most of the verbs in newspapers and magazines, the kinds of writing we like to read.
> *Patient:* Well, it is believed by me that most verbs are made passive by naval writers. In the letters and directives that have been prepared by this speaker, passive verbs have been utilized extensively. Are problems caused? (Department of the Navy 1983, 1–19).

UNIVERSITY OF CHICAGO: A MANUAL FOR WRITERS OF TERM PAPERS, THESES, AND DISSERTATIONS

Chicago style gives a format for a reference list that differs in some respects from that for bibliographic entries. We offer reference list format in both exhibit and discussion. Chicago style permits either in-text notes or endnotes.

- Chicago style sets endnotes flush left. It sets the first line of a reference list reference flush left and indents subsequent lines.
- Book titles are in italics or underlined and capitalized headline-style in both reference list note and endnote.
- In the reference list, items are alphabetized by last name of first author. Additional authors' names are in normal order, separated by commas, with *and* used to separate the last two.
- In parenthetical references, no comma separates author from date. If the reference contains author, date, and page, the page number, with no abbreviation for *page,* is separated from the date with a comma.
- If your instructor directs you to use endnotes, you quote or paraphrase your source in your text and mark the place with a superscript (a number raised half a line above the normal line). This number refers the reader to the similarly numbered endnote.

Book, One Author

Reference List Entry
Henze, Geraldine. 1992. *Winning Career Moves: A Complete Job Search Program for Managers and Professionals.* Homewood, Ill.: Business One Irwin.

In-Text Note
Among techniques for overcoming job-search anxiety is generating, on paper, a long list of "worst-case" possibilities. Because many of them are far-fetched and improbable, they begin to seem ridiculous. The anxiety tends to diminish, and the job seeker's worries assume more sensible proportions (Henze 1992, 42).

Endnote
3. Geraldine Henze, *Winning Career Moves: A Complete Job Search Program for Managers and Professionals* (Homewood, Ill.: Business One Irwin, 1992), 42.

Journal Article, Two Authors

Reference List Entry
Lewis, Phillip V., and Henry E. Speck, III. 1990. "Ethical Orientations for Understanding Business Ethics." *Journal of Business Communication* 27, no. 3: 213–32.

In-Text Note
A recent discussion of business ethics helpfully lists the many subsets of ethical theory (Lewis and Speck 1990, 215).
> *or*

Lewis and Speck (1990) offer an exhibit dividing the subsets of ethical theory into teleological theories and deontological theories (215).

Endnote
5. Phillip V. Lewis and Henry E. Speck, III, "Ethical Orientations for Understanding Business Ethics," *Journal of Business Communication* 27 (1990): 215.

Work Contained within Another Work

Reference List Entry
Dumaine, Brian. 1992. "Creating a New Company Culture." *Fortune,* 15 January 1990, 127–31. In *Organizational Reality: Reports from the Firing Line,* ed. Peter J. Frost, Vance Mitchell, and Walter R. Nord. 4th ed., 443–48. New York: HarperCollins Publishers Inc.

In-Text Note
Change in corporate culture can take five to ten years, but without change, the organization might die (Dumaine 1992, 444).

Endnote
1. Brian Dumaine, "Creating a New Company Culture," *Fortune,* 15 January 1990, 127–31, in *Organizational Reality: Reports from the Firing Line,* ed. Peter J. Frost, Vance Mitchell, and Walter R. Nord, 4th ed. (New York: HarperCollins Publishers Inc., 1992), 444.

Newspaper Article, One Author

Reference List Entry

Applegate, Jane. 1990. "Service without a Smile Can Be Deadly." *Los Angeles Times,*
15 June, D3, D7.

In-Text Note

Small businesses, many having to depend on word of mouth in place of expensive
advertising, can least afford to send customers away unhappy, a recent *Los Angeles
Times* article said. "Customer service experts say the average unhappy customer
complains to about half a dozen friends, neighbors and colleagues about poor
service. Imagine the impact that 10 unhappy customers could have on your
earnings" (Applegate 1990, D3).

Endnote

10. Jane Applegate, "Service without a Smile Can Be Deadly," *Los Angeles Times,* 15
June 1990, D3, D7.

Newspaper Article, No Author

Reference List Entry

"Overseas Work Appeals to More U.S. Managers as a Wise Career Move." 1983. *The
Wall Street Journal,* 19 July, 1.

In-Text Note

Despite encountering difficulties on both leaving and re-entering the American
culture, ambitious executives seek overseas assignments eagerly, according to a
survey ("Overseas work" 1983, 1).

Endnote

8. "Overseas Work Appeals to More U.S. Managers as a Wise Career Move," *The
Wall Street Journal,* 19 July 1983, 1.

Magazine Article, Multiple Authors

Reference List Entry

Begley, Sharon, Lynda Wright, Vernon Church, and Mary Hager. 1992. "Mapping the
Brain." *Newsweek,* 20 April, 66–70.

In-Text Note

Neuroscientists, using an array of new imaging technologies, are able to map
different areas of the human brain that become active upon the person's engaging in
different activities (Begley, Wright, Church, and Hager 1992, 66). The brain is
compared to "a society of specialists" (70).

Endnote

5. Sharon Begley, Lynda Wright, Vernon Church, and Mary Hager, "Mapping the
Brain," *Newsweek,* 20 April 1992, 70.

Unpublished Paper Presented at a Meeting

Reference List Entry

Hellweg, Susan A., and Steven L. Phillips. 1983, March. Communication policies and practices in American corporations. Paper presented at the Western Regional Meeting of the American Business Communication Association, Marina del Rey, Calif.

In-Text Note

Though Hellweg and Phillips (1983) reported that 53 percent of their 98 Fortune 500 respondents had a corporate communication policy, respondents did not specify form and coverage.

Endnote

11. Susan A. Hellweg and Steven L. Phillips, "Communication Policies and Practices in American Corporations," Paper presented at the Western Regional Meeting of the American Business Communication Association, Marina del Rey, Calif., March 1983.

Interview

Reference List Entry

Garcia, Howard, partner, Ibanez and Garcia, CPA, Inc. 1993. Interview by Margaret Fox, 22 March. Burbank, Calif.

In-Text Note

Still another interviewee commented on the substantial amounts of writing required of CPAs (Garcia 1993)

Endnote

3. Howard Garcia, partner, Ibanez and Garcia, CPA, Inc., interview by Margaret Fox, 22 March 1993, Burbank, Calif.

Government Document

Reference List Entry

Department of the Navy. 1983. *Correspondence Manual* (SECNAVINST 5216.5C). Washington, DC: U.S. Government Printing Office.

In-Text Note

In the following mock exchange, the U.S. Navy's *Correspondence Manual* reduces to absurdity the timeworn military preference for passive voice:

Doctor: When did you first notice your use of verbs in the passive voice?
Patient: The utilization was first noticed by me shortly after the Navy was entered. The Marine Corps has been joined by my brother. The same condition has been remarked on by him.
Doctor: Did you know that most of the verbs we speak with are active? So are most of the verbs in newspapers and magazines, the kinds of writing we like to read.
Patient: Well, it is believed by me that most verbs are made passive by naval writers. In the letters and directives that have been prepared by this speaker, passive verbs have been utilized extensively. Are problems caused? (Department of the Navy 1983, 1–19).

Endnote

21. Department of the Navy, *Correspondence Manual* (Washington, D.C.: U.S. Government Printing Office, 1983), 1–19.

REFERENCING, COMMON SENSE, AND ODD AND NONPRINT INFORMATION FORMATS

The preceding examples do not begin to cover all the kinds of secondary sources in which you might find information. Each of the style manuals on which these examples are based is more than 200 pages long.

You might encounter a source you cannot format using these examples. If you do, recall why we reference sources: for our readers' convenience and further reading and for our own credibility.

With that in mind, format the note intelligently. For instance, let's say you are using an eight-page fact sheet provided by TRW, a large corporation. What will the reader want to know about the source? Give as much of the expected information as you can locate. If no author is given, reference the corporation as author. Use whatever title appears at the head of the fact sheet.

Any publication or printing information you believe the reader would find helpful you may give within square brackets. These brackets tell the reader that this information is factual but not printed in the source itself.

Often no publisher, city of publication, or date will be listed. If you can determine what the year of publication is, give it in square brackets: [1989]. If you are concerned that the reader will think you were careless, you can use, in square brackets, the abbreviations [n.p.] for no publisher and no place, [n.d.] for no date, and [n.pag.] for no pagination. If the piece does not have page numbers but you can easily count eight pages, say [8 pages].

For unusual formats, open a bracket at the end of your bibliography citation and tell the reader what kind of source you are using: for example, [Fact sheet] or [Monthly newsletter].

A sensible approach to documenting TRW's information sheet might be this one:

TRW. [1989]. Components of a credit rating. [Fact sheet provided by TRW], [8 pages].

In your in-text reference, you can say (TRW, [p. 7]).

When you cannot go to an original printed source but have the contents of the source in full text, as often occurs in online or CD/ROM sources, your bibliographic citation might be

Acquisition development. (1991, November). *Dairy Foods,* p. 24 [CD/Corporate].

Dreyer's Grand Ice Cream sees 1q pretax net below year ago. (1992, March 4). [Dow Jones News].

You give as much information as you can find using that source. The bracketed part of the note tells the reader what kind of source you used and shows why full publication information is not available.

The examples in this section follow APA style as nearly as possible, but the APA manual lacks examples of these kinds of sources. If your instructor has directed you to use MLA or Chicago, try to conform the style for your odd-format citations as closely as possible to that style.

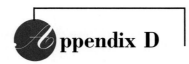

ppendix D | SPECIALIZED PERSUASION: COLLECTING

Businesses must collect the money for the products or services they sell on credit. Most buyers honor their agreement to pay. Such buyers never receive any collection messages except the initial bill. Other buyers postpone or evade payment for various reasons. Some forget; some procrastinate; some have bad luck; and a few never intend to pay.[1] To all these individuals, businesses send collection messages.

Although larger businesses have collection departments that employ and train workers solely for the job of collecting, you might work for or run a small business in which collections is only one of your many writing tasks.

Collectors have two goals: to collect the money and to retain the buyer's goodwill. Continued business *makes* money. A customer lost means a new one the business must attract—and doing so *costs* money.

ELEMENTS OF PERSUASION IN COLLECTIONS

Collection messages are another form of persuasive writing.   This section will discuss some of the elements of persuasion that influence the effectiveness of a collection message.

People are influenced by emotion.   Prior to the mild-appeal stage of the collection series, the use of emotional appeal is minimal and subtle. The writer establishes a businesslike, firm, yet friendly and considerate tone. Beginning with the mild-appeal stage, though, the writer attempts to engage the reader's emotions more seriously. Emotion—stronger emotions and heavier use—increases as the collection series progresses.

Communicators need to present a credible, sincere image to persuade well.   Writers of collection letters need to know exactly where the firm stands with respect to law and to its own collection policies. They best present themselves as forthright yet courteous. They must appear determined to collect what is due, yet unthreatening and, at least in the early collection stages, willing to adapt to a reader's reasonable needs.

Communicators need to understand and control their own emotions before they can effectively move the emotions of others.   Anyone who feels personally hostile toward debtors should not write collection letters. Probably the most useful emotion to motivate a collector is a spirit of helpfulness.

Communicators should not disrupt readers' expectations.   A debtor knows for sure that the creditor will ask for payment. Sometimes creditors feel apologetic asking for payment. But *not* asking for payment would disrupt the debtor's expectations (although it might please the debtor). Another of a debtor's expectations is that he or she will be treated like a human being. A collector should never fail to be courteous and humane.

People dislike dissonance, that is, lack of closure.   People do not like to have their affairs out of balance. Getting a matter closed feels good and is a most useful emotional appeal in collections.

A given message will not have the same effect on every recipient.   Some debtors respond unfavorably to friendly reminders to pay. If these debtors become known to

---

[1]Some debtors withhold payment because they genuinely believe they do not owe. Sometimes businesses make errors; sometimes delivery services cause breakage or loss. If a sum is disputed, it is not yet the collector's affair. Customer service should address these cases.

the collector, some stages in the progression from inquiry to mild appeal to urgent appeal to ultimatum can be skipped. Similarly, some debtors always intend to pay but are just very slow. These people might react best to a spaced series of reminders and mild appeals. "Overkill" is best avoided. The right amount of persuasion is the amount that will do the job—and no more.

People's opinions and actions are influenced by the opinions and actions of others whose opinions they value. The appeals to pride and to fair play have deep cultural roots. What others think of a person's honesty strongly affects that person's self-esteem. The fair-play appeal also hits a cultural value—that of sportsmanly conduct.

Word choice strongly affects the success of a persuasive effort. Early stages in the collection series call for words that create pleasant, cooperative feelings: *appreciate, cooperation, convenient, overlooked, prompt, mark your bill PAID IN FULL,* and the like. If necessary, later in the series different, more serious, and perhaps more motivating feelings can be created by words like *legal obligation, legal remedies, credit reputation, forced to take steps,* and so forth. At the end of the series, the writer selects—carefully—words that create considerable uneasiness: words like *an early settlement* (this expression smacks of the courtroom), *other means of enforcing collection, long past due, last opportunity to prevent legal action.* You will be able to add many more. *Avoid any words that could be used against you in a suit or countersuit.*

Actions (following through) must reinforce words. Once into a collection series, the writer must keep up the pressure until the money is collected or until further efforts to collect it would be futile. The writer needs to begin the collection effort as soon as the need appears and to keep sending the letters in the series at regular intervals. A firm should not hesitate to follow through on an ultimatum. Failure to do so will damage the firm's credibility and cost the business heavily in the long run.

THE COLLECTION SERIES

Collectors usually use a five-step series of messages. (The series stops, of course, as soon as the buyer pays the bill.) The steps are reminder, inquiry, mild appeal, urgent appeal, and ultimatum. The collector sends a different kind of message depending on the stage in the collection effort and the assumption about the debtor's intentions (see Exhibit D–1).

If the firm has not been paid by a bill's due date, the collection series should **begin promptly.** No more than about 10 days should pass before the collector sends the first message—the reminder—which is often no more than a phone call or a second copy of the bill itself stamped *past due.* The series should **proceed systematically.** If one message does not bring payment, additional messages should follow within a few days. Regularity and persistence show the debtor that the business intends to follow through.

Early collection messages are low key. Collectors need to exert the least pressure needed to collect the debt. If earlier, softer messages do not work, the messages should **become sterner.** Even at later stages of the series, however, the messages should show the business to **be humane and flexible.**

Because debtors fall into categories, collection letters tend to be standardized, computer-stored form letters or letter parts, and phone collections tend to follow fairly set scripts for different situations. Because wording is important, businesses work up a courteous but effective series and keep to it.

At each successive stage of collection, the collector's assumptions about the debtor grow less optimistic. The assumptions give rise to the gist of each message. Each message to the debtor should state the dollar balance and amount past due and should request payment. At no stage should the message be insulting, nor should the business ever make any threat that is illegal or that it does not intend to carry out. Collectors should at all times put themselves in the place of the debtor and work to do the right thing by all.

EXHIBIT D–1 Stages in the Collection Series

Stage	Assumption	Kind of Message	Content
Notification	Will pay promptly	Usual statement	Amount due, due date, terms
Reminder	Will pay; overlooked	Statement, perhaps with rubber stamp, penned note, or sticker; or form letter or brief reference in other letter or phone call	Same as above, perhaps with indication that this is not first notice
Inquiry	Something unusual; needs special consideration	One letter or phone call	Asks for payment or explanation and offers consideration and helpfulness
Appeal	Needs to be persuaded	One or more letters or phone calls	Selected appropriate and increasingly forceful appeals, well developed
Urgency	May be scared into paying	Phone call or letter, sometimes from high executive or special collector	Grave tone of something getting out of hand; may review case; still a chance to come through clean
Ultimatum	Must be squeezed	Letter, mailgram, telegram	Pay by set date or we'll report to credit bureau (or sue, now illegal to threaten and not do); may review case to retain goodwill by showing reasonableness

Source: Gretchen N. Vik, C. W. Wilkinson, and Dorothy C. Wilkinson, *Writing and Speaking in Business*, 10th ed. (Homewood, Ill.: Richard D. Irwin, 1990), p. 195.

COLLECTING BY LETTER

Remember that unlike phone calls, letters are one-directional. Clarity and completeness are essential. If readers do not understand something in the letter, they may take the message less seriously, assuming the business does not have its act together.

Examples of letters for each stage of the collection process follow.

Reminder

Dear Mr. Laverty:

Perhaps you overlooked your balance of $155.92 when it came due April 30.

We'll appreciate your sending payment in the enclosed postpaid envelope. Or drop it off when you visit the store to check the summer preseason sales. Thanks for shopping at Portman's.

Inquiry

Dear Mr. Laverty:

We're wondering why your balance of $155.92 has gone unpaid for almost a month.

We need to hear from you, either in the form of a check for the amount due or in the form of an explanation. If there's a problem, maybe we can help solve it. Please send your balance right away, or call us.

Mild Appeal

Dear Mr. Laverty:

Your excellent payment record up till now has been something to be proud of. We're getting concerned, though. We haven't had a response from you to our previous messages. Please show us that responsible attention to your obligations is still very important to you.

Please send $155.92 in the enclosed envelope right away.

Urgent Appeal

Dear Mr. Laverty:

Several messages to you have not brought payment of your balance of $155.92, past due now for almost 60 days.

Our concern has grown to worry, not just about the debt we have not collected but also about the problem you're creating for yourself. If you do not send payment now, collection is turned over to a collection agency and your nonpayment becomes part of your credit record. Future credit might be much less easy to get.

An envelope is enclosed for your use. Send $155.92 today and prevent any further steps.

Ultimatum

Dear Mr. Laverty:

By 5 P.M. Friday, July 15, we must receive your payment of $155.92, which has been past due since April 30.

If we do not receive this sum by that deadline, you will next hear from Juggernaut Collection Agency. Law and precedent entitle us to recover this sum, and we intend to pursue it.

We also intend to notify the Dallas Merchants' Credit Association. Businesses to whom you apply for future credit will routinely access the Credit Association's computerized database and will find there the record of your nonpayment.

This can still be avoided, but only by your immediate payment.

Letters such as these can be computer stored and modified to contain information appropriate to each debtor, the amount owed, and so on.

COLLECTING BY TELEPHONE

When collecting by phone, you have a chance to interact and change what you say, depending on what the debtor says.

Phone collectors are trained to handle a variety of negative reactions from the debtors they call, especially at later stages in the collection series. Even if debtors curse, weep, threaten, or slam down the receiver, the caller must remember that the emotion is not directed at them personally. Much of it is reaction to stress or the debtors' displaced anger at themselves for getting into debt in the first place. The collectors remind themselves of their dual purpose—collecting the money and retaining good-will—and do their best to persuade debtors to pay.

At the reminder or inquiry stage, the conversation usually does not become heated. An *inquiry-stage* exchange might go like this:

> *Customer:* Hello.
> *Collector:* Good morning, Mrs. Canby. How are you?
> *Customer:* Fine, how are you?
> *Collector:* Fine, thank you. Mrs. Canby, I'm Roger Mars, calling from Directors Equity Bank, where you have your homeowner's loan. Our records show that your mortgage payment of $986 due June 30 hasn't arrived yet. We have a grace period of seven days, but your payment was due fully four weeks ago, and we're expecting

	your check for July 31 now also. Can you give us some explanation of why your June 30 payment hasn't arrived?
Customer:	But I sent it on June 30. I pay all my bills right around the first of the month. It always gets there by the end of the grace period.
Collector:	We haven't received it, though. Would you look at your checkbook log and make sure you sent it?
Customer:	[Looks at checkbook log.] I wrote the check. It's number 1172, June 30, for $986.
Collector:	Did your last bank statement show it as having cleared the bank?
Customer:	Um. No. Hmmmm. I *know* I wrote it!!! You must have lost it in your office.
Collector:	Actually that's unlikely, but I'll tell you what. Let's talk again in another week, and if the check hasn't surfaced then, I'll ask you to write us another.
Customer:	Well, all right, but I mailed you that check.
Collector:	Thanks, Mrs. Canby. Have a pleasant day.
Customer:	You too. Bye.

This collector remains pleasant, nonaccusatory, reasonable, cooperative, and flexible. He does not respond to Mrs. Canby's attempt to blame the problem on the bank. His flexibility calls for the same response from Mrs. Canby.

A week later, however, the check has not appeared. The collector calls again. This time, he uses a *mild appeal:*

Customer:	Hello.
Collector:	Hello, Mrs. Canby. This is Roger Mars, from Directors Equity Bank, calling again about your overdue June 30 mortgage payment of $986. Last week we agreed to wait another week for it to appear. Your check for the July 31 payment came on the fourth, but the June 30 check is still missing.
Customer:	How exasperating! I *wrote* the check. I'm sure it's there in your office somewhere.
Collector:	We supervise our clerical and data entry workers closely, because we know how important our customers' accounts are and how unfair it would be if any of them got a bad mark on their credit ratings because of us. We double-checked [puts a smile in his voice]—we even looked under deskmats—but the check didn't arrive here.
Customer:	Hmph!
Collector:	Would you do this, Mrs. Canby: Send us another check for the amount of $986. Since the other check hasn't cleared your bank, the funds are still there and your balance should cover it easily. Then we'll continue to watch for the original check—your number 1172—and if it comes, we'll phone you immediately and either return it to you or apply it to a future month's mortgage payment. If you do this, we can put the whole problem behind us. Things will be back in balance this way.
Customer:	Oh, all right, but I *wrote that check!*
Collector:	Then it's bound to turn up. Meanwhile, thanks for being so cooperative. You're helping us both. Hope your day is a good one.
Customer:	Thanks. You too.

Because the previous week Mrs. Canby had agreed to write another check if the first one did not appear, she now feels she must be consistent and do so. She isn't overjoyed about it, but she has the distinct sense that if she does not, she will continue to hear from the (so far) pleasant collector.

These two collection phone call scripts are real. They succeeded. Mrs. Canby sent the payment that same day and continued as a satisfied customer of Directors Equity Bank. What about the lost check? About seven months after this incident, Mrs. Canby received an envelope from the power company. In it, with no note or explanation, was a very crumpled check numbered 1172. She had written it but had mistakenly picked it up along with the check for the power company, where it lay for six months because handling it was no one's priority. When they got around to it, they sent it to the address printed on the check.

COLLECTIONS AND THE LAW

Many businesses use paper-copy messages for some collections and the telephone for others. Some use telegrams or faxes as well. At late stages, sometimes a collector visits the debtor at his or her home or office.

In the past, some collectors' persistence turned into downright harassment. Occasional violence or other illegal action occurred. Clearly, the fact that a debt is owed does not justify abuse. To curb abuses, the Fair Debt Practices Act, passed by Congress in 1978, put restrictions on bill collectors. Many states too have passed laws protecting debtors from harassment. In some states, for instance, creditors may not

- Telephone a debtor before 8 A.M. or after 9 P.M.
- Tell a debtor's neighbors, friends, employers, or co-workers about the debt.
- Misrepresent themselves as someone else—a lawyer, for instance.
- Telephone more than twice in one 24-hour period.
- Threaten violence or public humiliation.
- Threaten legal action that the creditor cannot legally take or does not intend to follow through on.
- Telephone the debtor if the debtor has sent the creditor a letter saying not to.

Laws vary from state to state. If your firm retains legal counsel, consult that lawyer. If not, consult your local Legal Aid Society or check an appropriate library for the latest revision of your state's statutes. If a debtor's rights are violated, he or she can bring suit.

USING A COMPUTER-ASSISTED COLLECTION SYSTEM/SERVICE

Firms with high-volume collections sometimes use automated credit collection systems. They set up records in the database when customers apply for credit. The records hold data such as the credit applicant's employment history and credit history. The automated systems use programmed decision criteria and credit-scoring models to decide, on the basis of the firm's business strategy and acceptable level of risk, whether to offer credit and, if so, to what limit. If certain customers are influential or high-dollar accounts, the system can flag these for special handling. Vik, Wilkinson, and Wilkinson show the greatly increased efficiency such systems offer:

Through these systems, the store can identify customers who are over the credit limit and get them in touch with a collector. Using the systems, a collector can talk to about 75–100 people a day, whereas a collector using the phone and manual systems can talk to only 25–35 people a day.[2]

Whether a firm uses manual or computer-assisted collection practices, the same rationale underlies the series of messages to the debtor. They must be prompt, persistent, humane, clear, and credible; and each message in the series should be firmer than the last.

---

[2]Gretchen N. Vik, C. W. Wilkinson, and Dorothy C. Wilkinson, *Writing and Speaking in Business,* 10th ed. (Homewood, Ill.: Richard D. Irwin, 1990), p. 191.

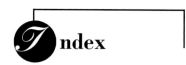

Index

A

ABI/Inform, bibliographic database, 140
Abilities, job search, 382
Accomplishments, job search, 382
Activities and honors
  and job search, 389
  questions concerning, job interview, 439–40
  on résumé, 400–401
Ad hoc videoconferencing, 514
Adjustments and compromises and complaints, 310–15
Administering research survey, 168–70
Agenda, communicators, 464
Agenda in interpersonal communication, 464–65
AIDA Sequence, 365
Altercasting, 356
Ambiguity and multiple meaning, 469–71
Analytical report, 133
Answering help-wanted ads, 427
Apparel for job interview, 433, 436
Appendixes or exhibits, reports, 243
Applying information, cover letter, 414
Area charts, 196
Articulation, 280
Ask for interview, cover letter, 415
Asking for information directly, 38
Assembling information on self, job search, 386–89
Atypical questions, job interview, 442–44
Audience analysis, 5–6, 56, 56–57
Audiences in general, 274–75
Audiotape recordings, 290
Audit reports, 117
Avoiding
  communication pitfalls, non-native employees, 483–84
  isms, 81–85
  negative language, 328–29
  noun clumps, 77–78
  outdated expressions, 72–73
Awareness and control of verbal sending, 472

B

Back orders, 317–20
Bar charts, 190–94
Barriers to effective organizational communication, 502–4
Baseline behavior establishment, 471–72
Beginning, middle, and end of oral presentation, 275–76
Behavioral baseline, 471
Bell-shaped curve, 172

Benefits, 452
Bias against handicapped workers, 84–85
Bibliographic styles, 592–601
Bibliography, 146
Bona fide occupational qualification, interviews, 525
Boolean operator, 136–37
Boundary spanning, 497
Business Periodicals Index, 138
Business reports contrasted with other research reports, 134
Business writer's self-analysis, 95
Business writing style
  avoidance of isms, 81–85
  clarity, 69
  coherence and transition, 79–81
  computer aids to revising, 93–94
  conciseness, 69
  correctness and naturalness, 71–74
  courtesy, 70–71
  credibility, 70
  effective emphasis, 81
  goal, mature business writing style, 91–92
  inconspicuousness, 69
  interest, 75
  positiveness, 74–75
  readability, 75–79
  suitability, 70
  variables and judgment calls, 88–91
  word choice, general principles, 85–88
  writing for readers in other countries, 92–93

C

Campus career-planning office, 383–84
Categories of nonverbals, 473–83
CD/ROM, 141, 141
Census, survey, 160, 162
Chalkboards or whiteboards, 289
Changing face, business library, 135–36
Channel defined, 11
Choosing physical surroundings, small meetings, 509
Chronological versus functional approach, résumé, 406–9
Clarifying concepts, slides and, 209
Clarity
  business writing, 69
  visuals and, 184
Clip art, 204–6
Clique, 504
Closed question, 428
Coaching, correcting, and supporting, discipline, 533
Coherence and transition, business writing, 79–81

Collection messages, 602–7
College recruiting system, 324–25
Column charts, 190
Communicating as part of a business
  audience analysis, 5, 6
  globalization of communication, 9–10
  multiple audiences and multiple writers, 9
  "you" attitude, 5
Communicating in organizations
  corporate cuture, 494–96
  organizational communication networks, 499–505
  power, politics, and influence, 496–99
  small-group meetings, 506–15
Communicating interpersonally
  active listening, 465–69
  common ground and trust, 463–65
  informing and influencing and teamwork, 462–63
  nonverbal communication, 489–84
  perception and attitude, 462
Communicating to motivate, 535–36
Communicating to resolve conflict, 538–42
Communicating with publics and stakeholders, 542–48
Communication, managing and supervising
  communicating to motivate, 535–36
  communicating with publics and stakeholders, 542–48
  communication and conflict, 536–42
  disciplinary communication, 532–35
  interviewing, from organizational side of desk, 522–29
  performance appraisals, 529–32
Communication and conflict, 536–42
Communication audit, 547–48
Communications model
  cultural differences, as barriers to communication, 13–14
  encoding and decoding language, 12–14
  sender, channel, feedback, filter, noise, 10–12
Company research, and job interview, 425
Company tours and lunches, job candidates, 448–49
Component bar graph, 194, 195
Compromise, as conflict resolution, 536, 540–41
Compromise adjustments, 315–17
Computer aids to revising, 93–94
Computer interviews, 429–30
Computerized, online catalog, library, 136

609